AF478349

# INFORMATION SYSTEMS DESIGN METHODOLOGIES:
## A Comparative Review

IFIP WG 8.1 Working Conference on
Comparative Review of
Information Systems Design Methodologies
Noordwijkerhout, The Netherlands, 10-14 May, 1982

NORTH-HOLLAND PUBLISHING COMPANY
AMSTERDAM • NEW YORK • OXFORD

# INFORMATION SYSTEMS DESIGN METHODOLOGIES:

## A Comparative Review

Proceedings of the IFIP WG 8.1 Working Conference on
Comparative Review of Information Systems Design Methodologies
Noordwijkerhout, The Netherlands, 10-14 May, 1982


*edited by*

**T. W. OLLE**
*T. William Olle Associates*
*Walton-on-Thames, Surrey*
*U.K.*

**H. G. SOL**
*University of Groningen*
*Groningen*
*The Netherlands*

**A. A. VERRIJN-STUART**
*University of Leiden*
*Leiden*
*The Netherlands*

1982


NORTH-HOLLAND PUBLISHING COMPANY
AMSTERDAM • NEW YORK • OXFORD

ISBN: 0 444 86407 5

Published by:
NORTH-HOLLAND PUBLISHING COMPANY – AMSTERDAM • NEW YORK • OXFORD

Sole distributors for the U.S.A. and Canada:
ELSEVIER SCIENCE PUBLISHING COMPANY, INC.
52 Vanderbilt Avenue
New York, N.Y. 10017

PRINTED IN THE NETHERLANDS

# CRIS:
## An Introduction

Being in the business of designing information systems in this second half of the 20th century, one tends to forget that this has been an age-old activity. For ever since mankind started speaking and, especially, devised useful sign conventions, we have been engaged in the design of systems that serve some form of organizational communication and control. This may not be the place for conjectures on the evolution of prehistoric practice, but the fact remains that even today a large part of decision making in organizations is supported more by informal (or "soft") than by formal (or "hard") information. Conversations, rumours, memo's and personal notes play such a prominent role that one might well ask how much progress has really been made by computerising most routine and a number of non-standard systems. Our achievements as such are certainly impressive, yet serve a limited purpose only. Why?

One of the reasons may be that we find it very difficult truly to "design" such abstract constructs. The nature of the difficulties is at least two-fold. Firstly, there is the intrinsic conflict of flexible requirements versus the rather rigid systems one is capable of building. Secondly, even if a suitable end-product might be conceived, it is often impossible for the designer to find out what is needed because of the extent of the potential changes in the organization, because of a lack of understanding of, and communication with the "user", and possibly because of downright resistance.

The way I am putting it is the pragmatic systems-oriented one: "I know what things might be constructed, so what would you, the user, like me to develop for you?". Putting it thus one considers the building opportunities first and the requirements analysis (with this technological knowledge at the back of one's mind) second.

It is not realistic to sequence the two in reverse order. For information analysis without guiding the user as to the possibilities (and impossibilities) is meaningless. It is realistic to alternate between analysis and design. It is realistic to make the user participate as much as possible. And it is essential continually to remain critical regarding one's own knowledge and ideas ....

One of the limitations to extend our capabilities is the lack of "comparative" information concerning the abundant information systems design "methodologies". The situation is very much one where a clever designer has developed a particular approach and then makes a living teaching seminars on his invention. If he has a charismatic personality his ideas will be picked up by a certain following, who will hallow the formalism offered as gospel. Since a number of such methodologies have already become enshrined in dogma, but the sets of disciples hardly overlap, many interested people only know and understand one or at best two of them.

Now, information systems design for organizations being a rather creative activity, it is clear that there cannot be a "best" methodology in any general sense. Even if some might be "better" than others for particular situations, the lack of true comparative knowledge makes it impossible as yet categorically to state in what way that would be so. And finally, I believe that we may just be in a position to suggest some methodologies vaguely being "good" (i.e. satisficing), but to this we should immediately add that this does not cover the full range.

A contribution to remedy the restricted knowledge and understanding of what one has to offer is CRIS. As explained in Bill Olle's background paper the idea is that a three-stage exercise might resolve some of our problems: first by comparing what is there, next by analyzing what the essential features appear to be and lastly, in a sort of synthesis, possibly finding appropriate approaches for given environments. Appropriate, or "more" appropriate, for "most" appropriate is impossible, as we agreed. Straightforward though this sequence of studies seems to be, it poses a number of problems in connection with the comparison process. What are suitable criteria, for instance? Just inviting papers explaining methodologies is obviously not the way to get them truly side by side. This is where Bill Olle deserves full credit for suggesting the format of the first study: by actually applying an information systems design methodology to one standard case its strong and weak points will emerge on a basis which does allow comparison with other methodologies similarly applied.

Remained the choice of problem case. The one adopted is closely related to our own (IFIP) environment: how to support a Working Conference organized by an IFIP Working Group. Even a superficial consideration will reveal that, whilst it certainly is not an over-complex case, it is very far from trivial. The reactions of the members of the TC8 family varied enormously. Some thought it so well defined that the problem statement, in their view, amounted to a full systems requirement definition, i.e. there seemed nothing more to be "designed". On the other hand there were those who considered it so ill-structured that an extensive formalization would be required before even the first design step might be dreamt of ....

The review committee had no easy task. Originally, it was thought that the spectrum to be covered would be one-dimensional. Process-orientation on the one hand ("which processes will serve to provide our organization with the information it needs") and data-orientation on the other ("how do we design such a flexible database that any information needed may be derived easily") seemed to be the two poles. As the reader will find out the world of information systems is more complex. Apart from the information requirement side there are the organizational repercussions that keep interfering with the design process (as reflected in the formalism and the nature of the documentation insisted on), there is the shift of emphasis on different aspects in different phases, there is the varying importance attached to the logical flow, the efficiency, the data independance, the process independance, and so forth. But it is up to the reader to illuminate himself from the pages that follow.

A working conference of this kind would have been impossible without the assistance of a number of persons. Of these I will mention only two. One, in fact, I have already introduced: Bill Olle, who came up with the idea in the first place and then saw it through all of its painstaking steps to realization. The other is Henk Sol, who was never deterred by his normally (or rather abnormally) busy life to do what is required of an Organizing Committee Chairman. All this without the aid of a computer-supported system ....


Alex Verrijn-Stuart
WC General Chairman

# TABLE OF CONTENTS


CRIS:  An Introduction     v
A.A. VERRIJN-STUART

Comparative Review of Information Systems Design Methodologies -
Stage 1: Taking Stock
T.W. OLLE     1

IFIP WG 8.1 Case Solved using Sysdoc and Systemator
F. ASCHIM and B.M. MOSTUE     15

Active and Passive Component Modelling: ACM/PCM
M.L. BRODIE and E. SILVA     41

A Declarative Approach to Conceptual Information Modeling
M.R. GUSTAFSSON, T. KARLSSON and J.A. BUBENKO, JR.     93

SDLA, System Descriptor and Logical Analyzer
E. KNUTH, F. HÁLASZ and P. RADÓ     143

The ISAC Approach to Specification of Information Systems
and its Application to the Organization of an IFIP
Working Conference
M. LUNDEBERG     173

System Development in a Shared Data Environment,
the D2S2 Methodology
I.G. MACDONALD and I.R. PALMER     235

DADES: A Methodology for Specification and Design of
Information Systems
A. OLIVÉ     285

IML-Inscribed High-Level Petri Nets
G. RICHTER and R. DURCHHOLZ     335

The Remora Methodology for Information Systems Design and Management
C. ROLLAND and C. RICHARD 369

The Evolutionary Design Methodology applied to Information Systems
G. RZEVSKI, D.B. TRAFFORD and M. WELLS 427

A Draft Proposal for Integrating System Specification Models
A. SØLVBERG 475

NIAM: An Information Analysis Method
G.M.A. VERHEIJEN and J. VAN BEKKUM 537

The User Software Engineering Methodology:  An Overview
A.I. WASSERMAN 591

EPILOGUE 629

Active and Passive Component Modelling: ACM/PCM
by M.L. Brodie and E. Silva
Reviewed by R. TRAUNMÜLLER 631

The ISAC Approach to Specification of Information Systems and its
Application to the Organization of an IFIP Working Conference
by M. Lundeberg
Reviewed by A.G. DALE 633

System Development in a Shared Data Environment,
the D2S2 Methodology,  by I.G. MacDonald and I.R. Palmer
Reviewed by T. SKOUSEN 635

The Remora Methodology for Information Systems Design
and Management,  by C. Rolland and C. Richard
Reviewed by C. TULLY 639

A Draft Proposal for Integrating System Specification Models
by A. Sølvberg
Reviewed by B.K. BRUSSAARD 641

NIAM: An Information Analysis Method, by G.M.A. Verheijen
and J. van Bekkum
Reviewed by J.R.S. KISTRUCK 643

The User Software Engineering Methodology: An Overview
by A.I. Wasserman
Reviewed by P.J.H. KING 647

*INFORMATION SYSTEMS DESIGN METHODOLOGIES: A Comparative Review*
*T.W. Olle, H.G. Sol, A.A. Verrijn-Stuart (editors)*
*North-Holland Publishing Company*
© *IFIP, 1982*

COMPARATIVE REVIEW OF INFORMATION SYSTEMS DESIGN METHODOLOGIES
Stage 1: Taking Stock

Dr. T. William Olle

T. William Olle Associates Ltd.
2 Ashley Park Road
Walton-on-Thames
Surrey KT12 1JU
England

This paper serves to explain the aims of the first stage of
the IFIP WG8.1 exercise organized in support of the aims of
that group.  The paper outlines the various parts of the
first stage with emphasis on the in-depth review process
which was performed.


BACKGROUND

The Comparative Review of Information Systems Design Methodologies was first
discussed at the June 1979 meeting of IFIP WG8.1 held in Bonn.

IFIP WG8.1 whose title is "Design and Evaluation of Information Systems" has as
its approved scope of work the following:

> "the development of approaches for the analysis, design, specification
> and evaluation of computer assisted information systems".

In view of the fact that there are already innumerable approaches of the kind
which the scope of work suggests should be developed, it seemed inappropriate
for the Working Group to develop further such approaches without first undertaking
some kind of systematic study of the existing state of the art.

The idea was put forward of organizing an exercise around some kind of standard
test case.  It was felt that it might be ill-advised to launch a test case on the
information systems design community without some kind of a dry run.

A test case was developed concerned with conference organisation.  It seemed high
time to get away from purchasing systems and from course and classroom scheduling
systems which have been the mainstay of everyone's presentation of their design
methodology for many years.

Members of Working Group 8.1 volunteered to prepare and present a methodology at
the following meeting of the group held near Paris in 1980.  These presentations
occupied most of the two day meeting.  As a result of the dry runs, the test case
was refined and it was agreed that there must be some kind of question and answer
possibility available to participants.

The IFIP TC8 Committee of National Representatives approved the first stage of
the exercise at their meeting held also in June 1980 immediately after the WG8.1
meeting.  Approval by the IFIP General Assembly followed in October 1980 and this
introduced the period of publicity.

The first stage of the exercise can be broken down into four periods as follows:

1.  October 1980 to March 1981          Publicity
2.  March 1981 to September 1981        Prepare submissions
3.  September 1981 to January 1982      Review submissions
4.  January 1982 to May 1982            Conference registration.

PUBLICITY AND LETTERS OF INTENT

The Publicity period was more than just publicity and a call for contributions.
All who wrote to the Secretariat about the exercise were sent a copy of the
Problem Definition for the test case (see Appendix 1 to this paper) and some preliminary instructions.  The need for a Letter of Intent by 15 March 1981 was
emphasized.  By this date, over 50 Letters of Intent had been received from many
countries.

This number gave cause for concern.  One of the aims of the exercise was to ensure
that each submission was thoroughly reviewed.  Since a submission was intended to
be around 20,000 words, it was hard to expect any reviewer to handle more than 5
or 6 submissions.  In addition, there was a necessary limit on the size of the
Review Committee.

The Review Committee held its first meeting in March 1981 in San Francisco in conjunction with a meeting of WG8.1.  The main purpose of the meeting was to develop
a first draft of the Review Format.

At this meeting also, the all-important review philosophy was discussed at length.
It was agreed that the Review Committee should not approach the review process
with some agreed concept of an ideal methodology against which all submissions
should be measured.  The aim of the review process was rather to select a number
of methodologies which best represented the spectrum of information systems design
methodologies.

QUESTIONS AND ANSWERS

As agreed at the 1980 meeting of WG8.1, provision was included in the exercise for
the prospective submitters to ask the questions they would like to be able to ask
of a real life information user for whom the system was to be designed.

A surprisingly small number of those who had sent in a Letter of Intent took advantage of this opportunity.  Only eleven submitters asked questions about the
test case problem definition.  Some asked one or two fairly innocent questions.
Other submitters sent in several pages of in-depth questions about IFIP, about
Working Conferences and all kinds of related topics.  It was clear that many of
the potential submitters were not too well informed about IFIP as an organisation.

As a matter of policy, all questions and all answers were sent to all who had sent
in a Letter of Intent.

BOUNDARIES OF THE EXERCISE

Some of the discussions during the dry run and several of the questions brought
out a fairly significant problem.  There are clearly very different scopes assigned to the term "information systems design methodology".  When the exercise
was initially conceived, it was with the aim of reviewing methodologies for designing information systems, once it has been clearly agreed that a system is
needed and indeed what kind of system (in broad lines) is needed.

It was clearly brought out that some methodologies embody procedures and techniques for ascertaining whether or not a system is needed and, if so, what kind of system.  Every attempt was made to clarify that such considerations were outside the scope of the exercise.  Even so, some submitters obviously felt that these considerations were an inherent part of their methodology quite independently of whether they were part of the exercise or not and chose not to draw the line between "establishing need" and "design".


SUBMISSION PREPARATION

The submitters were allowed the five summer months of 1981 to prepare their submissions.  Again it must be emphasised they were being asked for 20,000 words and not the typical 5,000 words requested for most papers submitted for conferences.

During the submission period, another 26 Letters of Intent were received, making a total of 76.  Had this number of submissions been received, the effect on the exercise would have been nothing short of disasterous!

Clearly, many of the submitters of Letters of Intent balked at the task of preparing a 20,000 word paper.  The number of submissions which was finally received, namely 25, was just about ideal.  Each submission could be given five thorough reviews and the reviewers agreed to handle six submissions each.


REVIEW COMMITTEE

The Review Committee was chosen partly from among the WG8.1 membership, avoiding all who seemed likely to want to prepare a submission and one or two who were involved with some other WG8.1 activity.  In accordance with the IFIP TC8 practice on these matters, individuals from outside WG8.1 were invited as well. The final Review Committee contained 11 members of WG8.1 and 11 non-members (one of whom was a WG8.2 member).

An effort was made to ensure that the Review Committee membership was not drawn only from academic affiliations, and 9 of the 22 were from other affiliations than universities.  The group was, of course, highly international with members from 11 different countries.

The Review Committee worked extremely hard and its role in the exercise was considerably more than that of a typical Programme Committee.  It would be inappropriate to bury their names in an appendix and for this reason they are listed in Figure 1.


REVIEW PROCESS

It was agreed at the first meeting of the Review Committee that the aim of the review process was not to select the "seven best methodologies" for the simple reason that it was not clear how it would be possible at such an early stage to define what "best" meant.  While individuals might have opinions, the problem of reaching a committee concensus seemed insurmountable.

The aim then was to select "seven methodologies which best cover the existing spectrum of methodologies".  Inevitably, this gives rise to the problem of how to define the spectrum.  It was not clear that the spectrum had only one dimension, but it did seem apparent already from the dry runs in WG8.1 that some methodologies placed emphasis on the processes (or functions) to be performed by the system while others (influenced largely by the developments over the past two decades in data base technology) placed the emphasis on an analysis of the data

| | |
|---|---|
| Prof. T.M.A. Bemelmans | University of Eindhoven, Netherlands |
| Prof. F. Bodart | Institut d'Informatique, Namur, Belgium |
| Prof. G. Bracchi | Politecnic di Milano, Italy |
| Prof. B.K. Brussaard | Ministry of the Interior, The Hague, Netherlands |
| Prof. A.G. Dale | University of Texas at Austin, USA |
| Mr. K.-H. Dreckmann | ADV/ORGA F.A. Meyer GmbH, Wiesbaden, FR Germany |
| Mr. H. Kangassalo | University of Tampere, Finland |
| Prof. P. Kerola | University of Oulu, Finland |
| Prof. P.J.H. King | Birkbeck College, London, UK |
| Dr. R. Kistruck | SRI-Europe, Croydon, UK |
| Prof. M. Klein | CESA, Jouy-en-Josas, France |
| Mr. E.T. Lundquist | Infologigruppen, Stockholm, Sweden |
| Dr. S. Navathe | University of Florida, Gainsville, USA |
| Mr. M.A. Newton | Open University, Milton Keynes, UK |
| Dr. T.W. Olle (Chairman) | T. William Olle Assoc. Ltd., Walton-on-Thames, UK |
| Mr. A. Rochfeld | Societe d'Informatique et des Systemes, Paris, France |
| Dr. T. Skousen | Handelshøjskolen i København, Denmark |
| Dr. H.G. Sol | University of Groningen, Netherlands |
| Mr. J.M. Sykes | Imperial Chemical Industries Ltd., Wilmslow,UK |
| Dr. R. Traunmüller | Johannes Kepler Universität, Linz, Austria |
| Mr. C. Tully | University of York, UK |
| Dr. K. Voss | GMD, St. Augustin, FR Germany |

Figure 1.   Members of Review Committee for CRIS I

to be used in the system being designed.  In no way was this even regarded as a
black and white distinction.  This will be amplified later in this paper.

The Review Form used in the review process evolved into a form with five parts.
Parts 3 to 5 are included in their entirety in Appendix 2.  Part 1 of the form
was for each reviewer to summarise his ratings for all the submissions he reviewed
and Part 2 contained identification, overall recommended rating and general
questions on format.

Part 3 of the form was intended to help the Review Committee to place the submission in the overall spectrum.  The most important question was probably that
asking the reviewer to place the submission in one of five categories on the
process analysis/data analysis spectrum.  The second question in this part probed
into aspects of the methodology which could not be categorised as data analysis
or process analysis.  The third question examined how the overall design activity
was to be partitioned by the methodology into clearly defined disjoint sub-tasks.

Further questions in Part 3 sought the reviewers' opinion on unique features,
methodologies to which the object methodolgy was felt to be similar, applicability

to a wide range of information systems, and whether the methodology was commercial or research and whether it was computerised in any way.

Part 4 of the form contained sixteen questions on the methodology and Part 5 contained 20 questions on the handling of the test case. The 20 questions on the handling of the test case included one question on each of the 13 activities the information system was intended to support. It should be noted that these 13 correspond to those in the Problem Definition (Appendix 1).

A brief scan of the questions in Parts 4 and 5 will indicate that many of these questions might  well be open to interpretation by a reviewer who had not been able to attend the meeting at which the rationale for the questions had been discussed and identified. (The two initial meetings of the Review Committee had each attracted about half of the members.)

In order to counteract this effect to some extent, a set of notes on the questions was prepared and circulated to each reviewer.

The reviewers were asked to answer the questions in Parts 4 and 5 by means of a rating between 0 and 10. The following list cites the interpretation of each of the 11 possible ratings.

        10    Perfect
         9    Almost perfect
         8    Good
         7    Better than average
         6    Just above average
         5    Average
         4    Just less than average
         3    Rather less than average
         2    Poor
         1    Negligible or token support
         0    No evidence of any support.

A few reviewers found difficulty in assigning ratings to the handling of the test case, specifically the 13 questions dealing with how the activities were handled.


RESULTS OF THE REVIEW PROCESS

In this section presenting the results of the review process, it must be emphasized that only general trends are discussed and that every attempt is made to preserve the anonymity of the submitters and the reviewers.

The first most striking aspect of the review process was the variation in assigning ratings to submissions by the reviewers. For the methodology only, the following figures emerged:

| | |
|---|---|
| Possible maximum | 160 |
| Highest average by a reviewer | 111 |
| Observed mean | 84.6 |
| "All fives" | 80 |
| Lowest average by a reviewer | 64 |
| Minimum | 0 |

For the test case, the figures were even more extreme,

| | |
|---|---|
| Possible maximum | 200 |
| Highest average by a reviewer | 180 |
| Observed mean | 113 |
| "All fives" | 100 |
| Lowest average by a reviewer | 77 |
| Minimum | 0 |

It would clearly have been unfair on certain submitters to have simply accepted the markings and based any judgments on the aggregate marks for each submission.

The marks were therefore normalised about the observed means in each case. This has the effect of clustering the marks more closely about the means such that the maximum and minimum normalised ratings for the methodology were 100 and 86 respectively and for the test case 114 and 44 respectively.

Several quite highly rated methodologies were noted in submissions with very lowly rated test cases and the number of submissions which had done a good job in these quantitative terms in presenting the methodology and handling the test case was quite small. However, it is important to note that the quantitative ratings on methodology and test case were taken as advisory only by the Review Committee during the deliberations at its final meeting. Several other factors were also taken into account, not least of which was the recommendation of each reviewer in Part 2 of the Review Form.

On the question of the "spectrum" discussed earlier in this paper, the results of this analysis were quite interesting. Once again there was a disparity among the reviewers with only one submission receiving a unanimous classification by all five reviewers involved.

It was possible to summarise the categorisations in such a way that a submission could be placed in one of three broad categories. These categories with the number of different submissions in each were as follows:

| | |
|---|---|
| Emphasis on data analysis | 11 |
| Equal emphasis | 6 |
| Emphasis on process analysis | 8 |

When the results of this broad categorisation were co-related with the ratings of the methodology, it was very clear that the methodologies with an emphasis on data analysis were in general more highly rated than those in the other two categories. Furthermore, those with equal emphasis were somewhat less clearly more highly rated than those in which the emphasis was on process analysis.

The two extreme categories (see Question 1.1 in Part 3 of the Review Form) were hardly used at all by the reviewers and the most used category was the middle one. This seems to indicate an emerging recognition that a methodology needs to provide for both data analysis and process analysis and cannot be successful if it is restricted to one or the other.

Another factor taken into account was the uniqueness of a methodology. In one or two cases the Review Committee felt that a methodology should be included because it offered something unusual even though the methodology might not have been so highly rated.

The third and final meeting of the Review Committee was a two day one and there
was considerable discussion about the best way to select the methodologies for
presentation at the Working Conference and for inclusion in the proceedings.
The Committee's final decision was also influenced by the size and related cost
of the proceedings.  Thirteen of the twentyfive submissions were in fact selected.
Seven of the thirteen were selected for presentation at a half day plenary session.
The other six were selected for presentation at an evening session.  All thirteen
are included in this proceedings.

Apart from a few general comments in this paper, the first stage has been restricted to taking stock.  Some comparative assessment by the Review Committee
has been inevitable in order to make the selection.


FUTURE WORK

Having taken stock of available methodologies, the next step has been to organise
the next stage with the theme of "comparative feature analysis".  This has been
planned for July 1983 in York in England.  Papers have been invited which make a
comparative analysis of the features to be found in several methodologies.  The
methodologies analysed are expected to include several of those included in this
proceedings.

COMPARATIVE REVIEW OF INFORMATION SYSTEMS DESIGN METHODOLOGIES

<u>Problem Definition</u>

## 1.  Background

An IFIP Working Conference is an international conference intended to bring together experts from all IFIP countries to discuss some technical topic of specific interest to one or more IFIP Working Groups. The usual procedure, and that
to be considered for the present purposes, is an invited conference which is not
open to everyone. For such conferences it is something of a problem to ensure that
members of the involved IFIP Working Group(s) and Technical Committee(s) are invited even if they do not come. Furthermore, it is important to ensure that sufficient people attend the conference so that the financial break-even point is
reached without exceeding the maximum dictated by the facilities available.

IFIP Policy on Working Conferences suggest the appointment of a Program Committee
to deal with the technical content of the conference and an Organising Committee
to handle financial matters, local arrangements, and invitations and/or publicity.
These committees clearly need to work together closely and have a need for common
information and to keep their recorded information consistent and up to date.

## 2.  Information system to be designed

The information system which is to be designed is that necessary to support the
activities of both a Program Committee and an Organising Committee involved in
arranging an IFIP Working Conference. The involvementof the two committees is seen
as analogous to two organisational entities within a corporate structure using
some common information.

The following activities of the committees should be supported.

<u>Program Committee:</u>

1.      Preparing a list to whom the call for papers is to be sent.

2.      Registering the letters of intent received in response to the call.

3.      Registering the contributed papers on receipt.

4.      Distributing the papers among those undertaking the refereeing.

5.      Collecting the referees´reports and selecting the papers for inclusion
        in the program.

6.      Grouping selected papers into sessions for presentation and selecting
        chairman for each session.

<u>Organising Committee</u>:

1.      Preparing a list of people to invite to the conference.

2.      Issuing priority invitations to National Representatives, Working
        Group members and members of associated working groups.

3.      Ensuring all authors of each selected paper receive an invitation.

4.      Ensuring authors of rejected papers receive an invitation.

5.      Avoiding sending duplicate invitations to any individual.

6.      Registering acceptance of invitations.

7.      Generating finallist of attendees.


## 3.   Boundaries of system

It should be noted that budgeting and financial aspects of the Organising Commit-
tee´s work, meeting plans of both committees, hotel accomodation for attendees and
the matter of preparing camera ready copy of the proceedings have been omitted
from this exercise, although a submission may include some or all of these extra
aspects if the authors feel so motivated.

COMPARATIVE REVIEW OF INFORMATION SYSTEMS DESIGN METHODOLOGIES

<u>REVIEW FORM</u>

General questions to place submission in overall spectrum.

1.      Data analysis and process analysis.
1.1.  In which of the following five categories would you place the
       methodology (tick one).
       A. Pure process analysis
       B. Process analysis with some data analysis   ____
       C. Equal weight
       D. Data analysis with some process analysis   ____
       E. Pure data analysis

1.2.  In a case where B or D is selected, what is your estimate of
       the percentage of the methodology concerned with process
       analysis (B should be more than 50, D should be less that 50).   ________

2.      List aspects of methodology as presented which cannot be
       classified as process analysis or data analysis.

       1. ________________________________________________________
       2. ________________________________________________________
       3. ________________________________________________________

3.      Partitioning the design activity.
3.1.  Does the methodology require partitioning of the overall design
       activity into disjoint sub-tasks which are clearly defined in the
       submission? (Answer Yes or No) ______________

3.2.  If so, list these sub-tasks, using the sequence and terminology
       of the submission.

       1. ________________________________________________________
       2. ________________________________________________________
       3. ________________________________________________________
       4. ________________________________________________________
       5. ________________________________________________________
       6. ________________________________________________________
       7. ________________________________________________________

4.      Is the methodology as described implemented on a computer? ____________

5.      Unique and non-unique factors.
5.1.  Is the methodology unique in some sense compared with other
       methodologies known to you (not only those submitted for the
       exercise)? If so, state how.

_______________________________________________
_______________________________________________
_______________________________________________
_______________________________________________

5.2.	If the methodology is similar to one or more other known
	methodologies, then list these using the acronym assigned by
	the submitter for this exercise where appropriate.

	___________________	___________________	___________________
	___________________	___________________	___________________
	___________________	___________________	___________________

5.3.	Is the methodology a combination of other known methodologies?
	If so, which?

	___________________	___________________	___________________


6.	Applicability.
6.1.	Is the methodology applicable to a wide range of information
	systems? ___________

6.2.	If not, what kinds of information system do you feel it would
	not be useful for? _________________________________________


7.	Commercial or research.
7.1.	Does the submission give the impression that the methodology
	is commercially available? _________________________________

## Methodology ratings

How do you rate the following aspects of the part of the submission presenting the methodology? (See notes on assigning ratings).

1. Comprehensibility and clarity.

2. Conciseness.

3. Quality of terminology used in the methodology.

4. Ease of use in an average systems development environment.

5. Justification for the methodology explained.

6. Basis for the methodology sound.

7. Extent to which methodology leaves problem oriented design decisions to the application programmer responsible for constructing the system (0 high, 10 low).

8. Extent to which methodology provides a specification at one or two early stages which can be used to evaluate the advisability of continuing with the subsequent stages.

9. Extent to which methodology provides methods and tools for a requirements analysis.

10. Quality of system specification produced using the methodology.

11. Quality of partitioning into sub-tasks listed in General Questions 3.2.

12. Extent to which methodology supports the detection of design flaws.

13. Extent to which methodology supports the detection on incomplete design.

14. Extent to which methodology allows for quantitive estimates of aspects relevant to data system performance.

15. Extent to which methodology provides tools and means to check whether the specifications produced using the methodology meet the requirements input to it.

16. Extent to which the methodology is cost effective in terms of the designer's daily salary.

<u>Rating of handling of test case</u>

How do you rate the following aspects of the part of the submission presenting the handling of the test case?

1.   Comprehensibility and clarity.

2.   Conciseness.

3.   Extent to which methodology handles test case <u>without</u> contrived tricks.

4.   Extent to which results presented in the treatment of the test case arise from strict application of the methodology as described in the first part of the submission versus the part which appears to be based on the author's own intuition and experience.

5.   Extent to which resulting specifications are usable by individuals involved in constructing the system, including the average application programmer.

6.   Extent to which the resulting specifications are understandable by the responsible end user who may want to have the system modified to meet new requirements.

7.   Extent to which an average application programmer can rapidly learn to read and use the kind of specifications illustrated in the handling of the test case.

8.   To what extent does the system as designed support the following activities of the Programma Committee of an IFIP Working Conference.

8.1. Preparing a list of persons to whom the call for papers is to be sent.

8.2. Registering the letters of intent received in response to the call.

8.3. Registering contributed papers on receipt.

8.4. Distributing papers among those undertaking the refereeing.

8.5. Collecting the referees' reports and selecting the papers for inclusion in the programme.

8.6. Grouping selected papers into sessions for presentation and selecting a chairman for each session.

9.   To what extent does the system as designed support the following activities of the Organising Committee of an IFIP Working Conference.

9.1. Preparing a list of people to invite to the conference.

Page 5.

9.2. Issuing priority invitations to National Representatives, Working Group members and members of associated Working Groups.          _________

9.3. Ensuring all authors of each selected paper receive an invitation.          _________

9.4. Ensuring authors of rejected papers receive an invitation.          _________

9.5. Avoid sending duplicate invitations to any individual.          _________

9.6. Registering acceptance of invitations.          _________

9.7. Generating final list of attendees.          _________

*INFORMATION SYSTEMS DESIGN METHODOLOGIES: A Comparative Review*
*T.W. Olle, H.G. Sol, A.A. Verrijn-Stuart (editors)*
*North-Holland Publishing Company*
© *IFIP, 1982*

# IFIP WG 8.1 CASE SOLVED USING SYSDOC AND SYSTEMATOR

Frode Aschim
SYSDECO A/S, P.O. Box 138 - Taasen, Oslo 8, Norway

Bernt M. Mostue
Central Institute for Industrial Research
Forskningsvn. 1, P.O. Box 350, Blindern, Oslo 3, Norway

This paper gives a brief overview of SYSDOC and SYSTEMATOR. SYSDOC
is an information system design methodology while SYSTEMATOR is a
unique software tool which gives computer aid for all phases of the
information system development process. In the second half of the
paper we outline how SYSDOC and SYSTEMATOR can be used for solving
the IFIP WG 8.1 Conference Organization case.

## INTRODUCTION

SYSDOC®  is an information system design methodology developed in 1974 by
Frode Aschim and K.A. Braaten from the Central Institute for Industrial Research,
Oslo, Norway. The initial development was done in cooperation with the Norwegian
State Railways. Since then the SYSDOC methodology has been extended and improved
based on practical experience with the methodology in a large number of projects
in industry and in the public sector.

In 1975 work was started to develop a computer aid in the information system
development process. This work resulted in SYSTEMATOR which is a unique software
tool which gives computer aid to all phases of the information system development
process. One of the unique features of SYSTEMATOR is that it contains the complete mapping of the requirements into the design. SYSTEMATOR also contains
modules for proposing designs from the requirements.

SYSTEMATOR was developed at the Central Institute for Industrial Research with
Frode Aschim (until 1980) and later Bernt Mostue as project leader.

SYSDOC® and SYSTEMATOR® are commercially available products marketed by
SYSDECO A/S, P.O. Box 138 - Taasen, Oslo 8, Norway.


## SYSDOC METHODOLOGY AND SYSTEMATOR OVERVIEW

The SYSDOC methodology is primarily data-oriented (while most available methodologies are primarily functionally-oriented) with emphasis on information system
requirement specification. Functions are primarily described by describing their
processing rules in a very high level language.

The conceptual datamodel using the concepts found in natural language is the
focal point of the SYSDOC methodology. In addition the methodology is used for
designing and describing the user interface. All this is done in an implementation independent manner.

---

SYSDOC® is a registered trade mark belonging to Central Institute for Industrial
Research, Blindern, Oslo 3, Norway.

                     *F. Aschim and B.M. Mostue*

The starting point in the system life cycle for the SYSDOC methodology is a
problem definition giving the main objectives of a proposed system. The SYSDOC
methodology is then used for describing the concepts and the terminology to be
used by the end user, and the relationships between the concepts. The result is
an integrated conceptual datamodel. This is supplemented with a complete
description of the user interface including data content, layout, user dialog
and processing rules for all the inputs, reports and screen-displays in the
system. The user dialog and processing rules are expressed in a formal, very
high level language (SYSDUL).

The resulting system specification is thus a complete specification where transactions have been "abstract programmed" in SYSDUL using the conceptual datamodel
as the database. Such high level programs which are completely implementation
independent are called "Abstract programs" (term invented by Christer Jaderlund).

SYSTEMATOR is a collection of computer programs which are used together with the
SYSDOC methodology. It contains modules for storing, modifying, documenting and
analysing system requirements. Thus it has the type of analysis capability found
in systems like PSL/PSA [1] and SREM [2] allowing identification of data which
are stored, but never used, used but never stored, etc.

SYSTEMATOR is capable of producing a large number of requirement reports and can
also document the conceptual datamodel or subsets of it using graphical tools.
Resource estimates and database design aid reports may also be produced [5]. But
unlike other specification systems on the market, SYSTEMATOR can also be used
for the physical design process.

The mapping from conceptual datamodel to physical datamodel(s) is described in
a mapping language and SYSTEMATOR generates the DDL for the database. This mapping information is then used by the SYSTEMATOR program generator to produce
COBOL or FORTRAN programs from the "Abstract programs".

How transactions should be combined into modules are also described in a special
language. SYSTEMATOR then generates the necessary files and programs.


BRIEF DESCRIPTION OF THE SYSDOC METHODOLOGY

The SYSDOC methodology is basically a methodology for arriving at a requirement
specification expressed in an implementation independent manner. This requirement
specification may automatically or under designer control be transformed into a
complete system using SYSTEMATOR. The requirement specification can be divided
into three main parts:

    a)  The description of the conceptual datamodel.
    b)  The description of the information system user interface.
    c)  The description of the manual procedures.

All three are described using diagrams to give an overview and forms to record
detail. In addition the first two of these are partly described in a formal
language. This section describes the main concepts used for describing a) and
b) above while the steps to go through in applying the methodology are outlined
in the case study in the second half of this paper.

SYSDOC CONCEPTUAL DATAMODELLING CONCEPTS
A SYSDOC conceptual datamodel contains three main types of concepts; entity
types, relationship types and data element types. These concepts can however be
elementary, derived, generalized or grouped. These main concepts and their
different categories will be described in this section.

ELEMENTARY CONCEPTS.  <u>Entity type</u>. An entity type description is a description
of the general rules that apply and the properties which the entities of that
type may have. An entity may be a physical object, an abstract object or an
event. The entity type description also includes cardinality information such
as the maximum number of entities of the type.

An entity occurrence corresponds roughly to nouns in natural language.

<u>Relationship type</u>.  A relationship type description is a description of one
particular type of relationship that may exist between the entity occurrences.
A relationship type may be of degree one to one, one to many or many to many.

The relationship type description contains information regarding what entity
types the relationship may involve, whether the relationship membership is
optional or mandatory for entity occurrences of the type and cardinality
information.

A relationship type corresponds roughly to a verb or predicate in natural
language. The "inverse" of a relationship is handled in SYSDOC by giving
context dependent names to a relationship where the context is given by the
starting point of a sentence (the subject).

        Example:
            "The Person X owns the Car Y"
              is equivalent (informationwise) to the sentence
            "The Car Y has-as-owner Person X"

In SYSDOC these two sentences are considered to describe the same relationship
(Say R1). In the context of a PERSON (Person is Subject) this relationship is
called "owns" and in the context of a CAR it is called "has-as-owner". (The
hyphen "between" the words has been introduced to simplify syntax analysis.)

<u>Note</u>! Relationships in SYSDOC do <u>not</u> have any attributes as opposed to for
instance the ERA model [3]. A "relationship" having attributes is by definition
an entity. (All entity types may, however, be made invisible to certain users
who may <u>view</u> such entities as relationships.)

<u>Data element type</u>.  A data element type description contains a definition of its
type and description of length, integrity constraints, default report and screen
headings, etc. The type of information given is similar to what is found in most
data dictionary systems with the exception that no implementation dependent
information is given, only description of the format as it appears on a screen
or a piece of paper to an external user.

A data element type normally describes an attribute of one entity type, but may
apply to several. The same data element type may also describe several attributes of one entity type by using "concept-qualifiers". For instance

        PLANNED.DEPARTURE-TIME
and
        REAL.DEPARTURE-TIME

are an example of the same data element type used with different concept-
qualifiers to describe two different attributes of possibly the same entity
type (e.g. FLIGHT).

An occurrence of a data element type has meaning only in the context of an entity
or if it is global (describing a global entity) such as DATE. A data element
occurrence thus can not stand alone. It is therefore not surprising that a data
element type roughly corresponds to what follows after a "transitive verb" in
natural language.

DERIVED CONCEPT TYPES.  The three concepts described in the previous section may be elementary or derived.

<u>Elementary concept</u>.  An elementary concept is a concept for which an occurrence of the concept must be given to the information system from the outside.

<u>Derived concept</u>.  A derived concept is a concept for which an occurrence of the concept may be derived by the information system from elementary concepts given to the information system from the outside.

<u>Derived data element type</u>. The average weight of a group of PERSONS may be derived (calculated) by the information system if the weight of the different persons exists in the information system. Average weight is therefore a derived data element type in an information base containing the weight of the persons.

<u>Derived entity type</u>. A derived entity is an entity made up of information from two or more entity occurrences (of the same or a different entity type). For instance is it possible to define MARRIED-COUPLE as a derived entity type in an information base containing information about PERSON's and their BIRTH, DEATH, MARRIAGE and DIVORCE.

<u>Derived relationship type</u>. A derived relationship type is a relationship which can be derived using one elementary relationship and one or more dataelements or two or more elementary relationships.

An example of a derived relationship type is shown on the diagram below:

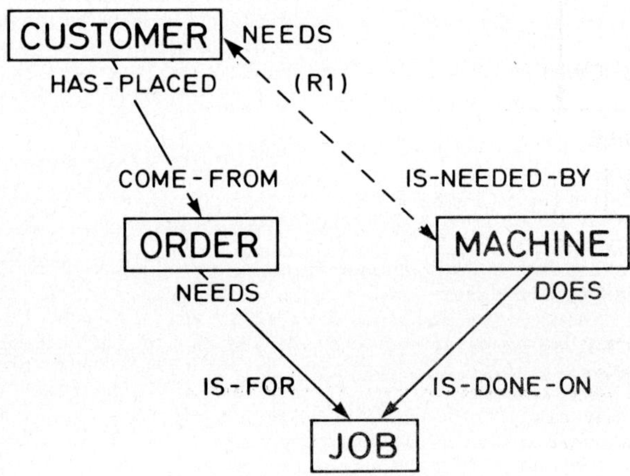


Fig. 1.   Example showing a derived relationship type.

The relationship type marked R1 and drawn with a dotted line is a derived relationship type. It may be used to answer questions such as which customers may be effected by a breakdown of a particular MACHINE, information which may be derived using the three elementary relationship types on the diagram.

<u>Description of derivation rules</u>. The derivation rules for derived entity types, derived relationship types and derived data element types are described in the same very high level language used for making the Abstract programs (SYSDUL). An example of derivation rule for a derived data item type, which is an attribute of CUSTOMER in the example in Figure 1 is given below:

```
NO-OF OPEN ORDERS =
      NUMBER OF ORDERS WITH STATUS-CODE EQ ˆOPENˆ WHICH CUSTOMER HAS PLACED
```

CONCEPTS USED TO DESCRIBE ALTERNATIVES AND GENERALIZATION.  It is useful to
have a way of describing alternatives in conceptual datamodels just like in
computer programming. It is also very convenient to describe common information
only once. The concepts used to do this with SYSDOC are briefly described in the
rest of this section.

<u>Generalized entity type</u>. The "generalized entity type" concept is used in SYSDOC
to express that a given entity occurrence may be considered as being of different type in different contexts (overlapping types). An example showing two
generalized entity types are shown on the diagram in Figure 2.

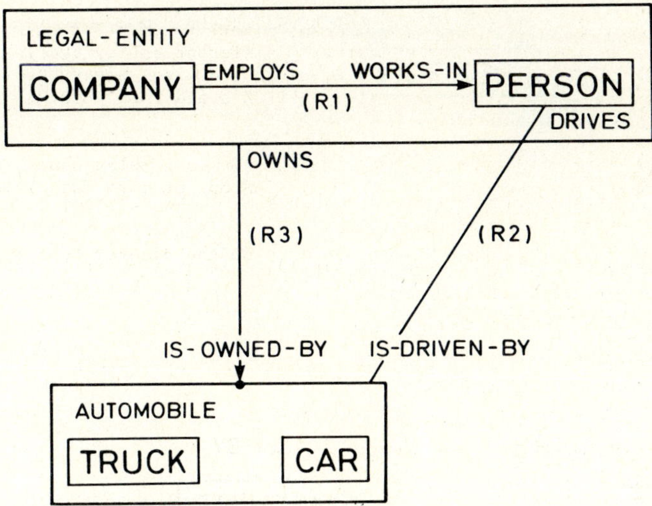


Fig. 2.  Example showing two generalized entity types.

Corporations and persons may both own cars (they are both LEGAL ENTITY), but
only persons may drive cars.

Generalized entity types may also be viewed as a mechanism for describing alternatives. In the example above a legal entity is either a company or a person.

The concept of generalized entity types is similar to what Smith and Smith [4]
in 1979 called generalization. This concept was introduced in SYSDOC in 1974 and
experience has shown that this is a very useful concept especially in applications concerning complex datastructures (eg. CAD). An elementary entity type may
be part of many generalized entity types not necessarily overlapping and not
necessarily organized in a hierarchical fashion.

An entity occurrence which is part of a generalized entity type has all the
attributes of its elementary entity type and all attributes of the generalized
entity types it is part of. (E.g. a CAR may have the data element types defined
for CAR and the data element types defined for automobiles and may participate in
all relationship types a car or an automobile may participate in.)

<u>Generalized relationship type</u>. A generalized relationship type is describing
that two relationship types are alternatives for a pair of entity occurrences
participating. The example in Figure 3 illustrates this:

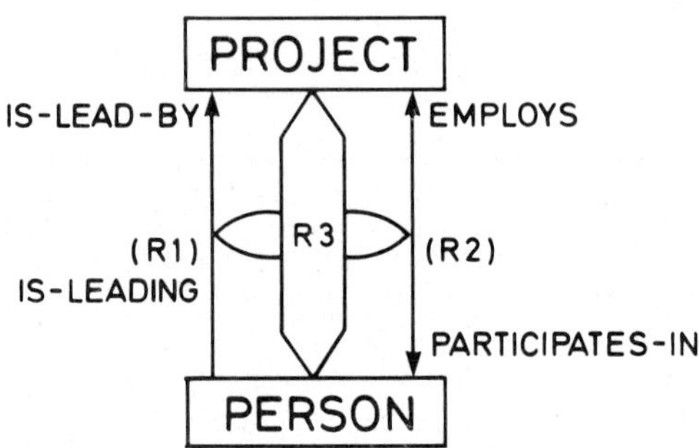


Fig. 3.   Example illustrating a composite relationship type.

The project leader (relationship R1) of a project should not at the same time
also be an ordinary participant in the project (relationship R2). To express
this constraint a generalized relationship (R3) can be introduced. This relationship can also be used to find all persons engaged on a project (i.e. the union
of R1 and R2).

<u>Alternative data element type</u>. An alternative data element type is simply a name
given to two or more data element types which are alternatives in the sense that
only one of them may exist for one entity occurrence or an input/report.

The "general" information given for an alternative data element type is whether
the alternative may or must exist in a certain context.

NAMED SUBSETS OF ENTITY TYPES.  It is often practical to name certain subsets
of an entity type. For instance the entity type PERSON may be subdivided into
married, divorced, pensioned, etc., often with complex rules to define them
(e.g. pensioned). With SYSDOC such subsets may be given a name and used just
like other entity types by users of the information base. But they may not be
stored. In the example above only persons may be stored (never pensioned, they
become pensioned when they fulfill the condition of becoming one e.g. the day
they become 67 years).

The subsets are defined by giving a subsetting criterion expressed in SYSDUL,
and may overlap.

<u>EXAMPLE</u>
      PENSIONED ARE:
      PERSONS (WITH AGE GE 67) OR
      (WITH AGE GE 60 AND PROFESSION EQ FIREMAN)


CONCEPTS FOR GROUPS

<u>Group of data element types</u>. A group of individual data element types may be
given a name. The main purpose is ease of reference.

<u>Subsets of the conceptual datamodels</u>. Subsets of the datamodel may be defined by giving a "scope". This is a criterion to be met by the elements to be included and/or a listing of elements to include/exclude. This is used for defining user views (always a strict subset) and subsets of the documentation.


SUMMARY OF CONCEPTS

Table 1.  Summary of SYSDOC main datamodelling concepts.

TYPE OF CONCEPT

| Basic concept name | Elementary | Derived | Generalized (alternatives) | Named subset | Named group |
|---|---|---|---|---|---|
| Entity type | X | X | X | X | |
| Relationship type | X | X | X | | |
| Data element type | X | X | X | | X |
| Mixture of above | | | | | X |


USER INTERFACE DESCRIPTION
The user interface description may be done with varying degree of detail. On the most detailed level of description the user interface description contains:

a)   Description of the end users of the system.
b)   Description of data content, data structure and layout of screens,
     reports and inputs (transactions in short).
c)   Time and volume information showing how often and when
     the different transactions are used.
d)   Description of the processing rules (those not already defined
     as part of the conceptual datamodel) and the user dialog for
     the transactions.

The languages used for this are a mixture of forms (with corresponding screens for data entry) and the SYSDUL language.

Space does not permit a thorough description of this in this paper. The reader is referred to the solution of the IFIP WG 8.1 case study for further details.


BRIEF DESCRIPTION OF THE SYSTEMATOR MODULES

The SYSTEMATOR modules can roughly be divided into two main parts:

   a)   Modules for requirements specification.
   b)   Modules for system implementation.

All modules are accessible through SYSTEMATOR's common user interface where the user gets access to the required module by selecting from simple menues or answering questions. All modules which require dialogue with the user are on-line and use SYSTEMATOR's own screenhandling system. All other modules are run as separate jobs generated and initiated by SYSTEMATOR.

All information given to SYSTEMATOR is stored in SYSTEMATOR's internal database for later use. SYSTEMATOR is one of the few development tools using a database system for storing and retrieving data. The data base system used is portable. How the modules are integrated through the SYSTEMATOR database (integrated data dictionary) is illustrated on the diagram, Figure 4.

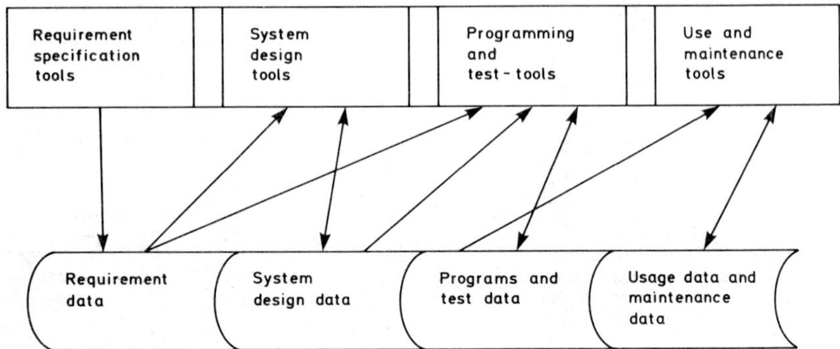


Fig. 4.   Integration of SYSTEMATOR modules through the database.

REQUIREMENT SPECIFICATION
There are modules for storing, modifying, documenting and analysing system
requirements.

DATAMODEL UPDATE  is an interactive module for storing and modifying detailed
descriptions of entity types, relationship types and data element types
(elementary, derived, composite or grouped).

USER INTERFACE UPDATE  is an interactive module for storing and modifying
descriptions of the inputs and outputs of the system. This includes descriptions
of data content, user dialogue, lay-out (screens) and the processing rules
"abstract programmed" in SYSDUL.

REQUIREMENT DOCUMENTATION.  A large number of reports can be requested including
specification-documentation reports, key-word reports and various specification-
analysis reports. The specification-analysis reports include syntax-analysis
reports for the "Abstract programs", reports showing data which are stored but
never used, used but never stored, etc. The datamodel or subsets of it may also
be documented using graphical tools. The required reports are requested interactively from SYSTEMATOR that initiates a separate job which produces the reports.

MODULES FOR SYSTEM IMPLEMENTATION
There are modules for describing and documenting an implemented system and
modules for generating one.

DATABASE DESIGN AND CREATION.  This module accepts as input a description of the
mapping from the conceptual datamodel to the physical datamodel(s), and stores
this information in the SYSTEMATOR database. Based on this information plus the
description of the conceptual datamodel, SYSTEMATOR generates the DDL for the
database. Everything  which is not mentioned in the mapping description is
implemented using default rules. The mapping description can be "empty". In that
case a functionally correct default database is generated based solely on the
description of the conceptual datamodel.

PROGRAM DESIGN, GENERATION AND TESTING.  The information given in the implementation description is used by the SYSTEMATOR program generator to produce
COBOL or FORTRAN programs from the "Abstract programs". One useful feature is
that a generated program can be run, and thus tested, initially under SYSTEMATOR
control without loading it separately.

DEFAULT SYSTEM DESIGN.  As mentioned in the section "DATABASE DESIGN AND
CREATION" SYSTEMATOR is capable of generating a functionally correct, but not
necessary optimal default database. SYSTEMATOR can also automatically generate
screen descriptions and programs for handling standard storing/changing/reading
of entity types. One can thus use SYSTEMATOR to generate a default prototype
system which can be used for experimenting with user-dialogues, etc.

SYSTEM DOCUMENTATION.  This module includes many of the same type of reports
mentioned in section "REQUIREMENT DOCUMENTATION", but they now document the
implemented system. It also includes maintenance reports such as which modules
have to be regenerated when a data element type is changed, which program has
to be reloaded, etc.

DEFINE SUBSYSTEM (SCOPE) OF INTEREST.  The user may define subsets of the datamodel which are to be included when the documentation or the actual system(s)
is generated. One can for instance divide the model in two and use two different
implementation descriptions to generate two databases using different Database
Management Systems.

SYSTEMATOR USAGE ADMINISTRATION.  This module keeps track of the users allowed
to update the SYSTEMATOR database, users allowed to regenerate programs, etc.
This module can also produce reports describing the use of SYSTEMATOR, such as
who was the last to update what, at what time, etc.


SYSDOC AND SYSTEMATOR USED FOR SOLVING THE IFIP WG 8.1 DESIGN CASE

The problem description was available and all interviews with users are considered done through answering the written questions. The case therefore starts
later in the system development process than is the case in normal projects. The
steps we went through to arrive at a running system is outlined in the following.

IDENTIFY THE USERS OF THE PROPOSED SYSTEM
The users may be divided into two main groups.

Direct users
Those users of a proposed information system who enter or retrieve data from
terminals.

Indirect Users
Those users who receive reports from or supply input to the system.

This gave the following lists:

Direct Users
Organizing Committee
Program Committee

Indirect Users
    Authors          Both Potential
    Referees        and
    Attendees     Real
    Chairmen
    IFIP board

Some of the indirect users are possible candidates for direct use (e.g. Referees).

The most important users in this case are the direct users, especially the
Program Committee.

MAKE LIST OF THE ENTITIES INVOLVED

A preliminary list of the entities involved was then made on a piece of paper where we added new entity types as we discovered them in the problem description or in the answers to questions. The method for doing this is primarily to read the problem description looking for nouns. If the noun referred to in a sentence is an occurrence of an object or event, we generalize the sentence by instead substituting the entity type.

This shall be illustrated by an example.

The first sentence in the problem definition is:

> "An IFIP Working conference is an international conference intended to bring together experts from all IFIP countries to discuss some technical topic of specific interest to one or more IFIP Working Group."

Analysing the different parts of this sentence is done as follows:

a)     "An IFIP Working Conference"

The pronoun An indicates that an entity type follows. IFIP-WORKING-CONFERENCE could be considered an entity type, but could also be generalized further by saying that CONFERENCE is the entity type. In that case conferences may have an attribute, for instance called conference-type, which has as one of its values WORKING, and another attribute type or relationship type the organizing organization of the conference (in this case IFIP).

The purpose of this information system is IFIP-WORKING-CONFERENCES and therefore in this particular case we will choose this as the entity type. But the same sentence analysed for the needs of a different information system might have given different results.

b)    - "is an international conference"

International may be considered an attribute of the entity type CONFERENCE but since in this case all IFIP-WORKING-CONFERENCES are international, it is not necessary to record this fact in the information base and therefore not include it in the datamodel.

c)    - "intended to bring together experts from all IFIP countries"

EXPERT could be considered to be an entity type but we chose to generalize the entity type by calling the entity type PERSON. Some persons will then have the attribute of being an expert.

COUNTRY may be considered as an entity type with one of its attributes being whether or not the country is an IFIP-country. As far as we could see, the information base only contains persons from IFIP-countries. Therefore we decided to use the less general entity type IFIP-COUNTRY as our entity type.

The rest of this part of the sentence refers to the relationship types between IFIP-WORKING-CONFERENCE and PERSON called "are intended to bring together" and between PERSON and IFIP-COUNTRY called "is from". The first of these relationships is a general description of the objective of WORKING-CONFERENCE and needs not be recorded in the information base. Instead the more specific relationship type between an IFIP-WORKING-CONFERENCE and those persons actually participating in the conference, will be recorded in the information base.

d)    - "to discuss some technical topics of specific
       interest to one or more IFIP working groups".

The entity types referred to in this part of the sentence are TECHNICAL-TOPIC and IFIP-WORKING-GROUP. Technical topic could have been replaced by the more general entity type TOPIC but since all topics referred to in the problem description seemed to be technical topics, we chosed to use TECHNICAL-TOPIC as the entity type. Similarly, we could have chosen the more general entity type GROUP but we chosed to use the more specific IFIP-WORKING-GROUP since all entity occurrences in the information base will be IFIP working groups.

The relationship types referred to are the relationship between IFIP-WORKING-CONFERENCE and TECHNICAL-TOPIC. We gave it the name "covers" in direction from IFIP-WORKING-group ("Discusses" is the word used in the problem description). This part of the sentence also contains reference to the relationship type between TECHNICAL-TOPIC and IFIP-WORKING-GROUP which is called "is-of-interest-to" in the direction from TECHNICAL-TOPIC. The problem statement also includes some information regarding the degree of the relationship type since one TECHNICAL-TOPIC may be of interest to several IFIP-WORKING-GROUPS.

The analysis of the sentences has to be supplemented with information (interview of users) to find if the degree of a relationship type is one to one, one to many, etc. The resulting "sentence datamodel" is shown in Figure 5.

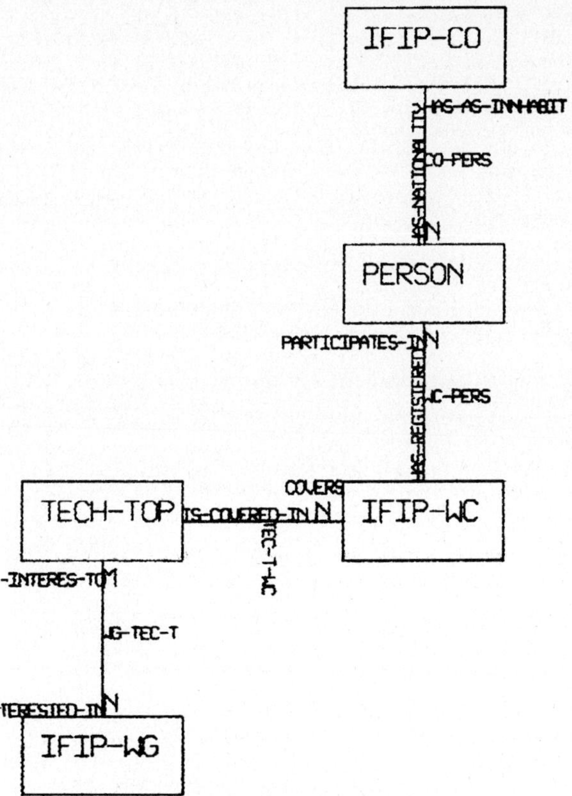


Fig. 5. Datamodel for first sentence of IFIP WG 8.1 case problem description.

As it is clear from the above discussion, alternative models more or less
general than the model above, do exist. The consequence for the users is that
a more general datamodel requires more data to be input. For example using the
datamodel above a user entering new countries into the information base only has
to give the country name. If the more general entity type COUNTRY is chosen,
the user entering data also has to supply a code saying whether the country is
an IFIP country or not. However, if this solution was chosen the system would
be more flexible which would be required for example if persons from non-IFIP
countries were allowed to working conferences.

FIND RELATIONSHIP TYPES AND DRAW CONCEPTUAL DATAMODEL DIAGRAMS
After having made a preliminary list of entity types we started the process of
making conceptual datamodel diagrams. For medium and large systems it is most
practical to do this by several user group oriented and/or function oriented
conceptual data submodels.

It was clear from the list of entity types that one single model would be
unpractical to work with. Our experience is that user group oriented models are
convenient to use, especially for communication with users. We therefore made
one submodel for each of the two primary user groups. In addition we made a
separate conceptual data submodel showing the IFIP organization. This part of
the model is special as only a small fraction of its entity occurrences is of
relevance for the arrangement of one conference. It is a part of the system
which could have been convenient to get as a starting point from IFIP, for
committees arranging working conferences. But it would otherwise hardly be worth
the work of entering this information into the information base, as it is only
used to find which persons to invite to the conference by the organizing
committee.

The submodels were sketched on paper while reading through the problem description for the second time, this time also looking for the relationship types.

Note that no user view integration is necessary afterwards since this is done
continuously during the development process by storing all parts of the model
in the same database. For large projects this may necessitate that one of the
system analysists participates in several working groups.

The entity types and relationship types thus defined were then entered into
SYSTEMATOR's database interactively. The information given was the short name,
the descriptive name and the definition of both entity types and relationship
types. For relationship types, the type, the context dependent names and the
participating entity types were also given. SYSTEMATOR documentation reports
giving lists of the entity types and the relationship types were produced, and
the conceptual datamodel and submodels were plotted using the automatic datamodel drawing facilities of SYSTEMATOR. From this point on all documentations
were always up to date in SYSTEMATOR's database and no manual lists or sketches
were made.

The submodels produced are shown and briefly explained in the rest of this
section. The entity types drawn, contain only the short (Max 8 characters)
name of the entity types. The reader is therefore referred to the list of entity
types (produced by SYSTEMATOR) shown on Table 2 (TABLE OF CONTENT FOR ENTITY
TYPES). This list or more commonly an equivalent list also containing definitions is often used together with the datamodel diagrams when we interview users.

DRAWING CONVENTIONS.  The conventions for drawing used by the SYSTEMATOR
automatic datamodel drawing module are:

| SHORT NAME | DESCRIPTIVE NAME | DOCNO PAGE |
|---|---|---|
| ABSTRACT | PAPER-ABSTRACT | 1 |
| CFP-GRP | CALL-FOR-PAPER-GROUP | 2 |
| IFIP-CO | IFIP-COUNTRY | 3 |
| IFIP-OC | IFIP-CONFERENCE-ORG-COMMITTEE | 4 |
| IFIP-PC | IFIP-PROGRAM-COMITTEE | 5 |
| IFIP-TC | IFIP-TECHNICAL-COMMITTEE | 6 |
| IFIP-WC | IFIP-WORKING-CONFERENCE | 7 |
| IFIP-WG | IFIP-WORKING-GROUP | 8 |
| INV-GRP | GROUP-TO-RECEIVE-INVITATION | 9 |
| INVITAT | INVITATION | 10 |
| L-OF-INT | LETTER-OF-INTENT | 11 |
| ORGANS | ORGANISATION | 12 |
| PAPER | SUBMITTED-PAPER | 13 |
| PERSON | PERSON | 14 |
| PROGRAM | CONFERENCE-PROGRAM | 15 |
| REF-GRP | REFEREE-GROUP | 16 |
| REFERIN | CONTRIBUTION-REFEREEING-ASIGNMENT | 17 |
| SESSION | PROGRAM-SESSION | 18 |
| SOC-EV | SOCIAL-EVENT | 19 |
| TECH-TOP | TECHNICAL-TOPIC | 20 |

Table 2.  Short and descriptive names of entity types
          (sorted on short name).


-   Entity types are designated rectangels with the short name
    inside the rectangle.
-   Relationship types are drawn as lines between rectangles
    (recursive relationship types with a circle).
-   The degree of the relationship type is given by:

    many to many  The letter N is written on one end and the
    letter M at the other.

    one to many  The letter N is written in that end of the
    relationship type where several entities may be found.

    one to one  No special letter used (none of above).

-   The context dependent relationship names are written
    near the entity type where the name is to be used.
-   The short unique name of the relationship type is written on
    the middle and perpendicular to the relationship type line.
-   Composite entity types are designated as rectangles
    with double horizontal lines.

IFIP ORGANIZATION SUBMODEL.  Figure 6 shows a conceptual datamodel showing
IFIP's organization and IFIP's connection with Working Conferences. It contains
one recursive relationship (drawn with a small circle) showing which IFIP working groups are associated with each other. The rest of the datamodel is fairly
straight forward.

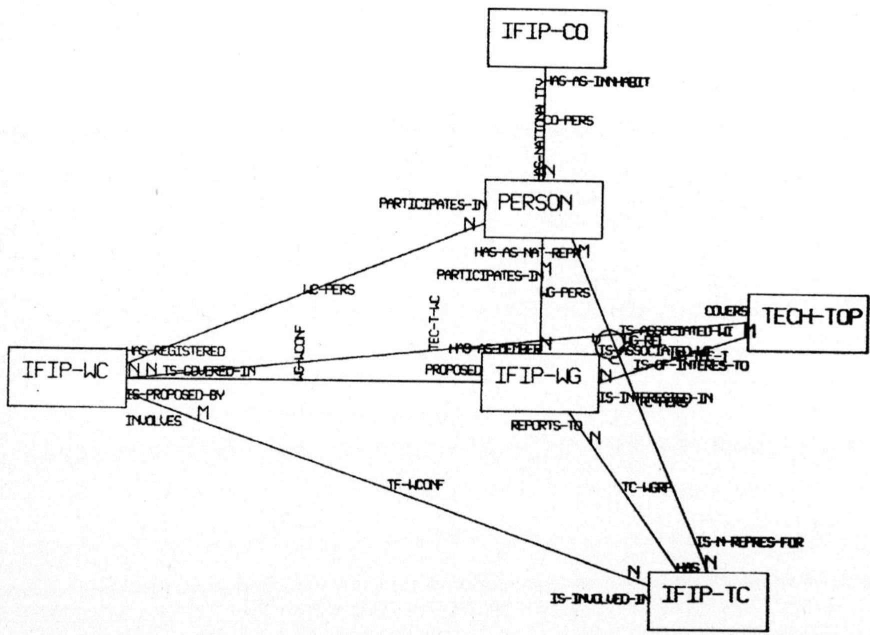


Fig. 6.  The IFIP organization conceptual datamodel.


THE ORGANIZING COMMITTEE SUBMODEL.  The organizing committee submodel is shown
on Figure 7.

This model contains some interesting aspects. Some of the entity types on the
diagram will only contain one entity occurrence since only one conference will
be stored in the information base. This is true for

    INV-GRP   The group of people who will receive or have
                received invitation to the conference.

    IFIP-OC   The IFIP organizing committee.

    CFP-GRP   The group of persons and organizations which
                will or have received a call for paper.

This form of entity type is called "Unary" entity type in SYSDOC. The attributes
of such entities can be used (read/updated) without prior localization of the
entity occurrence. Except for this they are described like other entity types.
No special convention is used on the automatically drawn diagram to designate
these, but this ought to be done as this is important information to both the
users and systems analysts.

We decided to have INVITATION as an entity type. This entity type has the data
element types date-invitation-was-sent, invitation number, date-answer-was-
received and a code telling whether answer received was positive or negative.
We also considered letting CALL-FOR-PAPER be an entity type. This is definitely
an entity type but it seems unnecessary including it in the information base

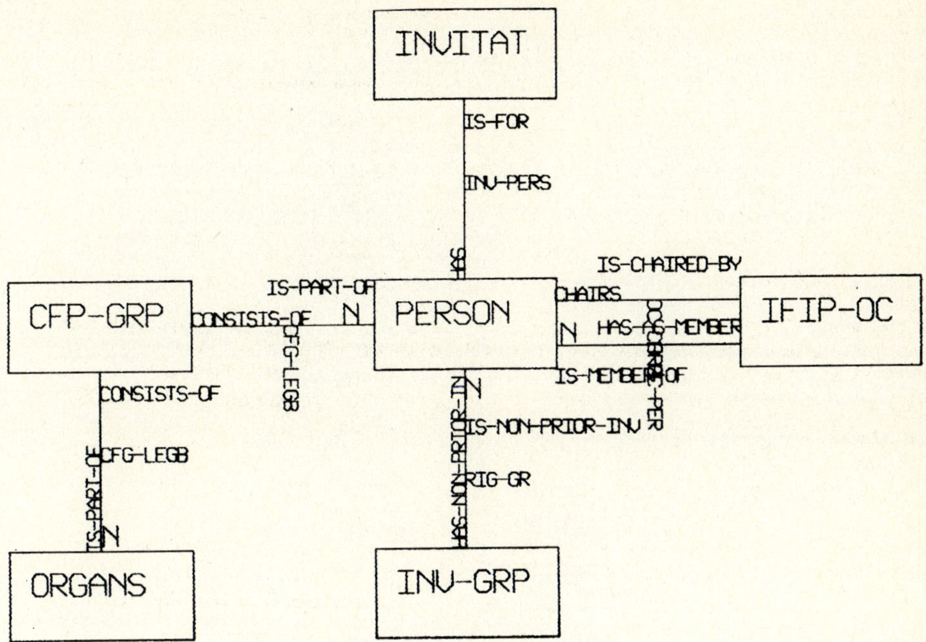

Fig. 7.  The organizing committee submodel.

since the call for papers probably is sent out as one batch so that no information tion needs to be collected regarding the individual CALL-FOR-PAPER. If that is true the information needed by the information system is contained in the relationship between the CALL-FOR-PAPER-GROUP (CFP-GRP) and PERSON and it is unnecessary to enter already known facts into the information base. We therefore decided not to include CALL-FOR-PAPER in the conceptual datamodel, as the conceptual model in our view should not contain other entity types than those that need to be stored in the information base (when the purpose of the model is to build an information system).

However, this is partly a matter of taste. We did include CALL-FOR-PAPER as an entity type initially and only left it out when we felt certain there was no need for it. As a general rule in the analysis phase it is better to include (and later remove) too much than too little. The rule we use is: Include if you are in doubt.

Note! The relationships from CFP-GRP define which legal bodies shall receive calls for paper. Due to a restriction in the drawing program, the generalized entity type LEGAL BODY is not drawn with the participating entity types drawn within it as we did on the manually drawn examples shown earlier. Instead the relationships to the generalized entity type are drawn to both of the constituent entity types. Thus the relationship CFG-LEGB is drawn twice on the diagram, once from CFP-GRP to PERSON and once from CFP-GRP to ORGANS.

By defining a subsetting criterion it is possible to define subsets of persons from this datamodel such as

1)    <u>INVITED</u> IS PERSON'S WHO HAS ANY INVITATION
2)    <u>COMING</u>  IS PERSON'S WHO HAS INVITATION WITH ANSW-CODE EQ 'ACCEPTED'

These subsets are not normally shown on the conceptual datamodel diagrams.

One of the more complex tasks in this problem description is the sending of
invitations to those persons that should get one. This we solved by introducing
a named subset of the entity type PERSON.

TO-BE-INVITED-ARE:
      PERSON'S (WHO HAS SUBMITTED ANY PAPER) OR (IS-NATIONAL-REPRESENTATIVE-
      IN ANY TECHN-COMMITTEE WHO IS-INVOLVED-IN THE WORKING CONFERENCE) OR
      PARTICIPATES-IN (THE WORKING-GROUP OR ANY WORKING-GROUP ASSOCIATED-
      WITH THE WORKING GROUP)) OR (IS-NON-PRIORITY-INVITED IN THE INV-GRP)

The relationship called RIG-GR between INV-GRP and PERSON is thus used just for
entering which persons are to receive an invitation in addition to those covered
by the general IFIP rules. The abstract program for writing out invitations is
thus just a few statements reading PERSONS-TO-BE-INVITED by a simple FOR EACH
statement, then writing the invitation and registering in the database that the
invitation has been sent.

THE PROGRAM COMMITTEE SUBMODEL.  The Program Committee submodel is shown in
Figure 8.

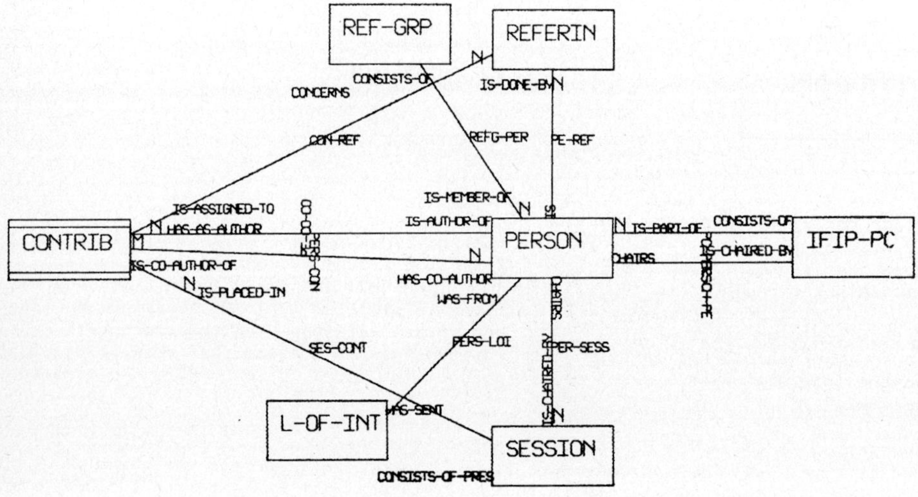


Fig. 8.   The Program Committee submodel.

The entity types IFIP-PROGRAM-COMMITTEE (short name IFIP-PC) and REFEREE-GROUP
(short REF-GRP) are also unary. CONTRIBUTION is a generalized entity type whose
occurrences may be either PAPER or ABSTRACT. We have made the assumption that
CONTRIBUTION must have one author (mandatory relationship membership for
CONTRIBUTION) and possibly several co-authors. REFERIN is the name given to the
refereeing of one CONTRIBUTION by one PERSON. The integrity constraint enforcing
that only a PERSON who is-member-of the REFEREE-GROUP will be refereeing is
handled by a derived relationship type going from REF-GRP via PERSON to REFERIN.
(Note! not shown on the diagram.) By defining that this derived relationship type
is mandatory for all REFERIN is equivalent to saying that there for all REFERIN s
will be possible to follow the relationship PE-REF from REFERIN to PERSON and then
the relationship REFG-PER to REF-GRP. Thus the integrity constraint is enforced.

THE COMPLETE CONCEPTUAL DATAMODEL.  The following diagram shows the complete
datamodel automatically drawn (from the same database as previous submodels).
This is difficult to read on the scale used even though a few entity types have
been left out to make the diagram easier to read, but it is quite easy to read
drawn in colours in a scale twice as big than the scale used here.

Our experience is that system analysts familiar with a conceptual datamodel
normally prefer to work with the complete model. But when talking to users such
diagrams tend to become too complex for users and sometimes also for the
analysts. Subdatamodels are better to use but since it is timeconsuming to draw
and update such submodels they are seldom made if produced manually. We have
therefore found that the capability SYSTEMATOR has to draw submodels fast and
neatly is very important.

It is possible when using SYSTEMATOR interactively from a graphics terminal to
manually modify drawn datamodels. The user at the graphics terminal may zoom,
change window and move the different parts of the datamodel around. An entity
type symbol may be moved by pointing at it (with a tablet-pen or light-pen) and
pulling it to a new position. All texts and relationship types to or from the
entity type will then follow (rubber band), but it is up to the user to control
that no collisions results from the move. But the automatically drawn diagrams
have been of such quality that so far we have not used the interactive drawing
editor on practical problems (all diagrams in this paper have been left unchanged by human hand).

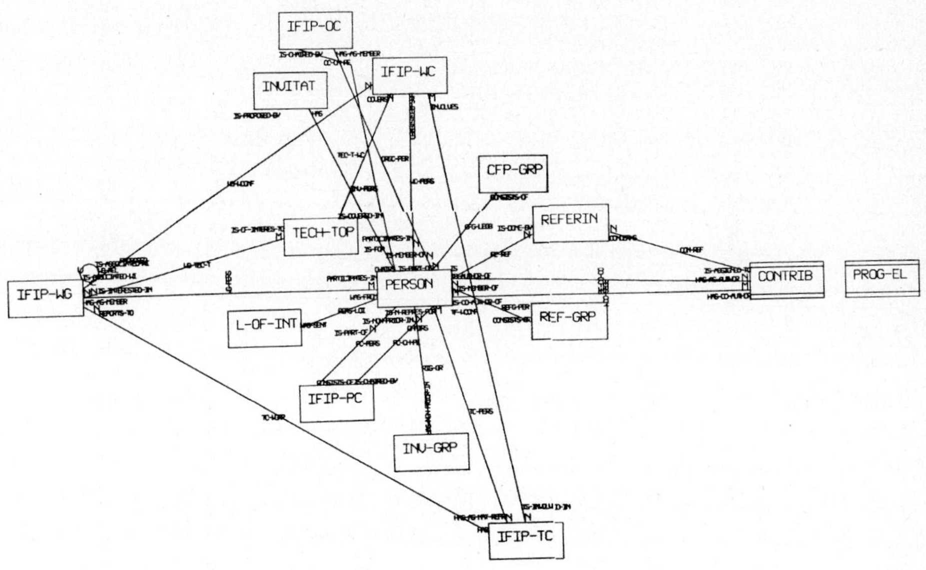

Fig. 9.  The almost complete conceptual datamodel.

MAKE INPUT/REPORT LISTS
Before the conceptual datamodel is detailed further, it is useful to obtain
better knowledge about the information needs of users of the proposed system.
This is done first by making lists of the most important functions the system

is to perform and the most important inputs to and outputs from the system and the datacontent needed for these functions. This list was entered into SYSTEMATOR's database. All trivial transactions (such as storing new technical-topic, IFIP-WG, etc.) were not included. The reason for this is that all the normal types of transactions for updating and retrieving information concerning one entity type may be generated automatically by SYSTEMATOR.

The resulting list of transactions is given in the following table.


INPUTS

| SHORT NAME | DESCRIPTIVE NAME | DOCNO | PAGE |
|---|---|---|---|
| CONTR-RE | CONTRIBUTION-REFEREEING-ASSIGNMENT | | 1 |
| CONTR-RE | CONTRIBUTION-REFEREEING-ASSIGNMENT | | 1 |
| LOI-REG | REGISTRATION-OF-LETTER-OF-INTENT | PCIN | 2 |
| LOI-REG | REGISTRATION-OF-LETTER-OF-INTENT | PCIN | 2 |
| PC-CHAIR | PROGRAM-CHAIRMAN-APPOINTMENT | PCIN | 3 |
| PC-CHAIR | PROGRAM-CHAIRMAN-APPOINTMENT | PCIN | 3 |
| RE-CO-UP | RECEIPT-CODE-FOR-INVITATION-UPDATE | OCIN | 4 |
| RE-CO-UP | RECEIPT-CODE-FOR-INVITATION-UPDATE | OCIN | 4 |
| REG-CONT | REGISTRATION-OF-CONTRIBUTIONS | | 5 |
| REG-CONT | REGISTRATION-OF-CONTRIBUTIONS | | 5 |
| REG-OC | REGISTRATION-OF-ORG-COMMITEE-MEMBER | OCIN | 6 |
| REG-OC | REGISTRATION-OF-ORG-COMMITEE-MEMBER | OCIN | 6 |
| REG-OC-C | REG-ORGANIZING-COMMITTEE-CHAIRMAN | OCIN | 7 |
| REG-OC-C | REG-ORGANIZING-COMMITTEE-CHAIRMAN | OCIN | 7 |
| REG-REFF | REGISTER-REFFEREEING | | 8 |
| REG-REFF | REGISTER-REFFEREEING | | 8 |
| REG-SESS | REGISTRATION-OF-SESSIONS | | 9 |
| REG-SESS | REGISTRATION-OF-SESSIONS | | 9 |
| REM-CONT | REMOVAL-OF-CONTRIBUTIONS | | 10 |
| REM-CONT | REMOVAL-OF-CONTRIBUTIONS | | 10 |
| REM-OC | REMOVAL-OF-ORG-COMMITEE-MEMBER | OCIN | 11 |
| REM-OC | REMOVAL-OF-ORG-COMMITEE-MEMBER | OCIN | 11 |
| UP-REF-S | UPDATE-REFEREEING-STATUS | | 12 |
| UP-REF-S | UPDATE-REFEREEING-STATUS | | 12 |


REPORTS

| SHORT NAME | DESCRIPTIVE NAME | DOCNO | PAGE |
|---|---|---|---|
| ADDR-LAB | ADRESS-LABELS-FOR-INVITATIONS | OCRE | 1 |
| CFP-LIST | LIST-OF-WHO-ARETO-RECEIVE-CALL-FOR-P | PCRE | 2 |
| CONT-REF | CONTRIBUTION-REFEREE-REPORT | PCRE | 3 |
| INV-TO-B | LIST-WHO-ARE-TO-BE-INVITED | OCRE | 4 |
| INVIT-GR | LIST-WHO-HAS-RECEIVED-INVITATION | OCRE | 5 |
| LIST-ATT | LIST-OF-ATTENDEES | OCRE | 6 |
| LOI-REC | LETTERS-OF-INTENT-RECEIVED | PCRE | 7 |
| PAPER-LI | PAPERS-NOT-RECEIVED-FROM-REFFEREE | PCRE | 8 |
| PAPER-RE | PAPERS-RECEIVED-LISTED-BY-STATUS | PCRE | 9 |
| REFFREP | REFEREE-REPORTS-RECEIVED | PCRE | 10 |
| SESS-LI | SESSIONS-WITH-CHAIRMAN | PCRE | 11 |


Table 3. List of important transactions.

DEFINE HOW ENTITIES ARE TO BE IDENTIFIED AND THE DATAELEMENTS NEEDED
At this stage after having obtained a better knowledge of the information needs
of the users we returned to the conceptual datamodel.

First we went through all the entity types previously entered into the
SYSTEMATOR database, this time defining the data element types needed to describe
the entities of the type. At the same time we tried to find out how entities
could be uniquely identified and if it was practical to introduce new data element types for ease of reference. For instance we decided to introduce the data
element type invitation number to uniquely identify INVITATION's and contribu-
tion-number to uniquely identify CONTRIBUTION's. Both of these could have been
left out and was introduced to simplify the use of the proposed information
system. This type of decisions may have practical consequences and must be discussed with the users.

The way we in practice went about doing this was first to list the name of the
data element types describing each entity type interactively on a screen, at the
same time also giving the data element (or dataelements) chosen for identifier.
At the same time we recorded cardinality information if this was known (maximum-
and average-number of entities of the type and integrity constraints). Afterwards
the description of the data element types was entered. Before doing this, a list
of all undefined data element types (data element types describing an entity type
with no description entered into the SYSTEMATOR database) was produced by
SYSTEMATOR. An example of such a report is shown in Figure 10 where the letter U
would appear to the right of concepts referred to in the requirement specification but not yet described. (Note! Not shown in the figure.)

The main statistics for datamodel elements entered into SYSTEMATOR's database
were:

        No of Elementary entity types  =  20
        No of Data element types       =  50
        No of Relationship types       =  26

DETAIL IMPORTANT TRANSACTIONS
Having defined the conceptual datamodel we started to make detailed description
of the most important transactions. How this was done shall be illustrated with
one input transaction and one report.

One of the transactions needed is that of storing the assignment of refereeing
a paper to a referee and later recording or changing date received, the evaluation code, grade given, etc.

The first thing to do when manually defining a transaction is to define the
datalayout and the datacontent of the screen. This may be done with SYSTEMATOR's
interactive screen editor. The user then has full control over layout. Length
and integrity control information for dataelements is taken from the SYSTEMATOR
database and also, if wanted, standard screen texts.

The layout can, however, also be made automatically by SYSTEMATOR and may later
be edited by the user. The diagram below shows the screen layout proposal
produced automatically by SYSTEMATOR.

The screen contains all data element types defined for the entity type with the
specified data element screen heading if one is defined. Otherwise the short name
of the data element type is used as screen heading. The screen also contains
fields for connecting the entity type to the relationship types it participates
in. The screen headings used are the context dependent relationship type name
followed by the screen heading of the unique identifier of the entity at the
other end. Thus the last line is used to give the contribution title (the

```
ABST-PAP    ABSTRACT-DESCRIBES-PAPER                        RL
ABSTRACT    PAPER-ABSTRACT                                  EN
AC-RE-DA    ACCEPTANCE-REJECTION-DATE                       DA
ADDR-LAB    ADRESS-LABELS-FOR-INVITATIONS           OCRE    RE
ARR-PLAC    PLACE-OF-ARRANGEMENT                            DA

C-NAME      COUNTRY-NAME                                    DA
C-TITLE     CONTRIBUTION-TITLE                              DA
CAPACITY    CAPACITY                                        DA
CFG-LEGB    CALL-FOR-PAPER-GR-LEGAL-ENTITY                  RL
CFP-GRP     CALL-FOR-PAPER-GROUP                            EN
CFP-LIST    LIST-OF-WHO-ARETO-RECEIVE-CALL-FOR-P    PCRE    RE
CFP-STAT    CALL-FOR-PAPER-STATUS                           DA
CO-PERS     IFIP-COUNTRY-HAS-PERSONS                        RL
CON-REF     CONTRIBUTION-IS-ASSIGNED-TO-REFEREEN            RL
CONT-REF    CONTRIBUTION-REFEREE-REPORT             PCRE    RE
CONTR-RE    CONTRIBUTION-REFEREEING-ASSIGNMENT              IN
CONTR-ST    CONTRIBUTION-STATUS                             DA
CONTRIB     CONTRIBUTION                                    EN

D-REC       DATE-RECEIVED                                   DA
D-REMAIN    DATE-WHEN-LAST-REMAINDED                        DA
D-SENT      DATE-SENT                                       DA
DA-ANSW     DATE-OF-ANSWER                                  DA
DA-END      END-DATE-FOR-A-WORKING-CONFERENCE               DA
DA-SENT     DATE-SENT                                       DA
DA-START    STARTING-DATE-OF-A-CONFERENCE                   DA
DATE-REC    DATE-RECEIVED                                   DA

EL-NAME     PROGRAM-ELEMENT-NAME                            DA
END-T       END-TIME-OF-A-PROGRAM-ELEMENT                   DA
EVAL-COD    EVALUATION-CODE                                 DA

FIN-BREA    FINANCIAL-BREAK-EVEN-POINT                      DA

GRADE       REFEREE-GRADE                                   DA
GTRI-PER    GRP-TO-RECEIVE-INV-HAS-PERS                     RL
```

Fig. 10.  List of all used short names (First page).

unique key of contribution as we have defined it) and the context dependent
relationship name (CONCERNS) of the relationship type being connected.

After having produced the screen layout (manual or automatic) for the transactions abstract programs in SYSDUL were written manually for "difficult"
transactions and generated automatically for "simple" transactions. How a
fairly simple abstract program could look like is illustrated in Figure 13.

```
     R E F E R I N        CONTRIBUTION-REFEREEING-ASIGNMENT


--------------------------------------------------------------------

                                   WRIT.BY      BM
                                   WRIT.DATE    110881
                                   CHANG.DATE   170881

NO OF ENTITIES IN THE CLASS:
INITIALY =
MIN      =                         INCREASAGE PR YEAR=
MAX      =        300              DECREASAGE PR YEAR=
AVER.    =                         AVER.STORAGETIME  =      0


           DEFINITION
             250 WORK DONE BY ONE PERSON ON ONE CONTRIBUTION
             251 COULD BE IN ONE OF 3 STATES:
             252 1 : PLANNED
             253 2 : FINISHED
             254 3 : CURRENTLY BEEING WORKED AT


SEQ.  ELEMENTNAME-SHORT   DESCRIPTIVE NAME                  NO.CHAR
--------------------------------------------------------------------
 30    REFR-NO             REFEREEING-NUMBER                    -3N
                    UNIQUE NUMBER ASSOCIATED WITH THE WORK DONE BY ONE
                    PERSON ON ONE CONTRIBUTION

           UNIQUE KEY

 31    D-SENT             DATE-SENT                             -6N
                    DATE WHEN A CONTRIBUTION WAS SENT TO ONE REFEREE


 32    D-REC              DATE-RECEIVED                         -6N
                    DATE WHEN THE REFEREEING OF ONE CONTRIBUTION FROM
                    ONE REFEREE IS RECEIVED


 33    D-REMAIN           DATE-WHEN-LAST-REMAINDED              -6N
                    DATE WHEN A REFEREE WAS LAST REMAINDED TO REPORT
                    ON ONE CONTRIBUTION

 34    EVAL-COD           EVALUATION-CODE                       -8A
                    CODE WHICH ARE USED BY REFEREES TO EXPRESS THEIR
                    OPINION OF A CONTRIBUTION


 35    GRADE              REFEREE-GRADE                         -2N
                    GRADE GIVEN TO A CONTRIBUTION BY A REFEREE


                                                   ----
                                           SUM =   31
                                                   ========
                APPROX SPACE REQ. IN THOUSAND CHAR=    9.300
```

Fig. 11.  Example of entity type report.

```
        ENTITY    CONTRIBUTION-REFEREEING-ASIGNMENT
        -----------------------------------------------

REFR-NO  :... DATE-SENT :......  DATE-REC :......  DATE-REMAIN :......
EVAL-COD :........  GRADE :..

IS-DONE-BY PERS-COD :....
CONCERNS C-TITLE   :..........................................................
```

Fig. 12.  Screen layout proposal automatically produced by SYSTEMATOR.


```
        R E F - A S S        CONTRIBUTION-REFEREEING-ASSIGNMENT

                              WRIT.BY      BM
                              WRIT.DATE    140881
---------PROCEDURE-STATEMENTS-----------------------------------------------


              OBTAIN REFR-NO
              FIND REFERIN WITH REFR-NO
              IF NOT FOUND
              C
              C     NEW REFERIN
              C
                DISPLAY 'NEW ASSIGNMENT OF REFERIN'
                STORE REFERIN WITH REFR-NO
              ELSE
              C
              C     EXISTS ALREADY
              C
                GET AND DISPLAY D-SENT,D-REC,D-REMAIN,EVAL-COD AND GRADE
              END IF
              OBTAIN D-SENT,D-REC,D-REMAIN,EVAL-COD AND GRADE
              REMEMBER THAT REFERIN HAS D-SENT,D-REC,D-REMAIN :
                  EVAL-COD AND GRADE
              OBTAIN PERS-COD
              REMEMBER THAT REFERIN IS-DONE-BY PERSON WITH PERS-COD
              OBTAIN C-TITLE
              REMEMBER THAT REFERIN CONCERNS CONTRIB WITH C-TITLE
```

Fig. 13.  Example of abstract program.


The transaction is used both for storing new REFERIN's and later entering or
reading the attributes of the individual REFERIN's. The program does not contain
a description of how to handle all errors that may occur (e.g. referring to a
non existent PERSON) but code for handling this in a standardized way may be
added automatically by SYSTEMATOR.

The abstract programming may also to a large extent, be completely automated
by SYSTEMATOR. Thus an equivalent abstract program could have been generated
automatically by SYSTEMATOR. The resulting abstract program could have been
modified by the user. The abstract program for producing the report (Fig. 15)
may also be written manually or generated automatically.

Figure 14 shows an example of one of the reports the system shall produce. This
layout was entered interactively with SYSTEMATOR's screen editor which may also
be used to define layout for reports.

```
                    CONTRIBUTION REFEREE REPORT

  TITLE : ........................................................

  AUTHOR :
  ..........................     ..............................
  CO-AUTHOR(S) :
  ..........................     ..............................
  ..........................     ..............................

  CONTRIBUTION STATUS : .........

  REFEREE REPORTS :
                          DATE    DATE    DATE  EVALUATION GRADE
              NAME        SENT    REC   REMAIN     CODE
     .......................  ......  ......  ......  ........  ..
     .......................  ......  ......  ......  ........  ..
     .......................  ......  ......  ......  ........  ..
     .......................  ......  ......  ......  ........  ..
     .......................  ......  ......  ......  ........  ..
     .......................  ......  ......  ......  ........  ..
     .......................  ......  ......  ......  ........  ..
```

Fig. 14.  Example of report layout.

The abstract program below shows how this report could be abstractly programmed.

```
        R E F - R A P P        CONTRIBUTION-REFEREE-REPORT

                               WRIT.BY      BM
                               WRIT.DATE    150881
-----------PROCEDURE-STATEMENTS------------------------------------------


              OBTAIN C-TITLE
              FIND AND DISPLAY CONTR-ST OF CONTRIB WITH GIVEN C-TITLE
              FIND AND DISPLAY P-NAME AND P-ADRESS OF PERSON WHO :
                   IS-AUTHOR-OF CONTRIB
              FIND AND DISPLAY P-NAME AND P-ADRESS OF ALL PERSON´S :
                   WHO IS-CO-AUTHOR-OF CONTRIB
              FOR ALL REFERIN WHICH CONCERNS CONTRIB
                  GET AND DISPLAY D-SENT,D-REC,D-REMAIN,EVAL-COD :
                       AND GRADE
                  FIND AND DISPLAY P-NAME OF PERSON WHICH REFERIN IS-DONE-BY
              END FOR
```

Fig. 15.  Abstract program giving report shown on Figure 14.

In this particular case almost every screen and abstract program could satis-
factorily be produced automatically by SYSTEMATOR.

To get statistics on the number of people who e.g. have accepted invitations is obtained by defining the derivation rule for the derived data element describing this. This could be defined as follows: NO-OF-PEOPLE-ACCEPTED =: NUMBER OF INVITATION'S WITH REPCODE EQ "YES". By saying that this data element type is an attribute of the entity type organizing-committee and generating a default screen and an abstract program for this entity type such statistics can be produced without any programming.

Similar arguments are true for most of the other functions needed in the described case. They may simply be performed using the automatically designed screens and abstract programs. Our solution to the case problem is therefore rather short.

Thus traditional programming disappears and even most of the abstract programs and layouts may be generated automatically by SYSTEMATOR.

GENERATE PROTOTYPE SYSTEM
Thus having defined the datamodel and user interface partly manually but mostly automatically, the next step is to produce a running system. To do this the following steps have to be followed.

GENERATE A DATABASE.  One of the SYSTEMATOR menu selections is generation of a default database. The SYSTEMATOR schema-generator will then make a database design automatically. This includes determination of internal storage format, calculation of file size based on cardinality information and choosing a database design that gets around the restrictions of the databasesystem. Generalized entity types and many to many relationships are among the facilities not normally found in currently available databasesystems.

The result is a mapping description stored in the SYSTEMATOR database showing the mapping from the datamodel to the database and a complete DDL is also generated. This may automatically be sent to the databasesystem schema-description processor to get a physical database. All necessary JCL is generated automatically. Reports are also produced to give an overview of the physical database.

GENERATE THE PROGRAMS.  When the physical database design is known to SYSTEMATOR (it was stored during schema-generation by the SYSTEMATOR schema-generator) the abstract programs are used to generate COBOL or FORTRAN program modules by the SYSTEMATOR program generator.

The last step is to collect the generated modules into programs. This may also be done automatically by SYSTEMATOR or the user chooses from a menu which module to include in the different programs.

EXPERIMENTATION, EVALUATION AND MODIFICATION
After having gone through the preceeding steps there now eixsts a system which can be used by the users. Changes can be made to previously defined abstract programs or screens and the changed programs can be regenerated. It is also possible to define new transactions. These may be tested immediately after they have been generated, since at this stage an information system database exists. This testing may be done from SYSTEMATOR (the generated program is loaded with the help of SYSTEMATOR).

If changes are made to the datamodel the database has to be regenerated and all program modules affected by the change also have to be regenerated. SYSTEMATOR reports show which modules that need to be regenerated and the regeneration may also be done automatically. (Note! Regeneration is necessary since no interpretation is done at runtime to get small and efficient programs.)

If the user has stored much data in the database, it is desirable to dump data
from the old database to the new database. A SYSTEMATOR module for doing this
is currently being developed.

SYSTEMATOR'S database design aid (SYDADA [5]) may be used to produce rough cost
and performance estimates to help in the evaluation of whether to continue the
development or perform any reevaluations. The primary use of SYDADA is, however,
to collect information for the database designer.

PHYSICAL SYSTEM DESIGN
After experimentation and trial the next step is the physical system design.
The important job left for the designer is the database design. The chosen
design is given as a mapping description showing the mapping from datamodel to
physical database. Parts not being decided by the database designer are done by
the default database design algorithms in the schema generator. The complete
system is then regenerated according to the new database design.

PRACTICAL USE AND MAINTENANCE
New transactions may be added or old ones modified as described above.

Database design is very important for the performance of database oriented
systems. It is difficult to estimate how a proposed system is to be used.
Therefore we plan to include in SYSTEMATOR the capability of collecting
statistics on how often and when the different transactions are run. This
information can be used to get detailed reports from SYSTEMATOR's database
design aid (SYDADA [5]) showing how and when the different parts of the
conceptual datamodel are used. Based on this information and measurements
of response-times a new system design may be made. This is done by giving
a new database design mapping description. This may be followed by new
measurements and regenerations if desired. Thus system maintenance with
SYSTEMATOR is done either by changing the specification or the design
description and then regenerating the effected parts of a system.


CONCLUSION

In this particular case, and with such a powerful tool as SYSTEMATOR, the information system was essentially build when the conceptual datamodel had been made.
The reason is that the inputs were quite simple (default update transactions are
probably satisfactory) and few special reports were defined (default transactions and a few derived dataelements handle the rest of the information needs).
In a more typical information system a larger number of abstract programs have
to be written but typically between 60 and 80 percent of the transactions can
be automatically generated.

This shows what central role a datamodel has to play in the system development
process with modern tools. Conceptual data modelling is the main technique used
in requirements specification and decisive in discussions with users. The conceptual datamodel is also the dominant factor controlling the user interface of a
system. Information system development is thus essentially conceptual data
modelling with sufficiently strong tools available.

But this form of description normally has to be supplemented with a more
functionally oriented description technique. For some types of systems (e.g.
systems with much hardware) the function oriented description is the central
part. No formal language has been made in SYSDOC to give functionally oriented
description (other than abstract programs). We therefore often supplement a
SYSDOC description with a functional description done with a description
technique familiar to the user. The IFIP case (as many administrative systems)

is so data oriented that we felt no need for using a functionally oriented
technique to supplement the description.

The SYSTEMATOR software is operational on NORD 10/NORD 100 (16 Bits mini) with
minimum 156 Kb memory. Most of the modules are also operational on UNIVAC 1100,
and DEC 10/20. The software is written in METAFORTRAN which is translated to
standard FORTRAN when the software is implemented on new computers. The current
SYSTEMATOR version generates code for the SIBAS DBMS (CODASYL type of DBMS)
which is the most commonly used DBMS in Scandinavia (approx. 150 installations).
Limited versions of SYSTEMATOR have been made which generates COBOL programs
using CINCOM's TOTAL or IBM's DL/1.


REFERENCES

[1]   Alford, M., SREM, Symposium on Formal Design Methodology,
      Cambridge, England, 9-12 April 1979.

[2]   PSL/PSA, ISDOS Working Paper 98,99, Michigan Univ., USA.

[3]   Chen, P., The Entity-Relationship Model Toward a unified View of Data.
      ACM Transactions on Database Systems, Volume 1, No. 1, March 1976, pp 9-36.

[4]   Smith and Smith, Database Abstractions: Aggregation and Generalization,
      ACM Transactions on Database Systems, Volume 2, No. 2, June 1977.

[5]   Øren, A., Aschim, F., Statistics for the usage of a conceptual data-
      model as basis for logical Data Base Design, 5th Int. Conf. on Very
      Large Databases. Rio de Janeiro, Brazil, Oct. 3-5, 1979.

[6]   Aschim, F., Computer aided System development with MADDS.
      Data No. 12, 1978.

*INFORMATION SYSTEMS DESIGN METHODOLOGIES: A Comparative Review*
*T.W. Olle, H.G. Sol, A.A. Verrijn-Stuart (editors)*
*North-Holland Publishing Company*
© *IFIP, 1982*


# ACTIVE AND PASSIVE COMPONENT MODELLING: ACM/PCM*

Michael L. Brodie                    Erico Silva

Department of Computer Science
University of Maryland
College Park, MD 20742

ACM/PCM is a modelling methodology for the design and development of
moderate to large size database-intensive applications.  Unlike some
methodologies with similar goals, structural (date or static) and behavioral (process or dynamic) properties are treated explicitly and
abstractly.  Database design and program (transaction) design are
fully integrated.  This integration and many other benefits are gained based on the principle of abstraction.  In particular ACM/PCM
takes advantage of data, procedure, and control abstractions.

ACM/PCM provides concepts, tools, and techniques for each stage of
the database life cycle.  This paper presents the methodology for
only the logical design and specification stage.  The methodology
results in a complete, precise specification of the objects, actions,
and transactions that constitute an application.  The methodology is
illustrated in the specification of an information system to be used
to organize IFIP conferences.

## 1.  INTRODUCTION

ACM/PCM provides means for the design and development of complex, object-oriented
information systems that make extensive use of interactive database transactions.
The complexity of these systems arises from complicated structural and behavioral
properties that change through time; concurrent, interactive access by users with
different processing needs over a large, shared database; and multiple, but distinct database views (external schemas).  Large information systems with these
characteristics that have been successfully designed and developed using ACM/PCM
include: criminal court scheduling, university  registration, hotel reservation,
real estate management, and soccer team management.

The principle of abstraction is the suppression of some detail in order to emphasize more appropriate detail.  ACM/PCM makes extensive use of abstraction to address two main problems in the design, development, and evolution of information
systems, namely:

- managing complexity

- defining and ensuring a high degree of semantic integrity

Abstraction provides an approach to reasoning about databases, programs, and
their development.  Three significant consequences of this approach are: equal
emphasis on and integrity of structural and behavioral properties of an application, a complete life cycle for information system design and development, and
modelling through levels of abstraction.

---

*This work was supported, in part, by the national Science Foundation under grant
number MCS 77-22509, by the National Bureau of Standards, and by Brasilian Corporation for Agricultural Research (EMBRAPA).

The first consequence recognizes that database applications have both structural and behavioral properties. <u>Structure</u> refers to states and static properties, i.e., entities and their relationships. <u>Behavior</u> refers to state transitions and dynamic properties, i.e., operations and their relationships. A complete design and specification of a database application must include both structure and behavior. Using abstraction, an application can be decomposed into small, meaningful objects. Both structural and behavioral properties of objects can be designed in isolation resulting in a data abstraction. A <u>data abstraction</u> defines the structure of an object and meaningful operations (actions) which provide the only means of altering the object. The decomposition aids in managing complexity. Data abstractions can be related in simple ways to compose higher level objects and operations (transactions) that reflect the inherent complexity of the application.

ACM/PCM takes advantage of database and programming language research results in abstraction. A principal objective of database design has been to extract as many structural properties as possible from programs that will access the database to define conceptual and external schemas. Consequently, many excellent concepts, such as semantic data models, were developed to deal with structure explicitly and abstractly. Some behavioural properties are defined implicitly by structural properties. The remaining behavioral properties are defined using insert, update and delete primitives and procedural abstractions not included in data models. The separate treatment of structure and behavior complicates design, specification, and modification and semantic integrity analysis. Increasingly, the database emphasis on structure is shifting to include behavior. In the programming language area, behavioral properties are considered to be more abstract (i.e., representation-free) than structural properties. As a result many excellent concepts, such as procedural and control abstractions, have been developed to deal explicitly and abstractly with behavior. Structural properties are specified implicitly. The emphasis on behavior is currently shifting in light of recent interest in data abstractions and object-oriented programming. In ACM/PCM as many properties as possible are extracted from potential transactions and are specified as structural or behavioral, whichever is the most appropriate.

The name "Active and Passive Component Modelling" emphasizes that each object is a data abstraction that can be realized in a software component. Data abstractions are highly interrelated. An operation invoked on one object may result in operations being invoked on others. Each object can play active and passive roles. In a <u>passive role</u>, an object has operations invoked on it. In an <u>active role</u>, an object can invoke meaningful operations over related objects to complete a transaction (e.g., invoking *order-part* may cause the *part* abstraction to invoke *reduce-part-inventory*, *create-shipping-bill*, and *create-invoice*).

Typically, systems are passive; users are the agents or invokers of operations. Using ACM/PCM, active roles can be divided amongst interactive users and objects. Active roles are important in alerting and monitoring applications (e.g., office automation, command and control, and critical patient care) and in interactive systems providing intelligent responses (e.g., high level query, transaction and exception handling).

The second consequence of the abstraction approach is related to software engineering. In ACM/PCM, the database life cycle is decomposed into descrete steps each of which deals with distinct aspects of the design and development process. There are six steps.

1.  Requirements Formulation and Analysis.
        'Real World' knowledge of the application is informally described and analyzed.

2.  Logical Design and Specification
        A precise, abstract model of the application is specified in terms of

a semantic data model.

3.  Implementation Design
        An implementation model (e.g., schemas and programs) is defined in terms
    of the data model of the target implementation system.

4.  Implementation
        The implementation model  is encoded and tested to produce an executable
    system.

5.  Operation, Monitoring and Maintenance
        Install and operate the system.

6.  Evolution, Adaptation and Modification
        Modify the system to meet changing requirements.

Each stage requires verification for completeness and consistency.

The ACM/PCM database life cycle provides a complete framework for information
system design and development.  This paper describes the concepts, tools, and
techniques for the logical design and specification step only.

The third consequence of the abstraction approach is design and development in
levels of abstraction.  In ACM/PCM, three levels are distinguished: the transaction level, the conceptual level and the database level.  The levels are similar
to those in the ANSI/SPARC architecture.  The transaction level, like the external schema level, is designed for specific application and end user needs.  Transaction modelling involves the design and specification of structural and behavioral properties of transactions, queries, and reports.  The conceptual level, like
the conceptual schema level, is designed to meet the common needs of all known
transactions.  Conceptual modelling involves the design and specification of a
data abstraction (i.e., structure and actions) for each application object.  The
database level, like the internal schema level, involves the implementation and
maintenance of the properties specified at the other levels using existing software (e.g., DBMSes, programming languages).  Modelling at all three levels involves behavior and structure.  This paper focuses on the conceptual and transaction levels.

Modelling at all three levels proceeds in a two step abstraction process.  First,
the gross structural and behavioral properties of objects are identified and related.  This (gross) design is done with the aid of diagramatic tools called
object schemes and action schemes.  In the second step, the properties are specified precisely.  This (fine) design is done using the specification language
BETA.  The syntax of BETA is given in the appendix.

The  five year development of ACM/PCM has been directed at producing concepts,
tools, and techniques for each step of a comprehensive database life cycle.  The
development has concentrated on simplicity.  The approach is based on one
principle, abstraction, and its related theories.  For each step, concepts, tools
and techniques were developed in parallel.  The main concepts are embodied in
a semantic data model.  Tools and techniques have been developed to support its
application.  The results were tested and refined by applying them in the design
and development of large, complex information systems.  Due to the importance of
structure in databases, the structural aspects of SHM+ were defined first [1, 2].
Next, the database life cycle and the role of data design in the cycle was investigated [3].  After the ACM/PCM approach was formulated [4], SHM+ was extended
to accomodate behavioral concepts and associated tools and techniques were
developed [5].  Finally, the concept of association was added [6] to complete the
set of primitive concepts needed to deal with all structural and behavioral
properties of database-intensive applications.

## 2.   ACM/PCM:   CONCEPTS, TOOLS and TECHNIQUES

The structure and behavior modelling concepts of ACM/PCM are defined in the Extended Sematic Hierarchy Model (SHM+).  Before presenting the ACM/PCM logical design and specification methodology, first the means for structure modelling are presented, followed by the means for behaviour modelling.

### 2.1  Structure Modelling Concepts and Tools

For the design and specification of structural properties of database applications, SHM+ provides one structural concept, the object, and four forms of structural abstraction for relating objects.  SHM+ extends the semantic hierarchy model [7,8] by adding the association abstraction to the three forms of abstraction:  classification, aggregation and generalization.

<u>Classification</u> is a form of abstraction in which a collection of objects is considered as a higher level object class.  An <u>object class</u> is a precise characterization of all properties shared by each object in the collection.  An <u>object</u> is an instance of an object class if it has the properties defined in the class. Classification represents an *instance-of* relationship between an object class in a schema and an object in a database.  For example, an object class *employee* with properties *employee-name, employee-number,* and *salary* may have as an instance the object with property values 'John Smith', 402 and $20,000.  Classification is used in structure modelling to identify, classify and describe objects in terms of object classes.  In the remainder of the paper, 'object' is used to refer to object classes and the associated objects except when the two concepts must be distinguished.

Aggregation, generalization and association are used to relate objects.  Some properties of an object are determined by the role it plays in one or more of these relationships.  <u>Aggregation</u> is a form of abstraction in which a relationship between <u>component objects</u> is considered as a higher level <u>aggregate</u> object. This is the *part-of* relationship.  For example, an *employee* may be an aggregate of components *employee-number, employee-name,* and *salary.*  <u>Generalization</u> is a form of abstraction in which a relationship between category objects is considered as a higher level <u>generic object</u>.  This is the *is-a* relationship.  For example, the generic *employee* may be a generalization of categories *secretary* and *manager,* i.e., *secretary is-a employee* and *manager is-a employee.*  <u>Association</u> is a form of abstraction in which a relationship between <u>member objects</u> is considered as a higher level <u>set object</u>.  This is the *member-of* relationship.  For example, the set *union* is an association of *employee* members and the set *management* is a set of *employee* members.

The three forms of abstraction provide techniques for structure modelling.  The main techniques, composition/decomposition and generalization/specialization, take advantage of property inheritance.  Aggregation and association support upward inheritance in which properties of the components or members are inherited by the aggregate or set.  For example, the properties of the components *employee-name, employee-number,* and *salary* are inherited as properties of the aggregate *employee.*  Aggregates and sets are designed by <u>decomposition</u> into, or <u>composition from</u>, components or members without concern for their properties.  <u>Generalization</u> supports downward inheritance in which all properties of a generic object are inherited by each of its category objects.  For example, the categories *secretary* and *manager* inherit all properties of the generic *employee.* Categories are designed by <u>specialization</u> in which only those properties that distinguish the category object from the generic object are defined.  For example, a *secretary* is defined as an *employee* with the distinguishing property of *typing-speed.*  Alternatively, a generic object can be generalized from the common properties of distinct objects.  Property inheritance supports abstraction, modularity and consistancy, since essential properties of an object are defined once and are inherited in all relationships in which it takes part.

Structure modelling at the conceptual level involves the identification and relationship of all objects required for an application.  Aggregation, generalization and association can be applied to compose objects to form aggregates,
generics and sets, and to decompose objects into components, categories and members.  Repeated application of composition/decomposition results in aggregation
and association hierarchies.  The repeated applications of generalization/spe-
cialization results in generalization hierarchies.  An object can simultaneously
take part in all three kinds of hierarchies.  The combined result is a conceptual model of the application which reflects the complexity of the application
being modelled.  The complexity can be reduced by ignoring particular details to
consider each object independently as an aggregate, component, generic, category,
set or member.

Structure modelling at the transaction level involves identifying objects and relationships needed by a transaction.  Those common to other transactions are
selected from the conceptual model.  Additional objects and relationships may be
introduced as local to the transaction.

Object schemes are diagramatic tools that aid gross structure design.  An object
scheme, like a data structure diagram and an E-R diagram, graphically represents
the objects and structural relationships of a database application.  An <u>object
scheme</u> is a directed graph in which nodes are strings denoting objects and edges
identify aggregation, generalization and association relationships between objects.  The graphic notation for the three forms of abstraction are given in
Figure 1.

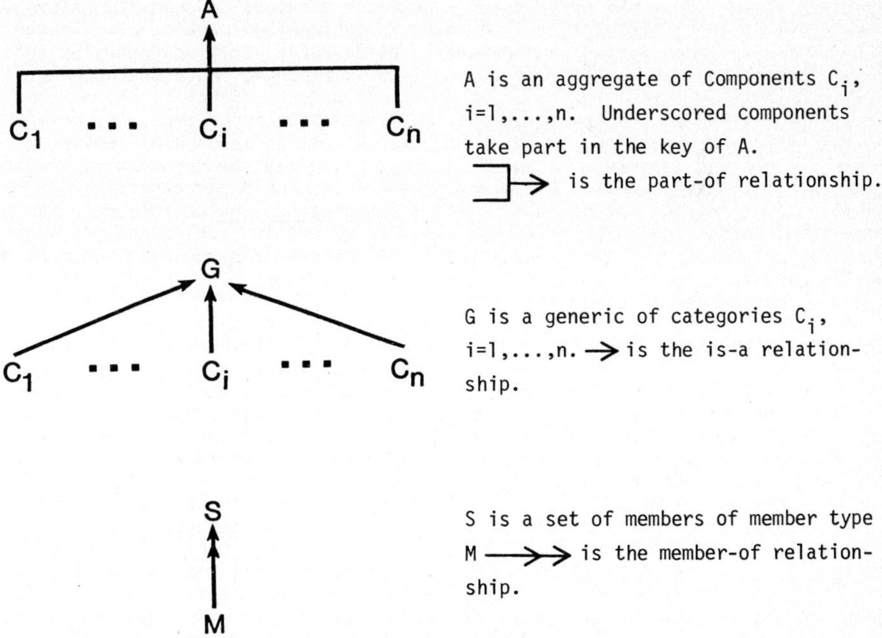


Figure 1:  Object Scheme Notational Conventions

Using object schemes, the gross design of structure takes advantage of abstraction and modularity.  Detailed information about constituent objects can be ignored when designing an object.  Many structural properties can be assumed through property inheritance.

## 2.2  Behavior Modelling Concepts and Tools

For the design and specification of behavioral properties of database applications, SHM+ provides primitive database operations on objects, three forms of control abstraction with which to compose application-oriented operations and two forms of procedural abstraction:  actions for conceptual modelling and transactions for transaction modelling.

Each database operation is either an altering or a retrieval operation over a single instance of an object class.  The altering operations are INSERT, DELETE and UPDATE, e.g., INSERT *employee*, UPDATE *employee-salary* and DELETE *employee-group*.  Altering operations ensure SHM+ semantics for each role an objects plays, e.g., an aggregate can be inserted only if the essential components exist; deleting a generic causes its categories to be deleted.  Retrieval operations for object values are:  FIND an object in the database, CREATE an object using a defined procedure and REQUEST an object (interactively) from the user.

Control abstractions are used to relate operations to form higher-level, composite operations.  The three forms of control abstraction sequence, choice and repetition are behavioral analogs of the three forms of structural abstraction. Aggregation corresponds to <u>sequence</u>.  An operation on an aggregate is composed of a sequence of operations, one of each component.  Generalization corresponds to <u>choice</u>, e.g., <u>if</u> <u>then</u> <u>else</u> or <u>case</u> control structures.  An operation on a generic is composed of an operation on the generic category.  Association corresponds to repetition, e.g., <u>do</u> <u>while</u> or <u>for each</u> control structures.  An operation on a set is composed of an operation that is applied to each member of the set.  The three forms of control abstraction can be used to define all primitive recursive functions.  Hence, they are sufficient for most application-oriented operations.

Behavior modelling at the conceptual level involves the identification, design and specification of actions for each object.  An <u>action</u> is an application-oriented operation designed for one object to ensure that all properties of the object are satisfied.  An action is designed from a single database altering operation by providing the necessary invocation context.  Before invoking the database operation, certain pre-conditions must be met and actions on other objects may be necessary.  After the actions are invoked, a post-condition must be checked and the database operation is executed.  For both pre- and post-conditions, exception handling must be designed.

Actions provide the only means of altering an object.  This ensures the semantic integrity of an object since all constraints on the object must be satisfied by all attempts to alter it.  The <u>scope</u> of an action includes the object of interest and all objects immediately related by aggregation, generalization or association.  The database operation can alter only the object of interest.  All other objects are accessed by means of actions.  Actions provide a degree of modularity which aids design and re-design.  The behavior of an object is completely defined by its actions.  The objective of designing actions for an object is that they may be used to construct any legal, application-oriented operation.

The behavioral and structural properties of an object constitute a data abstraction which completely defines the semantics of the object.  The result of conceptual modelling, the conceptual model of the application, is a network of data abstractions related by the three forms of abstraction.  The objective of conceptual modelling is to provide an adequate basis for the design of all application-oriented objects and operations, e.g., queries and transactions.

Behavior modelling at the transaction level involves the identification, design and specification of transactions. Transactions are designed to fulfill specific user requirements. A <u>transaction</u> is an application-oriented operation which alters one or more objects. A <u>transaction scope</u> includes all objects accessed in the transaction. A transaction is designed from actions on objects in the scope by providing an appropriate invocation context. The invocation context of a transaction provides a particular <u>behavioral view</u> of the underlying conceptual model just as derivation rules and constraints provide particular <u>structural views</u>. Pre-conditions, action invocations, post-conditions and exception-handling are required, as is the case with actions. However, unlike actions there is no database operation.

To ensure the semantic integrity of database applications there is a strict invocation hierarchy. Transactions are the only means for end users to alter the database. Transactions invoke actions which are the only means of altering objects. Each action invokes a single database operation to alter a single object. Both actions and transactions are well-defined logical units with well-defined scopes, pre- and post-conditions and effects on the database. Typically, transactions have been used as a unit of physical integrity. Design using the SHM+ treats actions and transactions as units of semantic integrity.

Behavior modelling is done, together with structure modelling, in a two step process which reduces the amount of detail to be considered at one tiem. First the gross behavioral properties are designed. Actions and transactions are identified and related to objects. Then, aided by the gross designs, actions and the fine details of actions and transactions are specified.

SHM+ provides design aids for the design of gross behavioral properties. A <u>behavior scheme</u> is an explicit graphical representation of the gross properties of a single action or transaction. Three forms of control abstraction, (i.e., sequence, choice and repetition) are used to represent the behavioral relationships between action (or transaction) and its constituent operations. There is a constituent operation for each object in the action or transaction scope. The constituent operations and their relationships are represented by adding behavioral information to an object scheme. This facilitates the explicit modelling of behavior at a gross level of detail. Behavior schemes integrate structural and behavioral properties in one representation.

A <u>behavior scheme</u> for an action or transaction is an object scheme which includes each object in the scope plus an operation label on each edge, one lable for each constituent operation. An operation label indicates the nature of a constituent operation by naming the database operation(s) on which it is based and by giving an invocation context by means of an arrow ($\longrightarrow$). The arrow points to the object on which the operation is invoked and points from the object that invoked it. A double arrow ($\Longrightarrow$) is used to distinguish the action or transaction from the constituent operations. The relationship between operations is given by the forms of abstraction.

Figure 2 gives the notation for behavioral relationships and invocation contexts for behavior schemes by adding operation edge notation to the object scheme notation given in Figure 1. In Figure 2, $T_1$, $T_2$, and $T_3$ are the names of actions or transactions; $O_1$, $O_2$, ..., $O_n$ are the names of constituent operations.

Although most constituent operations are based on one action, they can be composed by sequence, choice and repetition of one or more actions. Operation edges name the database operations on which the action is based. The syntax for operation names is given by the grammar,

OP ::= *insert*|*update*|*delete*|*find*|*request*|*create*|*null*|
     OP ∨ OP|OP ∧ OP|OP*

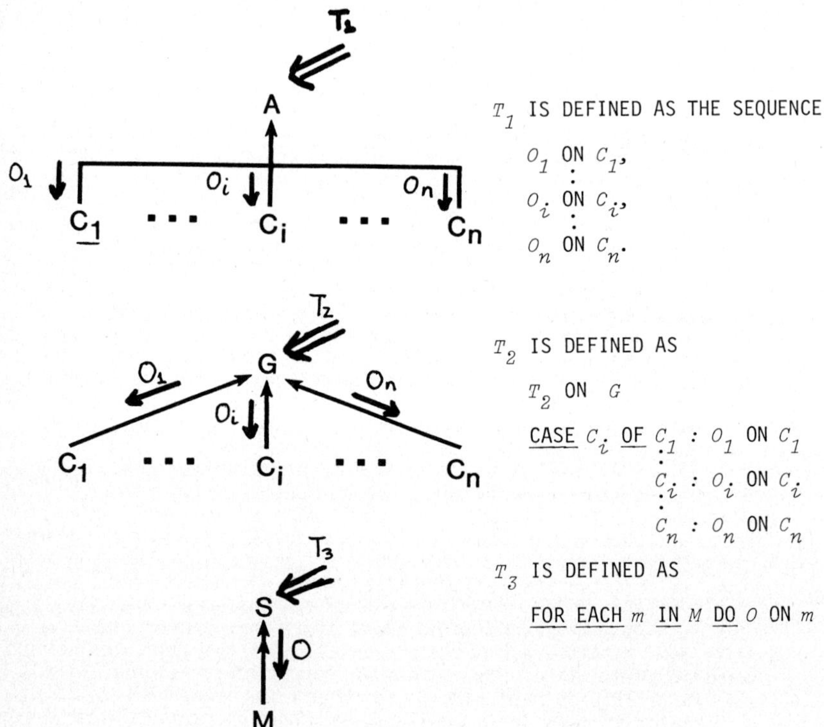



Figure 2:  Behavioral Relationships in Behavior Schemes

where 'Λ' indicates <u>and</u> (for sequence); 'V' indicates <u>or</u> (for choice); and '*' indicates zero or more repetitions.

Using behavior schemes, the design of gross behavioral properties of actions and transactions can be done explicitly and abstractly taking advantage of modularity. The effect of an operation is considered explicitly in terms of constitutent operations, their relationship and invocation context.  Detailed information about constituent objects, hence parameters, can be ignored as can the details of actions on those objects.  Those actions can be designed using separate behavior schemes and can be invoked by any object to which the object is related.  This modularity simplifies the design process and ensures the semantic integrity of the object.

Due to the abstraction and modularity inherent in object and behavior schemes, gross conceptual modelling can precede or follow gross transaction modelling. Experience with SHM+ has shown that neither transaction nor conceptual modelling should be complete independently, but that design is an iterative process. Generally, a preliminary design of transaction schemes aids substantially in conceptual modelling which is then followed by complete transaction modelling.

Gross structural and behavioral properties designed using object and action schemes can be specified precisely using an extension of BETA [1,2].  Structure specification is straightforward and is illustrated in the next section.  Behavior specification, less conventional in database methodologies, are described briefly.

A behavior specification is a complete definition of the behavioral properties of
an action or transaction.  Such specifications should be precise, abstract, formal
and easy to use and modify.  To be complete, all properties must be defined precisely and explicitly.  Typically this means many constraints on each operation.
A specification is abstract if it gives a minimum amount of detail should be
excluded.  Formal (possibly automated) techniques can be applied for semantic
integrity analysis of formal specifications.  Finally, due to the size, complexity
and evolutionary nature of database applications, specifications should be easily
constructed, understood and modified.

BETA behavior specifications are based on the axiomatic and predicate transformer
techniques.  A behavior specification is given in terms of constraints expressed
as predicates, hence, they can be both abstract and precise.  They are readily
constructed and modified by adding and deleting predicates.

Actions and transactions have similar components based on the form:

$$N (V) I, O, L:  P\{A\} Q, D$$

$N$ is the operation name and $V$ is a parameter list.  $I, O, L$ defines the operation's scope by naming: $I$, the objects accessed through actions and retrieval
operations; $O$, the object altered through the database operation, $D$; and, $L$, the
objects local to the operation.  The effect of the operation is specified in terms
of: a pre-condition, $P$; an active role, $A$; a post-condition, $Q$; and possibly a
database operation $D$.  $P$ and $Q$ are lists of  predicates and $A$ is composed of zero
or more action invocations.

An action alters one object, $O$, directly by means of an SHM+ primitive INSERT,
UPDATE or DELETE operation, $D$, and can access objects, $I$, that are or will be
immediately related to $O$ by means of actions in $A$.  $P\{A\}Q$ constitutes the pre-
condition to be satisfied to ensure the successful execution of $D$.  $P\{A\}Q$  must
check or establish every relationship between $O$ and objects in $I$.  The optential
complexity of $P\{A\}Q$ warrants considering it in three parts.  $P$ ensures that $A$ can
proceed.  The actions in $A$ appropriately alter the object in $I$ to ensure the desired relationships and $Q$ checks the success of $A$.

A transaction can access any collection of objects only by means of their actions,
hence, $O$ and $D$ are empty.  $I$ and $L$ define the transaction scope.  $P$ is the pre-
condition that determines whether $A$ can proceed.  $A$ is composed of actions that
achieve the desired effects of the transaction which are then checked by the post-
condition $Q$.

The active role of an action consists of invocation of actions on related objects.
An action invoked in an active role is called a <u>dependent</u> action.  Unlike an action in the active role of a transaction, a dependent action must ignore properties of the object that invoked it.  Otherwise, the dependent action may invoke
the invoking action resulting in circularity.

A behavior specification has the form:

$$N (V) I, O, L:  P\{ \}Q, D$$

The effect of an action or transaction, i.e., exactly <u>what</u> it does, is completely
defined by $P\{ \}Q, D$.  The active role $A$ defines <u>how</u> the effect is achieved and is
therefore excluded as inappropriate detail for a specification.  The effect of an
operation is specified in terms of simple predicates in $P$ and $Q$ that can be precise, abstract, formal and easy to specify and modify.


## 2.3  The ACM/PCM Technique

Conceptual and Transaction Modelling are divided into the following
steps and result in the named products:

A. CONCEPTUAL MODELLING
   A.1  CONCEPTUAL MODELLING OF STRUCTURE
      A.1.1 Structure Design
         An _object scheme_ for each object and an integrated object
         scheme for the entire application.
      A.1.2 Structure Specification
         A structure specification for each object.
   A.2  CONCEPTUAL MODELLING OF BEHAVIOR
      A.2.1 Behavior Design
         One insert, one delete and at least one update _action scheme_
         for each object.
      A.2.2 Behavior Specification
         A _behavior specification_ for each action scheme.
   A.3  ENCAPSULATION
      One data abstraction for each object consisting of its structure
      and behavior specifications.
B. TRANSACTION MODELLING
   B.1 TRANSACTION DESIGN
      A _transaction scheme_ for each identified transaction
   B.2 TRANSACTION SPECIFICATION
      A _transaction specification_ for each identified transaction

Each step is now outlined in detail.

A. CONCEPTUAL MODELLING
   A.1 CONCEPTUAL MODELLING OF STRUCTURE
      A.1.1.  Structure Design
      A.1.1.1.  Object identification:
         Identify and name the basic objects to be represented.
      A.1.1.2.  Object classification:
         Classify each object as either _permanent_ or _temporary_ and
         as _independent_ or _dependent_.
      A.1.1.3.  Construct individual object schemes:
         Considering permanent objects first, apply the aggregation/
         decomposition, generalization/specialization and associa-
         tion/membership to each identified object.  Consider first
         the independent objects and then dependent objects. this step
         results in identifying the _basic objects_.
      A.1.1.4.  Object Scheme integration:
         Connect all object schemes to form an integrated _object
         scheme_.  The integrated  object scheme should include all
         objects (basic and composite) and all structure relation-
         ships.
      A.1.1.5.  Object scheme refinement and verification:
         Ensure that all information and structural properties as
         defined in the requirements and previous steps, are
         represented in the integrated object scheme.
      A.1.1.6.  Constraints identification:
         Express any required constraint not implicitly stated in
         the object scheme representation.

Examples of Structure Design (A.1.1.)
    ex: A.1.1.1.  TECHNICAL-COMMITTEE
              WORKING-GROUP

              REFEREE
              PAPER

    ex: A.1.1.2.  Technical Committee is considered permanent and independent,
            while a working-group is considered permanent and dependent
            (depends on technical-committee).

ex:   A.1.1.3.

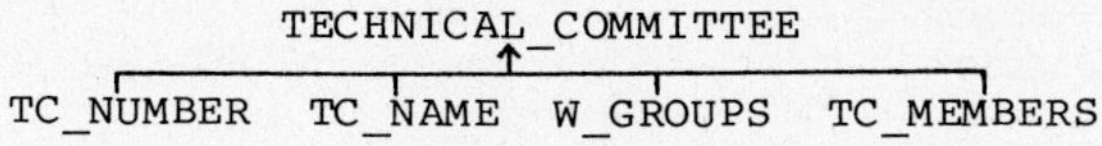

<pre>
                      TECHNICAL_COMMITTEE
           ┌──────────────────┴──────────────────┐
      TC_NUMBER    TC_NAME   W_GROUPS    TC_MEMBERS
</pre>

        Figure 3 : TECHNICAL_COMMITTEE Object Scheme

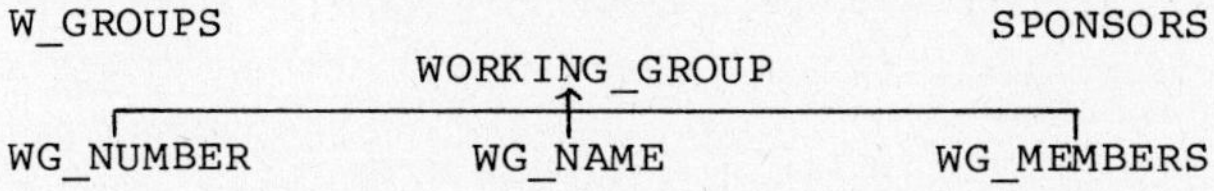

<pre>
  W_GROUPS                                    SPONSORS
                    WORKING_GROUP
           ┌──────────────┴──────────────┐
      WG_NUMBER          WG_NAME          WG_MEMBERS
</pre>

        Figure 4 : WORKING_GROUP Object Scheme


ex:   A.1.1.4.  see integrated object scheme diagram. Figure 17.

ex:   A.1.1.6  "Each technical committee should have at least one working
               group".
A.1.2. STRUCTURE SPECIFICATION:
       A.1.2.1.   Identify Fine Structural Detail
                  For each aggregate, identify key components and essential
                  (cannot be null) components.  Identify the domain (type) of
                  each object.  For each category of a generic object, deter-
                  mine whether the category is exclusive (an object of that
                  category can be in only one category for the same generic).

                  For each association object, determine whether membership is
                  automatic or manual.  Membership is automatic when the members
                  of one association are identified through a predicate calculus
                  expression.  Membership is manual when objects become members
                  of an association through explicit database operations.

                  In order to perform this step, one must consider the object
                  schemes, the requirements, SHM+ and BETA, the specification
                  language.

       A.1.2.2.  Structure Specification (using BETA)
                 For each object specify its structural properties based on
                 previously designed object schemes.
       A.1.2.3.  Assertion Specification
                 Specify each constraint identified in the step A.1.1.6 as an
                 assertion over the integrated object scheme.
       A.].2.4.  Verify the Specification
                 Insure that all specifications are consistent by considering
                 the semantics of the SHM+, the requirements and the integrated
                 object scheme.  Insure users and management understand and
                 approve the specification.

Examples of Structure Specification (A.1.2.)
      ex:   A.1.2.1.   Consider the object scheme in example A.1.1.3.
                       TC-NAME and TC-NUMBER are both keys for technical-committee.

TC-MEMBERS and W-GROUPS were considered essential components,
since each technical-committee should have both.  The basic
components here are TC-NUMBER and TC-NAME which were identified to belong to the domains INTEGER4 and STR160 respectively.  The type INTEGER4 is defined as being integers in the
range from 1 to 9999, while STR160 is defined as being any
alfanumeric string 160 characters.

```
ex:  A.1.2.2.  (a)   the specification of TECHNICAL-COMMITTEE:
                     type
                          integer4 = 1..9999;
                          str160   = STRING OF 160 CHARACTERS;
                     technical-committee =   OBJECT
                        AGGREGATE OF
                             tc-members:ESSENTIAL;
                             tc-number;
                             tc-name;
                             w-groups:ESSENTIAL;
                                 KEY Tc-name;
                                 PRIMARY KEY tc-number;
                     END OBJECT;
              (b)   manual association object specification:
                    w-groups = OBJECT
                       AGGREGATE OF
                            tc-number;
                            PRIMARY KEY tc-number;
                       ASSOCIATION OF working-group:
                            MANUAL MEMBERSHIP;
                       END OBJECT
              (c)   automatic association object specification:
                    referees = OBJECT
                       AGGREGATE OF
                            wc-name;
                            PRIMARY KEY wc-name;
                       ASSOCIATION OF referee:
                            AUTOMATIC MEMBERSHIP (each r in referee);
                       END OBJECT;
```

The above specify that each referee occurrence belongs to the referee
association.

```
              (d)   a category object specification:
                    person = OBJECT
                       AGGREGATE OF
                            person-number;
                            person-name;
                            address:essential;
                              KEY person-name;
                              PRIMARY KEY person-number;
                       GENERIC OF
                            national-representative;
                            cfp-invitee : NONEXCLUSIVE;
                            conference-invitee : NONEXCLUSIVE;
                            tc-member : NONEXCLUSIVE;
                            referee : NONEXCLUSIVE:
                            ws-member : NONEXCLUSIVE;
                            oc-member : NONEXCLUSIVE;
                            pc-member : NONEXCLUSIVE;
                            pc-chairperson : NONEXCLUSIVE;
                            oc-chairperson : NONEXCLUSIVE;
```

```
            session-chairperson : NONEXCLUSIVE;
            attendee : NONEXCLUSIVE;
        END OBJECT;
```

ex:  A.1.2.3.  The constraint example can be expressed in BETA in the following assertions:

ALL tc IN technical-committee (SOME tcms IN tc-members (tcms PART OF tc));

ALL tcms IN tc-members (SOME tc IN technical-committee (tcms PART OF tc));

ALL tcms IN tc-members (SOME tcm IN tc-member (tcm MEMBER OF tcms));

A.2.  <u>CONCEPTUAL MODELLING OF BEHAVIOR</u>
In this step, actions and dependent actions are designed for each object.  One insert, one delete and one or more update actions are designed for each object.  Insert and update actions are considered first.
A.2.1.  Design of Gross Behavior Detail.
The following steps are to be applied to each independent, composite object in the object scheme using classification done in the step A.1.1.2.  Objects that cannot be manipulated directly (i.e. those strictly dependent on other objects) need not be considered for action schemes.  They will be inserted, updated and deleted through dependent actions (to be considered in 2.1.4).
A.2.1.1  Object abstraction
Consider the complete object scheme for the object, i.e. the object and all immediately related objects (aggregates, components, generics, categories, associations and members connected to it by one edge.)
A.2.1.2.  Action schemes design
Design  the insert, update and delete action schemes by considering the requirements, the object scheme and the SHM+ action scheme template given in section 2.2.
A.2.1.2.1.  Insert and Delete action scheme design:
Insert and delete action schemes are constructed by considering the effect of the object insertion or deletion on all other objects in the object scheme.  The action over the object is decomposed into <u>insert</u>, <u>delete</u>, <u>update</u>, <u>find</u>, <u>create</u>, or <u>null</u> dependent actions over each one of the objects in the object scheme.  The requirements, the SHM+ data model constraints and the assertions will determine what dependent actions should be used.  The insert or delete action of an object must enforce all desirable properties of the object with respect to the other objects connected to it.
A.2.1.2.2.  Update Action Schemes Design
For each updatable combination of properties, construct an update action scheme by determining the dependent actions necessary to have the desired effect on each related object.

Examples of Behavior Design
ex:  A.2.1.1.  insert technical-committee action scheme:
Object abstraction is achieved by considering only the technical-committee object scheme (see ex: A.1.1.3).
Insert action scheme design:  in order to perform an insert technical-committee operation we should insert the key components (tc-number and tc-name which are basic objects) and insert the essential components tc-members and w-groups which are associate objects.  The action scheme becomes:

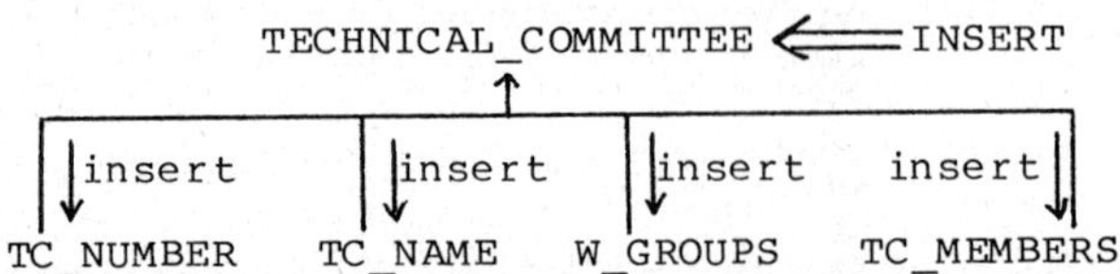

Figure 5: Insert TECHNICAL_COMMITEE

A.2.1.2.  Dependent Action Design
This step is to be followed after all action schemes are
constructed.  For each object, collect all dependent actions
invoked on it by immediately related objects.  Dependent
actions are either inserts, deletes, updates, finds, create,
or null.  Find, create and null are primitive operations
requiring no action scheme.  Design action schemes for the
remaining dependent actions by (1) specializing the corresponding, existing action schemes, i.e., adding and deleting
properties to account for the context in which the action is
invoked or (2) if the action does not exist, follow steps
A.2.1.2.1 or A.2.1.2.2.

ex:  A.2.1.3.  Dependent Action Insert w-groups:
The object scheme is

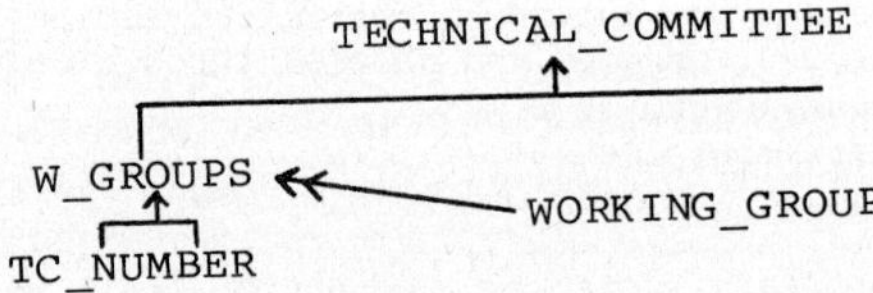

Figure 6: W_GROUPS Object Scheme

As a design decision, the dependent action of insertion w-
groups upon the insertion of technical-committee should
yield an association with no members (initially empty).  The
association will be populated by insert working-group action.
The dependent action scheme is:

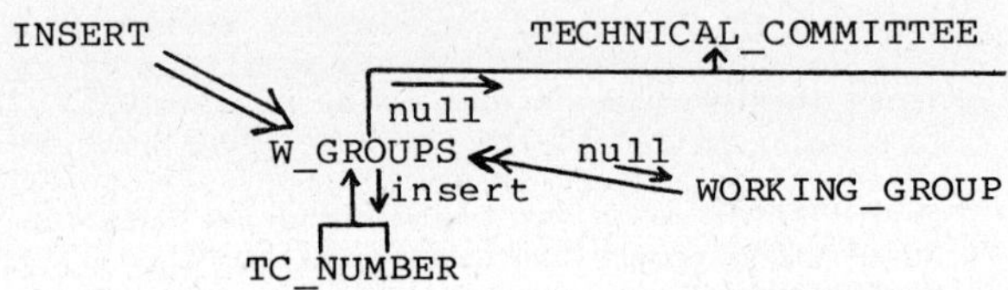

Figure 7: INSERT W_GROUPS Dependent Action Scheme

A.2.2  BEHAVIOR SPECIFICATION
Each action and dependent action is specified using BETA.  The following steps should be performed for each action and dependent action.
A.2.2.1.  Scope specification:
Specify information to be passed as parameters to the action;
to be obtained through user interaction; and which objects to
be inserted/updated/deleted by the action.  Specify objects
in the action scheme on which a dependent action will be pre-
formed.

A.2.2.2.  Pre/post condition specification:
    Define pre-conditions and post-conditions that complete the behavior
    specification for the action (or dependent action). The following
    guidelines aid pre/post-condition specifications:
    - The pre/post-condition of an action over an object must enforce
      all properties of that object with respect to its neighbors.
      Notice that the conditions cannot refer to objects outside action
      scheme.
    - Insert actions should test whether object occurrences with the
      same key exist in the database.
    - Insert actions must check the existence of essential, composite
      components.
    - Check, in the post-condition of insert member-object actions, if
      the occurrence is a member of the related manual association oc-
      curence.
    - Check, in the post-condition of delete member-object actions, if
      the occurrence is not a member of the related manual association
      occurrence.
    - Check, in the pre-condition of insert member-object actions, if
      the related association occurrence exist.
    - Do not check membership of a member object in automatic associa-
      tions.
    - Check, in the post-condition of delete aggregate-object actions,
      if the composite components that do not stand by themselves (when
      all object occurrences are part of some aggregate-object occur-
      rence) were deleted.
    - Check, in the post-condition of delete associate-object actions
      if the association occurrence has no members.
    - Check, in delete actions, the existence of the object being
      deleted.
A.2.2.3. Database operation specification:
    Specify which database operation, if any, will be executed over
    the object.
ex: A.2.2.3:  insert-technical-committee specification

```
ACTION insert-technical-committee (name, number);
   IN (name:tc-name, number: tc-number)
   OUT (tc: technical-committee)
   LOCAL (tcms: tc-members, wgs: w-groups)
   PRE-CONDITION:
      tc-doesnt-exist(number, name)?
   POST-CONDITION: tc-members-exist (number)?
      w-groups-exist (number)?
   DB-OPERATION: INSERT technical-committee (name, number tcms, wgs)
```

Notice that as a result of a design decision, the technical committee's name and
number are passed to the action as parameters.  Technical-committee is the object
being operated on (OUT specification).  There are two objects in the object
scheme, tc-members and w-groups, over which dependent actions will be performed.

    The pre-condition for this action is that there is no
    technical-committee with some name or number as the one
    being inserted.  The post-condition ensures that the
    corresponding tc-members and w-groups were inserted, before
    the database operation INSERT is performed on the techni-
    cal-committee.
    The specification of the pre and post condditions are the
    following:

```
tc-doesn't-exist(x) = NO tc IN technical-committee
   (tc.tc-number = x OR tc.tc-name = y);
tc-members-exist(x) = SOME tcms in tc-members
   (tcms.tc-number = x);
w-groups-exist(x) = SOME wgs IN w-groups
   (wgs.tc-number = x);
```

A.2.2.4.    Verify the Specification:
            Ensure that all specifications are not inconsistent by
            considering the semantics of SHM+, the requirements and the
            action schemes.  Ensure users and managers understand and
            approve the specification.


B.   TRANSACTION MODELLING

Transactions are the outermost integrity layer.  All integrity constraints
specified over the database must be enforced.  Transactions are built
on  top of existing actions.  For each transaction identified in the
requirements, carry out the following steps:
B.1.  Transaction Design:
      B.1.1.  Scope design:
              Identify all objects to be accessed in the transaction,
              i.e., those read, those over which insert, update of delete
              actions will be performed, and those referenced by any of
              the transactions pre and post conditions.
      B.1.2.  Transaction scheme design:
              Create a TRANSACTION object to connect all objects read,
              inserted or deleted.  Over the resulting scheme, specify
              the actions to be performed over each one of the objects.
              This yields the transaction scheme.
ex: B.1.2.    The Transaction to define a conference:
              Insert a working-conference object together with the tech-
              nical committees and working-groups envolved in organizing
              the conference.  The Transaction scheme is:

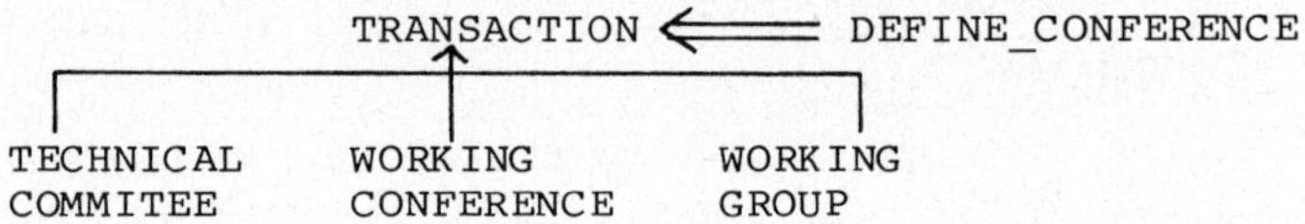


Figure 8: DEFINE_CONFERENCE Transaction Scheme


B.2.  TRANSACTION SPECIFICATION (using BETA)
      Specify each Transaction, by naming it, declaring its parameters,
      including the scope specification and defining the transactions
      behavior through pre and post conditions.
      The scope declaration must include the objects identified in B.1.1.
      and all information passed as parameters to  the transaction's
      actions.  The transaction behavior specification can be based on the
      behavior specifications of its actions.  According to this, the pre-
      conditions are the conditions required to correctly initiate the
      sequence of actions (they are obtained from the actions pre-
      conditions).  The post-conditions must check conditions that ensures
      the correct execution of actions.  The pre and post conditions
      should verify any other condition required to ensure database
      semantic integrity that is not verified at the actions pre and post
      conditions nor enforced by the actions execution.
ex: B.2.    The define-conference transaction specification is
            TRANSACTION define-conference
                SCOPE (wc: working-conference, wg: working-group,
                      tc: technical-committee, wgs: w-groups)
                PRE-CONDITION: no-wc?
                POST-CONDITION: wc-exist?
                   at-least-1-sponsor?
                   all-tc-have-at-least-1-wg?

The pre/post conditions are:

```
no-wc = NO wc IN working-conference;
wc-exist = SOME wc IN working-conference;
at-least-1-sponsor = AT LEAST 1 wg IN working-group
all-tc-have-at-least-1-wg = ALL tc IN technical-committee
      (SOME wgs IN wg-groups
      (SOME wg IN working-group
      (wgs PART of tc AND wgs MEMBER OF wgs)));
```

## 3.  ACM/PCM:  IFIP WORKING CONFERENCE EXAMPLE

A logical design of a database system was developed using the ACM/PCM technique
on IFIP Working Conference organization application system.  The problem was proposed and defined by the IFIP working group WG8.1 for a comparative review of
information systems design methodologies (CRIS Conference).

The final database specification is 70 pages long; has 42 transactions, 63 actions, 48 dependent actions, 50 basic objects (data elements) and 30 composite
objects.  Due to the size of specification, only a small part is presented here
with some of the design decisions involved. Next the ACM/PCM technique is followed with some results and decisions presented for each step.

> A.   CONCEPTUAL MODELLING OF STRUCTURE
>      The following objects were identified.
>      A.1.1.1.  To represent the basic concepts of the application (DEF identi-
>                fies the defined object, DESC is its description):

```
DEF accepted
  DESC paper accepted for presentation at the conference;
DEF assigned_to_session;
  DESC paper that is enrolled for presentation in one session
DEF attendee
  DESC a person who will be present at the conference;
DEF author
  DESC person who submitted a paper;
DEF cfp_divulgation
  DESC technical publisher or association who will get conference
       announcements for publication in their magazines;
DEF cfp_invitee
  DESC a person who will get an invitation to submit a technical
       paper to the conference;
DEF conference_invitee
  DESC person who got an invitation to attend the conference;
DEF dropped
  DESC paper withdrawn from the conference by the author;
DEF intended_attendee
  DESC person who sent a registration to attend the conference;
DEF letter_of_intent
  DESC a correspondence that indicate that an individual or more wishe
       to present one or more papers at this conference;
DEF national_representative
  DESC IFIP national representative;
DEF not_assigned_to_session
  DESC accepted paper that is currently not enrolled in any session;
DEF oc_chairperson
  DESC organizing committee chairperson;
DEF oc_member
  DESC person that belongs to the working conference
       organization committee;
DEF paper
  DESC a technical report submitted to be presented at conference;
```

```
DEF paper_referee_assignment
  DESC refers to transfering a paper to a referee for evaluation,
        consist of person, comments, date of assignment,
        deadline, date comments received, and paper;
DEF pc_chairperson
  DESC program committee chairperson;
DEF pc_member
  DESC person involved in the working conference paper
        selection;
DEF referee
  DESC appointed person to review submitted papers;
DEF rejected
  DESC technical paper not accepted by the technical committee;
DEF session
  DESC a technical meeting where  technical papers are present to
        people attending the conference;
DEF session_chairperson
  DESC individual that will be chairing the session;
DEF subscriber
  DESC person who sent a letter showing interest in presenting a paper;
DEF tc_member
  DESC representive of IFIP member society to a technical
        committee;
DEF technical_committee
  DESC IFIP technical committee;
DEF wg_member
  DESC working group member;
DEF working_conference
  DESC a IFIP technical conference to discuss and debate a specific
        issue;
```

The objects TECHNICAL-COMMITTEE, WORKING-GROUP, NATIONAL-REPRESENTATIVE, TC-MEMBER and WG-MEMBER are considered the most permanent while WORKING-CONFERENCE, CFP-INVITEE, CFT-DICULGATION, PC-CHAIRMAN, OC-CHAIRMAN nad REFEREE are considered more permanent than the others.  TECHNICAL-COMMITTEE is an independent object; WORKING-GROUP depends on TECHNICAL-COMMITTEE; WORKING-CONFERENCE depends on WORKING-GROUP; AUTHOR, ACCEPTED, REJECTED and DROPPED depends on PAPER; ASSIGNED-TO-SESSION and NOT-ASSIGNED-TO-SESSION depends on ACCEPTED.  ATTENDEE, CFP-DIVULGATION, CFP-INVITEE, PAPER, SESSION, CONFERENCE-INVITEE, INTENDED-ATTENDEE, LETTER-OF-INTENT REFEREE, PC-CHAIRPERSON, OC-CHAIRPERSON, PC-MEMBER and OC-MEMBER depends on WORKING-CONFERENCE.  ASSIGNED-TO-SESSION and SESSION-CHAIRPERSON depend on SESSION; and SUBSCRIBER depends on LETTER-OF-INTENT (step A.1.1.2).


Now object schemes are designed for each identified object.  (Step A.1.1.3)  New objects are introduced whenever necessary.  The TECHNICAL-COMMITTEE object (from the problem definition) has a unique number (assigned by IFIP), a name, at least one working group and members.  The TECHNICAL-COMMITTEE is modelled as an aggregate of TC-NUMBER, TC-NAME, TC-MEMBERS and W-GROUPS; where TC-MEMBERS and W-GROUPS are associations of TC-MEMBERS and WORKING-GROUP respectivelly.  (See Figure 3). WORKING-GROUP has a unique number, a name and members; and is modelled as an aggregate of WG-NUMBER, WG-NAME and WG-MEMBERS, associate of wg-member.  (See Figure 4) A WORKING-CONFERENCE has a name, a place where held, a start date, an end date, several sessions, a PC-CHAIRPERSON, a OC-CHAIRPERSON, zero or more REFEREES several PC and OC members, at least one sponsoring WORKING-GROUP, and eventually several of the following: ATTENDEE, CFP-INVITEE, SUBMITTED-PAPER and CFP-DIVULGATION. The Figure 9 shows  how WORKING-CONFERENCE is modelled.  The association ATTENDEES is defined as having a component, capacity, which states the maximum number of conference attendees.

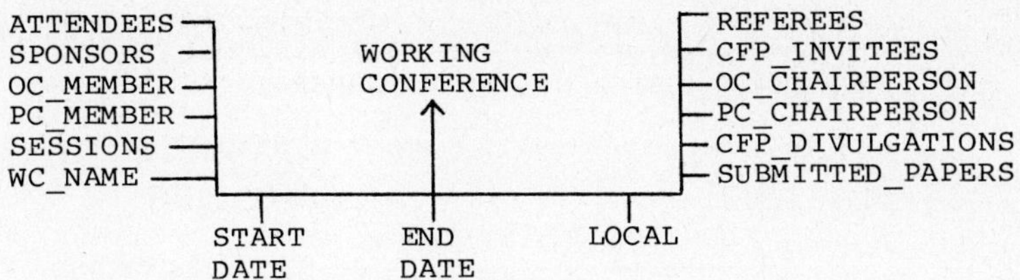

Figure 9: WORKING_CONFERENCE Object Scheme

The application requires that name and address should be stored for TC-MEMBER, WG-MEMBER, OC-MEMBER, PC-MEMBER, PC-CHAIRPERSON, OC-CHAIRPERSON, NATIONAL-REPRESENTA-TIVE, REFEREE, AUTHOR, SUBSCRIBER, SESSION-CHAIRPERSON and CFT-INVITEE (they will eventually receive a letter).  Those objects are naturally modelled as being categories of an object PERSON, which is an aggregate of name, address and an unique number (system's internal key).  CFP-INVITEE has one component that is the date when the invitation was sent (used to keep track of who got call-for-paper invitation and who still has to get one).  AUTHOR should have, as additional information, what paper he/she sent and also his/her relative position in a list of co-authors (when the paper has more than one author); this informaion is called order-number.  Instead of using AUTHOR as a category of PERSON, the fact that a person is a paper author is modelled as an aggregate AUTHORSHIP of components PAPER, PERSON (one of the authors) and order-number, with PAPER and PERSON as being the key.  SUBSCRIBER is modelled following similar reasoning.  CONFERENCE-INVITEE is defined as being the persons who get invitation to attend the confer-ence, this object is modelled as (in addition to its category role) an aggregation of invitation priority and invitation date to help keep track to whom and when invitation was sent.   An INTENDED-ATTENDEE is a person who got a conference in-vitation and wants to attend the conference (sent a registration form), the registration may or may not be accepted (the person enrolled as an attendee) due to capacity limitations.  CONFERENCE-INVITEE is modelled as a category of CONFER-ENCE-INVITEE (only conference-invitees can send registrations) having as addition-al information (aggregate) the registration date, the date when the decision whether or not enroll him as an ATTENDEE was reached and when the letter communi-cating the decision was sent.  This modelling allows great flexibility in proces-sing conference registrations.  (See Figures 10-14).

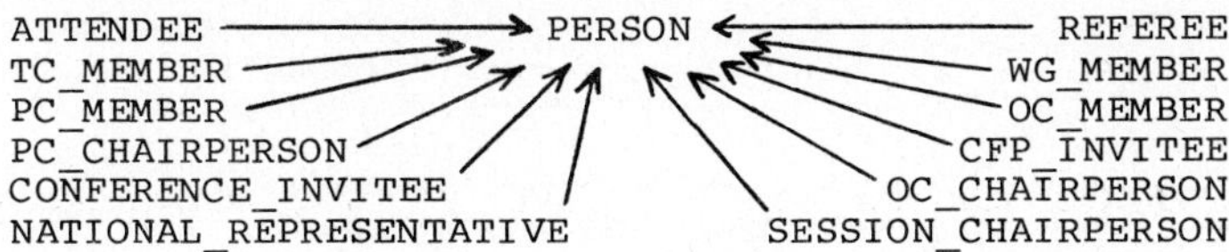

Figure 10: PERSON Object Scheme

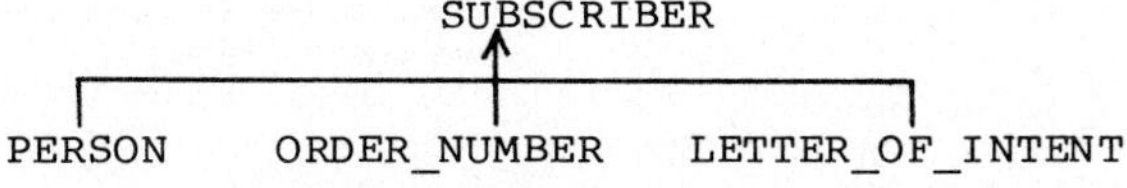

Figure 11: SUBSCRIBER Object Scheme

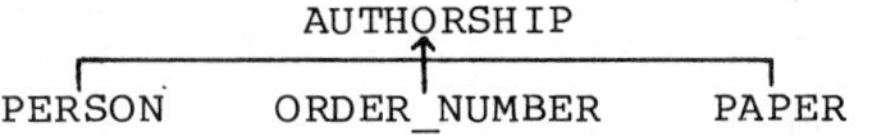

Figure 12: AUTHORSHIP Object Scheme

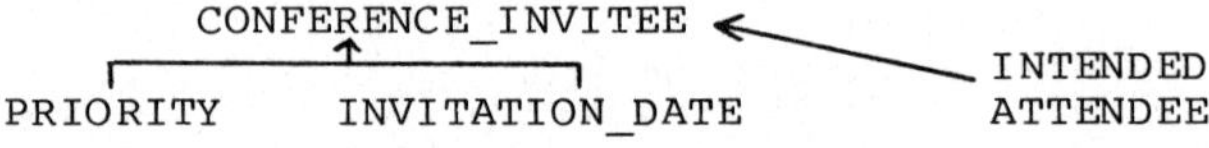

Figure 13: CONFERENCE_INVITEE Object Scheme

Figure 14: INTENDED_ATTENDEE Object Scheme

It is clear that REJECTED, ACCEPTED and DROPPED are categories of PAPER.  A RE-
JECTED paper has a component reason, that records why the program committee didn't
accept the paper.  An ACCEPTED paper is classified as being ASSIGNED-TO-SESSION or
NOT-ASSIGNED-TO-SESSION, in order to help the process of assigning papers to
session (see Figures  15-16).    All technical committees should have at least one
working group and one member; there is at most 1 working conference in the system;
up to papers can be assigned to a referee; the number of attendees cannot exceed
the capacity; all letters of intent should have at least one subscriber; all
papers should have at least one author; working groups should have at least one
member; the working conference should have at least one sponsoring working group;
no pc member can submit a paper; a session chairperson cannot have a paper authored by him (if any) in his session.  The SESSION object has a chairperson, a title,
a date when held, a meeting place, start and end times, and a set of papers that
will be presented at the session.  SESSION is modelled as an aggregate of SESSION-
CHAIRPERSON, SESSSION-TITLE, DATE, LOCAL, START-TIME, END-TIME and PAPERS-TO-BE-
PRESENTED (associate of ASSIGNED-TO-SESSION).

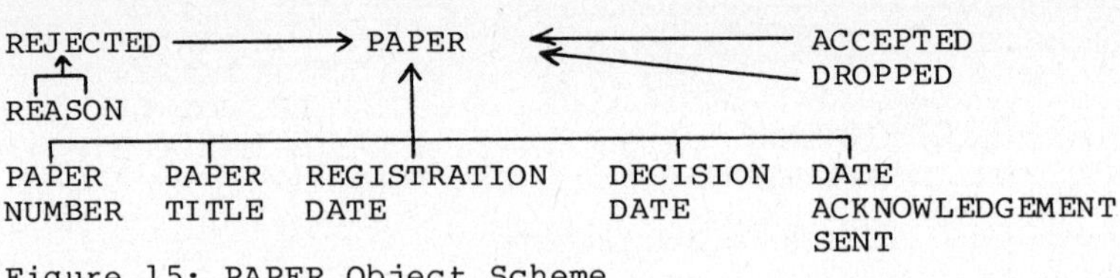

Figure 15: PAPER Object Scheme

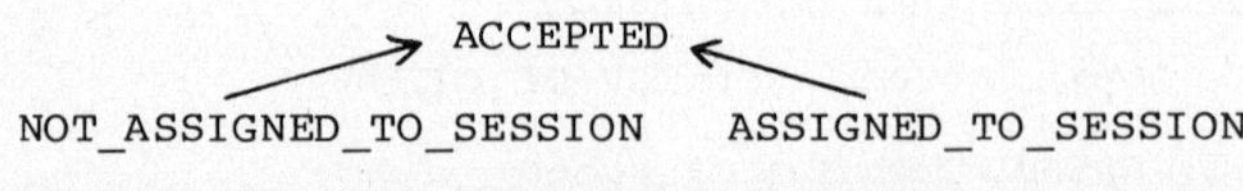

Figure 16: ACCEPTED Object Scheme

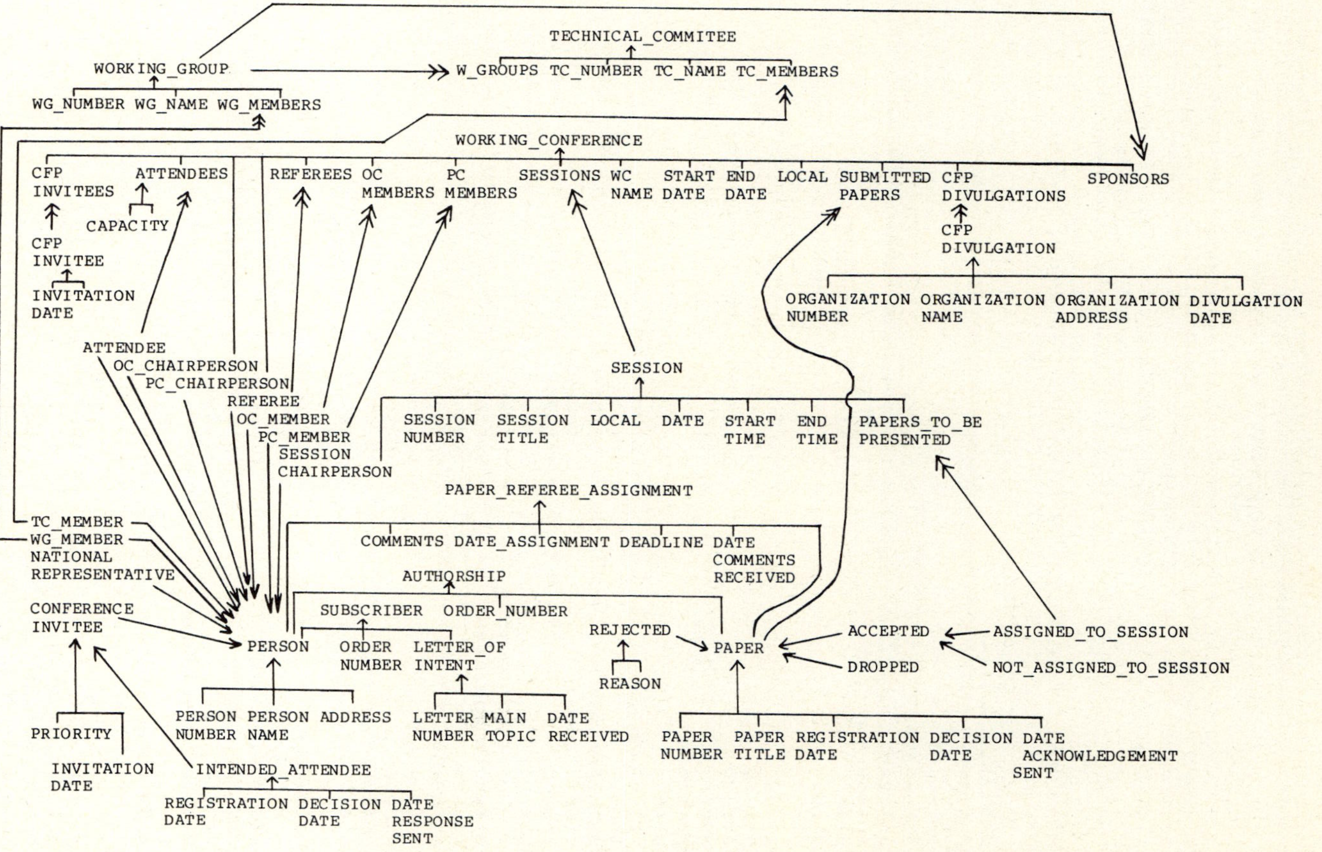


Figure 17: Integrated Object Scheme

The integated object scheme (step A.1.1.4) is shown at Figure  17.   The scheme
was refined and the resulting decisions are shown in the object scheme specification.  The following constraints were identified from the problem statement: the
next assertions are introduced to restrict the databases modelled by the integrated object scheme in order to better represent the application: the associations
TC-MEMBERS and W-GROUPS exist only if the corresponding TECHNICAL-COMMITTEE objects exist (they depend on TECHNICAL-COMMITTEE); the association objects ATTEN-
DEES, SPONSORS, PC-MEMBERS, OC-MEMBERS, REFEREES, CFP-INVITEES, SESSIONS, SUBMIT-
TED-PAPERS and DIVULGATIONS exist only if the corresponding WORKING-CONFERENCE
object exist.  Similarly, there is no PAPERS-TO-BE-PRESENT object without the corresponding SESSION; all PERSON objects belong to at least one of the categories
INTENDED-AUTHOR, CFP-INVITEE, REFEREE, TC-MEMBER, WG-MEMBER, OC-MEMBER, PC-MEMBER,
PC-CHAIRPERSON, OC-CHAIRPERSON, SESSION-CHAIRPERSON or is an author of a paper or
subscriber of a letter of intent.  The following is the resulting structure specification (step A.1.2).

```
TYPE
        integer1                        = 1..9;
        integer2                        = 1..99;
        integer3                        = 1..999;
        integer4                        = 1..9999;
        str6                            = STRING OF  6 CHARACTERS
        str8                            = STRING OF  8 CHARACTERS;
        str20                           = STRING OF 20 CHARACTERS;
        str60                           = STRING OF 60 CHARACTERS;
        str160                          = STRING OF 160 CHARACTERS;
        str400                          = STRING OF 400 CHARACTERS;
        address                         = str60;
        comments                        = str400;
        date                            = str6;
        letter_number                   = interger4;
        local                           = str20;
        main_topic                      = str20;
        order_number                    = integer1;
        reason                          = str400;
        time                            = str8;
        organization_number             = integer4;
        organization_name               = str20;
        tc_name                         = str160;
        ws_number                       = integer4;
        tc_number                       = integer2;
        ws_name                         = str160;
        end_date                        = date;
        start_date                      = date;
        place                           = address;
        wc_name                         = str160;
        end_time                        = time;
        start_time                      = time;
        session_number                  = integer2;
        session_title                   = str20;
        date_of_assignmaent             = date;
        deadline                        = date;
        date_comments_received          = date;
        paper_title                     = str160;
        paper_number                    = integer4;
        registration_date               = date;
        date_ack_sent                   = date;
        decision_date                   = date;
        date_received                   = date;
        divulgation_date                = str6;
        person_name                     = str20;
```

```
  person_number                  = integer4;
  invitation_date                = date;
  priority                       = integer1;
  date_res_received              = date;
  date_response_sent             = date;
  capacity                       = integer3;
cfp_invitee = OBJECT
  AGGREGATE OF
    invitation_date:ESSENTIAL;
  END OBJECT;

intended_attendee = OBJECT;
  AGGREGATE OF
    date_res_received:ESSENTIAL;
    decision_date;
    date_response_sent;
END OBJECT;
conference_invitee = OBJECT
  AGGREGATE OF
    priority:ESSENTIAL;
    invitation_date;
  GENERIC OF
    intended_attendee;
END OBJECT;
person = OBJECT
  AGGREGATE OF
    person_number;
    person_name;
    address:ESSENTIAL;
     KEY person_name;
     PRIMARY KEY person_number;
  GENERIC OF
    national_representative;
    cfp_invitee : NONEXCLUSIVE;
    conference_invitee : NONEXCLUSIVE;
    tc_member : NONEXCLUSIVE;
    referee : NONEXCLUSIVE;
    ws_member : NONEXCLUSIVE;
    oc_member : NONEXCLUSIVE;
    pc_member : NONEXCLUSIVE;
    pc_chairperson : NONEXCLUSIVE;
    oc_chairperson : NONEXCLUSIVE;
    session_chairperson : NONEXCLUSIVE;
    attendee : NONEXCLUSIVE;
END OBJECT;
letter_of_intent = OBJECT
  AGGREGATE OF
    date_received:ESSENTIAL;
    main_topic:ESSENTIAL;
    letter_number;
     PRIMARY KEY letter_number;
END OBJECT;
subscriber = OBJECT
  AGGREGATE OF
    person;
    letter_of_intent;
    order_number:ESSENTIAL;
     PRIMARY KEY person, letter_of_intent;
END OBJECT;
rejected = OBJECT
  AGGREGATE OF
    reason:ESSENTIAL;
  END OBJECT;
```

```
accepted = OBJECT
  GENERIC OF
    assigned_to_session : EXCLUSIVE;
    not_assigned_to_session : EXCLUSIVE;
  END OBJECT;
paper = OBJECT
  AGGREGATE OF
    paper_title:ESSENTIAL;
    paper_number;
    registration_date:ESSENTIAL;
    date_ack_sent;
    decision_date;
      KEY paper_title;
      PRIMARY KEY paper_number;
  GENERIC OF
    accepted : EXCLUSIVE;
    rejected : EXCLUSIVE;
    dropped : EXCLUSIVE;
END OBJECT;
authorship = OBJECT
  AGGREGATE OF
    person;
    paper;
    order_number:ESSENTIAL;
      PRIMARY KEY person, paper;
END OBJECT;
paper_referee_assignment = OBJECT
  AGGREGATE OF
    person;
    comments;
    date_of_assignment:ESSENTIAL;
    deadline:ESSENTIAL;
    date_comments_received;
    paper;
      PRIMARY KEY person, paper;
END OBJECT;
papers_to_be_presented = OBJECT
  AGGREGATE OF
    session_number;
      PRIMARY KEY session_number;
  ASSOCIATION OF assigned_to_session :
    MANUAL membership;
END OBJECT;
session = OBJECT
  AGGREGATE OF
    date;
    end_time;
    LOCAL;
    papers_to_be_presented:ESSENTIAL;
    session_chairperson;
    start_time;
    session_number;
    session_title:ESSENTIAL;
      PRIMARY KEY session_number;
END OBJECT;
cfp_divulgation = OBJECT
  AGGREGATE OF
    organization_number;
    organization_name:ESSENTIAL;
    address:ESSENTIAL;
    divulgation_date;
      PRIMARY KEY organization_number;
END OBJECT;
```

```
attendees = OBJECT
  AGGREGATE OF
    wc_name;
    capacity:ESSENTIAL;
      PRIMARY KEY wc_name;
  ASSOCIATION OF attendee :
    AUTOMATIC membership(EACH att IN attendee);
END OBJECT;
cfp_invitees = OBJECT
  AGGREGATE OF
    wc_name;
      PRIMARY KEY wc_name;
  ASSOCIATION OF cfp_invitee :
    AUTOMATIC membership(EACH cfp_inv IN cfp_invitee);
END OBJECT;
referees = OBJECT
  AGGREGATE OF
    wc_name;
      PRIMARY KEY wc_name;
  ASSOCIATION OF referee :
    AUTOMATIC membership(EACH r IN referee);
END OBJECT;
oc_members = OBJECT
  AGGREGATE OF
    wc_name;
      PRIMARY KEY wc_name;
  ASSOCIATION OF oc_member :
    AUTOMATIC membership(EACH oc_m IN oc_member);
END OBJECT;
pc_members = OBJECT
  AGGREGATE OF
    wc_name;
      PRIMARY KEY wc_name;
  ASSOCIATION OF pc_member :
    AUTOMATIC membership(EACH pc_m IN pc_member);
END OBJECT;
conference_invitees = OBJECT
  AGGREGATE OF
    wc_name;
      PRIMARY KEY wc_name;
  ASSOCIATION OF conference_invitee :
    AUTOMATIC membership(EACH c_i IN conference_invittee);
END OBJECT;
ws_members = OBJECT
  AGGREGATE OF
    ws_number;
      PRIMARY KEY ws_number;
  ASSOCIATION OF ws_member :
    MANUAL membership;
END OBJECT;
working_group = OBJECT
  AGGREGATE OF
    ws_members:ESSENTIAL;
    ws_number;
    ws_name;
    KEY ws_name;
      PRIMARY KEY ws_number;
END OBJECT;
```

```
sponsors = OBJECT
  AGGREGATE OF
    wc_name;
      PRIMARY KEY wc_name;
  ASSOCIATION OF working_group :
    AUTOMATIC membership(EACH ws IN working_group);
END OBJECT;
sessions = OBJECT;
  AGGREGATE OF
    wc_name;
      PRIMARY KEY wc_name;
  ASSOCIATION OF session :
    AUTOMATIC membership(EACH s IN session);
END OBJECT;
submitted_papers = OBJECT
  AGGREGATE OF
    wc_name;
      PRIMARY KEY wc_name;
  ASSOCIATION OF paper :
    AUTOMATIC membership(EACH p IN paper);
END OBJECT;
divulgations = OBJECT
  AGGREGATE OF
    wc_name;
      PRIMARY KEY wc_name;
  ASSOCIATION OF cfp_divulgation :
    AUTOMATIC membership(EACH cfp_d IN cfp_divulgation);
END OBJECT;
working_conference = OBJECT
  AGGREGATE OF
    attendees:ESSENTIAL;
    divulgations:ESSENTIAL;
    cfp_invitees:ESSENTIAL;
    conference_invittees:ESSENTIAL;
    end_date:ESSENTIAL;
    pc_members:ESSENTIAL;
    pc_chairperson:ESSENTIAL;
    place:ESSENTIAL;
    wc_name:ESSENTIAL;
    oc_members
    oc_chairperson:ESSENTIAL;
    referees:ESSENTIAL;
    sessions:ESSENTIAL;
    sponsors:ESSENTIAL;
    start_date:ESSENTIAL;
    submitted_papers:ESSENTIAL;
      PRIMARY KEY wc_name;
END OBJECT;
w_groups = OBJECT
  AGGREGATE OF
    tc_number;
      PRIMARY KEY tc_number;
  ASSOCIATION OF working_group :
    MANUAL membership;
END OBJECT;
tc_members = OBJECT
  AGGREGATE OF
    tc_number;
  PRIMARY KEY tc_number;
  ASSOCIATION OF tc_member :
    MANUAL membership;
END OBJECT;
```

```
   technical_committee = OBJECT
     AGGREGATE OF
        tc_members:ESSENTIAL;
        tc_number;
        w_groups:ESSENTIAL;
        tc_name;
        KEY tc_name;
          PRIMARY KEY tc_number;
   END OBJECT;


ASSERT


ALL tc IN technical_committee (SOME tcms IN tc_members
                                 (tcms PART OF tc));
ALL tcms IN tc_members(SOME tc IN technical_committee
                         (tcms PART OF tc));
ALL tcms IN tc_members (SOME tcm IN tc_member (tcm MEMBER OF tcms));
ALL wgs IN w_groups(SOME tc IN technical_committee
                      (wgs PART OF tc));
ALL tc IN technical_commitee (SOME wgs IN w_groups (wgs PART OF tc));
ALL wgs IN w_groups (SOME wg IN working_group (wg MEMBER OF wgs));
ALL wgms IN wg_members (SOME wg IN working_group(wgms PART OF wg));
AT MOST 1 wc IN working_conference;
AT MOST 10 pra IN paper_referee_assignment
                         (SOME p IN person (pra.person = p));
ALL as IN attendees (SOME wc IN working_conference (as PART OF wc));
ALL as IN attendees (as.capacity >= COUNT [ EACH a IN attendee])
ALL cfpis IN cfp_invitees (SOME wc IN working_conference
                                      (cfpis PART OF wc));
ALL rs IN referees (SOME wc IN working_conference (rs PART OF wc));
ALL ocms IN oc_members (SOME wc IN working_conference
                         (ocms PART OF wc));
ALL pcms IN pc_members (SOME wc IN working_conference
                         (pcms PART OF wc));
ALL cfis IN conference_invitees (SOME wc IN working_conference
                                    (cfis PART OF wc));
ALL li IN letter_of_intent (SOME s IN subscriber (li PART OF s));
ALL p IN paper (SOME a IN authorship (p PART OF a));
ALL s IN sponsors (SOME wc IN working_conference
                     (s PART OF wc));
ALL s IN sponsors (AT LEAST 1 wg IN working_group (wg MEMBER OF s));
ALL s IN sessions (SOME wc IN working_conference
                    (s PART OF wc));
ALL sps IN submitted_papers (SOME wc IN working_conference
                               (sps PART OF wc));
ALL ds IN divulgations (SOME wc IN working_conference
                          (ds PART OF wc));
ALL ptbp IN papers_to_be_presented (SOME s IN session
                                      (ptbp PART OF s));
ALL a IN accepted (SOME nats IN not_assigned_to_session (a IS nats) OR
                   (SOME ats IN assigned_to_section (a IS ats));
ALL s IN sponsors (SOME ws IN working_conference (ws MEMBER OF s));
ALL p IN person
   (SOME a IN authorship (a.person_number = p.person_number) OR
    SOME ia IN intended_author (p IS ia) OR
    SOME cfpi IN cfp_invitee (p IS cfpi) OR
    SOME r IN referee (p IS r) OR
    SOME tcm IN tc_member (p IS tcm) OR
    SOME wsm IN ws_member (p IS wsm) OR
    SOME ocm IN oc_member (p IS ocm) OR
    SOME pcm IN pc_member (p IS pcm) OR
    SOME occ IN oc_chairperson (p IS occ) OR
    SOME pcc IN pc_chairperson (p IS pcc) OR
    SOME sc IN session_chairperson (p IS sc));
```

```
NO a IN authorship (SOME p IN person ((SOME r IN referee (p IS r)) OR
                    (SOME pcm IN pc_member (p IS pcm)) AND p PART OF a);
NO s IN session (SOME ptb IN papers_to_be_presented
                (SOME as IN assigned_to_session
                (SOME ac IN accepted
                (SOME p IN paper
                (SOME a IN authorship (ptb PART OF s AND
                as MEMBER OF ptb AND ac IS as AND p IS ac AND
                p PART OF a AND s.chairperson = a.person))))));
```

Only the technical committees and working groups involved in the conference organization are stored in the system.  This decision is reflected by the SPONSORS membership of WORKING-GROUP (i.e., following association semantics, all WORKING-GROUP
objects must belong to SPONSORS).  No information about IFIP itself is stored in
the system, since this was not required in the problem definition and is not needed.  The national representative is modelled as a simple category of person, with
no further information, since their affiliation and fact that they are representatives to IFIP are not required in the system.  Technical committee and working group are represented to help the handling of TC and WG member invitations.

WORKING-CONFERENCE has several components, most of them associations.  Since the
system is a single conference system, those associations are not strictly required
(e.g., all attendees are attendees of the one conference).  The associations were
used to give more meaning to the WORKING-CONFERENCE object.  They state explicitly the relationships between the conference and the attendees, referees, OC-members and PC-members.  The problem definition stated that call-for-papers are sent
to individuals and technical magazines.  Although the handling the call-for-papers
mailing list is the same in both cases (name, address and date sent) they are
modelled by different objects because they are different real world objects, with
different semantics.  The modelling of REFEREE, PC-CHAIRPERSON, OC-CHAIRPERSON,
SESSION-CHAIRPERSON, PC-MEMBER, OC-MEMBER, TC-MEMBER, WG-MEMBER, NATIONAL-REPRE-
SENTATIVE and CFP-INVITEE as categories of PERSON allows an individual to have
different roles in the working conference system but ensures that the name and
address are the same, without redundancy.  The problem definition stated that only
authors, TC and WG members, and NATIONAL REPRESENTATIVES get invitations to attend
the conference, and that only invited persons can attend.  In order to register,
and keep track of the attendance of both conference invitees and organizers (PC
and OC members, session chairpersons), ATTENDEE was defined as being a category
of PERSON, instead of a category of conference invitee.  The INTENDED-ATTENDEE
object was identified when the problem of registration handling was analyzed.  An
organizing committee may want to wait until all registrations are received to decide who can attend when the number of persons waiting to attend exceed the capacity.  This could have been modelled using only ATTENDEE and a flag : CONFIRMED
or NOT CONFIRMED.  The former was chosen  as it is more precise.

The problem definition stated that a working-conference may or may not have referees appointed.  PC members can also "referee" papers.  The assignment of papers
for refereeing to either PC members or referees is modelled by the aggregate
PAPER-REFEREE-ASSIGNMENT with components PERSON, PAPER, COMMENTS, DATE-ASSIGNMENT,
DEADLINE, and DATE-COMMENTS-RECEIVED.  The behaviour specification makes sure that
the PERSON component belongs to one of the categories REFEREE or PC-MEMBER.  This
restricts the assignment of papers for refereeing to persons that are either PC
members or appointed referees.  The modelling of session and session chairperson
was based on the design decisions that the only restriction to the appointing of
a person to chair a session is that the person cannot have one of its papers (if
any) in the session.  The session chairperson is not required to have any other
role in the system (i.e., author, PC or OC member, WG or TC member).  DEADLINE
is in PAPER-REFEREE-ASSIGNMENT to allow the due date of the referees report to be
(1)  dependent on the date the paper was sent (say 30 days later) or (2)  a fixed
date for all papers to be returned.  The first alternative allows flexibility in
controlling the paper refereeing process.  However, the traditional approach,
alternative 2, is also permitted.

Actions and dependent actions were designed for each one of the composite objects
in the integrated object scheme.  The development of insert, update and delete
actions for an object is shown here (steps A.2.1 and A.2.2).  Consider the PAPER
OBJECT scheme (figure 18).

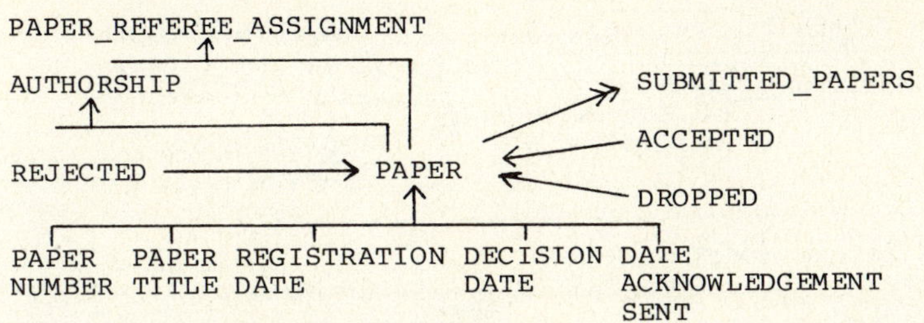

Figure 18: PAPER Object Scheme

The INSERT-PAPER action is designed as follows, considering each one of the
objects in the PAPER object scheme  PAPER x AUTHORSHIP: when the paper is inserted the associated AUTHORSHIP objects should also be inserted (each paper has at
least one author); this requires an INSERT dependent action over AUTHORSHIP.  No
dependent actions are required over the objects ACCEPTED, REJECTED and DROPPED
since the paper is judged only after its insertion.  Similarly no dependent action
is done on PAPER-REFEREE-ASSIGNMENT.  The PAPER aggregate has no composite objects
and the basic conponents are inserted with the INSERT PAPER database operation.
The figure  19  shows the insert action scheme.

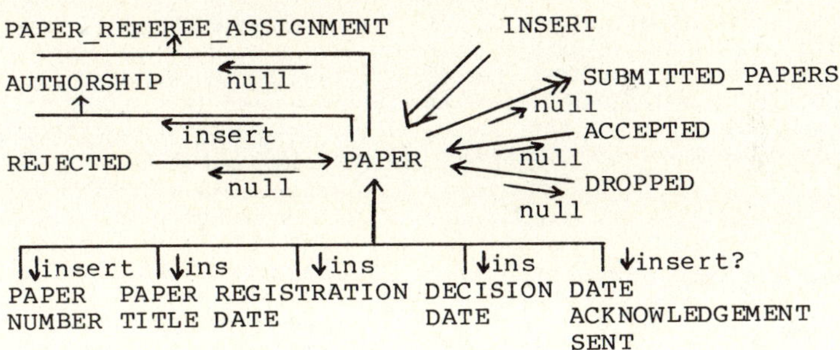

Figure 19:  INSERT_PAPER Action Scheme

The PAPER deletion requires that its authorship information should be removed from
the database, so a DELETE dependent action scheme is required for AUTHORSHIP.  As
a design decision, the paper deletion is allowed only when it has no referee assigned and is not accepted or rejected.

The design decisions for the DELETE-PAPER action are: delete the corrected AUTHOR-
SHIP and PAPER-REFEREE-ASSIGNMENT (they cannot stay in the database when PAPER is
removed since PAPER is part of the key of both objects).  No dependent action is
needed to remove the paper from the SUBMITTED-PAPERS association since the membership is automatic.  The PAPER categories should also be deleted (if the object belongs to any of them) since a category object cannot stay in the database when the

corresponding generic is deleted (SHM+ semantics).  The PAPER components are basic objects, they are removed with the database operation DELETE ACTION.  The action scheme is shown in the figure 20.

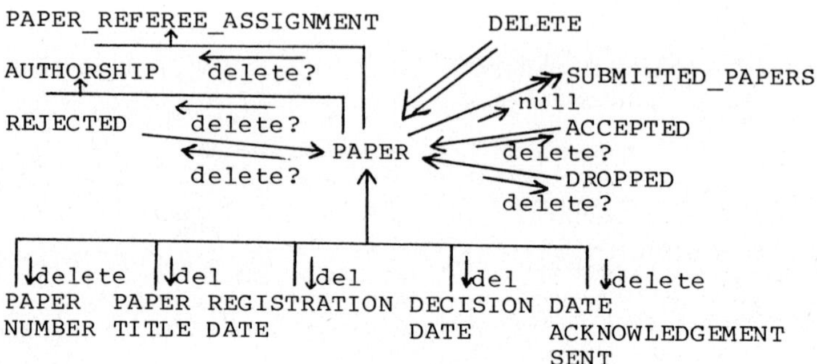


Figure 20:  INSERT_PAPER Action Scheme

The update action that is developed here allows the PAPER object be updated to correct any wrong information in the components PAPER-TITLE, REGISTRATION-DATE and DATE-ACKNOWLEDGEMENT-SENT.  This is a very simple update action, with no dependent actions (see figure 21).  The next step (A.2.1.3) is to design the dependent action schemes.  The development of 8 dependent actions (INSERT-PAPER-INSERT-AUTHORSHIP, DELETE-PAPER-DELETE-AUTHORSHIP, DELETE-PAPER-DELETE-DROPPED, DELETE-PAPER-DELETE-ACCEPTED, DELETE-PAPER-DELETE-REJECTED and DELETE-PAPER-DELETE-PAPER-REFEREE-ASSIGNMENT) is required to support the actions shown before.  The INSERT-PAPER-INSERT-AUTHORSHIP design is illustrated here (figure 22 is the AUTHORSHIP object scheme).  This dependent action (DA) is triggered by the INSERT-PAPER action, so the connection of PAPER to AUTHORSHIP is not considered here.  The AUTHORSHIP insertion requires that the corresponding person exist in the database, as a design decision we chose to insert the PERSON object if it doesn't already exist in the database (i.e. if this is the first time that information about the person is entered to the system).  Figure 22 has the DA scheme.

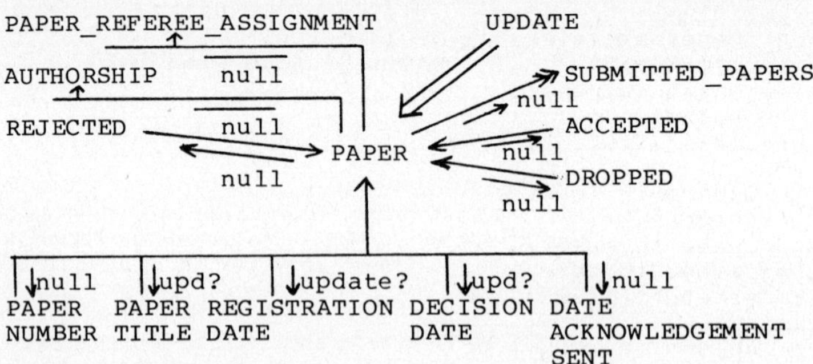


Figure 21:  INSERT_PAPER Action Scheme

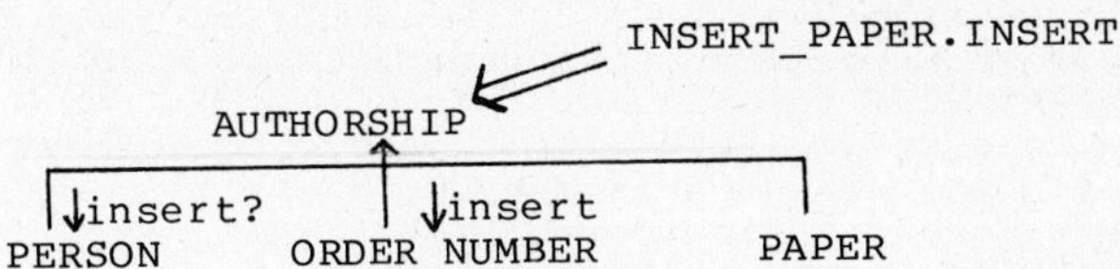


Figure 22: INSERT_AUTHORSHIP Dependent Action Scheme

The specification of the actions and transactions previously described is shown
next.  The INSERT-PAPER action specification shows that the paper number and
title are received as parameters while the other input informations (described
in IN) are obtained through user interaction.  SUBMITTED-PAPERS object is local
to the action since it's not an input nor output object and is required by the
action for correct paper insertion; this object must exist before the action is
called.  The pre-conditions require that there is no paper with the same title
or number in the system (they are the PAPER'S keys), and that the association
SUBMITTED-PAPERS exist.  The post-condition ensure that there is at least one
AUTHORSHIP object in the system for the paper being inserted before the DB-
OPERATION is performed, inserting the PAPER object with its basic components.
This is, clearly, the correct specification for the action modelled before.  To
satisfy the post-condition a dependent action to insert AUTHORSHIP must be executed; the basic objects are inserted by the db-operation (see following text).
The DELETE-PAPER action requires that a paper exist before it can be deleted
and the active role's post-condition verifies whether the appropriate dependent
actions were executed, deleting the objects that cannot exist after the db-
operation DELETE PAPER is executed.

```
paper_exist(x) =
   SOME p IN paper (p.paper_number = x);
wc_exist =
   SOME wc IN working_conference;
no_paper (x, y) =
   NO p IN paper (p.paper_number = x OR p.paper_title = y);
no_author_is_pc_member (x) =
   NO p IN person (SOME pcm IN pc_member (SOME a IN authorship
                   ((a.paper = x AND p PART OF a) AND p IS pcm)));
submitted_papers_exist =
   SOME subp IN submitted_papers;
authors_exist(x) =
   SOME a IN authorship(a.paper_number = x);
paper_not_accepted(x) =
   NO a IN accepted (a.paper_number = x);
paper_not_rejected(x) =
   NO r IN rejected (r.paper_number = x);
no_authors(x) =
    NO a IN authorship (a.paper_number = x);
paper_not_dropped(x) =
    NO d IN dropped (d.paper_number = x);
paper_not_assigned_to_referee(x) =
   NO pra IN paper_referee_assignment (pra.paper = x);
person_exist(x) =
   SOME p IN person (p.person_name = x);
isnt_assigned_to_session(x) =
   NO as IN assigned_to_session (as.paper_number = x);
```

```
isnt_not_assigned_to_session(x) =
  NO nas IN not_assigned_to_session (nas.paper_number = x);
paper_not_to_be_presented_in_any_session (x) =
  NO as IN assigned_to_session (SOME ptb IN papers_to_be_presented
            (as.paper_number = x AND as MEMBER OF ptb));
DEPENDENT ACTION isrt_paper_isrt_authorship(pen, pan)
  IN (pen:person_name, pan:paper_number, o:order_number)
  OUT (a:authorship)
  LOCAL (p:person)
  PRE-CONDITION: true?
  POST-CONDITION: person_exist(pen)?
  DB-OPERATION: INSERT authorship(pen, pan);
DEPENDENT ACTION isrt_authorship_isrt_person(pn)
  IN (pen:person_name, num:person_number, a:address)
  OUT (p:person)
  PRE-CONDITION: true?
  POST-CONDITION: true?
  DB-OPERATION: INSERT person(pn, num, a);
DEPENDENT ACTION del_paper_del_authorship(pen, pan)
  IN (pen:person_name, pan:paper_number)
  OUT (a:authorship)
  PRE-CONDITION: true?
  POST-CONDITION: true?
  DB-OPERATION: DELETE authorship(pen, pan);
DEPENDENT ACTION del_paper_del_referee_assignment(pen, pan)
  IN (pen:person_name, pan:paper_number)
  OUT (a:authorship)
  PRE-CONDITION: true?
  POST-CONDITION: true?
  DB-OPERATION: DELETE paper_referee_assignment(pen, pan);
DEPENDENT ACTION del_paper_del_dropped(pn)
  IN (pn:paper_number)
  OUT (d:dropped)
  PRE-CONDITION: true?
  POST-CONDITION: true?
  DB-OPERATION: DELETE dropped(pn);
DEPENDENT ACTION del_paper_del_accepted(pn)
  IN (pn:paper_number)
  OUT (a:accepted)
  LOCAL (as:assigned_to_session, nas:not_assigned_to_session)
  PRE-CONDITION: true?
  POST-CONDITION: isnt_assigned_to_session(pn)?
    isnt_not_assigned_to_session(pn)?
  DB-OPERATION: DELETE accepted(pn);
DEPENDENT ACTION del_paper_del_rejected(pn)
  IN (pn:paper_number)
  OUT (r:rejected)
  PRE-CONDITION: true?
  POST-CONDITION: true?
  DB-OPERATION: DELETE rejected(pn);
DEPENDENT ACTION del_accepted_del_not_assigned(pn)
  IN (pn:paper_number)
  OUT (nas:not_assigned_to_session)
  PRE-CONDITION: true?
  POST-CONDITION: true?
  DB-OPERATION: DELETE not_assigned_to_session(pn);
```

```
DEPENDENT ACTION del_accepted_del_assigned(pn)
  IN (pn:paper_number)
  OUT (as:assigned_to_session)
  LOCAL (ptb:papers_to_be_presented)
  PRE-CONDITION: true?
  POST-CONDITION: paper_not_to_be_presented_in_any_session(pn)?
  DB-OPERATION: DELETE assigned_to_session(pn);
DEPENDENT ACTION del_assigned_upd_papers_to_be_presented(pn)
  IN (pn:paper_number)
  OUT (ptb:papers_to_be_presented)
  LOCAL (sn:session_number)
  PRE-CONDITION: paper_to_be_presented(pn)?
  POST-CONDITION: true?
  DB-OPERATION: UPDATE paper_to_be_presented(sn,-pn);
ACTION insert_paper(pn, title)
  IN (a:authorship, title:paper_title, d:registration_date,
        pn:paper_number)
  OUT (p:paper)
  LOCAL (sp:submitted_papers)
  PRE-CONDITION :
    no_paper(pn, title)?
    submitted_papers_exist?
  POST-CONDITION: authors_exist(pn)?
  DB-OPERATION : INSERT paper(title, pn, d);
ACTION delete_paper(pn)
  IN (pn:paper_number)
  OUT (p:paper)
  LOCAL (a:accepted, r:rejected, d:dropped,
          a:authorship, pra:paper_referee_assignment)
  PRE-CONDITION: paper_exist(pn)?
    paper_exist(pn)?
  POST-CONDITION :
    no_authors(pn)?
    paper_not_dropped(pn)?
    paper_not_accepted(pn)?
    paper_not_rejected(pn)?
  DB-OPERATION : DELETE paper(pn);
ACTION update_paper (pn)
  IN (pn:paper_number, t:paper_title,
        rd:registration_date, dd:decision_date)
  OUT (p:paper)
  PRE-CONDITION: paper_exist(pn)?
  POST-CONDITION: true?
  DB-OPERATION: UPDATE paper(pn, t, rd, dd);
```

Consider now the design of a REGISTER-PAPER transaction. From the user viewpoint, this transaction should record in the database information about the paper
and authors. The action INSERT-PAPER does this, so all the transaction must do is
use the INSERT-PAPER action (figure 23 is the transaction scheme). The transaction specification should check in the pre-condition the non-existence of any
other paper with the same number or title (to ensure that the action can be called) and the post-condition should check if the paper now exists in the database
and if no author is pc-member (restriction stated in the problem definition);
specifying, this way, that the action INSERT-PAPER has to be used (the pre/post
condition specify that a paper with the given name and number that didn't exist
before the transaction, exist after the transaction execution, so a PAPER object
was inserted and the only way to do this is using the defined INSERT action).

```
TRANSACTION  <=======  REGISTER_PAPER
      ↑↓insert
    ┌──┴──┐
    PAPER
```

Figure 23 : REGISTER_PAPER Transaction Scheme

```
TRANSACTION register_paper(t)
  SCOPE (t:paper_title, pn:paper_number, p:paper,
         wc:working_conference, a:authorship, pcm:pc_member)
  PRE-CONDITION: wc_exist?
    no_paper(pn, t)?
  POST-CONDITION: paper_exist(pn)?
    no_author_is_pc_member(pn)?
```

Design decisions for some other actions and transactions are discussed next. See the specification of the end of the discussion.

The insertion of PAPER-REFEREE-ASSIGNMENT requires that both the PERSON who will referee and the PAPER be already stored in the system. The assignment is recorded in the database together with the date the assignment was made and the deadline (see INSERT-PAPER-REFEREE-ASSIGNMENT action). The referee's comments about a paper are recorded through the UPDATE-PAPER-REFEREE-ASSIGNMENT action, which requires that the assignment of the paper to the person refereeing was previously recorded. The transactions ASSIGN-REFEREE-TO-PAPER and REGISTER-REFEREE-COMMENTS use the above actions. To insert a PC-MEMBER object is necessary to have the corresponding generic object PERSON in the database. It was decided that such PERSON object need not exist before the action is performed. If the object doesn't exist an insert PERSON dependent action is executed to satisfy the SHM+ semantics. The person cannot already be a PC-MEMBER object. Similar decisions were made in the design of insert actions for all other categories of PERSON. The PERSON object is never inserted directly, only through one of its role (i.e., all persons in the system must have at least one role). The dependent action insert PERSON is not executed if the person already exist in the system. Notice that no dependent action to make the PC-MEMBER a member of the PC-MEMBERS association is required since this association is defined as having an automatic membership (all PC-MEMBER are members of the PC-MEMBERS association). The transaciton APPOINT-PC-MEMBER uses this action. A similar design approach was taken in the specification of actions and transactions to insert OC-MEMBERS, CFP-INVITEE, REFEREE, PC-CHAIRPERSON, and OC-CHAIRPERSON. The insertion of OC-CHAIRPERSON or PC-CHAIRPERSON require that no other such object exist, since there is only one conference in the system.

The insertion of WG-MEMBER or TC-MEMBER objects allows the person to exist already in the system as a WG or TC member respectively. The person cannot exist for the same working group or technical committee into which the person is being inserted as a member. Instead of defining INSERT WG-MEMBER or INSERT TC-MEMBER action a decision was made to model the insertions through actions ADD-MEMBER-TO-WG-MEMBERS and ADD-MEMBER-TO-TC-MEMBERS actions. They verify that the person is not already a member of the WG-MEMBERS or TC-MEMBERS associations that belong to the WORKING-GROUP, or TECHNICAL-COMMITTEE, being considered. Those actions call dependent actions to insert WG-MEMBER (or TC-MEMBER) object if the person doesn't already belong to the proper category and perform UPDATE database operations to include the member in the correct association. The problem definition stated that a person can be a member of several working groups or technical committees. The dependent actions INSERT-WG-MEMBER and INSERT-TC-MEMBER, if necessary, use the dependent action INSERT-PERSON. The dismissal of a WG-MEMBER is accomplished

by removing the person from the proper WG-MEMBERS association and by executing
a DELETE-WG-MEMBER dependent action if the person is not a member of another working-group (see action REMOVE-MEMBER-FROM-WG-MEMBERS and Transaction DROP-WG-
MEMBER). The transaction DROP-TC-MEMBER and ACTION REMOVE-MEMBER-FROM-TC-MEMBERS
were designed and specified similarly.

The action INSERT-ATTENDEE checks, before the action is started, if the capacity
is reached, if the person already exists in the system, if the person is not already registered as an ATTENDEE and if the association ATTENDEES exist (i.e., if
there is one WORKING-CONFERENCE). The Transaction REGISTER-ATTENDEE makes sure
that the person can attend the conference (i.e., is a INTEND-ATTENDEE object or a
OC or PC member, or chairperson). The transaction DROP-ATTENDEE is used to remove a person from the attendees and/or intended attendees lists, it used the
actions DELETE-ATTENDEE and DELETE-INTENDED-ATTENDEE to perform this. The reasoning is that a person can ask that his registration be withdrawn before a decision
was reached whether accept or reject the registration. When a registration is
sent the transaction REGISTER-INTENDED-ATTENDEE must be used to insert the proper
INTEND-ATTENDEE object. Several other transactions and actions were designed and
their specification follows. Only a few predicates are given.


## PREDICATE

```
has_no_paper_assigned(x) =
  NO pra IN paper_referee_assignment
          (SOME p IN person (p.person_name = x AND p PART OF pra));
ws_members_exist(x) =
  SOME wsms IN ws_members (wsms.ws_number = x);
person_not_ws_member(x, y) =
  NO wsm IN ws_member (SOME wsms IN ws_members
          (wsm.person_name = x AND wsms.ws_number = y AND
          wsm MEMBER OF wsms));
ws_member(x, y) =
    SOME wsms IN ws_members (SOME wsm IN ws_member (wsm MEMBER OF wsms
              AND wsm.person_name = x AND wsms.ws_number = y));

tc_member(x, y) =
    SOME tcms IN tc_members (SOME tcm IN tc_member (tcm MEMBER OF tcms
              AND tcm.person_name = x AND tcms.tc_number = y));
not_tc_member(x, y) =
    NO tcm IN tc_member (SOME tcms IN tc_members (tcm.person_name = x
              AND tcms.tc_number = y AND tcm MEMBER OF tcms));
person_not_pc_member(x) =
    NO pcm IN pc_member (pcm.person_name = x);

referees_exist =
    SOME rs IN referees;
member_w_groups(x, y) =
    SOME ws IN working_group (SOME wss IN w_groups (ws.ws_number = x
              AND wss.tc_number = y AND ws MEMBER OF wss));
session_chairperson_exist_if_any(x) =
    SOME sc IN session_chairperson (sc.person_name = x OR x = null);
not_ws_member(x, y) =
    NO wsm IN ws_member (SOME wsms IN ws_members (wsm.person_name = x
              AND wsms.ws_number = y AND wsm MEMBER OF wsms));
not_conference_invitee(x) =
    NO ci IN conference_invitee (ci.person_name = x);
not_intended_attendee(x) =
    NO ia IN intended_attendee (ia.person_name = x);
capacity_not_reached =
    ALL as IN attendees (COUNT [ EACH a IN attendee] < as.capacity);
```

```
ACTION insert_technical_committee(name, number);
  IN (name:tc_name, number:tc_number)
  OUT (tc:technical_committee)
  LOCAL (tcms:tc_members,wss:w_groups)
  PRE-CONDITION:
    tc_doesnt_exist(number, name)?
  POST-CONDITION : tc_members_exist(number)?
    w_groups_exist(number)?
  DB-OPERATION : INSERT technical_committee (name, number, tcms, w

ACTION delete_technical_committee(number)
  IN (number:tc_number)
  OUT (tc:technical_committee)
  LOCAL(tc_ms:tc_members, w_ss:w_groups)
  PRE-CONDITION : tc_exist(number)?
  POST-CONDITION : no_tc_members(number)?
    no_w_groups(number)?
  DB-OPERATION : DELETE technical_committtee(number)

ACTION INSERT working_conference(name, pc_c, oc_c, place, s, e)
  IN (name:wc_name, pc_c:pc_chairperson, oc_c:oc_chairperson,
       place:place, s:start_date, e:end_date)
  OUT (wc:working_conference)
  LOCAL (as:attendees, ds:divulgations, cfpis:cfp_invitees,
         cis:conference_invitees, pcms:pc_members, ocms:oc_members,
         s:sessions, sps:sponsors, subp:submitted_papers, r:referee
  PRE-CONDITION : no_wc?
  POST-CONDITION:
    attendees_exist?
    divulgations_exist?
    cfp_invitees_exist?
    conference_invitees_exist?
    pc_members_exist?
    oc_members_exist?
    sessions_exist?
    sponsors_exist?
    submitted_papers_exist?
    referees_exist?
    pc_chairperson_exist?
    oc_chairperson_exist?
  DB-OPERATION : INSERT working_conference(name, pc_c, oc_c, place
                                       s, e, as, ds, cfpis, ci
                                       pcms, ocms, ss, sps, su

ACTION delete_working_conference
  OUT (wc:working_conference)
  LOCAL (as:attendees, cfps:cfp_invitees, rs:referees, ocms:oc_mem
         pcms:pc_members, occ:oc_chairperson, pcc:pc_chairperson,
         sps:sponsors, ds:divulgations, cis:conference_invitees)
  PRE-CONDITION : wc_exist?
  POST-CONDITION :
    attendees_doesnt_exist?
    cfp_invitees_doesnt_exist?
    referees_doesnt_exist?
    oc_members_doesnt_exist?
    oc_chairperson_doesnt_exist?
    pc_chairperson_doesnt_exist?
    pc_members_doesnt_exist?
    sponsors_doesnt_exist?
    sessions_doesnt_exist?
    submitted_papers_doesnt_exist?
    divulgations_doesnt_exist?
    conference_invitees_doesnt_exist?
  DB-OPERATION : DELETE working_conference
```

```
ACTION insert_working_group(name, number, tc)
  IN (name:ws_name, number:ws_number, tc:tc_number)
  OUT(ws:working_group)
  LOCAL (wgs:w_groups, wsms:ws_members, sps:sponsors)
  PRE-CONDITION : ws_doesnt_exist(number, name)?
     sponsors_exist?
     w_groups_exist(tc)?
  POST-CONDITION : member_w_groups(number, tc)?
     ws_member_exist(number)?
  DB-OPERATION : INSERT working_group(name, number, wgs)

ACTION delete_working_group(ws_n)
  IN (ws_n:ws_number)
  OUT (ws:working_group)
  LOCAL (wgs:w_groups, wsms:ws_members)
  PRE-CONDITION : ws_exist(ws_n)?
  POST-CONDITION :
     not_member_w_groups(ws_n)?
     ws_members_doesnt_exist(ws_n)?
  DB-OPERATION : DELETE working_group(ws_n)

ACTION insert_session(s_n, s_t)
  IN (s_c:session_chairperson, s_n:session_number, s_t:session_tit
        d:date, l:LOCAL, s_time:start_time, e_time:end_time)
  OUT (s:session)
  LOCAL (p:papers_to_be_presented, ss:sessions)
  PRE-CONDITION : session_doesnt_exist(s_n)?
     sessions_exist?
  POST-CONDITION : papers_to_be_presented_exist(s_n)?
     session_chairperson_exist_if_any(sc)?
  DB-OPERATION : INSERT session(s_c, s_n, s_t, d, l, s_time, e_tim

ACTION delete_session(s_n)
  IN (s_n:session_number)
  OUT (s:session)
  LOCAL (ptb:papers_to_be_presented, sc:session_chairperson)
  PRE-CONDITION : session_exist(s_n)?
  POST-CONDITION :
     session_has_no_chairperson(s_n)?
     session_has_no_papers(s_n)?
  DB-OPERATION : DELETE session(s_n)

ACTION insert_paper_referee_assignment(pe_n, d_a, dlne, pa_n)
  IN (pe_n:person_number, d_a:date_assignment, dlne:deadline,
        pa_n:paper_number)
  OUT (pra:paper_referee_assignment)
  LOCAL (pe:person, pa:paper)
  PRE-CONDITION :
     paper_exist(pa_n)?
     person_exist(pe_n)?
     the_person_is_not_refereeing_the_paper(pe_n, pa_n)?
  POST-CONDITION : true?
  DB-OPERATION : INSERT paper_referee_assignment(pe, d_a, dlne, pa

ACTION delete_paper_referee_assignment(pe_n, pa_n)
  IN (pe_n:person_number, pa_n:paper_number)
  OUT (pra:paper_referee_assignment)
  PRE-CONDITION :
     paper_referee_assignment_exist(pe_n, pa_n)?
  POST-CONDITION : true?
  DB-OPERATION : DELETE paper_referee_assignment(pe_n, pa_n)
```

```
ACTION insert_letter_of_intent(ln)
  IN (s:subscriber, d:date_received, m:main_topic, ln:letter_number)
  OUT (l:letter_of_intent)
  PRE-CONDITION: letter_of_intent_doesnt_exist(ln)?
  POST-CONDITION: subscriber_exist(ln)?
  DB-OPERATION: INSERT letter_of_intend(d, m, ln)

ACTION delete_letter_of_intent(ln)
  IN (ln:letter_number)
  OUT (l:letter_of_intent)
  LOCAL (s:subscriber)
  PRE-CONDITION: letter_of_intent_exist(ln)?
  POST-CONDITION: no_subscriber(ln)?
  DB-OPERATION: DELETE letter_of_intent(ln);

ACTION delete_sessions
  OUT (ss:sessions)
  LOCAL (s:session)
  PRE-CONDITION: sessions_exist?
  POST-CONDITION: no_session?
  DB-OPERATION: DELETE sessions;


ACTION insert_referee (n)
  IN (n:person_name, a:address, pn:person_number)
  OUT (r:referee)
  LOCAL (p:person, rs:referees)
  PRE-CONDITION: person_not_referee(n)?
    referees_exist?
  POST-CONDITION: person_exist(n)?
  DB-OPERATION: INSERT referee(n);

ACTION delete_referee(n)
  IN (n:person_name)
  OUT (r:referee)
  LOCAL (pra:paper_referee_assignment)
  PRE-CONDITION: person_referee(n)?
    has_no_paper_assigned(n)?
  POST-CONDITION: true?
  DB-OPERATION: DELETE referee(n)

ACTION insert_tc_member(n, tc)
  IN (n:person_name, tc:tc_number, a:address, pn:person_number)
  OUT (tcm:tc_member)
  LOCAL (p:person, tcms:tc_members)
  PRE-CONDITION: tc_members_exist(tc)?
    not_tc_member(n, tc)?
  POST-CONDITION: person_exist(n)?
    tc_member(n, tc)?
  DB-OPERATION: INSERT tc_member(n);

ACTION delete_tc_member(n, tc)
  IN (n:person_name, tc:tc_number)
  OUT (tcm:tc_member)
  LOCAL (tcms:tc_members)
  PRE-CONDITION:
    tc_member(n, tc)?
  POST-CONDITION: not_tc_member(n, tc)?
  DB-OPERATION: DELETE tc_member(n);
```

```
ACTION insert_pc_member(n)
  IN (n:person_name, a:address, pn:person_number)
  OUT (pcm:pc_member)
  LOCAL (p:person, pcms:pc_members)
  PRE-CONDITION: person_not_pc_member(n)?
    pc_members_exist?
  POST-CONDITION: person_exist(n)?
  DB-OPERATION: INSERT pc_member(n)?

ACTION delete_pc_member(n)
  IN (n:person_name)
  OUT (pcm:pc_member)
  PRE-CONDITION: pc_member(n)?
  POST-CONDITION: true?
  DB-OPERATION: DELETE pc_member(n);

ACTION insert_oc_member(n)
  IN (n:person_name, a:address, pn:person_number)
  OUT (ocm:oc_member)
  LOCAL (p:person, ocms:oc_members)
  PRE-CONDITION: person_not_oc_member(n)?
    oc_members_exist?
  POST-CONDITION: person_exist(n)?
  DB-OPERATION: INSERT oc_member(n);

ACTION delete_oc_member(n)
  IN (n:person_name)
  OUT (ocm:oc_member)
  PRE-CONDITION: oc_member(n)?
  POST-CONDITION: true?
  DB-OPERATION: DELETE oc_member(n);

ACTION insert_accepted_paper(pn)
  IN (pn:paper_number)
  OUT (a:accepted)
  LOCAL (na:not_assigned_to_session)
  PRE-CONDITION: paper_not_accepted(pn)?
    paper_exist(pn)?
  POST-CONDITION: is_not_assigned_to_session(pn)?
  DB-OPERATION: INSERT accepted(pn);

ACTION delete_accepted_paper(pn)
  IN (pn:paper_number)
  OUT (a:accepted)
  LOCAL (a:assigned_to_session, na:not_assigned_to_session)
  PRE-CONDITION: accepted_paper(pn)?
  POST-CONDITION: isnt_assigned_to_session(pn)?
    isnt_not_assigned_to_session(pn)?
  DB-OPERATION: DELETE accepted_paper(pn);

ACTION insert_assigned_to_session(pn, sn)
  IN (pn:paper_number, sn:session_number)
  OUT (as:assigned_to_session)
  LOCAL (p:papers_to_be_presented, a:accepted)
  PRE-CONDITION: accepted_paper(pn)?
    isnt_assigned_to_session(pn)?
    papers_to_be_presented_exist(sn)?
  POST-CONDITION: paper_to_be_presented(pn,sn)?
  DB-OPERATION: INSERT assigned_to_session(pn);
```

```
ACTION delete_assigned_to_session(pn)
  IN (pn:paper_number)
  OUT (as:assigned_to_session)
  PRE-CONDITION: is_assigned_to_session(pn)?
  POST-CONDITION: isnt_assigned_to_session(pn)?
  DB-OPERATION: DELETE assigned_to_session(pn);

ACTION delete_divulgations
  OUT (ds:divulgations)
  LOCAL (wc:working_conference, d:cfp_divulgation)
  PRE-CONDITION: divulgations_exist?
  POST-CONDITION: no_cfp_divulgation?
  DB-OPERATION: DELETE divulgations;

ACTION insert_cfp_divulgation(n,a)
  IN (nr:organization_number, n:organization_name, a:address)
  OUT (d:cfp_divulgation)
  LOCAL (ds:divulgations)
  PRE-CONDITION: cfp_divulgation_doesnt_exist(n)?
    divulgations_exist?
  POST-CONDITION: true?
  DB-OPERATION: INSERT cfp_divulgation(nr, n, a)

ACTION delete_cfp_divulgation(n)
  IN (n:organization_number)
  LOCAL (d:cfp_divulgation)
  PRE-CONDITION: cfp_divulgation_exist(n)?
  POST-CONDITION: true?
  DB-OPERATION: DELETE cfp_divulgation(n);

ACTION insert_conference_invitee(n, d)
  IN (n:person_name, d:invitation_date, p:priority)
  OUT (c:conference_invitee)
  PRE-CONDITION: true?
    not_conference_invitee(n)?
  POST-CONDITION: true?
  DB-OPERATION: INSERT conference_invitee(n, d, p);


ACTION delete_conference_invitee(n)
  IN (n:person_name)
  OUT (c:conference_invitee)
  LOCAL (ia:intended_attendee)
  PRE-CONDITION:
    conference_invitee(n)?
  POST-CONDITION: not_intended_attendee(n)?
  DB-OPERATION: DELETE conference_attendee(n);

ACTION insert_intended_attendee(n)
  IN (n:person_name, d:registration_date)
  OUT (ia:intended_attendee)
  LOCAL (ci:conference_invitee)
  PRE-CONDITION: conference_invitee(n)?
    not_intended_attendee(n)?
  POST-CONDITION: true?
  DB-OPERATION: INSERT intended_attendee(n, d);

ACTION delete_intended_attendee(n)
  IN (n:person_name)
  OUT (ia:intended_attendee)
  PRE-CONDITION: intended_attendee(n)?
  POST-CONDITION: true?
  DB-OPERATION: DELETE intended_attendee(n);
```

```
ACTION insert_attendee(n)
  IN (n:person_name)
  OUT (a:attendee)
  LOCAL (p:person, as:attendees)
  PRE-CONDITION:
    person_exist(n)?
    attendees_exist?
    capacity_not_reached?
    not_attendee(n)?
  POST-CONDITION: true?
  DB-OPERATION: INSERT attendee(n);

ACTION delete_attendee(n)
  IN (n:person_name)
  OUT (a:attendee)
  PRE-CONDITION: attendee(n)?
  POST-CONDITION: true?
  DB-OPERATION: DELETE attendee(n);

ACTION insert_not_assigned_to_session(pn)
  IN (pn:paper_number)
  OUT (nas:not_assigned_to_session)
  LOCAL (a:accepted)
  PRE-CONDITION: isnt_not_assigned_to_session(pn)?
    accepted_paper(pn)?
  POST-CONDITION: true?
  DB-OPERATION: INSERT not_assigned_to_session(pn);

ACTION delete_not_assigned_to_session(pn)
  IN (pn:paper_number)
  OUT (nas:not_assigned_to_session)
  PRE-CONDITION: is_not_assigned_to_session(pn)?
  POST-CONDITION: true?
  DB-OPERATION: DELETE not_assigned_to_session(pn);

ACTION insert_dropped_paper(pn)
  IN (pn:paper_number)
  OUT (d:dropped)
  LOCAL (p:paper)
  PRE-CONDITION: paper_not_dropped(pn)?
    paper_exist(pn)?
  POST-CONDITION: true?
  DB-OPERATION: INSERT dropped(pn);

ACTION delete_dropped_paper(pn)
  IN (pn:paper_number)
  OUT (d:dropped)
  LOCAL (p:paper)
  PRE-CONDITION: dropped(pn)?
  POST-CONDITION: true?
  DB-OPERATION: DELETE dropped(pn);

ACTION insert_cfp_invitee(n)
  IN (n:person_name, a:address, pn:person_number)
  OUT (cfpi:cfp_invitee)
  LOCAL (p:person, cfpis:cfp_invitees)
  PRE-CONDITION: not_cfp_invitee(n)?
    cfp_invitees_exist?
  POST-CONDITION: person_exist(n)?
  DB-OPERATION: INSERT cfp_invitee(n);
```

```
ACTION delete_cfp_invitee(n)
  IN (n:person_name)
  OUT (cfpi:cfp_invitee)
  PRE-CONDITION: cfp_invitee(n)?
  POST-OPERATION: true?
  DB-OPERATION: DELETE cfp_invitee(n);

ACTION remove_member_from_ws_members(pn, wsn)
  IN (pn:person_number, wsn:ws_number)
  OUT (wsms:ws_members)
  LOCAL (wsm:ws_member)
  PRE-CONDITION: ws_member(pn, wsn)?
  POST-CONDITION: not_ws_member_or_member_another_ws(pn, wsn)?
  DB-OPERATION: UPDATE ws_members(wsn, -pn);

ACTION include_session_chairperson(pn, sn)
  IN (pn:person_name, sn:session_number)
  OUT (s:session)
  LOCAL (sc:session_chairperson)
  PRE-CONDITION: session_exist(sn)?
    session_has_no_chairperson(sn)?
  POST-CONDITION: session_chairperson(pn)?
  DB-OPERATION: UPDATE session(sn, +pn);

ACTION remove_session_chairperson(sn)
  IN (sn:session_number)
  OUT (s:session)
  LOCAL (pn:person_number, sc:session_chairperson)
  PRE-CONDITION: has_session_chairperson(sn)?
  POST-CONDITION:
    not_session_chairperson_or_chairs_another_session(pn, sn)?
  DB-OPERATION: UPDATE session(sn, -sc);

ACTION add_member_to_tc_members(pn, tcn)
  IN (pn:person_name, tcn:tc_number)
  OUT (tcms:tc_members)
  LOCAL (tcm:tc_member)
  PRE-CONDITION: tc_members_exist(tcn)?
    not_tc_member(pn, tcn)?
  POST-CONDITION: person_tc_member(pn)?
  DB-OPERATION: UPDATE tc_members(tcn, +pn);

ACTION remove_member_from_tc_members(pn, tcn)
  IN (pn:person_name, tcn:tc_number)
  OUT (tcms:tc_members)
  LOCAL (tcm:tc_member)
  PRE-CONDITION: tc_member(pn, tcn)?
  POST-CONDITION:
    not_tc_member_or_member_another_tc(pn, tcn)?
  DB-OPERATION: UPDATE tc_members (tcn, -pn);

ACTION add_member_to_ws_members(pn, wsn)
  IN (pn:person_name, wsn:ws_number)
  OUT (wsms:ws_members)
  LOCAL (wsm:ws_member)
  PRE-CONDITION: ws_members_exist(wsn)?
    not_ws_member(pn, wsn)?
  POST-CONDITION: person_ws_member(pn)?
  DB-OPERATION: tc_members (wsn, +pn);
```

```
ACTION insert_rejected_paper(pn)
  IN (pn:paper_number)
  OUT (r:rejected)
  LOCAL (p:paper)
  PRE-CONDITION: paper_exist(pn)?
    paper_not_dropped(pn)?
    paper_not_accepted(pn)?
    paper_not_rejected(pn)?
  POST-CONDITION: true?
  DB-OPERATION: INSERT rejected (pn);

ACTION delete_rejected_paper(pn)
  IN (pn:paper_number)
  OUT (r:rejected)
  LOCAL (p:paper)
  PRE-CONDITION: paper_rejected(pn)?
  POST-CONDITION: true?
  DB-OPERATION: DELETE rejected(pn)?

ACTION insert_national_representative(n)
  IN (n:person_name, a:address, pn:person_number)
  OUT (nr:national_representative)
  LOCAL (p:person)
  PRE-CONDITION: not_national_representative(n)?
  POST-CONDITION: person_exist(n)?
  DB-OPERATION INSERT national_representative(n);

ACTION delete_national_representative(n)
  IN (n:person_name)
  OUT (nr:national_representative)
  LOCAL (p:person)
  PRE-CONDITION: national_representative(n)?
  POST-CONDITION: true?
  DB-OPERATION: DELETE national_representative(n);

ACTION update_referee_assignment(pen, pan, c, d)
  IN (pen:person_number, pan:paper_number, c:comments,
    d:date_comments_received)
  OUT (pra:paper_referee_assignment)
  PRE-CONDITION: paper_referee_assignment_exist(pen, pan)?
    pra_has_no_comments(pen, pan)?
  POST-CONDITION: true?
  DB-OPERATION: UPDATE paper_referee_assignment(pen, pan, c, d);

TRANSACTION assign_referee_to_paper(pan, pen)
  SCOPE (pan:paper_number, pen:person_number, r:referee,
        pcm:pc_member, pa:paper, pe:person,
        pra:paper_referee_assignment)
  PRE-CONDITION:paper_exist(pan)?
    person_can_referee(pan)?
    workload_not_exceeded(pen)?
    the_person_is_not_refereeing_the_paper(pen, pan)?
  POST-CONDITION: paper_referee_assignment_exist(pen, pan)?

TRANSACTION accept_paper(pn)
  SCOPE (pn:paper_number, a:accepted, r:rejected,
        d:dropped, p:paper)
  PRE-CONDITION: paper_exist(pn)?
    paper_not_accepted(pn)?
    paper_not_rejected(pn)?
    paper_not_dropped(pn)?
  POST-CONDITION: accepted_paper(pn)?
```

```
TRANSACTION define_conference
  SCOPE (wc:working_conference, ws:working_group,
         tc:technical_commitee, wgs:w_groups)
  PRE-CONDITION: no_wc?
  POST-CONDITION: wc_exist?
    at_least_1_sponsor?
    all_tc_have_at_least_1_ws?

TRANSACTION appoint_pc_member(n)
  SCOPE (n:person_name, pcm:pc_member, wc:working_conference,
         a:authorship, p:person)
  PRE-CONDITION: wc_exist?
    person_not_pc_member(n)?
    person_not_author(x)?
  POST-CONDITION: pc_member(n)?

TRANSACTION drop_pc_member(n)
  SCOPE (n:person_name, pcm:pc_member, p:person, tcm:tc_member,
         ocm:oc_member, pcc:pc_chairperson, occ:oc_chairperson,
         sc:session_chairperson, cfpi:cfp_invitee, r:referee,
         a:authorship, s:subscriber, wsm:ws_member,
         nr:national_representative)
  PRE-CONDITION: pc_member(n)?
    pc_member_not_refereeing_or_is_also_referee(n)?
  POST-CONDITION: person_not_pc_member(n)?
    not_person_or_has_another_role(n)?

TRANSACTION insert_call_for_paper_invitee(n)
  SCOPE (n:person_name, cfpi:cfp_invitee, wc:working_conference)
  PRE-CONDITION: wc_exist?
    not_cfp_invitee(n)?
  POST-CONDITION: cfp_invitee(n)?

TRANSACTION drop_call_for_paper_invitee(n)
  SCOPE (n:person_name, pcm:pc_member, p:person, tcm:tc_member,
         ocm:oc_member, pcc:pc_chairperson, occ:oc_chairperson,
         sc:session_chairperson, cfpi:cfp_invitee, r:referee,
         a:authorship, s:subscriber, wsm:ws_member,
         nr:national_representative)
  PRE-CONDITION: cfp_invitee(n)?
  POST-CONDITION: not_cfp_invitee(n)?
    not_person_or_has_another_role(n)?

TRANSACTION appoint_referee(n)
  SCOPE (n:person_name, r:referee, wc:working_conference)
  PRE-CONDITION: wc_exist?
    person_not_referee(n)?
  POST-CONDITION: person_referee(n)?

TRANSACTION drop_referee(n)
  SCOPE (n:person_name, pcm:pc_member, p:person, tcm:tc_member,
         ocm:oc_member, pcc:pc_chairperson, occ:oc_chairperson,
         sc:session_chairperson, cfpi:cfp_invitee, r:referee,
         a:authorship, s:subscriber, wsm:ws_member,
         nr:national_representative)
  PRE-CONDITION: person_referee(n)?
  POST-CONDITION: person_not_referee(n)?
    not_person_or_has_another_role(n)?
```

```
TRANSACTION reject_paper(pn)
  SCOPE (pn:paper_number, a:accepted, r:rejected,
         d:dropped, p:paper)
  PRE-CONDITION: paper_exist(pn)?
    paper_not_rejected(pn)?
    paper_not_dropped(pn)?
    paper_not_accepted(pn)?
  POST-CONDITION: rejected_paper(pn)?

TRANSACTION register_referee_comments(pen, pan)
  SCOPE (pen:person_number, pan:paper_number, c:comments,
         pra:paper_referee_assignment, d:date_comments_received)
  PRE-CONDITION: paper_referee_assignment_exist(pen, pan)?
    pra_has_no_comments(pen, pan)?
  POST-CONDITION: comments_updated(pen, pan, c, d)?

TRANSACTION define_session
  SCOPE (sn:session_number, s:session, st:session_title,
         wc:working_conference)
  PRE-CONDITION: wc_exist?
    no_session_has_this_number_and_title(sn, st)?
  POST-CONDITION: session_exist(sn)?

TRANSACTION assign_paper_to_session(pn, sn)
  SCOPE (pn:paper_number, sn:session_number, p:paper,
         a:assigned_to_session, nas:not_assigned_to_session,
         au:authorship, s:session)
  PRE-CONDITION: is_not_assigned_to_session(pn)?
    session_chairperson_if_any_is_not_paper_author(pn, sn)?
  POST-CONDITION: is_assigned_to_this_session(pn, sn)?
    isnt_assigned_to_session(pn)?

TRANSACTION drop_paper_from_session(pn)
  SCOPE (pn:paper_number, p:paper, a:assigned_to_session,
         nas:not_assigned_to_session)
  PRE-CONDITION: is_assigned_to_session(pn)?
  POST-CONDITION: isnt_assigned_to_session(pn)?
    is_not_assigned_to_session(pn)?

TRANSACTION drop_paper_from_referee(pen, pan)
  SCOPE (pen:person_number, pan:paper_number,
         pra:paper_referee_assignment)
  PRE-CONDITION: paper_referee_assignment_exist(pen, pan)?
  POST-CONDITION:
    the_person_is_not_refereeing_the_paper(pen, pan)?

TRANSACTION drop_session(sn)
  SCOPE (sn:session_number, s:session)
  PRE-CONDITION: session_exist(sn)?
  POST-CONDITION: session_doesnt_exist(sn)?

TRANSACTION register_letter_of_intent
  SCOPE (ln:letter_number, li:letter_of_intent,
         wc:working_conference)
  PRE-CONDITION:wc_exist?
    letter_of_intent_doesnt_exist(ln)?
  POST-CONDITION: letter_of_intent_exist(ln)?

TRANSACTION drop_letter_of_intent(ln)
  SCOPE (ln:letter_number, li:letter_of_intent)
  PRE-CONDITION: letter_of_intent_exist(ln)?
  POST-CONDITION: letter_of_intent_doesnt_exist(ln)?
    all_persons_have_at_least_1_role?
```

```
TRANSACTION appoint_ws_member(pn, wsn)
  SCOPE (pn:person_name, wsn:ws_number, wsm:ws_member, wsms:ws_members)
  PRE-CONDITION: ws_members_exist(wsn)?
    person_not_ws_member(pn, wsn)?
  POST-CONDITION: ws_member(pn, wsn)?

TRANSACTION drop_ws_member (pn, wsn)
  SCOPE(pn:person_name, wsn:ws_number, p:person, pcc:pc_chairperson,
        occ:oc_chairperson, sc:session_chairperson, pcm:pc_member,
        ocm:oc_member, wsm:ws_member, tcm:tc_member, r:referee,
        a:authorship, s:subscriber, cfpi:cfp_invitee,
        nr:national_representative)
  PRE-CONDITION: ws_member(pn, wsn)?
  POST-CONDITION: person_not_ws_member(pn, wsn)?
    not_person_or_has_another_role(pn)?

TRANSACTION register_attendee(pn)
  SCOPE (pn:person_name, a:attendee, pcc:pc_chairperson,
         occ:oc_chairperson, pcm_pc_member, ocm:oc_member,
         ia:intended_attendee)
  PRE-CONDITION: intended_attendee_or_conference_organizer(pn)?
  POST-CONDITION: attendee(pn)?

TRANSACTION register_intended_attendee(pn)
  SCOPE (pn:person_name, ia:intended_attendee, ci:conference_invitee)
  PRE-CONDITION: conference_invitee(pn)?
    not_intended_attendee(pn)?
  POST-CONDITION: intended_attendee(pn)?

TRANSACTION drop_attendee(pn)
  SCOPE (pn:person_name, a:attendee,
         p:person, ia:intended_attendee)
  PRE-CONDITION: attendee_or_intended_attendee(pn)?
  POST-CONDITION: not_attendee_nor_intended_attendee(pn)?

TRANSACTION appoint_oc_member(pn)
  SCOPE (pn:person_name, ocm:oc_member, wc:working_conference)
  PRE-CONDITION: wc_exist?
    person_not_oc_member(pn)?
  POST-CONDITION: oc_member(pn)?

TRANSACTION drop_oc_member(pn)
  SCOPE(pn:person_name, p:person, pcc:pc_chairperson,
        occ:oc_chairperson, sc:session_chairperson, pcm:pc_member,
        ocm:oc_member, wsm:ws_member, tcm:tc_member, r:referee,
        a:authorship, s:subscriber, cfpi:cfp_invitee,
        nr:national_representative)
PRE-CONDITION: oc_member(pn)?
  POST-CONDITION: person_not_oc_member(pn)?
    not_person_or_has_another_role(pn)?

TRANSACTION drop_conference
  SCOPE (wc:working_conference)
  PRE-CONDITION: wc_exist?
  POST-CONDITION: no_wc?
    no_tc_exist?

TRANSACTION drop_paper(pn)
  SCOPE (pn:paper_number, p:paper)
  PRE-CONDITION: paper_exist(pn)?
    paper_not_assigned_to_referee(pn)?
  POST-CONDITION: paper_doesnt_exist(pn)?
    all_persons_have_at_least_1_role?
```

```
TRANSACTION withdraw_paper(pn)
  SCOPE (pn:paper_number, p:paper, a:accepted, r:rejected, d:dropped)
  PRE-CONDITION: paper_exist(pn)?
    paper_not_dropped(pn)?
    paper_not_rejected(pn)?
  POST-CONDITION: dropped(pn)?
    paper_not_accepted(pn)?

TRANSACTION include cfp_divulgation(n)
  SCOPE (n:organization_name, cfpd:cfp:divulgation,
         wc:working_conference)
  PRE-CONDITION: wc_exist?
    cfp_divulgation_doesnt_exist(n)?
  POST-CONDITION: cfp_divulgation_exist(n)?

TRANSACTION drop_cfp_divulgation(n)
  SCOPE (n:organization_name, cfpd:cfp_divulgation)
  PRE-CONDITION: cfp_divulgation_exist(n)?
  POST-CONDITION: cfp_divulgation_doesnt_exist(n)?

TRANSACTION appoint_tc_member(pn, tcn)
  SCOPE(pn:person_name, tcn:tc_number, tcms:tc_members)
  PRE-CONDITION: tc_members_exist(tcn)?
    not_tc_member(pn, tcn)?
  POST-CONDITION: tc_member(pn, tcn)?

TRANSACTION drop_tc_member(pn, tcn)
  SCOPE(pn:person_name, tcn:tc_number, p:person, pcc:pc_chairperson,
        occ:oc_chairperson, sc:session_chairperson, pcm:pc_member,
        ocm:oc_member, wsm:ws_member, tcm:tc_member, r:referee,
        a:authorship, s:subscriber, cfpi:cfp_invitee,
        nr:national_representative)
  PRE-CONDITION: tc_member(pn, tcn)?
  POST-CONDITION: not_tc_member(pn, tcn)?
    not_person_or_has_another_role(pn)?

TRANSACTION appoint_session_chairperson(pn, sn)
  SCOPE (pn:person_number, sn:session_number, sc:session_chairperson,
         s:session, ptb:papers_to_be_presented, as:assigned_to_session,
         a:authorship)
  PRE-CONDITION: session_exist(sn)?
    session_has_no_chairperson(sn)?
    session_has_no_papers_from_this_person(pn, sn)?
  POST-CONDITION: session_has_this_chairperson(pn, sn)?

TRANSACTION drop_session_chairperson(sn)
  SCOPE(pn:person_name, pn:person_name, p:person, pcc:pc_chairperson,
        occ:oc_chairperson, sc:session_chairperson, pcm:pc_member,
        ocm:oc_member, wsm:ws_member, tcm:tc_member, r:referee,
        a:authorship, s:subscriber, cfpi:cfp_invitee,
        nr:national_representative)
  PRE-CONDITION: has_session_chairperson(sn)?
  POST-CONDITION: session_has_no_chairperson(sn)?
    not_person_or_has_another_role(pn)?

TRANSACTION include_national_representative(n)
  SCOPE (n:person_name, nr:national_representative)
  PRE-CONDITION: not_national_representative(n)?
  POST-CONDITION: national_representative(n)?
```

```
TRANSACTION drop_national_representative(n)
  SCOPE (n:person_name, nr:national_representative, p:person,
         tcm:tc_member, wsm_ws_member, ocm:oc_member, pcm:pc_member,
         pcc:pc_chairperson, occ:oc_chairperson, sc:session_chairperson,
         r:referee, a:authorship, s:subscriber, cfpi:cfp_invitee)
  PRE-CONDITION: national_representative(n)?
  POST-CONDITION: not_national_representative(n)?
    not_person_or_has_another_role(n)?

TRANSACTION issue_invitations
  SCOPE (d:invitation_date, p:person, nr:national_representative,
         tcm:tc_member, wsm:ws_member, a:authorship,
         ci:conference_invitee);
  PRE-CONDITION: there_is_person_to_receive_invitation?
  POST-CONDITION: there_is_no_person_to_receive_invitation?

TRANSACTION issue_announcements
  SCOPE (d:divulgation_date, cfpd:cfp_divulgation)
  PRE-CONDITION: there_is_organization-to-set-divulgation?
  POST-CONDITION: there_is_no_organization_to_set_divulgation?
```

## Acknowledgement

The authors gratefully acknowledge the contribution of Dzenan
Ridjanovic to SHM+ and to ACM/PCM as well as his helpfull comments
on this work and also the contribution of Donald Swaab to the
design and specification of the IFIP working conference system.

REFERENCES

1.  Brodie, M.L., Specification and Verification of Database Semantic Integrity.
    CSRG-91, University of Toronto, April 1978.

2.  Brodie, M.L., "The Application of Data Types to Database Semantic Integrity",
    Information Systems 5, 4 (1980).

3.  Brodie, M.L., "Data Quality in Information Systems", Information and Manage-
    ment 3, (1980).

4.  Brodie, M.L., "Data Abstraction for Designing Database-Intensive Applica-
    tions", in Brodie, M.L. and Zilles, S.N. (Eds.) Proc. Workshop on Data
    Abstraction, Databases, and Conceptual Modelling.  SIGPLAN Notices 16, 1
    (January 1981).

5.  Brodie, M.L., On Modelling Behavioral Semantics of Databases.  Proc. 1981
    International Conference on Very Large Databases, Connes, France, September
    1981.

6.  Brodie, M.L., Association:  A Database Abstraction for Semantic Modelling,
    Proc. 2nd International Entity-Relationship Conference, Washington, D.C.,
    October 1981.

7.  Smith, J.M. and D.C.P. Smith, "Database Abstraction:  Aggregation and Gen-
    eralization", ACM TODS 2, 2 (June 1977).

8.  Smith, J.M. and D.C.P. Smith, "A Database Approach to Software Specifica-
    tions", in W.E. Riddle and R.E. Fairley (Eds.), Software Development Tools,
    Springer-Verlag, New York (1980).

## APPENDIX  : SYNTAX OF THE BETA LANGUAGE

- NOTATION:

The syntax is given in a modification of Backus-Naur form. The meta
symbols ::= | { } < > {. .} are not part of the language. < > enclose
English words that denote a syntactic construct. { } enclose construct
to indicate zero or more repetitions. {. .} indicate zero or one
occurrence of the enclosed sequence.

- IDENTIFIERS, NUMBERS, STRINGS AND CONSTANTS:

```
<letter> ::= A|...|Z|a|...|z
<digit> ::= 0|1|2|3|4|5|6|7|8|9

<identifier> ::= <letter>{<letter or digit>}
<letter or digit> ::= <letter>|<digit>
<unsigned integer> ::= <digit>{<digit>}
<sign> ::= +|-
<string> ::= '<character>{<character>}'
<character> ::= <letter or digit>|<special symbol>
<constant> ::= {.<sign>.}<unsigned integer>|<string>
        |<character>|{.<sign>.}<constant identifier>
        |<enumerated value>
<constant identifier> ::= <identifier>
<enumerated value> ::= <identifier>
```

- DATABASE SCHEMA SPECIFICATION :
  --------------------------------

```
<database schema specification> ::= <database identifier>= DATABASE
        {.<constant definition part>.}
        {.<type definition part>.}
        {.<assertion specification part>.}
        {.<behaviour specification part>.}
        END DATABASE.
<database identifier> ::= <identifier>
<constant definition part> ::= CONST <constant definition>;
        {<constant definition>;}
<constant definition> ::= <constant identifier>=<constant>


<type definition part> ::= TYPE <type definition>;
          {<type definition>;}
<type definition> ::= <type identifier>=<type>
<type identifier> ::= <identifier>
<type> ::= CHAR | BOOLEAN | <enumerated type>|<subrange type>
        |<string type>|<composite type>|<type identifier>
<enumerated type> ::= (<enumerated value>{,<enumerated value>})
<subrange type> ::= <constant>..<constant>
<string type> ::= STRING OF <constant> CHARS
<composite type> ::= OBJECT
        {.<aggregate definition>.}
        {.<generic definition>.}
        {.<associate definition>.}
        END OBJECT
<aggregate definition> ::= AGGREGATE OF <component definition part>
        {.<key definition>.}
<component definition part> ::= <component definition>;
        {<component definition>;}
<component definition> ::= <type>{.: ESSENTIAL.}
<key definition> ::= {<candidate key>;}<primary key>
<candidate key> ::= KEY <key component>{,<key component>};
<key component> ::= <type identifier>
<primary key> ::= PRIMARY KEY <key component>{,<key component>};
<generic definition> ::= GENERIC OF <category definition part>
<category definition part> ::= <category definition>;
        |<category definition>;}
<category definition> ::= <type identifier>:
        <exclusiviness classification>
<exclusiviness classification> ::= EXCLUSIVE | NONEXCLUSIVE
<associate definition> :: ASSOCIATE OF <member>:<membership>;
<member> ::= <type identifier>
<membership> ::= MANUAL {.MEMBERSHIP.} | AUTOMATIC {.MEMBERSHIP.}
        (<object occurrence selector>)
<assertion specification part> ::= ASSERT <assertion>;{<assertion>;}
<assertion> ::= <quantifier><assertion variable> IN <type identifier>
        {.(<logical expression>).}
<quantifier> ::= ALL | SOME | NO | EXACTLY <constant>
        | AT MOST <constant> | AT LEAST <constant>
<assertion variable> ::= <identifier>
<logical expression> ::= <logical term>{<boolean operator>
        <logical term>}|(<logical expression>)
<logical term> ::= <join term>|<restriction term>|<assertion>
        | NOT <logical term>|<abstraction term>
<join term> ::= <basic component designator><relational operator>
        <basic component designator>
<basic component designator> ::= <assertion variable>.
        <type identifier>
```

```
<relational operator> ::= < | <= | = | >= | > | <>
<restriction term> ::= <basic component designator>
          <relational operator><scalar term>
          |<scalar term><relational operator><scalar term>
<scalar term> ::= <arithmetic function> [<object expression>]
          |<constant>|<constant identifier>
<arithmetic function> ::= MAX | MIN | AVERAGE | SUM | COUNT
<object expression> ::= <type identifier>
          |<basic component designator>|<object occurrence selector>
<object occurrence selector> ::= EACH <assertion variable>
          IN <object identifier>{, WHERE (<logical expression>).}
<abstraction term> ::= <assertion variable><abstraction type identifier>
          <assertion variable>
<abstraction type identifier> ::= IS | PART OF | MEMBER OF
<boolean operator> ::= AND | OR
<behaviour specification part> ::=
          {,<predicate specification part>.}
          {,<dependent action specification part>.}
          {,<action specification part>.}
          {,<transaction specification part>.}
<predicate specification part> ::= PREDICATE <predicate specification>;
          {<predicate specification>;}
<predicate specification> ::= <predicate> = <assertion>
<predicate> ::= <predicate identifier>{,(<parameter list>).}
<predicate identifier> ::= <identifier>
<dependent action specification part> ::= DEPENDENT ACTIONS
          <dependent action specification>;
          {<dependent action specification>;}
          END DEPENDENT ACTIONS;
<dependent action specification> ::=
          DEPENDENT ACTION <action definition>
<action definition> ::=
          <action identifier>{,(<parameter list>).}
          {,IN (<scope definition>).}
          {,OUT (<scope definition>).}
          {,LOCAL (<scope definition>).}
          PRE-CONDITION : <predicate use part>
          POST-CONDITION : <predicate use part>
          DB-OPERATION : <db-operation>;
<action identifier> ::= <identifier>
<parameter list> ::= <scope identifier>{,<scope identifier>}
<scope identifier> ::= <identifier>
<scope definition> ::= <scope element>{,<scope element>}
<scope element> ::= <scope identifier>:<type>
<predicate use part> ::= <predicate>?{<predicate>?}
<db-operation> ::= INSERT | UPDATE | DELETE
<action specification part> ::= ACTIONS
          <action specification>;{<action specification>;}
          END ACTIONS;
<action specification> ::=
          ACTION <action definition>
<transaction specification part> ::= TRANSACTIONS
          <transaction specification>;{<transaction specification>;}
          END TRANSACTIONS;
<transaction specification> ::= TRANSACTION <transaction identifier>
          {,(<parameter list>).}
          SCOPE (<scope definition>)
          PRE-CONDITION : <predicate use part>
          POST-CONDITION : <predicate use part>
```

*INFORMATION SYSTEMS DESIGN METHODOLOGIES: A Comparative Review*
*T.W. Olle, H.G. Sol, A.A. Verrijn-Stuart (editors)*
*North-Holland Publishing Company*
© *IFIP, 1982*

# A DECLARATIVE APPROACH TO CONCEPTUAL INFORMATION MODELING

Mats R. Gustafsson, Terttu Karlsson, Janis A. Bubenko jr
The Systems Development Laboratory (SYSLAB)
Department of Computer Sciences
Chalmers University of Technology and
The University of Göteborg
S-412 96 Göteborg, Sweden

This report demonstrates a Declarative Approach to Conceptual
Information Modeling applied to a case defined by IFIP TC 8,
Working Group 8.1. The report is submitted to the WG 8.1 Working
Conference "Comparative Review of Information Systems Design
Methodologies", to be held in the Netherlands in the Spring of
1982. The approach focuses on the conceptual information modeling and analysis parts of the systems development process. We
show how conceptual modeling is integrated in the early phases
of systems development work and how a declarative conceptual information model is used as a basis for the design of a procedural specification of an information processing system model.

## INTRODUCTION

The approach to information system development and specification described in this
paper differs in one fundamental respect from most other approaches reported in
the literature. The unifying and fundamental task during the early, problem- and
application analysis stages is to create and specify a "theory" - an unrestricted
"conceptual model" - of the perceived application discourse. In contrast to other
approaches this approach arrives at a "declarative" conceptual specification of
the application, which together with operational information requirements constitutes the basis for designing a procedural information system model. Most approaches by-pass the declarative phase and more or less directly go from analysis of
corporate problems, needs etc to a procedural information system model. This
"short-cut" implies that most assumptions, rules and constraints about the perceived reality are implicit and "hidden" in the procedures of the information system.

Our approach aims at an _explicit_ specification of them. This brings it very close
to the conceptual modeling framework recently described in the preliminary report
by ISO/TC97/SC5/WG3 [ 9 ]. Our approach thus introduces several concepts, principles and a way of thinking and reasoning about a perceived application reality
which differs from the more traditional and practically established approaches.
While we believe that our philosophy is more natural, logically sound and "user-
friendly" (non-data processing expert friendly) than traditional approaches, experience has shown that persons with a strong background in information _systems_
work or in software engineering and data bases have difficulties in changing their
thinking habits from procedural to declarative. In this respect our approach lies
closer to work which concerns "knowledge representation" in the field of Artificial Intelligence.

This is the main reason why we have included in this report a substantial amount
of description of basic concepts, principles, methodological assumptions and rules.
Chapter 1 presents a popular and informal introduction to the concept of a "declarative" specification and discusses its role in the systems development process -
the system life cycle.

Chapter 2 discusses more in-depth- but still informally - the fundamental concepts
and underlying principles of our approach.  Illustrations are presented using the
IFIP WG8.1 case (the case in included in the editorial). Also the method of designing a conceptual model is outlined.

Chapter 3 introduces and illustrates, using the IFIP WG8.1 case, particular formal concepts and specification constructs (a specification language) applied in
this approach. A language to specify entity types, attributes functions, events,
various types of constraints etc is introduced. Due to space limitations it is not
possible to present the full, detailed "solution" to the case in this paper. We
do, however, present in Appendix 1 a complete compact listing of the components of
the solution, i e the conceptual application model arrived at after a thorough a-
nalysis using our approach (entity types, functions, event types and constraints).
We feel that this demonstrates the strength of our approach - to force the user
and/or the analyst to arrive at a model, which is as complete as possible.

Chapter 4 focuses on the problem of designing a procedural information system model for this particular case. The basis for this design is the declarative model
plus stated information **requirements (batch and/or interactive)**.
The information model is described by a conceptual data base schema (using a binary relational data model) and a set of processing procedures - a conceptual processing model. The next design step - to transform (if necessary) this solution to
a model utilizing a particular, traditional data base management system (such as
a CODASYL/DBTG type DBMS) - is also briefly outlined.

The paper is concluded by a discussion which summarizes the major traits of our
approach.


## 1.  A NEW LOOK AT THE DEVELOPMENT PROCESS

It is an established principle in all scientific or engineering disciplines that
equations (rules, assumptions) about a model of some phenomenon are set-up before
an attempt is made to solve them. The solution implies devising numerical and/or
symbolic processing procedures, making data storage considerations and designing
input/output schemes. Clearly, many solution alternatives are feasible and they
all must satisfy the stated requirements concerning information about the particular model. But the set of "equations" always constitutes a basis for the various
processing solutions.

Somewhat drastically, we might say that most approaches to information system design proceed from an informal discussion about the application to a procedural solution without explicitly stating the "application equations". In our approach the
task of explicitly specifying the "equations" - we call it the declarative conceptual information model - is included. This causes some changes to the system development process, which will be discussed in the sequel. First we will describe
the background of this approach and give an illustration of the concept "declarative".

It is evident that in order to describe a dynamic, perceived reality the concept
of time - a "temporal dimension" - is needed just as setting up equations for
dynamic phenomena in engineering requires a time argument. The first researchers
to consider time in information system specifications were Young and Kent [15] and
Langefors [11]. Bubenko worked further on this "temporal problem" [ 3 ] and presented an approach - IAM [ 4 ] which to a large extent constitutes the early basis of
this paper. IAM was influenced by ideas of Langefors [11] and contemporary ideas
on information and data modeling.  It turned out, however, that the primitives
and constructs of IAM for structuring of the "perceived" reality should be elabo-

rated. Above all, it lacked good ways to describe generalization, existence and
various other types of constraints. Further research led to the approach described
in [5]. It also constitutes the basis for this paper.

In order to describe the distinction between the declarative and the procedural
approach consider the assignment statement in an Algol-like language.

        a:= a + b;

This means that, when this statement is executed, the value of variable  a  is updated (its old value is replaced by the sum of the old value and the value of variable  b  at execution time). We see that the values of the variables (storage
locations, if you wish) change only when the procedure is executed, that the variables reflect the "current" values with respect to execution and that by assignment statements we cannot represent time dependent conditions (such as for instance: a  is at some time interval greater than  b ). To write the assigment statement as an equation  a = a + b  is, of course, senseless. In order to describe the
dynamics of this model, we need to refer to the values of the variables as a function of time, i. e.  a(t), b(t). Then  a(t)  represents the value of variable  a
at time  t.  An "updating" of a variable could now be specified as, e.g.

        a(t) = a(t-1) + b(t)

and  a   condition as

        $a(t) > b(t) \; ; \quad t_1 \le t \le t_2$

Note that by the latter, declarative approach we may "conceptually" refer to the
value of variable  a  at any point in time. For instance, we can define the average value of  "a"  in a time interval  (t1, t2), t2 > t1, as,

$$\text{average } (t_1, t_2) = \frac{1}{t_2 - t_1} \int_{t_1}^{t_2} a(t)dt$$

The inventory status example from the area of business data processing is often
used to illustrate modeling and specification approaches. A typical specification
would view the quantity-on-hand information as a relation

        QOH(ARTICLE-NO, QUANTITY)

which is maintained and updated by transactions signalling deliveries from vendors
(DEL) and shipments to customers (SHIP) as in figure 1.1.

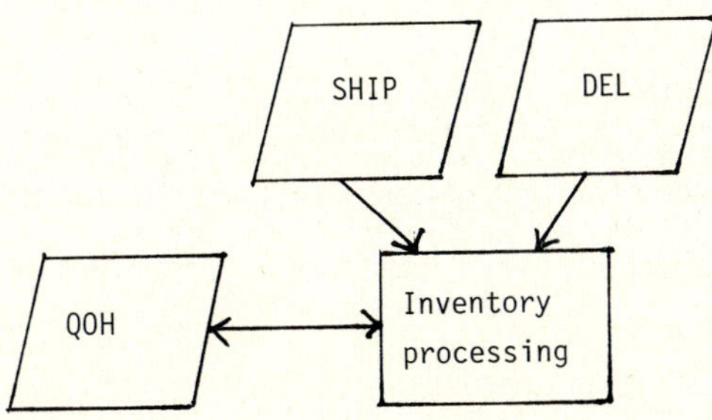


Figure 1.1

The inventory <u>processing</u> model would be described informally as (several solutions exist!)

> <u>when</u> SHIP-transaction, subtract SHIP-quantity from quantity in QOH <u>for</u> corresponding article type

> <u>when</u> DEL-transaction, increase quantity in  QOH  by  DEL-quantity.

This is analogous to treating  QOH  as a variable which is updated. It is probably a perfect solution to an information systems design problem <u>if</u> the requirements dictate that only the current, or the most recent, QOH-<u>values</u> are of interest. It is, by this model, however, not possible to "reason about"  QOH  in an extended time perspective.

An improvement in this direction would be to collect in  QOH  "time-stamped" mes-<u>sages</u> about quantity-on-hand values when changes occur, represented by the re<u>la</u>-tion

> QOH (ARTICLE-NO, TIME-POINT, QUANTITY)

Then <u>each</u> article type would have the number of tuples in this relation correspon-ding <u>to the</u> sum of  SHIP  and  DEL  transactions for that article type. The exten-sion of the relation would be ever increasing and we would have no concept of "up-dating a value" (rather: <u>inserting</u> a new tuple). Note, however, that without addi-tional information, we <u>cannot here</u> refer to quantity-on-hand values at time points which are not represented by the tuples of  QOH.  This additional information is, of course, that a  QOH-value   is unchanged between transactions. It follows im-plicitly from figure 1 and the processing description, but it does <u>not</u> follow from the  QOH-schema.

Our approach is an extension to this approach as we would view the "quantity-on-hand" as a function which is dependent on the arguments 'article' and 'time' (its domains). The range of the function is a suitably bounded value set of non-negative integers. We would thus define it as

> qoh: ARTICLE, T --- > VQOH

where qoh is the name of the function and ARTICLE, T and VQOH denote domains. In order to refer to a particular article´s  x  quantity-on-hand at a time point  t, we write  qoh(x,t).  Let  $QDEL(x,t_i)$  resp  $QSHIP(x,t_j)$  denote quantities delivered resp shipped at time points  $t_i$ ,  $t_j$.  If these are the only functions affecting the function "qoh" then we can write an <u>equation</u> which defines  qoh

$$qoh(x,t) = \sum_{\forall t_i \leq t} QDEL(x,t_i) - \sum_{\forall t_j \leq t} QSHIP(x,t_j)$$

This is a rule, an invariant , that is assumed to hold for our perceived reality. Observe that it is independent of any processing solution. We can, furthermore, "reason about" the quantity-on-hand in a time perspective without bringing on ques-tions about processing, storage, etc. For instance, we can introduce the constraint that bounds the function´s value as  $0 \leq qoh(x,t) \leq 5000$. Or we can define a new, three argument function $avgqoh(x,t_1,t_2)$ which gives us the average  qoh  in the interval $(t_1,t_2)$  as

$$avgqoh(x,t_1,t_2) = \frac{1}{t_2 - t_1} \int_{t_1}^{t_2} qoh(x,t)dt$$

In a similar way, using standard mathematical notation, we can define occurence times of events when the quantity-on-hand drops below or exceeds certain inventory levels [5].

In summary, this "time- and storage- unrestricted" view of the percived application reality is what we earlier described as "setting up the equations" about an application. In fact, the "equations" reflect a "theory" about some application - a perceived universe of discourse (UoD). We will demonstrate that this our "unrestricted" modeling approach gives us absolute freedom from processing, storage and other technical considerations to reason about true application problems, assumptions and constraints of the UoD.

Our basic view of a formalized information system is then, to be a vehicle, a mechanism, which is able to store, communicate and process assertions or propositions [9] about some application discourse. The assertions are of certain predefined types and they are processed according to a set of predefined procedures. The logic of these procedures is determined by operative requirements stated for the system and by a set of rules and constraints specified (or rather assumed or agreed-upon) for the application discourse. The set of rules and constraints thus specify how certain assertions are related (e.g. how one assertion logically follows from other assertions) and what we may assert (i.e. which is the permissible collection of assertions). For instance, we may assert that "a country  C  is represented in an IFIP Working Conference  W" (now follows the rule) "if the IFIP Working Conference  W  has an accepted paper  P  which has one of its authors living in country  C".  An example of a rule constraining the set of permissible assertions would be: "A person can be the chairman of at most one conference session". This would restrict the number of sentences (assertions) of the type  "Person  P is the chairman of session  S"  we were permitted to make.

In our approach we define a Conceptual Information Model (CIM) to be

> - a collection of definitions of permissible assertion types

> - a collection of rules and constraints which govern how assertions
>   are related and what may be asserted.

Theoretically, we may view also rules and constraints as assertions. Extensions of the CIM are then concrete facts asserted about the UoD.

Combining the CIM and its extension, we can view it as our "theory" about the application discourse and further partition the set of assertions in axioms or theorems. A theorem is a concrete fact or a rule or constraint which logically follows from a set of axioms (concrete facts and rules). For instance, given the information (assertions) above plus the assertions

> - a session  S  is scheduled for a particular day  D

> - the set of chairmen serving some sessions  S  on a particular
>   day  D  form the set  CHM(D)

From this logically follows the rule that "for any two days  $D_1$  and  $D_2$  the sets CHM($D_1$)  and  CHM($D_2$)  are disjoint".

The question what to consider as an axiom or a theorem is a matter of where we draw the outer boundary of our discourse. From a practical, infological point of view the axioms which are rules and constraints correspond to our initial assumptions about the perceived application and the axioms which are concrete facts correspond to initial information ("transactions" - if you wish).

The concept of an "information requirement" can now be more precisely defined

having presented the concept of a theory of an application. The semantic part of
an information requirement always expresses <u>what</u> one wants to know <u>about</u> some
"topic". This is equivalent to presenting a <u>set</u> of assertions about <u>something</u>. If
we disregard information requirements concerning rules and constraints (while it
is theoretically feasible,conventional information systems cannot handle it) then
the following may happen as we analyze requirements with respect to a theory  T

1.        The requirement is considered to correspond to an axiom in  T

2.        The requirement is considered to correspond to a theorem in  T

3.        Neither (1) or (2) holds

In the latter case we have to reexamine the theory  T  and extend it.  If the requirement is assumed to correspond to initial information then an axiom is added
to  T.  Otherwise it will correspond to a theorem. The theorem and proper rules
for its derivation must then be introduced and added to  T.

Thus, our conceptual information model (CIM) and its extensions correspond to a
description of a time varying theory about an application discourse. <u>When</u> and <u>how</u>
is the CIM developed?

Figure 1.2 presents a crude outline of our development approach. It shows that a
conceptual information model (CIM) plays a role already in the <u>very early phases</u>
of development work. During the phases (the exact structuring of them is not <u>essen</u>-
tial)

1.        goal, problem & decision analysis,

2.        activity analysis & design and

3.        specification of requirements

the CIM is gradually, incrementally established and <u>used</u>. Its major <u>use</u> in these
phases is to act as a common frame of reference concerning the "topic" of the information system to be developed. An information system will serve the needs of a
large number of individuals and groups. Their views, languages and assumptions
about a perceived application reality will differ. Their views etc, will be - by
negotiations - integrated into a common base - the CIM. This does not mean that
the users will "sacrifice" their views. Rather, it will be possible to relate one
view to another.

Clearly, the scope and contents of a CIM is determined by the scope of problems,
decisions, activities and their information requirements (existing or anticipated).
Conversely, an information requirement can be precisely and formally defined only
if a CIM is defined.

So, <u>one</u> role of CIM is to support the initial activities 1,2,3 (figure 1.2) of the
system development process. When fully developed, it presents the "equations" of
our application discourse. The dashed line in figure 1.2 indicates this state. The
<u>other</u> role of a CIM, together with requirements (indicating lay-outs, response-
time and timeliness requirements, interaction patterns etc), is to act as a detailed, formal and precise base from which an information system model (box nr 4 in
figure) can be designed. This design step is analogous to devising a set of numerical solution procedures for a set of mathematical equations. It involves several
storage and processing efficiency decisions as will be discussed in chapter 4.

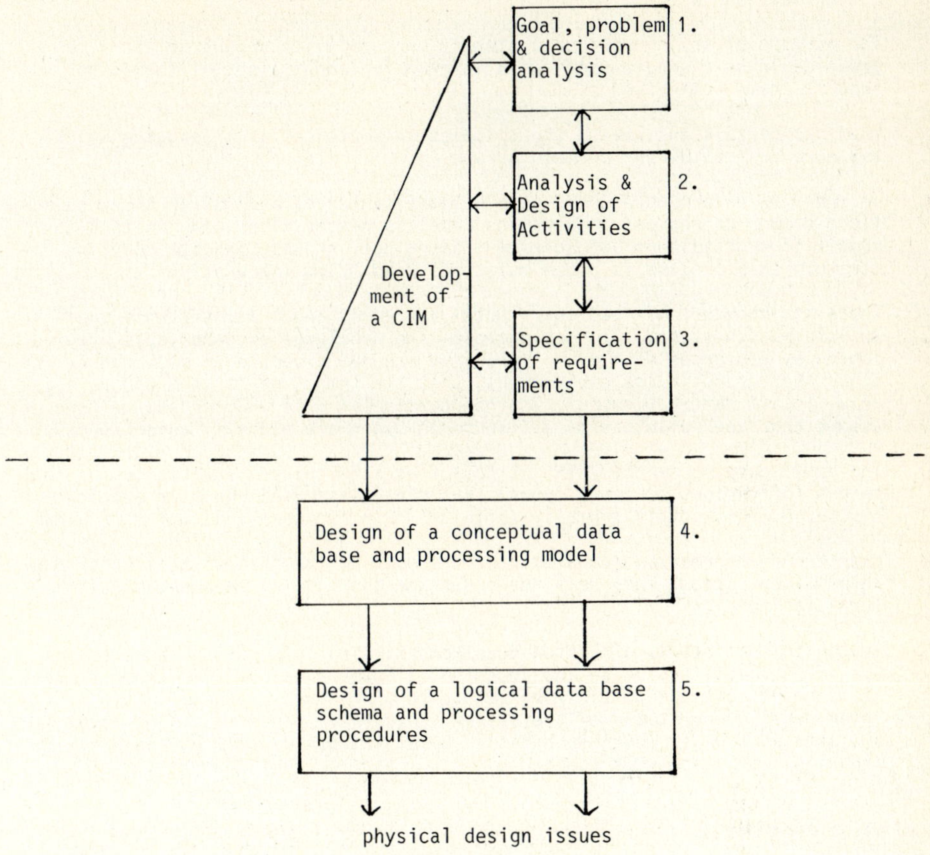


Figure 1.2

In the next chapter we will more in depth discuss some basic principles of developing a conceptual information model.


2.  FUNDAMENTAL CONCEPTS, PRINCIPLES AND THE METHOD OF DESIGNING A CIM

Before going into a discussion of concepts, principles and methodology,our views
and assumptions on system development and information system users will be given.

## 2.1  Basic views and assumptions

1. The purpose of an information system is to supply its groups of users (a group could be a single user) with information about a set of topics to support their activities

2. User groups talk and reason about topics in sentences of a language which may more or less differ between groups

3. In order to determine equivalences between sentences and define their semantic a common conceptual information model is needed. The  CIM  is thus the result of negotiations and agreement among user groups. In data modeling literature this process is often referred to as "view integration".

4. There is, however, no need for a total agreement about all sentence types in an information system. If, for example, the knowledge of some topic, represented by sentences of type  S  are (and are not expected to be) used by any other user group in the environment, then the semantics of them can be a purely "local" matter (comment: In this particular IFIP WG8.1 case, we however, assume that the semantics of all sentence types are globally agreed upon).

5. The basic purpose of the  CIM  is to act as a definition for the set of sentences (of various sentence types) that can be asserted about an application discourse. This set is normally infinite (from a theoretical point of view).

6. User group information requirements thus dictate the "set of topics" of the information system. This sets the scope and contents of the conceptual information model.

7. In the initial stages of system development, user information requirements are often vague, unprecise and incomplete. However, already in these stages it is beneficial and possible to recognize and introduce the main types of 'phenomena' of the topic of the system. This facilitates reasoning about it and acts as a basis which is extended by additional details as the activity and requirement analysis proceeds.


## 2.2  Basic concepts

In order to be able to carry out a reasonably precise discussion about methodological principles and the analysis and design steps of our approach, a brief introduction to basic concepts used is needed. Formal representation and specification issues are presented in chapter 3[1]).

We assume that the application universe of discourse is considered as consisting of a time varying set of entities. An entity is of one or more entity types. An entity population of type, say, AUTHOR, at time  t  is the set of entities which at time  t  belong to that type (are considered authors). Type membership may vary with time.

Entities are characterized by attributes. Attribute values may vary with time. Entity attributes are specified by attribute functions. For instance, an author's address can be viewed as an attribute function with name "address-of-author"

    address-of-author: AUTHOR, D ---> ADDRESS

(where  ADDRESS  is another entity type or a data type[2])which states that the address may vary from day to day and that on a particular day an author has one and only one address.

Assume now that we also wish to introduce the entity type  REFEREE  and the attribute function "address-of-referee". A negotiation with users may now lead to a generalization of the  AUTHOR  and  REFEREE  entity types to a type named  PERSON. Also the attribute functions may now (if their semantics are assumed equivalent) be "moved up" to the  PERSON  type and named, say, "mailing-address". We can now either define the former functions as equivalent to "mailing-address" and/or to apply the "inheritance rule":

> "if entity  x  is at time  t  of type  $E_1$  and  $E_1$  is a subtype of  $E_2$ and an attribute function  $f_2$  is defined for  $E_2$  then  $f_2$  applies also to  x".

In the above paragraph we thus have informally illustrated fragments of the problem of "view integration" which sometimes may lead to an extended structure of structure of entity types.

Another concept which is associated with entities is their <u>existence</u>. An existence criterion will state under which conditions an entity of type, say  PERSON, will be considered as "existing in the universe of discourse at a particular time  t. In this case we may assert, for instance, that a person exists as long as an author <u>or</u> a referee exists.

The existence criteria for authors may be defined in terms of <u>events</u> which signal the arrival of a submitted paper (introduces authors) or the withdrawal of a paper. Other kinds of conditions may hold for referee existence.

The above discussion introduced the <u>event</u> concept which is another fundamental notion of our modeling approach. Events are of different <u>event types</u> and introduce <u>dynamics</u> in the model. We use events to define existence of entities. However, they are also fundamental in our model for defining entity population membership, attribute value and relationship variations over time. The conceptual extension of our model would be "empty" without events. The basic property of an event is that it is a phenomenon that occurs only once and that it has no attributes which vary with time. Each event has an associated <u>occurrence condition</u>. Events are further categorized as <u>external</u> or <u>internal</u>. An <u>internal</u> event (to the information system) has a formal occurrence rule specified. External events do not have such rules and their occurrence is dependent on conditions outside the formal scope of the system.

Relationships may hold at time  t  between entities of various types. Relationships and "relationship attributes" are modeled by <u>relationship functions</u>. For instance, if an author can be the author of several papers and a paper can be authored by several authors, then this can be modeled by the relationship function defined by:

> co-authorship: AUTHOR, PAPER, T ---> Boolean

The expression below (applied to an extension of the model)

> co-authorship(a,p,t)

where  a,p  at time  t  belong to the  AUTHOR  resp the  PAPER  populations, will return the value <u>true</u> if such a relationship can be derived from other information about authors, papers etc.

This brings us to the concept  of <u>derivable information</u>. As pointed out in chapter 1, derivable information corresponds to <u>theorems</u>. This means that if we consider, say, an attribute function "mailing-address" to be derivable then a <u>derivation rule</u> must be specified. It will define the 'formula' and other **information to be** used to derive a mailing-address. In this particular case we may assume that the

value of mailing-address(p,d) (p ∈ PERSON, d ∈ DAY) is derived from the latest
"address-change-message" event. So, derivation analysis brings us to examine our
model, developed so far, for information which can be used in specifying derivation rules (the same holds for existence rules!). If no such information can be
found, we have to extend the model by introducing suitable functions or events so
that a derivation rule can be defined. Normally, the "address-change-message"
event type would not be part of our model in an initial stage.Derivation analysis
thus forces us to design such an event (design is a matter of agreement and negotiations) in order to define how mailing addresses vary with time.

Another basic concept has to be mentioned. In order to define the sets of "permissible sentences" of various types we need constraint definitions. These may be
more or less complex and have a more or less global scope. In the simple case a
constraint would restrict  the set of permissible values of the domain of a function to, for example, the set of positive integers less than 100. A more complex
constraint would, for instance, express the condition that "a person  p  cannot
be the chairman of a session  s  if during the time of session  s  another session
s' is scheduled which contains a paper of which  p  is a co-author".

We will say that a conceptual information model is consistent if its set of rules
and constraints does not contain a contradiction[3].


## 2.3  The development of a CIM

The main idea is that the CIM is incrementally developed during the initial phases
of the systems life-cycle (figure 1.2). Already in the initial phase (goal and
problem analysis) some decisions are made and restrictions of the scope of the
topic are agreed upon and introduced. A subset of the major entity types, and possibly also event types (e.g. AUTHORS, PAPERS, ...,  CALL-FOR-PAPERS, ACCEPTANCE-
NOTICE, ...etc) will be introduced. There is no reason to delay the specification
of them to a later stage. On the contrary, our hypothesis (confirmed in several
practical experiments) is that the "skeleton" of the CIM should be introduced as
early as possible as it forms the "back-bone" of further problem analysis, activity analysis and requirement specification. Also generic relationships should be
discussed, negotiated and specified as early as possible.

The conceptual information model is then elaborated (and quite possibly changed!)
in subsequent stages. In analyzing and/or designing **activities** of an enterprise we
examine their needs for information support.

Detailed analysis of each information requirement (see next section 2.4) will
further incrementally extend the model by introducing new entity types and, above
all, various attribute and relationship functions.

When all output information requirements are considered and their corresponding
information is included in the CIM,the next step is to make it complete by defining and specifying all existence, generalization, derivation and occurrence rules.
We denote this set of activities as "inference analysis". Each inference analysis
step may - and often will - introduce new information requirements. This will,
in its turn, further extend the CIM. It should be pointed out that introduction
of a new requirement actually is a design step. It is here we make the (practical)
decision where to draw the external boundary of the system, i.e. which event types
to consider external.

When the inference analysis phase is finished we can guarantee that our CIM is
complete in the sense that each existing or anticipated information requirement
can be satisfied and that each element of a CIM-extension either is initial information or can be derived from initial information (cf precedence analysis in [11]).

What we cannot guarantee (and which no existing method can do) is the <u>validity</u> of the CIM respect to the users´ "real" requirements and their perception of the application discourse. Experimental, "prototyping" techniques [ 2 ] have been found a good help in this respect and our approach in no way excludes the use of such techniques.

In summary, the CIM is successively, incrementally and to some extent iteratively developed in the early phases of the system development process. Major components of it are introduced already by reasoning about the "topic" of the information system. Refinements, details and new elements are introduced by careful corporate activity analysis and by performing a thorough inference analysis starting with those parts of a CIM which correspond to output requirements.


2.4   Information requirements and the conceptual information model

The various information handling activities of an organization can be more or less programmable and more or less well-structured. In an ideal situation we can hope to be able to specify in an algorithm how a decision is reached, how an information set is produced out of other information sets (which is the purpose of the activity) and to specify a logical flow of documents. Another ideal situation is if we can specify a straight forward man-machine dialogue how to deal with certain administrative tasks. In the above cases the number of "kinds" of information an activity needs is limited and the way it deals with it is a relatively simple and well defined matter.

Consider, as an example, the activity "Call-for-papers distribution". Its information requirements at time  t  consist of a list of persons (with names, titles and addresses) who should be sent a "Call-for-papers" invitation. This activity has possibly also the information requirement "Which persons have been "called" so far?". Anyway, it is an extremely simple situation compared to the needs of the activity "Paper selection process" carried out by the Program Committee.

Anyone familiar with the work of a Program Committee (PC) would agree that it is unrealistic to attempt to draw a nice information flow-graph of the activities of the PC-activity "selecting papers for acceptance". At best, the PC-activities and information needs can be described by a (large) set of various types of documents and listings and a (large) set of queries the PC-members <u>may</u> wish to ask about their discourse (which of course is AUTHORS, REFEREES, PAPERS, REFEREE-REPORTS, etc). The order between requirements of different kinds is, however, not possible to predict.

Our approach focuses on the semantic contents of information requirements (documents, queries) and <u>not</u> on <u>flows</u> of documents (which is a data processing system implementation design problem). This means that when we analyze a corporate activity we are focusing on what requirements (documents, queries) the activity has and not on the flow of documents within and between activities.

Each document type is composed of sentences, of different types, about a topic. The way a document is arranged also expresses certain (implicit) assumptions of the application discourse (such as functionality, M:N relationships, etc). So, by analyzing a document a <u>local</u>, conceptual view of a <u>part</u> of the application can be established. It can be expressed in the same "language" and notation as the "global" CIM created so far by analyzing other activities and their requirements. The next step is then to "integrate" this new "local view" (LV) with the CIM established so far. The integration step can imply several things

1.   the LV is contained in CIM

2.   the LV is not contained in CIM but no inconsistencies can be detected for

CIM' = CIM $\cup$ LV

3.    the LV is not contained in CIM and CIM' = CIM $\cup$ LV contains contradictions.

Case (1) simply says that the LW does not contribute anything new to the CIM and that the local requirement corresponding to LW can be satisfied with the "existing" CIM.

Case (2) implies that an (marginal, if the set (L -CIM) is "small") enlargement of CIM must be made in order for it to satisfy LV.

Case (3) is more problematic and may imply a partial redesign of CIM reconsidering assumptions and constraints introduced so far. It should be pointed out that case (2) does in no way guarantee that CIM' is from a practical point of view free from contradictions. A "forgotten constraint" C , introduced later, may very well make the set C    CIM' inconsistent

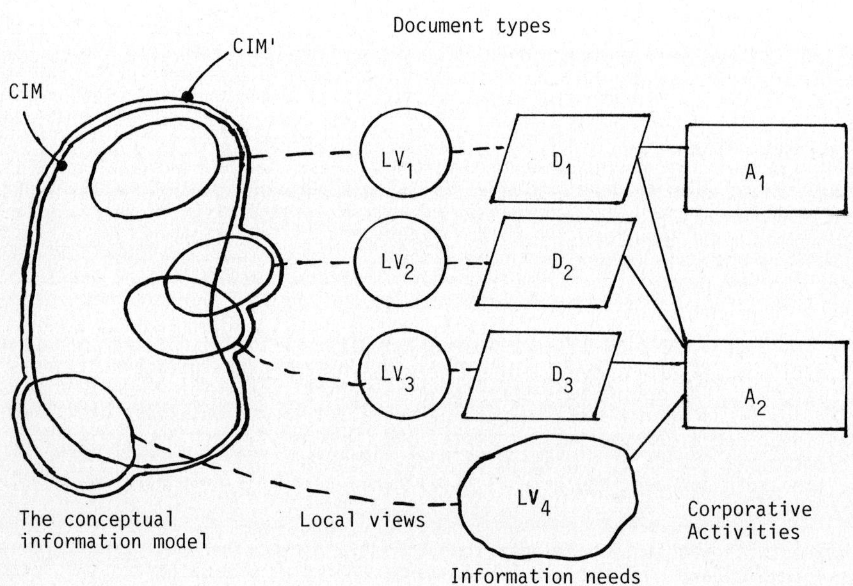


Figure 2.1

Figure 2.1 illustrates a situation where a local view $LW_1$ is fully contained in a CIM while $LW_2$ and $LW_3$ partly overlap each other and also extend the CIM.

In figure 2.1 also another common information requirement situation is illustrated, namely the case when the users are not capable to exactly specify the conceptual contents of a "document" in terms of sentence types etc. What the users instead are assumed to have is a "mental image" of a "topic" of their interest and concern. With reference to our case, this may be true for certain parts of the PC "paper selection" task, where you do not know which kinds of queries may come up but where you are reasonably sure of the "discourse" of the queries. This situation corresponds to  $LW_4$  in figure 2.1.

Figure 2.1 clearly indicates that the contribution to  CIM  from each new activity considered and analyzed is decreasing. Experiments have confirmed this property [2] of the  CIM  design process. In figure 2.2a it is shown that the  CIM  "stabilizes" after a relatively short time and that new requirements only marginally change or extend it. Experience shows, however, that the design of activities and man/machine interaction takes considerably longer time to reach a stable state (figure 2.2b).

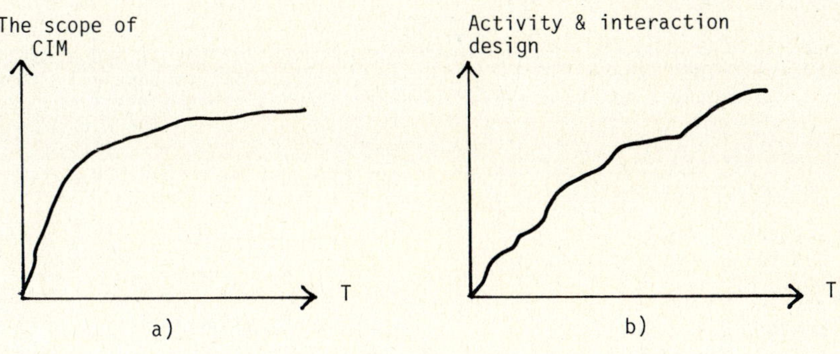


Figure 2.2

This observation indicates that it is advantageous to develop the conceptual information model as early as possible. Detailed design of corporate activities and man-machine interaction can then be carried out using the  CIM  as a 'stable' frame of reference.


## 3.   THE CIAM (CONCEPTUAL INFORMATION ANALYSIS METHODOLOGY) APPROACH

In this chapter the basic specification constructs of the specification language used in the CIAM approach are introduced. These constructs, which are further described in [5] and [6], use the basic modeling principles as described in chapter 2.

The process of developing a conceptual information model (CIM), previously outlined in section 2.3, is here further elaborated and illustrated by examples from the IFIP WG8.1 case. Appendices 1 through 3, which comprise a very compact summary of the conceptual application model we have arrived at, are referenced.


### 3.1  Basic specification constructs

The concept of time is essential in the CIAM approach. We need to refer to time points and sets thereof, as well as intervals between time points, when defining function value variations, existence criteria, generalization and various other constraints and rules. Thus we need a time model.

Four basic constructs are used when specifying a  CIM:

1.   The <u>entity type</u> specification

2.   The <u>event type</u> specification

3.   The <u>relationship function</u> specification

4.   The <u>data type</u> declaration.

This will be illustrated in the sequel.


### 3.1.1     A time model

A time model in CIAM consists of an infinite set  $T$  of time points and a set  $TI$ of time interval types, where  $TI = \{ TI_1, \ldots\ldots, TI_N \}$. $TI$  is partially ordered according to a component function, which is total and has the semantics of "part-of".

As an example, let the time model consist of the sets  $T$, $TI = \{S,MIN,H,D,M,Y\}$ and the "part-of" functions:

         second: T ---> S
         minute: S ---> MIN
         hour: MIN ---> H
         day:    H ---> D
         month:  D ---> M
         year:   M ---> Y

The "part-of" function holds an "inheritence" property i.e. if  $X$  and  $Y$  are two time interval types and "part-of: X ---> Y"  holds, then  $X$  "inherits" all functions defined for  $Y$.

All individual time points and intervals are considered to be events.

For different applications the specific components of the time model may, of course, vary according to what is found to be relevant for the application at hand.

For the "IFIP case" we have found no need for a very sophisticated time model. The information requirements analyzed indicate the need for the following time concepts

         - the set  T
         - the set  TI = {D}
         - the "part-of" function "day: T ---> D"

Given a particular time point  $t \in T$  we can now determine the day  $d \in D$  it is a part of by the reference  "day(t)".

To be able to refer to days by name, we introduce the simple data type

         DAYNO:  (1,.........)

and the name function

         dayno:  D ---> DAYNO


### 3.1.2     The entity type specification

The entity type specification scheme consists of

- the entity type name
- the entity existence assertion
- the generalization assertion
- the attribute function specification including definition of the
  function characteristics total/partial and into/onto[4] In case the
  function is found derivable, one or more (alternative) derivation
  rule specifications are included.
- the identifier assertion.

The entity existence specification asserts the conditions that must be fulfilled
for an entity to be considered as a member of the entity population at time  t .
The generics entry defines which other entity type(s) the type is generalized into. The identifier assertion indicates the set of attribute functions (alternatives are possible) which uniquely point out any individual entity belonging to the
particular type.

To illustrate this construct, consider the specification of the entity type
REFEREE[5].

```
entity       REFEREE;
existence    ∀x∀ d∃z(REFEREE-SELECTION(z) ∧ referee(z) = x ∧
             day(z)≤d ---> REFEREE(x,d));
generics     ∀x∀d (REFEREE(x,d) ---> PERSON(x,d));
attribute functions
             pf no-of-papers(D) : NUMBER;
                 derivation rule {number of events of type
                 PAPER-TO-REFEREE-ALLOCATION for that referee}
identifier {inherited from PERSON}
end;
```

The existence rule asserts that an entity  x  is of type  REFEREE  at day  d  if
there has occured "referee selection event" at a day less than or equal to  d .
The attribute function is a mapping

$$no\text{-}of\text{-}papers: REFEREE, D \to NUMBER$$

and indicates the total number of papers allocated to a particular referee at day
$d \in D$.


## 3.1.3    The event type specification

The event type specification comprises

- the event type name
- the attribute specification
- the occurrence time assertion
- the identifier assertion
- the occurrence condition specification(in the case the event is
  considered external this condition **is not specified**).

The attribute specification indicates which other entity, data or event types a
particular event type is functionally associated to. The attributes of an event
type are not time dependent. This is the major distinction between considering
a phenomenon as an entity or as an event. The occurrence time assertion functionally relates the event type to a suitably chosen time event type. The identifier entry specifies which attributes, including the occurrence time **attribute**, uniquely
identify the event.

An example from the "IFIP case":

```
event   PAPER-ARRIVAL;
    paper-no: PAPER-NO;
    paper: PAPER;
    patitle: PATITLE;
    principal-author: AUTHOR;
    pname: PNAME;
    petitle: PETITLE;
    mailing-address: MAIL-ADDRESS;
    affiliation: AFFILIATION;
    day: D;
identifier paper;
occurrence condition external;
end;
```

However, as we assume that submissions also contain a definition of the author´s opinion of which (one or more) subject areas the submitted paper covers, there is another event simultaneous with a  PAPER-ARRIVAL  event:

```
event AUTHORS-SUBJECT-AREA-DEFINITION;
    paper: PAPER;
    subject-area: SUBJECT-AREA;
    day: D;
identifier paper;
occurrence condition external;{any event of this type is
    simultaneous with a corresponding PAPER-ARRIVAL event}
end;
```

The requirement for this event to occur simultaneously with the PAPER-ARRIVAL event can formally be expressed as

$$\forall x \; (\text{PAPER-ARRIVAL}(x) \rightarrow \exists y \; (\text{AUTHORS-SUBJECT-AREA-DEFINITION} \; (y) \wedge$$
$$\text{paper} \; (y) = \text{paper} \; (x) \wedge \text{day} \; (y) = \text{day} \; (x) \; ))$$

As, further, any submitted paper may have one or more co-authors in addition to the principal author, there is another set of concurrent events:

```
event   CO-AUTHORSHIP-MSG;
    paper: PAPER;
    co-author: AUTHOR;
    co-name: PNAME;
    co-title: PETITLE;
    co-address: MAIL-ADDRESS;
    co-affiliation: AFFILIATION;
    day: D;
identifier paper, co-author;
occurrence condition external;{any event of this type is
    simultaneous with a corresponding PAPER-ARRIVAL event}
end;
```

Another example of an event type, whose occurrence is constrained by a rule, is the ARRIVAL-CONFIRMATION event:

```
event  ARRIVAL-CONFIRMATION;  { confirmation of paper-arrival }
    paper: PAPER;
    day: D;
identifier paper;
occurrence condition external; {at most  x  days after the occurrence of
    the PAPER-ARRIVAL event, an ARRIVAL-CONFIRMATION event of the
    corresponding paper must occur}
end;
```

### 3.1.4   The relationship function specification

The relationship function specification includes

- the relationship function name
- the domain specification
- the range specification
- the derivation rule definition.

Relationship functions in CIAM are multiargument functions defined in more than
two domains. The domains of the argument, which can be entity, data or time event
types, are specified in the domain entry and the range domain in the range entry.
The def entry specifies the derivation rule(s).

Consider the relationship between papers and referees. One paper may be sent to several referees for reviewing and one referee may review more than one paper. This
is then modeled by the boolean relationship function (predicate)[6)]

```
function paper-referee;
domain   p: PAPER;
         r: REFEREE;
         d: D;
range    Boolean;
def      ∀p∀r∀d (PAPER(p,d) ∧ REFEREE(r,d) ∧ D(d) ∧
         (∃y) (PAPER-TO-REFEREE-ALLOCATION(y) ∧ paper(y) = p ∧
         referee(y) = r ∧ day(y) ≤ d ∧
         (∄z) (PAPER-TO-REFEREE-WITHDRAWAL(z)∧paper(z) = p ∧
         referee(z) = r ∧ day(z) > day(y) --->
         paper-referee(p,r,d))));
```

The predicate "paper-referee(p,r,d)" is true at a particular day if the actual pa-
per has been earlier allocated to the actual referee by a PAPER-TO-REFEREE-ALLOCA-
TION event and has not after that been withdrawn by any PAPER-TO-REFEREE-WITHDRA-
WAL event.

### 3.1.5   The data type declaration

CIAM uses data types to describe individual phenomena. As opposed to entities, data values have no independent, own existence.

Data types can be base types and simple or aggregated interpreted types.

As an example of a data type declaration consider the aggregated type MAIL-
ADDRESS:

```
data MAIL-ADDRESS;
      street-addr:    STRADDR;
      postal-code:    ZIP;
      city:           string[1...30] of char;
      state:          string[1...25] of char;
      country:        string[1...30] of char;
      identifier      (street-addr, postal-code),
                      (street-addr, city, state, country);

data STRADDR;
      street#:        (1....1000);
      street-name:    string [1...30] of char;
      identifier      street#, street-name;

data ZIP;
      country-code:   (A,B,......Y);
      zip#:           string [1...12] of char;
      identifier      country-code, zip#;
```

As another example, let us take the ACC-CODE data type defining the set of possible values of the time-varying acceptance-code attribute function of PAPER:

```
data ACC-CODE;
      acc-code: (ACC,REJ,PEND,REV);
```

where the codes, in order, mean that a paper at time point  t  is either accepted, rejected, has a pending status or is in need of additional reviewing.

Some of the data types used are interpretations of the boolean base type, e.g.:

```
data CONFIRM-SUB;
      confirm-sub: Boolean;
```

The corresponding attribute is used to keep track of whether a submitted paper has yet been confirmed or not.


3.2   The CIM development process

In this section the CIM development process is elaborated and illustrated. The development process includes five major design steps. In the first step an initial, partial CIM "skeleton" is outlined merely by reasoning about the application discourse. In the subsequent steps, this initial CIM skeleton is, successively, further elaborated and extended. The last step involves a final test of the consistency/completeness of the model and a check that the stated information requirements are satisfied.

The five design steps are:

1.   Development of an initial, partial CIM through reasoning about the application discourse.

2.   Further function and activity analysis and extension of the model by detailed information requirements.

3.   Inference analysis.

4.   Global constraint specification.

5.   Consistency/completeness and requirement satisfiability test.

With regard to the IFIP WG8.1 case,step number 1 of the design process is carried out by reasoning about the case description.


3.2.1   Developing an initial, partial CIM by reasoning of the application
        discourse

By reasoning about the application discourse it is possible, already in the very early phases of the development cycle, to distinguish and identify major "concepts" and "phenomena" of the application. Thus obvious and important entity types, generic relationships between entity types and existence criteria can be discussed, agreed upon and introduced. The existence criteria can often be expressed by means of "birth" - and "death" - events for entities. By doing this various other major application relevant event types are often recognized.

Thus, initially approaching the "IFIP case" application discourse, as described in the original problem definition, by subsequent clarifications and by adding our own knowledge and assumptions, this could suggest a preliminary set of entity types like: REFEREE, AUTHOR, ATTENDEE, PAPER, CONFERENCE, SESSION, CHAIRMAN, PC-MEMBER, OC-MEMBER etc.

As the discussions proceed, generic relationships between these entity types are likely to be taken into account. Thus, matters of synthesis (new types can be created by generalization of other types) and of decomposition (forming new lower level types) are considered.

There are several "kinds" of "humans" (persons) involved in this particular application - they are acting in different roles and sometimes the same person can play several roles at different or at the same time (from the viewpoint of one conference). A particular person may be a PERSON-TO-CALL, a CHAIRMAN of session, an AUTHOR of a paper, an ATTENDEE etc. Presumably, persons in different roles have some attributes in common like names, addresses, affiliations etc. Thus,this reasoning may lead to the introduction of a "super-type" PERSON with which these common attributes later can be associated.  So, generic relationships like "PERSON-TO-CALL is a PERSON" are agreed upon and formally described by:

$$\forall x \forall d (PERSON\text{-}TO\text{-}CALL(x,d) ---> PERSON(x,d));$$

which says that "for all  x  and for all  d, if  x  is a PERSON-TO-CALL at day  d then  x  is also a PERSON at day  d".

At this point considerations must also be made about which constraints (global rules) apply to persons in various roles. This is further discussed in section 3.2.4.

In Appendix 3.2 the finally chosen generalization hierarchy of a subset of the entity types of the "IFIP case" is shown. In this case the hierarchy is tree-structured [7].
The discussion of existence criteria for the specified entity types suggests the consideration and introduction of various event types.

For instance, what is the condition for a referee to exist? Referees are more or less informally selected by the program committee members among people they know have a professional background and skill in subject areas relevant to the particular conference. An external event type REFEREE-SELECTION may then be added to the CIM already at this stage and defined as:

```
event REFEREE-SELECTION;
   referee: REFEREE;
   pname: PNAME;
   petitle: PETITLE;
   mailing-address: MAIL-ADDRESS;
   affiliation: AFFILIATION;
   day: D;
identifier referee;
occurrence condition external;
end;
```

Simultaneous with this event is a set of REFEREE-SUBJECT-AREA-PREFERENCES events, which tell about in which subject areas, the referee prefers to make his/hers reviewing. The important thing at this stage, however, is not to arrive at a complete specification of the event types - it is important to recognize them and reason about them.

Then, the existence assertion of REFEREE can be defined as:

$$\forall x \forall d \exists z (\text{REFEREE-SELECTION}(z) \wedge referee(z) = x \wedge$$
$$day(z) \leq d \dashrightarrow \text{REFEREE}(x,d));$$

In this case, as apparent, the decision was taken not to introduce any "death" - event of referees, i.e. once selected as a referee, the person remains a referee during the entire relevant time scope of the conference.

Existence criteria for generalized entity types are, if applicable, expressed by means of generics, e.g. :

$$\forall x \forall d (\text{PERSON-TO-INVITE}(x,d) \vee \text{REFEREE}(x,d) \vee$$
$$\text{PERSON-TO-CALL}(x,d) \vee \text{OC-MEMBER}(x,d) \vee \text{PC-MEMBER}(x,d)$$
$$\dashrightarrow \text{PERSON}(x,d));$$

To further illustrate the reasoning in this initial step let us put the question: How to deal with papers and their authors? Submitted papers are going to be either accepted for the conference or rejected. Authors of accepted as well as rejected papers will be invited to the conference. As a constraint we should avoid "sending duplicate invitations to any individual". A paper may have one or more authors (of which one is considered the principal author and the others are co-authors) and a person may be the author of one or more papers. And there are still more knowledge and assumptions in this connection, which influence the modeling and must be taken into account. From this some example modeling issues arise:

- introduce entity types ACC-AUTHOR and REJ-AUTHOR
- suggest existence criteria e.g.

    <u>existence</u> ACC-AUTHOR
    {A person is an accepted author at time  t  if,at that time, an accepted
    paper exists of which  x  is an author}

- introduce AUTHOR as a generalization of ACC-AUTHOR and REJ-AUTHOR and
  suggest

    <u>existence</u> AUTHOR

$$\forall x \forall t (\text{ACC-AUTHOR}(x,t) \vee \text{REJ-AUTHOR}(x,t) \dashrightarrow \text{AUTHOR}(x,day(t)));$$

    <u>generics</u> AUTHOR

$$\forall x \forall d (\text{AUTHOR}(x,d) \dashrightarrow \text{PERSON-TO-INVITE}(x,d));$$

Suppose  PERSON-TO-INVITE was previously introduced and

> generics PERSON-TO-INVITE
>
> ∀x∀d(PERSON-TO-INVITE(x,d) ---> PERSON(x,d));

- if we now assume that there are persons (INVITED-SPEAKER), who are especially invited to write a paper for the conference - are these persons to be considered as authors? If the answer is yes, then the existence criterion of AUTHOR must be modified

- introduce entity type PAPER

- should we introduce types ACC-PAPER and REJ-PAPER decomposing PAPER? How about invited papers (as opposed to submitted papers)? Let us instead introduce an attribute function "acc-code" of PAPER. Then the existence of ACC-AUTHOR can be made more precise

> existence ACC-AUTHOR
>
> {An author is an accepted author at time  t  if he is an author of a paper the acceptance-code of which is "ACC" at that time}

- but when is an AUTHOR really "born" in our system? At the time he becomes either an accepted or rejected author or both, he already exists as an author. This leads us to the LETTER-OF-INTENT and PAPER-ARRIVAL event types. Assuming that (as a simplification) the letter of intent contains information about the principal author and that simultaneous with the PAPER-ARRIVAL event there is the CO-AUTHORSHIP-MSG event (see section 3.1.3) one would, possibly not in this design step but during the inference analysis step, arrive at

> existence AUTHOR
>
> ∀x∀d(∃y) (LETTER-OF-INTENT(y) ∧ principal-author(y) = x ∧ day(y) ≤ d) ∨ (∃q) (PAPER-ARRIVAL(q)  ∧ principal - author(q) = x ∧ day(q) ≤ d) ∨ (∃z) (CO-AUTHORSHIP-MSG(z) ∧ co-author(z) = x ∧ day(z) ≤ d) ∨ INVITED-SPEAKER(x,d) ---> AUTHOR (x,d));

However, this specification, which tells that an author's existence may start with the LETTER-OF-INTENT event or with the PAPER-ARRIVAL event (a submission needs not to have been preceded by a letter of intent) if he is a principal author or by the CO-AUTHORSHIP-MSG event if he is a co-author (in which case he may very well be the principal author of another paper) or if he is an invited speaker, needs not to be the final one - a paper may be withdrawn, which suggests the PAPER-WITHDRAWAL event type, and if the paper withdrawn is the only paper the author(s) is authoring he (they) will end his (their) existence.

The time resolution levels used must be co-ordinated with time and up-to-date requirements. It is assumed above that an author exists "on a daily basis"; papers arrive and can be withdrawn from one day to another. During the paper selection process, however, a paper may have its acceptance-code changed from one time point to another, which determines whether the author is an accepted or rejected author at a particular timepoint.

### 3.2.2     Further function/activity analysis and extension of the model
         by considering detailed information requirements

The initial, partial CIM arrived at by reasoning about the application discourse
now serves as a basis for further analysis of problems, activities and for detailed requirement specification.

The "IFIP case" includes operations of two major committees, the Program Committee
and the Organizing Committee. For these committees there are a number of tasks defined and within these tasks it is possible to distinguish several more or less
well-structured activities.


The activities need information to fulfil their tasks and put requirements on the
information system to be designed. Sometimes these information requirements are
quite easy for the users to specify in detail. Examples of such requirements are
form oriented reports, listings and queries of different kinds e.g. a list of persons to whom the Call-for-papers is to be sent, with name, title and mailing address. However, sometimes it is not possible to state in detail the exact information content - what can be said is that one needs various information about some
discourse.

Consider, for instance, the work of the Program Committee when selecting papers
for acceptance and allocating them into sessions. This is a very ill-structured
process, where the information support, which would be of help, is hard to detail.
Yet one knows it concerns papers, authors, referee review reports, subject areas
etc. The information can be assembled and presented in various and numerous ways.
One has here merely a "conceptual image" of information. Very likely, though, many
such requirements would be derivable from knowledge already in the CIM - they need
not imply any extension of it.

It is possible to list the informal information requirements arrived at after
problem and activity analysis, which are not included in this report.

To illustrate the extension of the CIM by detailed information requirements, consider the REFEREE DISTRIBUTION LIST (Q7):

    " A list of program committee members with title, name, mailing address and
    for each PC-member a list of referee-persons, with title, name, mailing add-
    ress and preferred subject areas, which papers have been sent to that referee
    and total number of papers sent."

This list is required at any time  t  and should correctly reflect the situation
the day before.

The receiver of this **information** is the activity "Distribution to referees",
which needs this information in order to accomplish a good and fair distribution
of submitted papers among existing referees with respect to subject area interests
and workload.

Analyzing this requirement closer, the intrinsic "local conceptual view" revealed
could informally be stated as:

    - there are program committee members, each having a title, a name and a
      mailing address

    - there are referees, each having a title, a name and a mailing address

    - there are papers, which are sent to referees for reviewing

- a referee can have several papers sent to him

- there are subject areas (of the conference) and a referee may prefer to
  review papers, which lie within one or more of these subject areas

- a PC-member has a "pool" of referees.

Four entity types are suggested by this: PC-MEMBER, REFEREE, PAPER and SUBJECT-
AREA. At this stage there is a high probability that they have been introduced
already. However, the generics of PC-MEMBER and REFEREE must be checked in order
to assure that they have the attributes needed by inheritance. The extensions this
requirement is likely to give rise to are:

- the boolean type relationship functions

        paper-referee: PAPER,REFEREE,D ---> Boolean
        pc-member-referee: PC-MEMBER,REFEREE,D ---> Boolean
        referee-preferred-subject-areas:
            REFEREE,SUBJECT-AREA,D ---> Boolean

- a time-varying (daily) attribute function of the entity type REFEREE

        no-of-papers: REFEREE,D ---> NUMBER

The decision to model the PC-MEMBER - REFEREE relationship as a relationship function instead of as an attribute function of referee was based on the additional
knowledge (assumption) that a referee may be part of more than one PC-member referee pool.

The meaning of "total numbers of papers sent", which is part of the requirement,
was then concluded to mean the total number sent so far independent of PC-member.


3.2.3 Inference analysis

So far, we have considered all output information requirements and some 'input'
requirements reflected by events, when discussing existence criteria of entities.
The inference analysis step involves further detailed specification of rules of
- existence
- generalization
- derivation and
- occurrence.

The specification of existence and generalization rules has been treated earlier.
During this step these rules must be completely specified.

For all specified attribute functions, which have been assumed derivable i.e. include a time domain, derivation rules must be set up. This may lead to new information requirements i.e. to the extension of the model by new functions and by new
external and possibly internal event types.

Consider, for example, the attribute function "affiliation" of entity type PERSON.
Persons change their affiliations and this fact has been judged to be of relevence
to our application. Therefore it has been modeled by specifying that this attribute is time varying. The chosen resolution level is "day". How then can we derive the affiliation of a particular person at a particular day? Of course, the
system puts a requirement on its environment to be informed when a person changes
his affiliation; at this stage such an "affiliation-change-message" event type is
not likely to have already been made part of our model.Then we have to extend it by:

```
┌─────────────────────────────────────────────┐
│  event AFFILIATION-MSG;                      │
│    person: PERSON;                           │
│    affiliation: AFFILIATION;                 │
│    day: D;                                    │
│  identifier person,day;                      │
│  occurrence condition external;             │
│  end;                                        │
└─────────────────────────────────────────────┘
```

Then we can specify the derivation rule verbally as:

> {A person´s affiliation at a particular day is the affiliation of the
> latest AFFILIATION-MSG event for that particular person}

and more formally:

```
tf affiliation (D): AFFILIATION;
   derivation rule ∀x∀d∃y(PERSON(x,d)  ∧  D(d)  ∧
   (AFFILIATION-MSG(y)  ∧  person(y) = x  ∧  day(y) ≤ d  ∧
   ( ∄z(AFFILIATION-MSG(z)  ∧  person(x) = z  ∧  day(z̄) > day(y)))
   ---> affiliation(x,d) = affiliation(y));
```

"Values" of the attributes specified as not time-varying, e.g. "pname" of PERSON,
must be initially supplied when an entity starts an existence period in the model.
As PERSON is a generalization of other types, all "birth" event types refered to
in the existence criteria of all its "sub types" must have the attribute "pname"
as well. Of course, one may argue, that persons change their names as they do
change affiliations and addresses. However, during the relevant time interval of
one conference, this has been assumed not to be the case and the decision was taken to consider names of persons as "stable".

Derivation rules must also be specified for all relationship function types. Consider the relationship function "paper-referee", mentioned in the foregoing  section. Papers are distributed to referees for reviewing and how this decision making is actually performed is an ill-structured process. This process is therefore not formalized and included in the model. However, some decision support are
left by the "REFEREE DISTRIBUTION LIST". These considerations resulted in the extension of the model by two external event types: PAPER-TO-REFEREE-ALLOCATION and
PAPER-TO REFEREE-WITHDRAWAL (a referee may, for some reason, return a paper he
thinks he is not able or interested in to review). The completed specification of
the "paper-referee" relationship function then is:

```
┌──────────────────────────────────────────────────────────┐
│  function paper-referee;                                  │
│  domain    p: PAPER;                                      │
│            r: REFEREE;                                    │
│            d: D;                                          │
│  range     Boolean;                                       │
│  def       ∀p∀r∀d(PAPER(p,d) ∧ REFEREE(r,d) ∧ D(d) ∧     │
│            (∃y) (PAPER-TO-REFEREE-ALLOCATION(y) ∧         │
│            paper(y) = p ∧ referee(y) = r ∧ day(y) ≤ d ∧   │
│            (∄ z) (PAPER-TO-REFEREE-WITHDRAWAL(z) ∧        │
│            paper(z) = p ∧ referee(z) = r ∧ day(z) > day(y)│
│            ---> paper-referee(p,r,d)));                   │
└──────────────────────────────────────────────────────────┘
```

During this phase,the occurrence conditions of all specified event types, must be
further analyzed and specified. The event types considered external are just marked "external", while the internal type events need a detailed formal definition.
Consider, for example, the internal event type

```
event PERSON-INVITATION;
   invitee: PERSON-TO-INVITE;
   invitation-category: INVITATION-CATEGORY;
   day: D;
identifier invitee, invitation-category;
```

The persons to invite day  D  are the members of the population PERSON-TO-INVITE(D).
Let us recall the existence assertion of PERSON-TO-INVITE

```
existence PERSON-TO-INVITE
∀x∀d (AUTHOR(x,d) ∨ NAT-REP(x,d) ∨ RELEVANT-WG-
MEMBER(x,d) ∨ CHAIRMAN(x,d) ∨ CO-CHAIRMAN(x,d)
---> PERSON-TO-INVITE(x,d));
```

The members of the arranging working group and the members of associated working
groups are the entities of the entity type RELEVANT-WG-MEMBER, the national representatives (NAT-REP) are, we assume, the members of the corresponding technical
committees. Further, we assume that each session is lead by one chairman and one
co-chairman.

However, when should we start to invite people to attend the conference? This
is an "external" decision, which is taken by the Organizing Committee. The event
type

```
event INVITATION-DECISION;
   inv-start-day: D;
   day: D;
identifier day;
occurrence condition external;
end;
```

is then introduced as a triggering event of PERSON-INVITATION.

The occurrence rule for PERSON-INVITATION is now formulated as

$$\forall z \forall x \forall t \ (\text{INVITATION-DECISION}(z) \land \text{day}(z) = d \land \text{PERSON-TO-INVITE}(x,t)$$
$$\land \ \text{day}(t) = d \rightarrow \exists y (\text{PERSON-INVITATION}(y) \land \text{day}(y) \geq d$$
$$\land \ \text{invitee}(y) = x));$$

The global rule stated as: "Avoiding sending duplicate invitations to any individual" is now expressed as

$$\forall x \forall y \ (\text{PERSON-INVITATION}(x) \land \text{PERSON-INVITATION}(y) \rightarrow$$
$$\text{invitee}(x) \neq \text{invitee}(y) )$$

However, a "person-to-invite" can be invited at one conference for more than one
reason; he may be the chairman of one session, the co-chairman of another session,
the author of an accepted paper, the co-author of a rejected paper etc. To handle
this situation we have introduced the 'relationship attribute' "invitation-catego-
ry" modeled by

```
function  inv-cat-of-person-to-invite;
domain    ip: PERSON-TO-INVITE;
          ic: INVITATION-CATEGORY;
          d:  D ;
range     Boolean;
def       ∀ip∀ic ∀d(PERSON-TO-INVITE(ip,d) ∧ D(d) ∧
          (∃y) (PERSON-INVITATION(y) ∧ invitee(y) = ip ∧
          invitation-category(y) = ic ∧ day(y) ≤ d)
          ---> inv-cat-of-person-to-invite(ip,ic,d));
end;
```

In Appendix 1.6 an example of an inference graph, showing the part of the conceptual model which concerns the entity type PAPER, is shown.


### 3.2.4  Global constraints

Constraint definitions are used to define the sets of "permissable sentences" of
various types. Constraints can have a more or less global scope.

<u>Local constraints</u>.

Certain types of constraints are, in CIAM, defined in close connection to the specification constructs.

In the entity type specification there are the

- existence assertion
- generalization assertion
- attribute function derivation rule specification and the function characteristics (total/partial, into/onto)
- identifier assertion.

Further, the event type specification includes the

- identifier assertion
- **occurrence assertion**

and, the relationship function specification the

- derivation rule specification.

The data type declaration contains the

- identifier declaration and the
- value-set declaration.

Consider e.g. the assumption (for a list of informal basic assumptions see Appendix 2).

"One referee can review several papers and one paper can be reviewed
by several referees."

How is this assumption modeled? The assumption indicates that there is a many-to-
many relationship between papers and referees and then the modeling of this assumption as a boolean-type relationship function is appropriate in this case
i.e.

paper-referee: PAPER,REFEREE,D ---> Boolean

The semantics of this function (obvious by the derivation rule specification) is
that it is true for a particular paper, a particular referee and a particular
day if, at any time before that day, the paper has been sent to the referee for
reviewing and if, thereafter,the referee has not returned the paper unreviewed.
Consider another assumption

> "A session has one chairman and a person can be the chairman
> of several sessions."

Then, chairman is made an attribute function of session. This function is time-dependent, partial and onto. Each chairman must be the chairman of at least one session. However, the totality aspect of this function is time-dependent. During session design time, there may well be that a particular session not yet has been given a chairman. However, at some point in time and latest at the deadline of the final Program, each session must have a chairman selected.

<u>Global constraints</u>.

In addition to the more local type constraints, there are constraints, which have a more global scope and which cannot be modeled locally in connection with any specification construct.

Considering the informal basic assumptions there are some examples of such constraints:

(A10)  "A session chairman or co-chairman does not need to be a member of the Program Committee. In addition all PC-members need not be chairmen or co-chairmen."

(A11)  "An author of an accepted paper must not be the chairman or co-chairman of the session in which his paper is to be presented."

(A13)  "A person must not review a paper if he is an author or a co-author."

(A23)  "A PC-member must not be an author or co-author."

Often the members of the Program Committee act as session chairmen. To make it clear that others than PC-members can be chairmen (A10) was explicitly written down. However, this assumption, which actually is not a constraint, is modeled in the CIM by the absence of any generic relationship involving PC-MEMBER and CHAIRMAN/CO-CHAIRMAN.

The constraints (A13) and (A23) can be formally specified as

$$\forall x \forall d\ (\text{PAPER-TO-REFEREE-ALLOCATION}(x) \land \text{paper}(x) = a \land$$
$$\text{referee}(x) = b \rightarrow \neg(\text{co-authorship}(a,b,d) \lor \text{principal-author}(a) = b));$$

$$\forall x \forall d\ (\text{AUTHOR}(x,d) \rightarrow \neg\,\text{PC-MEMBER}(x,d));$$

As an invited-speaker is an author this excludes the possibility of an invited-speaker being a PC-member or a referee.

(A11)  is a bit more complicated to express by formal notation

$$\forall x \forall t \forall y \forall z\ (\text{SESSION}(x,t) \land \text{chairman}(x,t) = y \land$$
$$\text{co-chairman}(x,t) = z \rightarrow$$
$$\nexists a(\text{PAPER-TO-SESSION-ALLOCATION}(a) \land \text{SESSION}(a) = x$$
$$\land\ (\text{co-authorship}(\text{paper}(a),y,\text{day}(t)) \lor$$
$$\text{co-authorship}(\text{paper}(a),z,\text{day}(t)) \lor$$
$$\text{principal-author}(\text{paper}(a)) = y\ \lor$$
$$\text{principal-author}(\text{paper}(a)) = z\ )));$$

### 3.2.5 Consistency/completeness and requirement satisfiability test

As pointed out in chapter 2, it is not possible, of course, to formally veri**fy** the validity of the CIM. The question of whether the formulation of a specific rule in CIM 'adequately' reflects and abstracts the users´perception of some part of the application discourse must be a matter for the user/designer community to agree upon and decide.

As an example, consider the question of the subject area of a submitted paper. How is this going to be modeled? Sometimes it is required of a submitter of a paper to indicate the subject area of his paper by checking one out of a given set of prede- fined areas. If this is the user´s perception of this topic (more adequate would probably be to allow more than one alternative  to be checked as this will happen anyway  we model it by the attribute function "subject-area:  PAPER ---> SUBJECT- AREA". Assume there is a new requirement: "In which subject areas has a particular referee performed reviewing so far?" modeled by: "referee-subject-area: REFEREE, SUBJECT-AREA,D ---> Boolean". The relationship function: "paper-referee: PAPER, REFEREE,D ---> Boolean" is already a part of the model and "referee-subject-area" is then, one might think, derivable from "subject-area" and "paper-referee". However, the result is then based on the authors´opinion of subject area classifi- cation - the referees may have different opinions. So which is the more adequate (valid) choice in this situation?

Our solution allows several subject areas to be defined for a paper and, further- more, clarifies the origin of these definitions:

        author-defined-subject-areas:
          PAPER,SUBJECT-AREA,D ---> Boolean
        referee-defined-dubject-areas:
          REFEREE,PAPER,SUBJECT-AREA,D ---> Boolean
        final-paper-subject-areas:
          PAPER,SUBJECT-AREA,D ---> Boolean

The last function is defined by decisions made by the program committee based on information modeled by the first two functions.

In the view integration process, when successively integrating the 'local views' in the information requirements and assumptions into the global CIM established, so far, there may, of course, appear inconsistencies and contradictions. An incon- sistent theory is, by definition, a theory which contains both a theorem and its negation.

Consider the following set of assertions:

1.    An author is either an accepted author or a rejected author, but not both.

2.    An accepted author is an author who has an accepted paper.

3.    A rejected author is an author who has a rejected paper.

4.    An author may be the author of several papers.

Taking a 'pragmatic' viewpoint, one would agree that this set of assertions is not free from contradictions; as an author may be the author of, say, two papers, it may certainly be the case that he has one paper accepted and the other one rejec- ted. He is then both an accepted and a rejected author. However, as there is no explicit statement that there really exist authors, who are authors of more than one paper, the set of assertions is formally not inconsistent (confer [12] and [13])

Thus, in order to detect 'pragmatically' inconsistent assertions our model has to be extended by assertions stating the existence of certain state of affairs.

Next we turn our attention to checking the satisfyability of information requirements. The informal information requirements each inherently presents a set of assertions about some topic of the IFIP conference application. When analyzing an information requirement, trying to define the intrinsic local conceptual view, each such assertion must correspond to either an axiom or a theorem of our theory (the CIM). If it does not, our theory has to be extended with additional theorems or axioms.

An accurate inference analysis should ensure that all theorems are derivable from other theorems and/or axioms of our theory i.e. each element of an extension of our CIM can be derived from initial information.

However, the informal information requirements are not very precisely and unambiguously formulated. By using the components of the CIM, it is not possible to reach a precise and complete specification of them. This, of course, is also a prerequisite of showing that the requirements really are satisfied by our theory. This shows the strong mutual dependency between the information requirements and CIM. The information requirements dictate the contents and scope of the CIM, but the CIM is necessary to precisely define the information requirements.

As an example of a formally expressed information requirement consider the "REFEREE DISTRIBUTION LIST" (Q7) previously discussed in section 3.2.3:

```
at any time point  t
for each {x: PC-MEMBER(x,day(t)) }
display petitle(x,day(t)), pname (x),
        mailing-address(x,day(t));
   for each {y: REFEREE(y,day(t)) ∧
            pc-member-referee(x,y,day(t))}
   display petitle(y,day(t)), pname(y),
           mailing-address(y,day(t)),
           no-of-papers(y,day(t));
      for each {z: PAPER(z,day(t)) ∧
              paper-referee(z,y,day(t)) }
      display paper-no(z), pname(principal-author(z)),
              petitle(z);
```

This specification, using the concepts defined in our CIM, now verifies that CIM satisfies requirement Q7.


3.3 Assessment


In this section some concluding remarks about the CIAM development procedure are made. This is followed by an evaluation of the approach according to the "check list" of [9].

### 3.3.1  Concluding remarks about the development procedure

The CIAM development procedure, as described earlier, prescribes that the CIM is incrementally developed. By reasoning about the application discourse, there is an initial, partial CIM agreed upon. This 'basic' CIM is then, stepwise, further incrementally extended, elaborated and formalized.

Each step in the procedure has a well-defined purpose and concentrates on establishing and elaborating those parts of the CIM, which are relevant for the design decisions to be taken in that step. In the very early phases, for example, one concentrates on discussing major entity and event types. Even if main derivable attributes of the entity types sometimes can be distinguisted (and specified) during these discussions, the detailed specification of the derivation rules should, preferably, be postponed to the inference analysis step.

During the work solving the IFIP WG8.1 case, some of our major experiences of the CIAM approach were :

- it was very valuable initially to be able to reason about the application discourse in terms of major entity and event types, existence and generalization rules. The 'basic' CIM arrived at after this step and the deeper understanding of the application it gave us was really felt to be of great help when specifying the information requirements

- the specification constructs summarizing the characteristics and assertions to be specified for the major model type-concepts gave a 'stability' to the work. At each stage they told what was known about any particular entity or event type so far and what remained to be specified

- the stepwise approach where each step concentrates on predefined parts of the CIM to be established and elaborated was found advantageous

- the inference analysis step demands of the user/designer the complete specification of all existence, generalization, occurrence and derivation rules. In this way, we were forced by the procedure to introduce new requirements to ensure the satisfiability of the user information requirements.

### 3.3.2  Assessment of the conceptual modeling language

The 'power' of a modeling language cannot be measured in quantitative terms and no common agreement exists as to what should characterize a 'powerful' modeling language. However, in the ISO preliminary report[9] a "check list" is presented which tests if a particular modeling language has the power to express and 'capture' in the conceptual schema certain types of assertions about an application discourse. The check list comprises 47 different assertions about an example universe of discourse which has to do with registration of cars and which is limited to the scope of interest of the registration authority. We have generalized the 47 different assertions into 13 assertion classes, which express assumption types, state of affairs and types of rules as follows.

1.  Permissible types of facts, which delimit  the scope of the 'topic'.

2.  Separation of 'objects' and names, which are used to refer to objects (entities,events). Specification of unique identifiers.

3.  The concept of events and event occurrence rules, i.e. conditions which must hold for an event to occur.

4.  Event occurrence constraints, i.e. rules which constrain event occurrence for instance that an event must not happen later than day  d  if condition  c  holds, etc.

5.  Attributes, functionalities, totalities/partialities, into/onto - mappings.

6.   Attribute value derivation rules; time dependent rules (for instance: if in time interval $T_1$ then use rule $R_1$ else use rule $R_2$).

7.   Relationships between n, n > 2, objects; relationship functions.

8.   Relationship value derivation rules; time dependent rules.

9.   Constraints on attribute and relationship values; time dependent constraints.

10.  Existence criteria and constraints (for instance that an entity of type E and associated information is considered 'existing' until x years after the latest event of type V which concerned the entity).

11.  Entity populations, constraints on entity populations (for instance: the numbers of chairmen should never exceed the number of sessions).

12.  Generic relationships, rules and constraints (for instance: referees are persons, so are PC-members, only referees and PC-members may review a paper).

13.  Conceptual model - organization couplings and constraints (for instance: events of type x can only be triggered by organizational function F ).

The ISO-report further analyzes four classes of modeling approaches and tests their expressive power with respect to the above types of assertions. Only one of the four classes of approaches, the "Interpreted Predicate Logic Approach" (IPL) is found to have the power to deal with all 13 types of assertions. It is easy to see that our approach lies very close to the IPL-approach and that it has the power to deal with all of the above listed types of assertions, provided that adequate entity and event types are introduced.


## 4.   DESIGN OF A CONCEPTUAL INFORMATION PROCESSING SYSTEM

When the design of the CIM and the checking of its correctness and consistency is completed, there is a "time- and storage- unrestricted" model of the perceived application. Such an "unrestricted" model is, however, unrealistic to implement in its full generality. Therefore, the next step in the design is to develop an implementable, time-restricted model.

Several approaches to logical design are presented in the literature [1,7,8,14]. The approaches often include  a tool, using which an efficient, DBMS dependent data structure can be created starting from a fixed conceptual data structure and fixed processes which operate on that structure.

CIM is not a description of a fixed data structure, neither does it contain any processes. At the CIM level, it is not decided which data will be <u>explicitly</u> stored in the data base or which processes will be operating on that data.

To our knowledge, there is no method for logical design, which accepts as a starting point a time- and storage-unrestricted model such as CIM.

Therefore, the next step in the CIAM approach is to create a fixed data structure and fixed processes on that structure. This design activity is called the conceptual information processing system (CIPS) design.

In this section, the decisions involved in the CIPS design are discussed. The subsequent design step, the logical, DBMS dependent design is also discussed shortly. The CIPS for the IFIP WG8.1 case is presented in Appendix 4.

### 4.1  Models at the CIPS level

The conceptual information processing system consists of two models: a conceptual data base model (CDBM) and a conceptual processing model (CPM). The CDBM is a mo-

del describing the information which will be stored in the data base. The CPM describes the processes for the maintenance of the data described in CDBM. The information retrieval as stated in the IRQ is assumed to be done using a suitable query language and is not included as a part of CPM, but must, of course, be dealt with when defining the CDBM.
The CIPS level is independent of the DBMS which eventually will be used. Several data models and their languages can therefore be used at this level. In this approach, the binary approach according to CS [10] is chosen for compatibility reasons (see chapter 4.3).


## 4.2  Design decisions

A main problem in this design phase is the "time-restriction" activity. This activity involves design decision for each of the time-varying attribute and relationship functions defined in CIM.

In order to describe the meaning of the time-restriction concept, we show an example of a time-varying attribute function in CIM:

```
entity PERSON;
.

.

.
attribute functions:
tf mailing-address (D): MAIL-ADDRESS;
derivation rule: (∀x∀d∃y(PERSON(x,d) ∧ D(d) ∧ ADDR-STATUS-MSG(y)
& person(y) = x ∧ day(y) ≤ d ∧ (∃z)(ADDR-STATUS-MSG(z) ∧
person(z) = x ∧ day(z) > day(y) ---> mailing-address(x,d) =
mailing-address (y))));
.

.
end;
```

The above derivation rule specifies that the mailing-address for a person on a particular day is the mailing-address in the latest address-status-message (ADDR-STATUS-MSG) for that person. The rule describes the behaviour of a person´s mailing-address from the start time of the enterprise, until "now" because the variable  d describing "days" is universally quantified. An arbitrary day in the life-time of the enterprise can be substituted for the variable  d.

For example, the following "days" can be substituted for it:

- the day exactly one week ago from "now"
- the first day of the current year
- the current day.

Time-expressions, as the above, are called time-slices. The question is about which one or several of all the possible time-slices of a function should we maintain information of in the data base?

The activity of deciding these time-slices is called the time-restriction decision. The time-slices, for which it is decided to maintain information about, are called relevant time-slices.

In order to make the time-restriction decision for a function, the first task is to study the information requirements and find out on which time-slices there is an output requirement concerning the function. Those time-slices are then the relevant time-slices for the function in case. For example, in case of the "mailing-address", there is an information requirement for the current mailing-address. The current day, i.e. the day of the request, is a relevant time-slice for the function mailing-address.

There can, however, be additional relevant time-slices for a function. Assume that in an application, there is a derivation rule defined for a function denoting yearly salary (YSAL) as follows. (The IFIP WG8.1 case contains no functions with these properties. The example is from another universe of discourse.)

$$(\forall x \forall y (YSAL(x,y) = \Sigma \ MSAL(x,m)))$$
$$\forall m:year(m) = y$$

where MSAL(x,m)  denotes the monthly salary for a person  x  in month  m.  If a function  f  appears in a derivation rule for a function  g, we say that the function  g  is <u>dependent</u> on the function  f.  Here, the function YSAL is dependent on the function MSAL.

One would like to state that, in order to be able to derive YSAL, it is necessary to choose the months in the current year as relevant time-slices for MSAL. It is, however, not necessarily the correct decision. Assume that we aim to manage the process for deriving YSAL by accumulating YSAL by MSAL at the end of each month. In this case, it would not be necessary to maintain information about MSAL for each month during the year, only MSAL for the current month would be required. Therefore, the current month would be a relevant time-slice for MSAL. In the case that yearly salary would be computed only at the end of the year then all months during the current year would be relevant time-slices for MSAL.

The above example shows that before the time-restriction decision for a function can be made, it must be decided <u>how the functions which are dependent on that function will be processed</u>. This decision is called <u>the decision of processing policy</u>. The processing policy can be, as examplified above, an instant updating or computing at request time. It can also be something between these two 'extreme' alternatives.

There is, however, an additional "degree of freedom" in the CIM, which makes the time-restriction decision even more complicated. In CIM, <u>alternative</u> derivation rules can be specified for a function. For example, one <u>could specify</u> the following derivation rules for yearly salary function (YSAL):

$$(\forall x \forall y (YSAL(x,y) = \Sigma \ MSAL(x,m)))$$
$$\forall m:year(m) = y$$

and

$$(\forall x \forall y (YSAL(x,y) = \Sigma \ DSAL(x,d)))$$
$$\forall d:year(d) = y$$

where DSAL(x,d)  denotes daily salary for a person  x  on day  d .

Before relevant time-slices for DSAL and MSAL can be decided, it must be decided which of these rules will be used for derivation of YSAL <u>and</u> how YSAL will be processed. Choosing one of the alternative derivation rules  is called the <u>derivation rule decision</u>.

As we have seen, the time-restriction decision for a function  f  is dependent on

- decision concerning processing policy for all functions which are dependent on  f
- derivation rule decision for all functions which are dependent on  f
- information requirements concerning the function  f.

The examples above have been concerned with time-restriction of time-varying attribute functions. Exactly the same reasoning can be performed for relationship functions with a non-Boolean range.

In the IFIP WG8.1 case, the above described design decisions are not very complicated. First, we have not identified any function which is dependent on another function. Further, there is at most one derivation rule defined for every function. Therefore, the relevant time-slices for each function are those stated in information requirements.

Representation of CIPS

As mentioned already, the CIPS in CIAM approach is described using CS 4- concepts [10]. The discussion in the following concerns CIPS design when using these concepts. If another language were used for representation of CIPS, the designed structure would very probably be quite different.

A CS4 data structure consists of a set of e-records. An e-record includes two entities and a binary association between them. An e-record type is in this paper represented as follows:

        NODE --- association name ---> NODE (TYPE)

where NODE is an entity type and TYPE stands for the type of the association which can be one-to-one (1:1), one-to-many (1:M), many-to-one (M:1) or many-to-many (M:M).

There is, to some extent, a natural correspondence between CIM concepts and the concepts in CS4. For example, an entity type in CIM is quite natural to describe as an entity type in CDBM. Also, a data type, defined as a range for a function, which is decided to be explicitly stored, is natural to describe as an entity type. If there is a need to represent a time domain in CDBM, it will also be an entity type.

A relationship function with a Boolean range represents a set of relationship of a particular type. The set of relationship types will be a natural entity type in CDBM, represented by functional associations to its domains.

Example:

CIM

```
 ┌──────────────────────────────────┐
 │ function  paper-referee;          │
 │ domain    p: PAPER;               │
 │           r: REFEREE;             │
 │           d: D;                   │
 │ range     Boolean;                │
 │ .                                 │
 │ .                                 │
 │ .                                 │
 │ end;                              │
 └──────────────────────────────────┘
```

The entity type PAPER-REFEREE and the following associations are introduced.

CDBM

```
 ┌─────────────────────────────────────────────────────────────┐
 │ PAPER-REFEREE --- paper-of-paper-referee ---> PAPER (M:1)    │
 │ PAPER-REFEREE --- ref-of-paper-referee ---> PERSON (M:1)     │
 └─────────────────────────────────────────────────────────────┘
```

The above example requires some explanation.  For the relationship paper-referee, the only relevant time-slice is the one appearing in IRQ, in this case the current day. Therefore, there is no need to represent the time domain in CDBM.

An <u>attribute function</u> in CIM, which is not time-varying, has an entity type as domain and a data type, another entity type or a time domain as range. If the function is decided to be stored in the data base, i.e. represented in CDBM, then it will be represented as an association between the CDBM entities which correspond with the domain and range types in CIM.

Example:

CIM

```
entity SUBJECT-AREA;
.
.
attribute functions:
tf subject-area-description: SUBJ-AREA-DESCR ;
.
.
end;
```

CDBM

```
SUBJ-AREA --- subject-area-description ---> SUBJ-AREA-DESCR (M:1)
```

For a time-varying attribute function, if there is need for representing the time domain in CDBM, an entity describing the relationship between the entity type and time domain must be created.

Assume that for the entity type PERSON-TO-INVITE, we have decided to store the invitation-status (inv-status) and also that we have a need to store not only the current invitation status, but also the next most recent invitation-status.

CIM

```
entity PERSON-TO-INVITE;
.
.
attribute functions:
pf  inv-status (D): INV-STATUS;
.
.
end;
```

Then we create a new entity INV-STATUS-DAY denoting the person's invitation status history.

CDBM

```
INV-STATUS-DAY --- person-of-inv-status-day ---> PERSON-TO-INVITE (M:1)
INV-STATUS-DAY --- day-of-inv-status-day ---> DAY                 (M:1)
INV-STATUS-DAY --- inv-status ---> INV-STATUS                     (M:1)
```

Of course, it is also possible to create two new entity types denoting the current and the next current invitation status.

CDBM

```
PERSON --- curr-inv-status ---> CURR-INV-STATUS (M:1)
PERSON --- next-curr-inv-status ---> NEXT-CURR-INV-STATUS (M:1)
```

Because of the nature of the function, the attribute function descriptions in
CDBM will always be either one-to-one (1:1) or many-to-one (M:1). A prerequisite
for a one-to-one characteristic for an association in CDBM is that it describes
an identifier function of an entity type in CIM.

CIM

```
entity PAPER;

.
.
attribute functions:
tf paper-no: PAPER-NO;

.
identifier paper-no;
end;
```

CDBM

```
PAPER --- paper-no ---> PAPER-NO (1:1)
```

Of course, it is also possible to represent in CDBM the entity type PAPER by the
entity type PAPER-NO. If entity types are represented by their identifier functions, then there will be no need for these (1:1) associations in CBBM.  As seen
in chapter 3, generalization hierarchies can be defined for entity types.  Attribute functions and also indentifiers are inherited from a higher level in the
generalization hierarchy. There is an example of such a hierarchy in the IFIP
WG8.1 case, namely the hierarchy for the entity type PERSON (see Appendix 1.2).

Such a hierarchy can be represented in CDBM in several ways. One possibility is
to define a new entity type CATEGORY, which is associated with the entity PERSON.
The entity CATEGORY would tell us which categories a particular person belongs to.
In case a subtype has local attributes, the subtype must be represented explicitly by an entity.

So far, we have discussed how the different concepts in CIM can be represented in
CDBM. We must, however, also deal with how information will be maintained in the
conceptual data base, i.e. we must develop a conceptual processing model. CPM will
be described using the following construct:

    When EVENT then
        OPERATION ('ASSOCIATION', NODE1, NODE2)

where NODE1 defines the node in CDBM from which the association ASSOCIATION originates, while NODE2 defines the node in CDBM to which ASSOCIATION is directed.
EVENT means that OPERATION on the defined e-record is performed at the occurrence
time of the event EVENT.

When dealing with the processing policy for each function, we assume that we already have decided when the function values will be updated. In the IFIP WG 8.1
case, an instant updating for each function is assumed, which means that the function is updated as soon a transaction affecting it arrives.

The following example shows how an instant updating processing policy is implemented in a CPM for the attribute function mailing address:

CIM

```
entity  PERSON;
  .
  .
  .
attribute functions:
tf mailing-address (D): MAIL-ADDRESS;
derivation rule: (∀x∀d∃y(PERSON(x,d) ∧ D(d) ∧ ADDR-STATUS-MSG(y)
& person(y) = x ∧ day(y) ≤ d ∧ (∄z) (ADDR-STATUS-MSG(z) ∧
person(z) = x ∧ day(z) > day(y) ---> mailing-address(x,d) =
mailing-address(y)));
  .
  .
  .
end;
```

The affecting event (transaction at the CIPS level) for the mailing-address is the ADDR-STATUS-MSG. An instant updating of mailing-address will be described in CPM as follows:

CPM

```
When ADDR-STATUS-MSG then
begin
        UPDATE ('ADDRESS', PERSON, MAIL-ADDRESS)
end;
```

There is, however, additional processes to be described in CPM, namely the processes describing how CIM-entities are introduced and possibly deleted. The information in CIM which defines this behaviour is the entity existence specification.

At some level of a generalization hierarchy, there must be an existence specification given, which describes by which event occurrences the entity type will begin its existence period and also possibly by which event occurrences it will end its existence period.

For example, for the entity type PAPER, there is the following existence specification in CIM:

```
entity PAPER;
existence  (∀x∀d∃y(PAPER-ARRIVAL(y) ∧ paper(y) = x ∧ day(y) ≤ d ∧
(∄z)(PAPER-WITHDRAWAL(z) ∧ paper(z) = x ∧ day(z) > day(y) -->
PAPER(x,d))));
  .
  .
  .
end;
```

The start and end points of the existence can now be described as follows in CPM:

```
When PAPER-ARRIVAL then
begin
        STORE (' ', , PAPER)
        STORE ('PAPER-NO', PAPER, PAPER-NO)
end;

When PAPER-WITHDRAWAL then
begin
        DELETE (*, PAPER,*)
        DELETE (*,*, PAPER)
end;
```

In the above description, the "empty" association and "empty" node mean that the entity type PAPER is operated alone. The construct (*,PAPER,*) implies deletion of all information associated with PAPER.

The above example concerns only the introduction of the entity type PAPER.

For an entity type, which has one or more subtypes defined, the existence specification describes which subtypes the entity type can consist of. The existence period for such an entity type can be assumed to start when an entity of a subtype is introduced in the model. For example, the entity type PERSON has the following existence specification in CIM:

CIM

```
entity  PERSON;
existence  (∀x∀d (PERSON-TO-INVITE(x,d) V REFEREE(x,d)
V  PERSON-TO-CALL(x,d) V OC-MEMBER(x,d) V PC-MEMBER(x,d)
---> PERSON(x,d))) ;
  :
  :
end;
```

This means that whenever some of the subtypes are introduced, then an entity of type PERSON is also introduced (if not already there). We must now study how the subtype entity types are specified for their existence.There is the following existence specification defined for PERSON-TO-INVITE in CIM:

CIM

```
entity PERSON-TO-INVITE;
existence  (∀x∀d(AUTHOR(x,d) V NATREP(x,d) V REL-WG-MEMBER(x,d)
V CHAIRMAN(x,d) V CO-CHAIRMAN(x,d)
---> PERSON-TO-INVITE(x,d)));
  :
  :
end;
```

The above existence specification tells us that a "person-to-invite" can be an "author", a "national representative", a "relevant-wg-member", a "chairman" or a "co-chairman". Now, the existence specifications for the entity types AUTHOR, NAT-REP, REL-WG-MEMBER, CHAIRMAN and CO-CHAIRMAN must be analyzed.

The existence specification for the entity type AUTHOR tells us that an entity type AUTHOR is assumed to be introduced by the event type LETTER-OF-INTENT, PAPER-ARRI-VAL and CO-AUTHORSHIP-MSG. Further, an AUTHOR can also be an INVITED-SPEAKER. The existence specification for the entity type INVITED-SPEAKER tells us that an INVI-TED-SPEAKER is introduced by the event type INVITED-SPEAKER-INTRODUCTION and the entity type ends its existence by the event type INVITED-SPEAKER-DELETE. When an event of type INVITED-SPEAKER-DELETE occurs, the entity type PERSON in the role of invited-speaker is assumed to be deleted. The person can still exist in the model in other roles.

The analysis of the generalization hierarchy for the entity type PERSON must proceed   until all of its subtype entity types are analyzed to their existence. Then, we have the following information about the existence of the entity type PERSON:

An entity of type PERSON is assumed to be introduced, if not already there, when an event of the following event types occurs:

```
    LETTER-OF-INTENT
    PAPER-ARRIVAL
    CO-AUTHORSHIP-MSG
    INVITED-SPEAKER-INTRODUCTION
    REFEREE-SELECTION
    PERSON-TO-CALL-INTRODUCTION
    OC-MEMBER-SELECTION
    PC-MEMBER-SELECTION
    WG-MEMBER-INTRODUCTION
    CHAIRMAN-INTRODUCTION
    CO-CHAIRMAN-INTRODUCTION
    NAT-REP-INTRODUCTION
```

We have also the following information about the existence of the entity type
PERSON-TO-INVITE:

> An entity of type PERSON-TO-INVITE is assumed to be introduced (if
> not already there), when an event of the following event types occurs:

```
    LETTER-OF-INTENT
    PAPER-ARRIVAL
    CO-AUTHORSHIP-MSG
    INVITED-SPEAKER-INTRODUCTION
    NAT-REP-INTRODUCTION
    WG-MEMBER-INTRODUCTION
    CHAIRMAN-INTRODUCTION
    CO-CHAIRMAN-INTRODUCTION
```

The declaration of a relationship function with a Boolean range includes a definition which describes by which event occurences the function value will be true and
/or false. In CDBM, 'true' is represented by the existence of a 'relationship entity'. The introduction of a 'relationship entity' is described in CPM in the same
way as the introduction of entity types.

The totality/partiality (tf/pf) and into/onto mappings for attribute functions affect the design of CPM. When an entity is stored, all of its associations describing total functions must also be stored. When an entity is deleted, all of its
associations must be deleted and for the associations describing functions with
onto mapping, also the associated entities must be deleted.

Above, we have described the decisions which are involved in the design of a conceptual information processing system. The design decisions done at the CIPS level
have impact on the performance of the future system, because a CIPS specification
is the starting point of the next step, the logical design. How great the impact
will be, varies from application to application. In the IFIP WG8.1 case, the design decisions were rather simple. However, for an application which involves several derivation rules for a function and/or  a complex inference structure, the
impact of the decisions made at the CIPS level can be rather high.

In order to make the above design decisions in a more optimal way, a formal procedure supported by a computer aid is desirable. Work towards such a tool is being
carried out.

## 4.3  The DBMS adaptation

The next task in the design work is to adapt the CIPS to the particular DBMS which is going to be used. The adaptation, i.e. the development of a logical data structure, is to be done with respect to the goals formulated for the total system, such as for instance, performance goals (minimal response times) or the desire for "user-friendly record structures", flexibility etc.

The number of logical data structures which can be created starting from a CDBM/CPM model, can be very high depending on the size of the application. Also different DBMS, having different properties, may result in many different implementation alternatives for an association. In order to find a structure which is optimal with respect to the goals, a lot of design and evaluation work is required. This work is too time-consuming if done manually. As already mentioned in chapter 4.1, there exist several approaches to logical data base design [1,7,8,14]. These approaches present computer aided tools.  The input requirement for all these tools is a binary data model structure and a description of processes which operate on that structure. The output consists of one or several DBTG-structures, which are in some sense 'optimal'.

The CIPS described in terms of a CS4-data structure and associated operations is, by simple modifications, compatible with the tools mentioned above. This is the main reason why a binary approach - according to CS4 - was chosen for description of the CIPS model.


## 5   CONCLUDING REMARKS

The CIAM system development approach partitions the information system specification work in two phases. In the first phase, which runs parallel with other organizational, problem and requirement analysis activities, 'equations' for the information system - represented by a declarative, conceptual information model CIM - are set up. In the second phase an information processing system model, which is procedural, is designed. This model conform to the 'equations' and to the requirements for information support as well as to efficiency, economy and other requirements.

In order to declaratively describe complex and dynamic relationships of an universe of discourse, adequate concepts and a powerful language is needed. In order to be able to develop automatic completeness and consistency checking algorithms, a good formalism is needed. In order not to be only a 'description technique' but also a 'method', the development approach must guide and force its users - they may be experts or non-experts - to detect problems, relationships, incomplete specifications and contradictions.

An example of such a completeness enforcing activity is the inference analysis which leads to the 'detection' and specification of a large set of 'events' (transactions) which affect the state of the extension of a conceptual information model. In other words - the approach should <u>force</u> its users to increase their understanding  of the 'statics' as well as 'dynamics' of the application and to arrive at valid agreements and assumptions about the universe of discourse. A method should also generate specifications which are 'design reviewable', i.e. it should be possible to explicitly see which design decisions have been made and why.

Our experience is that this approach meets the above goals. But there is a price for it. As we do not defe r decisions and specifications about complex application relationships to the 'programming phase', we include them <u>explicitly</u> in the conceptual information model. We feel that decisions and assumptions about application oriented matters should not be made by programmers and then 'hidden' in data structures and processing procedures. The consequence of this is, however, that the application oriented CIM becomes richer and more detailed. This requires increased work and "knowledge representation" activities in the early system development phases. Our opinion is, however, such a requirement is <u>logical</u> and - in the long run - <u>beneficial</u> to the users.

The notation and the description technique used in this report deserves a comment. In order to describe components, properties and relationships of a conceptual information model, we have to a large extent used a predicate calculus like language. This is, of course, necessary for being able to apply a computer aided tool for formal completeness and consistency checking (such a tool is currently being developed at SYSLAB).

It is, however, not at all necessary to force non-expert users to express their application knowledge and assumptions in such a formalism. The components of a CIM can just as well - though probably not unambigously - be described by using natural language. This can be done in the initial development phases by non-expert users; in this report we have included examples of 'informally formulated' conditions and constraints. The use of natural language does not change the basic assumptions, concepts and methodological steps of our approach. The natural language formulated model - or parts thereof - can thereafter be formally expressed by persons familiar with the formal notation. This will, of course, lead to detection of ambiguities, incomplete specifications and inconsistencies, which then have to be solved by negotiations with responsible persons which posess the required application knowledge.

We have not found it advantageous to use any <u>particular graphical</u> documentation and description technique  . A graphical technique normally depicts only <u>one</u> aspect of a complex model. It, further, makes the model less easy to <u>increment</u> and/ or to change. The process of developing a CIM is, actually, a complex decision and analysis activity. People working in this development process have 'information needs' much like people do have needs for information when making decisions in organizations. The 'information needs' here do, however, concern the model under development. Information about many different aspects of the model may be needed at different times. One single graphical or tabular representation would not suffice in this case. Different 'skeletons', 'projections' and 'pictures' of the model are needed depending on the design/analysis activity and problem at hand. While we are working towards such a CIM development environment, for this particular case, we have had great help by using a simple text editor (with pattern-searching capabilities) to incrementally develop and document the CIM. A full listing of the conceptual information model is presented in a supplement to this report. It has provided us with detailed information as well as sufficient overview of the model under development.

ACKNOWLEDGEMENT

The authors wish to thank their colleagues Stig Berild, Peder Brandt, Göran Goldkuhl, Ante Grubbström, Christer Hultén, Lars-Åke Johansson, Eva Lindencrona and Anita Sandin for many valuable comments and suggestions on the previous version of this report.

FOOTNOTES

1)
The concepts and constructs introduced are on a less primitive level than the formal language of logic and mathematics. Though it would be possible to describe an application discourse by the use of a primitive formalism based on logic and mathematics we introduce some slightly more complex constructs. These will have the 'normative' effect of guiding the user or designer in his work developing a conceptual model. It is also assumed that the 'higher-level' constructs will facilitate the use of the approach. A graphics formalism, covering the essential components of a conceptual model, could also be added to ease communication and discussions.

2)
The decision to represent a class of phenomena in the application discourse as an entity or a data type depends on the anticipated information requirements. Nothing prevents us to consider _everything_ as entities. If, however, the only anticipated role of a 'phenomena type' is to characterize other phenomena, then we would for convenience, model it as a data type.

3)
Our view of a conceptual information model and its extension is illustrated in the following figure

<table>
<tr><td colspan="3">(0) A description of permissible<br>     types of predicates</td></tr>
</table>

|                          | AXIOMS                                                      | THEOREMS                              |
|--------------------------|------------------------------------------------------------|---------------------------------------|
| General rules and constraints | (1) Basic assumptions about the discourse (closed Wff:s) | (2) Derivable assumptions (Wff:s)     |
| Concrete facts           | (3) Basic, initial facts about the discourse               | (4) Derivable facts                   |

The conceptual information model consists then of parts (0) and (1). The _extension_ of a conceptual information model is constituted by (3) and (4), where (3) is the set of initial information (analogous to transactions in a data processing system). Even if not explicitly stated, (1) should include relevant axioms of mathematics and logic and other general laws pertinent to the application universe of discourse [9].

4)
_tf_ or _pf_ immediately preceding an attribute function specifies that the function is total or partial, respectively. Totality means that all entities, which are members of the population underlying the type at any specific time point or interval (as specified for the type) are functionally associated with "entities" of the range type. When partial, there may be entities without such associations.

The into/onto characteristic is relevant only if the range is an entity or an event type (marked by _into_ or _onto_ immediately following the range type). _into_ means a mapping where not necessarily all members of the range type partakes, when _onto_ they all do.

5)
The language used in the following for the formulation of existence, generalization, derivation and occurrence rules is 1st order predicate calculus like. Some
additional research work is needed to arrive at a complete and detailed definition
of its alphabet and grammar.

Occasionally, for reason of simplification, the rules are formulated informally in
natural language. For further comments about the notation used, see chapter 5.

6)
In Appendix 1.3 the relationship functions of the "IFIP case" arrived at are
listed. One might argue that predicate type relationship functions could instead
be modeled as "relationship entities". Existence would then, however, be dependent
on the existence of other entities as seen from the definition of the example
immediately following.

7)
The generalization hierarchy of Appendix 1.2 is a tree, i.e. it has one root and no
shared nodes. There is, however, no general restriction in CIAM that a generalization hierarchy must be a tree.

The nodes of the hierarchy are types. The directed arcs have the semantics of
'is-a'. Thus, REFEREE 'is-a' PERSON, CHAIRMAN 'is-a' PERSON-TO-INVITE etc. Any
sub-type inherits all functions (attribute and relationship), identifiers and generalization rules from its super-type(s). Existence is not inherited. Further research is needed, however, for the detailed elaboration of inheritance rules.

Any entity can be an instance of several types e.g. the entity  x  may be one of
PERSON-TO-CALL and one of REFEREE and one of CHAIRMAN etc. Taking the dual look at
types as the sets of instance of the type (populations, which vary with time), the
types can be overlapping and any restrictions to this must be explicately stated
as global constraints (see section 3.2.4).

When there is a need to consider types as instances, higher-order-types can be introduced e.g. the number of attendees at time  t  can be represented as a time dependent attribute of the "high-order" type CONFERENCE (with the cardinality of 1):

        no-of-attendees: CONFERENCE, T → NUMBER

REFERENCES

[1]   Berelian, E., A Methodology for Data Base Design in a Paging Environment,
      The University of Michigan, Systems Engineering Laboratory, Ann Arbor,
      USA, 1977.

[2]   Berild, S. and Nachmens, S., CS4 - A Tool for Data Base Design by Infologic
      Simulation, Proc 3rd Int Conf on VLDB, Tokyo, 1977.

[3]   Bubenko jr, J.A., The Temporal Dimension in Information Modeling, IBM T.J.
      Watson Research Center, Yorktown Heights, N.Y. 10598, RC 6187, Aug 1976.

[4]   Bubenko jr, J.A., Inferential Abstract Modeling, IBM T.J Watson Research
      Center, Yorktown Heights, N.Y. 10598, RC 6343, Jan 1977.

[5]   Bubenko jr, J.A., Information Modeling in the Context of System Development,
      IFIP Congress 80, Tokyo and Melbourne, 1980.

[6]   Bubenko jr, J.A., On Concepts and Strategies for Requirements and Information
      Analysis, SYSLAB Report No 4, Dept of Computer Sciences, Chalmers University
      of Technology, Göteborg, Sweden, 1981.

[7]   Dahl, R., Interactive Data Base Designer, The Dept of Computer Sciences,
      Chalmers University of Technology, Göteborg, 1981.

[8]   Irani, K.B., Purkayastha, S., Teorey, T.J., A Designer for DBMS-Prossessable
      Logical Database Structures, Proc 5th Int Conf on VLDB, Rio de Janeiro,
      Brazil, 1979.

[9]   ISO TC97/SC5/WG3-81, Concepts and Terminology for the Conceptual Schema.

[10]  Janning, M., Nachemans, S., Berild, S., CS4 - An Introduction to Associative
      Databases and to the CS4-System, Studentlitteratur, Lund, Sweden, 1979 (in
      Swedish).

[11]  Langefors, B., Theoretical Analysis of Information Systems, Studentlitteratur,
      Lund, Sweden, 1966.

[12]  Lundberg, B., IMT - An Information Modeling Tool, SYSLAB Report No 3, Dept of
      Computer Sciences, Chalmers University of Technology, Göteborg, Sweden, 1981.

[13]  Lundberg, B., On Consistency of Information Models, SYSLAB Report No 6, Dept
      of Computer Sciences, Chalmers University of Technology, Göteborg, Sweden,
      1981.

[14]  Mitoma, M.F., Optimal Data Base Schema Design, University of Michigan, Ph.D
      Thesis, 1975.

[15]  Young, J.W. and Kent, H.K., Abstract Formulation of Data Processing Problems,
      Journal of Industrial Engineering, Nov-Dec, 1958, pp 471-479.

APPENDIX 1

CIM - THE CONCEPTUAL INFORMATION MODEL

This appendix documents the conceptual information model (CIM) of our solution of
the IFIP WG8.1 case. Because of the limited space we have chosen to show only very
compact listings of the major components under the following seven subheadings:

1.   Entity types

2.   Generalization hierarchy

3.   Relationship functions

4.   Event types

5.   Data types

6.   Example of an inference graph

7.   Global constraints

A full, detailed decription of entity types ( incl.derivation rules for attribute
functions, generalization and existence rules), event types (incl. occurence rules,
attribute functions), relationship functions (incl. derivation rules) and data types is presented in a supplement to this report. Interested readers can obtain this
supplement by writing to the authors.

APPENDIX 1.1

<u>Entity types</u>

Under each type its attribute functions are listed. Observe that types do inherit
attribute functions from associated supertypes.

ACC-AUTHOR

ATTENDEE

AUTHOR

CHAIRMAN

CO-CHAIRMAN

CONFERENCE
```
      tf confname: CONFNAME;
      tf confperiod: CONFPERIOD;
      tf no-of-invitations (T): NUMBER;
      tf no-of-attendees (T): NUMBER
```

INTENDED-PAPER
```
      tf principal-author: AUTHOR into;
      tf patitle: PATITLE;
      tf confirm-intent (D): CONFIRM-INTENT;
```

INVITED-SPEAKER
```
      pf main-intr-area: MAIN-INTR-AREA;
```

NAT-REP
```
      tf country-rep: COUNTRY;
```

OC-MEMBER

PAPER

```
        tf paper-no: PAPER-NO;
        tf principal-author: AUTHOR into;
        tf patitle (D): PATITLE;
        pf confirm-sub (D): CONFIRM-SUB;
        pf session (T): SESSION into;
        pf acc-code (T): ACC-CODE;
        pf invited (T): INVITED;
```

PC-MEMBER

PERSON

```
        tf petitle (D): PETITLE;
        tf pname: PNAME;
        tf mailing-address (D): MAIL-ADDRESS;
        tf affiliation (D): AFFILIATION;
```

PERSON-TO-CALL

PERSON-TO-INVITE

```
        pf inv-status (D): INV-STATUS;
```

REFEREE

```
        pf no-of-papers (D): NUMBER;
```

REJ-AUTHOR

RELEVANT-WG-MEMBER

SESSION

```
        tf session-name: SESS-NAME;
        pf chairman (T): CHAIRMAN onto;
        pf co-chairman (T): CO-CHAIRMAN onto;
        pf session-time (T): SESS-TIME;
```

SUBJECT-AREA

```
        tf subject-area-name: SUBJECT-AREA-NAME;
        tf area-description: SUBJECT-AREA-DESCRIPTION;
```

APPENDIX 1.2

Generalization hierarchy

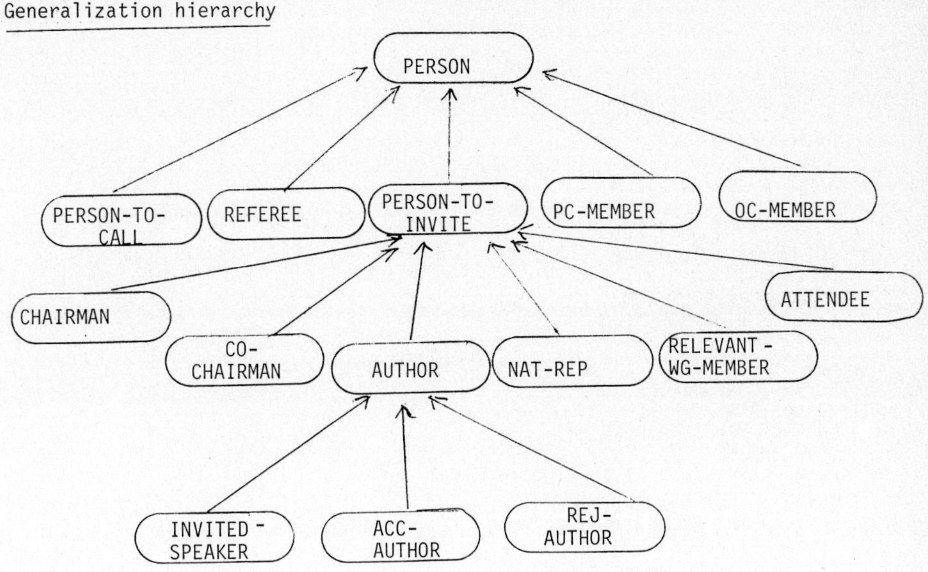


APPENDIX 1.3

Relationship functions

| Name: | Domains: | Range: |
|---|---|---|
| author-defined-subject-areas | PAPER,SUBJECT-AREA,D | Boolean |
| co-authorship | PAPER,AUTHOR,D | Boolean |
| final-paper-subject-areas | PAPER,SUBJECT-AREA,D | Boolean |
| inv-cat-of-person-to-invite | PERSON-TO-INVITE,INVITATION-CATEGORY,D | Boolean |
| paper-referee | PAPER,REFEREE,D | Boolean |
| pc-member-referee | PC-MEMBER,REFEREE,D | Boolean |
| referee-defined-subject-areas | REFEREE,PAPER,SUBJECT-AREA,D | Boolean |
| referee-paper-return | REFEREE,PAPER,D | Boolean |
| referee-preferred-subject-areas | REFEREE,SUBJECT-AREA,D | Boolean |
| session-subject-areas | SESSION,SUBJECT-AREA,T | Boolean |

APPENDIX 1.4

<u>Event types</u>

<u>External event types</u>

```
        ACCEPTANCE-DECISION
        ACCEPTANCE-OF-INVITATION
        ADDR-STATUS-MSG
        AFFILIATION-MSG
        ARRIVAL-CONFIRMATION
            occurence condition {at most  x  days after the occurence
            of PAPER-ARRIVAL}
        AUTHORS-SUBJECT-AREA-DEFINITION {simultaneous with PAPER-ARRIVAL}
        CALL-DECISION
        CHAIRMAN-ALLOCATION
        CHAIRMAN-INTRODUCTION
        CHAIRMAN-DELETE
        CO-AUTHORSHIP-MSG {simultaneous with PAPER ARRIVAL}
        CO-CHAIRMAN-ALLOCATION
        CO-CHAIRMAN-DELETE
        CO-CHAIRMAN-INTRODUCTION
        CONF-INIT
        FINAL-PAPER-SUBJECT-AREA-DEFINITION
        INTENT-CONFIRMATION
            occurence condition {at most  x  days after the occurence
            of LETTER-OF-INTENT}
        INVITATION-DECISION
        INVITED-SPEAKER-INTRODUCTION
        INVITED-SPEAKER-DELETE
        LETTER-OF-INTENT
        NAT-REP-INTRODUCTION
        OC-MEMBER-SELECTION
        PAPER-ARRIVAL
        PAPER-REFEREE-REVIEW
        PAPER-TO-REFEREE-ALLOCATION
        PAPER-TO-REFEREE-WITHDRAWAL
        PAPER-TO-SESSION-ALLOCATION
        PAPER-WITHDRAWAL
        PATITLE-MSG
        PC-MEMBER-SELECTION
        PERSON-TO-CALL-INTRODUCTION
        PETITLE-MSG
        REFEREE-SELECTION
        REFEREE-SUBJECT-AREA-DEFINITION {simultaneous with PAPER-REFEREE-REVIEW}
        REFEREE-SUBJECT-AREA-PREFERENCES {simultaneous with REFEREE-SECELTION}
        REFEREE-TO-PC-MEMBER-ALLOCATION
        SESSION-INTRODUCTION
        SESSION-DELETE
        SESSION-SUBJECT-AREA-MSG
        SESSION-TIME-MSG
        SUBJECT-AREA-DEFINITION
        SUBMISSION-CONFIRMATION
        WG-MEMBER-INTRODUCTION
```

<u>Internal event types</u>

```
        PERSON-INVITATION
            occurence condition {this set of events, one for each invitee, is
            triggered by the INVITATION-DECISION event to start inviting at the
```

        day specified as inv-start-day in that event}
    PERSON-CALLING
        occurence condition {this set of events, one for each PERSON-TO-CALL,
        is triggered by the CALL-DECISION event to start calling at the day
        specified as call-start-day in that event}


APPENDIX 1.5

<u>Data types</u>


        ACC-CODE
        AFFILIATION
        CONFIRM-INTENT
        CONFNAME
        CONFPERIOD
        CONFIRM-SUB
        COUNTRY
        COV-OF-PAPER
        INVITATION-CATEGORY
        INVITED
        INV-STATUS
        MAIL-ADDRESS
        MAIN-INTR-AREA
        NUMBER
        NUM-SC-ORI
        NUM-SC-PRE
        NUM-SC-SIG
        OVER-IMPR
        PAPER-NO
        PATITLE
        PETITLE
        PNAME
        RATE-REF-FAM
        SESS-NAME
        SESS-TIME
        SUBJECT-AREA-DESCRIPTION
        SUBJECT-AREA-NAME
        TIME-PERIOD
        TOT-REC-SC
        TYPE-OF-PAPER
        WEI-SC-ORI
        WEI-SC-PRE
        WEI-SC-SIG

## APPENDIX 1.6

### Inference graph

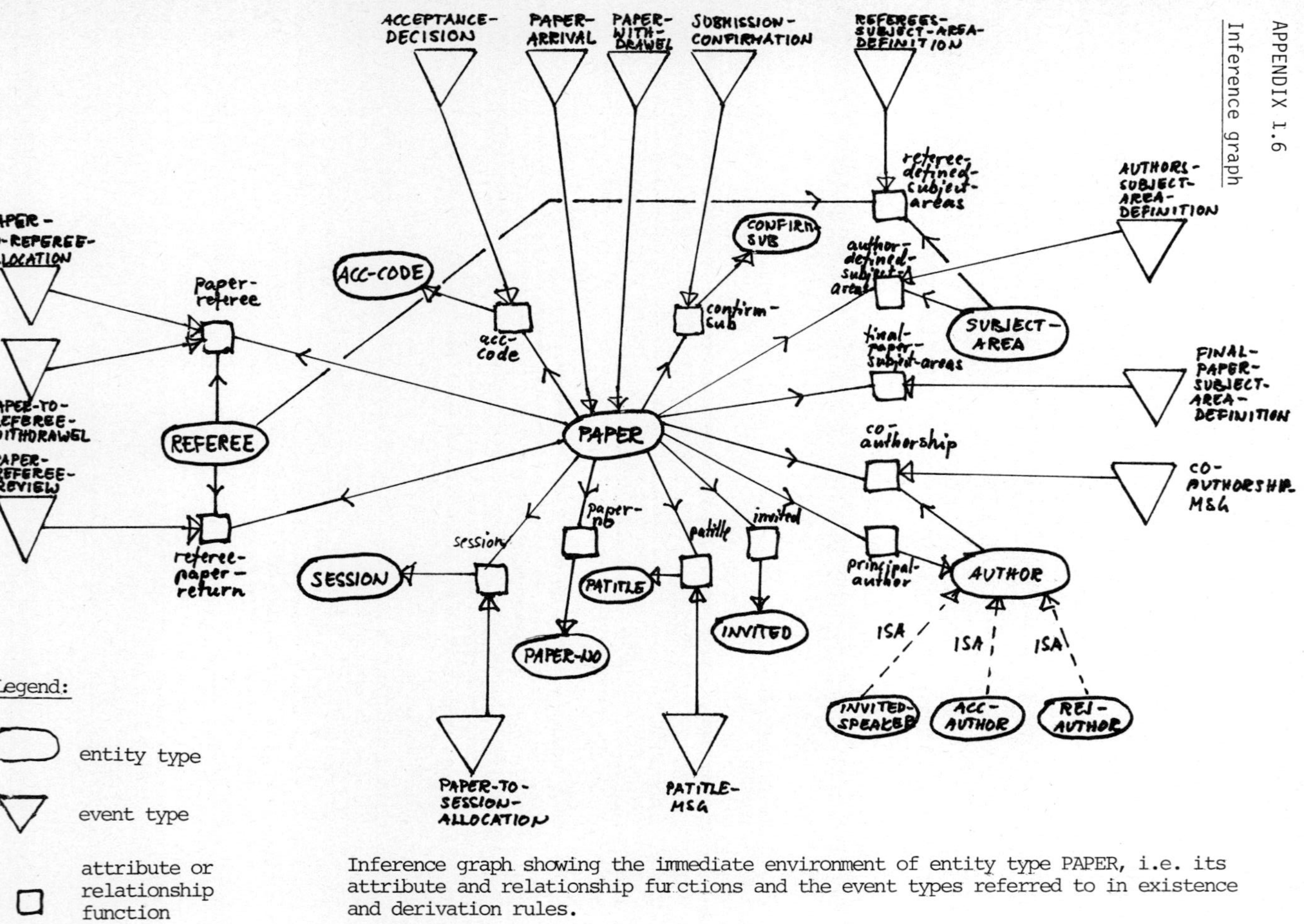


Inference graph showing the immediate environment of entity type PAPER, i.e. its attribute and relationship functions and the event types referred to in existence and derivation rules.

*INFORMATION SYSTEMS DESIGN METHODOLOGIES: A Comparative Review*
*T.W. Olle, H.G. Sol, A.A. Verrijn-Stuart (editors)*
*North-Holland Publishing Company*
© *IFIP, 1982*

SDLA

SYSTEM DESCRIPTOR AND LOGICAL ANALYZER

E. Knuth, F. Halász, P. Radó

Computer & Automation Institute
Hungarian Academy of Sciences
H-1502, P.O.B. 63, Budapest
HUNGARY

SDLA is tool for recording system descriptions in machine-processable
form, storing them in a database, carrying out various analysis functions, and producing structured documents. The descriptive language
of SDLA is *not fixed* in advance, it is *formed by the user* himself
in order to match properly his conceptual world with permissible
language terms.

## 1. GENERAL BACKROUND

The major problem of information systems design methodologies is finding those
adequate computerized tools which can support or replace the enormous clerical
and organization work induced by the growing complexity of today's computer based
systems to be implemented. Such a tool usually consists of a "project-database",
an "input-processor" which can interpret a certain descriptive language transforming it to computerized data, and a "query processor". The latter may itself
be pretty complex containing selection algorithms, facilities for logical analysis, mechanisms for formatted report generation, etc. Descriptions which are incrementally entering into the database can be checked with respect to various
completness and consistence criteria. These criteria are usually also fixed in
advance in accordance with the descriptive language selected. (The most succesful
system of this kind has been the PSL/PSA [1] developed by the ISDOS project at
the University of Michigan.)

When applying a particular computer aided methodology with a given descriptive
language it frequently turns out, however, that it is hard to match the predefined concepts of the language with those derivable from the problem we are faced.
That is, the diversity of various application fields can not be easily captured
by fixed languages constructed in advance. On the other hand, it turned out that
any of the software tools supporting particular descriptive languages has essentially the *same structure*. It has been recognized, therefore, that it is possible
to construct a set of computer aided tools *independently* of the application language and then these can be supplemented with those mechanisms facilitating
language definitions.

In this way, so-called *meta systems* can be built providing the same capabilities
as those of "convential" computer aided methodologies, but these are free of
language restrictions for it is the user himself who designates his own conceptual
world and language terms.

The approach of SDLA [2] is one of the possible ways to reach the goals outlined
above. (Another possible way is the one suggested by the System Encyclopedia
Management System (SEMS) [3] of the ISDOS project. SEMS is based essentially on

Chen's Entity-Relationship-Attribute model [4] while SDLA concentrates slightly
more on semantic issues concerning its data model. The development of SDLA has
also been done in cooperation with the ISDOS project at the University of
Michigan.)

It should be noted that system SDLA is a set of fundamental tools for information
systems design, but not a technology itself. The capabilities of SDLA are comprised in *part 2.* in this paper. SDLA can serve, however, as a computerized basis
for various technologies. *Part 3.* outlines one of the possible application methodologies which can be suggested for a wide range of practical problems. Finally,
*part 4.* demonstrates it by the *Conference Organization Example* using the
features of SDLA.


## 2. FEATURES OF SDLA

### 2.1 *SYSTEM ARCHITECTURE*

Figure 1. shown below recalls the simplified structure of conventional computer
based supporting methodologies built for predefined descriptive languages.

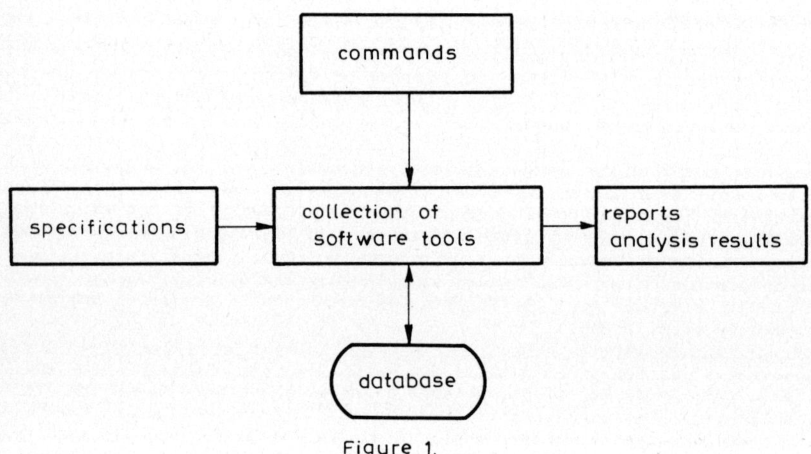


Figure 1.


The functional scheme of SDLA is slightly more compound as a consequence of the
language independency, see figure 2. As it can be seen the software system is
divided into two major parts namely the *language independent part* and the
*language definition facility.* From the viewpoint of realization the fundamental
part is the former. This is built upon an appropriately chosen general scheme
onto which each potential descriptive language can be mapped later. The *language
definition facility* or *meta interpreter* is somewhat simpler, its major function
is the generation of those tables which will control the operation of the language independent part. Besides, it have some additional functions too as the
automatic generation of language manuals, reference cards, etc.

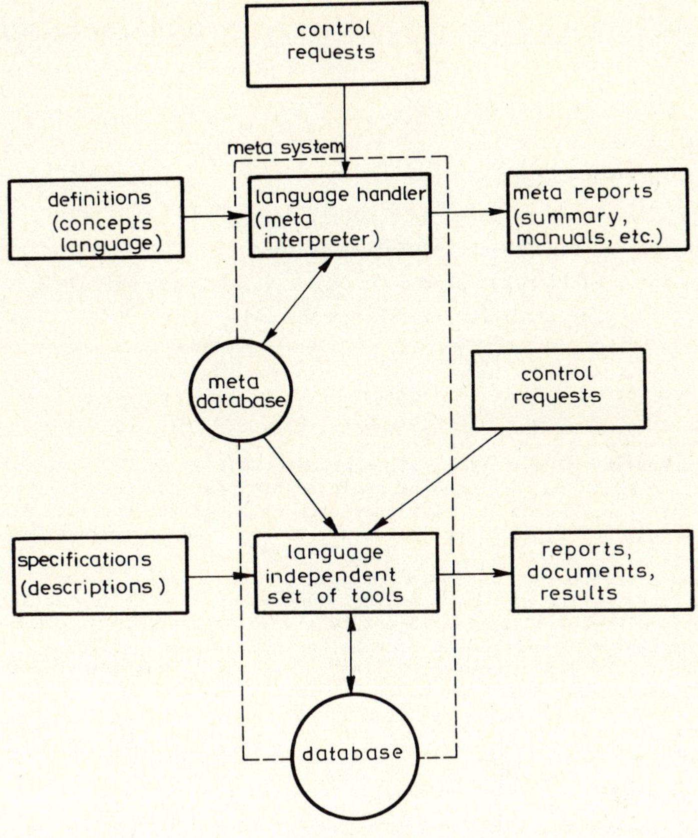


Figure 2.

## 2.2 *INTERNAL DATA MODEL*

When it was found that a computer aid for system analysis may be developed without resorting to a particular methodology, it was also recognized that the computer aid should be developed based on a particular data model which would affect the way an area of real world problems is conceptualized (see also [5]).

The data model of SDLA is derived from SIMULA 67 [6] with slight extensions (and further additions for language definition purposes). The model is a simple uniform one having just one kind of data type termed "concept" (which may represent "entities", "relationships", or even "attributes" in Chen's [4] sense as well).

Our fundamental scheme is the following. In the data base we store *objects*, each of which is an *instance of an abstract concept*. Objects are described by attrributes. An abstract concept is characterized by its *associated set of attributes*, to which the attributes of its instances correspond in their number and types. (The actual set of objects as instances to a given concept can always be considered as a *relation* i.e. the subset of the Carthesian product of the attribute value ranges. This viewpoint is useful, as it is known, for formalizing operations in a data base.)

Instead of going into syntactic details we illustrate the definition formalism of concepts by example 1.


    concept modul;

    concept data(part-of:data);

    concept condition(associated-data:data);

    concept precondition(to-activate:modul,when:condition);

    concept postcondition(termination-of:modul,resulting:condition);

    concept invariant(condition,associated:modul);


Example 1.


For each concept (type) any number of  *subtypes* can also be defined. Subtypes inherit all the attributes possessed by their supertypes, however, they may have extra attributes too, which are characteristic only for the special. Example 2. shows a collection of typical applications for this kind of type refinements.

The primary aim of the type refinement mechanism is capturing semantic aspects by a generalized version of *type checking*. Namely, during the instatiation at the descriptive level any special object is always accepted in a role of a more general. (For instance, any object of type "printfile" can participate a relationship declared for "files", however, "files", in general, may not attend any relationship declared explicitely for only "printfiles".)


    concept process;

    concept manual-process is  process;

    concept computerized-processes is  process;


    concept file (opening:procedure,blocked:boolean);

    concept printfile is  file(pagesize:integer,line-length: integer);


    concept input (process, data);

    concept usage is input;

    concept control is input;


Example 2.


We remark that each concept definition in SDLA can be supplemented with so-called "semantic constraints" and "integrity constraints" too. The former serves for automatic generation of statements derivable from the input descriptions, the latter ensures ways to declare compound checking considerations (being invariant throughout the whole life cycle). (These will not be detailed here, the reader can find it in [7].)


## 2.3  LANGUAGE DEFINITION

Sentence form declarations constitute the second major function of the definition processor (meta interpreter). For each concept any number of "forms" can be attached which will tell us how the concept can be stated (and then instantial-ized) from contexts throughout the information system description. We illustrate this facility by Example 3. only. For exact details we refer to the document [7].


> **concept** data-derivation(process,used:data,derived:data);
>
>    **form** used:  **used-by** process **to-derive** derived;
>
>    **form** derived:  **derived-by** process  using  used;
>
>    **form** process:  **uses** used  **to-derive** derived;

Example 3.


Declarations contained in Example 3. tell us that whenever being in a process context (process-section or process-subsection) during the description phase we may write the third sentence form, or when in a data context (data-section, data--subsection) we may use the first and second forms as well.

In this sense equivalent statements can be said in various forms as it is shown in Example 4.


> **process**  P;
>
>    **uses**  D   **to-derive**  E;
>
> **data**  D;
>
>    **used-by**  P   **to-derive**  E;
>
> **data**  E;
>
>    **derived-by**  P   using  D;

Example 4.


Whatever context form appears in the input text, the conceptual data representa-tion is the same, and a so called "totalreport" would return it in all possible contexts (regardless of the origin).

## 2.4  DESCRIPTIVE PHASE

as a whole is a serie of sentences entered incrementally and given by sentences
stated in those forms declared at the meta level. They constitute sections and
subsections of an arbitrary level of nesting. Example 5. shows a typical piece of
a description of such fashion.


        modul M;
             belongs to subsystem S;
             uses data D1,D2;
                to derive entity  E;
                    under condition  C;
             uses data D3;
                via interface  F;
             utilizes system   WP;
       data  D4;
         created by M1;
         accessible for  M2, M3   read only;
         etc.


Example 5.


Sentences in such a description are in juxtapositioned or in subordinated relationships with each other shown by the positioning of lines. The positioning itself
is made automatically by the input processor (controlled by a so called context-
-stack see [7]) which ensures a very important correctness checking facility (the
so called "context-checking") for the input descriptions.

A description like above is acceptable if all its subordination contexts correspond exactly to those declared at the (meta) form definitions, and the object
names appearing in the description coincide in their type (in the generalized
sense concerning subtypes) to the type specifications of attribute definitions.
(For more details we refer to [7].)



## 2.5. FORMATTED REPORT SYSTEM

is one of the important query facilities in SDLA. (We remark that as a consequence of the relational nature of the logical storage scheme a kind of relational
query is also available. This, however, will not be detailed here. We refer to
[7] concerning its heuristic description and to [8] concerning its exact theoretical basis.)

The formatted report system communicates in the *user defined* descriptive language.
Therefore, the user has to know only one language (the very one defined himself).
Example 6. shows such a report specification. This specification is acceptable if
all

```
            REPORT

          modul M;

              submodul any;

                    dependent submodules any;

                    related data any access any;

          ENDREPORT
```

Example 6.


the sentence forms contained in it are declared at the meta level and their subordination contexts are proper. The symbol "any" (used in places of object names)
serves as the so called "free variables". These are to be filled according to the
current contents of the database. (There are further possibilities too, such as
"named free variables", "set names" referring to previous selections, etc. For
exact details we refer to [9].


```
          DOCUMENT

          module M;

              submodule M1;

                  dependent submodules  A,B,X;
                  related data D1  acess  immediate;
                               D2  acess  via interface F;

              submodule M;

                  related data D3 acess read only;

          END
```


Example 7.


Example 7. shows a possible output concerning the report specification expressed
in Example 6. It demonstrates that the structure of the generated document corresponds exactly to the one given by the report specification, while free variables are replaced by actual names from the database.

The report generation facility (illustrated by this oversimplified example) is
very important in the sense that

      a) its results can be *accepted* as input descriptions too;
      b) it is logically *complete*.

At the same time, the formatted report generation facility (together with the selection facilities not dealt with here) serves as a basis for further (more structured, more edited, etc.) reports, dumps, or graphic outputs generated by special routines.


# 3. DESIGN METHODOLOGY

The project database belonging to SDLA is intended to be used throughhout the designed system's whole life cycle and, therefore, it can be asked or updated at any time later on. A full technology including all project management aspects should refer to this whole cycle. In this paper we concentrate on its most crital phase, starting with the *interview process* and ending with a complete (logical) *system design* which is sufficient for an average ability implementor to realize the system designed.


## 3.1  ENVIRONMENT SPECIFICATION

Before starting the design process it is strongly advised to record a complete environment specification and enter it to the SDLA database. This description should include the following major parts:

A. *Activity descriptions*.  Their characteristic data should contain at least the following:

- who executes them;
- what sources are used;
- what do they produce;
- what kind of tools are utilized.

(Activities should be classified in the way shown in Figure 3.)

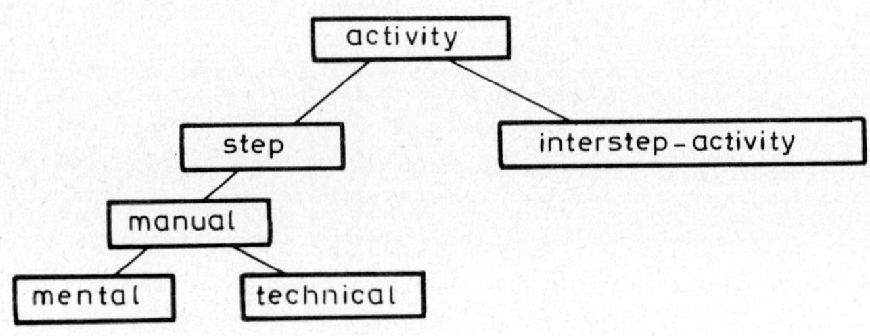


Figure 3.

The ordering among activities can be represented in several ways. In the simplest case serial numbers could be sufficient (as it is applied in our formalization of the Conference Organization Example in part 4. of this paper). In general, however, more complex models, Pert-graphs, Petri-nets, etc. can be used, see e.g. out proposals at [10].

B. *Corporation description*.  This should include the organizational structure of the bodies, staff, personnel incorporated with the information system to be designed. The desctiption should contain

- the activities they are involved;
- information they are using;
- documents they produce;
- their responsibility;
- their access limitations.

C. *Description of documents.* This part should concern to the content of those
manual documents (vouchers, acknowledgements, protocols, minutes) which serve
as a basis of the work of different bodies, and to those what they produce.
In addition to the structure of the document the following details should be
described.

- who produces it;
- who uses it;
- which activities concern to it;
- access restrictions;
- validity limitations.

D. *Description of data* to be computerized. This description should be made in the
same way as of the manual documents. Note that in *this phase we are not at all
interested in storage mechanisms,* and data representation ways but concentrate
only on functional structures!

E. *List of tools* which can be utilized by the participating personnel. This list
can contain both kinds of devices which are available at present and which are
to be implemented by the information system being under development. In general,
the description, however need not cover other aspects than the overall function
and structure.

*Note* that during the description process statements having the same logical content need not be said more than once. E.g. if we have specified that during a
certain activity a particular document is produced, then when that document is
specified it is unnecessary state its originating activity again. *It is the
function of the report system* to structure and reproduce all implicite specifications automatically.

*Note,* also, that the *process of description* need not follow the list given above
from A. to E. Information gained from the *successive interview process* can immediately be described formally and entered incrementally in *any order*. Again,
it is the function of SDLA to group them systematically.


*3.2 LOGICAL DESIGN*

Having the environment analysis finished, the so called logical design of the
information system to be developed can be started. We use a top-down approach
with successive refinements of the plan. At each step, during the design process,
the system can be decomposed further until a final level. This final level should
satisfy the following requirements:

i.  The description still *must not contain implementation details.*
    Therefore, it may well be implemented by conventional file-systems,
    or by any kind of database management systems equally.

    ii.    It is *complete* in the sense that using the information contained in it an average programmer can easily realize it (or, what is the same, an average designer can easily produce its implementation--level plan).

The logical-level system-specification should cover the following major parts:

A.  *Information structures to be stored.*  Recall that we do have already data descriptions listed during the environment analysis. Now our task is to form top-down hierarchic structures from them in accordance with the hierarchy of program modules handling them. Data structures at the description may include the following aspects:

- type definitions (set, list, element, etc.),
- inclusion relationships with other data,
- initialization, usage, update, and derivation
relationships

- activization and timing conditions,
- access limitations and security considerations,
- restorability constraints,
- integrity properties.

B.  *I/O specifications.*  These are the data structures consumed or produced by software components. Their description should also be made by hierachic refinement steps.

C.  *System functions.*  In this part software components (processes, proce- dures, routines, functional modules) are specified. The following data should at least be given:

- the function's input data,
- the functions's output data,
- other data utilized,
- description of the function.

The process of successively refining descriptions is done in the following way. We start with a level-0 description which is usually the same for all information systems, see Figure 4.

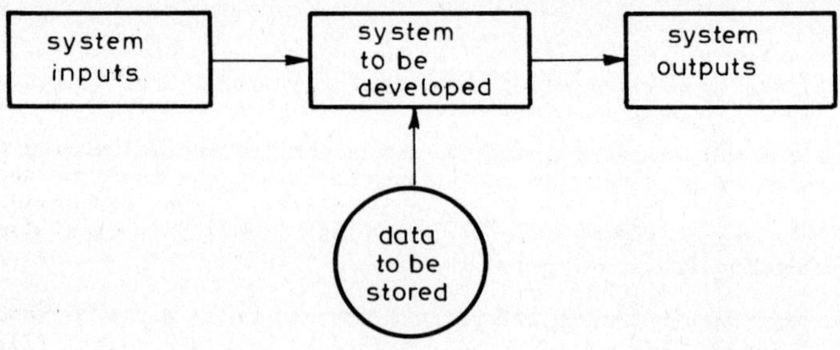


Figure 4.

Then all four components shown in Figure 4. are decomposed into a level-1 description containing newly specified relationships between the parts. Etc.

Note that interfaces receiving and generating I/O-s are embodied in the environment description. Remark, that final notes at point 3.1 apply here too.

### 3.3 IMPLEMENTATION DESIGN

We only mention here that an implementation level system design can also be produced using SDLA but we do not believe its necessity. The logical design should be fine enough to tell us all what is really fundamental and functional. Implementation documentations should preferably be made using standard utilities possessed by the implementation device applied. (Such documentation supports can be find in most of the up-to-date systems such as PROTE, METACOBOL, IDMS, ADABAS, etc.) Anyway, it is possible to make implementation level descriptions using appropriate concepts to represent storage mechanisms and program structures if needed. We do not go into such details here, the reader can find proposals in the work [10].

## 4. THE CONFERENCE ORGANIZATION EXERCISE

This part illustrates the applications of the principles given in part 3. using the tools summarized in part 2. For better readability we disregard of starting with a boring sequence of sentence form definitions, but give their main parts as an appendix.

To obtain a better quality we do not give computer printouts here. The description written below is fully computer processable supposing the necessary definitions contained by the appendix is entered previously.

### 4.1. ENVIRONMENT DESCRIPTION

A. THE ENVIRONMENTAL PROCESS

step 1 'p r o p o s a l' manual mental;

   made by WG;

   produces   conference-organization-proposal;


step 2 'r a t i f i c a t i o n' manual mental;

   made by TC;

       using   conference-organization-proposal;

   produces   founding-document;


step 3 'c o m m i t t e e s   f o r m a t i o n'   manual mental;

   parallel substep       'PC formation';

      made by PC-chairman;

          using   conference-organization-proposal,

                  founding-document;

      produces   PC-member-list;

                  PC-invitation-letter-form;

```
parallel substep 'OC formation';
   made by   OC-chairman;
       using  conference-organization-proposal,
              founding-document;
   produces  OC-member-list,
             OC-invitation-letter-form;
step 4 'd a t a b a s e   i n i t i a l i z a t i o n'  manual technical;
   device  conference-supporting-system;
   actions;
       enter  conference-head-information;
          into  conference-database;
          based on  founding document;
       enter  PC-members,
             OC-members;
          into  conference-database;
          based on  PC-member-list,
                 OC-member-list;
       enter  PC-invitation-letter-form,
             OC-invitation-letter-form;
          by word-processing;

step 5 'c o m m i t t e e s   i n v i t a t i o n'  manual technical;
   at request of   PC-chairman,
                OC-chairman;
   action;
       mail  PC-invitations,
            OC-invitations;
          by electronic-mail;
          using  PC-invitation-letter-form,
                OC-invitation-letter-form,
                PC-member-list,
                OC-member-list;
          utilizing   word-processing,
                   conference-supporing-system;
```

step 6 'f i r s t    P C    m e e t i n g'  manual mental;
    produces   call-for-address-list,
                announcement-text,
                deadlines,
                minutes-PC1;
    made by  PC;
        using  founding-document;


step 7 'm a i l    o f    a n n o u n c e m e n t s'  manual technical;
    actions;
        enter  deadline-data;
            into  conference-database;
            based on  minutes-PC1;
        enter  call-for-list;
            into  conference-database;
            based on  call-for-address-list;
        enter  announcement-text;
            by word - processing;
        mail  announcement-text;
            by  electronic-mail;
            using  call-for-list;
            utilizing  word-processing;
                    conference-supporting-system;


interstep activity from 9 'p r e r e g i s t r a t i o n'  manual technical;
    made by  conference-secretariat;
        using  conference-mail-received;
        utilizing  conference-supporting-system;
    actions;
        update  list-to-be-informed,
                list-to-participate,
                list-to-lecture,
                invitation-data;

interstep activity from 9 to 10 'p a p e r s    r e g i s t r a t i o n';
    made by  conference-secretariat;
        using  conference-mail-received;
        utilizing  conference-supporting-system;
    action;
        update  submission-head-information;

```
step 10 'd e s i g n a t i o n    o f    r e f e r e e s'  manual mental;
  made by PC-chairman;
      using  submission-head-information;
      utilizing conference-supporting-system
   timed at  submission-deadline;
   produces  referation-designations,
             referation-viewpoints;

step  11 'm a i l    t o    r e f e r e e s' manual technical;
    actions;
        enter referation-information;
           into conference-database;
           based on  referation-designations;
         enter  referation-viewpoints;
            by  word-processing;
         mail  paper-received,
              referation-viewpoints;
            by  electronic-mail;
           using conference-mail-received,
                reference-information:
           utilizing  word-processing,
                conference-supporting-system;

interstep activity from 11   to   12  'r e f e r e n c e   r e g i s t r a t i o n'
                                                       manual technical;
    made by conference-secretariat;
       using  conference-mail-received;
       utilizing conference-supporting-system;
     action;
        update  referation-information;

step  12  's e c o n d   P C   m e e t i n g' manual mental;
   produces acceptance-text,
             refusion-text,
             acceptance-list,
             session-designation,
             program-table,
             chairman-list,
             chairman-appointment-text;
```

```
    made by PC;
        using  referation-information,
               submission-head-information,
               list-to-lecture,
               invitation-data;
        utilizing    conference-supporting-system;


step 13 'a u t h o r    n o t i f i c a t i o n' manual technical
    actions;
        update referee-information;
            using acceptance-list;
            utilizing conference-supporting-system;
        enter acceptance-text,
              refusion-text;
            by word-processing;
        mail author-notification;
            by electronic-mail;
            using referee-information;
            utilising word-processing,
                      conference-supporting-system;


step 14 'c h a i r m a n   a p p o i n t m e n t'  manual technical;
    actions;
        enter chairman-appointment-text;
          by word-processing;
        enter  chairman-list;
        mail chairman-appointment-text;
          by electronic-mail;
          using  chairman-list;


step 15 's e c o n d   O C  m e e t i n g'  manual mental;
    produces list-of-accepted-participants,
             participants-reply-card-text;
             sorry-to-say-text;
    made by OC;
        using list-to-participate,
              invitation-data,
              call-for-list;
```

**step** 16 'second announcement' manual technical;
  **actions;**
      **enter** list-of-accepted-participants,
          program-table;
        **into** conference-database;
      **enter** participants-reply-card-text,
           sorry-to-say-text;
        **by** word-processing;
     **mail** program-table,
         participants-reply-card-text;
        **by** electronic-mail;
        **using** list-of-accepted-participants;
      **mail** program-table;
         **by** electronic-mail;
         **utilizing** ptc-selection-program;
            **comment** to those priority invited
            persons not intended to participate;


**interstep activity from** 16 **to** 17 'card registration'
                                **manual technical;**

  **made by** conference-secretariat;
    **using** conference-mail-received!
    **utilizing** conference-supporting-system!
  **action;**
    **update** participant-list;


**step** 17 'final documents' **manual technical;**
  **action;**
    **print** participant-list,
        program-table,
        general-information;
     **by** conference-supporting-system;

B. DOCUMENT STRUCTURES

**manual document**  conference-organization-proposal;
   **parts** topic,
        approximate-date,
        proposed-place,
        proposing-WG,
        PC-chairman-name,
        OC-chairman-name,
        reasoning;
   **optional parts** list-of-topic-subdirections,
           list-of-PC-members,

           list-of-OC-members;
           list-of-participating-WGs;

**manual document**  founding-document;
   **parts** conference-title,
        conference-date,
        conference-place,
        proposing-WG,
        PC-chairman-name,
        OC-chairman-name,
        discussion;

**manual document**  PC-invitation-letter-form;
   **parts** conference-topic,
        conference-data,
        conference-place,
        PC-chairman-name,
        OC-chairman-name,
        date-of-first-PC-meeting,
        place-of-first-PC-meeting,
        polite-embedding-text;

## C. DATA STRUCTURES

```
computerized data conference-database;

    part   conference-head-information;
      containing  qualification;
                data,
                place,
                WG no,
                TC no,
                PC-chairman-data,
                OC-chairman-data;


    part  PC-members,
        OC-members;
      consisting of records of type  personal-data;

    part deadline-data;
      containing date-of-submission,
              date-of-notification,
              final-copies-deadline,
              participation-deadline;

    part  call-for-list;
      consisting of records of type  institution-address,
                                 personal-data;

    part  invitation-data;
      consisting of records of type  inv-pers-data;
      subsetting criteria priority-invited,
                    participates,
                    lectures,
                    rejects,
                    deputy-delegates;


    part  list-to-be-informed,
        list-to-participate,
        list-to-lecture;


    part submission-head-information;
      consisting of records of type  submission-entry;
```

```
part referation-information;
   elements referee-data,
            paper-reference,
            return-date,
            qualification-data,
            textual-remarks,


part program-table;
   consisting of groups of type   session-data;
   consisting of  session-heading,
              records of type    lecture-data;
part list-of-accepted-participants,
    participant-list;
part repedly-card;
   element name,
           hoteling-data,
           arrival-data,
           other-requests;
```

## D. RECORD TYPES

```
record type  personal-data;
   used in  conference-database;
   elements distinction,
            name,
            status,
            affiliation,
            address,
            phone,
            telex;


record type  submission-entry;
   elements author-names,
            author-reference,
            title,
            institution,
            country,
            classification,
            qualification-data;
etc. ...
```

                                  *E. Knuth et al.*

E. PERSONNEL

communities involved   WG,

                       TC,

                       PC, PC-chairman,

                       OC, OC-chairman,

                       conference-secretariat;


F. COMPUTER AIDS

system   conference-supporting-system;

   connected systems   word-processing,

                       electronic-mail;

etc. ...


The whole specification given above can be entered into the SDLA database supposing that the corresponding concepts and sentence forms have adequately been given
at the meta level. These are listed in appendix A.

Having the specification entered the database various reports can be produced
using the selective report generator facilities. For instance the simple request

> REPORT 'COMMUNITIES ACTIVITIES';
>
> community  any;
>     makes step any;
> END

will result in a document consisting of  lists of steps grouped according to the
communities making them as it is shown below

> COMMUNTIES ACTIVITIES
>
> community WG;
>     makes step 1 'proposal';
>
> community PC;
>     makes step 6 'first PC meeting',
>         step 10 'designation of refers';
>
>             .
>             .
>
>     etc.

Or, as another example, the request

```
            REPORT  'DATA HANDLING';
         computerized data any;
              part any;

                   entered by any;
                   updated by any;
                   used in any;


         END
```

will list all computerized data together with their "entering", "updating", and
"usage" associations:

```
     DATA HANDLING

        computerized data conference-database;
            part conference-head-information;
                entered by initialization-procedure;
            part PC-members;
                entered by initialization-procedure;

               .
               .
               .

            part submission-information;

                entered by papers-reg-proc;

                updated by referation-proc;


               .
               .
               .

            etc.
```

Queries like above can reveal and make explicit several connections and relationships specified implicitely. Within the limits of the language defined the structure of the queries are free, therefore documents reflecting quite different
aspects than the original description entered can well be generated.

These reports serve as vehicles for *environment analysis* providing a firm basis
for the succeeding logical system design.


## 4.2. LOGICAL SYSTEM DESIGN

According to 3.2 this part of the description deals only with the software complex
to be implemented. Therefore, the specification and any document derivable from
it by SDLA queries are dedicated to the *implementors* (in contrast to the environment specification which is dedicated to the designers).

As it is mentioned, the design is made by stepwise refinement of the scheme shown
in figure 4. To decrease the extent we shall terminate only the main branches at
the description.

A. FUNCTIONS AND I/O RELATIONSHIPS


```
function conference-support;
    subfunction dedicated-functions;
        subfunction initialization,
                PC-functions,
                OC-functions,
                mail-input-registration,
                mail-output-automatism;
        end;

    subfunction standarized-mechanisms;
        subfunction word-processing,
                electronic-mail;


function initialization;
    receives head-information,
            PC-member-list,
            OC-member-list;

    creates head-information-set;
    creates committees-subset;
        in personal-set;


function PC-functions;
    subfunction set-deadlines,
            enter-call-forlist,
            create-referee-set;
    end;

    subfunction referation-consumption;
        subfunction update-refereee-set,
                update-submission-set;


function mail-output-automatism;
    parameters name-of-text-to-be-mailed,
    utilizes set-of-addresses;
            word-processing,
            electronic-mail;
```

```
function mail-input-registration;
    subfunction registrate-first-reply-card,
               registrate-papers,
               registrate-referee-replices,
               registrate-second-reply-card;


function registrate-first-reply-card;
    receives personal-data;
    receives desired-status-description;
            deduced by conference-secratariat;
                based on first-reply-card;
    updates personal-status,information;
            in personal-set;


function registrate-papers;
    receives submission-head-information
    updates submission-set;
etc. ...
```

The process of functional decomposition can be continued in the same way rather mechanically based on the environment specification. Having finished this design step the designer may ask some useful reports to support his further work. For instance, he may ask for a list of data which occured in the description entered so far. It will result in the following report:


```
REPORT

data head-information-set;
data personal-set;
    parts committees-subset,
          personal-status-information;
data submission-set;
    :
    :
    etc.

END
```

This document can help the system designer when elaborating his data structures.

B.  INFORMATION STRUCTURES

```
  set conference-information;
    subset head-information-set;
    subset personal-set;
          subset committees-subset,
                  call-for-address-set,
                  invited-persons-set,
                  submitters-set,
                  referees-set,
                  participants-set;
              subsetting criteria personal-status-information;
    subset submission-set;

  input conference-input;
      subpart head-information,
              PC-member-list,
              OC-member-list;
      end;

      subpart minutes-PC1-data;
          subpart deadlines,
                  call-for-list;

          end;

      subpart minutes-OC1-data;
          subpart invitation-list;
              subpart priority-invitation-list;

  output conference-output;
      subpart address-list;
              call-for-addresses,
              invited-addresses,
              submitters-addresses
              referees-addresses,
              participants-list;
          subsetting criteria personal-status-information;
      end;
```

```
        subpart general-information;
            subpart headline,
                deadlines-designated,
                responsibilities;
        subpart program;
            subpart program-head-information,
                schedule,
                social-part;
```

## C. DATA STRUCTURES

```
entity personal-data;
    contained in   personal-set,
                   PC-member-list,
                   OC-member-list,
                   call-for-list,
                   invitation-list,
                   address-list;
    consists of    personal-identification,
                   personal-status-information;


entity personal-identification;
    consists of    distinction,
                   name,
                   affiliation,
                   address,
                   phone,
                   telex;


entity personal-status-information;
                   status-designations,
                   status-functions;

      :
      :
    etc.
```

Data elements can now be automatically derived from this kind of rough description
by appropriate queries. The exact representation of data elements belongs to the
implementation level plan. We do not detail it here.

*APPENDIX–A.     CONCEPTS FOR ENVIRONMENTAL DESCRIPTION*

This is a partial list containing  only the main concepts. The reader could easily
supplement it with the omitted details.

```
concept phase (name:text)
concept step is phase (no:integer);
concept manual-step is  step;
concept manual-mental-step is manual-step;
     form absolute: step no name manual mental;
concept manual-technical-step is  manual-step;
     form absolute: step no name manual technical;
concept computerized-step is step;
concept substep is step (part-of:step);
concept parallel-substep is substep;
   form part-of: parallel substep;
concept mental-activity (in:manual-mental-step);
concept making is mental-activity (personnel);
   form in: made by personnel;
   form personnel: makes step in;
concept source (information,of:mental-activity);
   form of:  using information;
   form information: used by of;
concept production is mental-activity (document);
   form in: produces document;
   form document:  produced at step in;
concept selection is  mental-activity (information, from: information);
   form in: selects  information from from;
concept information;
concept document is information;
concept manual-document is document;
concept computerized-data is information;
concept device (is:system,for:manual-technical-step);
concept action (in: manual-technical-step);
concept entering is action (in: action, entered: data);
    form in: enter data;
concept mail is  action (in: action, document);
concept update is action (in:action, information);
concept print is action (in:action, information);
etc. ...
```

APPENDIX-B.   CONCEPTS FOR LOGICAL DESIGN

(Partial list.)


```
concept function (part-of:function);
    form part-of: subfunction;

concept data-activity (function);
concept data-flow is data-activity;
concept reception is data-flow (input);
    form function: receives input;
    form input: received by function;

concept generate is data-flow (output);
    form function: generates output;
    form output; generated by function;

concept data-action is data-activity;

concept create is data-action (set);
    form function: creates set;
    form set: created by function;

concept update is data-action (set);
    form function: updates set;
    form set: updated by function;

concept deduce (reception,staff);
    form reception:deduced by staff;
    from staff: deduces reception;

concept basis (deduce, information);
    form deduce: based on information;

concept inclusion (data-activity,data);
    form data-activity: in data;

concept prm-to-func (function,data);
    form function: parameters data;
```

```
concept utilize (function,utilized-function:function);
    form function: utilizes  utilized-function;
    form utilized-function: utilized by function;

concept data;

concept set is  data (part-of: set);
    form part-of: subset;

concept input is; data (part-of:input);

concept output is data (part-of:output);

concept subsetting-criterion (data,is:data);
    form data: subsetting criteria  is;
    form is: subsetting criterion for data;

concept entity (owner:entity);

  e.t.c.
```

## REFERENCES

[1]   Teichroew, D. and Hershey, E.A. III, PSL/PSA a computer aided technique for structured documentation and analysis of information processing systems, IEEE Trans. SE-J, 1(1977).

[2]   Knuth, E., Radó, P., Tóth, Á., Preliminary Description of SDLA, Studies 105/1980, Computer and Automation Institute Hungarian Academy of Science (December 1979).

[3]   Teichroew, D., Macasovic, P., Hershey, E.A. III, and Yamamoto, Y., Application of the Entity-Relationship Approach to Information Processing Systems Modelling, Proceedings, International Conference on Entity-Relationship Approach to System Analysis and Design, Los Angeles (December 10-12, 1979.)

[4]   Chen, P., The Entity-Relationship Model - Toward a Unified View of Data, ACM TODS 1 (1976) 9-36.

[5]   Teichroew, D., Knuth, E., Radó, P., Kang, K.C., Concept Refinement Approach (CRA), a System Specification Technique, CRA, Draft Paper, ISDOS Project The university of Michigan Ann Arbor (January 1981).

[6]   Dahl, O.J. Myhrhang, B., Nygaard, K., SIMULA 67 Common Base Language, NCC (1970).

[7]   Radó, P., Kiss, O., Knuth, E., Szilléry, A., SDLA 1.0 Users Manual, Working Papers II/14, Computer and Automation Institute Hungarian Academy of Science (November 1980).

[8] Knuth, E., Rónyai, L.,   Closed Convex Reference Schemes,
Working Papers II/12, Computer and Automation Institute Hungarian Academy of
Sciences (October 1980).

[9] Knuth, E., Radó, P., Halász, F.,   Formatted Report System of SDLA,
Working Papers II/18, Computer and Automation Institute Hungarian Academy of
Sciences  (July 1981).

[10] Knuth, E., Radó, P.,   Principles of Computer Aided System Description,
Studies 117/1981, Computer and Automation Institute Hungarian Academy of
Sciences (November 1980).

*INFORMATION SYSTEMS DESIGN METHODOLOGIES: A Comparative Review*
*T.W. Olle, H.G. Sol, A.A. Verrijn-Stuart (editors)*
*North-Holland Publishing Company*
© *IFIP, 1982*

# THE ISAC APPROACH TO SPECIFICATION OF INFORMATION SYSTEMS AND ITS APPLICATION TO THE ORGANIZATION OF AN IFIP WORKING CONFERENCE

Mats Lundeberg

The Institute for Development of Activities in Organizations
Birger Jarlsgatan 18, 4 tr
S-114 34 STOCKHOLM
Sweden

This report presents the ISAC approach to information systems specification and its application to a case concerning support to the
activities of programme and organizing committees for an IFIP Working
Conference.  The specification has been prepared on three levels:
(i) change analysis, (ii) activity studies, and (iii) information
analysis. By using the ISAC approach, information systems can be
specified in a number of small, manageable, and connected steps in
such a manner that both users and designers understand the contents.

## 1    INTRODUCTION

### 1.1    WHAT DO I WANT TO OFFER YOU WITH THIS REPORT?

This report presents the ISAC approach to information systems specification and
its application to a standard case study. The ISAC approach to information systems
specification has been presented in [2,3]. The case has been defined by IFIP's
Working Group 8.1 [4]. The case concerns support to the activities of programme and
organizing committees for  an IFIP Working Conference.  IFIP's Working Group 8.1
has proposed to compare different work methods and description techniques in the
information systems specification area by means of this case.

The significance of this report is thus that it offers you an integrated presentation of the ISAC approach to information systems specification and its application
in order to be able to

1       Understand the ISAC approach
2       Compare the ISAC approach with other approaches
3       Evaluate the usefulness of the ISAC approach in your own environment

Please note that no such comparison or evaluation will be made in this report,
since it is only intended to be a starting-point for such activities.

In the ISAC approach, information systems are specified on three levels:

1       Change analysis
2       Activity studies
3       Information analysis

The report is structured according to these levels, treating each of them separately. Before that, the introduction will in the next sections continue with overview
presentations of the possibilities of the ISAC approach and of the approach itself.

### 1.2    WHAT POSSIBILITIES DOES THE ISAC APPROACH OFFER?

The ISAC approach to information systems specification consists of a work methodology from the needs, problems, and ideas experienced by the users to a detailed
user-oriented information systems specification. By methodology we mean a number

of manageable and coherent work steps including rules for what types of documentation that are produced during these work steps. We thus distinguish between description techniques and method steps, where method steps are part of work methods.
Work methods and method steps concern the work manners, while description techniques concern the way of documentation.

In this report, I want to emphasize the following possibilities of the ISAC
approach.

Information systems can be specified in a number of small, manageable, and connected steps
________________________________________________________________________________

Many problems have to be analyzed and solved in connection with the specification
of information systems. We think that a good way to solve complex problems is to
divide them into subproblems until they become manageable. A prerequisite for this
work is that the division in subproblems is coherent. The ISAC approach specifies
information systems on three levels, change analysis, activity studies, and information analysis. In each of these three levels a number of method steps are performed. Each method step uses the results from the preceding method steps. Together these method steps form an integrated methodology.

Information systems can be specified when there really is a need for them
________________________________________________________________________________

This is the important thing with change analysis from an information systems perspective. A professional information systems analyst should only participate in
the specification of information systems when there really is a need for them.
Even when the user says he is sure information systems are needed, a change analysis will put this in a proper perspective without much extra effort because of
the three-level specification approach.

Information systems can be specified to contribute to the activities of the organization
________________________________________________________________________________

This is the important thing with activity studies. Information systems have value
only if they contribute to improve the situation for people in the organization.
They have no value of their own. We must therefore study the activities that
people perform in the organization and that somehow should be improved. This part
of the work is a natural continuation of parts of change analysis, but now performed on a more detailed level.

Information systems can be specified in such a manner that both users and designers understand the contents
________________________________________________________________________________

This is the important thing with information analysis. One does not need any data
technical background or knowledge in order to specify what information systems
should do. At the same time the information analysis specifications can be so
exact that they can form the direct starting point for subsequent data system
design.

1.3     WHAT DOES THE ISAC APPROACH LOOK LIKE IN SHORT?

The purpose of change analysis is to study what changes that you should strive for
in order to do something about the problems and needs you experience in the activities of your organization. It is important to try and find the reasons behind the
problems and not just the symptoms. Change analysis starts with analysis of problems and needs.This includes description of the current situation, description of
goals as well as analysis of needs for changes. Change analysis then continues
with study of change alternatives and ends with choice of change approach (a number of development measures). We would decide on systems development as the suitable development measure only if the change  analysis indicated  that there
are problems and needs in the information systems area. In other situations we

would choose other development measures, e.g. development of the direct business activities (production, marketing, etc.), organizational development or development of personal relations.

The purpose of activity studies is to delimit future information systems in the activities of the organization. The information system should be delimited in such a way that they contribute to solving the problems of the different interest groups involved. In order to delimit information systems, one usually has to describe the activities in more detail than in change analysis. Delimitation of future information systems should be made from the specific problems and needs that the users have and not from existing technical aids. Apart from delimitation, different ambition levels of information systems are studied in activity studies.

The purpose of information analysis is to describe what the thus delimited future information systems will contain and perform. The description is used in two different connections. On one hand, it represents a means of communication for the affected interest groups in their discussion of the information contents. On the other hand, it constitutes an exact basis for the succeeding data system design. The information analysis starts from the desired results from the information system. One then studies what is needed in order to arrive at these results (precedence analysis). The structure of the information sets is also studied (component analysis). Finally, necessary processes in the information system are described (process analysis).

## 2      CHANGE ANALYSIS

### 2.1    METHOD STEPS USED IN CHANGE ANALYSIS

We shall now describe the work methods used in change analysis. The different method steps are described chronologically. In practical work, however, we must always count on the need for iterations, since later steps can give rise to new knowledge and perspectives on earlier steps. At the highest level, change analysis (C) is divided into the following:

C1      Analysis of problems, current situation, and needs
C2      Study of change alternatives
C3      Choice of change approach

### 2.11    Analysis of problems, current situation, and needs (C1)

The change analysis begins with a description, analysis, and evaluation of the current activities and the current situation. Among other things the interest groups involved and the problems and needs for changes that they experience are studied. The following method steps are used:

1      Problem listing

Experienced and expected future problems and possibilities are investigated. This gives a first indication of the potential needs for changes that may improve the situation in the activities of the organization. The problems are documented in a problem table. There is no structure requirement in this table.

2      Analysis of interest groups

The next step is to identify the interest groups (personnel categories) that are affected by the listed problems. Examples of different interest groups are: (i) end users who are affected by the change in their daily work, (ii) public users, i.e., persons in the environment who are affected by the change, e.g., customers and deliverers, (iii) funders, i.e., persons with responsibility for the results of the department of the organization affected by the change.

The interest groups are documented in a list of interest groups. During the analysis of interest groups new interest groups with additional problems may be found. The problem table is supplemented with these new problems if such are found.

3        Problem grouping

It is not convenient to work with too many problems at the same time. Therefore, the problems in the problem table are divided into a number of problem groups. These problem groups can represent an embryo for a subsequent definition of subprojects later on. The problem groups are documented in a problem group table.

4        Description of current activities

It is now possible to illustrate the relevant activities in connection with the problems and interest groups at hand. This is done in a description of current activities and their environment. A crude activity model, consisting of (i) activity graphs (A-graphs), (ii) text pages for A-graphs, and (iii) property tables is produced. The description technique for A-graphs will be described in section 2.2. The description of current activities should be carried so far that all problems can be related to some activities or sets in the A-graphs.

5        Description of objectives

When the development starts there is seldom an exact description of the objectives for the activities that have been described and delimited in the description of current activities. Usually, different interest groups have different desires. These desires are often vague and some of them may be in conflict with each other. During this work step the desires are described more concisely in a number of realistic objectives. The result is documented in a table of objectives.

6        Evaluation of current situation and analysis of needs for changes

Now it is possible to compare what is wanted (the table of objectives) with what is available (the problem table and its illustration in the description of current activities). The differences are the needs for changes. All problems imply potential needs for changes. By studying the table of objectives, the problems can be transformed to needs for changes and then given priority according to the values of the different interest groups. The needs for changes are documented in one table of needs for changes for each problem group. The result of the analysis of problems and needs is thus needs for changes with given priority that can be used as a basis for the subsequent study of change alternatives.

2.12    <u>Study of change alternatives (C2)</u>

We shall now generate (create) and describe different change alternatives. The alternatives are evaluated from human, social, and economic viewpoints with regard to their workability and realizability, confer [1]. A study of change alternatives is normally made for each problem group. The following method steps are used:

1        Generation of change alternatives

This is a creative part of the work. Therefore, no exact guidelines can be given. Sometimes it may be of help to systematically investigate what flows and activities could be changed and the consequences of such changes. The change ideas are summarized in a table of change alternatives.

2        Description of change alternatives

In order to be able to analyze and evaluate the consequences of the alternatives, each change alternative is described in a new activity model (A-graphs with text pages and property tables). Very often the A-graphs for the different alternatives

have a similar structure, but the contents of the text pages and property tables
vary.

3        Evaluation of change alternatives

The change alternatives are analyzed and evaluated from different viewpoints, e.g.,
human, social, and economical. The purpose is to get enough basis to choose
between the alternatives. Thus detailed calculi do not have to be made at this
stage.

2.13    Choice of change approach (C3)

The last part of the change analysis is to choose a change approach, i.e., change
alternative and suitable development measures, for each problem group. The relation between parallel development measures is also analyzed. The following method
steps are used:

1        Choice of change alternative

The reason for the choice is documented.

2        Choice of development measures

A change alternative usually results in a combination of development measures.
Examples are: (i) information systems development, (ii) organizational development
including development of personal relations, (iii) development of direct business
activities, e.g., development of the production, the products, or the distribution.

3        Analysis of parallel development measures

An analysis is made of how parallel development measures effect each other.

2.2      DESCRIPTION TECHNIQUES USED IN CHANGE ANALYSIS

2.21     A-graphs

An A-graph or activity graph is a picture of some activity. The legend for A-
graphs is found in figure 2.1. The symbols are of three kinds: (i) sets, (ii) activities, and (iii) flows. A-graphs have a hierarchical structure in order to give
an overview of complex activities and at the same time give details on lower
levels. This means that overview graphs are detailed in a number of new A-graphs.
A reference system is used in order to relate the different parts of the description to each other. The overview graph always has reference code 0. Each activity
in the overview graph is referenced with a one-digit number. In detailing an activity the subactivities have the same reference code with the addition of another
digit. In detailing graphs an abbreviated notation is often used. The reference
code for the activity is given in the upper-left corner of the graph frame. A dash
is used to replace the sign for this reference code. Output sets from an activity
have the same reference code with the addition of a capital letter. Input sets to
the overview graph have reference codes as if they came from imagined activities
in the environment. Subsets have the same  reference codes as the corresponding
main sets with the addition of a digit.

2.22     Text pages

There is not space for much text in the symbols in A-graphs. Therefore, the graphs
may have to be supplemented with text pages. Text pages permit more detailed descriptions and explanations of abbreviations as well as indication of subsets. The
text page contains reference codes and names for all sets and activities of the A-
graph. The contents of a text page are divided into three parts: (i) input sets,
(ii) sets/activities inside the frame of the graph, and (iii) output sets. Many

SYMBOLS IN A-GRAPHS              CORRESPONDENCE IN DESCRIBED ACTIVITY

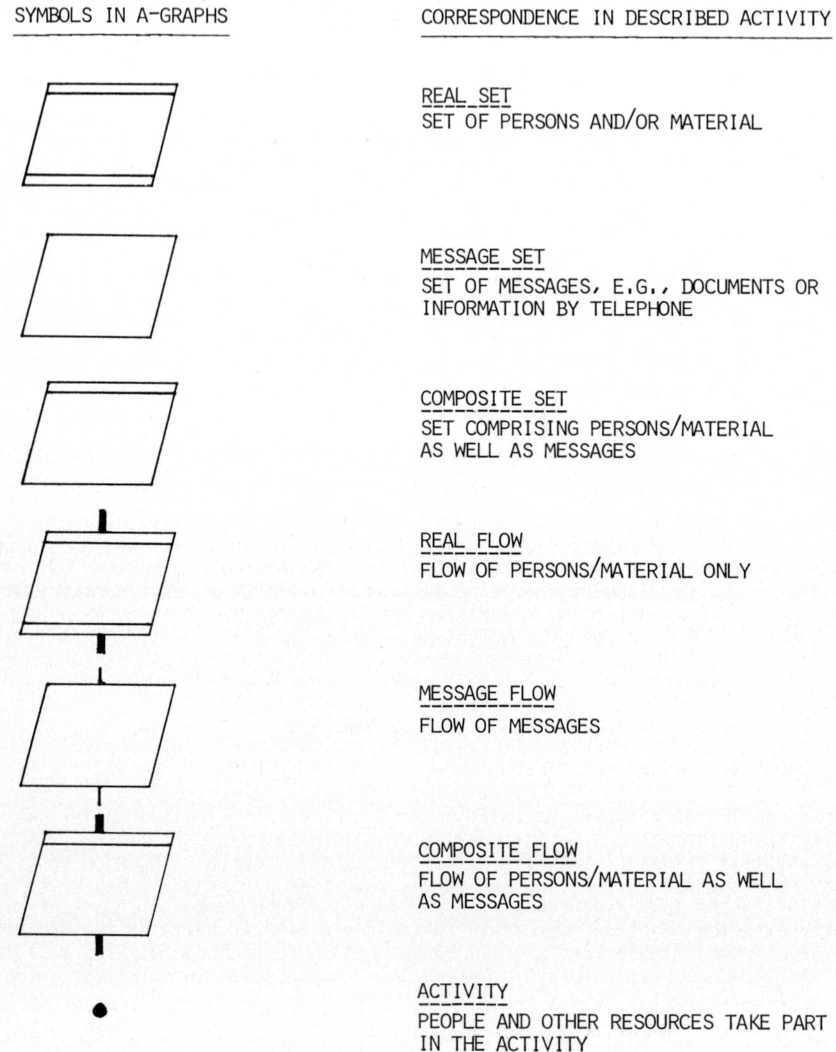


ALL FLOWS ARE ASSUMED TO GO FROM TOP TO BOTTOM ON THE GRAPHS, ARROWS ARE
NEEDED ON UPWARD AND (POSSIBLY) HORIZONTAL FLOWS ONLY.

Figure 2.1   Explanation of symbols used in A-graphs


sets have to be described in many A-graphs. They are therefore also described in
several text pages. In preparing A-graphs it is therefore often simpler to work
with one list of sets and activities for all A-graphs in a graph series. The text
pages are then written when the final documentation of the work is prepared.

2.23    Property tables

The graphical part of a description of activities is general in character. The A-graphs must be supplemented with qualitative and quantitative information in order to obtain a description of specific activities. This is done in property tables, which can be constructed for flows and for activities. Reference to A-graphs is made through reference codes and names.

2.3    CHANGE ANALYSIS OF THE ORGANIZATION OF AN IFIP WORKING CONFERENCE

2.31    Analysis of problems, current situation, and needs

1    Problem listing

The purpose of problem listing is to investigate experienced problems as well as expected future problems and possibilities. The problems are documented in a prob-lem table. There is no requirement of structure in this table. The problem table in figure 2.2 (except the right column) is the result of a dialogue with the users as organized by the review committee of the comparative review of information systems design methodologies.

2    Analysis of interest groups

In this step, the interest groups that are affected by the listed problems are identified. The list of interest groups is documented in figure 2.3. It should be noted that one person in this case may belong to several interest groups. The list of interest groups is also the result of a dialogue with the users. Normally, the problem table is supplemented with additional problems of new interest groups. In this case, this iteration has not been documented explicitly. Instead, figure 2.2 contains all the problems thought of so far.

3    Problem grouping

Not applicable in this application. Problem grouping is used when too many prob-lems have been found, so that they must be grouped to be manageable.

4    Description of current activities

The relevant activities in connection with the problems and interest groups at hand are now described. Figure 2.5 shows an A-graph with an overview of the activ-ities in connection with the organization of an IFIP Working Conference. The A-graph has been prepared using the symbols shown in figure 2.1 above. The A-graph illustrates five main activities:

4        Initiation
5        Programme  Committee Activities
6        Organization Committee Activities
7        Working Conference
8        Evaluation

and the corresponding input and output sets to these activities. Figure 2.4 shows a text page to this A-graph. A-graphs for the programme committee activities are found in figures 2.7, and 2.9 with corresponding text pages in figures 2.6, and 2.8. Figures 2.10 and 2.11 illustrate a text page and an A-graph describing the organizing committee activities. Figure 2.12 finally illustrates a property table describing numbers of elements in some of the sets of the A-graphs.

The description of the current situation can now be evaluated against the problem table. The criterion for evaluating whether the current description has been car-ried far enough or not is whether all (relevant) problems can be related to the current description. The right column of figure 2.2 relates the problems in the problem table to the activities and sets of the A-graphs. The right column of

IFIP

Analyst
Mats Lundeberg
Subject
Organization of an IFIP Working Conference

PROBLEM TABLE
Date
1981-07-28

| PROBLEMS | | DESCRIPTION | RELATED ACTIVITIES/ SETS IN A-GRAPHS |
|---|---|---|---|
| NO | NAME | | |
| P1 | DIFFICULTY IN INVITING INVOLVED COMMITTEE/ GROUP MEMBERS | IT IS DIFFICULT TO ENSURE THAT MEMBERS OF THE INVOLVED IFIP WORK- ING GROUP(S) AND TECHNICAL COM- MITTEE(S) ARE INVITED EVEN IF THEY DO NOT COME | 62 |
| P2 | DIFFICULTY IN REACHING AND ATTRACTING ALL POTENTIAL AUTHORS | IT IS SOMETIMES DIFFICULT TO ENSURE THAT ALL POTENTIAL AUTHORS ARE REACHED WITH CALL FOR PAPERS AND TO GET THE "RIGHT" AUTHORS TO CONTRIBUTE PAPERS | 5A, 2B |
| P3 | DIFFICULTY IN REACHING AND PERSUADING REFEREES | IT IS SOMETIMES DIFFICULT TO FIND REFEREES AND TO PERSUADE THEM TO PARTICIPATE | 5B1, 2C1 |
| P4 | DIFFICULTY IN SELECT- ING PAPERS | IT IS DIFFICULT TO SELECT THE "BEST" PAPERS FOR A WORKING CONFERENCE | 531 |
| P5 | REFEREE REPORTS ARE OFTEN LATE | IT IS SOMETIMES DIFFICULT TO GET THE REFEREE REPORTS ON TIME | 52A |
| P6 | CONTRIBUTED PAPERS ARE OFTEN LATE | IT IS SOMETIMES DIFFICULT TO GET THE CONTRIBUTED PAPERS ON TIME | 2B2 |
| P7 | DIFFICULTY IN GROUPING PAPERS | IT IS DIFFICULT TO MAKE A "GOOD" GROUPING OF THE SELECTED PAPERS IN SESSIONS | 532 |
| P8 | DIFFICULTY IN SELECTING CHAIRMEN | IT IS SOMETIMES DIFFICULT TO SELECT CHAIRMEN FOR THE DIFFERENT SESSIONS | 534 |
| P9 | DIFFICULTY IN IN- VITING PARTICIPANTS | IT IS DIFFICULT TO ENSURE THAT ALL PEOPLE THAT ARE INTERESTED GET AN INVITATION | 62 |
| P10 | DIFFICULTY IN SELECT- ING PARTICIPANTS | IT IS DIFFICULT TO SELECT PARTICI- PANTS IN CASE OF LIMITED PARTICI- PATION | 63 |
| P11 | UNSTABLE REGISTRATION | REGISTRATION IS LATE, UNSTABLE AND WITH MANY LAST MINUTE CHANGES | 2D, 63 |
| P12 | DIFFICULTY IN TRACKING VIP'S | IT IS DIFFICULT TO KEEP TRACK OF INVITED GUESTS AND MAKE SURE THAT THEIR REGISTRATION IS UP TO DATE | 62A, 63 |

Figure 2.2  Problem table of problems in connection with the organization of an
          IFIP Working Conference

**IFIP**

Analyst                                               LIST OF INTEREST GROUPS
Mats Lundeberg                                        Date
Subject                                               1981-07-28
Organization of an IFIP Working Conference

| INTEREST GROUPS | PROBLEMS (SEE FIGURE 2.1) |
|---|---|
| **END USERS:** | |
| I1   PROGRAMME COMMITTEE CHAIRMAN | P2,P3,P4,P5,P6,P7,P8 |
| I2   PROGRAMME COMMITTEE MEMBERS | P2,P3,P4,P5,P6,P7,P8 |
| I3   PROGRAMME COMMITTEE SECRETARIES | P5,P6 |
| I4   ORGANIZING COMMITTEE CHAIRMAN | P1,P9,P10,P11,P12 |
| I5   ORGANIZING COMMITTEE MEMBERS | P1,P9,P10,P11,P12 |
| I6   ORGANIZING COMMITTEE STAFF | P11,P12 |
| **PUBLIC USERS:** | |
| I7   REFEREES | P3,P5 |
| I8   SESSION CHAIRMEN | P8 |
| I9   AUTHORS | P2,P6 |
| I10  ATTENDEES | P10,P11 |
| **FUNDERS (DECISION MAKERS):** | |
| I11  MEMBERS OF INVOLVED TECHNICAL COMMITTEES | P1 |
| I12  MEMBERS OF INVOLVED WORKING GROUPS | P1 |

Figure 2.3   List of interest groups affected by the organization of an IFIP Working Conference

figure 2.2 shows that it has been possible to relate all problems in the problem table to the description of the current situation. Hence we can continue with the next method step.

5        Description of objectives

The result of the description of objectives is documented in a table of objectives in figure 2.13. The table of objectives is the result of a dialogue with the users in the same manner as above.

6        Evaluation of current situation and analysis of needs for changes

The problems of the problem table are transformed to needs for changes by comparing with the table of objectives. The needs for changes are then given priority by the author of this paper. Ideally, this should have been done according to the preferences of the different interest groups. The needs for changes are documented

IFIP

Analyst                                TEXT PAGE
Mats Lundeberg                         A-GRAPH
Subject                                1981-07-28
Organization of an IFIP Working Conference: Overview


1A     Proposals for working conference
1A1    Proposed subjects and committees
1A2    Proposed distribution lists for invitations

2A     Accepted/rejected invitations from programme and organization committee
       members

2B     Letters of intent, contributed and revised papers from authors
2B1    Letters of intent from authors
2B2    Contributed papers from authors
2B3    Revised papers from authors
2B4    Cancellation of papers by authors

2C     Letters and reports from referees and chairmen
2C1    Letters and reports from referees
2C2    Accepted/rejected invitations from chairmen

2D     Accepted/rejected invitations from attendees

3A     Hotel confirmations from hotels

---

4      Initiation of a working conference

4B     Working conference plans including appointed committees
4B1    Working conference plans
4B2    Distribution lists for invitations
4B3    Appointed programme and organization committee members

5      Programme committee activities

5C     Programme. Pre-prints. Lists. Reports.
5C1    Programme
5C2    Pre-prints
5C3    Distribution lists
5C4    Reports on programme committee activities

6      Organization committee activities

6C     List of attendees. Reports.

7      Working conference

7A     Reports on presentations and discussions

8      Evaluation

---

4A     Invitations to programme and organization committee members

5A     Call for papers, and notices of accepted/rejected papers
5A1    Call for papers to potential authors
5A2    Notices of accepted/rejected papers to authors

5B     Invitations and papers to referees and chairmen
5B1    Invitations and papers to referees
5B2    Invitations to chairmen

6A     Invitations and confirmations to attendees
6B     Requests for hotel rooms

8A     Reports on working conference


Figure 2.4  Text page to A-graph WO

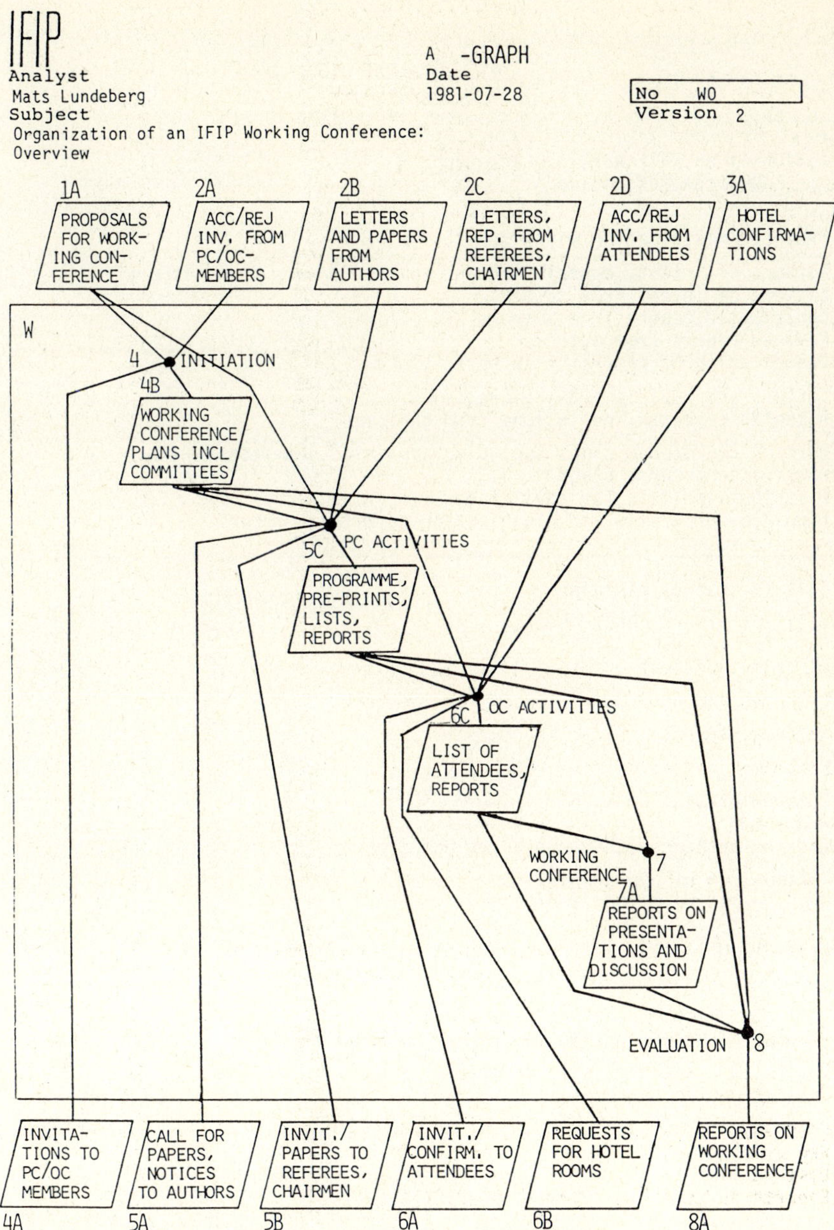


Figure 2.5  A-graph with overview of activities in connection with the organization of an IFIP Working Conference

# IFIP

Analyst                                    TEXT PAGE
Mats Lundeberg                             A-GRAPH
Subject                                    1981-07-28
Organization of an IFIP Working Conference:
Programme Committee Activities


1A2    Proposed distribution lists for invitations

2B     Letters of intent, contributed and revised papers from authors
2B1    Letters of intent from authors
2B2    Contributed papers from authors
2B3    Revised papers from authors
2B4    Cancellation of papers by authors

2C1    Letters and reports from referees
2C2    Accepted/rejected invitations from chairmen

4B     Working conference plans including appointed committees
4B1    Working conference plans
4B2    Distribution lists for invitations
4B3    Appointed programme and organization committee members

---

51     Call for papers planning

51A    Call for papers. Distribution list.
51A1   Call for papers
51A2   Distribution list

52     Planning and administration of referee work

52A    Referee reports

53     Programme design

53A    Programme. List of authors.
53A1   Programme
53A2   List of authors with accepted/rejected papers

54     Preparation of pre-prints

54A    Pre-prints

55     Evaluation

---

5A1    Call for papers to potential authors
5A2    Notices of accepted/rejected papers to authors

5B1    Invitations and papers to referees
5B2    Invitations to chairmen

5C1    Programme
5C2    Pre-prints
5C3    Distribution lists
5C4    Reports on programme committee activities


Figure 2.6   Text page to A-graph W5

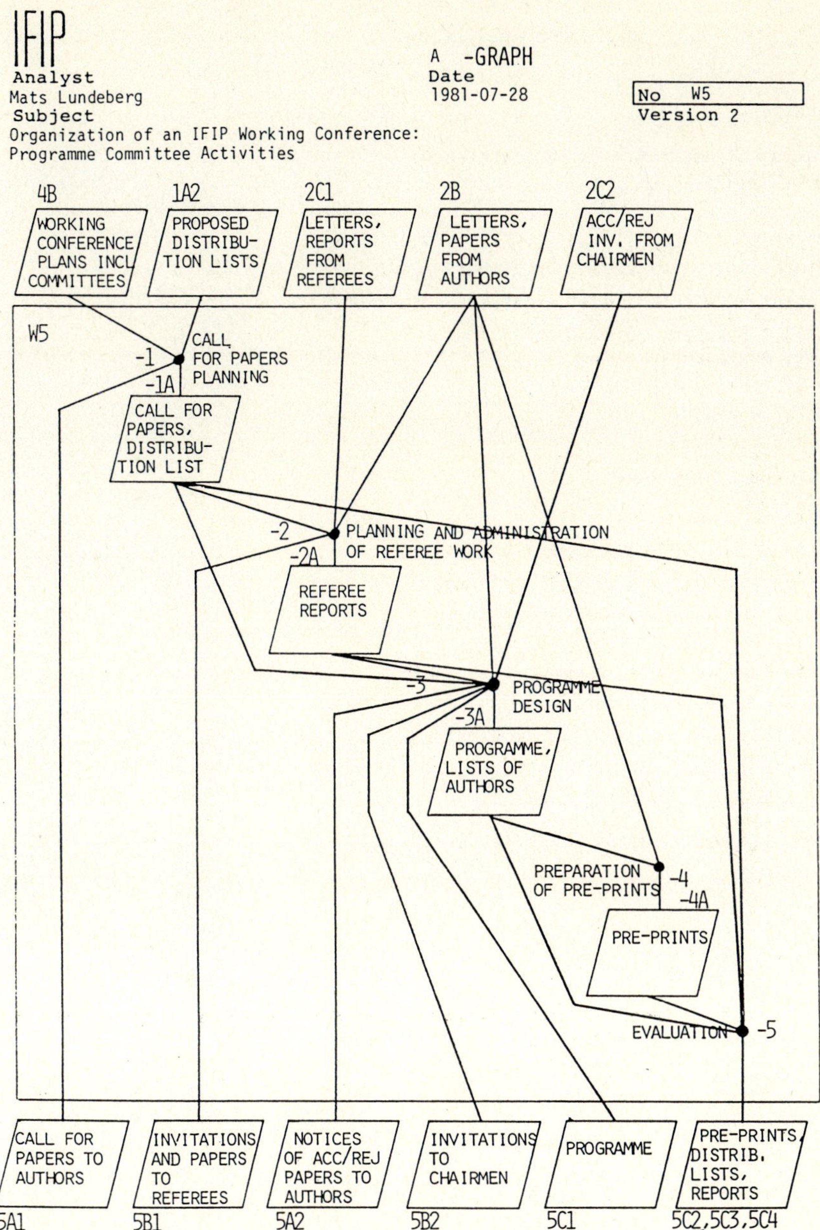


Figure 2.7  A-graph describing Programme Committee Activities

**IFIP**

Analyst                               TEXT PAGE
Mats Lundeberg                  A-GRAPH
Subject                              1981-07-28
Organization of an IFIP Working Conference:
Programme Design

| | |
|---|---|
| 2B2 | Contributed papers from authors |
| 2B4 | Cancellations of papers by authors |
| 2C2 | Accepted/rejected invitations from chairmen |
| 51A | Call for papers. Distribution list. |
| 51A1 | Call for papers |
| 51A2 | Distribution list |
| 52A | Referee reports |

---

| | |
|---|---|
| 531 | Selection of papers |
| 531A | Selected papers |
| 532 | Grouping of selected papers to sessions |
| 532A | Proposed programme without chairmen |
| 533 | Selection of programme |
| 533A | Suggestion for changes of selection |
| 533B | Programme without chairmen |
| 534 | Selection of chairmen |

---

| | |
|---|---|
| 53A | Programme |
| 5A2 | Notices of accepted/rejected papers to authors |
| 5B2 | Invitations to chairmen |
| 5C1 | Programme |

Figure 2.8   Text page to A-graph W53

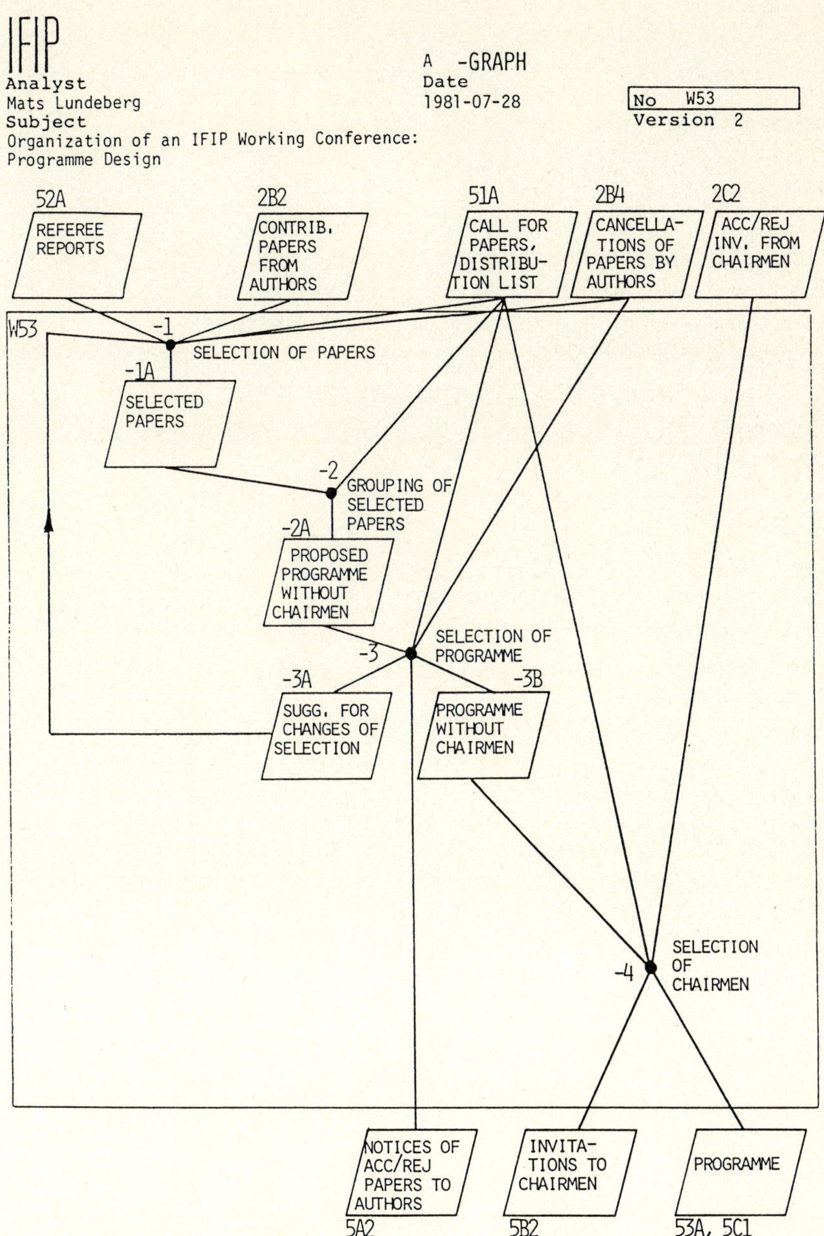


Figure 2.9   A-graph describing Programme Design

# IFIP

Analyst                                      TEXT PAGE
Mats Lundeberg                               A-GRAPH
Subject                                      1981-07-28
Organization of an IFIP Working Conference:
Organization Committee Activities


2D      Accepted/rejected invitations from attendees

3A      Hotel confirmations from hotels

4B      Working conference plans including appointed committees
4B1     Working conference plans
4B2     Distribution lists for invitations
4B3     Appointed programme and organization committee members

5C1     Programme

5C3     Distribution lists

---

61      Organization planning

61A     Conference organization plans

62      Invitation and participation planning

62A     List of attendees with requests

63      Hotel planning

63A     List of attendees

64      Evaluation

---

6A1     Invitations to attendees
6A2     Confirmations (positive/negative) to attendees

6B      Requests for hotel rooms

6C1     List of attendees
6C2     Reports on conference organization


Figure 2.10   Text page to A-graph W6

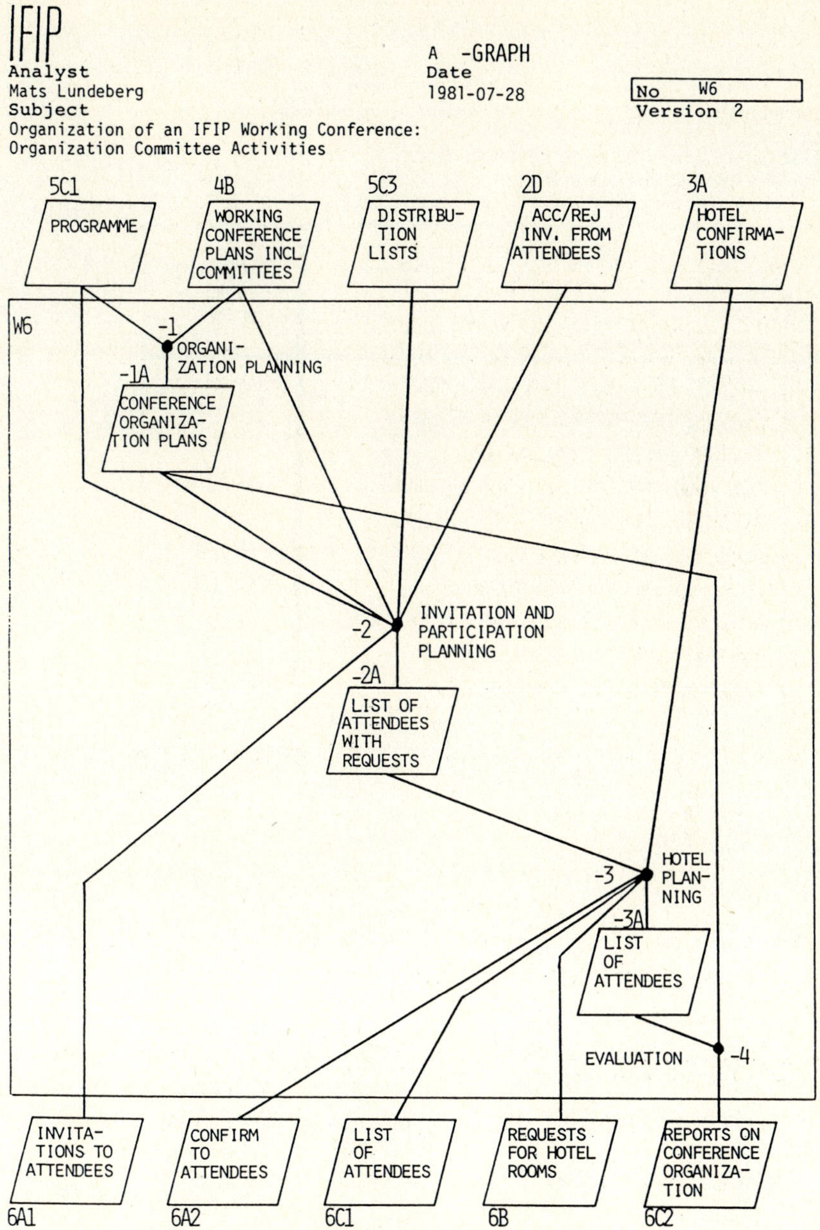


Figure 2.11   A-graph describing Organization Committee Activities

# IFIP

Analyst                                      PROPERTY TABLE
Mats Lundeberg                               Date
Subject                                      1981-07-28
Organization of an IFIP Working Conference:
Numbers of elements in some sets

| SETS | | NUMBER OF ELEMENTS IN SETS |
|---|---|---|
| REFER-ENCE CODE | NAME | |
| 2B1 | LETTERS OF INTENT FROM AUTHORS | 10-200 |
| 2B2 | CONTRIBUTED PAPERS FROM AUTHORS | 10-100 |
| 2B3 | REVISED PAPERS FROM AUTHORS | 10-20 |
| 2C111 | ACCEPTED INVITATIONS FROM REFEREES | 0-30 |
| 2C21 | ACCEPTED INVITATIONS FROM CHAIRMEN | 5-10 |
| 2D1 | ACCEPTED INVITATIONS FROM ATTENDEES | 50-120 |
| 5A1 | CALL FOR PAPERS TO AUTHORS | 100-600 |
| 5A21 | NOTICES OF ACCEPTED PAPERS TO AUTHORS | 10-20 |
| 6A1 | INVITATIONS TO ATTENDEES | 50-300 |
| 6A2 | CONFIRMATIONS TO ATTENDEES | 50-120 |

Figure 2.12   Property table describing numbers of elements in some of the sets
of the A-graphs in figures 2.5, 2.7, 2.9, and 2.11

# IFIP

Analyst                                      TABLE OF OBJECTIVES
Mats Lundeberg                               Date
Subject                                      1981-07-28
Organization of an IFIP Working Conference

| G1 | COVERAGE OF MOST INTERESTING FIELD ACTIVITIES | WORKING CONFERENCES SHALL REFLECT THE MOST INTERESTING ACTIVITIES IN THE FIELD RELATED TO THE THEMES OF THE CONFERENCES |
|---|---|---|
| G2 | ATTRACTION OF FOREMOST EXPERTS | WORKING CONFERENCES SHALL ATTRACT THE FOREMOST SPECIALISTS IN THE FIELD |
| G3 | HIGH QUALITY PROCEEDINGS | PROCEEDINGS SHALL BE OF A SATISFACTORILY HIGH QUALITY (SCIENTIFICALLY AS WELL AS PEDAGOGICALLY) |
| G4 | WORK SHALL NOT BE SALARIED | WORK IN A PROGRAMME OR ORGANIZATION COMMITTEE SHALL NOT BE SALARIED BY IFIP |

Figure 2.13   Table of objectives for an IFIP Working Conference

in figure 2.14. In the rest of this paper, we shall concentrate on the two needs for changes with the highest priority:

N5      Facilitate programme committee members work
N6      Facilitate organization committee members work

## 2.32     Study of change alternatives

### 1     Generation of change alternatives

The change ideas have been summarized in a table of change alternatives, see figure 2.15. They represent five different ideas of how to facilitate programme and organization committee members work (N5, N6).

### 2     Description of change alternatives

The change alternatives are described in new activity models. We will here concentrate on alternative A4 as advised by the review committee of the comparative review of information systems design methodologies. Figure 2.16 shows a property table that illustrates the difference between change alternative A4 and the current situation (AO). The structure of the A-graphs in figures 2.5, 2.7, and 2.11 remains the same.

### 3     Evaluation of change alternatives

The change alternatives are now analyzed and evaluated from different view points, e.g., human, social, and economic. The purpose is to get enough basis to choose between alternatives. In our case, because of the advised focus on information systems, we shall only note that alternative A4 has the advantage of clearly reducing the workload of committee members and the disadvantage of high investment costs in relation to possible gains.

## 2.33     Choice of change approach

### 1     Choice of change alternative

In our case, we choose alternative A4 Information systems because of the advised focus of the case.

### 2     Choice of development measures

In order to be able to develop and implement information systems to facilitate the work of committee members the following development measures will be needed:

DM1     Development of computer-based information systems to support an IFIP Working Conference
DM2     Development of related activities of the programme and organization committees

Because of the advised focus of the case, we shall only treat DM1.

### 3     Analysis of parallel development measures

Not applicable because of the advised focus of the case.

## 3     ACTIVITY STUDIES

### 3.1     METHOD STEPS USED IN ACTIVITY STUDIES

We shall now describe the work methods used in activity studies. At the highest level activity studies (A) in information systems development is divided into the following:

**IFIP**

Analyst
Mats Lundeberg
Subject
Organization of an IFIP Working Conference

TABLE OF
NEEDS FOR CHANGES
Date
1981-07-28

| NEEDS FOR CHANGES | PROBLEMS | OBJEC-TIVES | PRIORITY |
|---|---|---|---|
| N1  IMPROVE AVAILABLE INFORMATION ON INTERESTING FIELD ACTIVITIES | P2 | G1 | 4 |
| N2  IMPROVE GUIDELINES FOR SELECTION OF PAPERS | P4 | G3 | 3 |
| N3  IMPROVE QUALITY OF CALL FOR PAPERS, ETC. | P2 | G2 | 3 |
| N4  IMPROVE GUIDELINES FOR REFEREES | P3,P4 | G3 | 3 |
| N5  FACILITATE PROGRAMME COMMITTEE MEMBERS WORK | P2,P3,P4,P5, P6,P7,P8 | G4 | 1 |
| N6  FACILITATE ORGANIZING COMMITTEE MEMBERS WORK | P1,P9,P10, P11,P12 | G4 | 2 |

Figure 2.14   Table of needs for changes regarding organization of an IFIP Working Conference

**IFIP**

Analyst
Mats Lundeberg
Subject
Organization of an IFIP Working Conference

TABLE OF CHANGE
ALTERNATIVES
Date
1981-07-28

| | | |
|---|---|---|
| A0 | NO CHANGES | TO CONTINUE AS BEFORE (ZERO ALTERNATIVE) |
| A1 | CONSTITUTE ADDITIONAL COMMITTEES | THE COMMITTEE WORK IS SUBDIVIDED AND DISTRIBUTED AMONG ADDITIONAL COMMITTEES IN ORDER TO REDUCE THE TOTAL WORK LOAD OF INDIVIDUAL COMMITTEE MEMBERS |
| A2 | RAISE FEES AND HIRE PROFESSIONAL ASSISTANTS | PROFESSIONAL ASSISTANTS ARE HIRED TO DO MOST OF THE BACKGROUND WORK IN ORDER TO REDUCE THE TOTAL WORK LOAD OF INDIVIDUAL COMMITTEE MEMBERS. THIS IS FINANCED BY RAISING THE CONFERENCE FEES |
| A3 | DEVELOP INSTRUCTIONS FOR COMMITTEE WORK | INSTRUCTIONS FOR COMMITTEE WORK ARE DEVELOPED IN ORDER TO DECREASE UNNECESSARY COMMITTEE WORK AND SPEED UP NECESSARY COMMITTEE WORK |
| A4 | DEVELOP COMPUTER-BASED INFORMATION SYSTEMS | COMPUTER-BASED INFORMATION SYSTEMS ARE DEVELOPED IN ORDER TO SUPPORT AND FACILITATE COMMITTEE MEMBERS WORK |
| A5 | DEVELOP COURSES FOR COMMITTEE MEMBERS | COURSES FOR COMMITTEE MEMBERS ARE DEVELOPED IN ORDER TO GIVE COMMITTEE MEMBERS NECESSARY TRAINING BEFORE UNDERTAKING COMMITTEE WORK. THIS IS DONE IN ORDER TO FACILITATE THE ACTUAL COMMITTEE WORK |

Figure 2.15   Table of change alternatives regarding organization of an IFIP Working Conference

**IFIP**

Analyst
Mats Lundeberg
Subject
Organization of an IFIP Working Conference

PROPERTY TABLE
Date
1981-07-28

| ACTIVITIES IN A-GRAPHS | | A0: WORK DONE BY | A4: WORK DONE BY |
|---|---|---|---|
| REFER-ENCE CODE | NAME | | |
| 51 | CALL FOR PAPERS PLANNING | PROGRAMME COMMITTEE | PLANNING: PROGRAMME COMMITTEE<br>ADMINISTRATION: INFORMATION SYSTEM |
| 52 | PLANNING AND ADMINISTRATION OF REFEREE WORK | PROGRAMME COMMITTEE | PLANNING: PROGRAMME COMMITTEE<br>ADMINISTRATION: INFORMATION SYSTEM |
| 531 | SELECTION OF PAPERS | PROGRAMME COMMITTEE | SELECTION: PROGRAMME COMMITTEE<br>ADMINISTRATION: INFORMATION SYSTEM |
| 532 | GROUPING OF SELECTED PAPERS | PROGRAMME COMMITTEE | GROUPING: PROGRAMME COMMITTEE<br>ADMINISTRATION: INFORMATION SYSTEM |
| 534 | SELECTION OF CHAIRMEN | PROGRAMME COMMITTEE | SELECTION: PROGRAMME COMMITTEE<br>ADMINISTRATION: INFORMATION SYSTEM |
| 62 | INVITATION AND PARTICIPATION PLANNING | ORGANIZING COMMITTEE | PLANNING: ORGANIZING COMMITTEE<br>ADMINISTRATION: INFORMATION SYSTEM |

Figure 2.16   Property table illustrating the difference between change alternatives A0 and A4


A1        Partitioning in information subsystems
A2        Study of information subsystems
A3        Coordination of information subsystems

### 3.11    Partitioning in information subsystems

Activity studies in information systems development are only performed if information system needs have been identified during the change analysis. The activity studies start with describing the information processing parts of the activities (in the form of A-graphs, text pages, and property tables) in more detail. Among other things information subsystems are identified, classified, and delimited. The following method steps are used:

1        Detailed description of activities

The activity models that were produced during the change analysis describe the activities on a crude level for the change alternative that we decided to continue with. In this case, the result of change analysis is that information systems should be developed and/or modified. The task now is to describe these information systems as parts of the activities by means of A-graphs (including text pages) and property tables.

## 2        Identification of information subsystems

We now go through all A-graphs and search for potential information subsystems.
These are documented in a preliminary list of information systems. Our approach is
based on finding several information subsystems rather than one "total" information system. During the activity studies we should <u>not</u> decide on information
systems that are integrated via the utilization of <u>the</u> same technical aids, e.g.,
a computer, terminals, etc. Instead, we should identify the <u>specific</u> information
systems that produce relevant information for the users in <u>their</u> work.

## 3        Classification of information subsystems

We now classify the identified information subsystems according to their formalizability, and type of processing. We distinguish among four different information
processing activities in this connection:

IS1        Information systems that are impossible to formalize, e.g., including qua-
           lified decisions, informal contacts, and know-how. These information
           systems must necessarily be manual.

IS2        Formalizable information systems that are naturally manual in the sense
           that they are not suitable for automation. The manual tasks can be per-
           formed after given rules, e.g., standardized telephone calls and mail
           procedures.

IS3        Automatable information systems with calculations that can be performed
           after given rules. How these work tasks should be performed (manually or
           by using computers or other technical equipment) is decided during the
           data system design.

IS4        Automatable information systems with <u>only</u> message transport in time (stor-
           ing of messages) or space (switching <u>of</u> messages). This form of message
           transport is easy to formalize. Again, how it should be performed is de-
           cided during data system design.

IS4 contains <u>only</u> message transport. IS3 often contains parts of message storing
integrated with automatable calculations. This classification is the basis for:
(i) the subsequent study of information subsystems, (ii) the planning of the purpose and extent of the subsequent information analysis for the different types of
information processing activities.

## 4        Delimitation of information subsystems

The description of activities (A-graphs, text pages, and property tables) is elaborated once again, now to the point that the information subsystems occur as delimited activities in the A-graphs. The description of activities is carried so far
that the output message sets from an information subsystem: (i) are similar from
the user's point of view, i.e., involve similar objects and events in the activities of the organization, (ii) have similar time requirements (response time, frequency, timeliness, etc.). It is also practical to distinguish between manual and
automatable parts so that they form separate subsystems.

### 3.12    Study of information subsystems

Each information subsystem is now studied separately. Certain analyses are made
with regard to benefits and costs. A number of alternative ambition levels are
generated and tested for each subsystem. Finally, a suitable ambition level is
chosen. The following method steps are used:

1        Analysis of contributions

The analysis of the contribution from an information system is a renewed analysis
of the change analysis. An information system has no end in itself, but it must

contribute to the fulfillment of goals for the people involved in the various
activities. In order to locate different contributions (benefits) we may have to
make the activity description of the environment more elaborate. We need to study
how the environment uses the information produced by the information system. The
identified contributions (benefits) are documented in a property table.

2        Generation of alternative levels of ambition

Two conditions guide the choice of ambition level, namely, prerequisites such as:
(i) the quality of the information delivered to the information system, (ii) the
possibility of specifying calculation rules, (iii) the average and maximum workload. And requirements such as: (iv) response time, (v) timeliness, (vi) frequency,
(vii) volume, (viii) secrecy. The prerequisites and requirements are documented in
property tables. Then alternative ambition levels that fulfill specified prerequisites and requirements are generated. It is often practical to limit the study to
a few concrete levels of ambition that are sufficiently different. These are documented in a table of ambition levels.

3        Test of ambition levels

We must now check whether or not these ambition levels are realizable. If we find
similar information systems in use in other places, this is a good indication that
they are realizable. For other situations there are different possibilities, such
as: (i) desk tests, and (ii) field tests.

4        Cost/benefit analysis

The calculation of benefits is a refinement of the already stated contributions.
We note that activity studies is the last level of specification of information
systems in which the benefits are calculated. The costs can be estimated finer
during information analysis. The analysis of costs can only give crude estimates
during activity studies. We will not go further into cost/benefit calculus here.

5        Choice of ambition level

Using the human and social analysis from the change analysis and the results from
the cost/benefit analysis, we choose a suitable ambition level. One possible result may be that the information system specification is discontinued at this step.

## 3.13     Coordination of information subsystems

The activity studies conclude with an analysis of the relations between the different information subsystems, which then are given different priorities. The
following method steps are used:

1        Analysis of relations between different information subsystems

The subsystems on which work may continue are listed together. The relations
between these subsystems are described, analyzed, and documented.

2        Priority rating of different information subsystems

Development resources are always limited. We must therefore decide which information systems are to be developed and in which order.

## 3.2     DESCRIPTION TECHNIQUES USED IN ACTIVITY STUDIES

The same description technique for describing activities is used in activity
studies as in change analysis, see section 2.2 above.

## 3.3     ACTIVITY STUDIES OF THE ORGANIZATION OF AN IFIP WORKING CONFERENCE

### 3.31     Partitioning in information subsystems

1       Detailed description of activities

The activity studies start with adding such detail to the information processing
parts of the activity models that information subsystems can be identified in
accordance with change alternative A4 (figure 2.16). Figures 3.1-3.5 contain A-
graphs describing:

F51      Call for papers planning
F52      Planning and administration of referee work
F53      Programme design (modified from W53)
F537     Selection of chairmen
F62      Invitation and participation planning

The F stands for "Future" in order to distinguish the activity model for the
future situation from the activity model for the current situation.

2       Identification of subsystems

We now search for potantial information subsystems in the A-graphs. According to
the problem definition of the case [4] we limit ourselves to A-graphs 51, 52, 53,
and 62. The potential information subsystems found are documented in a preliminary
list of information systems (see left part of figure 3.6).

3       Classification of information subsystems

The identified information subsystems are now classified with regard to their
formalizability, automatibility, and type of processing (see section 3.11 above
and the right part of figure 3.6).

4       Delimitation of information subsystems

The description of activities is elaborated so far that the delimited information
systems occur as delimited activities in the A-graphs. In our case, no further description is necessary, since the existing descriptions in figure 3.1-3.5 are in
sufficient detail for this purpose already.

### 3.32     Study of information subsystems

Each information system is normally studied separately. In our case, we shall
study them somewhat in parallel because of their limited size. We shall restrict
the study to the "IS3" information systems in figure 3.6.

1       Analysis of contributions

The needs for changes from the change analysis (section 2.31 above) that the information systems shall fulfill are:

N5       Facilitate programme committee members work
N6       Facilitate organization committee members work

Figure 3.7 documents a property table with the identified contributions from the
"IS3" information systems to surrounding activities. We see that most contributions are of the type: "Facilitated planning through better information" and
"Quicker invitation through correct addresses". The only exception is information
system F527 Referee work administration with the contribution: "Facilitated planning through proposals about work distributions". The contributions in figure 3.7
can be seen as a first indication of to what degree the needs for changes will be
met by the specified information systems.

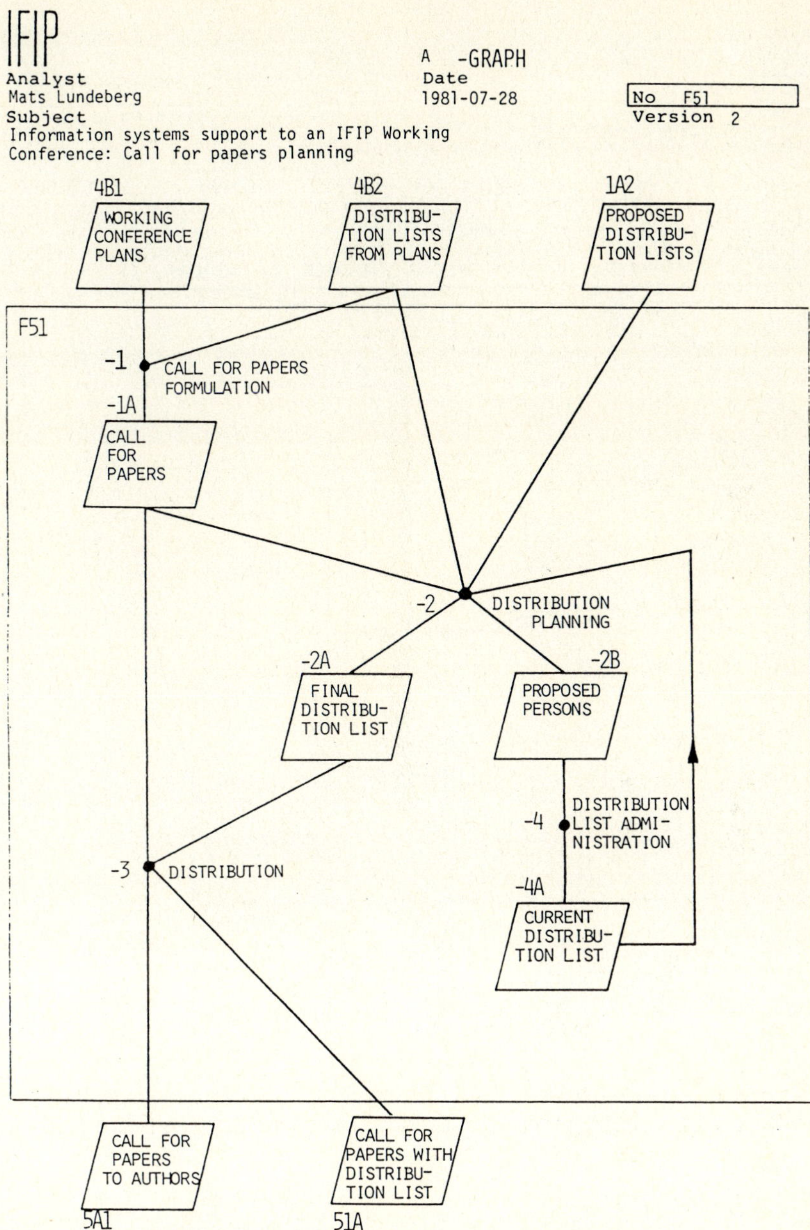


Figure 3.1  A-graph describing call for papers planning

*M. Lundeberg*

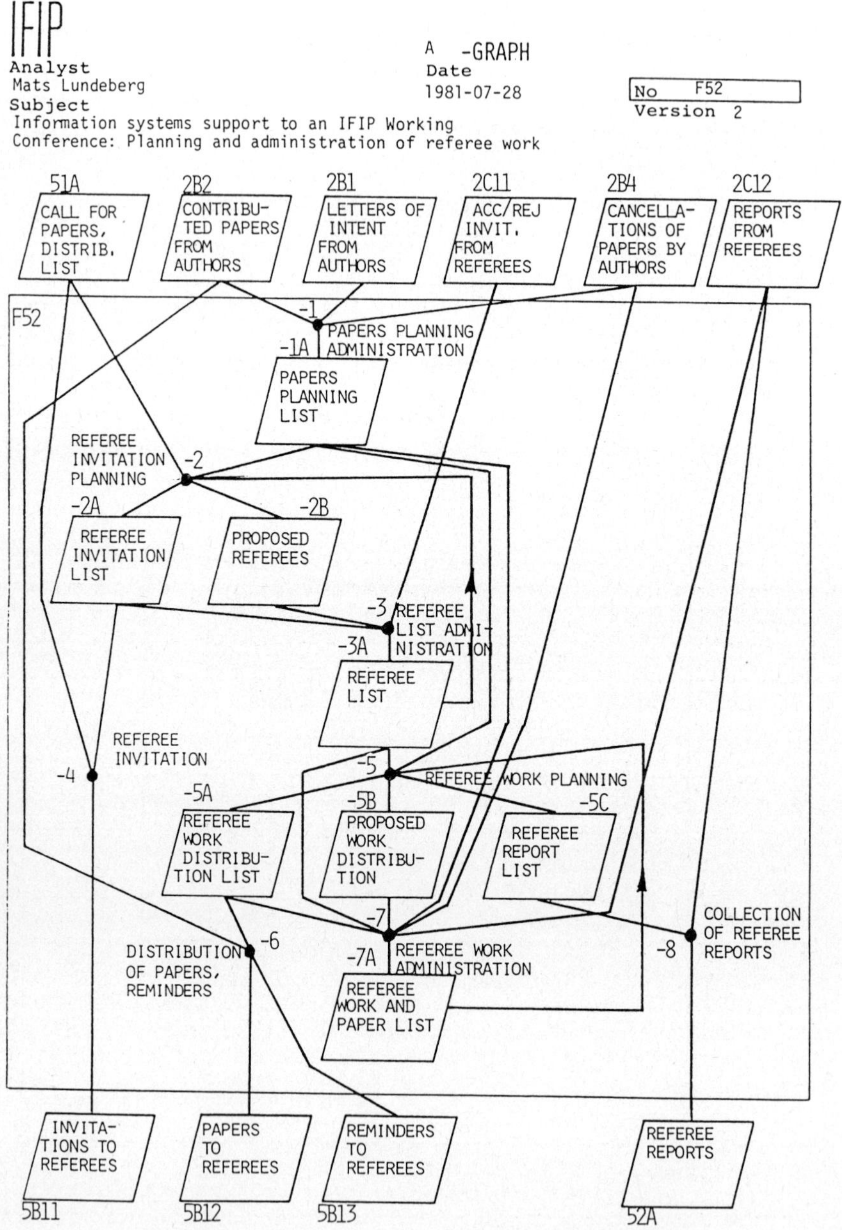


Figure 3.2  A-graph describing planning and administration of referee work

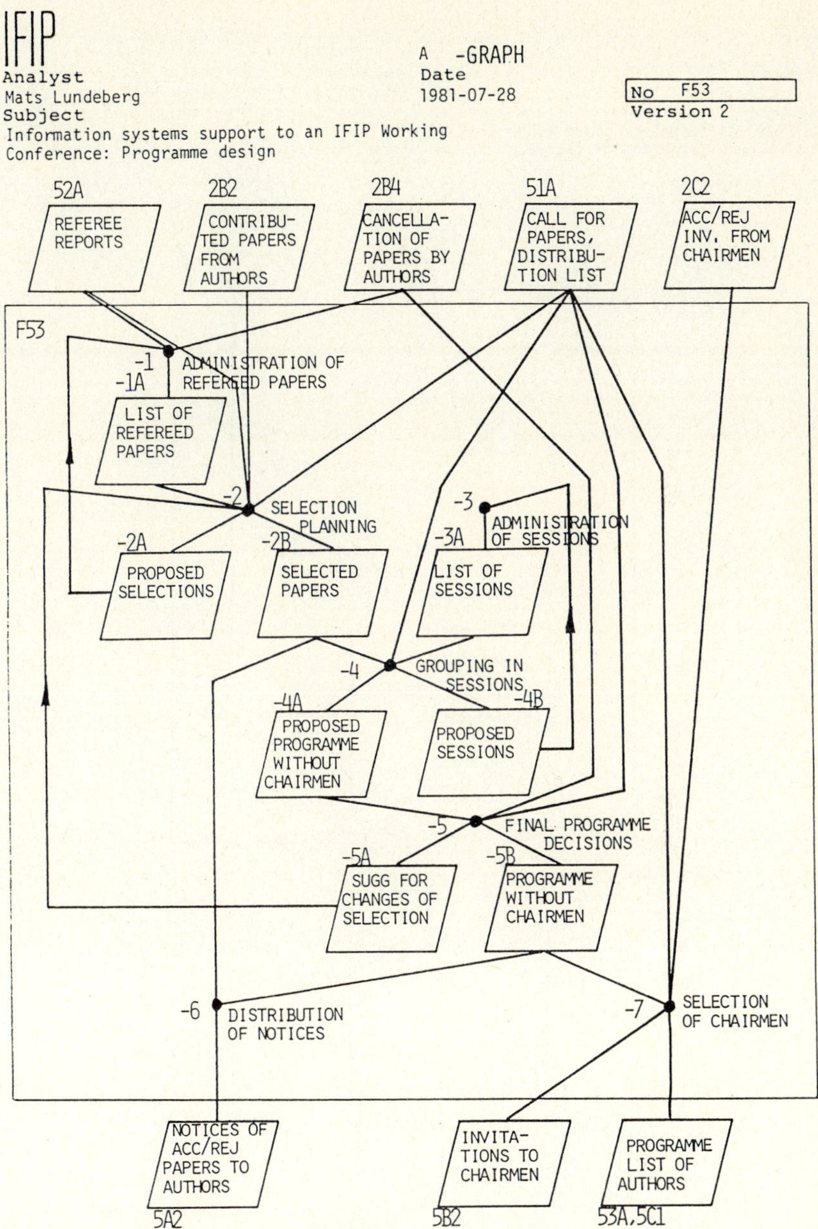


Figure 3.3  A-graph describing programme design

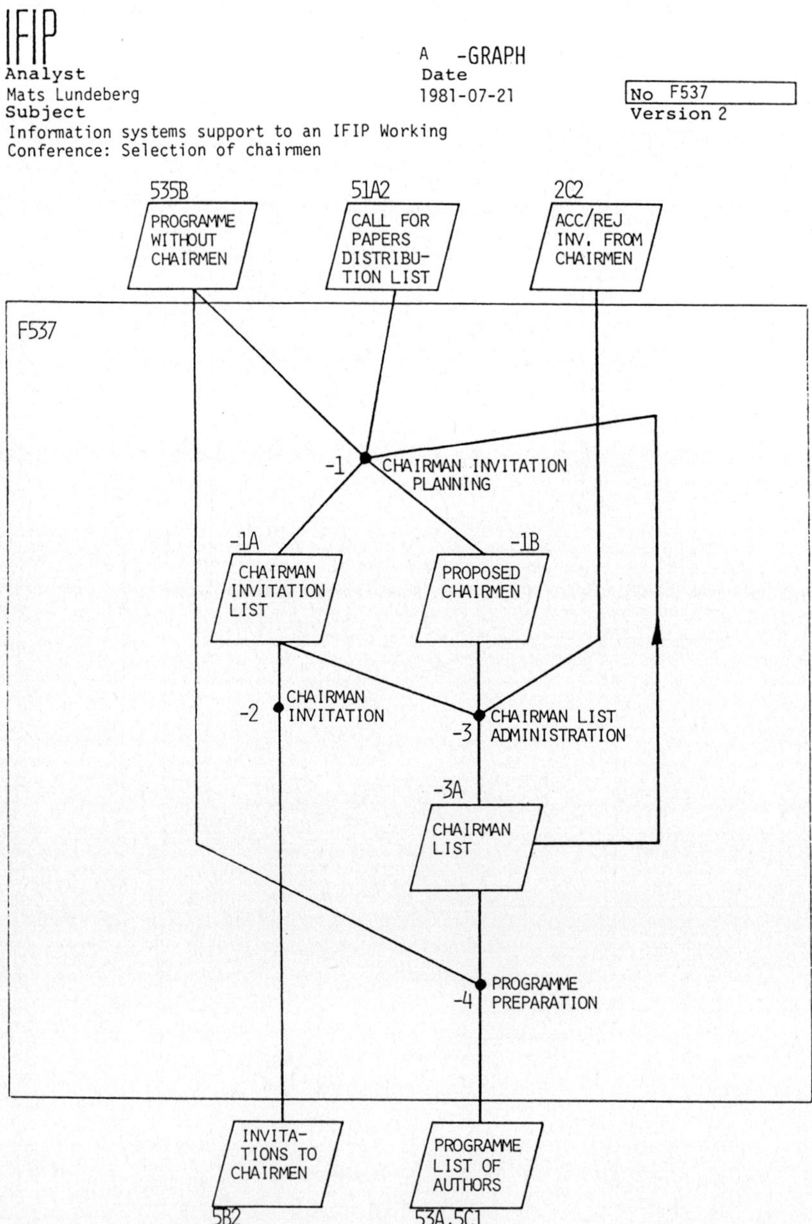


Figure 3.4  A-graph describing selection of chairmen

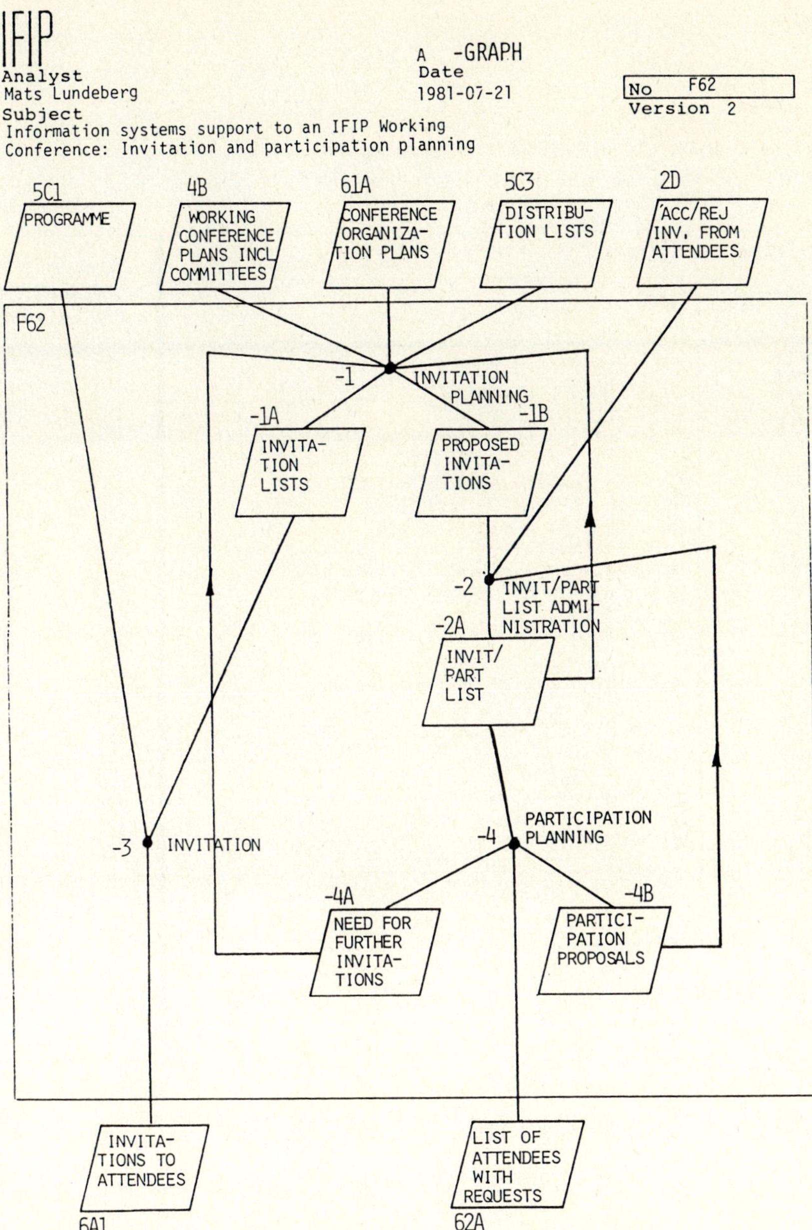


Figure 3.5  A-graphs describing invitation and participation planning

# IFIP

Analyst                                            PROPERTY TABLE
Mats Lundeberg                                     Date
Subject                                            1981-07-28
Information systems support to an IFIP Working
Conference: Classification of information subsystems

| INFORMATION SYSTEMS | | TYPE OF INFORMATION PROCESSING |
| REFERENCE CODE | NAME | |
| --- | --- | --- |
| F511 | CALL FOR PAPERS FORMULATION | IS1 |
| F512 | DISTRIBUTION PLANNING | IS1 |
| F513 | DISTRIBUTION | IS2 |
| F514 | DISTRIBUTION LIST ADMINISTRATION | IS3 |
| F521 | PAPERS PLANNING ADMINISTRATION | IS3 |
| F522 | REFEREE INVITATION PLANNING | IS1 |
| F523 | REFEREE LIST ADMINISTRATION | IS3 |
| F524 | REFEREE INVITATION | IS2 |
| F525 | REFEREE WORK PLANNING | IS1 |
| F526 | DISTRIBUTION OF PAPERS, REMINDERS | IS2 |
| F527 | REFEREE WORK ADMINISTRATION | IS3 |
| F528 | COLLECTION OF REFEREE REPORTS | IS2 |
| F531 | ADMINISTRATION OF REFEREED PAPERS | IS3 |
| F532 | SELECTION PLANNING | IS1 |
| F533 | ADMINISTRATION OF SESSIONS | IS3 |
| F534 | GROUPING IN SESSIONS | IS1 |
| F535 | FINAL PROGRAMME DECISIONS | IS1 |
| F536 | DISTRIBUTION OF NOTICES | IS2 |
| F5371 | CHAIRMAN INVITATION PLANNING | IS1 |
| F5372 | CHAIRMAN INVITATION | IS2 |
| F5373 | CHAIRMAN LIST ADMINISTRATION | IS3 |
| F5374 | PROGRAMME PREPARATION | IS2 |
| F621 | INVITATION PLANNING | IS1 |
| F622 | INVITATION/PARTICIPATION LIST ADMINISTRATION | IS3 |
| F623 | INVITATION | IS2 |
| F624 | PARTICIPATION PLANNING | IS1 |

Figure 3.6   List of information systems with types of information
             processing

IFIP

Analyst
Mats Lundeberg

Subject
Information systems support to an IFIP Working
Conference: Contributions

PROPERTY TABLE
Date
1981-07-28                    Version 2

| INFORMATION SYSTEMS | | CONTRIBUTIONS TO SURROUNDING ACTIVITIES | | |
|---|---|---|---|---|
| REFER-ENCE CODE | NAME | REFER-ENCE CODE | NAME | CONTRIBUTION |
| F514 | DISTRIBUTION LIST ADMINISTRATION | F512 | DISTRIBUTION PLANNING | FACILITATED PLANNING THROUGH ORDERED DISTRIBUTION LISTS |
| | | F513 | DISTRIBUTION | QUICKER DISTRIBUTION THROUGH PRINTED ADDRESSES |
| F521 | PAPERS PLANNING ADMINISTRATION | F522 | REFEREE INVITATION PLANNING | FACILITATED PLANNING THROUGH BETTER INFORMATION ABOUT CONTRIBUTED PAPERS |
| | | F525 | REFEREE WORK PLANNING | FACILITATED PLANNING THROUGH BETTER INFORMATION ABOUT CONTRIBUTED PAPERS |
| F523 | REFEREE LIST ADMINISTRATION | F522 | REFEREE INVITATION PLANNING | FACILITATED PLANNING THROUGH BETTER INFORMATION ABOUT REFEREES |
| | | F524 | REFEREE INVITATION | QUICKER INVITATION THROUGH CORRECT ADDRESSES |
| | | F525 | REFEREE WORK PLANNING | FACILITATED PLANNING THROUGH BETTER INFORMATION ABOUT REFEREES |
| F527 | REFEREE WORK ADMINISTRATION | F525 | REFEREE WORK PLANNING | FACILITATED PLANNING THROUGH PROPOSALS ABOUT WORK DISTRI-BUTIONS |
| | | F526 | DISTRIBUTION OF PAPERS, REMINDERS | QUICKER DISTRIBUTION THROUGH PRINTED ADDRESSES |
| | | F528 | COLLECTION OF REFEREE REPORTS | QUICKER COLLECTION THROUGH ORDERED WORK INFORMATION |
| F531 | ADMINISTRATION REFEREED OF PAPERS | F532 | SELECTION PLANNING | FACILITATED SELECTION THROUGH ORDERED INFORMATION |
| | | F536 | DISTRIBUTION OF NOTICES | QUICKER DISTRIBUTION THROUGH PRINTED ADDRESSES |
| F533 | ADMINISTRATION OF SESSIONS | F534 | GROUPING IN SESSIONS | FACILITATED GROUPING THROUGH ORDERED SESSION INFORMATION |
| F5373 | CHAIRMAN LIST ADMINISTRATION | F5371 | CHAIRMAN INVITATION PLANNING | FACILITATED PLANNING THROUGH BETTER INFORMATION ABOUT CHAIRMEN |
| | | F5372 | CHAIRMAN INVITATION | QUICKER INVITATION THROUGH CORRECT ADDRESSES |
| | | F5374 | PROGRAMME PREPARA-TION | QUICKER PREPARATION THROUGH CORRECT INFORMATION ABOUT CHAIRMEN |
| F622 | INVITATION/PARTI-CIPATION LIST ADMINISTRATION | F621 | INVITATION PLANNING | FACILITATED PLANNING THROUGH ORDERED INVITATION LISTS |
| | | F623 | INVITATION | QUICKER INVITATION THROUGH PRINTED ADDRESSES |
| | | F624 | PARTICIPATION PLANNING | FACILITATED PLANNING THROUGH ORDERED INVITATION LISTS |

Figure 3.7  Property table describing contributions to surrounding activities
            from the information systems

## 2        Generation of alternative levels of ambition

The prerequisites and requirements regarding characteristics such as
- workload
- response time
- frequency
- volume

are very limited. Hence only one ambition level is generated: As simple an ambition level as possible.

## 3        Test of ambition levels

Similar information systems are used in other situations. An explicit test of the
simple ambition level is therefore regarded as unnecessary.

## 4        Cost/benefit analysis

The problem definition of the case lacks sufficient information to make a detailed
cost/benefit analysis.

## 5        Choice of ambition level

We have two possible choices: (i) the simple ambition level or (ii) to discontinue
the information systems specification. Because of the advised focus of the case,
we choose to continue with the simple ambition level.

### 3.33    Coordination of information subsystems

The information systems F521 Papers planning administration and F523 Referee list
administration should be developed before F527 Referee work administration. F531

**IFIP**

Analyst
Mats Lundeberg
Subject
Information systems support to an IFIP Working
Conference: Priorities

PROPERTY TABLE
Date
1981-07-28                        Version 2

| PRIORITY | INFORMATION SYSTEMS | |
|---|---|---|
| | REFER-ENCE CODE | NAME |
| 1 | F514 F622 | DISTRIBUTION LIST ADMINISTRATION<br>INVITATION/PARTICIPATION LIST ADMINISTRATION |
| 2 | F521 F531 | PAPERS PLANNING ADMINISTRATION<br>ADMINISTRATION OF REFEREED PAPERS |
| 3 | F523 F527 | REFEREE LIST ADMINISTRATION<br>REFEREE WORK ADMINISTRATION |
| 4 | F533 F5373 | ADMINISTRATION OF SESSIONS<br>CHAIRMAN LIST ADMINISTRATION |

Figure 3.8  Priorities for information subsystems

Administration of refereed papers should be developed before F533 Administration of sessions. Based on these relations and the relative contributions from the different information subsystems, priorities are proposed in figure 3.8.

3.4    EVALUATION OF THE RESULTS FROM ACTIVITY STUDIES

Before continuing with information analysis, we shall make a short evaluation of the results from the activity studies against the chosen change approach. Are they in line with each other, i.e., are the results from the activity studies workable and realizable?

The chosen change approach is to facilitate programme and organization committee members work by developing computer-based information systems. The activity studies have identified more detailed contributions to the committee work (figure 3.7) well in accordance with the change approach idea. The activity studies have further indicated that such computer-based information systems are possible to realize (section 3.32). The decision is therefore taken to continue with the information analysis.

4       INFORMATION ANALYSIS

4.1    METHOD STEPS USED IN INFORMATION ANALYSIS

The different steps during information analysis (I) are:

I1      Precedence and component analyses
I2      Process analysis
I3      Property analysis

Precedence and component analyses precede process analysis, and property analysis is performed in parallel with these other steps. Of course, iterations may occur, exactly as in activity studies.

4.11    Precedence and component analyses

Precedence analysis involves the analysis of the information precedence relations in an information system. Here the information sets that are needed in order to derive a certain information set are analyzed. Component analysis involves the analysis of the structure of information sets. Here the message types (identification and property terms) that an information set is described by are analyzed. The following steps are used:

1       Transition from activity studies

The purpose and the extent of information analysis depend on the classification of the information subsystems made during the activity studies. If the information systems are automatable, information analysis must be performed. For nonautomatable information subsystems, the extent depends on the additional work and therefore varies from case to case.

The first step in information analysis is to decide on the suitable extent of the information analysis. This is documented in an information analysis planning table. The description of methods in information analysis given below is aimed at automatable information subsystems with calculations. For other types, only parts of these methods are used.

The following steps are performed for each subsystem:

T1      Extract input and output information sets from the A-graph of the subsystem and put these in a first outline of an overview I-graph (information precedence graph; the description technique for I-graphs will be described in section 4.2).

T2    Study the text pages of the A-graphs in order to start making a more pre-
      cise description of the input and output information sets.

T3    Refine the outline of the overview I-graph by means of precedence analysis
      (which will be described below). There will be one overview I-graph for
      each subsystem. These are distinguished by different prefixes (one or two
      letters) before the reference codes.

The continued precedence and component analyses are performed alternatingly. We
recommend starting with the component analysis of the output information sets in
order to obtain a better basis for the precedence analysis. We shall however start
our description with precedence analysis here.

2       Continued precedence analysis

Precedence analysis simply means analysis of information precedence relations.
These relations are documented in I-graphs and text pages. The documentation of
precedence analysis is hierarchical (just as in activity studies) and starts with
overview descriptions, which are elaborated and detailed successively.

The steps of precedence analysis for one level (I-graph) are:

P1    Start to identify the output information sets. These are found on the level
      above.

P2    Make a partitioning in information subsets if necessary (this corresponds
      to the first step of component analysis, see below).

P3    Analyze the precedents for each information set

P4    Repeat P3 until you reach the input sets.

During the precedence analysis the information processes in the information system
are disregarded because working with only one thing at the time simplifies the
analysis work.

3       Continued component analysis

In component analysis the structure of the information sets is studied. The component analysis is documented in C-graphs or in lists of components. The description
technique for C-graphs will be described in section 4.2. Component analysis is
performed in the following steps:

C1    Make a suitable partitioning of the information set in subsets.

C2    List all terms that should be in a message of the information set. One
      possibility is to draw a visual layout that shows the information contents
      but not the physical layout.

C3    Analyze the property terms and the identification terms to which they are
      related.

C4    Document the result in a C-graph.

## 4.12    Process analysis

Process analysis means making a detailed description of the information processes
in the information system. During the precedence analysis we disregarded processes.
The nodes of the I-graphs represent information precedence relations. We now take
information processes into account. The following method steps are used:

1       Identification of processes

The information processes are identified and documented in a list of processes.
The reference codes from the I-graphs are used. The processes are then named. When
several information sets have the same precedents, it may be suitable to divide

a precedence relation into several processes.

2        Detailed description of processes

Each process can now be described separately. The description is documented in process tables (decision tables) which consist of two parts: prerequisites and calculations. (Other description techniques such as Nassi-Schneidermann graphs can also be used). In the first part the prerequisites for the performance of the process are described. In the second part the conditions for alternative calculations and calculation rules are described. Here is described how the identification and property terms of the output information sets are derived from corresponding terms in the input information sets. It is not necessary to refer to other processes, since the relations between the processes are defined via the C-graphs.

4.13    Property analysis

The descriptions resulting from precedence and component analyses are structural descriptions. We also need property descriptions during the information analysis. The property analysis is a continuation of the property descriptions already made during change analysis and activity studies. The relevant property values are documented in property tables. We distinguish between quantitative and qualitative property analysis.

4.2    DESCRIPTION TECHNIQUES USED IN INFORMATION ANALYSIS

4.21    I-graphs

An I-graph or an information precedence graph is a picture of some part of the information system. An explanation of the different symbols used in I-graphs is given in figure 4.1. The number of symbols is small. In principle, I-graphs describe information sets and precedence relations among information sets. Figure 4.1 illustrates two special cases in addition to this: description of permanent information sets and of fictitious precedence relations. I-graphs are more precise than are A-graphs, which only show input and output sets without describing how these are related to each other. A permanent information set is an information set that exists in different generations in the same graph. These information sets have the same structure, but the information contents are from different points in time. When two information sets are identical and related it is shown by a fictitious precedence relation. The use of parentheses without reference codes indicates that a precedence relation is fictitious. The need to illustrate two identical information sets in the same graph is a consequence of the hierarchical way of description. Two sets are needed when one information set is an output set of a certain graph and at the same time a precedent to other information sets in the same graph. I-graphs are hierarchical in the same way as A-graphs are. The rules for the reference codes are similar to the rules for the reference codes of A-graphs (see section 2.21).

4.22    C-graphs

A C-graph or a component relation graph describes the contents and structure of an information set. An information set consists of a number of messages of the same type. A message consists of a message type and a value part. The message type is described by its terms: identification terms in the identification part and property terms in the property part. The purpose of the identification part of a message type is to identify an object/phenomenon and the purpose of the property part is to characterize this object/phenomenon. A message must consist of both an identification part and a property part; otherwise it contains no information. Figure 4.2 explains the symbols used in C-graphs. In a C-graph an information set is given an information set name followed by corresponding identification terms within parenteses. Composite information sets which have information subsets with different identification terms are not given identification terms on the highest

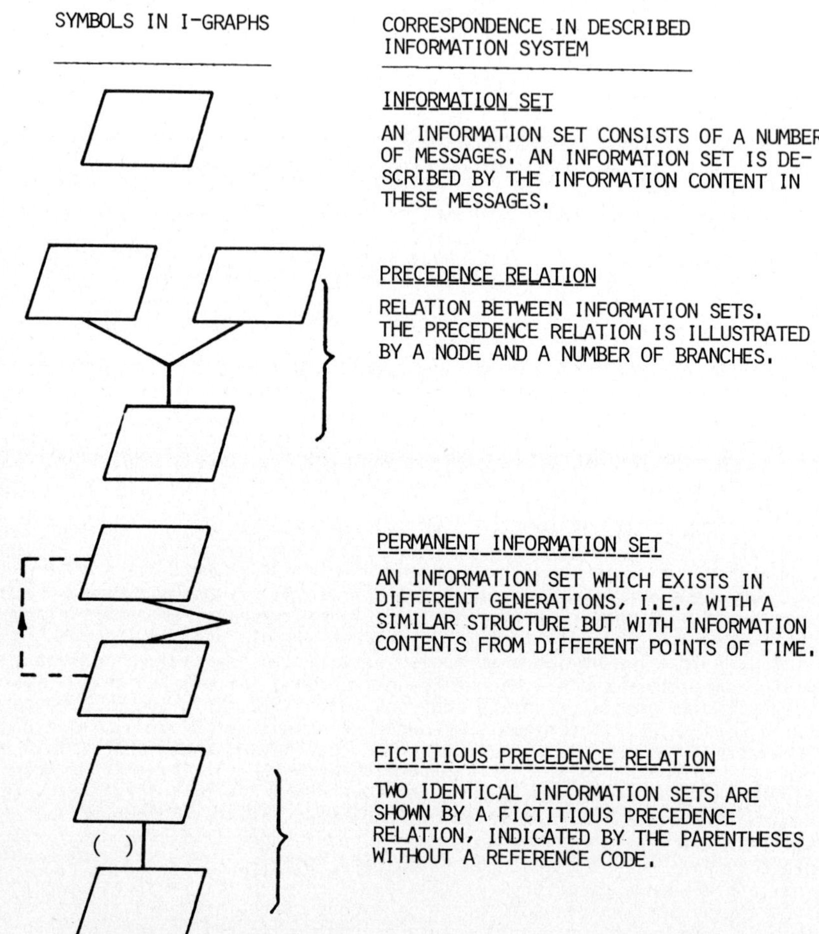


Figure 4.1  Explanation of symbols used in I-graphs

SYMBOLS IN C-GRAPHS

CORRESPONDENCE IN DESCRIBED
INFORMATION SYSTEM

INFORMATION SET

INFORMATION SET OR INFORMATION SUBSET.
IT IS GIVEN AN INFORMATION SET NAME
FOLLOWED BY AN IDENTIFICATION TERM IN
PARENTHESES. A TERM CAN CONSIST OF
SEVERAL SUBTERMS. AN INFORMATION SUBSET
IS IDENTIFIED BY THE IDENTIFICATION
TERM WITHIN PARENTHESES AND BY THE
IDENTIFICATION TERMS "HIGHER" UP IN
THE TREE STRUCTURE OF THE C-GRAPH.

(ID-TERM 1, ID-TERM 2*)

ITERATION

REPETITION OF SEVERAL MESSAGES WITH THE
SAME IDENTIFICATION OR PROPERTY TERM
BUT WITH DIFFERENT VALUES OF THIS TERM.
THE ASTERISK (*) INDICATES THE TERM THAT
HAS REPEATED OCCURENCES.

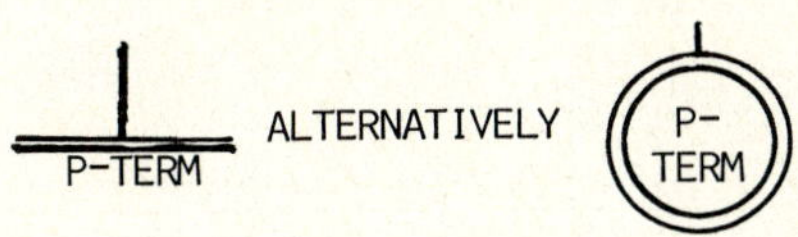


ELEMENTARY INFORMATION SET

AN INFORMATION SET WITH ONLY ONE PROPERTY
TERM. THE IDENTIFICATION TERMS ARE GIVEN
BY INFORMATION SETS "HIGHER" UP IN THE
STRUCTURE.

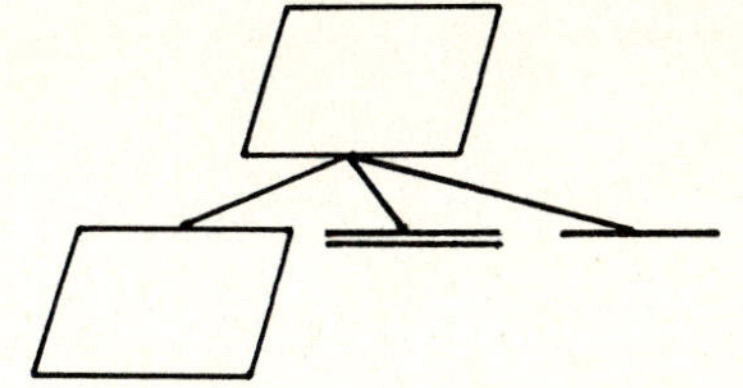


ALMOST ELEMENTARY INFORMATION SET

AN INFORMATION SET THAT CONSISTS OF A
NUMBER OF ELEMENTARY INFORMATION SETS
WITH COMMON IDENTIFICATION TERMS. IDENTI-
FICATION TERMS ARE GIVEN BY INFORMATION
SETS "HIGHER" UP IN THE STRUCTURE.

COMPONENT RELATION

DIVISION OF INFORMATION SET IN INFORMA-
TION SUBSETS. OTHER TYPES OF COMPONENT
RELATIONS (THE MESSAGE TYPES OF INFORMA-
TION SETS AND THE TERMS OF MESSAGE TYPES)
ARE INDICATED IMPLICITLY IN THE C-GRAPH.

Figure 4.2   Explanation of symbols used in C-graphs

level. An information subset is identified by the identification terms within
parentheses _and_ by the identification terms "higher" up in the tree structure of
the C-graph. Asterisks (*) are used in C-graphs to indicate the repetition of messages having the same message type. The asterisk is put after the term whose value
varies in the different messages.

An elementary information set consists of messages that have only one property
term (apart from necessary identification terms). An almost elementary information
set consists of a number of similar elementary information sets that have common
identification terms. Elementary and almost elementary information sets are indicated with one and two lines, respectively, in C-graphs. Component relations (relations between the parts of information sets) are illustrated explicitly. The other
types of component relations (the message types of information sets and the terms
of message types) are illustrated implicitly in the C-graph.

## 4.3     INFORMATION ANALYSIS OF INFORMATION SYSTEMS SUPPORT TO AN IFIP WORKING CONFERENCE

Information analysis is normally performed for each subsystem separately. For
reasons of presentation, we will have a mixture of separate and parallel information analysis of the information subsystems in this report.

### 4.31    Precedence and component analyses

The first step of information analysis is to decide on a suitable extent of the
information analysis. This is documented in an information analysis planning table,
see figure 4.3. We then continue with precedence and component analysis for each
subsystem separately.

### F514    Distribution list administration

The transition from activity studies is performed in the following steps:

T1      From A-graph F51 (figure 3.1) it follows that the input set is "Proposed
        persons" and the output set "Current distribution list".

T2      The output sets should consist of address lists, country distribution lists
        and total distribution lists. The input sets should contain information
        about new persons, about persons to be deleted and about changed informa-
        tion.

T3      An overview I-graph DLO is drawn in figure 4.4 by means of precedence
        analysis.

No continued precedence analysis is necessary (confer with the information analysis planning table in figure 4.3).

The continued component analysis for DL7A Total distribution list is performed in
the following steps:

C1      Total distribution list is subdivided into person information and summary
        distribution information.

C2      Person information should consist of the terms person, title, address,
        membership, country, and distribution date. Summary distribution informa-
        tion should consist of the terms conference, no. of national representa-
        tives, no. of working group members, no. of members of associate working
        groups, no. of priority persons and total no. of listed persons.

C3      In person information person is the identification term and the rest are
        property terms related to person. In summary distribution information con-
        ference is the identification term and the rest are property terms related
        to conference.

```
IFIP
Analyst                                    PLANNING TABLE
Mats Lundeberg                             Date
Subject                                    1981-07-28
Information systems support to an IFIP Working
Conference
```

| INFORMATION SYSTEM | | EXTENT OF INFORMATION ANALYSIS |
|---|---|---|
| REFERENCE CODE IN A-GRAPHS | NAME | |
| F514 | DISTRIBUTION LIST ADMINISTRATION | CRUDE PRECEDENCE ANALYSIS<br>COMPONENT ANALYSIS |
| F521 | PAPERS PLANNING ADMINISTRATION | CRUDE PRECEDENCE ANALYSIS<br>COMPONENT ANALYSIS |
| F523 | REFEREE LIST ADMINISTRATION | CRUDE PRECEDENCE ANALYSIS<br>COMPONENT ANALYSIS |
| F527 | REFEREE WORK ADMINISTRATION | PRECEDENCE ANALYSIS<br>COMPONENT ANALYSIS<br>PROCESS ANALYSIS |
| F531 | ADMINISTRATION OF REFEREED PAPERS | CRUDE PRECEDENCE ANALYSIS<br>COMPONENT ANALYSIS |
| F533 | ADMINISTRATION OF SESSIONS | CRUDE PRECEDENCE ANALYSIS<br>COMPONENT ANALYSIS |
| F5373 | CHAIRMAN LIST ADMINISTRATION | CRUDE PRECEDENCE ANALYSIS<br>COMPONENT ANALYSIS |
| F622 | INVITATION/PARTICIPATION LIST ADMINISTRATION | CRUDE PRECEDENCE ANALYSIS<br>COMPONENT ANALYSIS |

Figure 4.3   Information analysis planning table


C4      The result is documented in a C-graph in figure 4.5.

The rest of the information sets of distribution list administration follow directly in a similar manner.

### F622    Invitation/participation list administration

The overview I-graph IPO will have a similar structure as DLO in figure 4.4 and is
therefore not repeated here. The main difference is IP6A which apart from address
lists (IP6A1) also will contain status lists (IP6A2) and therefore is named address
and status lists. The C-graphs of invitation/participation list administration are
documented in figure 4.6.

### F521    Papers planning administration

The overview I-graph PPO is documented in figure 4.7. Corresponding C-graph is
found in figure 4.8.

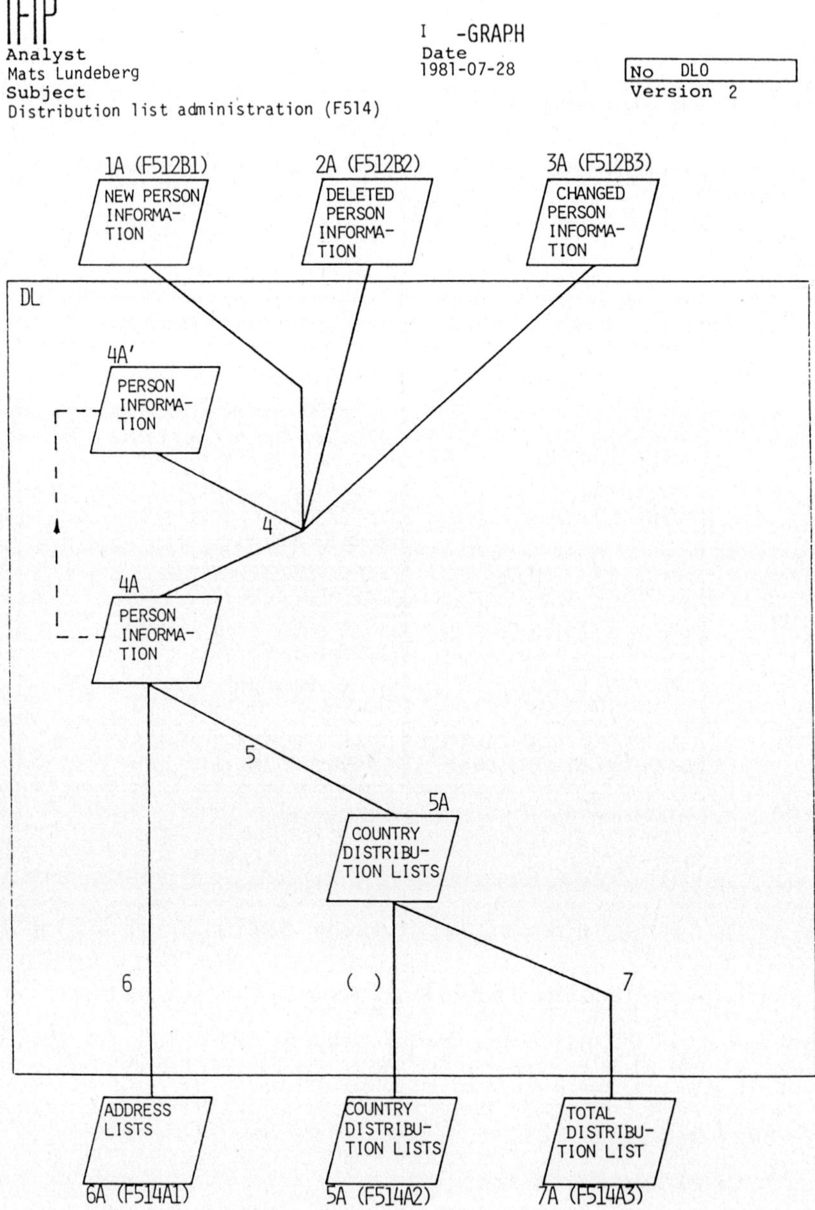


Figure 4.4  I-graph DLO

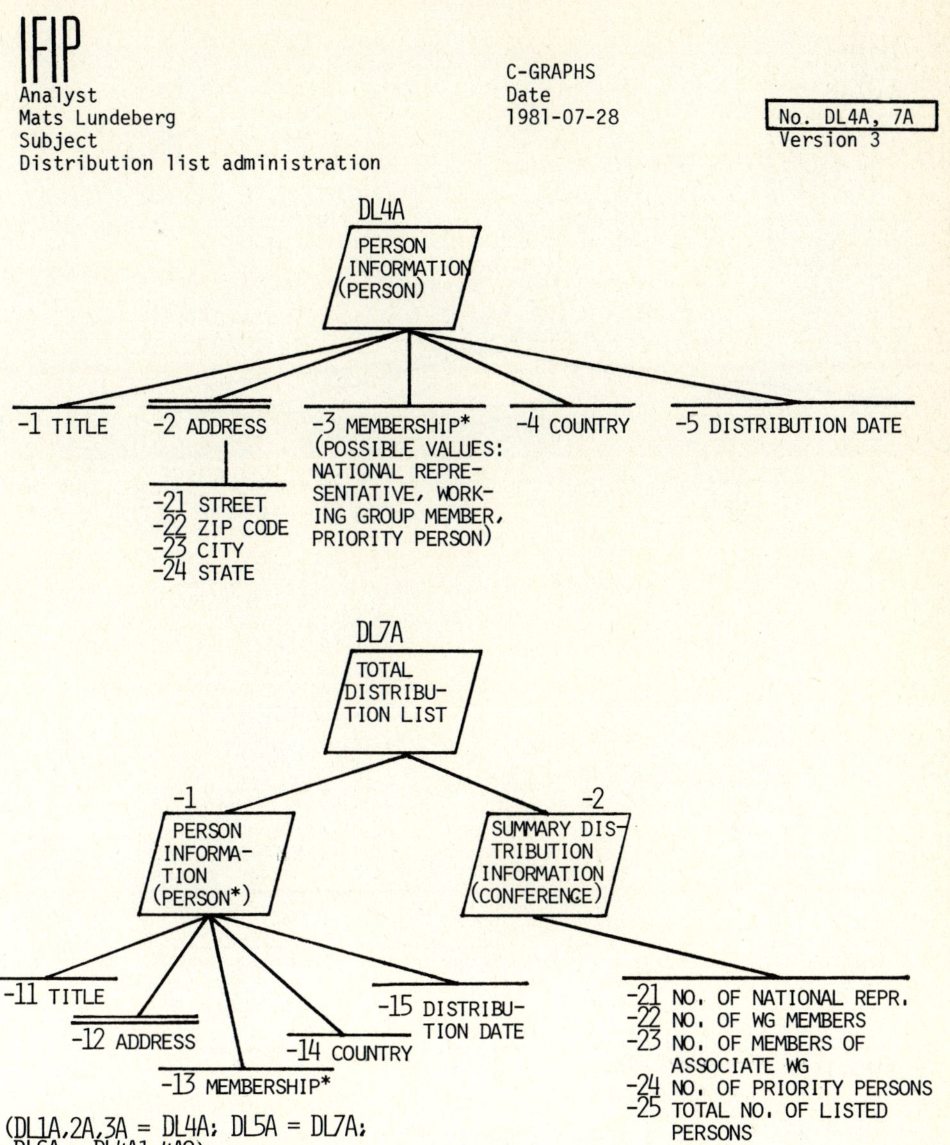


Figur 4.5  C-graphs for distribution list administration (DL4A,7A)

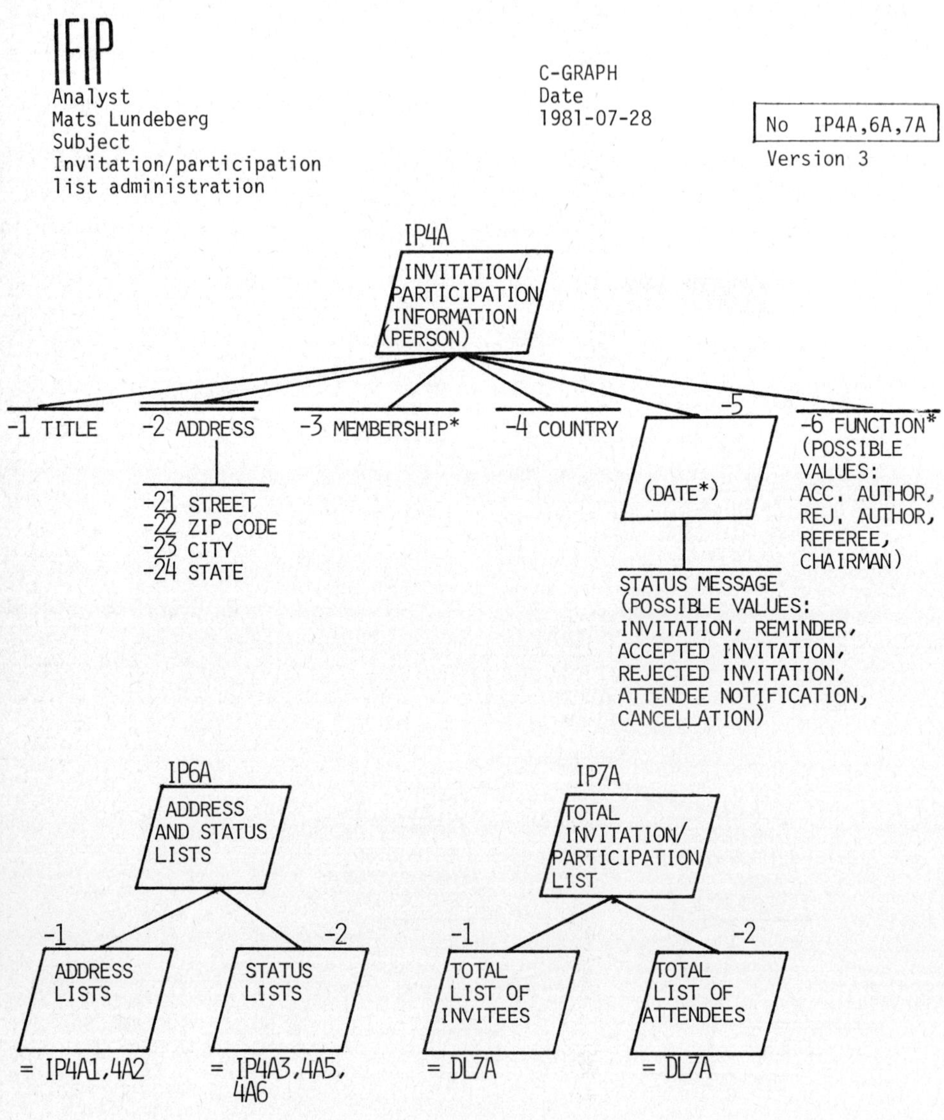


Figure 4.6   C-graphs for invitation/participation list administration
(IP4A,6A,7A)

### F531    Administration_of_refereed_papers

The overview I-graph APO will have a similar structure as PPO in figure 4.7 and is therefore not repeated here. Corresponding C-graph AP4A is found in figure 4.9.

### F523    Referee_list_administration

The overview I-graph RLO is documented in figure 4.10. Corresponding C-graph is found in figure 4.11.

### F527    Referee_work_administration

The overview I-graph RWO is documented in figure 4.12. A detailed I-graph RW7 is documented in figure 4.13. Corresponding C-graphs are found in figure 4.14.

### F533    Administration_of_sessions

The overview I-graph ASO is found in figure 4.15. Corresponding C-graph is documented in figure 4.16.

### F5373  Chairman_list_administration

The overview I-graph CLO will have a similar structure as RLO in figure 4.10 and is therefore not repeated here. Corresponding C-graph CL4A is found in figure 4.17.

### 4.32   Process_analysis

According to the planning table in figure 4.3, process analysis will only be performed for the subsystem Referee work administration. The processes for the other subsystems are regardes as well-defined through the precedence and component analyses.

### F527    Referee_work_administration

1       Identification of processes

The information processes are identified and documented in a list of processes in figure 4.18.

2       Detailed description of processes

Figure 4.19 illustrates process tables for processes RW73 and RW75. The other processes are regarded as well-defined through the precedence and component analysis.

### 4.33   Property_analysis

The property analysis in information analysis is a continuation of the property analysis already initiated in change analysis and activity studies. Due to the limited problem definition of the case, no further property tables are made here.

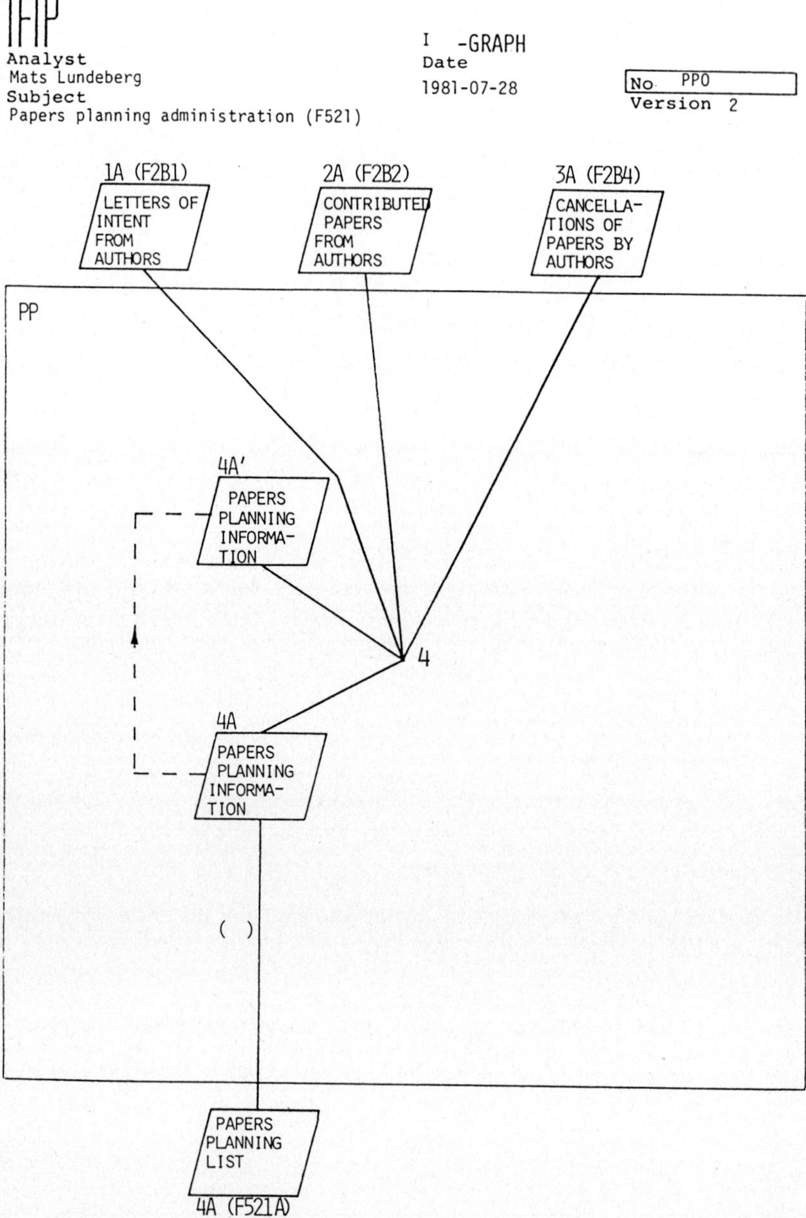


Figure 4.7  I-graph PPO

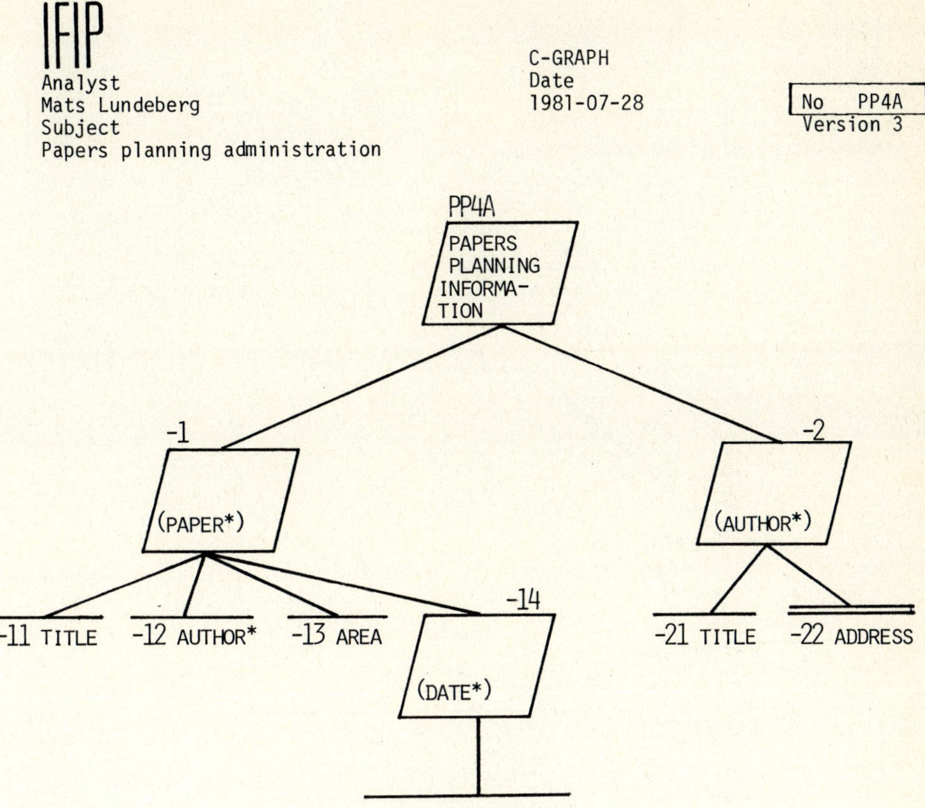


Figure 4.8   C-graph for papers planning administration (PP4A)

IFIP

Analyst
Mats Lundeberg
Subject
Administration of refereed papers

C-GRAPH
Date
1981-07-28

No AP4A

Version 3

(AP1A = AP4A EXCEPT AP4A15; AP2A = AP4A15; AP3A = AP4A15)

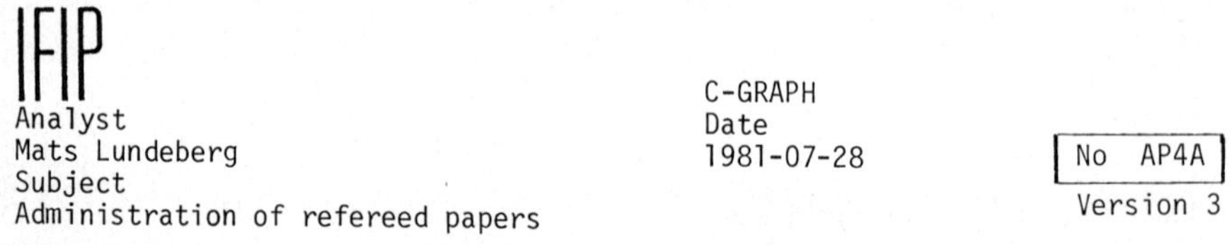

Figure 4.9 C-graph for administration of refereed papers (AP4A)

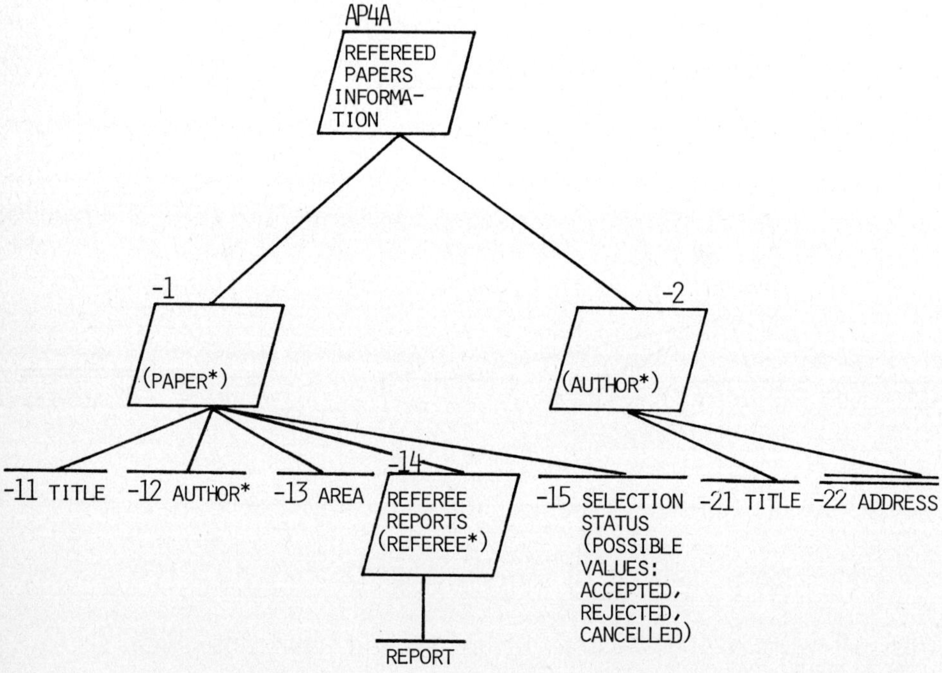

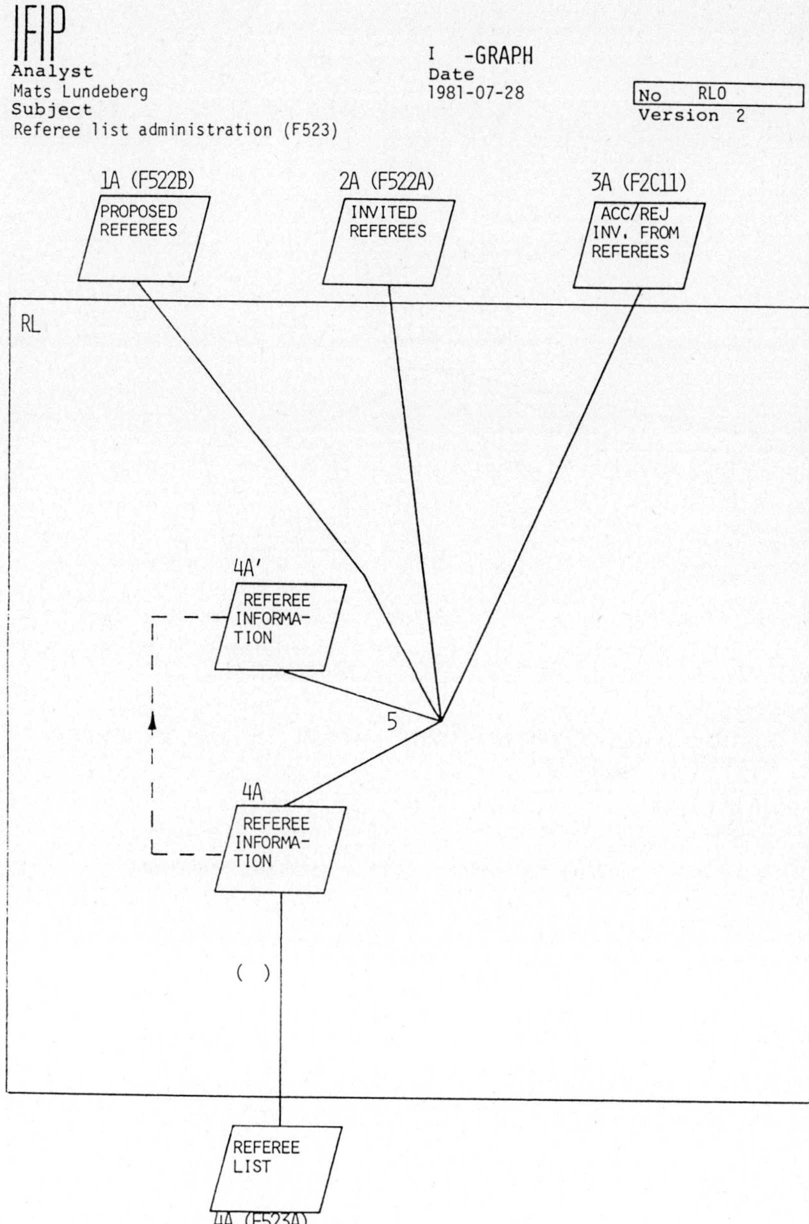


Figure 4.10   I-graph RLO

# IFIP

Analyst
Mats Lundeberg
Subject
Referee list administration

C-GRAPH
Date
1981-07-28

No   RL4A
Version 3

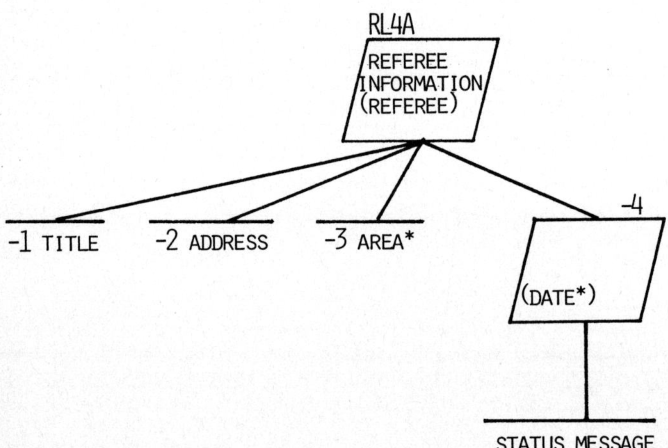


(POSSIBLE VALUES OF STATUS MESSAGE: PROPOSAL, INVITATION, REMINDER, ACCEPTANCE, REJECTION)

(RL1A = RL4A;      RL2A = RL4A4; RL3A = RL4A4)

Figure 4.11  C-graph for referee list administration (RL4A)

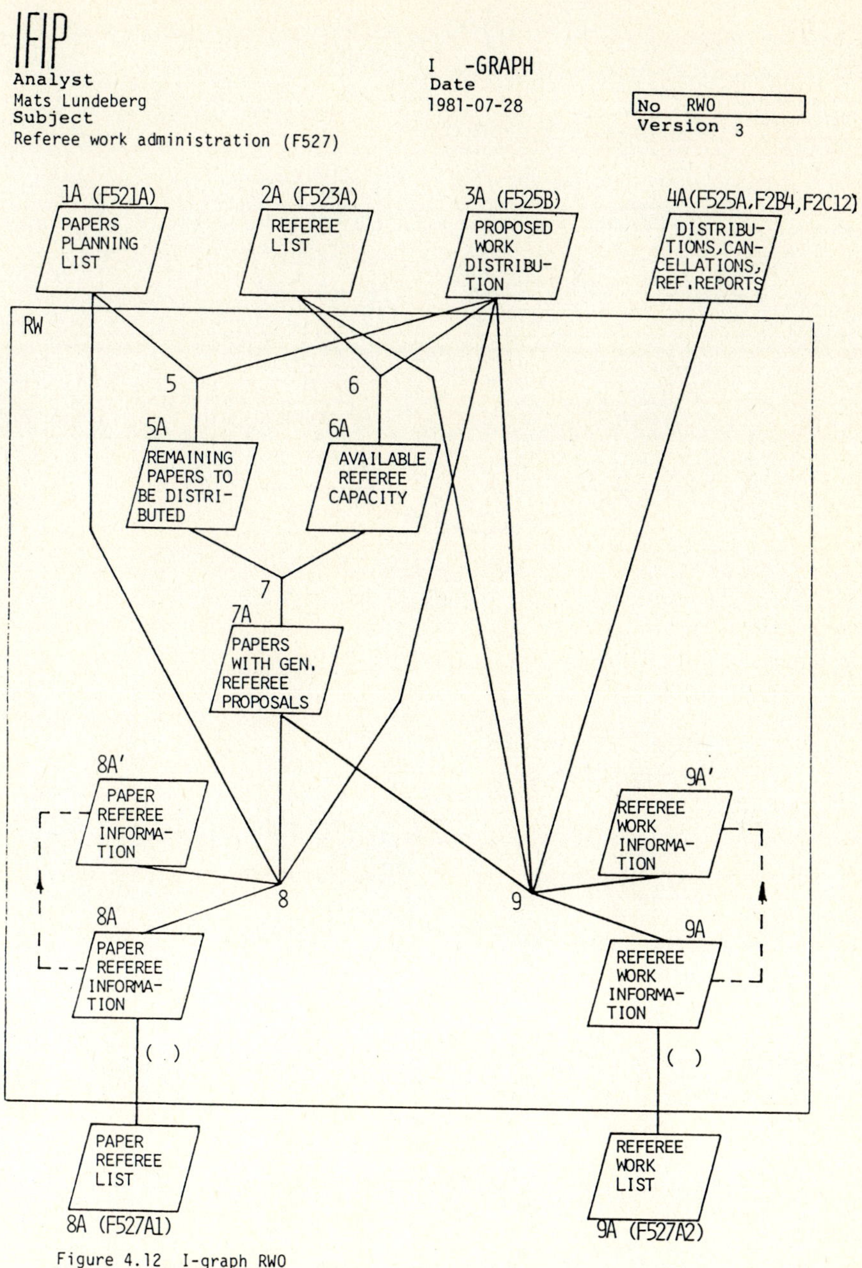


Figure 4.12  I-graph RWO

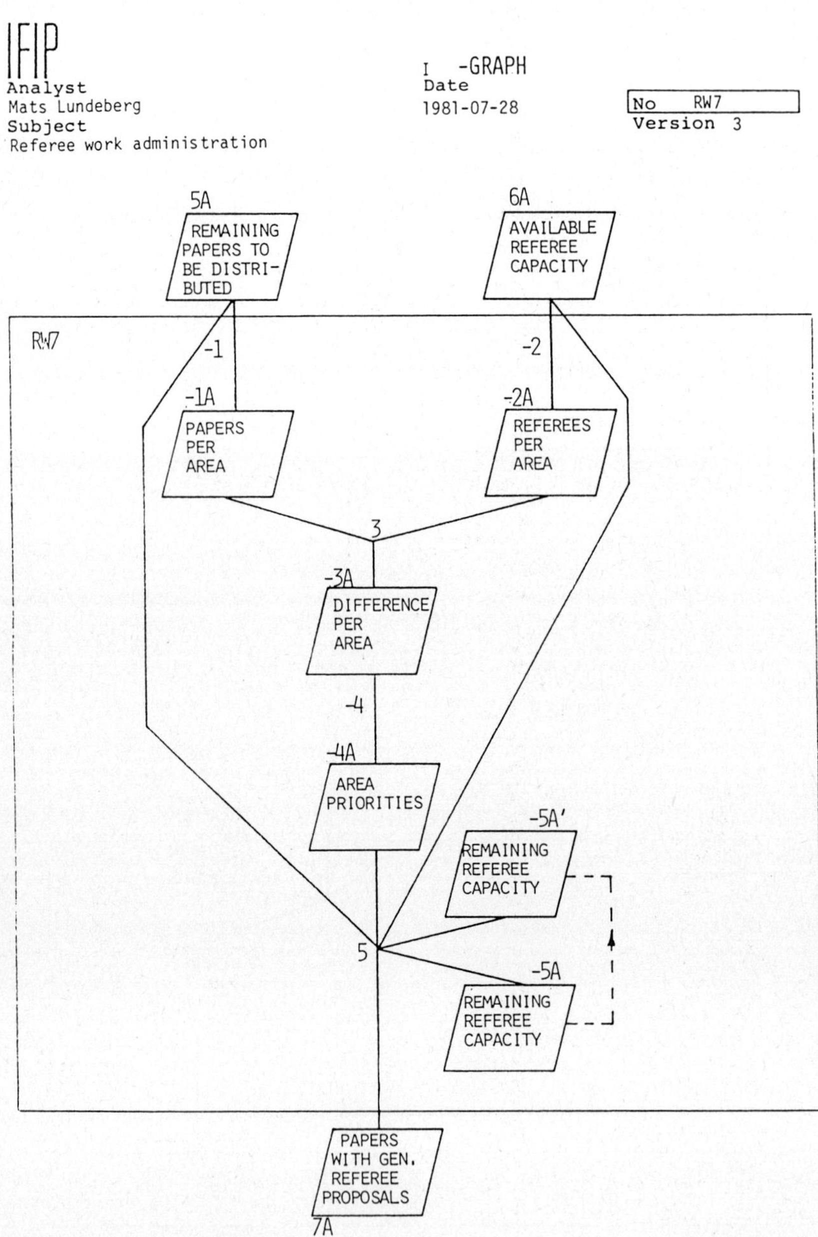


Figure 4.13   I-graph RW7

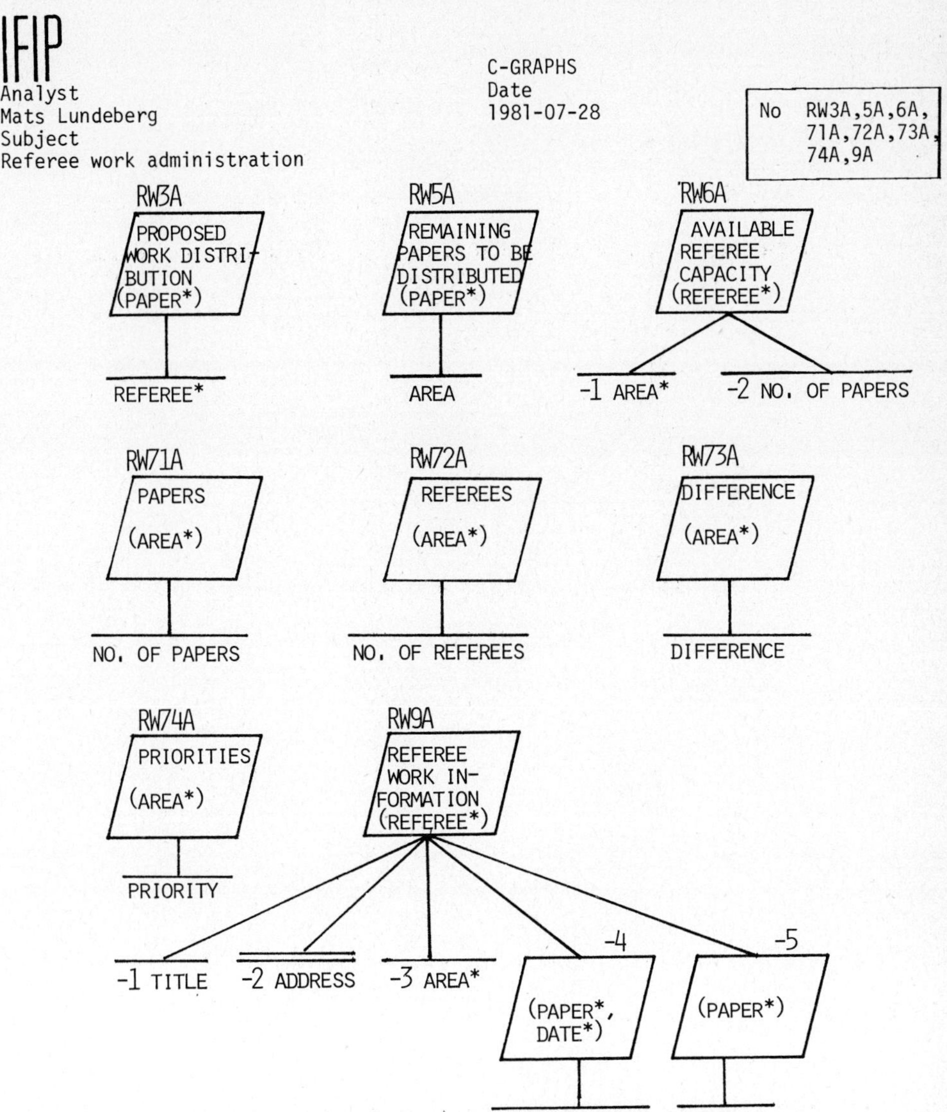


Figure 4.14   C-graphs for referee work administration (RW3A,5A,6A,71A, 72A,73A,74A,9A)

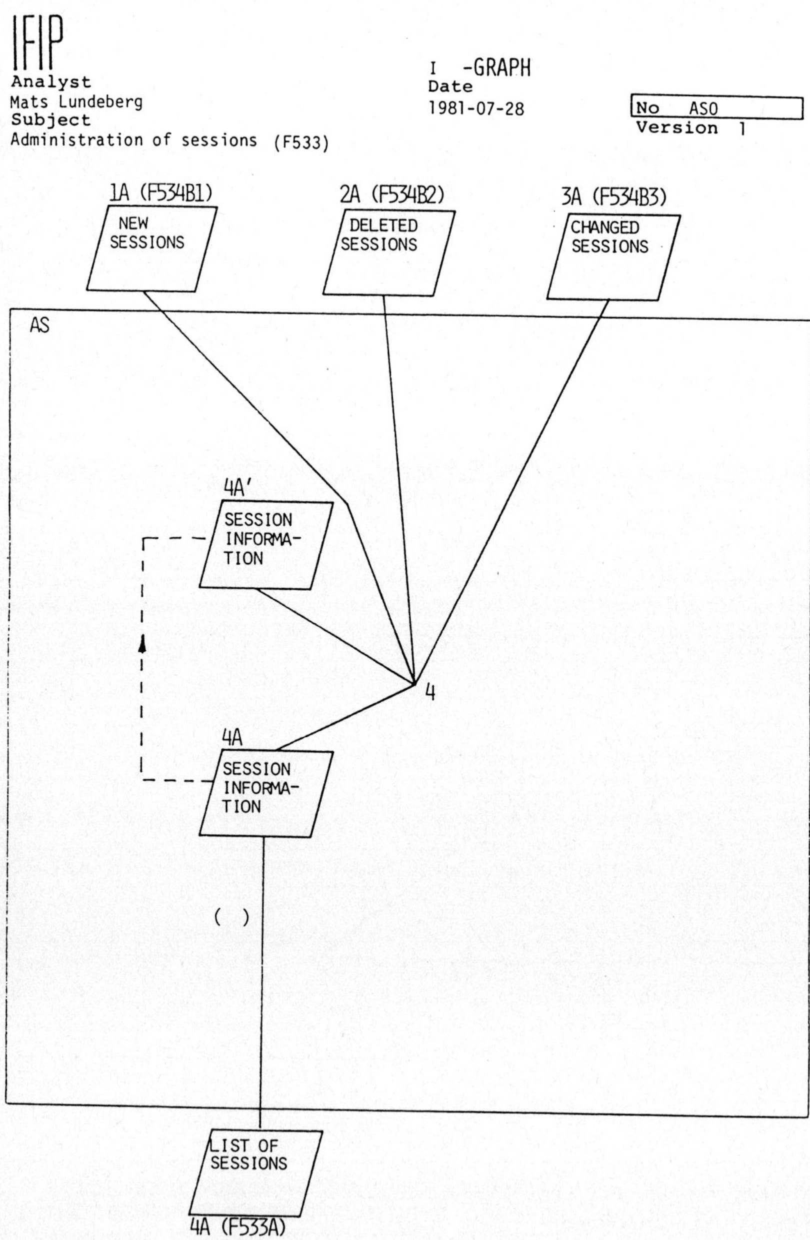


Figure 4.15   I-graph ASO

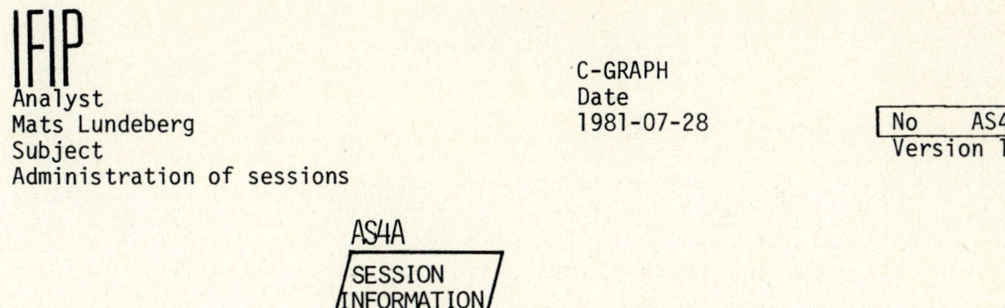


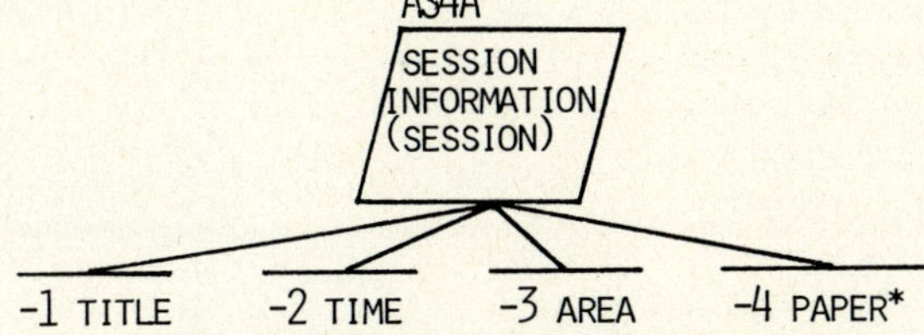


(AS1A = AS4A; AS2A = AS4A2; AS3A = AS4A)

Figur 4.16   C-graph for administration of sessions (AS4A)

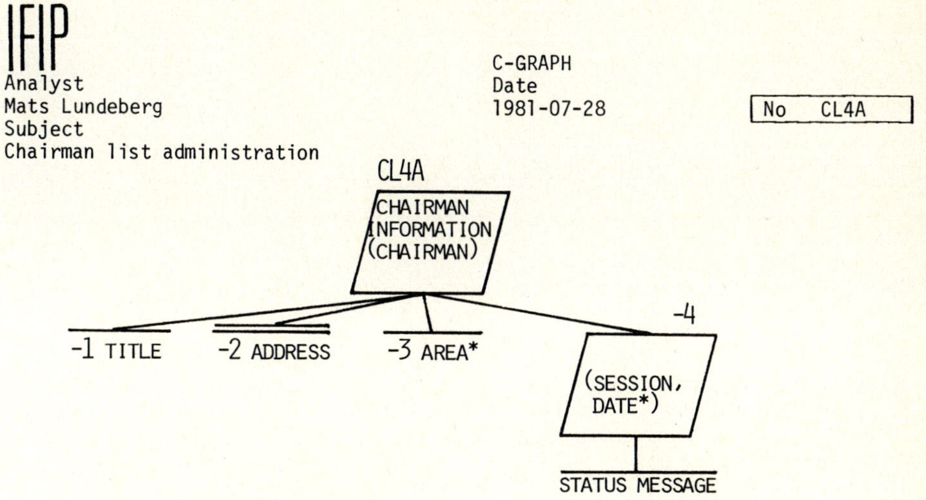


(POSSIBLE VALUES OF STATUS MESSAGE: PROPOSAL, INVITATION, ACCEPTANCE, REJECTION, REMINDER)

(CL1A = CL4A; CL2A = CL4A4; CL3A = CL4A4)

Figure 4.17   C-graph for chairman list administration (CL4A)

**IFIP**

Analyst                                          LIST OF PROCESSES
Mats Lundeberg                                   Date
Subject                                          1981-07-28                    Version 1
Referee work administration

| REFERENCE CODE | NAME |
|---|---|
| RW5 | DERIVATION OF REMAINING PAPERS TO BE DISTRIBUTED |
| RW6 | CALCULATION OF AVAILABLE REFEREE CAPACITY |
| RW71 | CALCULATION OF PAPERS PER AREA |
| RW72 | CALCULATION OF REFEREES PER AREA |
| RW73 | CALCULATION OF DIFFERENCE PER AREA |
| RW74 | CALCULATION OF AREA PRIORITIES |
| RW75 | GENERATION OF REFEREE PROPOSALS FOR PAPERS |
| RW8 | COLLECTION OF PAPER REFEREE INFORMATION |
| RW9 | COLLECTION OF REFEREE WORK INFORMATION |

Figure 4.18  List of processes for Referee work administration

**IFIP**

Analyst                                          PROCESS TABLES
Mats Lundeberg                                   Date
Subject                                          1981-07-28          No   RW73,75
Referee work administration                                          Version 2

PROCESS RW73

| PREREQUISITES |
|---|
| FIND MESSAGE IN 71A FOR ONE AREA |
| FIND MESSAGE IN 72A FOR THE SAME AREA |

| CALCULATIONS |
|---|
| AREA (73A) := AREA (71A) |
| DIFFERENCE (73A) := NO. OF REFEREES (72A) - NO. OF PAPERS (71A) |

PROCESS RW75

| PREREQUISITES |
|---|
| FIND AREA WITH THE HIGHEST PRIORITY IN 74A |
| FIND PAPER MESSAGE IN 5A FOR THIS AREA |
| FIND THREE POSSIBLE MESSAGES OF DIFFERENT REFEREES IN 6A AND 75A' FOR THIS AREA WITH REMAINING REFEREE CAPACITY >0 AND PERFORM THE CALCULATIONS PART THREE TIMES |

| CALCULATIONS | | |
|---|---|---|
| IS THERE A POSSIBLE REFEREE IN 6A AND 75A'? | N | Y |
| PAPER (7A) := PAPER (5A) | X | X |
| REFEREE (7A) := 'UNAVAILABLE' | X | |
| REFEREE (7A, 75A) := REFEREE (6A) | | X |
| NO. OF PAPERS (75A) := MIN {NO. OF PAPERS (6A, 75A')} -1 | | X |

Figure 4.19  Process tables RW73 and RW75

## 4.34　Evaluation of user oriented specifications

We have now documented user oriented specifications on three levels:

1　　Change analysis
2　　Activity studies
3　　Information analysis

These can be evaluated in different ways. The workability of the specification can be tested e.g. by use of experimental systems development. Conceptual analysis can be part of a realizability test in order to study possible integration between subsystems. I will in this report restrict myself to short workability and realizability tests.

Figure 4.20 shows a comparison between the problem definition of the case and the information systems specification in this report. Figure 4.20 thus documents a short workability test.

The conceptual analysis will follow a description technique picked from Sundgren [5,6], see figure 4.21. Figures 4.22-4.29 document conceptual submodels for each information subsystem. These submodels are derived from the corresponding C-graphs. The submodel in figure 4.24 is e.g. derived from the C-graph AP6A in figure 4.9. C-graph AP4A describes the following information subsets:

| Subsets | | Message types |
|---|---|---|
| AP4A11 | Paper title information | Title (paper) |
| AP4A12 | Paper author information | Author (paper) |
| AP4A13 | Paper area information | Area (paper) |
| AP4A14 | Referee reports | Report (paper, referee*) |
| AP4A15 | Paper selection information | Selection status (paper) |
| AP4A21 | Author title information | Title (author) |
| AP4A22 | Author address information | Address (author) |

The conceptual submodel in figure 4.25 describes these message types using the description technique in figure 4.21. The other submodels are derived in a similar manner. Figure 4.30 finally documents a conceptual model merged from all the conceptual submodels. Figure 4.30 thus documents a short realizability test in order to study possible integration between subsystems.

The conclusions of these illustrations are:

1　　The requirements of the problem definition of the case have been met, i.e., the specification is workable on a certain level

2　　The concepts used in the C-graphs are consistent

3　　It should be possible to realize an integrated database for the specified information subsystems

# IFIP

| Analyst | PROPERTY TABLE |
| Mats Lundeberg | Date |
| Subject | 1981-07-28 |
| Information systems support to an IFIP Working Conference | |

| ACTIVITY TO BE SUPPORTED ACCORDING TO PROBLEM DEFINITION OF THE CASE | SUPPORTING INFORMATION SYSTEM IN THIS REPORT | |
| --- | --- | --- |
| | A-GRAPH REFERENCE CODE | I-GRAPH REFERENCE CODE |
| **PROGRAMME COMMITTEE:** | | |
| 1  PREPARING A LIST TO WHOM THE CALL FOR PAPERS IS TO BE SENT | F514 | DLO |
| 2  REGISTERING THE LETTERS OF INTENT RECEIVED IN RESPONSE TO THE CALL | F521 | PPO |
| 3  REGISTERING THE CONTRIBUTED PAPERS ON RECEIPT | F521 | PPO |
| 4  DISTRIBUTING THE PAPERS AMONG THOSE UNDERTAKING THE REFEREEING | F527 (F523 | RWO RLO) |
| 5  COLLECTING THE REFEREES' REPORTS AND SELECTING THE PAPERS FOR INCLUSION IN THE PROGRAMME | F531 | APO |
| 6  GROUPING SELECTED PAPERS INTO SESSIONS FOR PRESENTATION AND SELECTING CHAIRMAN FOR EACH SESSION | F533 F5373 | ASO CLO |
| **ORGANIZING COMMITTEE:** | | |
| 1  PREPARING A LIST OF PEOPLE TO INVITE TO THE CONFERENCE | F622 | IPO |
| 2  ISSUING PRIORITY INVITATIONS TO NATIONAL REPRESENTATIVES, WORKING GROUP MEMBERS AND MEMBERS OF ASSOCIATED WORKING GROUPS | F622 | IPO |
| 3  ENSURING ALL AUTHORS OF EACH SELECTED PAPER RECEIVE AN INVITATION | F622 | IPO |
| 4  ENSURING AUTHORS OF REJECTED PAPERS RECEIVE AN INVITATION | F622 | IPO |
| 5  AVOIDING SENDING DUPLICATE INVITATIONS TO ANY INDIVIDUAL | F622 | IPO |
| 6  REGISTERING ACCEPTANCE OF INVITATIONS | F622 | IPO |
| 7  GENERATING FINAL LIST OF ATTENDEES | F622 | IPO |

Figure 4.20  Comparison between activities to be supported according to the problem definition and the supporting information systems in this report

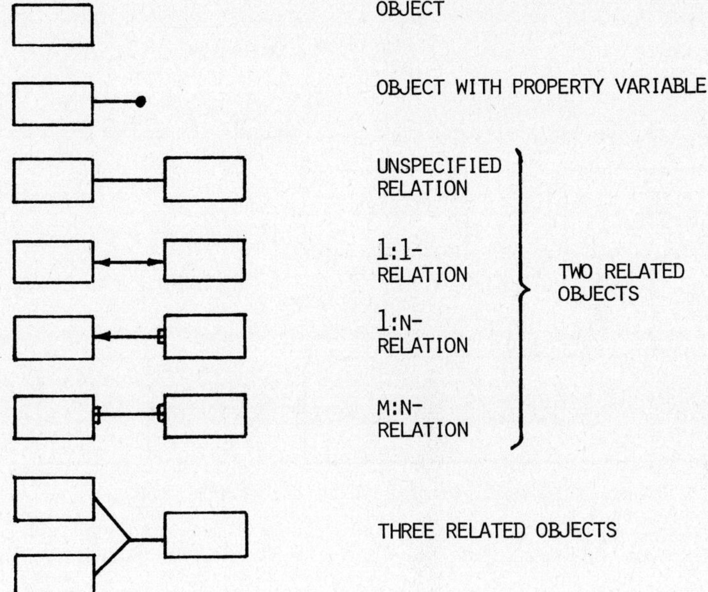


Figure 4.21   Symbols used in figures 4.22-4.30 (from Sundgren [5.6])

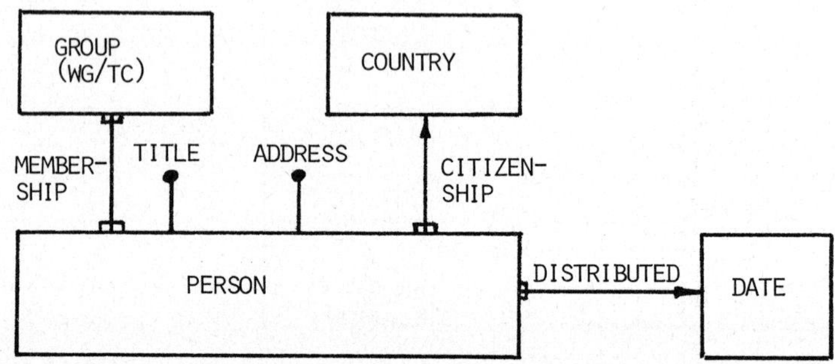


Figure 4.22   Conceptual submodel corresponding to C-graph DL4A
              (figure 4.5)

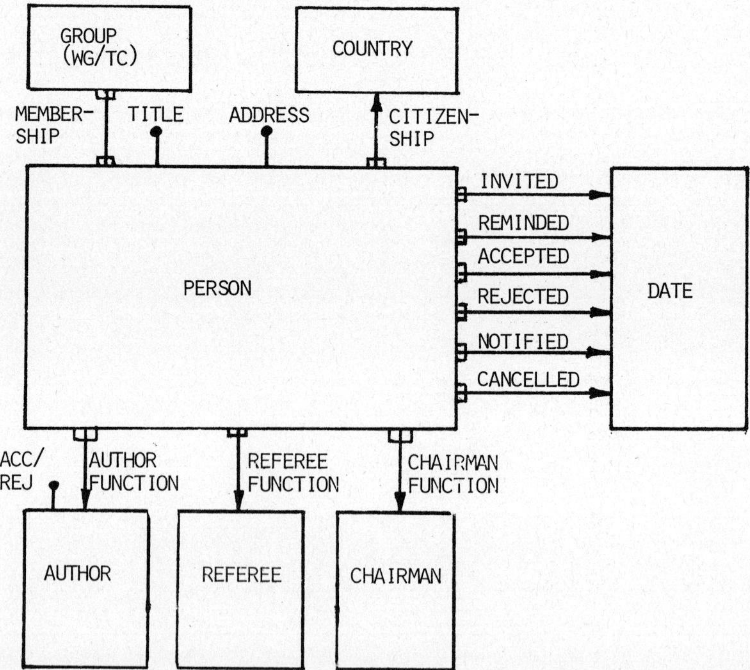


Figure 4.23   Conceptual submodel corresponding to C-graph IP4A
              (figure 4.6)

**IFIP**

Analyst
Mats Lundeberg
Subject
Information systems support to an IFIP
Working Conference

CONCEPTUAL SUBMODELS
Date
1981-07-28

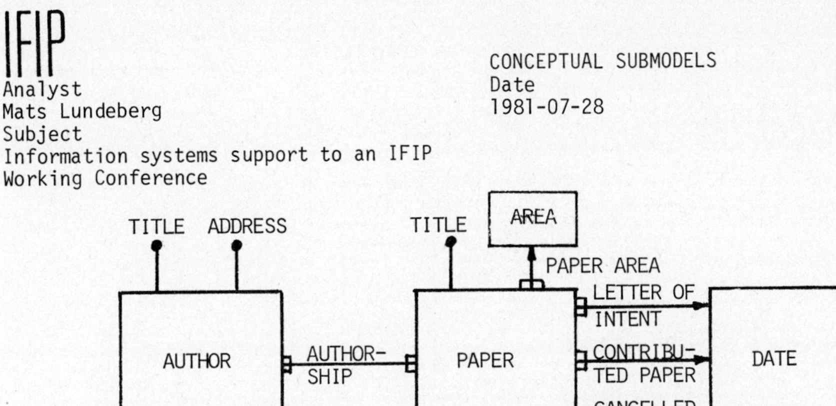


Figure 4.24  Conceptual submodel corresponding to C-graph PP4A (figure 4.8)

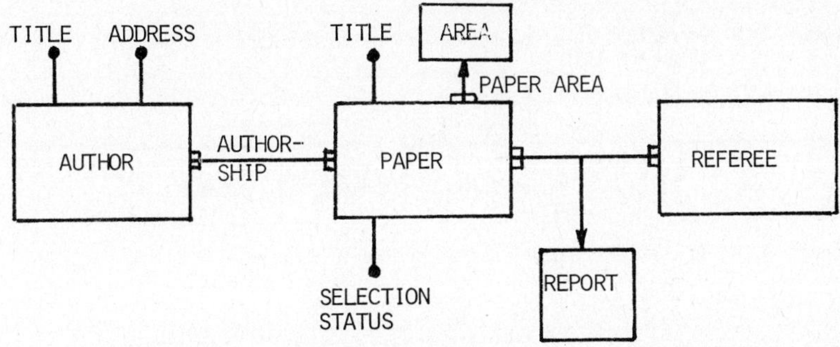


Figure 4.25  Conceptual submodel corresponding to C-graph AP4A (figure 4.9)

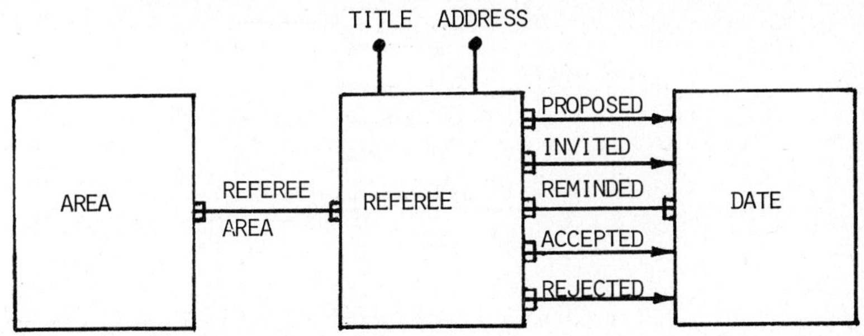


Figure 4.26  Conceptual submodel corresponding to C-graph RL4A (figure 4.11)

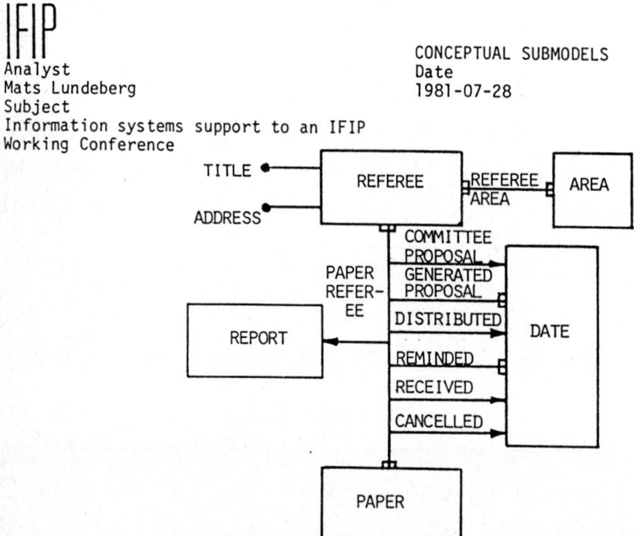


Figure 4.27   Conceptual submodel corresponding to C-graphs RW8A and RW9A
             (figure 4.14)

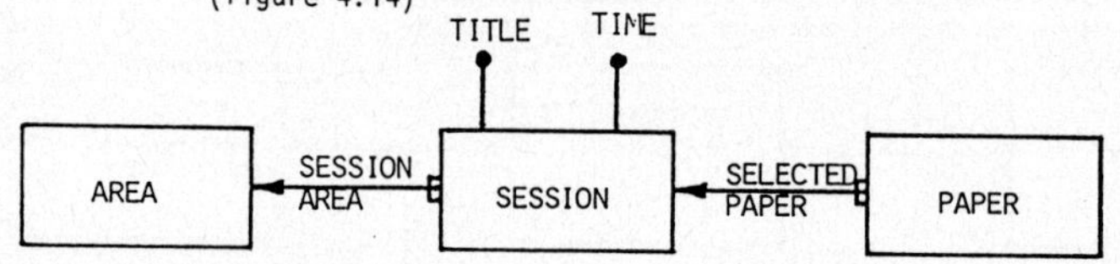


Figure 4.28   Conceptual submodel corresponding to C-graph AS4A (figure 4.16)

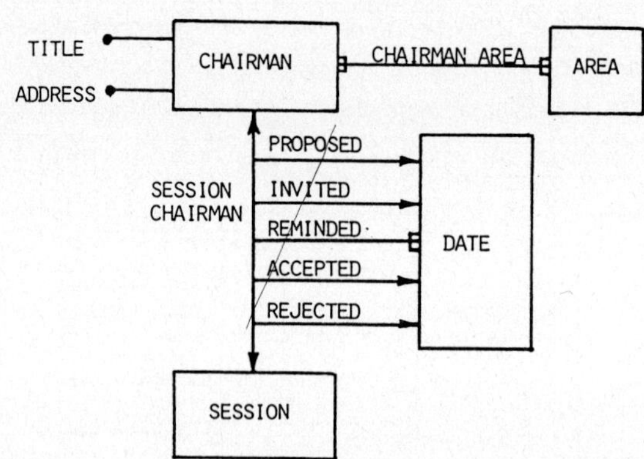


Figure 4.29   Conceptual submodel corresponding to C-graph CL4A (figure 4.17)

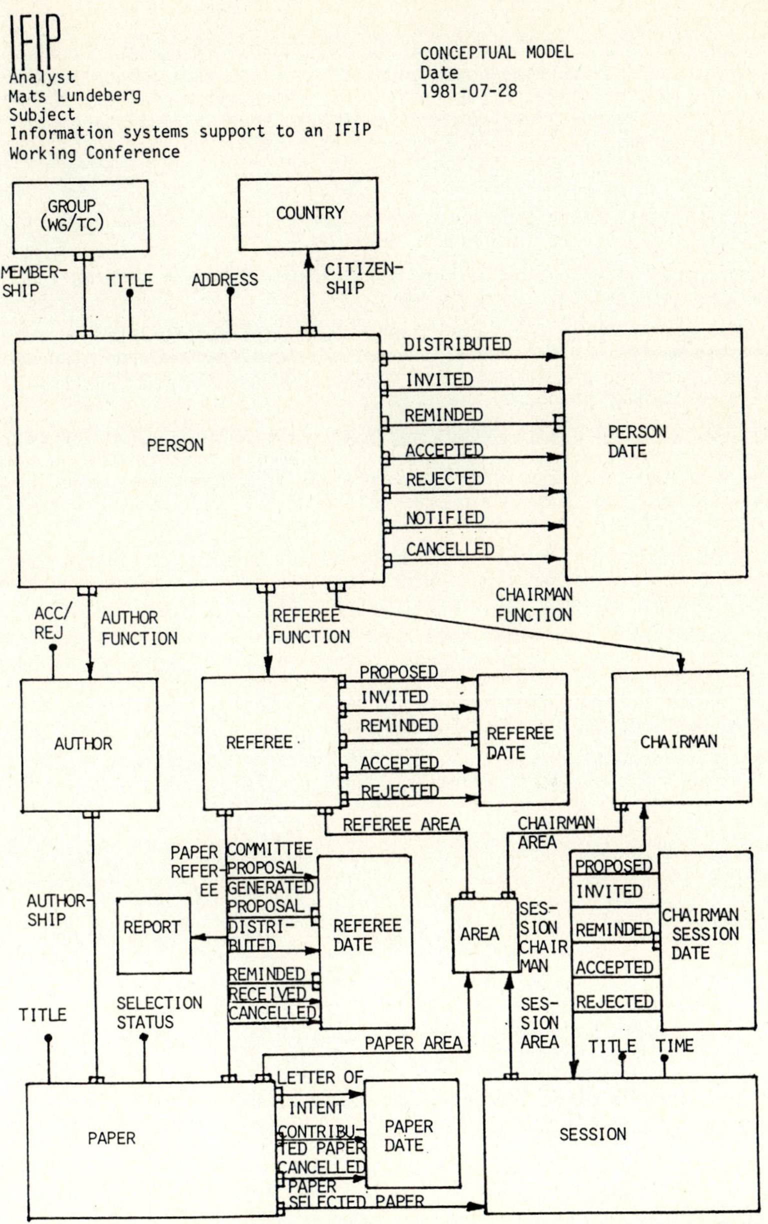


Figure 4.30  Conceptual model merged from conceptual submodels in figures
4.22-4.29

## 5    CONCLUSION

I have now documented a user oriented specification of information systems in order to support an IFIP Working Conference. I have also made a short conceptual analysis of the specification. I hope that this presentation of the ISAC approach to information systems specification and its application to a standard case study can help you to understand the ISAC approach. When comparing this specification with specifications using other approaches, the following points may be of interest:

1      The specification has been prepared on three levels: Change analysis, activity studies, and information analysis

2      A conceptual model can be derived very closely from the information analysis results

3      In each of the three levels mentioned above, the specification has been prepared by the use of a number of method steps. Each method step uses the results from the preceding method steps. Together these method steps form an integrated methodology

4      The important thing with change analysis  from an information systems perspective is to find out if there really is a need for information systems. Even when the user says he is sure information systems are needed, a change analysis will put this in a proper perspective without much extra effort because of the three-level specification approach

5      The ISAC approach is based on finding several information subsystems rather than one "total" information system. Specific information systems that produce relevant information for the users in their work are defined

6      Once information subsystems have been defined in the activity studies, the information analysis is facilitated because of clearly defined boundaries. The same phenomenon occurs on a lower level: The higher the degree of detail in the I-graphs, the easier the process analysis becomes because of clearly defined and detailed boundaries

7      The ISAC approach is result oriented in the sense that the users' needs determine the specifications rather than specifying invariant, neutral models separate from purpose

## REFERENCES

[1] Langefors, B., Theoretical Analysis of Information Systems (Studentlitteratur, Lund, 1966, 3rd edition 1973 and Auerbach, Philadelphia, Pa., 1973)

[2] Lundeberg, M., Goldkuhl, G., Nilsson, A., A Systematic Approach to Information Systems Development. Part I: Introduction, and Part II: Problem and Data Oriented Systems Work, Information Systems Volume 4 No. 1-2 (1979)

[3] Lundeberg, M., Goldkuhl, G., Nilsson, A., Information Systems Development - A Systematic Approach (Prentice-Hall, Inc., Englewood Cliffs, N.J., U.S.A., 1981)

[4] Olle, T.W. (editor), Comparative Review of Information Systems Design Methodologies: Problem Definition (IFIP Working Group 8.1, 1980)

[5] Sundgren, B., Five Examples of Infological Object System Analysis, SYS-INFORMATION 1977:52, The Swedish Central Bureau of Statistics, Stockholm, Sweden

[6] Sundgren, B., Data Base Design in Theory and Practice. Towards an integrated methodology, in: Yao, S. Bing (editor), Proceedings - Very Large Data Bases, Fourth International Conference on Very Large Data Bases, Berlin, September 13-15, 1978

*INFORMATION SYSTEMS DESIGN METHODOLOGIES: A Comparative Review*
*T.W. Olle, H.G. Sol, A.A. Verrijn-Stuart (editors)*
*North-Holland Publishing Company*
© IFIP, 1982

# SYSTEM DEVELOPMENT IN A SHARED DATA ENVIRONMENT

## THE D2S2 METHODOLOGY

I.G. MACDONALD [1] and I.R. PALMER [2]

1. DMW GROUP EUROPE *
   11, ALBERMARLE STREET
   LONDON W1X 3HE

2. INDEPENDENT CONSULTANT *

Since the early 1970's a number of consultants in Europe have, in association with Ian Palmer, been using and developing a pragmatic methodology for the analysis and development of systems. He has named it D2S2 since it is for the Development of Data Sharing Systems.

D2S2 is applicable in all systems environments, manual as well as computerised, and has been employed very widely particularly in areas where data sharing is required and where database solutions are appropriate. This paper describes the approach and shows how it would be used, particularly during the analysis stage, to meet the IFIP conferencing requirement.

## 1. GENERAL INTRODUCTION

## 1.1 INTRODUCTION

The purpose of this paper is to outline a methodology which has been found to be of real benefit when designing and implementing application systems; particularly those where related data is to be shared between several applications. No attempt will be made to survey the variety of other methodologies which have been developed in recent years, both commercially and from academic sources, although several of the concepts used in this methodology have been adapted from alternative approaches. What makes the methodology unique is its use of a variety of concepts in combination, with an emphasis on their value when applied to data sharing environments. Perhaps the greatest strength of this methodology is that it encourages the coordinated development of a series of applications. This is because the methodology was first developed for use with data base management systems where data sharing is a key criterion for success. By contrast with other approaches which have attempted to evolve upwards from programming into design, the methodology concentrated initially on analysis and strategic issues and has evolved downwards into design and towards programming. It has therefore been extended without difficulty from a database orientation to an effective means of supporting the development of any type of data handling or information system.
Aspects of the approach have been published by Davenport [1] Palmer [2] and Shave [3].

* Formerly with CACI Inc. International

## 1.2    IFIP CONFERENCING SYSTEM

Section 3 of this paper uses the IFIP conference organisation process as a means of illustrating the outcome from the application of many of the techniques included in the methodology.

The submission illustrates fairly fully the analysis approach and the documentation required to support it. However, as recognised in the WG8.1 note of 15 September 1980, dialogue with the users plays an important part in this type of approach to analysis since, particularly in the case of D2S2, it lays great stress on achieving an outcome which is suited to the fundamental business environment and is not one based on a refining of previously designed         clerical         or         computerised         systems.

In the absence of such a dialogue, the results in this case are therefore incomplete and suspect in their accuracy. This being so it is therefore not reasonable to put forward a design which carries with it any air of authority.  The process which is gone through is however discussed and illustrated with examples and documentation to show how a design may be achieved.

It is perhaps worth noting in this context that, in the absence of an automated data dictionary, the documentation of the analysis and design for this problem could extend to some 500 pages of standard forms.  Relatively little of this would however be required by the programmer since the major requirements are summarised succinctly in only a few diagrams.

The system requirements are themselves relatively simple . Data is structured around entities in the conference, paper, person and IFIP areas and the various forms of association that can develop between them.  There are only two significant users of the system, the programme committee and the organising committee and their requirements are largely concerned with maintenance of the data particularly on the associations and on displaying or listing it.  The scale of the problem therefore does not best illustrate the full power of the methodology and indeed means that it is susceptible to solution by means of almost any adequate data management sytem.  This being so then a major design consideration is likely to be the ease with which the system can support the more obvious clerical aspects of the task and provide word processing capabilities in combination with the data management.

## 1.3    ACKNOWLEDGMENTS

We wish to thank Geoffrey Baker, John Dodd, David Gradwell, Leslie Jennison, Rosemary Rock-Evans, Carl Rosenquist, Ed Tozer and the many others who have contributed to the development of D2S2.   ICL, Scicon, and CACI Inc. International are the companies most closely associated with the development and, in this paper, the CACI standard documentation has been used to illustrate the case study.

2.    THE METHODOLOGY

2.1    INTRODUCTION

The methodology has been developed to provide an adequate means of analysis and design in support of the development of systems, both manual and computer aided, in data sharing environments.

The development of the methodology has been governed by six fundamental principles.    These are that a methodology should provide:

   i. Clear    delineation,    during    the    analysis    and    design stages,    between    the    application    oriented    and    the    data oriented tasks.

     Without    such    delineation,    the    data    analysis,    and    eventual file    design,    is    inevitably    biased    towards    the    priority application    and    therefore    provides    little    flexibility    to enable    the    sharing    of    the    same    data with    applications    to    be developed    later.

  ii. Complete    separation    of    the    design    tasks    from    those    of analysis,    with    a    clear    interface    defined    in    terms    of    the information    which    must    be    passed    from    the    analysis    to    the design    stage.

     Without    such    a    separation    it    is    difficult    to    ensure    that changes    in    the    technology    of    data    processing    will    not    have    a major    impact    on    the    end-user's    systems.    It    becomes    equally difficult    to    provide    flexibility    in    the    system    design    to enable    it    to    respond    to    changes    in    the    business environment.

 iii. Orientation    towards    producing    a    strategy    for    system development    rather    than    towards    ad-hoc    problem    solving.

     A    disciplined    methodology    is    essential    when    the    development of    several    applications    is    required    to    be    coordinated    as part    of    a    long    term    plan.

  iv. Decomposition    into    small,    well    defined    and    controllable tasks.

     A    methodology    is    of    little    value    if    it    does    not    provide    a means    for    project    planning    and    progress    control.

   v. Emphasis    on    simple    diagrams    with    standard    specifications.

     Analysts    and    designers    can    gain    a    much    fuller    understanding of    a    complex    environment    using    complete    diagrammatic standards    rather    than    long    prose    descriptions.

vi. Interactive use of a data dictionary for all documentation
    and development work.

    The data dictionary thus becomes the focal point for all
    system development, rather than merely a list of data
    definitions and where-used linkages.

Each of these points has been borne in mind during the
development of the approach and the result has been an effective,
pragmatic methodology which continues to grow and develop along
with our increased understanding of the nature of information
systems.

2.2    THE METHODOLOGY IN THE SYSTEMS LIFE CYCLE

2.2.1 OVERVIEW

The methodology covers all stages of the systems life cycle and
includes techniques for approaching the tasks which make up each
stage.

The systems life cycle is seen to consist of the six phases shown
in figure 1 and described below:

  i.   The Strategy Stage, during which an overview is taken of
       the enterprise as a whole and documented in terms of its
       major entities and functions.    End user problems and
       priorities are considered and a data processing strategy
       for systems development in a number of applications areas
       is drawn up.

  ii.  The Analysis Stage, during which the selected area is
       analysed in more detail until its complexities are
       thoroughly understood and documented and the business
       requirement specification is prepared.

  iii. The Design Stage, during which the facts gathered from the
       previous stage are used to design files or databases,
       transactions, dialogues and batch runs, and eventually
       programs and operational procedures.

  iv.  The Construction Stage, during which programs are coded and
       tested, new files are loaded and verified, and the
       operational documentation is prepared.

  v.   The Transition Stage, during which the new system begins to
       go live, either in parallel operation or in a trial mode,
       until it passes the users acceptance tests.

  vi.  The Production Stage, during which the system is run
       operationally, and is maintained and tuned as necessary.
       It terminates when eventually the system becomes obsolete
       and has to be replaced.

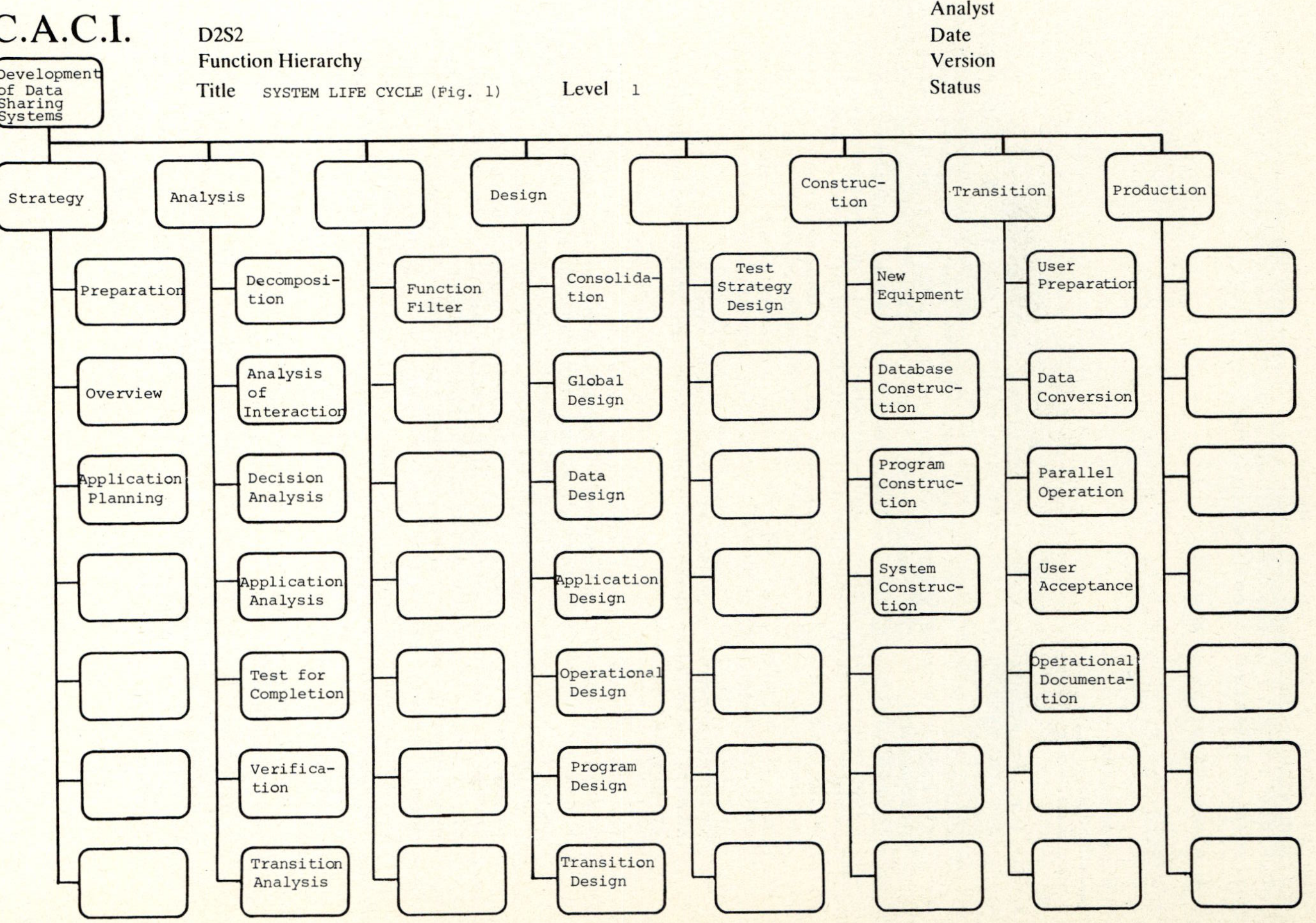

C.A.C.I.
D2S2
Function Hierarchy
Title  SYSTEM LIFE CYCLE (Fig. 1)    Level  1
Analyst
Date
Version
Status
Development of Data Sharing Systems
Strategy
Analysis
Design
Construction
Transition
Production
Preparation
Overview
Application Planning
Decomposition
Analysis of Interaction
Decision Analysis
Application Analysis
Test for Completion
Verification
Transition Analysis
Function Filter
Consolidation
Global Design
Data Design
Application Design
Operational Design
Program Design
Transition Design
Test Strategy Design
New Equipment
Database Construction
Program Construction
System Construction
User Preparation
Data Conversion
Parallel Operation
User Acceptance
Operational Documentation

Each of these stages can be decomposed into more detailed tasks
and activities as shown in figure 1. These are described in the
remainder of this paper though with particular emphasis on the
Analysis and Design stages.

2.2.2 THE STRATEGY STAGE

The Strategy Stage consists of three main tasks:

* Preparation
* Overview
* Applications Planning

a.      The <u>Preparation</u> task is critical to the success of the
        entire system development project.  First it is of prime
        importance to gain the commitment of the senior management
        whose world is to be analysed, of the user management who
        will be intimately involved in the project, and of the data
        processing staff who may not take kindly to the
        introduction of a new and different methodology.
        Education, both formal and informal, will be needed at all
        levels so that the people participating understand the
        objectives of the project and gain an appreciation of the
        methodology.  It is important to define clearly the scope
        and objectives of the project, together with any known
        constraints, to ensure that the project remains under
        control and that the analysis does not stray into other
        related areas.  A broad timescale can be set for each
        stage, with the tasks in this Strategy Stage being defined
        in greater detail.

b.      The objective of the <u>Overview</u> task is to provide a broad
        understanding of the enterprise as a whole and to identify
        those data and functional areas upon which attention needs
        to be focused.  The potential applications in the
        development strategy will be expressed in terms of those
        high level business functions which could benefit from
        computer support, and of those major entities about which
        data could usefully be held in the new system.  Hence, the
        overview is best expressed in terms of a global entity
        model identifying the major entities apparent in the
        business and showing the essential relationships between
        them, together with a function hierarchy showing the major
        business functions decomposed to about three levels of
        detail.  The entities involved with each of these functions
        are listed in order to draw up an entity-function matrix
        which, although lacking detail, is adequate to provide a
        good indication of the potential for data sharing.  To
        complete the overview, a function dependency diagram is
        necessary as both entity models and function hierarchies
        tend to provide only a static picture of the environment.
        This diagram portrays functional dependencies by showing
        which functions must preceed others in time and by
        indicating where the entities created or modified by one
        function become the input to another.

c.　　The overview task leads into the <u>Applications Planning</u> task which has an objective of determining which functions should be further decomposed and which areas of the entity model analysed in more detail. Functions are grouped into potential sub-systems based upon their similarity in terms of the entities involved (possibly by using cluster analysis techniques) and are refined in the light of dependencies revealed by the function dependency diagram. Each possible sub-system is then prioritised from the point of view of the possible benefits that could result from it being supported by a new computer system. The end product of this task is the application development strategy which defines the sub-systems to be designed and constructed during the timescale of the project and identifies the data areas with which each is concerned. The strategy will pay attention to the sequence of application development, first from the point of view of user benefits and current problems, and then from the logical dependencies revealed by the entity model and function dependency diagrams. The emphasis in the strategy stage is on the potential for computer support of business functions rather than on technical issues which are better left until the design stage.

## 2.2.3 THE ANALYSIS STAGE

The Strategy Stage in the systems life cycle is often the starting point for many systems or applications but subsequent stages may each be concerned with only one application. The next stage is that of analysis and it in turn consists of the following second level tasks:

* Decompostion of functions and of entities
* Analysis of interactions
* Decision analysis
* Application analysis
* Test for completion
* Verification
* Transition analysis
* Function filter

These, and their breakdown, are illustrated in figure 2.

a.　　The first task, <u>Decomposition</u>, is to break down into more detail those functions and entities which were selected during the Strategy Stage for further analysis. Each function is broken down into the constituent tasks necessary to achieve its purpose. Each of these is then broken down into its lower level tasks and this process of decomposition is continued until the analyst finds he is dealing with a level which is concerned more with the current mechanics of the function rather than with its purpose, i.e. of "how" rather than "what". The objective of function decomposition is to describe the business activities of an enterprise independently of its organisational structure and so to permit the design of a data processing system which directly

*I.G. MacDonald and I.R. Palmer*

C.A.C.I.

D2S2

Function Hierarchy

Title   SYSTEM LIFE CYCLE (Fig. 2)   Level   2

Analyst
Date
Version
Status

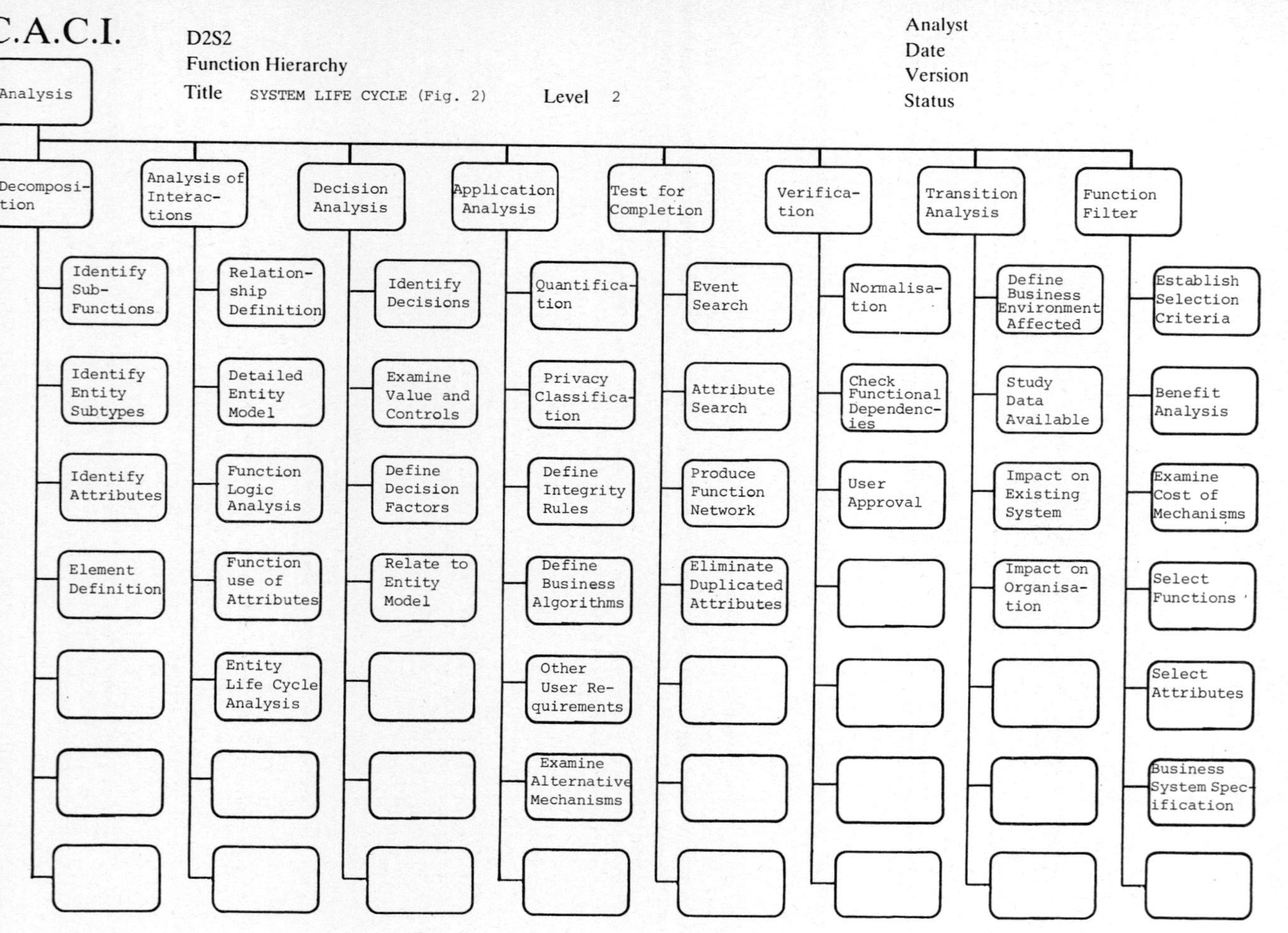

represents the business environment. The lowest level, or elementary, functions are likely to be represented as transactions during the subsequent design stage.

Similarly, the decomposition of entities increases the analyst's understanding of the business environment without biasing the analysis process towards any specific user requirements. Each major entity type is examined to determine whether it cannot be better defined as several slightly different types of entities which are sub-types of the first. This process leads also to the definition of further attributes because when entities are found to be different it is because attributes are identified also during the decomposition of the functions. Each relationship type is also scrutinised carefully to ensure that it is necessary and, in the case of many to many relationships, to determine whether any entities remain hidden.

A major part of this task, in terms of the work effort involved, is defining the meaning of all entities, attributes and functions identified, documenting this in the data dictionary and agreeing the meanings with all the users concerned. The usual problem is reconciling the different user viewpoints as to what each specific function or attribute really does mean to the business; an onerous task which is not necessary when there is no intention of sharing data.

b.    Once the entities and the functions have been defined it is possible to examine the interactions between them. In fact this task, the <u>Analysis of Interactions</u>, must be an iterative process as studying the interactions may well lead to a redefinition of the original entities or functions. Interactions between entities are known as relationships. These have their own properties and require to be defined precisely and be recorded in the data dictionary. The entities and their relationships are expressed as a detailed entity model which is progressively refined as the data area under analysis becomes increasingly understood.

The interactions between entities and functions are expressed in two converse ways. First for each of the most important elementary functions a function logic model is drawn showing the entity types and relationships necessary to support the function; a list of attributes used by the function is also compiled. Secondly each of the major entity types is considered from the point of view of its life cycle and all the states through which it passes, a change from one state to another being the result of some function. An entity life cycle diagram thus expresses all the functions in which an entity type can be involved and the life cycle states when it is valid for that function to take place. This latter process frequently pinpoints mistakes in the function hierarchy and causes a further reiteration in the analysis.

c.    The third analysis task is particularly relevant when working towards a management information system. This task, known as <u>Decision Analysis</u>, is concerned with identifying the decisions which each type of manager expects to take and the factors that he considers in making each decision. The entity life cycle diagrams are used as a prompt in this process, as a change of state in an entity is often the result of a formal or informal decision. Each decision factor must be classified as an attribute of some entity. Each type of decision may ultimately be supported by some transaction in a data processing system and each attribute must be available as information to the manager concerned. In addition the analyst needs to consider the value of the decision, the level of accuracy required, and how the results are monitored and controlled.

d.    Before the design stage can begin, further user involvement is necessary in a task termed <u>Application Analysis</u>, which is intended to ensure that all the facts are known on which to base subsequent designs. The various aspects of function and entity analysis may not necessarily unearth all the detailed user requirements. Specific business rules or algorithms, by which elementary functions are carried out, may need to be classified from the point of view of user privacy. The integrity rules, expressing the conditions under which an attribute or relationship may exist, need also to be defined. Of major importance too is the process of quantifying the frequency of functions and decisions, and the volumes of entities, attributes and relationships. These facts may come from the analysis of existing systems, but are almost certain to require user participation to allow for changes in activity patterns in the future. This also provides an opportunity for beginning to consider what mechanisms will be used to support the various elementary functions, at least at the level of the choice between on-line access and batch processing and between central and distributed systems.

e.    As a result of decompostion, analysis of interactions, decision analysis and application analysis a business area has been examined from several points of view and the analysts understanding and documentation ought to be complete. However, it is advisable to perform some tests, the <u>Test for Completion</u> task, to ensure that no functions or critical attributes have been missed from the analysis. To search for further possible attributes, forms, documentation and file layouts of existing systems are examined, as each field or box on a form should previously have been defined as the attribute of some entity. To search for missing functions, events which cause things to happen within the business area are analysed. Typically functions are triggered by events and a search for less frequent events, especially those whose origins are external to the enterprise, can lead to significant extensions to the models where exceptional functions have not been considered.

Once the analyst is confident that the entity model and function hierarchy are sufficiently complete he then searches for any redundancy. Typically, low level functions are found to be repeated in several previously independent function hierarchies. The elimination of this duplication converts the hierarchies into a function network. In data processing terms this indicates that the same transaction may form part of several applications or at least support several business functions. A final check needs to be made to eliminate duplicated attributes. This is normally a result of the same attribute being given different but similar names by different users.

f.    It then remains to verify in some way the now non-redundant entity model and function network; the <u>Verification</u> task. The technique of normalisation is used to check out the entity model, as this establishes that all attributes have been assigned correctly to entities and that there are no relationships hidden between the attributes of an entity type. To check if the function network has been correctly represented, function dependency diagrams are drawn for each level in the major function hierarchies. These diagrams indicate the time dependencies between functions and how the entities output from one function become input to others. It must be possible to draw a complete dependency diagram between all the functions at any one level in the hierarchy, otherwise the hierarchy cannot be valid. But the final and most important activity of the verification task is to gain user approval for the results of the analysis. This is most readily done by stepping through the relevant entity models and function hierarchies with each of the users. At this stage final acceptance should be gained for all the definitions and other properties documented in the data dictionary. The various models and diagrams are then frozen as representing an adequate and complete foundation for the design stage.

g.    The analysis stage is not complete without the <u>Transition Analysis</u> task, as the change from the existing system to the new system frequently poses major problems which need to be addressed before the design stage. The existing systems need to be analysed using function decomposition techniques to determine which of the elementary functions they support, either in whole or in part. The existing data files need to be analysed and described in terms of entity models in order to establish which entities, attributes and relationships they represent. The new system is bound to impact existing systems, replacing some of their routines and requiring interfaces, both temporary and permanent. The organisational impact also needs to be considered. It may be that the transition problems determine which of the elementary functions are to be supported on the new system.

h.      The final task is the <u>Function Filter</u> to weed out those
        functions for which a new system will not be designed.  The
        first step then must be to establish the filtering criteria,
        which ought to be related to long term objectives of the
        enterprise and to specific problems that are to be
        alleviated.  Benefit analysis can be conducted to establish
        for each elementary function the tangible and intangible
        benefits which could result from changing the mechanisms
        currently supporting them.  At the same time, costs of
        likely new mechanisms for each elementary function can be
        considered.  These costs ought to allow for the development
        work involved rather than only operational costs, and also
        for any constraints that have been placed upon the system
        design.  After considering the costs and benefits accruing
        for each of the functions in the traditional way, those to
        be supported by the new system design are then selected.
        Once this selection is complete, the results of function
        logic analysis can be used to select those relationships and
        attributes that will need to be represented in the system
        design.

The end point of the analysis stage is the business specification
which lists the selected functions, relationships and attributes.
This is not the traditional detailed specification, as these
elements and their properties have previously been defined in the
data dictionary.  The data dictionary ought by this time to
contain all integrity and consistency rules, privacy
specifications and quantification details.  The business system
specification need add only special user requirements and
business algorithms.  Even so, the objective is for this total
documentation to be adequate for the designers to design a system
with minimal further involvement of the end user.  The users
concern from this point onwards should be only with the details
of the dialogues, screen layouts and input documents; those
aspects assuring a sound man-machine interface.

## 2.2.4 THE DESIGN STAGE

The methodology makes it possible for the Design Stage to be
undertaken by different staff with different skills from those
used in the analysis stage.  The emphasis now is on applying data
processing techniques rather than understanding the business.  It
is not the intention of this paper to discuss the principles of
system design, but only to show how the facts gathered during the
Analysis Stage can now be applied to system design, particularly
where several applications share the same data.  The Design Stage
consists of the following secondary tasks:

*   Consolidation
*   Global Design
*   Data design
*   Application design
*   Operational design
*   Program design
*   Transition design
*   Test strategy design

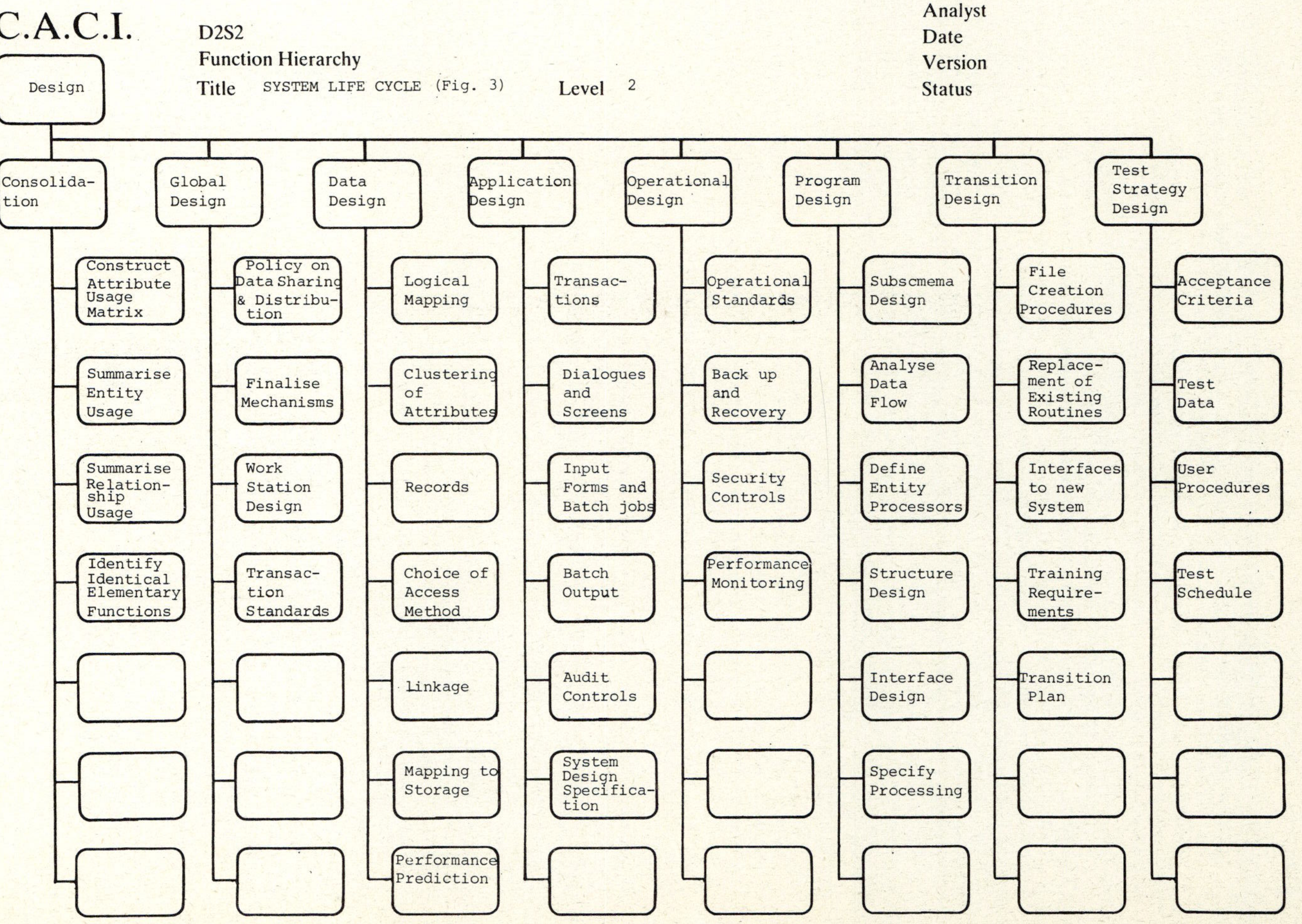
C.A.C.I.
D2S2
Function Hierarchy
Title   SYSTEM LIFE CYCLE (Fig. 3)   Level   2
Analyst
Date
Version
Status
Design
Consolidation
Global Design
Data Design
Application Design
Operational Design
Program Design
Transition Design
Test Strategy Design
Construct Attribute Usage Matrix
Summarise Entity Usage
Summarise Relationship Usage
Identify Identical Elementary Functions
Policy on Data Sharing & Distribution
Finalise Mechanisms
Work Station Design
Transaction Standards
Logical Mapping
Clustering of Attributes
Records
Choice of Access Method
Linkage
Mapping to Storage
Performance Prediction
Transactions
Dialogues and Screens
Input Forms and Batch jobs
Batch Output
Audit Controls
System Design Specification
Operational Standards
Back up and Recovery
Security Controls
Performance Monitoring
Subscmema Design
Analyse Data Flow
Define Entity Processors
Structure Design
Interface Design
Specify Processing
File Creation Procedures
Replacement of Existing Routines
Interfaces to new System
Training Requirements
Transition Plan
Acceptance Criteria
Test Data
User Procedures
Test Schedule

These are illustrated in figure 3.

a.     The task of <u>Consolidation</u> is ideally suited to automation, given a good data dictionary. We have found APL routines to be ideal for this purpose. What is required is simply a summary of the usage of each attribute, relationship and entity type, for all the elementary functions to be implemented.

A usage form is produced for each entity type showing the total number of creations, modifications and deletions, and the frequency with which an entity is selected by the value of different attributes or by membership of the relationships in which it participates. Similarly, a form is compiled for each relationship type summarising the frequency of its usage in both directions and of the connection and disconnection of entities. Attribute usage is summarised by a matrix for each entity type, showing the frequency of usage of each attribute against the elementary functions which may create, retrieve or delete them. All this information is quantitative in nature and is necessary for database or file design. In addition, the function logic models for the various elementary functions are compared to establish whether any are identical and hence could possibly be supported by the same transaction. Note however that even though the models are identical there may still be different patterns of attribute usage thus giving a need for completely different transactions.

b.     Before detailed Data and Application Design is possible several <u>Global Design</u> decisions need to be taken, based on the consolidated view of the application areas, together with such business considerations as overall costs, project timescales, degree of technical risk acceptable, and user attitudes. These decisions may include:

the extent of data sharing
the degree of distribution of functions and data
the timeliness of data

The mechanisms previously suggested for individual elementary functions may have to be reconsidered in the light of the overall policies.

The mixture of mechanisms chosen will largely determine how the users responsible will carry out each function, so that their physical environment or work stations can be designed. This is typically a global decision. Thus, for example, where several low volume elementary functions are to be supported by a remote online update mechanism, then they are likely to be carried out on the same terminal equipment. For each type of work station, whether online or batch, standards can then be set to enforce as much commonality as possible in the way users handle transactions, such as in layouts, error messages mand prompts.

c.  Once the global standards and the overall usage of all the selected types of entities, relationships and attributes is understood, the task of <u>Data Design</u> can commence.  This design will be biased towards the elementary functions selected so that it is wise to make the scope of the applications areas being implemented as broad as possible. However, to allow for maximum flexibility and thus future systems extension, the first task is simply to map the entity model into the structure of the selected database or file management system, ignoring the relative usage of the entities and relationships.  The result is a logical design, which may be constrained by the structuring limitations of the DBMS, but which should have no performance implications.

Performance is a reflection of the physical design, which in turn is a series of decisions on how the constructs in the logical design are to be implemented.  Most entity types must be mapped to record types depending on such considerations as size, frequency of access and privacy requirements.  Where an entity has many attributes, cluster analysis is performed upon the attribute usage matrix for that entity type in order to optimise the grouping of attributes into several record types.  Next the usage of each relationship type is examined to decide whether it is best represented by means of duplicated identifying attributes, chains of pointers, an index or any other facility provided by the DBMS.  The entity usage form should contain all the facts needed to choose the access method for the record types representing that entity type, whether these be one or more indexes, a randomising algorithm or simply a serial file.  The physical design of the database or files is complete once the various records, pointers and indexes have been mapped to disc or tape storage.  Because of the complexities of data sharing systems it is normally wise to subject this physical design to examination by some simulator or performance prediction system.  Ideally the performance simulator should interface with the data dictionary since this should by now contain all the consolidated usage figures and the details of the database or file designs.  Should the performance of some of the functions be shown to be unacceptable, some of the physical design decisions will need to be reconsidered, but these design iterations are greatly simplified if they can be made by amending the data dictionary and re-running the simulator.

d.  The <u>Application Design</u> task can be carried out parallel to that of data design.  Now the emphasis is on the function hierarchy rather than the construction of the entity model. Each of the selected elementary functions is considered as a transaction and the first design decision is whether each transaction should be handled as part of a batch job or in an online mode.  For batch transactions, input form design and output report layouts can be designed in the traditional way.  For online transactions, the function logic models are used to determine the necessary sequence for the online dialogue and to aid in the screen design. The entity life cycle diagrams also have a part to play in application design as they indicate the conditions under which it is valid to execute the transaction. This provides the basis for one of the audit and consistency controls that need to be built into the system design. It is expressed as a transaction control matrix showing, for each of the major entity types, the entity states valid for a transaction type and the entity states resulting from its execution. The end point of the application design task is a System Design Specification for that application, containing details of the dialogues, forms, output reports etc. It does not include the specification of the logical or physical data design from the previous task, as this design must not be tied to any one application.

e.    The task of <u>Operational Design</u> differs again from that of a traditional development project, in that it must reconcile the differing needs of several applications. The strategy to be adopted for data back-up and the recovery of files or online transactions is no longer the province of a single application. The security controls for protection of data and authorisation of retrieval or update, cannnot be designed effectively application by application. Data sharing implies also the design of a performance monitoring system both for data usage and for the response on individual transactions. This must be done before the system becomes operational rather than as an afterthought.

f.    The task of <u>Program Design</u>, should be left until the operational and data structuring issues are finalised. The structure of a program should be based on a decompostion of the elementary function that the program is to support. However, in most cases no further decomposition is meaningful and it is possible to base the program structure entirely on the equivalent function logic model. Thus there is a program module corresponding to each entity type in the model and where there are one to many relationships in the logic a module may be called many times during the execution of the transaction. Once the program structure has been defined, the interfaces between each of its modules must be defined in detail, in terms of the attributes of the entity types involved. Existing function dependency diagrams can be useful at this point and a diagram should be drawn to illustrate the data flow within the program. This in turn will lead to the design of the internal control of that program, bearing in mind the transaction control matrix and the ordered requirements from the system design specification. Finally, it may be necessary to write some processing specification for each module, although this should consist of no more than a reference to the input forms, report layouts and screen layouts defined in the

System Design Specification and to the business algorithms from the Business Systems Specification. Certainly the Program Specification should be expressed in terms of the diagramatic conventions already used, with a minimum of narrative.

g.    During the analysis stage the possibilities for transition were considered. This work is now applied in the <u>Transition Design</u> task. The attributes and relationships supported by the existing systems are already known, so that procedures can be defined for loading these into the new database structure. Similarly, procedures must be designed for the collection, verification, correction and loading of other data not available in the existing systems.

Where these systems already support elementary functions within the scope of the project, the effect of their being replaced must be determined. Interfaces must be designed between the old and the new systems detailing the data that will need to be passed between the two, its frequency and any time or other dependencies. These interfaces can first be defined in terms of attributes from the earlier transition analysis and then designed as records and communication files.

Transition design should be concerned with all the problems of using the new system alongside the old. This almost certainly will require user training to provide the skills and motivation needed to ensure their involvement, and to obtain the extra effort necessary while reconciling the two systems. The transition design task is complete only with a detailed plan encompassing data collection, interface programming and all end user activities and training.

h.    The final task in the Design Stage, all too often forgotten in conventional projects, is the <u>Test Strategy Design</u>. Where several applications and many programs, possibly both batch and online, are to share the same data, testing is more complex and the procedures must be more rigorous. To allow for any interaction problems between applications one common test database is needed. Test data cannot be the responsibility of each application, except in so far as they must incorporate special conditions found in only one application. The test strategy design must define the acceptance criteria for each application and for the data sharing system as a whole. The test plan should cover the creation, modification and deletion of every entity, attribute and relationship in the system. It must also consider every elementary function and the time dependencies between them. The testing plan will of course commence with the proving of individual modules and programs, but will lead to full user involvement in checking clerical procedures, interactive dialogues and the system under full volume stress conditions. Given that the tests will be proving such system constructs as records and transactions, the strategy is still expressed in terms of the entities and functions of the user environment

## 2.2.5   CONSTRUCTION STAGE

The fourth stage of the systems life cycle is known as the Construction Stage.    Previous stages were concerned with requirements in the architecture.   Now at last the system itself will be built.   Our approach to systems construction consists of the following tasks:

* Acquiring new hardware and software
* Database construction
* Program construction
* System construction

a.   The task of <u>Acquiring New Hardware and Software</u> covers the traditional activities of selection, contracting, installation, training and acceptance.   It may well include a large number of time consuming activities, ranging from the installation of purpose built remote user terminals to the acquisiton of specific software aids.   The impact of data sharing can place weight on the need for an overall strategy and its influence on purchasing decisions.

b.   The <u>Database Construction</u> task consists of schema coding and validation, the loading of test files and databases, and verification of the correctness of the desired physical storage structures and linkages between data.   A battery of proven test transactions is needed to check out the schema and the loaded database.

c.   The <u>Program Construction</u> task should involve by this point a relatively trivial process of module coding checked by such techniques as structured walk throughs and followed by compilation and then testing of the module in a test harness.

d.   During the <u>System Construction</u> task the job control statements must be written, and the individual programs integrated into one system.   The test database has already been proven and can be used at this stage to prove the application programs.   Testing of the integrated system ought to include its back-up and recovery procedures, the user procedures and the security provisions.   Performance monitoring should be undertaken at the same time.

It can be seen that apart from those activities concerning the database, data sharing does not introduce new activities into the Construction Stage.   It simply emphasises, in wishing to minimise the difficulties of systems implementation, the importance of clearly separating the design and construction stages and of taking account of all aspects of the operational system, not merely those related to application program coding and testing.

## 2.2.6 TRANSITION STAGE

The subsequent Transition Stage will of course differ markedly from system to system. However, the tasks of user preparation, data conversion, parallel operation and user acceptance apply as much in a shared data environment as with a conventional methodology. The stage is also not complete until the system includes the documentation necessary for its trouble free operation; both operational guides and the user manuals.

## 2.2.7 PRODUCTION STAGE

The final stage to which all this effort has been directed is the Production Stage in the systems life cycle. The first task, evaluation, is particularly important in a shared data environment. This is because it is necessary to evaluate each of the applications independently and also the benefits accruing from sharing data between them. Any evaluation of an operational system should include the adequacy of its documentation, its performance, the cost of running the system and the users reaction. Evaluation is likely to result in the identification of necessary improvements, both to meet user requirements and to improve its performance. It should be remembered that one of the main objectives of this disciplined methodology, basing the development on the user environment, and dividing the development into self contained stages, was to arrive at a flexible design that could be amended without great upheavals.

In our experience of developing and using this methodology, these objectives can and have been met. Even so it is fair to point out that we have been developing these ideas for less than ten years and that they continue to evolve as a result of new experiences in differing user situations. We do not claim that any one methodology can be suited unchanged to every user environment and level of analysis and design skill. The tasks briefly described in this paper must be used with discretion. At times it will be necessary to take short cuts, but this must be done only with a full understanding of the implications. As these concepts become more widely used, and as the utility of such aids as data dictionaries, simulators, and program generators improve, the methodology will continue to evolve.

## 2.3    TECHNIQUES AND CONVENTIONS

### 2.3.1 ENTITY MODELLING

Entity analysis provides a means of understanding and documenting the data framework supporting a complete business environment. Emphasis is placed on understanding the things which make up the environment rather than on detailing how these things are used. The results of entity analysis are summarised diagrammatically in an entity model and may be recorded in detail in a data dictionary. These results provide a description of an enterprise in terms of its types of entities, the types of relationships between them and the types of attributes which describe each entity. These concepts can be defined as follows:

a.    An _entity_ is a fundamental thing of interest to an enterprise.

   Hence, it is something about which information could be kept in a system. An entity may be a person, place, object, event or concept; entities do not necessarily have a physical existence in the environment.

b.    An _attribute_ is a descriptive value or property associated with an individual entity.

   One type of attribute may describe entities of more than one type. One descriptive value or attribute occurrence can be associated with only one entity occurrence. An entity can exist in its own right without having any attributes defined for it.

c.    A _relationship_ is an association between two or more entities.

   Different relationship occurrences of the same type may involve differing numbers of entities. All relationships of the one type are associations between entities of the same one or two types.

In the methodology each element in the environment must be classified as either an entity, an attribute or a relationship. No element may be classified in more than one way. At times decisions must be made based on the style of the enterprise being studied as to the most convenient way of representing certain aspects of the environment.

Unlike other methodologies we have found it convenient to introduce the restriction that only entities and not relationships may have attributes. Hence, anything which may have descriptive values must be treated as an entity. To allow the additional choice of it being treated as a relationship, adds even greater arbitrariness into the entity analysis process, increasing the number of iterations needed before an acceptable entity model is attained. Similarly, relationships may exist

only between entities and are restricted to associations of
entities of not more than two types.  Of course, all attributes
of an entity are related by virtue of the fact that they describe
that entity, but relationships are not defined between
attributes.

The entity model incorporates these concepts and uses a full set
of diagrammatic conventions to ensure that a complete description
of the environment can be provided.  These are as follows:

*   A 'soft' box is used to
    illustrate each entity type.
    This convention prevents
    confusion with diagrammatic
    techniques such as Bachman's
    where the boxes represent
    physical, designed
    structures.

    Entity
    Type

*   Boxes are linked by lines
    which represent the necessary
    relationship types between
    them.  These may be named
    along the lines in cases
    where their meaning may not
    be altogether clear.

Relationship Type

*   A broken line is used to
    indicate that a relationship
    type is optional and that
    occurrences of either of the
    entity types need not take
    part in such a relationship.

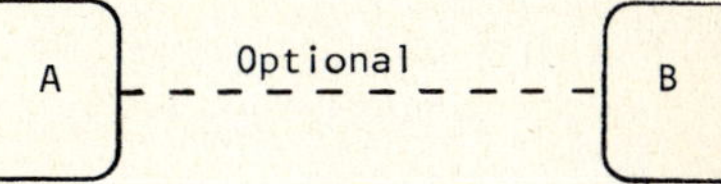


*   A line broken along one half
    of its length indicates that
    the relationship is
    contingent.  Thus occurrences
    of entity type B need not
    take part in such a
    relationship.  All
    occurrences of entity type A
    must however take part in
    such a relationship.

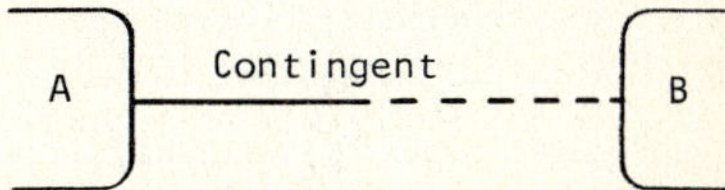


*   A solid line indicates that a
    relationship is mandatory.
    All occurrences of entity
    types A and B must take part
    in such a relationship.

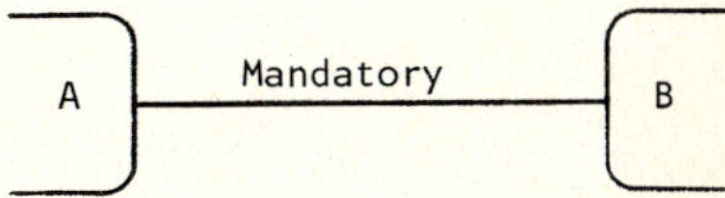

*   A 'crow's foot' on a relationship indicates a degree of many. Thus an occurrence of an A type entity can be associated with many occurrences of the B type.

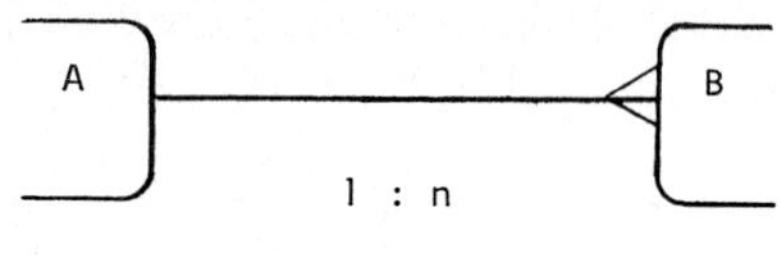


*   A 'crow's foot' at each end of a relationship indicates that the degree of the relationship is many-to-many. Thus an entity of type A can be related to many of type B and an entity of type B can be related to many of type A.

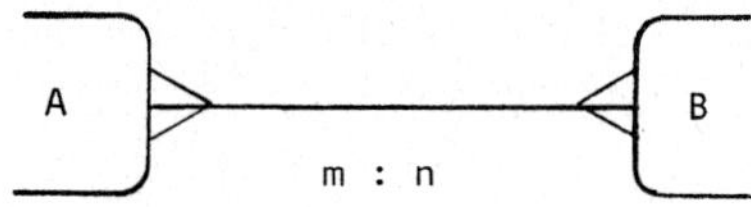


*   A one-to-one relationship where one occurrence of type A can be related to only one of type B and vice versa.

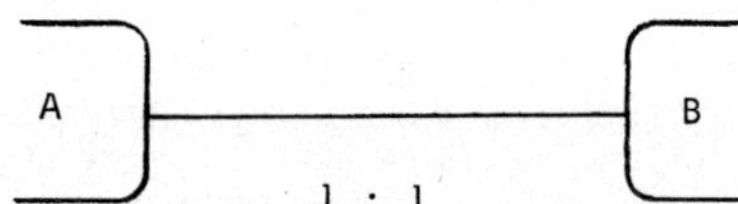


*   A relationship of fixed degree. One occurrence of entity type A is related to five and always five occurrences of entity type B.

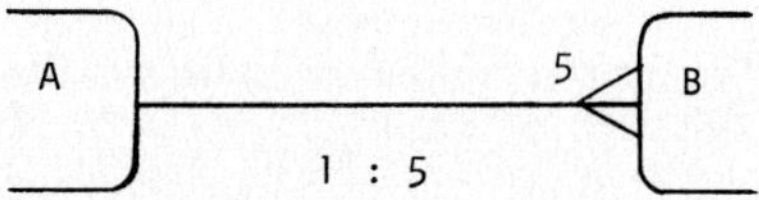


*   An arc through two relationships indicates exclusivity in respect of the entity type by the arc. Thus entities of type C can at any one time take part in either relationship A or B but not

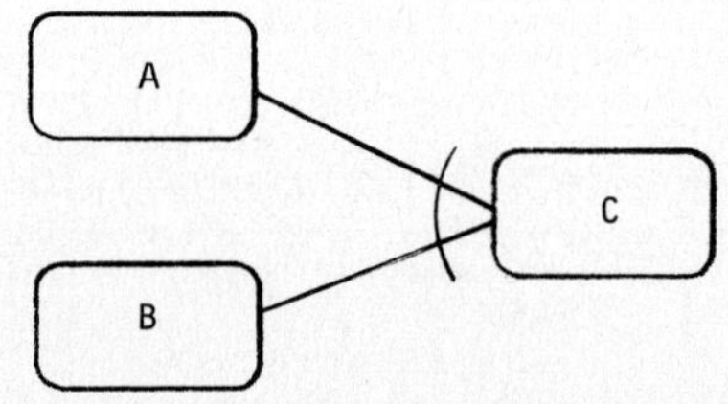


*   Entity sub-types may be recognised where the sub-types have some attributes of their own or take part in relationships in which the other sub-types are not concerned.

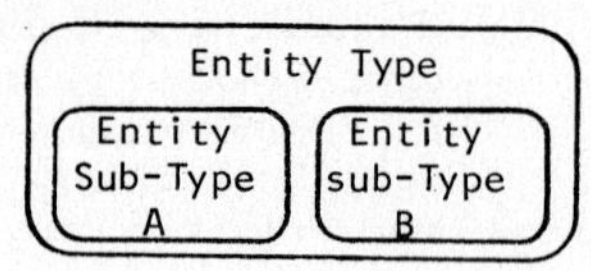

## 2.3.2 FUNCTION MODELLING

Function analysis concentrates on the functions or business processes which must be carried out for the enterprise to continue to operate and satisfy its objectives or achieve its goals. The analysis concentrates first on the identification of the major high-level business functions and then continues with their stepwise breakdown. The breakdown or function decomposition continues until the functions identified are at a sufficiently low level to correspond with transactions in a computer system, where appropriate. The results of the decomposition are presented pictorially as a function hierarchy.

Function analysis provides an understanding of what an enterprise does. It is carried out in a way which is independent of the organisational structure of the enterprise, with its political biases, and also of the currently designed systems used to support the functions.

A function is a type of business activity and an activity is itself an execution of the function. It is therefore what the enterprise does, not how it is done or who does it. Functions are performed as the result of an event and transform some input into output thus using or effecting a change to one or more entity types, attribute types or relationship types.

In documenting a function hierarchy the following conventions are employed:

*       The 'soft' box is used to indicate a function type at any level of the breakdown.

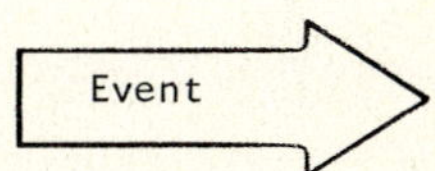


*       A solid arrow is used to identify a type of event acting as a trigger or stimulus to a particular function type.



*       The breakdown of a function is generally represented in a hierarchical form. Thus types B and C are lower level, more elementary functions than type A and make up type A. This representation is used to indicate that type A consists of type B and C.

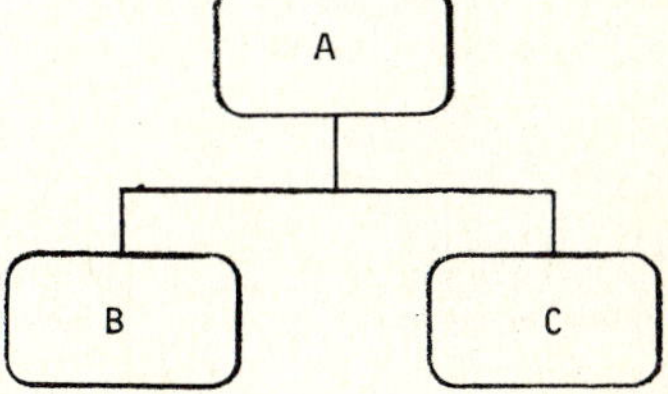

*       An arc is used to indicate
        exclusiveness.  Thus type A
        consists of type B and type
        C.

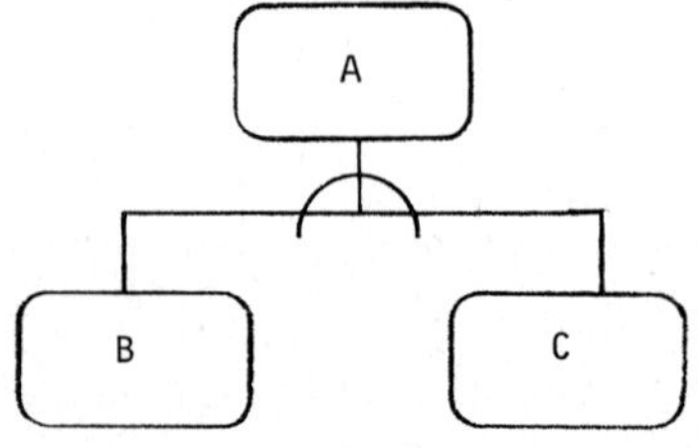

*       Optionality is shown by using
        a broken line.  Thus type A
        consists   of   type   B   and
        possibly   also   of   type   C.

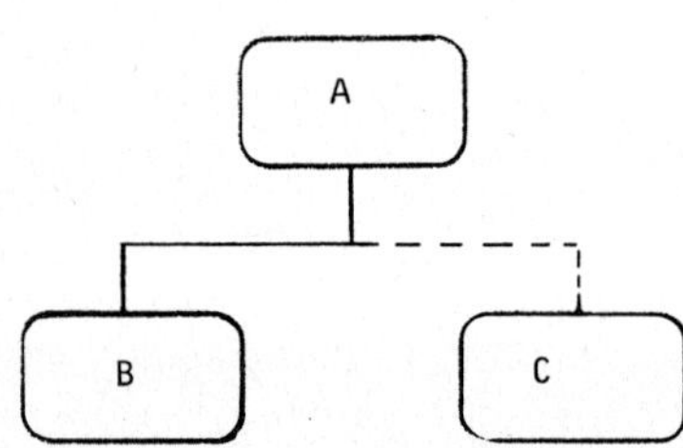

*       The 'crow's foot' is used to
        indicate that a function has
        to be performed several times
        before the higher-level
        function is complete.  Thus
        function type A consists of
        one   execution   of   type   B
        together with several of type
        C.

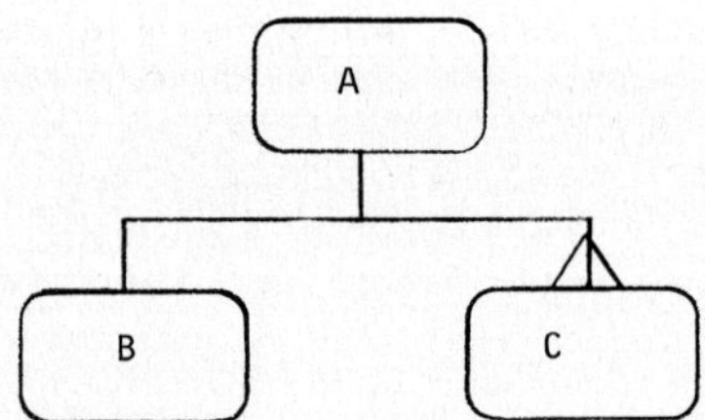

## 2.3.3 ENTITY LIFE CYCLE ANALYSIS

This analysis provides a state diagram which identifies each
state an entity can exist in during its life and shows what
events or functions cause it to change state or act on it in one
state.  This analysis provides a check on the completeness of the
function hierarchy and serves as a guide to the programmer,
leading to a complete logic in data handling operations.

The conventions used in drawing up an entity life cycle are as
follows:

*       The entity is initialised as
        the result of the event.

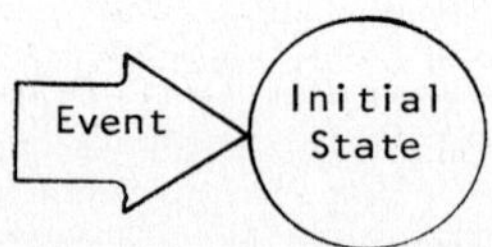

*   The state of the entity is
    changed as a result of the
    function.

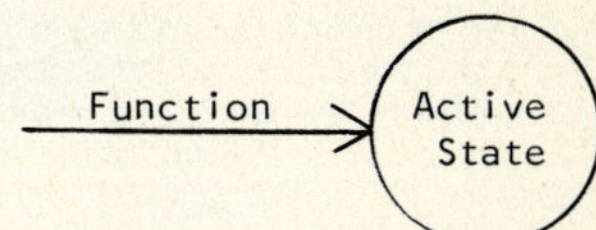


*   The entity is acted on or
    used by the function but it
    does not enter a new state.

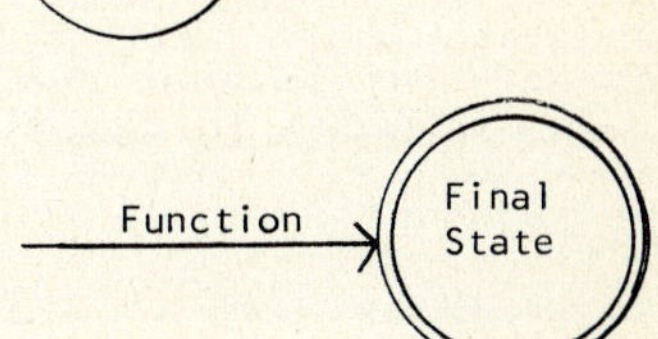


*   The entity ends its life
    cycle and is no longer
    available to the system.

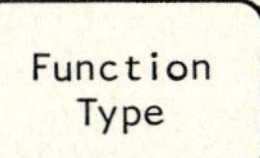


## 2.3.4 FUNCTION DEPENDENCY ANALYSIS

Function dependency analysis is used to show the logical 'data
flows' between functions.    It therefore illustrates major
dependencies between functions and shows what timing constraints
apply to the execution of functions as a result of their
dependence on others.

The conventions used in drawing a function dependency diagram are
as follows:

*   A 'soft' box is used to
    indicate a function type.

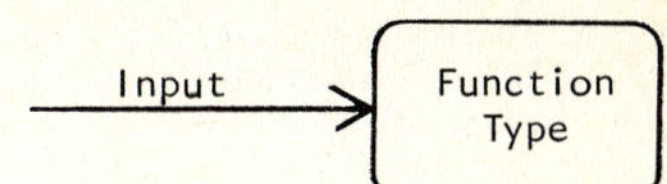


*   Input data to a function is
    represented by lines coming
    to the function on the left.



*   Output data from a function
    is represented by lines
    leaving the function on the
    right.

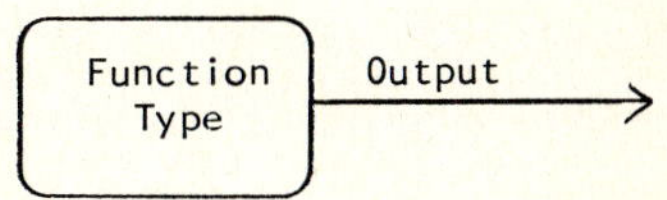

*      Data which serves to control
       or modify the function is
       shown on a line coming to the
       function from above or below.

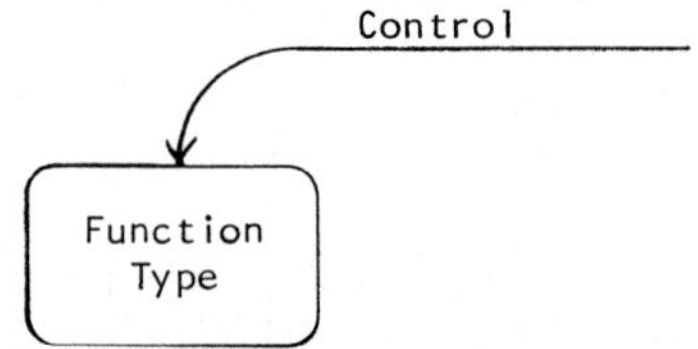


## 2.3.5 FUNCTION LOGIC ANALYSIS

Function logic analysis is a technique for studying the
interactions between functions and data.  It involves a diagram
or logic model for each elementary function showing the entity
types and relationship types needed to support the function and
the sequence in which they are required.

The criteria used to select particular entities are documented,
as are the actions performed by the function in creating,
modifying or deleting entities or relationships.  Volumetric
information is also associated with the analysis to provide usage
information necessary for subsequent design decisions.

The diagrammatic conventions employed are as follows:

*      This represents a starting
       point in the path where an
       entity occurrence is selected
       using a unique identifier.



*      A starting point where
       several or all entity
       occurrences are selected
       using search criteria or a
       general scan.

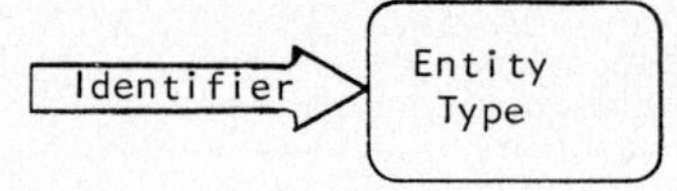


*      The next entity type is
       selected by following a
       relationship and applying
       some selection criteria.



*      An entity type C is selected
       at the intersection of two
       relationships which are
       selected by identifying
       specific occurrences of the
       other two entity types.

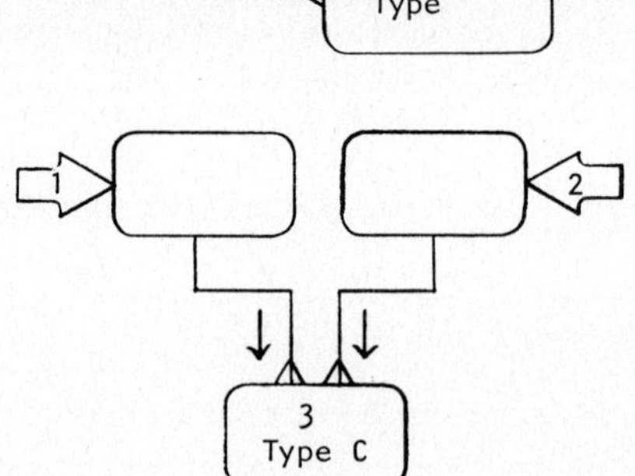

* The entity is retrieved but no attributes are modified or renewed.

* A new occurrence of the entity is created.

* The entity is modified. Thus attribute values, other than for the entity identifier, are changed.

* The entity occurrence is no longer of interest to the enterprise and is deleted.

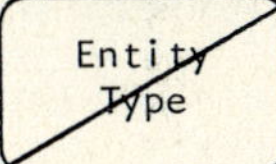

## 3.    IFIP CONFERENCING SYSTEM

### 3.1    GENERAL APPROACH

This section examines the problem posed by the IFIP WG8.1 and uses the problem to illustrate major aspects of the methodology for the design of data sharing systems.

The problem statement, the responses to questions, the material contained in the invitation to submit and the aims of WG8.1 in setting up the conference were the only sources of information on which to base this work.  They have provided a reasonable basis from which to identify the data existing within the conference area and have provided some insight into the major functions performed, though not a complete picture at the detailed level.

The analyses are therefore regarded as incomplete and unverified and, in the absence of any dialogue with users, would not normally serve as a basis for logical design.  A particular area of weakness lies in estimating the frequency with which functions may be performed.

Major aspects of the design process have however been illustrated and the means by which design decisions can be taken are discussed.

### 3.2    ANALYSIS

### 3.2.1 ENTITY MODELLING

Figure 4 illustrates the entity model for the conferencing system, the conventions used in drawing the model are given in 2.3.1 and examples of the ways in which the entities, attributes and relationships are documented are given in figures 6 and 7.

<u>Conference</u> is the IFIP working conference arranged under the auspices of one or possibly two technical committees.  It is identified by name and start date and possibly by some other code identifier and may include attributes describing the intended number of participants as a means of controlling the invitation process.

<u>Session</u> is one period within the conference and also is associated with a particular group of papers.  It has an identified chairman and could reasonably include other specially identified people as panellists for a discussion period.  It carries data on the date, time and topic for discussion.

<u>Conference Committee</u> is one of the two bodies of IFIP members who deal with the creation and arranging of the conference.

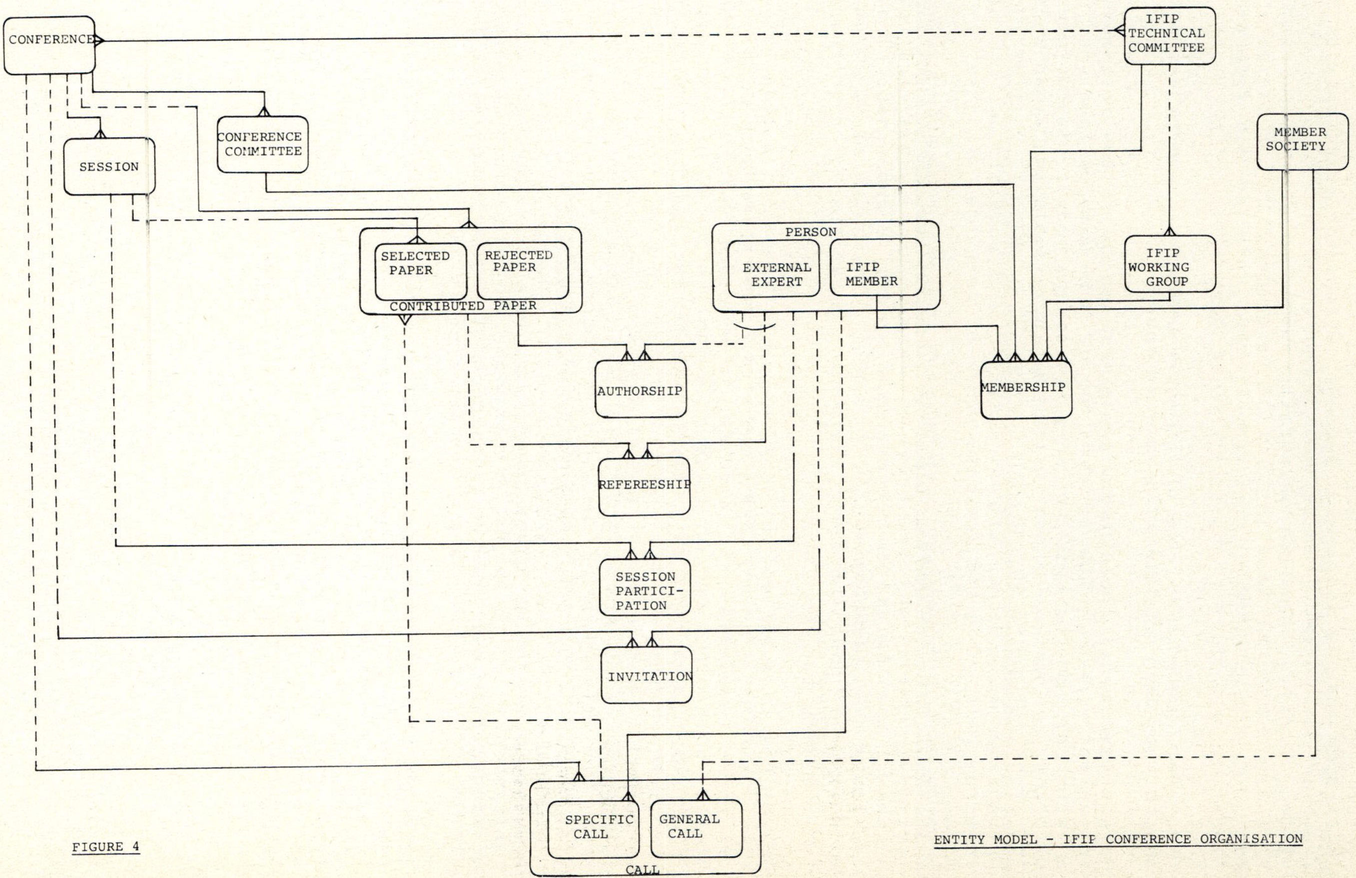


ENTITY MODEL – IFIP CONFERENCE ORGANISATION

FIGURE 4

<u>Contributed Paper</u> provides the potential content of the conference and its sessions. To begin with these exist only as a statement of intent from certain authors and consist only of a title. They may then be physically submitted after which time they are subjected to a process of assessment and, if selected for use, are grouped by session. Those selected and rejected thus form significant sub-types since only those selected take part in the relationship with session. It carries the name of the paper, possibly a list of keywords and possibly even a short abstract as well as details of its status.

<u>Person</u> covers all those individuals who may be of any relevance to the conference. Some of them may be IFIP members involved in a technical committee or society, others are people unassociated with IFIP but who are known to them as individuals concerned with the technical areas of interest to the TC or WG. It carries the person's name, address and affiliation and possibly a list of keywords indicating the person's areas of technical interest.

<u>IFIP Technical Committee, IFIP Working Group and Member Society</u> are all identified as entities simply for classification purposes, insofar as the conferencing system is concerned. They enable us to identify an IFIP member's association with the organisation and therefore help in prioritising conference invitations.

<u>Membership</u> is a period during which an IFIP member is associated with a conference committee, technical committee, working group or member society. It provides a means of controlling the invitation process and of preventing duplication of invitations. It is largely a form of cross-reference but carries the dates when membership started or ended.

<u>Authorship</u> is an occasion on which a person has been associated with the writing of a contributed paper. If a system were created which kept track of people for a period greater than that of the duration of a conference then this information could provide a valuable start when issuing calls for a future conference. It acts as little more than a cross-reference between person and paper but could contain information as to the status of the author and as to whether he is also a speaker.

<u>Refereeship</u> is a period during which a person may be acting as a referee in respect of a paper. Initially it exists as a request to be a referee, although this can only be done if the person is not intending to be an author. Following acceptance, an occurrence of refereeship will carry details of the invitation and acceptance dates and eventually the registration details and summary of the referee's report.

<u>Session Participation</u> is an occasion on which a person takes part in a conference session by special invitation to act as the session chairman.		The entity is essentially just a cross-reference between person and session.  It is however worth noting that its use would also cover instances where a panel discussion session was included in a conference and therefore where several participants were required.

<u>Invitation</u> covers details of a request sent to a person to attend a conference.  It also carries the date and nature of the person's response and, in the case of an acceptance, may also carry details of a subsequent decision not to attend.  This information is essential to those arranging the conference facilities.

<u>Call</u> covers the announcement of the conference and carries details of a request for potential authors to express their intention to submit papers.  The call may be associated with a specific person or may be a general request to a member society or even a published advertisement.  A specific call may become associated with an intention to contribute a paper and will certainly carry a closing date beyond which time letters of intent will not be accepted.

It should be noted that in an entity model only those things essential to the organisation are included.  Thus forms and documents are not normally taken to be entities since they are generally just aspects of one or more entities in an implemented fashion.  Details of call and invitation letters are therefore not included in the model though an implementation may wish to include a means of automatically duplicating and copying the text to any appropriate person.

## 3.2.2 FUNCTION MODELLING

Figures 5(1) - 5(3) illustrate the function model for the conferencing system.  The conventions used in drawing the model are given in 2.3.2 and an example of the documentation for a function is given in figure 7.

The breakdown has been taken to four levels where possible although the areas of facilities arrangement, the publishing of proceedings, publicity and finance have not been examined.  A significant number of the fourth level functions could clearly be decomposed to a fifth level but, in the absence of sufficient detail in the problem description, this has not been attempted.  Indeed, the fourth level also contains many assumptions about the functions required.  Because of this incompleteness no attempt has been made to fully annotate the model by including optionality, exclusivity and repetition though at the lowest levels this would normally be included.

*I.G. MacDonald and I.R. Palmer*

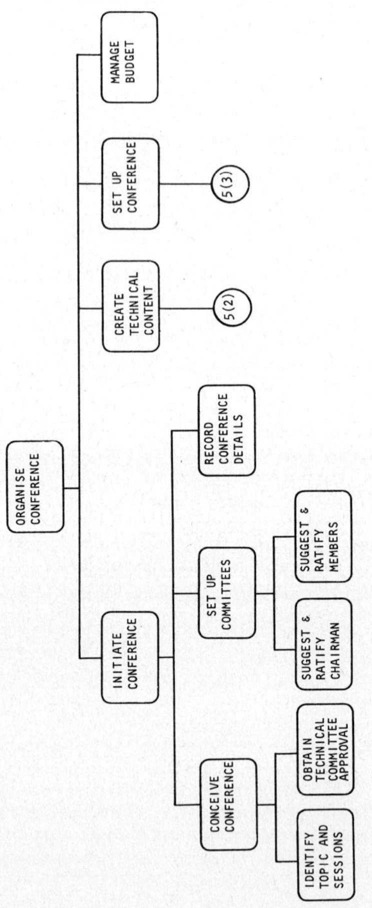


FIGURE 5(1)  IFIP CONFERENCE ORGANISATION FUNCTION MODEL

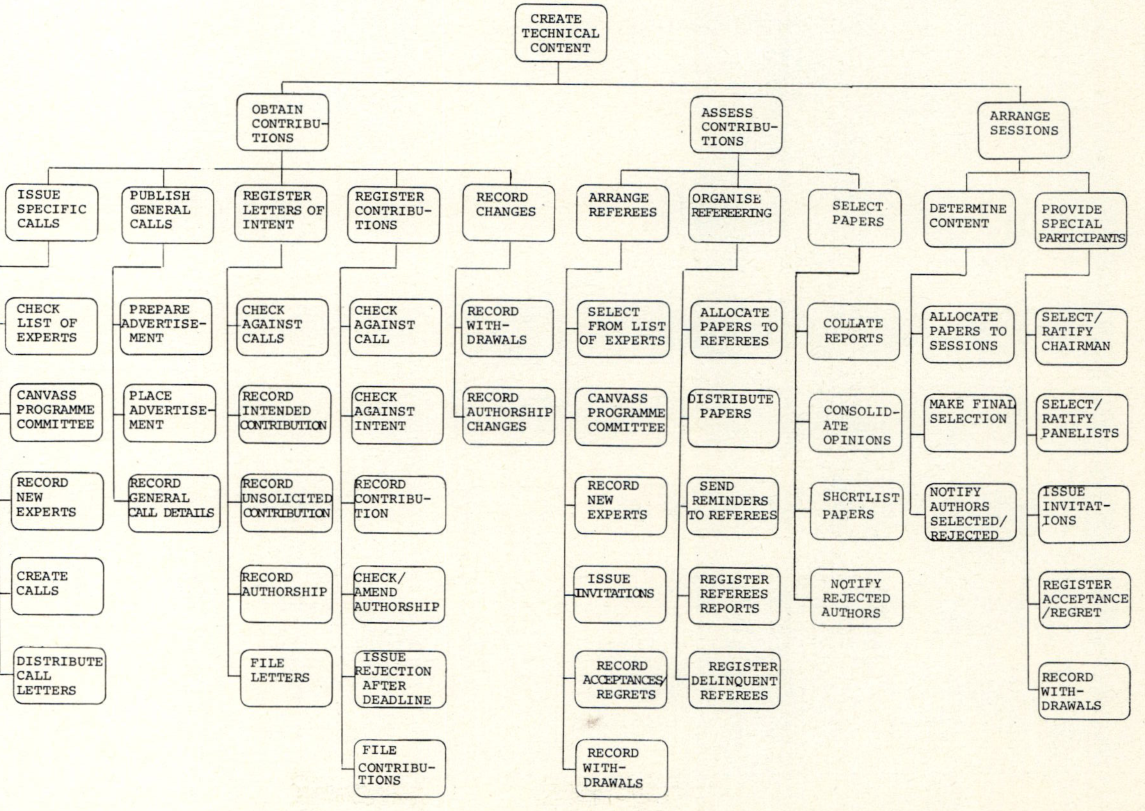



FIGURE 5(2)    IFIP CONFERENCE ORGANISATION FUNCTION MODEL

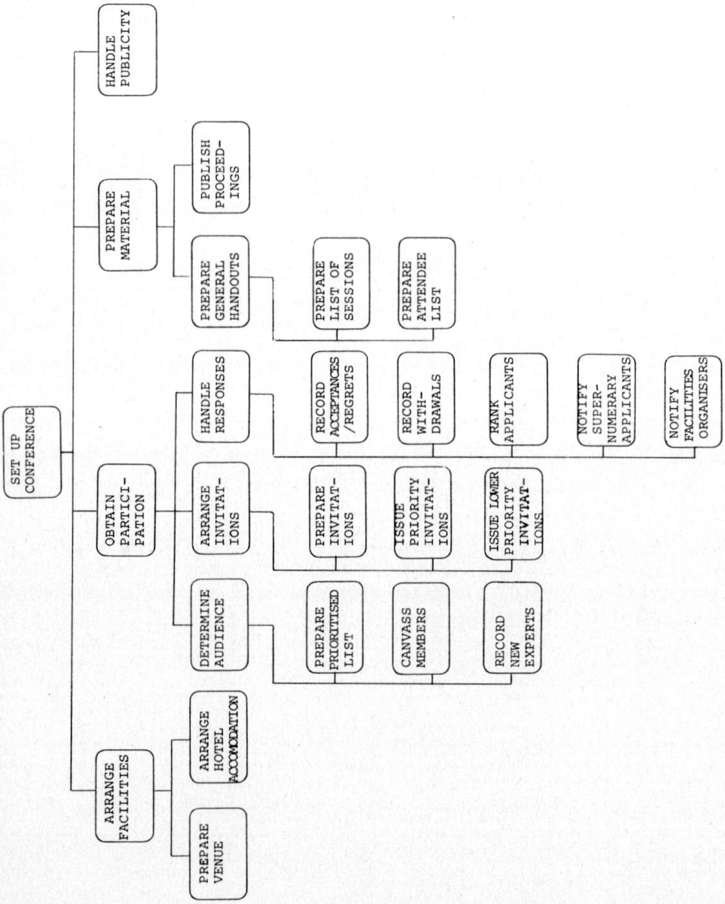

*I.G. MacDonald and I.R. Palmer*

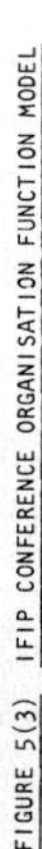


FIGURE 5(3)   IFIP CONFERENCE ORGANISATION FUNCTION MODEL

CACI
Entity Type
Specification Form

IFIP WG 8.1

| | |
|---|---|
| Entity Reference and Name | E03 : CONTRIBUTED PAPER |
| Synonym | |
| Definition | A written article on a pertinent technical topic submitted to the Programme Committee for their approval and for inclusion in a Conference Seminar. |
| Identified by | PAPER TITLE<br>REGISTRATION NUMBER |

| Number | Minimum | Average | Maximum | Rate of Growth | Date Applicable |
|---|---|---|---|---|---|
| | 10 | N/A | 100 | - | 1 Aug 81 |

| | |
|---|---|
| Owned by | Persons having Authorship |
| Available to | Programmee committee members |
| Consists of Entity Subtypes | E04 : SELECTED PAPER<br>E05 : REJECTED PAPER |
| Major Attribute Types | |
| Notes | |

IFIP

C.A.C.I.

CACI-01

Figure 6

CACI
Attribute Type
Specification Form

IFIP WG 8.1

| | |
|---|---|
| Attribute Reference and Name | A002 : CONFERENCE NAME |
| Synonym | CONFERENCE TITLE |
| Definition | The name by which the conference is formally known and which is used on all correspondence, advertising material and published proceedings. |
| Describes Entity | E01 : CONFERENCE |
| Domain | |

| Number | Minimum | Average | Maximum | Rate of Growth | Date Applicable |
|---|---|---|---|---|---|
| | 1 | 1 | 1 | - | 1 Aug 81 |

| | |
|---|---|
| Owned by | IFIP Working Group |
| Available to | Conference committees |

| Value | Meaning |
|---|---|
| N/A | |

Notes

IFIP

C.A.C.I.

CACI-03

**CACI**
**Relationship Type**
**Specification Form**

**IFIP**   WG 8.1

Relationship Reference and Name

| RO4 | CONTRIBUTION |

**Synonym**

**Definition**

The association between the conference and papers which have either been promised or received.

**Involves Entity**

| EO1 | CONFERENCE |

With Optionality of: ☐ always  ☑ sometimes (   %)   And With Degree of: ☑ one (1:)  ☐ many (n:)

| Minimum | Average | Maximum | Rate of Growth | Date Applicable |
|---|---|---|---|---|
| N/A | 1 | N/A | N/A | 1 Aug 81 |

**Involves Entity**

| EO3 | CONTRIBUTED PAPER |

With Optionality of: ☑ always  ☐ sometimes (   %)   And With Degree of: ☐ one (:1)  ☑ many (:n)

| Minimum | Average | Maximum | Rate of Growth | Date Applicable |
|---|---|---|---|---|
| 10 | N/A | 100 | N/A | 1 Aug 81 |

**Owned by**

Programme Committee

**Available to**

Programme Committee

**Interdependency**   ☐ exclusive with   ☐ inclusive with

**Relationship**

**Notes**

C.A.C.I.

CACI-02

---

**CACI**
**Function Type**
**Specification Form**

**IFIP**   WG 8.1

Function Reference and Name

| FOO8 | OBTAIN CONTRIBUTIONS |

**Synonym**

**Definition**

A process by which the programme committee first request that specialists in the topic of the conference submit for their approval papers considered suitable and then register details of those papers received.

**Purpose**

To provide technical material for the conference sessions

**Responsibility**

Programme committee

**Duration**

| Minimum | Average | Maximum | Rate of Growth | Date Applicable |
|---|---|---|---|---|
| – | 1 per conference | – | – | 1 Aug 81 |

**Location**

N/A

**Preceeding Function or Event**

SET UP CONFERENCE COMMITTEES

**Dependant Function or Event**

ASSESS CONTRIBUTIONS

**Consists of Sub Functions** | **With Number**

| FO19 | Prepare call list |
| FO20 | Send out calls |
| FO21 | Publish call |
| FO22 | Register letters of intent |
| FO23 | Register contributions |

**Notes**

C.A.C.I.

CACI-04

Figure 7

The analysis does cover most aspects of the conference including its initiation, the creation of the technical content and the means of ensuring an adequate audience. It is however worth noting that it contains no indication of how details about people associated with IFIP are handled although any system which may be set up will be heavily dependent on adequate input of data on such people.

Descriptions of individual functions are not provided. The hierarchy should in this case be reasonably self-explanatory.

## 3.2.3 ANALYSIS OF INTERACTIONS

Once the entity and function models have been constructed, their correctness can be confirmed in two ways, each involving an assessment of the way the two interact.

a. The entity state diagram identifies all of the states the entity can pass through and shows what functions cause a change of state or can use an entity without changing its state. Figure 8 provides an example for the Contributed Paper entity. This helps to identify any missing functions and can be used to construct a state-change matrix to guide programmers at the design and construction stage by demonstrating what actions are possible with that entity. The state-change matrix in this case will be as follows:

| Functions | I | II | III | IV | V | VI | VII | VIII | IX | X |
|---|---|---|---|---|---|---|---|---|---|---|
| Record against call | II | | | | | | | | | |
| Record unsolicited response | II | | | | | | | | | |
| Record contribution | | III | | | | | | | | |
| Failure to meet deadline | | X | | | | | | | | |
| Record authorship | | | III | | | | | | | |
| Record refereeship | | | III | | | | | | | |
| Change authorship | | | III | | | | | | | |
| Shortlist papers | | | IV / V | | | | | | | |
| Allocate to session | | | | V / VI | | | | | | |
| Record regrets | | | VII | | | VII | | | | |
| Read paper | | | | | | VIII | | | | |
| Publish proceedings | | | | | | | | IX | | |
| Archive | | | | | X | | X | | X | |

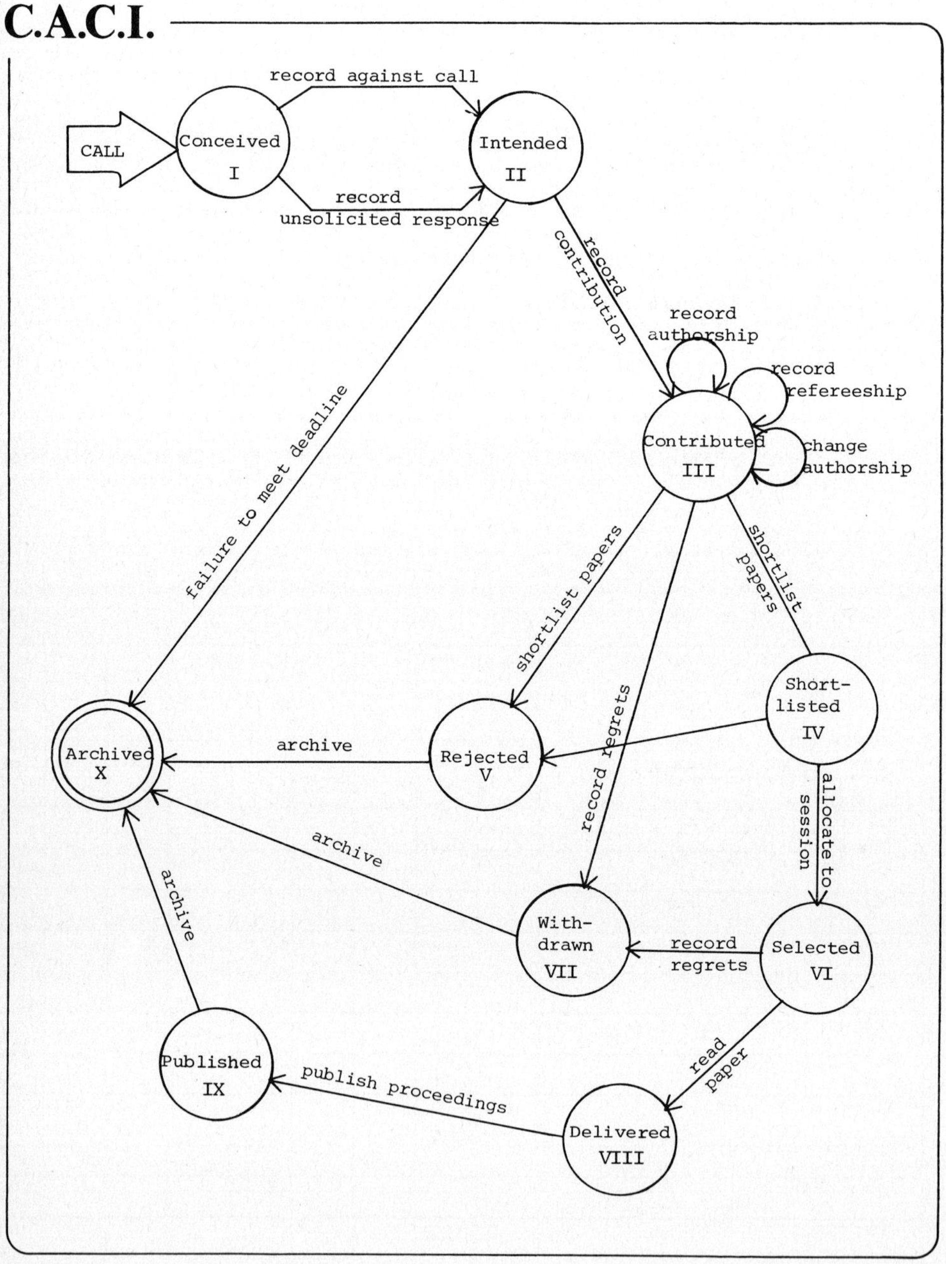

Contributed Paper
Entity Life Cycle     Figure 8

This clearly shows some functions such as 'read paper' which have not yet been included in the hierarchy and also 'archive' - an ill-defined function since it is not clear what happens to information gathered during conference organisation once the event is over.

b.   The function logic diagram (figure 9) and its associated documentation (figure 10) shows how a function type uses data and the route through the entity model it must follow, in logical terms, to obtain it.   By quantifying the frequency with which each function uses each part of the pathway a composite view can be built for all functions of the use of each entity type and relationship type.   This then provides guidance in developing the logical database.

The example given is that for the Prepare Prioritised List function.   This generates a list of people to be invited to the conference.   Authors, referees, committee members, members of the TC and WG involved and representatives of member societies are always invited.   Other specialists in the topics under discussion may also be invited, hence the use of selection by key word may be appropriate.   The selection logic required is probably as follows:

1.   Select person

2.   If authorship exists
     Then accept

3.   If refereeship exists and is not delinquent
     Then accept

4.   If person is an IFIP member

     4.1 Select membership

     4.2 If conference committee is associated
         Then accept

     4.3 If working group is associated and is WG8.1
         Then accept

     4.4 If technical committee is associated and is TC8
         Then acccept

     4.5 If member society is associated
         Then accept

5.   If keywords match
     Then accept

6.   Else reject

7.   List acceptances

C.A.C.I. 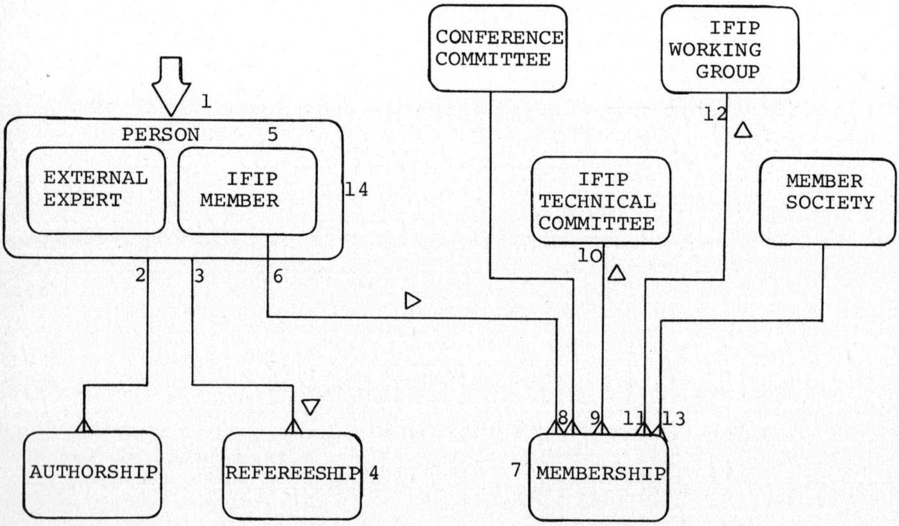
CONFERENCE COMMITTEE
IFIP WORKING GROUP
PERSON
EXTERNAL EXPERT
IFIP MEMBER
IFIP TECHNICAL COMMITTEE
MEMBER SOCIETY
AUTHORSHIP
REFEREESHIP
MEMBERSHIP
1
5
14
2
3
6
4
7
8
9
10
11
13
12
FUNCTION LOGIC MODEL - PREPARE PRIORITISED LIST
Figure 9
IFIP WG8.1

# C.A.C.I.

**IFIP**

CACI
Function Logic
Specification Form

**IFIP** WG 8.1

| Function Name | Prepare Prioritised List | | | | | | | |
|---|---|---|---|---|---|---|---|---|

Response Required

| Entity/Relationship Accessed | E/R | Selection Criteria | number R/F | C/C | M/T | D/C | Comments |
|---|---|---|---|---|---|---|---|
| E06 — PERSON | E | All, IFIP Member Status, Keywords | all | | | | |
| R12 — AUTHORING | R | Any | 1 | | | | per PERSON |
| R13 — REFEREEING | R | All | all | | | | |
| E14 — REFEREESHIP | E | All | all | | | | |
| R17 — IFIP MEMBERSHIP | R | All | all | | | | |
| E12 — MEMBERSHIP | E | All | all | | | | |
| R18 — COMMITTEE MEMBERSHIP | R | Any | 1 | | | | max/membership |
| R19 — TC MEMBERSHIP | R | Any | 1 | | | | max/membership |
| E09 — IFIP TECHNICAL COMMITTEE | E | | 1 | | | | per relation-ship |
| R20 — WG MEMBERSHIP | R | Any | 1 | | | | max/membership |
| E10 — IFIP WORKING GROUP | E | | 1 | | | | per relation-ship |
| R21 — SOCIETY/MEMBERSHIP | R | Any | 1 | | | | max/membership |

Notes

Actions - Entities : Retrieve ; Create ; Modify ; Delete
Relationships : Follow ; Connect ; Transfer ; Disconnect

CACI-05

Figure 10

c.   A third technique used is that of the function dependency
     diagram.  This illustrates dependencies between functions
     and shows the data input to and output from each.  Figure 11
     shows the dependencies among the fourth level functions
     making up Obtain Participation.

     This type of diagram is particularly valuable when carried
     out at the lowest level since it shows what the
     interdependencies between transactions will be in the
     designed system.

## 3.3    DESIGN

### 3.3.1 CLUSTER ANALYSIS

Once a logic model has been determined for each low level
function, it becomes possible to apply cluster analysis
techniques to determine the affinity between functions.  This can
be done manually by constructing a matrix, as in figure 12, of
entities against functions and manipulating it until reasonable
clusters of data usage are determined.  When operating at a
detailed level it is more practical to automate the process and
we have used APL systems to aid cluster analysis.

In figure 12 the functions included are largely at the third
level of breakdown and, although at this level the analysis
cannot be very sensitive, six possible groupings of functions
emerge.

Group 1 is hardly relevant to any computer system, being
concerned only with noting details of advertising calls.

Group 2 includes all those functions concerned with the direct
association between people and the conference while group 5 is
concerned with papers and their associated people.  These two
groups cover the main operations of the conference information
gathering system.  Groups 3 and 6 select from the information
gathered, one for papers, the other for people, and finally group
4 covers general reporting for the conference.

This analysis indicates the main areas of commonality between
functions and suggests that groups can be developed as
application areas.  In this case, the scope of the system is
sufficiently small for these to be regarded only as separate
programming tasks.

### 3.3.2 LOGICAL DATABASE DESIGN

The results from the quantification of usage in the function
logic analyses are consolidated onto usage summary forms for each
of the entities, relationships and attributes.  This information
is used to simplify the entity model by removing unnecessary
features.  Quantification has not been attempted here but by

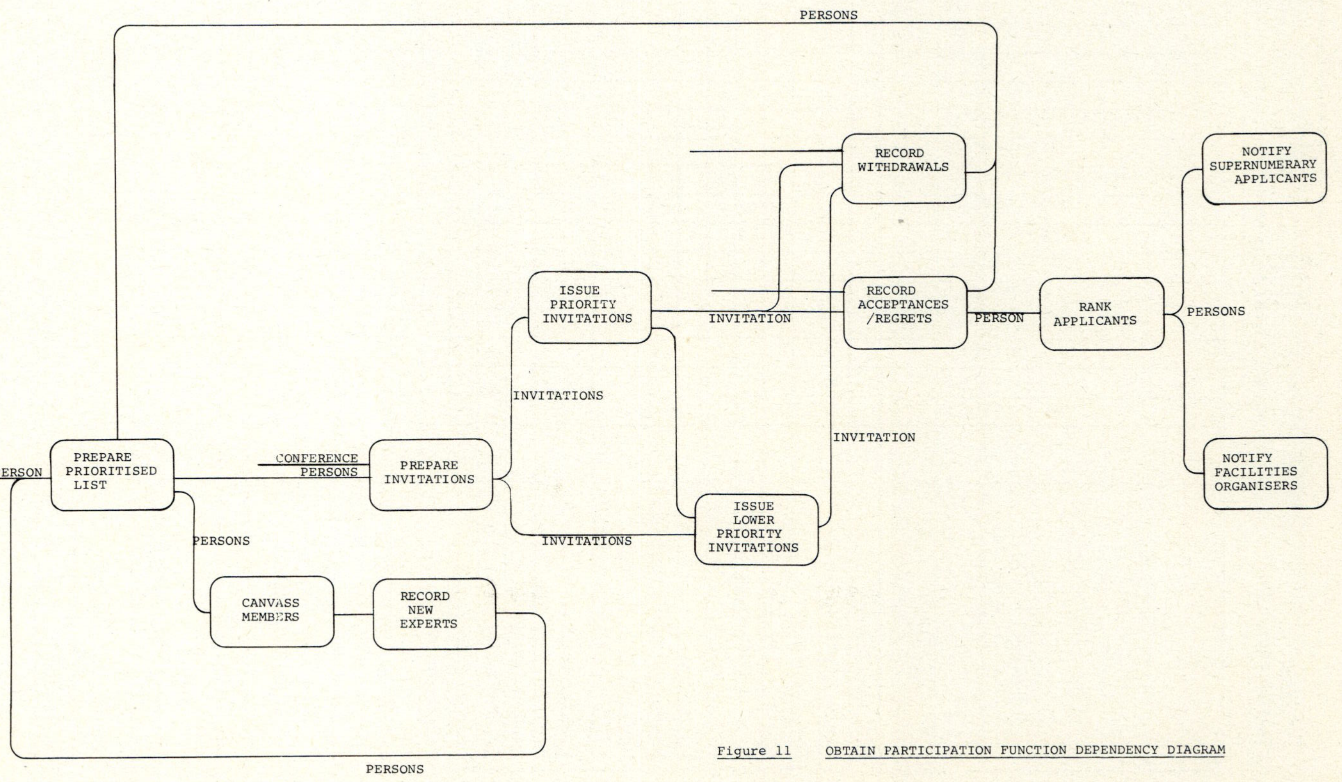


Figure 11     OBTAIN PARTICIPATION FUNCTION DEPENDENCY DIAGRAM

CACI
Matrix Form

**IFIP** · IFIP · C.A.C.I.

**IFIP**    WG 8.1

Entity / Function

| Function | Conference | Call | Session | Contributed Paper | Person | Authorship | Refereeship | Invitation | Session Participation | Membership | Conference Committee | IFIP TC | IFIP WG | Member Society | |
|---|---|---|---|---|---|---|---|---|---|---|---|---|---|---|---|
| Publish General Calls | X | X | | | | | | | | | | | | | 1 |
| Issue Specific Calls | X | X | | | X | | | | | | | | | | |
| Arrange Referees | X | | | | X | X | X | | | | | | | | 2 |
| Arrange Invitations | X | | | | X | | | X | | | | | | | |
| Handle Responses | X | | | | X | | | X | | | | | | | |
| Provide Special Participants | X | | X | | X | | | | X | | | | | | |
| Record Conference Details | X | | X | | X | | | | | | X | X | | | |
| Determine Session Content | | | X | X | | | | | | | | | | | 3 |
| Publish Proceedings | X | | X | X | X | X | | | | | | | | | |
| Prepare General Handouts | X | | X | X | X | X | X | X | X | | | | | | 4 |
| Register Letters Of Intent | | X | | X | X | X | | | | | | | | | |
| Register Contributions | | X | | X | X | X | | | | | | | | | |
| Record Changes | | | | X | X | X | | | | | | | | | 5 |
| Select Papers | | | | X | X | X | | | | | | | | | |
| Organise Refereeing | | | | X | X | | X | | | | | | | | |
| Determine Audience | | | | | X | X | X | | X | X | X | X | X | X | 6 |

CACI-14

Figure 12

making some assumptions and by reference to the matrix we can demonstrate the process.

Conference is probably used quite often but inspection may show that this is generally just to identify fully things such as calls, invitations and papers. This being so it is probably more appropriate simply to make the conference name an attribute, even redundantly, of these other entities. The same arguement can be applied to Session.

Conference Committee, IFIP TC, IFIP WG and Member Society are used very little and are there mainly to qualify the types of membership held by IFIP Member. As before, their identifiers could therefore be amalgamated with the attributes of Membership.

Call, Invitation and Session Participation are handled reasonably often under a variety of circumstances. The interest in them though is mainly in their existence and current state as a means of controlling functions such as the invitation process. They could however be of greater relevance if a general Person database was created since they could be retained as historical records of people's association with past conferences and therefore used as a guide to selection for calls, invitations and chairmanships.

Paper and Person are clearly the major entities and form the heart of the database. It cannot be easily determined from the problem statement whether there is any significant group of functions concerned with accessing single occurrences of these so it is not possible to determine any real need for indexes or means of immediate access. Selections are however made on the basis of technical characteristics or background which suggests that record types based on these entities should contain lists of keywords and be provided with a keyword retrieval mechanism. The entity subtypes could be dealt with simply by the use of status indicators in records. However, particularly in the case of Person, there may be justification for separating them into physically distinct subfiles.

Authorship and Refereeship each have a significant existence and usage and need to be implemented as logical record types acting as cross-references between Paper and Person. A shared Person file would also retain these as significant information on the individuals concerned.

The conclusion from this type of examination is likely to be that two alternative logical structures can be supported, as shown in Figure 13. One for the case where the system exists truly to serve single conferences and the other where a shareable database of people information is maintained. In the first case, information about calls, invitations and session participations can be reduced to status fields within the person record.

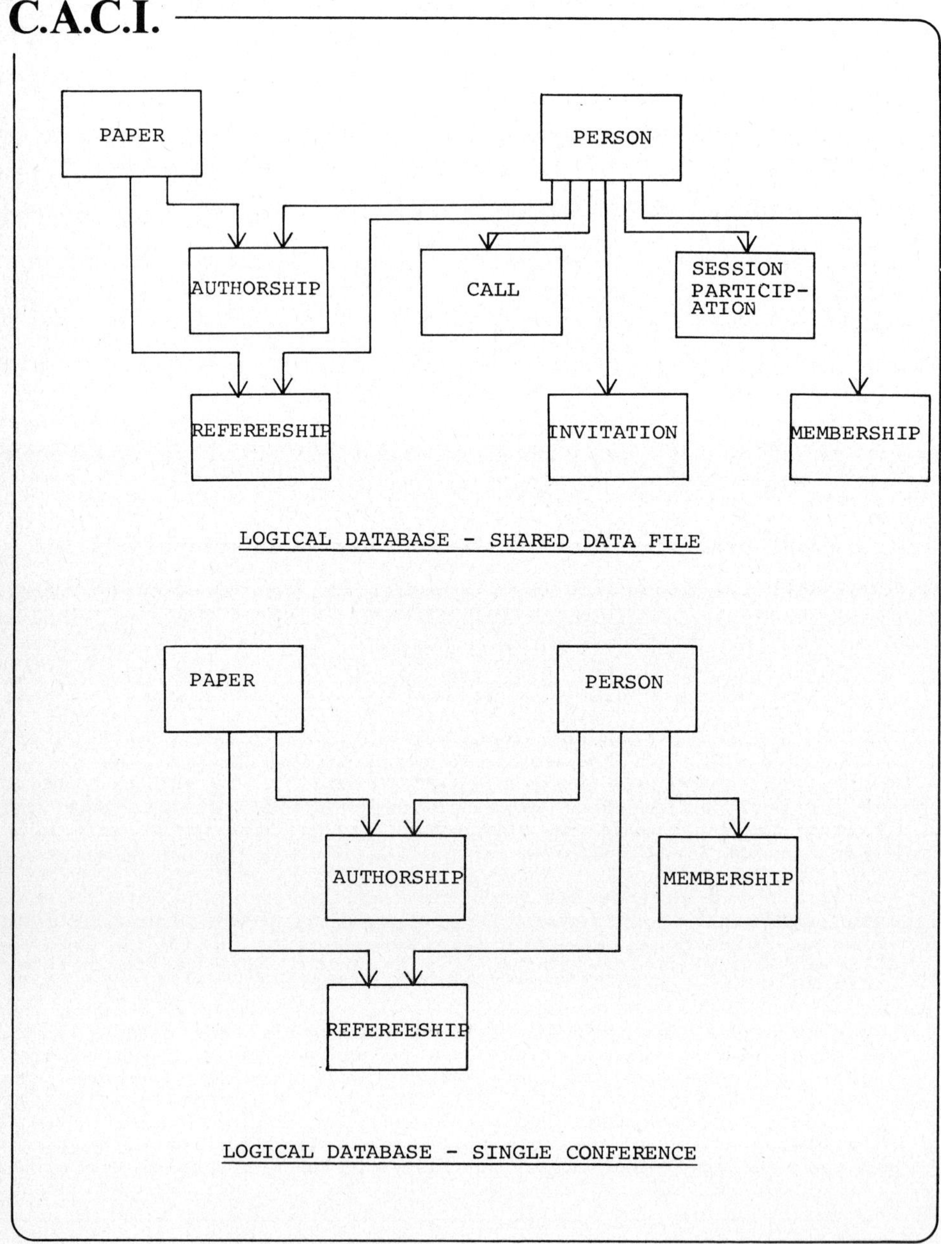
C.A.C.I.
PAPER
PERSON
AUTHORSHIP
CALL
SESSION
PARTICIP-
ATION
REFEREESHIP
INVITATION
MEMBERSHIP
LOGICAL DATABASE - SHARED DATA FILE
PAPER
PERSON
AUTHORSHIP
MEMBERSHIP
REFEREESHIP
LOGICAL DATABASE - SINGLE CONFERENCE
LOGICAL DATABASES      FIGURE 13
IFIP WG8.1

Possibly this process of collapsing records into one another could even be extended to include memberships. In the second case the maintenance of collections of past details implies that, at least in the logical database, separate records are maintained for each of a person's associations.

In either case, the resulting logical structure is quite simple and could be supported by most adequate data management systems.

### 3.3.3 APPLICATIONS DESIGN

The starting point for application design is the function hierarchy and the function logic diagrams. These indicate the transactions required at a logical level and are also used to determine the low-level transactions that will be needed to support them. Thus, registering a letter of intent requires elementary operations to create a contributed paper record, to identify persons who are authors, to create person records if the authors are not already known and to create authorship records. Reference to the entity model makes it clear that where mandatory relationships are present then operations to set them up will have to be provided by the logical transactions. The function logic indicates the program structure needed to support such logical transactions and the entity state diagrams indicate the low-level operations that can be performed on each entity type.

Together, these enable a system to be designed in which the low-level data handling is provided by a set of processors each handling one entity type, or more probably one logical record type. These processors are used by a set of transaction handlers, one for each logical transaction, which deal with the users input and supply the output. The structure envisaged is as shown below:

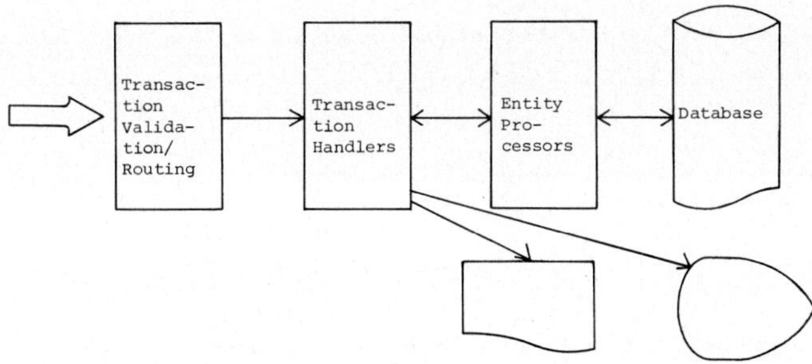

The main logical transactions that might need to be supported in this structure appear to be, from inspection of the function model and the entity model, the following:

Data Handling

> Record/Remove conference, committee membership
> Record new external expert, Update person details
> Record call
> Record invitation, acceptance/regret, withdrawal
> Record session participation invitation, acceptance/regret, withdrawal
> Record paper (on letter of intent or receipt of contribution)
> Update paper status
> Add/Remove authorship
> Record refereeship invitation, acceptance/ regret, withdrawal
> Update refereeship (with referee report)

Output Provision

> Select persons on keywords (for calls, refereeing, session participation)
> Select persons on invitation criteria
> Issue invitations
> Issue rejections after deadlines
> Allocate papers to referees
> Issue reminders to referees
> Issue list of collated referee's reports
> Issue notification to rejected authors
> Prepare ranked list of acceptances
> Issue notification to supernumerary applicants
> Prepare attendee list
> Prepare session list.

A range of other outputs would be required less regularly together with ad hoc requests for information, so any designed system may need to provide reasonable query handling and reporting facilities.

Missing from this is any proper set of transactions for handling IFIP members and their associations with areas of IFIP. This does not fall within the scope of conference organisation but clearly should be provided through some central, shareable capability within IFIP.

3.4    CONCLUSION

This examination of the IFIP conferencing system has served to illustrate major aspects of our development methodology although limitations of space have prevented a proper demonstration of all aspects.

The simplicity of the resulting logical database and the relatively small number of significant transactions provide an interesting contrast with the results of analysis. To an extent this is due to the 'single conference' constraint. A general system to handle all conferences for IFIP and to maintain information on past conferences would be significantly more elaborate. The logical database, for example, would probably be virtually the same as the entity model. However, the contrast is also due to the fact that the structured analysis methodology examines the whole of an area irrespective of which parts may be computerised. This is a major strength of the methodology since, once the functions to be computerised are selected, it is clear where and how they have to be integrated with the remaining manual functions. A complete systems development strategy can therefore be developed.

The methodology also serves to highlight both omissions in the analysis and areas where interfaces with other parts of the organisation are important. This is the case with information on IFIP members and other people and it is evident that before any efficient conferencing systems are built, IFIP is faced with a major decision on how best to satisfy the need for a common, shareable people database. Without this, the conferencing system becomes expensive to support since a significant effort must be made, whenever a conference is run, to create a specific people file. This course is not one we would recommend and instead we would wish to look for ways of creating a permanent people file which would then be available for use by the conferencing system whenever a conference is being arranged.

4.    REFERENCES

[1]    Davenport, R.A., Data analysis for database design, Australian Computer Journal 10 (1978) 122-137.

[2]    Palmer, I.R., Practicalities in applying a formal methodology to data analysis, in : Maddison, R.N. (ed), Data Analysis for Information System Design (British Computer Society, London, 1978).

[3]    Shave, M.J.R., Entities, functions and binary relations : steps to a conceptual schema, Computer Journal 24 (1981) 42-47.

*INFORMATION SYSTEMS DESIGN METHODOLOGIES: A Comparative Review*
*T.W. Olle, H.G. Sol, A.A. Verrijn-Stuart (editors)*
*North-Holland Publishing Company*
© *IFIP, 1982*

# DADES: A METHODOLOGY FOR SPECIFICATION AND DESIGN
## OF INFORMATION SYSTEMS

Antoni OLIVE

Facultat d'Informàtica
Universitat Politècnica de Barcelona
Jordi Girona Salgado, 31
BARCELONA (34). Catalonia.

In the first part of the paper we describe the DADES
methodology for the specification and design of informa
tion  systems (IS). DADES consists of three components: (i)
a formal language for the specification of IS requirements,
(ii) a method for validating the logical consistency of the
specifications, and (iii) a method for verifying the logical
correctness of some design decisions. These components may
be used in whole or in part in combination with several
existing  IS design methodologies. However, we have developed
a new methodology for IS design, using the DADES components
and other current methods. We believe that DADES includes
some features that may prove useful in some stages of IS
development.

In the second part, we illustrate DADES by designing an
"information system to be used to support the organising of
a technical conference, including the refereeing of papers",
as defined by the IFIP Working Group WG8.1.

## INTRODUCTION

The DADES methodology has evolved after some four years of research in the area
of logical design of information systems (IS) at the Facultat d'Informàtica of
the  Universitat Politècnica de Barcelona.

Despite the fact that the current version of DADES is still at a research stage
(it still lacks some adaptations and tools for practical use), we believe that
DADES includes some features that may prove useful in some stages of IS develop
ment and that they might be of interest to the research community. Such features
include the possibility of:

a) Specifying an IS without making any assumption about the system structure or
   the data base contents.

b) Validating the logical consistency of the specifications, in a formal way.

c) Formally verifying the logical correctness of some design decisions.

In what follows we briefly describe each of these features.

The need for specifying the requirements of an IS is broadly recognised. To be
useful, such specifications must have some properties, one of which is that they
must describe what the IS is intended to do, but not how the eventual system
will do it [14,30,36]. For example, specifications should not make assumptions
about the overall structure of the system  processes nor about the data base

contents, since these are design decisions that may be chosen among several
alternatives. DADES follows the approach of specification languages such as that
developed by Young&Kent [39] or SYSTEMATICS [12,13] in which a specification
consists basically of the definition of the conceptual schema of the IS and that
of the inputs and outputs.

Another desirable property of specifications is consistency. One aspect of this
property  is that the IS must be able to produce the specified outputs from the
inputs available. Most languages allow for the validation of this consistency
aspect only at the static level, while DADES can validate it at both static and
dynamic levels. Moreover, this validation is formal in DADES.

Finally, since specifications serve as a reference point from which alternative
design decisions can be developed and evaluated, it is important to be able of
verifying the consistency of such decisions with specifications, before proceed
ing to make further decisions. Although there has been important progress in the
area of program verification, it has not reached the area of IS verification
in the same degree. DADES attempts to make a contribution in this area, by
providing a formal method to verify the consistency of the design decisions
(about  the system structure or the data base contents) with specifications.

DADES is an acronym for "DAta oriented DESign" because it focusses on the data
that an IS collects, stores or produces, instead of focussing on the processes
that perform  the functions of a given IS.

DADES consists of: (i) a formal language for the specification of IS requirements,
(ii) a method for validating specifications, and (iii)  a method for the verifi
cation of some design decisions. These components may be used in whole or in
part in combination with several existing IS design methodologies, since DADES
is not restricted to a specific methodology. However, we have developed a new
methodology for IS design, using the DADES components and other current methods.

Any design methodology requires a data model and a data manipulation language
to describe the data to be treated by the IS under design. Although DADES can
be used with many of such models and languages, in this paper we will use the
relational model of data and the associated relational algebra, mainly due to
their broad diffusion; we call it the DADES/RM/RA version. However, it should
be noted that this is not an inherent limitation of DADES as such.

The research reported here is based in three main sources: the concept of
"precedence between information sets" [15,16], the Young&Kent language [39]
and the information algebras [6,38]. The precedence concept was originated by
Langefors and it has been used by several researchers in the area of informa
tion systems and data bases [3,5,22]. We use this concept mainly for the purpose
of specifications validation and design verification. As indicated above,
DADES takes an approach similar to that of the Young&Kent language. Despite
of the fact that this was probably the first published specification language,
it contains some interesting features not found in many later languages.
Finally, we use an algebraic notation for the definition of information sets
and processes.

In the first phase of our work [23,24] we used the precedence concept for the
derivability analysis of information sets, that is, the problem of determining
whether or not a given information set can be derived from others. We also
observed that this problem appears in several contexts. The original work used
as reference the informational model, but then we used the relational model,
with similar results [26]. An adaptation to the Solvberg's datalogical model
has been developed by Stavelin [33].

In a second phase we developed the approach of the DADES language [25] and we
compared it to the "Information Analysis" method of ISAC methodology [17].

These phases provided us confidence with the approach, so that we used it
[27,28,29] for the requirements specification and validation of data bases,
a subsystem of an IS, and finally for the complete specification of IS.

At present we are developing computerized tools and versions for practical use.

## PART I.  DESCRIPTION OF DADES

In this part of the paper we describe DADES. In the first section we present the
DADES language for the specification of requirements for information systems.
In the second section we describe the derivability analysis of information
sets. In the third, we use the derivability analysis to perform a formal valida
tion of the specifications, while in the fourth we show how to use it to
verify some design decisions. After describing the basic DADES components, we
propose, in section 5, a methodology for IS design.

1. THE DADES SPECIFICATION LANGUAGE.

In this section we describe the DADES language for the specification of IS.

1.1 The DADES approach.

According to the usual definition, an IS is a system that performs four functions:
collecting, storing, processing and distributing of information sets [15]. Using
this functional model, many specification languages consider, sometimes implicit
ly, that the definition of an IS must include the definition of these four
functions in some way.

However, we believe that to specify an IS it is sufficient to define the collect
ing and distributing functions, since if these definitions are complete then
the other two (storing, processing) can be deduced from them.

On the other hand, there are two reaons for not including the storing and
processing functions in the specifications. First, because decisions concerning
which informations are to be stored explicitly or how the processes are to be
structured are design decisions that should be delayed until later stages of
IS development. Second, because the collecting and distributing functions are
the only ones (or, at least, the most) relevant to end-users, since they define
which informations must be given  to the system (inputs) and which informations
will be derived by the system (outputs).

Therefore, the DADES approach to IS specification limits itself to the definition
of the inputs and outputs of the IS to be designed, without any reference to
which informations are to be stored explicitly nor to how the eventual processes
are to be structured.

For the definition of the informations that the IS must accept or must produce
to be complete, it has to include three aspects [35]: (1) Static, i.e. which
informations are input or output; (2) Dynamic, i.e. when will inputs arrive
or will outputs be produced; and (3) Spatial, i.e. where will inputs be generated
or outputs be received. In DADES, the first of these aspects is defined in
connection with the conceptual schema of the IS, while the second is defined
in connection with the life span of the IS.

The Universe of Discourse of an IS is the set of informations that the IS
receives, stores, processes or distributes during its life span. The definition
of the structure of the informations contained in the Universe of Discourse
is the IS conceptual schema. This schema is the basic element of the specifica
tion of an IS, since its inputs and outputs are defined in base to it (figure 1).

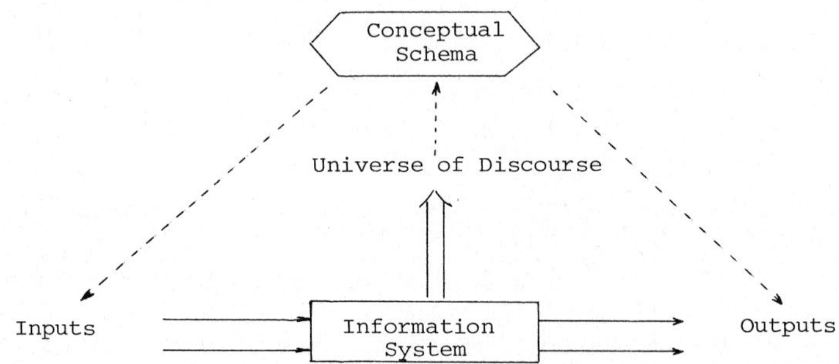


Figure 1.

Overview of the DADES approach to specifications.

In the following we describe the main features of the DADES language. We begin
with the definition of the "life span" (1.2) and "universe of discourse" (1.3)
concepts, that form the foundation for the conceptual schema (1.5). In 1.4 we
give a brief description of the relational model, to be used in this paper as
the data model for the conceptual schema. The associated relational algebra is
briefly described in the Appendix. Derivation rules, a part of the conceptual
schema, are described in section 1.6. Input and Output definition is explained
in 1.7. Finally, we give some concluding remarks. In a later section we consider
the validation of specifications.

To illustrate the main ideas and features of the language more clearly, we will
use a simple example throughout this part of the paper. The example is a simple
order processing system. During its normal operation, the system receives
replenishment notices and orders. When an order enters, the system tries to
fulfill it by consulting the corresponding stock level. If an order can not be
fulfilled then it automatically becomes a backorder. We assume that backorders
are processed daily, before normal operation starts. Other details of the exam
ple will be given as needed.

1.2 Life span of an IS.

In order to define the temporal aspects of informations and the dynamic aspects
of inputs and outputs we use as frame of reference the life span. By life span
L of an information system we mean the time interval in which the system
operates or exists.

References to a given instant or set of instants of L must be done in a time
scale, using some time unit. DADES defines a set of time units that can be used
in several parts of the specifications, such as domains of relations or input/
output definitions. The most usual are:

    - TIME, which will refer to a year/month/day/hour/minute/second.
    - DATE,        "        year/month/day
    - MONTH,      "        year/month.
    - YEAR,       "        year.

We denote by T the set of times comprised in L and by $t_0$ the initial time in T. Similarly, we denote by D (or M, Y) the set of dates (months, years) comprised in L and by $d_0$ ($m_0$,$y_0$) the first date (month, year) in L.

Due to the fact that in a specification time references may be done in several time units it is necessary to have functions to convert references from a time unit to another. DADES includes a set of such functions, some of which are depicted in Table 1. Each function has a name, a time unit as argument and a time unit as value. We indicate by P or I  whether the value of the function is a point in time or an interval. We also give the name of the inverse function. Note that in order to avoid a large number of function names, we assign the same name to functions with the same meaning giving the same time unit value, but with different arguments.

For example, the function MONTH gives the month of a time or the month of a date. In the first case, the inverse function is TIMES, while in the second case the inverse is DATES. In either case the value is a point (P).

Let $F(u)=v$ be one of the above functions. When applied to a given instant $u_i$, expressed in time unit u, F gives the instant $v_j$, expressed in time unit v, such that $F(u_i)=v_j$. F can also be applied to a set $U=\{u_1,....,u_n\}$ giving:

$$F(U)=\{v_j \mid \exists u_i (u_i \varepsilon U \wedge F(u_i)=v_j)\}$$

Using this notation, it can be shown that M=MONTH(T), D=DATE(T) and so on. Other properties will be given in later sections.

The above functions allow the designer to specify a given instant or set of instants. However, it may also be necessary to use other, non-standard functions to specify some particular instants of L. For this purpose, DADES allows the definition of user functions and specific points or intervals of time. The definition must include two aspects: the structure and the time ordering.

The structure of a user function is defined as follows:

FUNCTION: Function-name(time-unit1)=time-unit2 {POINT|INTERVAL};
   DOMAIN=Set of instants of time-unit1; RANGE=Name;
   INVERSE=Name of the inverse function;
   DESCRIPTION=Narrative description of the function.

DOMAIN defines the valid domain of the function, while RANGE gives a name to the set of values given by the function.

The definition of a point or interval is:

{POINT|INTERVAL}:Name=time-unit; DESCRIPTION=...

In the example, the definitions that may be required are:

FUNCTION: NEW-PRICES-TIME(date)=time POINT; DOMAIN=D; RANGE=NPTIMES;
   INVERSE=DATE; DESC=This function gives the point in time in which
   changes of prices of a date are entered to the system.

FUNCTION: NOP-TIMES(date)=time INTERVAL; DOMAIN=D; RANGE=NORMAL-TIMES;
   INVERSE=DATE; DESC=Gives the time interval of a date in which the new
   orders and the replenishments are entered.

FUNCTION: BOP-TIME(date)=time POINT; DOMAIN=D, RANGE=BOP-TIMES; INVERSE=DATE;
   DESC=Backorders are processed once a day. This function gives the
   time in which the process is performed.

POINT: INITIALIZATION=time; DESC=This point corresponds to the instant in which
  the system will be initializated.

A. Olivé

TABLE 1. Some standard time functions in DADES.

| FUNCTION | DESCRIPTION | ARGUMENT | VALUE | P/I | INVERSE | EXAMPLES |
|---|---|---|---|---|---|---|
| DATE | Date of a time | time | date | P | TIMES | DATE(1980/12/30/15/30/50) = 1980/12/30 |
| MONTH | Month of a time | time | month | P | TIMES | |
| | "      date | date | month | P | DATES | MONTH(1980/12/30) = 1980/12 |
| YEAR | Year of a time | time | year | P | TIMES | |
| | "      date | date | year | P | DATES | |
| | "      month | month | year | P | MONTHS | YEAR(1980/12) = 1980 |
| BEGN | First time of a date | date | time | P | DATE | BEGN(1980/12/30) = 1980/12/30/00/00/01 |
| | "   "     month | month | time | P | MONTH | |
| END | Last time of a date | date | time | P | DATE | END(1980/12/30) = 1980/12/30/24/00/00 |
| | "   "     month | month | time | P | MONTH | |
| PREVIOUS | Previous time of a time | time | time | P | NEXT | |
| | "      date of a date | date | date | P | NEXT | PREVIOUS(1981/01/01) = 1980/12/31 |
| NEXT | Next time of a time | time | time | P | PREVIOUS | |
| | "     date of a date | date | date | P | PREVIOUS | NEXT(1980/12/31) = 1981/01/01 |
| TIMES | Set of times comprised in a date | date | time | I | DATE | TIMES(1981/01/01) = { 1981/01/01/00/00/01 ÷ 1981/01/01/24/00/00 } |
| DATES | Set of dates comprised in a month | month | date | I | MONTH | DATES(1981/01) = { 1981/01/01 ÷ 1981/01/31 } |

We do not need to describe the process required to implement a function, nor the exact value of a point or interval. For our purposes, it suffices to define the relative ordering of the instants. For this reason, we supplement the definition by giving for each function, point or interval its lower and upper bounds.

In our example, the time ordering would be defined as follows:
TIME-ORDERING: FOR ALL d OF D: BEGN(d) < NEW-PRICES-TIME(d) ,
                               NEW-PRICES-TIME(d) < BOP-TIME(d) ,
                               BOP-TIME(d) < BEGN(NOP-TIMES(d)) ,
                               END(NOP-TIMES(d)) < END(d) ;
               INITIALIZATION < NEW-PRICES-TIME(d0) .

We omit here the complete description of this calculus-like notation, hoping that the examples will be self-explanatory. Note, however, the use of BEGN and END to refer to the first and last instant of an interval.

1.3 Universe of discourse of an IS.

We denote by Universe of Discourse (UD) of an IS the set of informations that the IS may receive, derive, store or distribute during its life span L. This definition is similar to the one given in [9,19] for data bases. We include in the UD not only base informations (i.e. given to the system), but also informations derived or implied by others. The same approach is taken in [3,5] for data bases.

As the UD is not limited to one instant of time, its informations must normally include a time reference [4,15,34]. Thus, informations such as stocks of products, age of people, sales, etc. must include a time reference, because without it the informations  would be meaningless in the context of the UD.

However, we distinguish between the intrinsic, extrinsic and assertion time of an information [4,39]. _Intrinsic_ time plays a role as part of the definition of an information, i.e. it constitutes part of its meaning. For example, in i1=THE TOTAL ORDERED OF PRODUCT p IN MONTH m IS x DOLLARS, m plays an intrinsic role. An information may or may not contain intrinsic time components. For example, in i2=THE AMOUNT OF ORDER o IS x DOLLARS there is no need of intrinsic time because the amount of an order is assumed to be stable and does not depend on time.

_Extrinsic_ time is the time when a particular information is asserted. For example, if we assert at time $t'>t$: i3=ORDER o ENTERS AT TIME t, $t'$ is the extrinsic time. If we can assert an information at time $t'$ then we can also assert it at any $t'' \geqslant t'$, provided that informations include the required intrinsic time components.

_Assertion_ time t of an information i, t=AT(i), is defined as the first valid extrinsic time of i. We can assert i at any $t' \geqslant t$. Usually, AT(i) depends on the intrinsic time of i. Thus, for example, in i4=THE PRICE OF PRODUCT p AT DATE d IS x DOLLARS  it could be AT(i4)=BEGN(d), or in the above i1, it could be AT(i1)=END(m) .

In other cases, assertion time may be a constant, as in i5=PRODUCT p HAS NAME n, where AT(i5)=t0 if the system knows i5 at the initial instant of L. Finally, assertion time may depend on intrinsic time of other informations, as in the above i2 and i3, where AT(i2)=AT(i3) and AT(i3)=t.

The assertion time of a set of informations I = $\{i1,...,in\}$ is defined  as AT(I)=MAX $[AT(i) \mid i \in I]$ .

The UD concept, as defined above, has two important properties for the specifi_cation of IS. First, it allows the non-ambigous definition of the information contents of an input or output, since it is simply a subset of the UD.

Second, using this approach the concept of information deletion or modification
is not necessary [32].   For example, if an information of the UD is i=QUANTITY
ON HAND OF PRODUCT p AT TIME t is q  and at time $t+1$ the quantity is q´, this
is not expressed as a modification (update) of i, but as another i´= QUANTITY
ON HAND OF PRODUCT p AT TIME $t+1$ IS q´.

1.4 The relational model.

In this paper, we use the relational model as the data model of DADES. For this
reason, in this section we briefly review the basic concepts and notation of
this model that are used in the rest of the paper. The relational algebra is
reviewed in the Appendix. For a more complete treatement see [7,8].

In the relational model of data, informations are represented by <u>relations</u>.
A relation consists of a set of tuples, each tuple having the same set of
attributes. For each attribute there is a set of possible values called the
domain of that attribute. Different attributes may share the same domain. A
<u>relation scheme</u>  R = NAME(A1:D1,...,An:Dn) is a description of a relation
consisting of a name and a set of attributes. When the names Ai,Di are the
same or when, for expository reasons, the domains can be ignored, only the
attribute names are given.

The set of all tuples of a given relation scheme that exists in a UD will be
called its <u>total relation</u>. A key is associated with each relation scheme R.
A <u>key</u> K of R is a minimal subset of the attributes of R such that no two tuples
of the total relation of R have the same K-component. As usual, we will under
line the attributes of K in R. A relation scheme is <u>elementary</u> if there
exists at most one non-key attribute.

We denote by A(R) the set of attributes of R, by K(R) the key of R, by $D(A_i)$
the domain of attribute $A_i$  and by $D(R,A_i) \subseteq D(A_i)$ the set of possible
values (or value set) for attribute $A_i$ in R.

1.5 Conceptual schema of an IS.

The descriptions of the classes of elements of the UD of an IS and the relations
among those classes, augmented with some additional constraints, is called
schema or conceptual schema of the IS (See [19]  for a similar definition at
the data base level). In section 5 we will discuss a design methodology for
this schema.

We assume that the informations of the UD have been modelled by means of the
relational model. Using this model, the IS schema is a set of relation schemes.
We impose two conditions on these relation schemes. First, as it is becoming
usual in conceptual models, they must be in <u>third normal form</u> [8] . Second,
the relation schemes should be <u>elementary</u>, since it is very suitable for the
specification and design of IS (other authors, such as [15,22],  use a similar
approach). However, the designer may define a non-elementary relation scheme
if he/she considers that it is a "natural" or practically non-decomposable
unit.

Relation schemes must be supplemented with the definition of the constraints
they must satisfy. There are many types of constraints [2] and a language must
select the most relevant, depending on the role they play in the design methodology
used. In the DADES language it suffices to define derivation rules (explained
in section 1.6) and the value set of the attributes.

In the following we give a conceptual schema for the example, excluding the
derivation rules. The first part of the conceptual schema is the definition of
the domains, and the second part is the definition of the relation schemes.

For every domain we specify its name, its type and, if required, a narrative description. We may omit the definition of the standard time domains, such as TIME, DATE, MONTH and YEAR. For every relation scheme R we specify its name, its attributes Al,...,An, its key, the assertion time AT(R), the value set of the attributes D(R,Ai), for i=1,...,n, and if required a narrative description. The definition of D(R,Ai) may be omitted if D(R,Ai) = D(Ai).

```
DOMAINS:   D1=PRODUCT; TYPE=NUM; DESC=Product serial number.
           D2=NAME; TYPE=CHAR(25).
           D3=DOLLARS; TYPE=NUM.
           D4=QUANTITY; TYPE=NUM.
           D5=ORDER; TYPE=NUM; DESC=Order serial number.
           D6=Y/N; TYPE=BOOLEAN; DESC = Yes or not.
```

RELATION-SCHEMES:

R1 = PRODUCTS(PRODUCT, NAME); AT=INITIALIZATION;
     DESC=Gives the name of a product. It is stable during the life span and it
     is known by the system at initialization time.

R2 = PRICE-CHANGES(PRODUCT, DATE, NEW-PRICE: DOLLARS); AT=BEGN(DATE); D(DATE)=D;
     DESC=Corresponds to the input transactions that specify price changes.
     They can be asserted at the beginning of their date. The value set of this
     date is D=DATE(L).

R3 = PRICES(PRODUCT, DATE, PRICE: DOLLARS); AT=BEGN(DATE); D(DATE)=D;
     DESC=Gives the price of a product in a given date. It is defined for every
     product and date D. It can be derived from R2.

R4 = STOCK(PRODUCT, TIME, QOH: QUANTITY); AT=TIME; D(TIME)=T;
     DESC=Gives the quantity on hand of a product in a given time. It is defined
     for every product and time T.

R5 = REPLENISHMENTS(PRODUCT, TIME, REPL: QUANTITY); AT=TIME;
     D(TIME)=NORMAL-TIMES; DESC=Corresponds to the input transactions that
     specify the replenishments. They enter the system during the NORMAL-TIMES.

R6 = ORDERS(ORDER, TIME, PRODUCT, QUANTITY); AT=TIME; D(TIME)=NORMAL-TIMES;
     DESC=Similar to R5 but for the orders. Note that it is non-elementary.
     An order is assumed to refer to only one product.

R7 = DATE-ENTERED(ORDER, DATE); AT=ORDERS; DESC=Gives the date when each order
     enters the system. This is derived from R6. Note that AT is the same as
     AT(ORDERS).

R8 = AMOUNT-ORDER(ORDER, AMOUNT: DOLLARS); AT=ORDERS;
     DESC=Gives the total amount of an order, in dollars.

R9 = TOTAL-QTY-ORDERED(PRODUCT, MONTH, TOTAL: QUANTITY);
     AT=END(MONTH); D(MONTH)=M; DESC=It is defined for every product and month.

R10= TOTAL-ORDERED (PRODUCT, MONTH, TOTAL: DOLLARS); AT=END(MONTH);
     D(MONTH)=M;DESC=Defined for every product and month M.

R11= DEL-INPUT-ORDERS(ORDER, DELIVERY: Y/N); AT=ORDERS;
     DESC=An order is served from stock if possible, otherwise, it becomes a
     backorder. This relation indicates whether each order is served from
     stock or not.

R12= BACKORDERS(ORDER, DATE); AT=BEGN(DATE); D(DATE)=D;
     DESC= An order is a backorder in date d if (1) it entered at date d-1
     and was not delivered, or (2) it was already a backorder in d-1 and was
     not delivered.

R13= DEL-BACKORDERS(ORDER, DATE, DELIVERY: Y/N); AT=BOP-TIME(DATE);
     D(DATE)=D; DESC=Similar to R11, for backorders.

## 1.6 Derivation rules.

In a given schema, a relation scheme is <u>base</u>  scheme if its tuples can not be
derived from the tuples of other relations of the schema. Otherwise, the relation
scheme is <u>derived</u>. We will postpone the problem of determining which relation
schemes are derived until section 5.

The set of operations of the relational algebra allows us to derive some relations
from others. However, there are relations, logically derivable from others,
which can not be obtained by means of the relational algebra. These relations
must be expressed as results of "user operations". Examples of user operations
may be arithmetic operations, statistical models, operations research models,
etc. Therefore, there are two classes of derived relation schemes: derived by
<u>model operation</u> (i.e. the relational algebra) and derived by <u>user operation</u>.

There must be a <u>derivation rule</u> for every derived relation scheme included in
the schema. If the relation scheme is derived by a model operation, then the
derivation rule is simply the corresponding relational algebra expression.

When a relation scheme is derived by a user operation, the corresponding deriva
tion rule is more complex, since in this case the inputs, outputs and the producing
relationship have to be specified.

The <u>producing relationship</u> (PR) concept is very similar to the one used in
[13,39]. Let R be the derived relation scheme, let K = K(R) and let DRi be
the derivation rule for R. Then, the producing relationship PRi of DRi,
PRi = PR(DRi), is a relation on K such that there exists a one-to-one correspon
dence between the tuples of PRi and the tuples of R. Every tuple of PRi "produces"
a tuple of R. We also say that there is an occurrence of DRi for every tuple
of PRi.

Let K = K(R) = {A1,...,Ai} and let <A1=p1,...,Ai=pi> be a tuple of PRi where
p1,...,pi are parameters instead of concrete values. This occurrence derives
the output R(A1=p1,...,Ai=pi). The inputs required for this derivation are
defined as relational expressions with p1,...,pi as parameters.

For example, let us consider the derivation rule for the price of a product. It
could be defined as follows:

DR1 = DERIVATION OF THE PRICE OF A PRODUCT;

PROD-REL : FOR EVERY PRODUCT AND DATE;
     PR = PRODUCTS[PRODUCT] x D;

PARAMETERS : PRODUCT=p, DATE=d;

OUTPUT : PRICE OF PRODUCT p AT DATE d;
   O1 = PRICES(PRODUCT=p, DATE=d);

INPUT : PRICE AT THE PREVIOUS DATE;
   I1 = PRICES(PRODUCT=p, DATE=PREVIOUS(d));

INPUT : CHANGE OF PRICE;
   I2 = PRICE-CHANGES(PRODUCT=p, DATE=d);

DESC = If I2 is present, then O1 is derived from I2, otherwise, it is derived
       from I1.

Note the simultaneous use of narrative and formal descriptions to improve readabi_
lity. There exists a tuple PRICES(PRODUCT=p, DATE=d) for every tuple in
PRODUCTS[PRODUCT] x D. The inputs required are the price at the previous date
and the changes of price. Notice that parameters allow us to relate the producing
relationship to inputs and output.

It may be surprising that we formalize the producing relationship and the input
output definitions of the derivation rule, while the process itself is not
formalized (rather we specify it in narrative form in the DESCRIPTION). The main
reasons for this are:

1) It is basic principle of DADES that the main design decisions of an IS
   (data base design, architectural design) are only influenced by the inputs,
   outputs and producing relationships of the derivation rules, and that they
   are not influenced by their internal structure (the computations they perform).

2) It would not make too practical sense to formalize the processes if there
   does not exist an automatic generator of programs and files, since in such
   a case it would be necessary to write them two times: first at the specifica_
   tion level and later at the program level.

Thus, although it would not be difficult to formalize the processes description
(using some existing or even new language) for the reasons given above we
prefer to describe them informally.

Another example is the derivation rule for R9:

DR2 = TOTAL QUANTITY ORDERED PER MONTH;

PROD-REL : FOR EVERY PRODUCT AND MONTH;
      PR = PRODUCTS[PRODUCT] x MONTH;

PARAMETERS : PRODUCT=p, MONTH=m;

OUTPUT : TOTAL QUANTITY ORDERED;
   O1 = TOTAL-QTY-ORDERED(PRODUCT=p, MONTH=m);

INPUT : ORDERS ENTERED DURING THE MONTH m;
   I1 = ORDERS(PRODUCT=p, TIME $\epsilon$ TIMES(m));

DESC = Sum of the order quantities ......

A necessary consistency condition for a derivation rule is that the assertion
time of the output must be greater than or equal to the assertion time of the
inputs. In this example, we see from the conceptual schema that AT(O1) = END(m),
AT(I1) = MAX(TIMES(m)). Using some obvious properties of the time  functions,
it can be easily shown that MAX(TIMES(m)) = END(m).

There is a graphical representation of the derivation rules that may be useful
at some stages of the IS development process. Figures 2 and 3 show this form
of representation for DR3, derivation of the amount of an order, and DR4,
derivation of date-entered of an order. The graphical representation can also
be used with narrative descriptions instead of formal descriptions. Figure 4
shows this form for DR5, derivation of stocks.

1.7 Input/output definition.

Once the users and designers have agreed on the conceptual schema of the IS, it
is possible to define the inputs and outputs of the IS. In the DADES language
each input or output is defined in base to the conceptual schema, independently
of other inputs or outputs, and it is not necessary to relate outputs with the
inputs required to derive them. This allows the persons involved (users and/or
designers) to work in parallel.

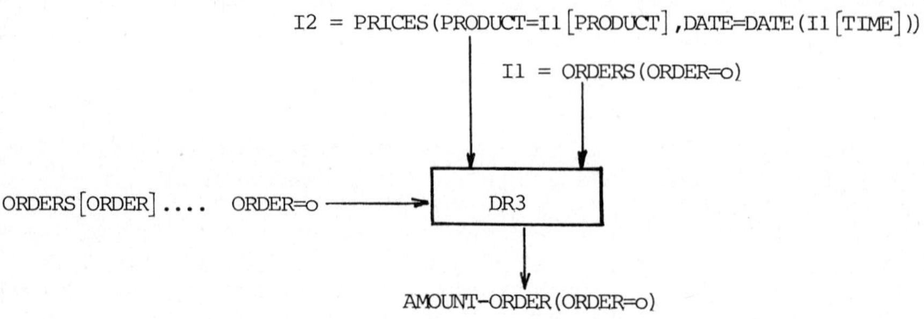

Figure 2. Graphical representation of DR3.

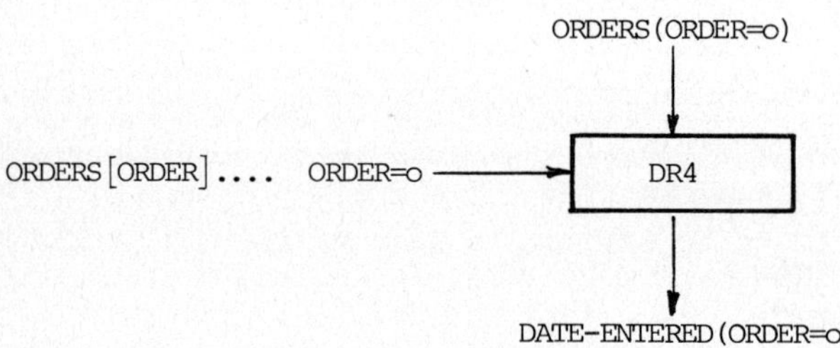

Figure 3. Graphical representation of DR4.

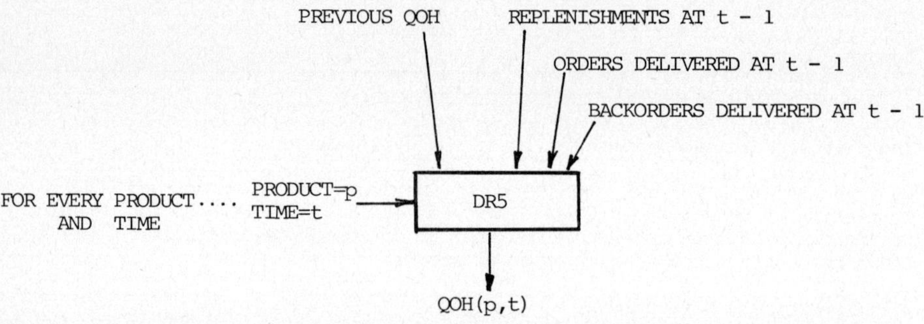

Figure 4. Graphical representation of DR5.

The description of an input or output must include four aspects:

        1) Static, or 'what'
        2) Dynamic, or 'when'
        3) Spatial, or 'where'
        4) Quantitative, or 'how many'

The static aspect is defined by means of a relational algebra expression corresponding to the UD informations that the input provides or the output requires. The dynamic aspect is defined by giving the arrival or production instant, referring it to the life span L, and using a time unit small enough to unambigously define when inputs arrive or when outputs should be produced. The spatial aspect is defined by giving the place of generation or reception of inputs or outputs, respectively. Finally, the quantitative aspect is defined by giving the volume and/or the frequence.

Let $I_1,\ldots,I_n$ be the input types, and let us assume that the time unit expressing input/output time is TIME. An input of type $I_j$ , $j=1,\ldots,n$, can arrive at any instant of a set $T(I_j) \subseteq T$. We denote by $I_j(t)$ the relational expression corresponding to the informations carried by the input of type $I_j$ arrived in t. If $t \notin T(I_j)$ then, by definition, $I_j(t) = \emptyset$. On the other hand, even in the case that $t \in T(I_j)$, if no input of type $I_j$ arrive at t, then $I_j(t) = \emptyset$.

The definition of an input of type Ij consists of the definition of the set $T(I_j)$, the relational expression $I_j(t)$, the location (LOC) where $I_j$ originates and the volume (VOL) and/or frequence (FREQ) per period. In $I_j(t)$, t refers to any instant of time $t \in T(I_j)$. For this reason, the $I_j(t)$ expression will normally have t as a parameter.

Additionally, the designer may define an "input checking procedure" to be executed for every input arrived at the system, as an input dialog and checking routine. These procedures would be defined in a way similar to that used for derivation rules.

Referring to our example, we will assume that there are the following input types:

I1 = SYSTEM INITIALIZATION;

    I1(t) = PRODUCTS; T(I1) = INITIALIZATION; LOC = MARKETING; VOL = 1000 PRODS;
    DESC = Specification, at initialization time, of the names for all
    products.

I2 = NEW ORDERS;

    I2(t) = ORDERS(TIME=t); T(I2) = NORMAL-TIMES;
    LOC = SALES-DEPT; FREQ = 200 PER DATE;
    DESC = Corresponds to the arrival of new orders. For every $t \in$ NORMAL-TIMES
    it enters the new orders produced in t.

I3 = REPLENISHMENTS;

    I3(t) = REPLENISHMENTS(TIME=t); T(I3) = NORMAL-TIMES;
    LOC = STORE-DEPT; FREQ = 100 PER DATE;
    DESC = Similar to I2.

I4 = CHANGES OF PRICE;

    I4(t) = PRICE-CHANGES(DATE=DATE(t)); T(I4) = NPTIMES;
    LOC = SALES-DEPT; VOL = 50 CHANGES;
    DESC = Enters the changes of price daily.

Note that these definitions are unambigous, since we define $I_j(t)$ and $T(I_j)$ in base to sets defined previously: the UD and the life span, respectively. Also note that $I_j(t)$ specifies the informations that are to enter to the system, without assuming any particular format. At the specifications level we are only concerned with the informational contents of inputs, delaying until later stages of IS development the assignments of formats to documents, displays, etc.

The definition of an output must also include the output information required, the instant when it should be produced, the location where it should be received and the volume estimates.

Let $O_1,...,O_m$ be the output types. The definition of a type $O_i$ output consists of the definition of the set $T(O_i)$, the relational expression $O_i(t)$, the location (LOC) and the volume (VOL) and/or frequence per period (FREQ). $T(O_i)$ is the set of instants at which outputs of type $O_i$ are to be produced. If $t \varepsilon T(O_i)$ then $O_i(t)$ is the relational expression corresponding to the information required by the output of type $O_i$, to be produced at t.

We assume that the outputs in our example are the following:

O1 = ORDERS TO BE DELIVERED;

    O1(t) = ORDERS(TIME=t) * DEL-INPUT-ORDERS(DELIVERY=YES) * PRODUCTS;
    T(O1) = NORMAL-TIMES; LOC = STORE-DEPT; FREQ = 150 PER DATE;
    DESC = Gives the new orders entered in t that are to be delivered in t.
    It includes the name of the product.

O2 = BACKORDERS TO BE DELIVERED;

    O2(t) = ORDERS * DEL-BACKORDERS(DELIVERY=YES,DATE=DATE(t)) * PRODUCTS;
    T(O2) = BOP-TIMES; LOC = STORE-DEPT; VOL = 5o ORDERS;
    DESC = Gives the backorders that are to be delivered in t. Similar to O1.

O3 = REPORT 1;

    O3(t) = TOTAL-QTY-ORDERED(MONTH=MONTH(t));
    T(O3) = END(M); LOC = STORE-DEPT; VOL = 1000 PRODUCTS;
    DESC = This report shows the total quantity ordered per product and month.

O4 = REPORT 2;

    O4(t) = TOTAL-ORDERED(MONTH=MONTH(t));
    T(O4) = END(M); LOC = MARKETING; VOL = 1000 PRODUCTS;
    DESC = Is a report showing the total amount ordered per product and month.
    It is required at the end of every month of the life span.

A necessary consistency condition for an input or output definition is that its instant of arrival or production must be greater than or equal to the assertion time of its informations. For example, we can see from the conceptual schema that for all $t \varepsilon$ END(M)  AT(O4(t)) = AT(TOTAL-ORDERED(MONTH=MONTH(t)) = END(MONTH(t)) = t.

1.8 Summary.

In this section we have described the main features of the DADES language for specification of information systems. In this language, a specification consists of:

    1. The conceptual schema of the UD

        a- Domains.
        b- Relation schemes.
        c- Assertion times.
        d- Value sets of attributes.
        e- Derivation rules.

    2. Input/Output definition.

        a- Information contents.
        b- Instants of arrival or production.
        c- Location.
        d- Volume estimates.
        e- Input checking procedures.

It is beyond the scope of this paper to compare the DADES language with other approaches. However, it may be useful to give some concluding remarks:

(1)- DADES allows a complete specification of an IS without requiring to define the data base contents nor the processes of the IS. These are design decisions that should not be included at the specifications stage.

(2)- DADES allows the unambigous, complete and formal description of the dynamic aspects of an IS; it considers all the roles that time plays in the informations and it explicitly defines when inputs will arrive or when outputs are to be produced.

(3)- The impact of changes upon the specification is likely to be quite restricted: in many cases they will be limited to local changes, such as addition, modification or deletion of an input/output definition. In other approaches a change may imply the modification of data base contents or some restructuring of the processes.

(4)- Finally, as we will see in the next sections, DADES allows the formal validation of specifications.

2. DERIVABILITY ANALYSIS.

In this section we describe derivability analysis, which will be used in following sections as the basis for the validation and verification methods. Derivability analysis focusses on the problem of determining whether or not an information set (iset) $\alpha$ can be derived from others isets $\alpha_1,...,\alpha_n$.

This problem can be approached from two equivalent points of view. The first is <u>precedence analysis</u> in which it is viewed as the problem of determining whether or not there exists a precedence relation between $\alpha$ and $\alpha_1,....,\alpha_n$. In the next section we briefly present this approach, showing that there exists a formal procedure to solve the problem. For a complete treatment see [28,29].

In this paper we will emphasize the more intuitive, practical-oriented <u>process-grouping</u> approach. Using this approach, derivability analysis can be viewed as the problem of building a process accepting $\alpha_1,...,\alpha_n$ as inputs and producing $\alpha$ as output. The basis for building such processes are the derivation rules and a set of process grouping operators. We present this approach in section 2.2.

2.1 Precedence analysis.

Let $\alpha_1,\ldots,\alpha_n$ be information sets (isets) and let A,B,... be sets of information sets (sis). A sis A is defined by simply giving its isets A $=\{\alpha_1,\ldots \alpha_i\}$.

We say that there is a <u>precedence</u> P[A,B] between a sis A $=\{\alpha_1,\ldots,\alpha_i\}$ and a sis B $= \{\alpha_j,\ldots,\alpha_n\}$ if there exists an information process such that its inputs are the isets $\alpha_j,\ldots,\alpha_n$ and its outputs are $\alpha_1,\ldots,\alpha_i$. The isets of B are sufficient to obtain the isets of A. Equivalently, we also say that sis B is a precedent of sis A.

The precedence concept is particularly useful for derivability analysis purposes because in order to analyse whether an iset can be derived from others it suffices to know its precedents. The specification about <u>how</u> the iset is obtained (that is, the information process) is irrelevant in this respect, thus simplifying the problem.

Given an UD, in order to define all its precedents it would be necessary and sufficient to define the direct precedents of every possible iset in this UD (indirect precedents and precedents between sets of isets can be derived using inference rules). Later on we will present the inference rules for precedences. However, it is impractical to define the direct precedents of every iset, because the number of isets in a UD can be very large. Instead, we will use precedence rules. A <u>precedence rule</u> is a rule that applied to a given iset gives its direct precedents.

There is a precedence rule for every derivation rule defined in the conceptual schema of the UD, and the precedence rule can be obtained from the definition of the derivation rule. For example, from DR1 (section 1.6) we obtain P[O1, {I1,I2}]. This is a precedence rule, since it can be applied to any product and date.

Given a set of precedence rules it is possible to infer additional precedences from it, using inference rules. There are several equivalent sets of inference rules and we present one of them here. In what follows A,B,C,D are arbitrary sets of isets.

IR.1 (Reflexivity). If A$\subseteq$B, then P[A,B].
IR.2 (Augmentation). If A$\subseteq$B and P[C,D], then P[AUC,BUD].
IR.3 (Transitivity). If P[A,B] and P[B,C], then P[A,C].
IR4. (Pseudotransitivity). If P[A,B] and P[C,AUD], then P[C,BUD].
IR.5 (Union). If P[A,B] and P[C,B], then P[AUC,B].
IR.6 (Decomposition). If P[AUB,C], then P[A,C] and P[B,C].

The rules IR.1 – IR.3 are sufficient, since the rules IR.4 – IR.6 are implied by them.

We say that a sis A is <u>derivable</u> from a sis B if, and only if, P[A,B]. It follows from rules IR.5 and IR.6 that P[$\{\alpha_1,\ldots,\alpha_n\}$,B] is equivalent to the set of precedences $\{P[\{\alpha_1,B],\ldots,P[\{\alpha_n,B]\}$. Thus, to show that $\{\alpha_1,\ldots,\alpha_n\}$ is derivable from B, it is enough to show that each of the isets $\alpha_1,\ldots,\alpha_n$ is derivable from B.

Normally, in the derivation process of a precedence it is not derived directly P[$\alpha$,B], but an intermediate precedence P[$\alpha$,C]. In such cases, the derivation is decomposed into as many steps as isets are in C, and $\alpha$ will be found derivable if all $\alpha_i\epsilon$C are so. If any $\alpha_i\epsilon$C is not derivable from C, then neither is $\alpha$.

Our derivability analysis is formally identical to the membership problem for
functional dependencies in data bases [1]. Beeri and Bernstein have shown
that the membership problem is decidable and that there exists an efficient
(linear time) algorithm to solve it. This algorithm is used for derivability
analysis, with only minor modifications.

2.2 Process grouping.

Derivation rules are elementary information processes, since they can not be
subdivided. Derivation rules may be grouped, producing non-elementary processes
which, in turn, may be grouped to produce other processes. We will describe
this grouping by means of <u>process grouping operators</u>.

Then, the problem of determining whether iset $\alpha$ can be derived from isets
$\alpha_1,\ldots,\alpha_n$ can be viewed as the problem of building a sequence of process
groupings that begins with derivation rules and terminates with a process
having $\alpha_1,\ldots,\alpha_n$ as inputs and $\alpha$ as output. The use of process groupings in
the context of IS design is described in [15,22].

This approach is in fact equivalent to precedence analysis, since derivation
rules are equivalent to precedence rules and process grouping operators
are equivalent to inference rules. We will not discuss in detail this equivalence
here.

The most important process grouping operators are described next. Other more
simple operators will be described in connection with examples given in the
following sections. We define an operator by indicating its operands, the
conditions they must satisfy and the process obtained as result. As for
derivation rules, a process P is characterized by its producing relationship
PR(P), the set of its inputs I(P) and the set of its outputs O(P). We also
say that there is an ocurrence of P for every tuple of PR(P).

<u>Horizontal grouping, $P = HG(P1,\ldots,Pn)$</u>

This operator groupes two or more processes $P1,\ldots,Pn$ with identical PR,
giving a process P with the same PR and such that its inputs and outputs
are the union of the inputs and outputs of $P1,\ldots,Pn$. Usually, $P1,\ldots,Pn$
will share some input, but this is not a necessary condition for this
operator to be employed. In the examples of section 1.6 it can be used
to group DR3 and DR4. The formal definition is:

    Conditions: $n \geqslant 2$,
             $PR(P1) = \ldots = PR(Pn)$

    Result: $PR(P) = PR(P1)$
            $O(P) = O(P1)U\ldots UO(Pn)$
            $I(P) = I(P1)U\ldots UI(Pn)$

<u>Vertical grouping, $P = VG(P1,P2,B)$</u>

Let us assume that a process P1 has iset $\alpha$ among its inputs and that a process
P2 has $\alpha$ among its outputs. The vertical grouping operator allows us to
group P1 and P2 into a single process P that eliminates the "writing out"
(production) and "reading in" of $\alpha$. More generally, the common input and
output of P1 and P2 may be a set B of isets. The definition of this operator is:

    Conditions: $B \subseteq I(P1)$,
             $B \subseteq O(P2)$,
             $A(PR(P2)) \subseteq A(PR(P1))$,
             $PR(P1)[X] \subseteq PR(P2)[X]$,   with $X = A(PR(P2))$

The two last conditions assure that there will be an occurrence of P2 for every occurrence of P1. This guarantees that B can be produced by P2.

    Result: PR(P) = PR(P1)
            O(P) = O(P1) U O(P2)
            I(P) = (I(P1) U I(P2)) - B

Projection, P = PJ(P1,X)

Let X be a set of attributes such that $X \subseteq A(PR(P1))$. This operator aggregates all occurrences of P1 corresponding to the same value of attributes X. The outputs of P are the union of the outputs produced by the aggregated occurrences of P1. Similarly, the inputs of P are the union of the inputs required by the aggregated occurrences of P1. The name of this operator is "projection" since it can be seen as a projection of relation PR(P1).

For example, an occurrence of DR1 (section 1.6) derives the price of a product in a given date. If we take X = {DATE} then an occurrence of PJ(DR1,X) aggregates all occurrences of DR1 corresponding to the same date. It will derive the set of prices for all products in a given date. The definition is:

    Condition: $X \subseteq A(PR(P1))$

Let $A(PR(P1)) = X \cup Y$, with $X \cap Y = \emptyset$ and let $X = \{ A_1, \ldots, A_i \}$.

    Result: PR(P) = PR(P1) $[X]$
            O(P) = $\Sigma$O(P1)
            I(P) = $\Sigma$I(P1) U {PR(P1)$(A_1 = p_1, \ldots, A_i = p_i)$}

where $p_1, \ldots, p_i$ are the parameters for the attributes of X.

The unions denoted by the symbols $\Sigma$O(P1) and $\Sigma$I(P1) can be easily obtained from the expressions of O(P1) and I(P1) by substituting the occurrences of all parameters of attributes $A_j$, $A_j \epsilon Y$, by relations PR(P1)$[A_j]$. For example, the result of P = PJ(DR1,DATE) is:

    PR(P) = D
    O(P) = PRICES(PRODUCT $\epsilon$PRODUCTS[PRODUCT], DATE = d)
    I(P) = {PRICES(PRODUCT $\epsilon$PRODUCTS[PRODUCT], DATE = PREVIOUS(d)),
            PRICE–CHANGES(PRODUCT $\epsilon$PRODUCTS[PRODUCT], DATE = d),
            (PRODUCTS[PRODUCT] x D) (DATE = d)}

In subsequent sections we will see that these expressions can be simplified.

Selection, P = S(P1,R)

The selection operator allows us to select some occurrences of process P1. Let R be a relation such that $R \subseteq PR(P1)$. Then, P = S(P1,R) is the same process as P1, but with PR(P) = R. The occurrences of P are a subset of occurrences of P1. The definition is:

    Condition: $R \subseteq PR(P1)$

    Result : PR(P) = R
             O(P) = O(P1)
             I(P) = I(P1)

Partition by relation grouping, P = PRG(P1,R)

Let X = A(PR(P1)) and let R be a relation such that K(R) = X and A(R) = X U A with attribute A  X. In this case, R defines a partition onto PR(P1). An element of this partition comprises all tuples of PR(P1) having the same value of attribute A in R. The PRG operator aggregates all occurrences of P1 of an

element of the partition. The outputs of P are the union of the outputs produced
by the aggregated occurrences of P1. Similarly, the inputs of P are the union
of the inputs required by the aggregated occurrences of P1.

In the examples of section 1.6 we can use R7 = DATE-ENTERED(ORDER,DATE) to group
all occurrences of DR3 with the same date, P = PRG(DR3,R7). The output of an
occurrence of P will be the iset AMOUNT-ORDER(ORDER$\varepsilon$R7(DATE=d)[ORDER]), that is
the amounts of all orders having date d. The definition of this operator is:

   Conditions: K(R) = X  with X = A(PR(P1)),
               A(R) = X U {$A_n$}  with $A_n \not\subset X$
   Result: PR(P) = (PR(P1) * R)[$A_n$]
           O(P) = $\Sigma$O(P1)
           I(P) = $\Sigma$I(P1) U {R($A_n$=$p_n$)}

The unions denoted by the symbols $\Sigma$O(P1) and $\Sigma$I(P1) can be easily obtained from
the expressions of O(P1) and I(P1) by substituting all occurrences of parameters
of attributes $A_j$, $A_j \varepsilon X$, by relations R($A_n$=$p_n$)[$A_j$], where $p_n$ is the parameter of P.

For example, the result of P = PRG(DR3,R7) is:

   PR(P) = (ORDERS[ORDER] * R7)[DATE]
    O(P) = {AMOUNT-ORDER(ORDER$\varepsilon$R7(DATE=d)[ORDER])}
    I(P) = {ORDERS(ORDER$\varepsilon$R7(DATE=d)[ORDER]= I1,
            PRICES(PRODUCT=I1[PRODUCT],DATE=DATE(I1[TIME]),
            R7(DATE=d)}

In subsequent sections we will also see that these expressions can be simplified.

   Partition by function grouping, P = PFG(P1,F)

This operator is equivalent to the previous PRG, but now the partition of PR(P1)
is done by a function F instead of a relation. Let X = A(PR(P1)) and let F be
a function with argument X, value Y and domain D(F). F defines a partition
onto PR(P1). An element of this partition comprises all tuples of PR(P1)
having the same value for Y in F. The PFG operator aggregates all occurrences
of P1 of an element of the partition. The definition is:

   Conditions: Argument of F = X, with X = A(PR(P1))

   Result: PR(P) = F(PR(P1)*D(F))
           O(P) = $\Sigma$O(P1)
           I(P) = $\Sigma$I(P1)

The unions denoted by the symbols $\Sigma$O(P1) and $\Sigma$I(P1) can be easily obtained
from the expression of O(P1) and I(P1) by substituting all occurrences of
parameters of attributes $A_j$, $A_j \varepsilon X$, by $F^{-1}$($p_n$), where $F^{-1}$ is the name of the
inverse function and $p_n$ is the parameter of P.

3. VALIDATION OF SPECIFICATIONS.

There are a number of requirements that an adequate requirements specification
must conform to. Among these there are completeness, consistency, unambiguity,
feasibility and others [14]. In this section we will consider the consistency
aspect of specifications.

In this respect, the main originality of DADES is that it provides a formal
method to validate the logical consistency of IS requirements. A necessary
condition for logical consistency of IS requirements is that the anticipated
outputs must be derivable from the inputs. (See [5] for a similar statement

at data base level). This condition can be stated in a simple and formal way
by using the concepts and notation introduced in the previous section.

## 3.1 Validation of logical consistency.

Let $I1,...,In$ be the input types of an IS. We denote by $Ij(t1,t2)$, $t2 \geqslant t1$, the
set of isets $\underset{t\epsilon\{t1\div t2\}}{U}\{Ij(t)\}$. Thus, $Ij(t1,t2)$ contains all inputs of type $Ij$
that have arrived between t1 and t2. Similarly, we denote by $I(t1,t2)$,
$t2 \geqslant t1$, the set of isets $\underset{j=1,n}{U} Ij(t1,t2)$.

Let $O1,..,Om$ be the output types to be produced by an IS. Let $Oi(t)$ be an iset
of type $Oi$ to be produced at time t. This iset must be derivable from the set
of inputs $I(t0,t)$ arrived between the initial time t0 and t.

Using precedence analysis, the condition for consistency is that for every
$Oi$, $i=1,m$, $\forall t\epsilon T(Oi)$, $P\left[Oi(t),I(t0,t)\right]$ must hold. Using the process grouping
approach, the condition is that for every $Oi$, $i=1,m$, it must exist a
sequence of process groupings that begins with derivation rules and terminates
with a process P such that $PR(P) = T(Oi)$, $O(P) = Oi(t)$ and $I(P) = I(t0,t)$.

In next section we use this later approach to validate the consistency of O3
in our example.

## 3.2 An example.

Let us take the O3 output type of the example of section 1. If specifications
are consistent, then it must be possible to build the process P indicated
in figure 5. An occurrence of P must exist for every t such that $t\epsilon END(M)$.
The output of the t-occurrence must be $O3(t)=TOTAL-QTY-ORDERED(MONTH=MONTH(t))$.

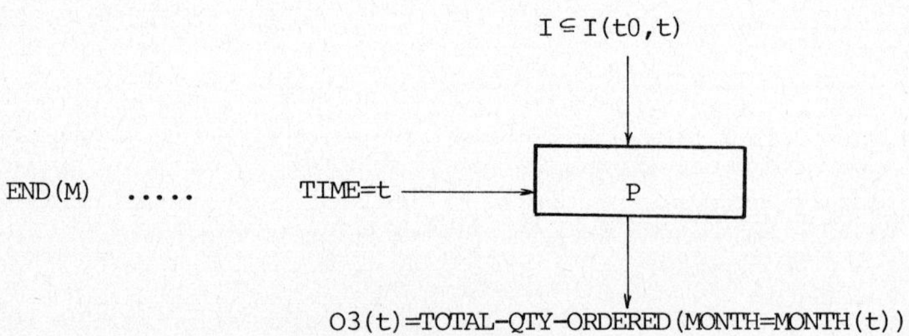


Figure 5. Validation of O3.

TOTAL-QTY-ORDERED is an user derived relation scheme. DR2, figure 6, is the
corresponding derivation rule, as defined in section 1.6. If we project DR2
into attribute MONTH we obtain $P1 = PJ(DR2,MONTH)$, as shown in figure 7. The
resulting relational expressions have been simplified by applying the
following equivalences:

1.- $(PRODUCTS\left[PRODUCT\right] \times M)\left[MONTH\right] = M$
2.- $(PRODUCTS\left[PRODUCT\right] \times M)\left[PRODUCT\right] = PRODUCTS\left[PRODUCT\right]$
3.- $ORDERS(PRODUCT\epsilon PRODUCTS\left[PRODUCT\right],TIME\epsilon TIMES(m)) = ORDERS(TIME\epsilon TIMES(m))$
    Since $D(ORDERS,PRODUCT) = PRODUCTS\left[PRODUCT\right]$
4.- $TOTAL-QTY-ORDERED(PRODUCT\epsilon PRODUCTS\left[PRODUCT\right],MONTH=m) =$
    $TOTAL-QTY-ORDERED(MONTH=m)$
    Since $D(TOTAL-QTY-ORDERED,PRODUCT) = PRODUCTS\left[PRODUCT\right]$

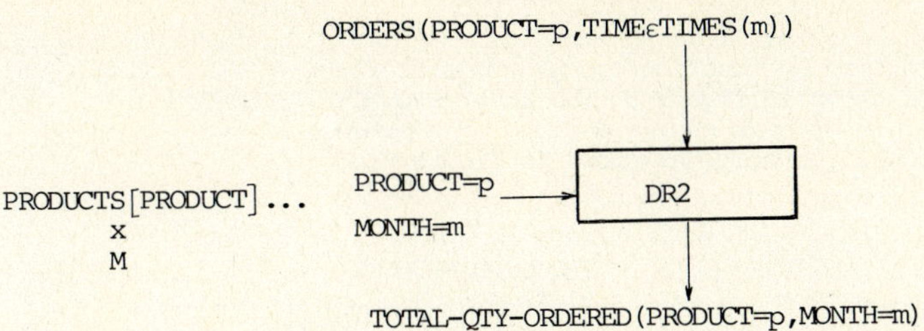

Figure 6. Derivation rule DR2.

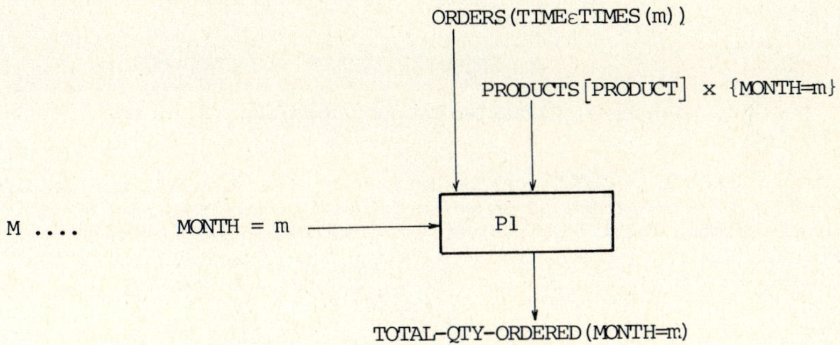

Figure 7. P1 = PJ(DR2,MONTH)

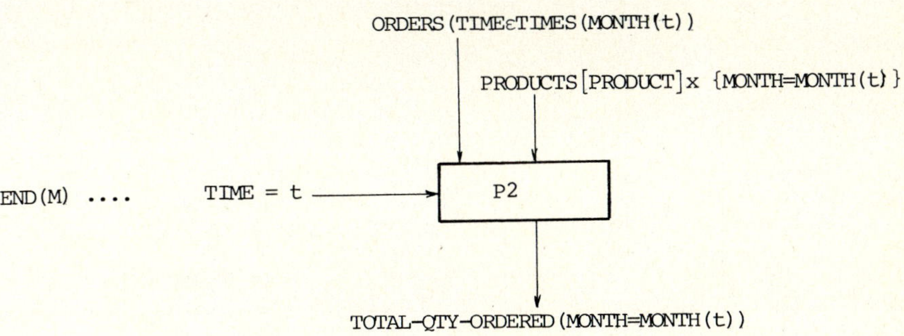

Figure 8. P2 = PFG(P1,END)

A. Olivé

5.-(PRODUCTS[PRODUCT] x M)(MONTH=m) = PRODUCTS[PRODUCT] x {MONTH=m}

We now apply the Partition by function grouping operator, P2 = PFG(P1,END), obtaining the process shown in figure 8. The input PRODUCTS[PRODUCT]x {MONTH=MONTH(t)} of this process can be derived by a process P3 corresponding to the Cartesian product operator, as shown in figure 9.

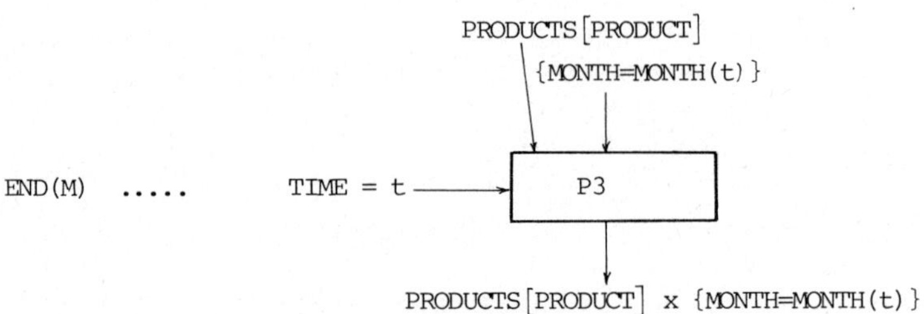

Figure 9. Cartesian product operator.

Similarly, input PRODUCTS[PRODUCT] can be derived by a process P4 corresponding to the projection of a relation, as shown in figure 10. Note the use of UNIQUE in the producing relationship since iset PRODUCTS[PRODUCT] has no parameters.

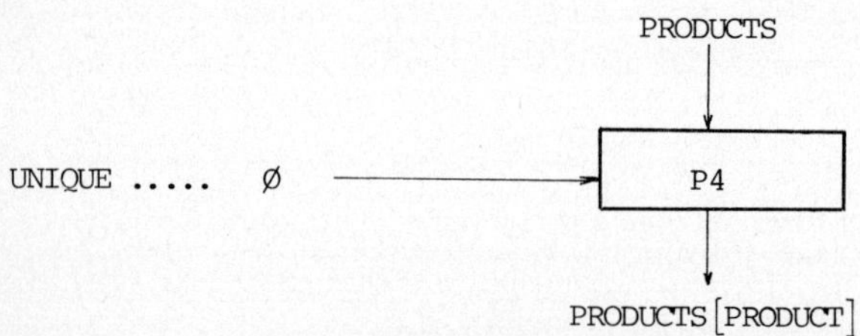

Figure 10. Relation projection operator.

Finally, grouping vertically P2, P3, and P4 we obtain  P5 = VG(P2,VG(P3,P4, PRODUCTS[PRODUCT]),B)  with B = PRODUCTS[PRODUCT] x {MONTH=MONTH(t)}. This result is shown in figure 11. P5 is the required process P (figure 5) if we can prove that $I(P5) \subseteq I(t0,t)$. The proof is easy because:

1) I1(t0,t) = PRODUCTS if $t \geq$ INITIALIZATION. From the TIME-ORDERING definition (section 1.2) we derive $\forall t \varepsilon$ END(M) : INITIALIZATION $<t$. Therefore PRODUCTS can be obtained from I1(t0,t).

2) {MONTH=MONTH(t)}  is a constant obtained by applying function MONTH to parameter t.

3)  I2(t0,t) = ORDERS(TIME$\varepsilon${t0$\div$t})   and
    ORDERS(TIME$\varepsilon$TIMES(MONTH(t)) $\subseteq$ I2(t0,t)   since if t corresponds to the end of month instant then it is obvious that TIMES(MONTH(t)) $\subseteq$ {t0$\div$t}.

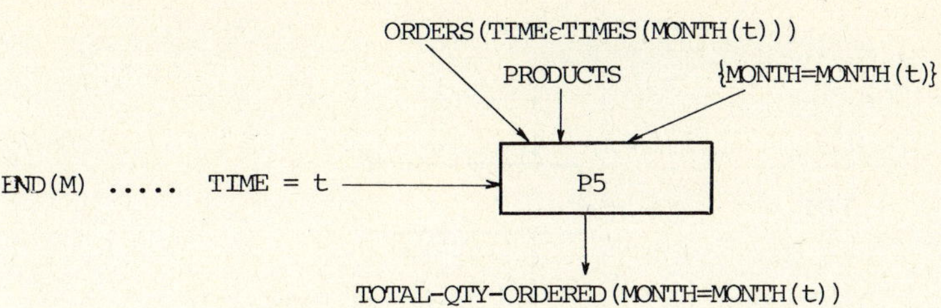


Figure 11.  P5 = VG(P2,P3,B)

## 4. VERIFICATION.

Specifications serve as a basis from which the designer develops alternative
design decisions. It  is widely recognised the need for verification of the
design correctness, before the IS is built. In this respect, the main originality
of DADES is that it provides a method for formally verifying some design
decisions corresponding to the architectural design of IS.

We can use the concepts and notation introduced in preceeding sections to model
an IS. Let L be the life span of the IS, expressed in a given time unit. Let us
assume that this unit is "time" and that T is the set of instants comprised
in L. Let $I1,...,In$ and $O1,...,Om$ be the defined input and output types. We
will denote by $I(t) = \bigcup_{j=1,n} Ij(t)$, $\forall t\varepsilon T$, the inputs at time t and by
$O(t) = \bigcup_{j=1,m} Oj(t)$, $\forall t\varepsilon T$, the outputs at time t. Both can be calculated from
the specifications.

Then the IS can be modeled as a process P such that its producing relationship
is T (figure 12). There is an occurrence of P for every $t\varepsilon T$. We denote by
$B^{-}(t)$ the contents of the data base at the beginning of the t-occurrence of
P and by $B(t)$ its contents at the end. Thus the t-occurrence receives $B^{-}(t)$ along
with input $I(t)$ and derives $B(t)$ together with output $O(t)$.

If for some $t1\varepsilon T$ we have $I(t1) = O(t1) = \emptyset$ and $B^{-}(t1) = B(t1)$ then P is
inactive in its t1-occurrence. On the other hand, if for some $t2\varepsilon T$ we have
$I(t2) = O(t2) = \emptyset$  but $B^{-}(t2) \neq B(t2)$ then the t2-occurrence only performs
a modification of the data base. In the general case, however, an occurrence
receives an input, derives an output and modifies the data base.

$B(t)$ will be the data base input at t+1. Thus, $B(t) = B^{-}(t+1)$ or, equivalently,
$B^{-}(t) = B(t-1)$. The addition to the data base in an occurrence is given by
$B(t) - B^{-}(t)$ and the deletion is given by $B^{-}(t) - B(t)$.

Usually, process  P is very complex, so for several reasons it is necessary to
decompose it into a number of smaller processes $P1,...,Pn$ in such a manner
that the composition of all of them be equivalent to P. We will call $P1,...,Pn$
subsystems of the IS. Other names used in the literature are system's
modules, programs, etc.

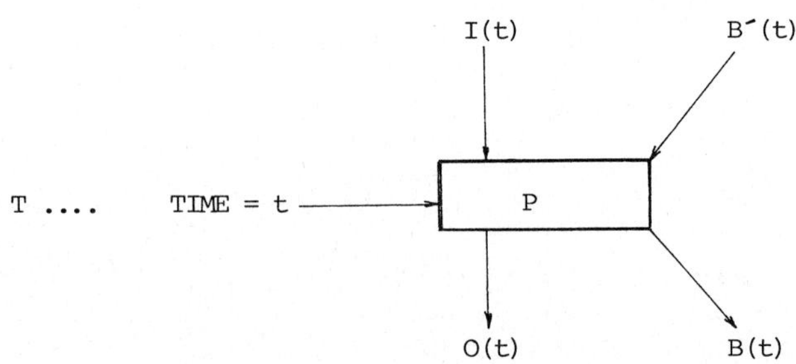



Figure 12. Model of an IS.

Our model allows us to highlight the two most important architectural design decisions. Both will be studied in the rest of this section. The first is to decide, for every $t \in T$, the data base contents of the IS, that is, the value of B(t), or alternatively B⁻(t). The second is to decide the subsystem structure, that is, the decomposition of P into subsystems P1,...,Pn. Although both decisions are related, for the purposes of verification they will be considered separately in this section.

## 4.1 Data base contents.

One of the most important tasks in architectural design of an IS is to decide which informations are to be explicitly stored in the data base. The task is complex because there exists a large number of alternatives and it is difficult to evaluate all of them. Tradeoffs have to be made among general criteria, such as retrieval time, update time, storage costs and others. Moreover, each of the alternatives must be logically consistent with the defined inputs and outputs of the IS.

This consistency can also be verified using derivability analysis. Let us assume that a specified alternative for data base contents is B(t), where B(t) is defined for every $t \in T$. B(t) is a set of isets, each defined as a relational expression from the conceptual schema, with t as parameter. From the model depicted in figure 12 we see that for all $t \in T$, B(t) must satisfy three conditions:

1) It must be derivable from the set of inputs I(t0,t) arrived between the initial time t0 and t.

2) It must be derivable from the set B⁻(t) U I(t) = B(t-1) U I(t), where I(t) is the input arrived at time t.

3) The outputs to be produced at time t, O(t), must be derivable from the set B⁻(t) U I(t) = B(t-1) U I(t).

All of these conditions can be verified using the precedence analysis or process grouping indicated in the preceeding sections.

In our example, one alternative for B(t) could be the following, where we give a name and a formal description for each iset of B(t):

```
B(t) = {PRODUCTS AND NAMES : PRODUCTS,
        STOCKS : STOCK(TIME=t),
        ORDERS RECEIVED : ORDERS(TIMEε{t0 ÷ t}) * AMOUNT-ORDER * DEL-INPUT-ORDERS,
        PRICES:  If t ≥ NEW-PRICES-TIME(DATE(t)) then
                    NEW PRICES : PRICES(DATE=DATE(t)),
                else OLD PRICES : PRICES(DATE=PREVIOUS(DATE(t))),
        BACKORDERS :  If t ≥ BOP-TIME(DATE(t)) then
                    NEW BACKORDERS : BACKORDERS(DATE=DATE(t)) * DEL-BACKORDERS,
                else PREVIOUS BACKORDERS :
                    BACKORDERS(DATE=PREVIOUS(DATE(t))) * DEL-BACKORDERS}
```

That is, this alternative contains the name of all products, the stock at time t
and all orders (with AMOUNT and DELIVERY attributes) entered between t0 and t.
Moreover, it contains the prices for date DATE(t) or PREVIOUS(DATE(t)),
depending on the value of t; and the backorders (with DELIVERY attribute) of
date DATE(t) or PREVIOUS(DATE(t)), depending on the value of t. It can be
shown that B(t) satisfies the stated conditions. However, we will not develop
the proofs here.

4.2 Overall process structure.

Another important task in the activity of architectural design of an IS is to
decide the overall process structure, that is, the decomposition of P into
its subsystems P1,...,Pn. The task is complex because of its relationship to
the design of the data base and because of its effects upon factors such as
efficiency, modifiability, understandability and reliability. Moreover, the
structure must be logically consistent with the specifications.

This consistency can also be verified using derivability analysis. For example,
let us assume that a specified alternative for subsystem structure is
P1,...,Pr. Every Pj, j=1,r, must be defined (figure 13) by giving its producing
relationship $PR(Pj) \subseteq T$ and specifying for any t-occurrence, $t \in PR(Pj)$:

    The input Ij(t) received
    The output Oj(t) produced
    The subset $B\overline{j}(t) \subseteq B^{\check{}}(t)$ read from the data base
    The subset $Bj(t) \subseteq B(t)$ added to the data base

where all values are relational expressions.

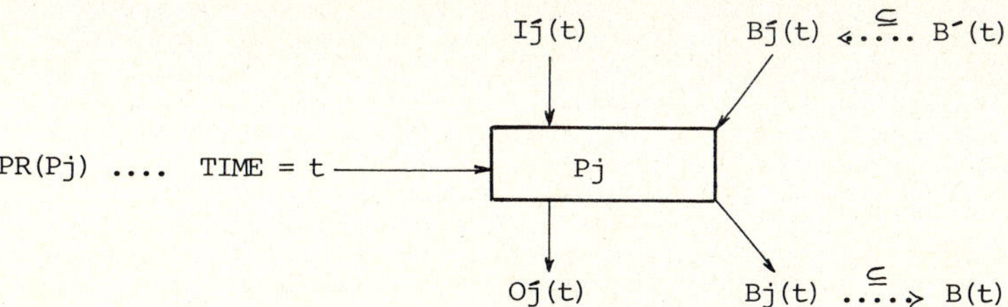


Figure 13. Definition of a process.

Besides $PR(Pj) \subseteq T$, $B\overline{j}(t) \subseteq B^{\check{}}(t)$ and $Bj(t) \subseteq B(t)$, any process Pj, j=1,r, must
satisfy the following conditions:

1) For all $t \in PR(Pj)$, $Bj(t)$ must be derivable from $Ij(t) \cup Bj(t)$.

2) For all $t \in PR(Pj)$, $Oj(t)$ must be derivable from $Ij(t) \cup Bj(t)$.

The two conditions ensure that Pj is logically consistent. Both can be verified using precedence analysis or process grouping.

In addition to being internally consistent, subsystems P1,...,Pr must be consistent with specifications. Let $\tilde{T} = \bigcup_{i=1,r} PR(Pj)$, $\tilde{I}(t) = \bigcup_{i=1,r} Ij(t)$, $\tilde{O}(t) = \bigcup_{i=1,r} Oj(t)$ and $\tilde{A}(t) = \bigcup_{i=1,r} Bj(t)$, for all $t \in \tilde{T}$. Thus, $\tilde{T}$, $\tilde{I}(t)$, $\tilde{O}(t)$ and $\tilde{A}(t)$ are calculated from the definitions of P1,...,Pr. Then, the necessary conditions for consistency can be stated as follows:

1) For all $t \in \tilde{T}$: $I(t) = \tilde{I}(t)$

2) For all $t \in \tilde{T}$: $O(t) = \tilde{O}(t)$

3) For all $t \in \tilde{T}$: $B(t) - \tilde{B}(t) = \tilde{A}(t)$

4) For all $t \in T$ and $t \notin \tilde{T}$: $I(t) = O(t) = \emptyset$

That is, the values calculated from specifications must be consistent with values calculated from design.

Figure 14 shows a possible set of subsystems for the order processing example. For the sake of clarity, we have used narrative descriptions (names) instead of formal expressions. It can be shown that each subsystem is consistent and that the whole set is consistent with specifications. However, we will not include the proofs here.

5. THE DADES METHODOLOGY.

In the previous sections, we have described the three basic components of DADES: a requirements specification language, a method for validation of specifications and a method for design verification. It is our belief that these components can be embedded, in whole or in part, in several design methodologies, or that they can complement other methods to form a coherent methodology. For example, the DADES language can be used for requirements specification of data bases [28] and the verification method can be used in many design methodologies.

However, we also have developed a methodology that integrates the DADES components with elements of other methodologies to form a coherent whole. It can be used in the specification and architectural design stages of the life of an IS [10]. It does not cover the full life cycle, since it does not address the needs analysis nor the detailed design and implementation stages. For this reason, a comprehensive IS development methodology should include methods to deal with these uncovered stages.

In this section we outline the steps, grouped into three phases, involved in the use of the DADES methodology. An example of its application will be given in the second part of this paper.

5.1 Preliminary specification phase.

This phase is mainly carried out at the end of the needs analysis stage. Its purpose is threefold: (1) To document the preliminary set of input/output requirements; (2) To develop a basic structure of the conceptual schema; and (3) To decide upon naming conventions to be used for referring to objects.

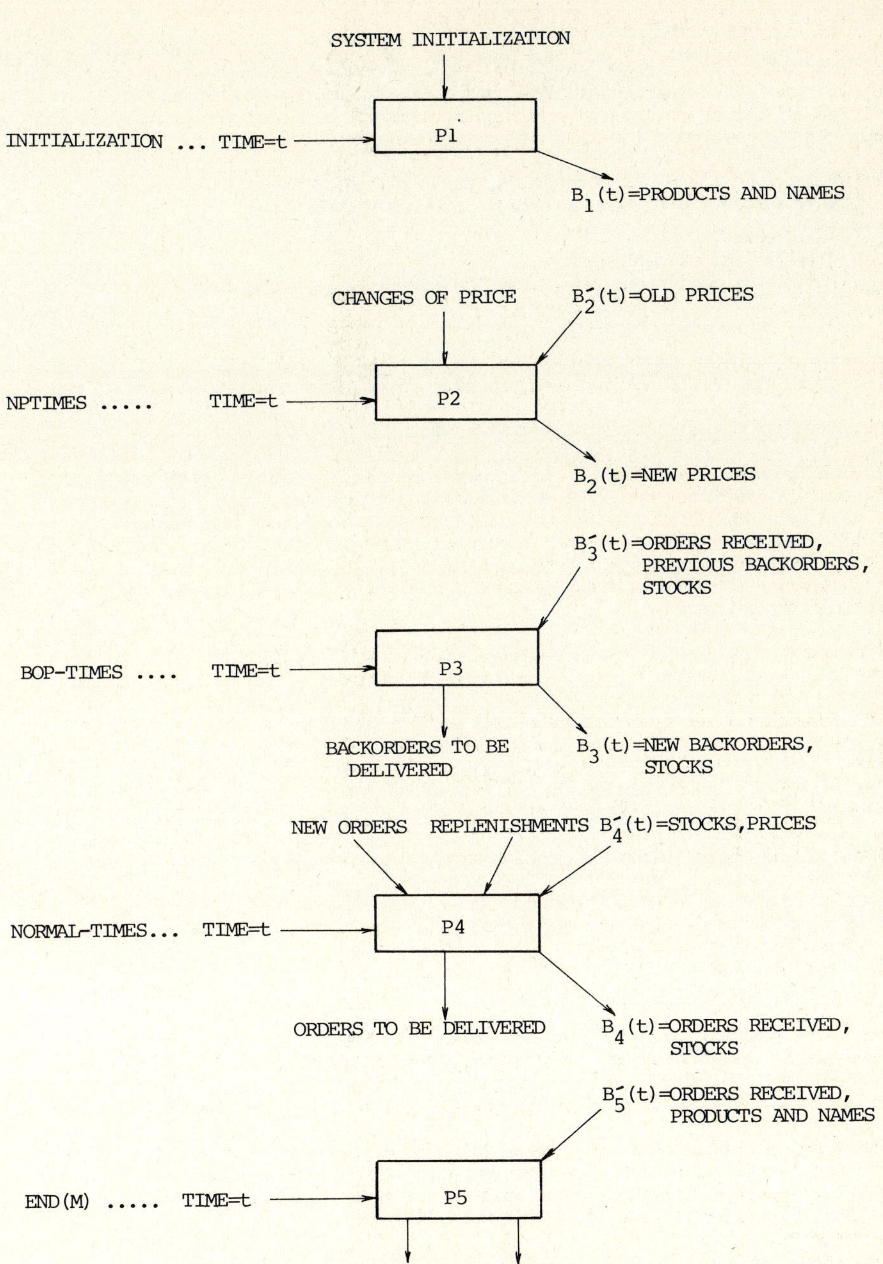


Figure 14. Subsystems for the example.

Step 1. <u>List input/output requirements.</u>

One of the tasks of the needs analysis stage is to determine the main input and output information requirements. The task is performed by analysing the activities in the object system and the information needs of the users. Several methods can be used to guide this task, such as [11,17] and others.

The first step of the DADES methodology is to document these input/output requirements. For each of them we give, in a narrative form:

>    - Its name
>    - Its origin or destination
>    - The main conditions governing the production of the outputs
>    - When inputs are available
>    - Its information contents.

These are preliminary specifications of requirements, that will be refined in a later step. So, it is not required to give formal and complete descriptions.

Step 2. <u>Develop the abstract conceptual schema.</u>

The conceptual schema of the IS, to be developed in the second phase, describes the classes of objects of the UD as well as the relations among them. However, there is a more abstract schema: the one that abstracts from the naming conventions with respect to object instances. The need to develop this abstract conceptual schema is increasingly recognised [5,21], mainly as a basis from which a conceptual schema can be derived and also as a basis for deciding the naming conventions.

Then the next step starts with an analysis of the information contents of each input/output requirement (step 1), in order to determine the set of entities, attributes and relationships that are of interest. These individual sets are then consolidated. The result is a selection of entities, entity attributes and relationships that comprise the UD of the IS.

Several methods, mainly developed in the data base area, can be used in this step, such as [5,34]. The outputs of these methods will be an abstract conceptual schema that describes the classes of elements of the UD (entities, attributes) and their relations, but abstracting from the naming conventions.

Although in the example of the second part of this paper we will use the relational model to describe this schema, other models might be used, depending on the specific method employed.

Step 3. <u>Decide the naming conventions.</u>

In order to be able to store, communicate and process information about the object system, it is necessary to assign names to the objects. Usually, the same object may be referred to in several ways and the users must be aware of the fact that they must take decisions about how names are assigned to objects.

The purpose of this step is to decide the naming conventions that will be used in the IS. It is performed by assigning a naming rule to each attribute of the abstract conceptual schema developed in the previous step. An analysis of the possible alternatives may be seen in [34].

5.2 Specification phase.

The purpose of this phase is to specify the requirements of the IS, using the DADES specification language. The four steps of this phase correspond very closely to the elements of the language and to the validation method as described in sections 1 and 3, respectively. For this reason, we will only give a brief description here.

It should be noted, however, that usually a number of iterations have to be made both within and between the four steps in a practical situation. This is common to almost all design methodologies.

Step 1. <u>Develop the conceptual schema.</u>

In the first step the conceptual schema is defined. The main inputs are the abstract conceptual schema and the naming conventions, both developed in the previuos phase. The result is the definition of the conceptual schema, as described in section 1.5.

In this step, as well as in the others, it may be necessary to define some time functions, points or intervals (section 1.2) in order to describe the time dimension of informations and the dynamic aspects of the system.

Step 2. <u>Define input/output requirements.</u>

The next step is to formalize and to complete the input/output requirements definition as described in section 1.7. The main inputs are the preliminary list of input/output requirements developed in the previous phase and the conceptual schema. Each input/output requirement is analysed and its narrative description is "translated" into a formal expression.

Step 3. <u>Define derivation rules.</u>

In this step the relation schemes of the conceptual schema are classified into either base or derived. Relation schemes whose informations (tuples) are given to the system (by means of inputs) are base, and the rest are derived.

For each derived relation scheme a derivation rule must be specified, as discussed in section 1.6. In trying to define a derivation rule the need for refining some relation scheme or for adding new inputs to the system may arise.

If a derived relation scheme is not used for the production of some output nor in some derivation rule, then it may be removed from the schema.

Step 4. <u>Validate specifications.</u>

At the end of the last step, specifications are complete. Now they must be validated for consistency, using the method described in section 3. The possible inconsistencies must be corrected. This, again, may imply the refinement of the conceptual schema or some of its derivation rules or the addition/modification of some input/output.

Even if performed manually, the validation task is worthwhile. The task is well structured and it is not difficult, although it is time-consuming. It is hoped that the use of an automated tool (at present under development) will be of great aid in this task.

5.3 Architectural design phase.

The purpose of this phase is to perform the logical design of the system data base and the design of the system structure.

We assume that the IS has to be implemented in a given centralized hardware/ software environment, with some data base management system (DBMS). The design of distributed systems (process or data base) will not be considered here.

We propose a bottom-up approach to architectural design, due to its recognised
advantages when a complete specification of the requirements is available. Our
choice has also been influenced by the availability of the verification method
that allows us to ensure the correctness of design decisions when they are made.

We start with an initial elementary system structure derived from specifications.
Then we perform the logical design of the data base for this structure, including
the verification of its consistency. In the next step we try to improve this
structure by grouping some processes. The data base design is then refined
and again we verify its consistency as well as the consistency of the new
system structure. The procedure is iterated a number of times until a satis
factory solution is reached.

The initial system structure is obtained by assuming that there is an independent
process for every input and output defined in the specifications. In this
structure, input processes read the inputs and update the data base, while
output processes produce the outputs from the information contained exclusively
in the data base. By successive refinements of this structure we will arrive
to processes with multiple inputs or outputs and such that outputs are produced
from information contained in the data base and in the inputs.

Step 1. <u>Logical data base design</u>.

In this step the logical design of the data base (DB) for the initial system
structure is performed, using some adequate methodology. A large number of
methodologies for DB design can be found in the literature. However, to be
useful in our context, a DB design methodology must be able to deal with:
(1) The dynamic aspects of a DB, including the temporal dimension of informations,
and (2) Base and derived informations, since both aspects must be considered
in an IS environment.

Some of the methodologies satisfying the above conditions are [3,37]. It can
be shown that the requirements specifications that these methodologies need
are included in, or can easily be derived from, a DADES specification. Thus,
in this respect, the DADES approach provides a smooth link between specifications
and DB design.

The result of the step is the design of the information contents of the DB
and its logical structure. This structure is specified in a data definition
language which is processable by the DBMS.

Step 2. <u>System structure design</u>.

In the previous step an initial system structure has been considered. In some
cases this structure may be quite satisfactory,  specially for fully data
base oriented systems. In other cases however this solution may be inacceptable
because of poor efficiency.

It may be possible to develop other feasible and more efficient structures
by grouping two or more processes into a single process. This may result in
a reduction of input/output transport. It may also reduce the volume of the
information to be stored in the data base.  For a complete treatment of
process grouping and its effects see [15,22].  Other possibilities may be
the delaying of inputs until they are required for the production of outputs
or the anticipation of outputs to the instant when the information required
to produce them is available. In both cases a reduction in the need for
information storage may result.

For each alternative to be considered it is necessary to refine the previous
logical data base design and to verify again its consistency. Moreover,
the consistency of the system structure with specifications must be verified,
using the method described in section 4.2. This ensures that the design is
correct.

The step  ends when, after a number of iterations, a satisfactory solution
is found.

PART II.  APPLICATION OF DADES TO THE CASE STUDY

In this part we illustrate the DADES methodology by applying it to the exercise
defined by the IFIP Working Group WG8.1. The exercise is about an "information
system to be used to support the organising of a technical conference, including
the refereeing of papers". Each of the following sections correspond to one
step of the DADES methodology described in the previous section.

We will not reproduce here the problem statement as defined in the Problem
Definition nor the information supplied in the responses to specific questions.
Rather, we will give the details as they are needed in the steps of our
methodology.

## 1. LIST INPUT/OUTPUT REQUIREMENTS.

The first step of the methodology is to document, in a narrative form, the
input/output requirements of the IS to be designed.

In order to arrive at the requirements for our case study, we have used an
ad hoc method, instead of a standard one, mainly due to the special characteris
tics of the exercise, such as the absence of a complete communication and
involvement of the users, and the lack of a complete knowledge about the
current system.

The activities that we have performed are:

1) Define the system boundary. The functions that are to be included as part
   of the system study are those defined in the Problem Definition. We
   have added to them the issuing of remainders to referees and the computer
   ising of the structured part of the referees' reports.

2) Develop an activity diagram of the current system, from the problem
   statement. Because of space limitations, we can not give here the complete
   diagram for our exercise, but we show a part of it in figure 15. This
   diagram depicts the system activities and their relationships.

3) Define objectives for the new system. We assume that the need for an IS
   to support the object system is established. The main objective is to
   support all the activities included in the system boundary, by providing
   computer support or the information required to perform the activities
   involved.

4) Develop an activity diagram for the new system. Working with the activity
   diagram of the current system and with the statement of objectives, we
   have produced an activity diagram of the new system. From this diagram
   (not included here) we have derived the list of input/output requirements
   shown in Tables 2 and 3.

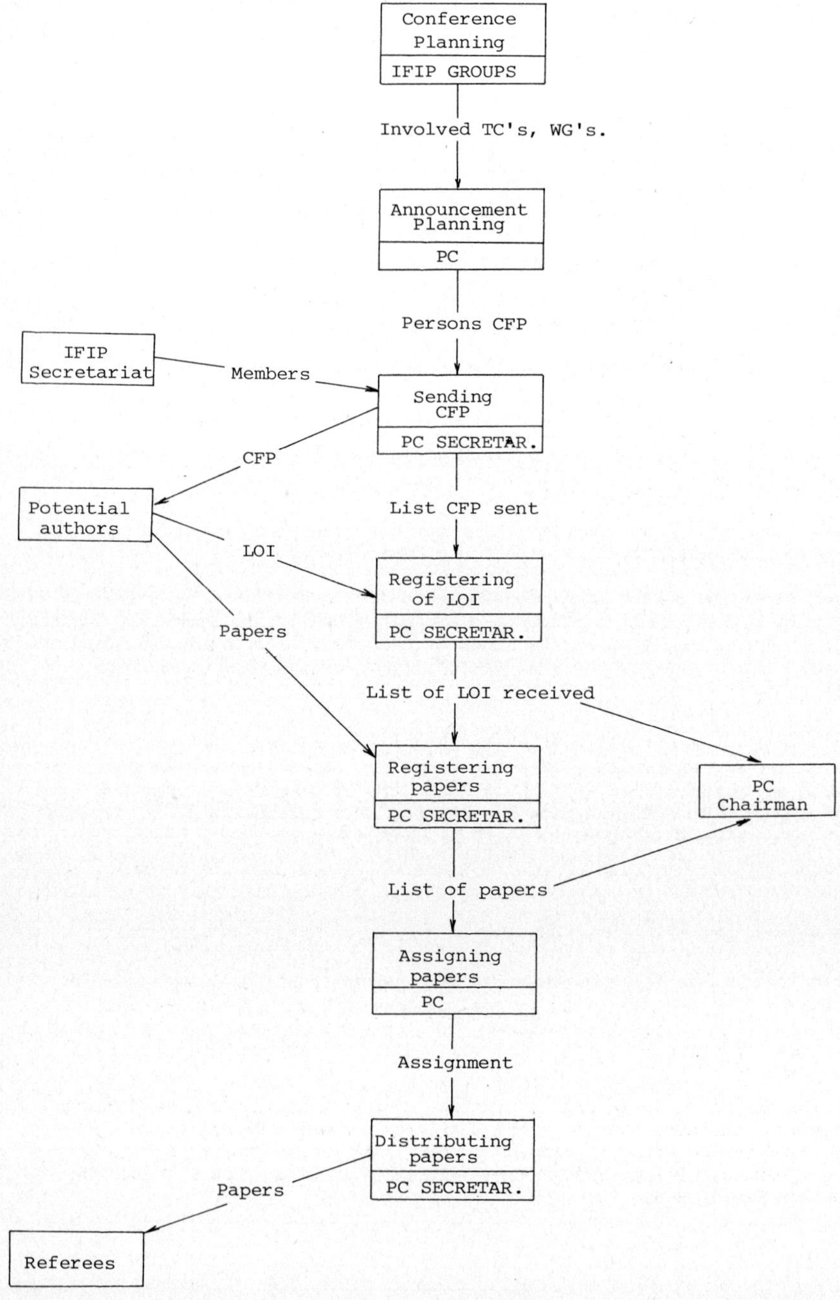


Figure 15. Activities of the system (partial).

Table 2. Input requirements.

| | NAME | CONTENTS | AVAILIBILITY/PRODUCTION | ORIGIN - DESTINATION |
|---|---|---|---|---|
| I1 | Involved groups | TC's and WG's involved in the Conference | After Conference planning | Diverse |
| I2 | Persons CFP | Person, affiliation, address | After Announcement planning | P. Committee |
| I3 | Members of involved groups | Group, person, affiliation, address | After Conference planning | IFIP Secretariat |
| I4 | Letter of intent | Title, author, affiliation, address, date received, coauthors | When received | Author |
| I5 | Paper | Title, author, affiliation, address, date received, coauthors | When received | Author |
| I6 | Referee's report | Referee, paper, attribute, qualification, date received | When received | Referee |
| I7 | Assignment of papers | Referee, paper | After assignment of referees | P. Committee |
| I8 | Selection of papers | Paper, Accepted/Rejected | After Selection of papers | P. Committee |
| I9 | Sessions | Session, title, date, hour, chairman, papers | After Conference organization | P. Committee |
| I10 | Invitation list | List of persons to invite to the Conference (except priority invitations). Contains persons, invitation date, closing date | After planning invitations | O. Committee |
| I11 | Registration | Person, date received, affiliation, address | When received | Invited persons |

Table 3. Output requirements.

| | NAME | CONTENTS | AVAILIBILITY/PRODUCTION | ORIGIN-DESTINATION |
|---|---|---|---|---|
| O1 | Call for papers | List of persons, affiliation, address to whom CFP is to be sent | When Sending CFP | Potential authors |
| O2 | List of LOI | List of letters of intent received | After deadline | P. Committee |
| O3 | List of papers | List of papers received | After deadline | P. Committee |
| O4 | Distributing papers | List for distributing papers among referees. | After assignment of referees | Referees |
| O5 | Remainders | Referee, paper for non-received reports | Some days before deadline | Referees |
| O6 | List of reports | List of referees' reports received | After deadline | P. Committee |
| O7 | Notification of acceptance | Author, affiliation, address, paper, coauthor, session, date, hour, chairman | After Conference organization | Authors |
| O8 | Notification of rejection | Author, affiliation, address, paper, coauthors | After Conference organization | Authors |
| O9 | Invitation | List of persons, affiliation, address, of invited persons, with closing date | As decided by O. Committee | Invited persons |
| O10 | List of registrations | Registered persons | When required | O. Committee |
| O11 | Attendance list | Person, affiliation, address | At the Conference | Attendees |
| O12 | Detailed inform. | Person, affiliation, address | When registration received | Registered persons |

## 2. DEVELOP AN ABSTRACT CONCEPTUAL SCHEMA.

Working with the input/output requirements we have arrived at the abstract conceptual schema shown in figure 16. We have specified the domains of AUTHOR, COAUTHOR and REFEREE in order to make clear that these attributes refer to PERSONS.

INVOLVED-GROUPS(GROUP)

PERSONS-CFP(PERSON)

PERSONS(PERSON,NAME,AFFILIATION,ADDRESS,DATE-CFP-SENT,DATE-INVITED,
        CLOSING-DATE)

MEMBERS(PERSON,GROUP)

LETTERS-OF-INTENT(LETTER,AUTHOR:PERSON,TITLE,DATE-RECEIVED)

LOI-COAUTHORS(LETTER,COAUTHOR:PERSON)

PAPERS(PAPER,AUTHOR:PERSON,TITLE,DATE-RECEIVED,ACC/REJ)

PAPERS-COAUTHORS(PAPER,COAUTHOR:PERSON)

ASSIGNMENTS(REFEREE:PERSON,PAPER)

REF-REPORTS(REPORT,REFEREE:PERSON,PAPER,DATE-RECEIVED)

QUALIFICATIONS(REPORT,ATTRIBUTE,QUALIFICATION)

SESSIONS(SESSION,DATE,HOUR,TITLE,CHAIRMAN)

PRESENTATIONS(PAPER,SESSION)

REGISTRATIONS(REGISTRATION,PERSON,DATE-RECEIVED,DATE-INF-SENT)

INVITATION-LIST(LIST,INVITATION-DATE,CLOSING-DATE)

INVITED-PERSONS(PERSON,LIST)

Figure 16. Abstract conceptual schema.

## 3. DECIDE THE NAMING CONVENTIONS.

In this step we assign a naming rule to each attribute of the abstract conceptual schema. We have decided the following naming conventions:

1) AFFILIATION, ADDRESS, TITLE, as usual.

2) PERSON, AUTHOR, COAUTHOR, REFEREE and CHAIRMAN by name.

3) GROUP, the usual IFIP code, such as TC8 or WG8.1.

4) DATE, as year/month/day.

5) HOUR, as hour/AM or PM.

6) ACC/REJ, by A (Accepted) or R (Rejected).

7) ATTRIBUTE, QUALIFICATION, codes assigned by the Program Committee.

8) SESSION, by number.

9) LETTER OF INTENT. We will use TITLE to refer to a letter. AUTHOR can not be used because we assume that the same person may be author of several letters of intent.

10) PAPER. We will assign a number to each paper. We do not use TITLE, as for letters, because it is too long and papers need to be referred to several times (assignments, reports and presentations).

11) REPORT. It will be identified by REFEREE and PAPER.

12) REGISTRATION. It will be identified by the PERSON registered.

13) LIST (of invited persons). It will be identified by number.

4. <u>DEVELOP THE CONCEPTUAL SCHEMA</u>.

In this step we define the conceptual schema of the IS. The activities that we
have performed are:

1) Define the domains of the attributes (figure 17). We assign a domain to
   each attribute included in the abstract conceptual schema, according to the
   naming conventions developed in the previous step. We also assign a type
   to each domain.

     DOMAINS:

       D1   = GROUP;TYPE=CHAR(6);DESC= IFIP Code.

       D2   = PERSON;TYPE=CHAR(20);DESC=Name of the person.

       D3   = AFFILIATION;TYPE=CHAR(30).

       D4   = ADDRESS;TYPE=CHAR(50).

       D5   = TITLE;TYPE=CHAR(50);DESC= Title of a paper or session.

       D6   = PAPER;TYPE=NUM;DESC=Paper serial number.

       D7   = ACC/REJ;TYPE=BOOLEAN;DESC=Accepted or rejected (a paper).

       D8   = ATTRIBUTE;TYPE=CHAR(10);DESC=Attribute for the refereeing and
              evaluation of papers, such as "Originality" and "Relevance".

       D9   = QUALIFICATION;TYPE=CHAR(10);DESC=Grade of an attribute in a
              paper, such as "High" or "Low".

       D10  = HOUR;TYPE=CHAR(7);DESC=Hour, minute, AM/PM.

       D11  = SESSION;TYPE=NUM;DESC=Session serial number.

       D12  = LIST;TYPE=NUM;DESC=Invitation list serial number.


                   Figure 17. Domains of the schema.

2) Analyse time attributes. For each time attribute included in the abstract
   conceptual schema we analyse its value set. From them, we define the
   specific points and intervals of the life span (figure 18). This definition
   will be refined in later steps.

3) Define relation schemes. We decompose each relation scheme of the abstract
   conceptual schema into elementary relation schemes and we introduce the
   naming conventions. We also define the assertion time and the value set
   of the attributes. In the example (figure 19), however, R3, R5, R7, R9
   R15 and R19 are defined as non-elementary since it is presumed that
   their attributes will always be used together. We have also included
   attribute DATE in R3 in order to be able to define its assertion time.

POINT : CONFERENCE-PLANNING = date; DESC=It corresponds to the date
when the Working Conference is planned.

POINT : ANNOUNCEMENT-PLANNING=date; DESC=It is the date when the
issuing of the Call for Papers (CFP) is planned.

POINT : CALL-FOR-PAPERS-SENT = date; DESC=Date when CFP is sent.

INTERVAL : RECEPTION-OF-LOI = date; DESC=Interval during which
letters of intent are received.

INTERVAL : RECEPTION-OF-PAPERS = date; DESC=Interval during which
papers are received.

POINT : ASSIGNMENT-OF-REFEREES = date.

INTERVAL : RECEPTION-OF-REPORTS = date; DESC=Interval during which
referees' reports are received.

POINT : SELECTION-OF-PAPERS = date; DESC=Date in which the Program
Committee selects the papers.

POINT : CONFERENCE-ORGANIZATION = date; DESC=Date in which the
Program Committee builds the Scientific Programme.

INTERVAL : INVITATIONS-PLANNING = date; DESC=Dates when invitations
are planned and issued.

INTERVAL : RECEPTION-OF-REGISTRATIONS = date.

INTERVAL : CONFERENCE = date.


Figure 18. Specific points and intervals
of the life span.


5. <u>DEFINE INPUT/OUTPUT REQUIREMENTS</u>.

In this step we define the input/output requirements developed in the first
step (Tables 2 and 3). For each input or output we define its information
contents as a relational expression of the relation schemes included in the
conceptual schema. We also define the set of instants of arrival or production,
the location and the volume estimates (figure 20). We omit here the definition
of the input checking procedures. The time unit that has been used is "date"
since it is small enough to describe the input/output occurrences of the
example.

In order to describe the instants of production of O7 and O8 it has been
necessary to define a new specific point:

POINT : NOTIFICATION = date; DESC = Date when authors are notified.

that should be added to the list of figure 18.

At this point, we can define the time ordering of the specific points and
intervals that have been used (figure 21). It is used in the validation
and verification activities.

RELATION-SCHEMES:

R1   = INVOLVED-GROUPS(GROUP); AT=CONFERENCE-PLANNING.

R2   = PERSONS-CFP(PERSON); AT=ANNOUNCEMENT-PLANNING; D(PERSON) ⊂ PERSON;
       DESC=Persons to whom a CFP is to be sent. IFIP Groups members not
       included.

R3   = PERSONS(PERSON,AFFILIATION,ADDRESS,DATE); AT=DATE; DESC=It includes
       all  known persons. Attribute DATE specifies when the person was
       known by the system.

R4   = CFP-SENT(PERSON); AT=CALL-FOR-PAPERS-SENT; D(PERSON) ⊆ PERSON; DESC=
       It includes all persons to whom CFP is sent. The date is not
       included since it is constant.

R5   = INV-SENT(PERSON, DATE,CLOSING-DATE:DATE); AT=DATE; D(PERSON) ⊆ PERSON;
       D(DATE) = D(CLOSING-DATE) = INVITATIONS-PLANNING; DESC=It includes
       the persons to whom an invitation is _sent as well as the date of
       invitation.

R6   = MEMBERS(GROUP,PERSON); AT=CONFERENCE-PLANNING; D(PERSON) ⊂ PERSON;
       DESC=It gives the members of the IFIP Groups. A person may be
       member of several groups.

R7   = LETTERS-OF-INTENT(TITLE,AUTHOR:PERSON,DATE-RECEIVED:DATE);
       AT=DATE-RECEIVED; D(PERSON) ⊂ PERSON; D(DATE-RECEIVED) = RECEPTION-
       OF-LOI.

R8   = LOI-COAUTHORS(TITLE,COAUTHOR:PERSON); AT=LETTERS-OF-INTENT;
       D(COAUTHOR) ⊂ PERSON.

R9   = PAPERS(PAPER,AUTHOR:PERSON,TITLE,DATE-RECEIVED:DATE);
       AT=DATE-RECEIVED; D(DATE-RECEIVED) = RECEPTION-OF-PAPERS;
       D(AUTHOR) ⊂ PERSON.

R10  = PAPERS-COAUTHORS(PAPER,COAUTHOR:PERSON); AT=PAPERS;
       D(COAUTHOR) ⊂ PERSON.

R11  = SELECTION(PAPER,ACC/REJ); AT=SELECTION-OF-PAPERS.

R12  = ASSIGNMENTS(REFEREE:PERSON,PAPER); AT=ASSIGNMENT-OF-REFEREES;
       D(REFEREE) ⊂ PERSON.

R13  = REF-REPORTS(REFEREE:PERSON,PAPER,DATE-RECEIVED:DATE);
       AT=DATE-RECEIVED; D(DATE-RECEIVED) = RECEPTION-OF-REPORTS;
       D(REFEREE) ⊂ PERSON.

R14  = QUALIFICATIONS(REFEREE:PERSON,PAPER,ATTRIBUTE,QUALIFICATION);
       AT=REF-REPORTS; D(REFEREE) ⊂ PERSON.

R15  = SESSIONS(SESSION,DATE,HOUR,TITLE,CHAIRMAN:PERSON); AT=CONFERENCE-
       ORGANIZATION; D(DATE) = CONFERENCE; D(CHAIRMAN) ⊂ PERSON.

R16  = PRESENTATIONS(PAPER,SESSION); AT=CONFERENCE-ORGANIZATION;
       D(PAPER) ⊂ PAPER; DESC=It gives the session at which an accepted
       paper is to be presented.

R17  = REGISTRATIONS(PERSON,DATE-RECEIVED:DATE); AT=DATE-RECEIVED;
       D(DATE-RECEIVED) = RECEPTION-OF-REGISTRATIONS; D(PERSON) ⊂ PERSON.


Figure 19. Relation schemes of the schema
(Part 1 of 2).

R18 = DATE-INF-SENT(<u>PERSON</u>,DATE); AT=DATE; D(DATE) = RECEPTION-OF-
REGISTRATIONS; D(PERSON)⊂ PERSON; DESC=It gives the date when
confirmation and detailed information is sent to registered persons.

R19 = INVITATION-LIST(<u>LIST</u>,INVITATION-DATE:DATE,CLOSING-DATE:DATE);
AT=INVITATION-DATE; D(INVITATION-DATE) = D(CLOSING-DATE) =
INVITATIONS-PLANNING; DESC=For each invitation list it gives the
date when invitations are issued as well as their closing date.

R20 = INVITED-PERSONS(<u>PERSON</u>,LIST); AT=INVITATION-LIST;D(PERSON)⊂ PERSON;
DESC=Persons included in an invitation list.


Figure 19. Relation schemes of the schema
(Part 2 of 2).


6. <u>DEFINE DERIVATION RULES</u>.

Now we classify the relation schemes into base or derived. Relation schemes
whose informations are given to the system by means of inputs are base.
Working with the list of input definitions of figure 20 we see that all
relation schemes are base, except R4, R5 and R18, which are derived. This is
a rather unusual result, since in most systems the proportion of derived to
base relation schemes is greater.

R6 = MEMBERS(GROUP,PERSON) is a special case that needs some refinement, since
input I3 enters the persons (along with affiliation, address and date) which
are members of IFIP groups, but without giving the group they belong. We
assume that I3 has to be modified to include these groups. According to this,
the new definition is I3(d) = MEMBERS * PERSONS. However, in other similar
situations it may be necessary to modify the schema.

R4 is derived by a model operation (section 1.6) since we assume that the
persons to whom a Call for Papers is sent are the members of the groups
involved and the persons given by R2. Thus we have:

        CFP-SENT = MEMBERS [PERSON] U PERSONS-CFP

We also assume that the confirmation and detailed information is sent the day
a registration is received. For this reason, R18 is also derived by a
model operation:

        DATE-INF-SENT = REGISTRATIONS

Finally, R5 is derived by user operation. The derivation rule is the following:

DR1 = INVITATIONS;

PROD-REL : FOR EACH MEMBER OF IFIP GROUPS, AUTHORS AND INVITED PERSONS;
     PR = MEMBERS [PERSON] U PAPERS [AUTHOR] U INVITED-PERSONS[PERSON];

OUTPUT : INVITATION;
   O1 = INV-SENT(PERSON=p);

 INPUT : MEMBERS OF IFIP GROUPS;
   I1 = MEMBERS(PERSON=p);

 INPUT : AUTHORS OF CONTRIBUTED PAPERS;
   I2 = PAPERS(AUTHOR=p) [AUTHOR];

 INPUT : INVITED PERSONS;
   I3 = INVITED-PERSONS(PERSON=p) * INVITATION-LIST;

DESC = If person p is in I1 or I2 then issue a priority invitation (with date
       of invitation and closing date given as constants to DR1). Otherwise, the
       date of invitation and the closing date are given in INVITATION-LIST.

INPUT-OUTPUT DEFINITION:

  TIME-UNIT = date.

    I1 == INVOLVED GROUPS; I1(d) = INVOLVED-GROUPS;
       T(I1) = CONFERENCE-PLANNING; LOC = DIVERSE; VOL = 3 GROUPS.

    I2 = PERSONS CFP; I2(d) = PERSONS(PERSONεPERSONS-CFP); T(I2) =
       ANNOUNCEMENT-PLANNING; LOC = PROGRAMM-COMMITTEE;
       VOL = 500 PERSONS.

    I3 = MEMBERS OF INVOLVED GROUPS; I3(d) = PERSONS(PERSONεMEMBERS[PERSON]);
       T(I3) = ANNOUNCEMENT-PLANNING; LOC = IFIP-SECRETARIAT;
       VOL = 75 PERSONS.

    I4 = LETTERS OF INTENT; I4(d) = LETTERS-OF-INTENT(DATE-RECEIVED=d) *
       LOI-COAUTHORS[AUTHOR* PERSON] PERSONS; T(I4) =
       RECEPTION-OF-LOI; LOC = AUTHORS; VOL = 200 LETTERS.

    I5 = PAPERS RECEIVED; I5(d) = PAPERS(DATE-RECEIVED=d)* PAPERS-COAUTHORS
       [AUTHOR* PERSON] PERSONS;
       T(O5) = RECEPTION-OF-PAPERS; LOC = AUTHORS; VOL = 100 PAPERS.

    I6 = REFEREES' REPORTS; I6(d) = REF-REPORTS(DATE-RECEIVED=d) *
       QUALIFICATIONS; T(I6) = RECEPTION-OF-REPORTS;
       LOC= REFEREES; VOL = 300 REPORTS.

    I7 = ASSIGNMENT OF PAPERS TO REFEREES; I7(d) = ASSIGNMENTS;
       LOC = PROGRAM-COMMITTEE; VOL = 300 ASSIGNMENTS.

    I8 = SELECTION OF PAPERS; I8(d) = SELECTION; T(I8) = SELECTION-OF-PAPERS;
       VOL = 20 ACCEPTED PAPERS.

    I9 = ORGANIZATION OF SESSIONS; I9(d) = SESSIONS*PRESENTATIONS;
       T(I9) = CONFERENCE-ORGANIZATION; LOC = PROGRAM-COMMITTEE;
       VOL = 10 SESSIONS.

    I10 = PERSONS TO INVITE; I10(d) = INVITATION-LIST(INVITATION-DATE=d) *
       INVITED-PERSONS * PERSONS; T(I10) = INVITATIONS-PLANNING;
       LOC = ORGANISING-COMMITTEE; VOL = 300 INVITATIONS.

    I11 = REGISTRATIONS; I11(d) = REGISTRATIONS(DATE-RECEIVED=d);
       T(I11) = RECEPTION-OF-REGISTRATIONS; LOC = INVITED-PERSONS;
       VOL = 120 REGISTRATIONS.

    O1 = CALL-FOR-PAPERS; O1(d) = CFP-SENT * PERSONS;
       T(O1) = CALL-FOR-PAPERS-SENT; LOC = POTENTIAL-AUTHORS;
       VOL = 500 PERSONS.

    O2 = LIST OF LETTERS OF INTENT; O2(d) = LETTERS-OF-INTENT
       [AUTHOR * PERSON] PERSONS * LOI-COAUTHORS;
       T(O2) = BEGN(RECEPTION-OF-PAPERS); LOC = PROGRAM-COMMITTEE;
       VOL = 200 LETTERS.

    O3 = LIST OF PAPERS; O3(d) = PAPERS[AUTHOR* PERSON] PERSONS *
       PAPERS-COAUTHORS; T(O3) = ASSIGNMENT-OF-REFEREES;
       LOC = PROGRAM-COMMITTEE,ORGANISING-COMMITTEE, VOL = 100 PAPERS.

    O4 = DISTRIBUTION OF PAPERS TO REFEREES; O4(d) = ASSIGNMENTS
       [REFEREE * PERSON] PERSONS * PAPERS; T(O3) = BEGN(RECEPTION-OF-REPORTS);
       LOC = REFEREES; VOL = 300 ASSIGNMENTS.

    O5 = REMAINDERS TO REFEREES; O5(d) = ASSIGNMENTS - (REF-REPORTS
       (DATE-RECEIVED ≤ d)[REFEREE,PAPER]); T(O5) = RECEPTION-OF-REPORTS;
       LOC = REFEREES; VOL = 50 REMAINDERS.


Figure 20. Input/Output definition (Part 1 of 2).

O6  = LIST-OF-REPORTS; O6(d) = PAPERS [AUTHOR * PERSON] PERSONS * QUALIFICATIONS;
      T(O6) = SELECTION-OF-PAPERS; LOC = PROGRAM-COMMITTEE; VOL =
      300 REPORTS.

O7  = NOTIFICATION OF ACCEPTANCE; O7(d) = SELECTION(ACC/REJ="A") * PAPERS
      [AUTHOR * PERSON] PERSONS * PAPERS-COAUTHORS * PRESENTATIONS *
      SESSIONS; T(O7) = NOTIFICATION; LOC = AUTHORS; VOL = 20 NOTIFICATIONS.

O8  = NOTIFICATION OF REJECTIONS; O8(d) = SELECTION(ACC/REJ="R") * PAPERS *
      PAPERS-COAUTHORS [AUTHOR * PERSON] PERSONS; T(O8) = NOTIFICATION;
      VOL = 80 NOTIFICATIONS.

O9  = INVITATIONS; O9(d) = INV-SENT(DATE=d) * PERSONS; T(O9) = INVITATIONS-
      PLANNING; LOC = INVITED-PERSONS; FREQ = 3 PER CONFERENCE.

O10 = LIST OF REGISTRATIONS; O10(d) = REGISTRATIONS(DATE-RECEIVED ≤ d) *
      PERSONS; T(O10) = RECEPTION-OF-REGISTRATIONS; LOC = ORGANISING-
      COMMITTEE; VOL = 100 REGISTRATIONS; FREQ = 5 PER CONFERENCE.

O11 = ATTENDANCE LIST; O11(d) = REGISTRATIONS [PERSON] * PERSONS;
      T(O11) = CONFERENCE; LOC = ATTENDEES; VOL = 120 REGISTRATIONS.

O12 = DETAILED INFORMATION; O12(d) = REGISTRATIONS(DATE-RECEIVED=d) *
      PERSONS; T(O12) = RECEPTION-OF-REGISTRATIONS; LOC = ATTENDEES,
      FREQ = 20 PER CONFERENCE.


Figure 20. Input/output definition (Part 2 of 2).


TIME-ORDERING:

          CONFERENCE-PLANNING < ANNOUNCEMENT-PLANNING,
          ANNOUNCEMENT-PLANNING < CALL-FOR-PAPERS-SENT,
          CALL-FOR-PAPERS-SENT < BEGN(RECEPTION-OF-LOI),
          END(RECEPTION-OF-LOI) < BEGN(RECEPTION-OF-PAPERS),
          END(RECEPTION-OF-PAPERS) < ASSIGNMENT-OF-REFEREES,
          ASSIGNMENT-OF-REFEREES < BEGN(RECEPTION-OF-REPORTS),
          END(RECEPTION-OF-REPORTS) < SELECTION-OF-PAPERS,
          SELECTION-OF-PAPERS < CONFERENCE-ORGANIZATION,
          CONFERENCE-ORGANIZATION < NOTIFICATION,
          CONFERENCE-ORGANIZATION < BEGN(RECEPTION-OF-REGISTRATIONS),
          BEGN(INVITATIONS-PLANNING) < BEGN(RECEPTION-OF-REGISTRATIONS),
          END(INVITATIONS-PLANNING) < END(RECEPTION-OF-REGISTRATIONS),
          END(RECEPTION-OF-REGISTRATIONS) < CONFERENCE.

Figure 21.  Time ordering.


## 7. VALIDATE SPECIFICATIONS.

In this step we validate the specifications, using the method described in
section 3. In our example, the proofs (not included here) are very simple,
since the system itself is simple, due to its low degree of elaboration of
information.

Once the proofs have been developed, we analyse whether all inputs are used
in the derivation of some output. In our example, although the system is
logically consistent, we see that I1 is not used in any case, so it may be
removed from the input/output definition.

## 8. ARCHITECTURAL DESIGN.

The hardware/software environment in which the system will be implemented has not
been specified. As it is necessary to know some characteristics of this
environment in order to perform an architectural design, we make the following
assumptions:

1) There are two small or medium size computer systems, one located at
   the Program Committee Secretariat (PCS system) and the other located
   at the Organising Committee Secretariat (OCS system).

2) It is possible to exchange information between both systems through
   magnetic files (tapes or diskettes).

3) Both systems are provided with some kind of relational DBMS. If this is
   not the case, in a later step we should adapt the design to the specific
   DBMS or file organization available.

### 8.1 Logical data base design for the initial system structure.

In the initial system structure there is a process for every input and output
defined in the specification (figure 20). We call PIj the process corresponding
to input Ij and POi the process corresponding to output Oi. Thus, there are
10 input processes PI2,...,PI11 (input I1 has been removed in the previous
step) and 12 output processes PO1,...,PO12. Processes PI2,...,PI9 and
PO1,...,PO8 belong to the PCS system and the rest to the OCS system.

For both systems, the logical design of their data base is simple, because of
the simplicity of the systems and the simplicity of the relational model.
For this reason, we have used again an ad hoc method consisting of:

1) Analyse the information contents of each output, in order to determine
   the required data base contents, B(d). Figure 22 shows this contents
   for our example.

2) Group into a single relation scheme the required relation schemes
   with the same key. Figure 23 shows the conceptual schema of the data
   base for our example.

3) Verify the correctness of B(d), according to the method described
   in section 4.1. Although we will not give here the proofs, it can be
   shown that the B(d) given in figure 22 is correct, since for all
   d$\varepsilon$D:

   > 1) B(d) is derivable from I(d0,d),
   > 2) B(d) is derivable from B(d-1) U I(d), and
   > 3) O(d) is derivable from B(d-1) U I(d).

### 8.2 System structure design.

The initial system structure developed in the previous step can be improved
by means of the following process groupings:

1) Processes PI2, PI3 and PO1 are grouped into a single process P1. In
   this manner we eliminate the need for storing the persons to whom
   a CFP is to be sent (I2), since the O1 (CFP) -that requires I2 and I3-
   is issued when I2 and I3 are input to the system.

2) Processes PI7 and PO4 are grouped into a single process P2. In this
   way we do not eliminate the need for storing the assignments (I7),
   since they are required for the production of the remainders (O5),
   but we reduce input/output transport.

$$B_{PCS}(d) = \{ \text{IFIP GROUPS MEMBERS: If } d \geqslant \text{ANNOUNCEMENT-PLANNING then}$$
$$\text{MEMBERS},$$

$$\text{PERSONS: If } d \geqslant \text{ANNOUNCEMENT-PLANNING then}$$
$$\text{PERSONS (PERSON} \epsilon X),$$

$$\text{LETTERS: LETTERS-OF-INTENT (DATE-RECEIVED} \leqslant d) * \text{LOI-COAUTHORS},$$

$$\text{PAPERS: PAPERS (DATE-RECEIVED} \leqslant d) * \text{PAPERS-COAUTHORS},$$

$$\text{ASSIGNMENTS: If } d \geqslant \text{ASSIGNMENT-OF-REFEREES then}$$
$$\text{ASSIGNMENTS},$$

$$\text{REPORTS: REF-REPORTS (DATE-RECEIVED} \leqslant d) * \text{QUALIFICATIONS},$$

$$\text{SELECTION: If } d \geqslant \text{SELECTION-OF-PAPERS then}$$
$$\text{SELECTION},$$

$$\text{SESSIONS: If } d \geqslant \text{CONFERENCE-ORGANIZATION then}$$
$$\text{SESSIONS} * \text{PRESENTATIONS} \}$$

$$B_{OCS}(d) = \{ \text{IFIP GROUPS MEMBERS: If } d \geqslant \text{BEGN (INVITATIONS-PLANNING) then}$$
$$\text{MEMBERS},$$

$$\text{PERSONS: If } d \geqslant \text{BEGN (INVITATIONS-PLANNING) then}$$
$$\text{PERSONS (PERSON} \epsilon X),$$

$$\text{AUTHORS: If } d \geqslant \text{BEGN (INVITATIONS-PLANNING) then}$$
$$\text{PAPERS [AUTHOR]},$$

$$\text{INVITATIONS: INVITATION-LIST (INVITATION-DATE} \leqslant d) *$$
$$\text{INVITED-PERSONS} * \text{PERSONS},$$

$$\text{REGISTRATIONS RECEIVED: REGISTRATIONS (DATE-RECEIVED} \leqslant d) \}$$

$$\text{with } X = \text{PERSONS-CFP U MEMBERS [PERSON] U}$$
$$\text{LETTERS-OF-INTENT (DATE-RECEIVED} \leqslant d) \text{ [AUTHOR] U}$$
$$\text{PAPERS (DATE-RECEIVED} \leqslant d) \text{ [AUTHOR]}$$

Figure 22. Data base contents.

MEMBERS (GROUP,PERSON)

PERSONS (PERSON,AFFILIATION,ADDRESS)

LETTERS-OF-INTENT (TITLE,AUTHOR,DATE-RECEIVED)

LOI-COAUTHORS (TITLE,COAUTHOR)

PAPERS (PAPER,AUTHOR,TITLE,DATE-RECEIVED,SELECTION,SESSION)

PAPERS-COAUTHORS (PAPER,COAUTHOR)

ASSIGNMENTS (REFEREE,PAPER)

REPORTS (REFEREE,PAPER,ATTRIBUTE,QUALIFICATION)

SESSIONS (SESSION,DATE,HOUR,TITLE,CHAIRMAN)

a) PCS system.

MEMBERS (GROUP,PERSON)

PERSONS (PERSON,AFFILIATION,ADDRESS,PAPER-AUTHOR,LIST,REGISTRATION-DATE)

INVITATION-LIST (LIST,INVITATION-DATE,CLOSING-DATE)

b) OCS system.

Figure 23. Conceptual schema of the data base.

3) Processes PI8, PI9, PO7 and PO8 are grouped into a single process P3. This grouping allows us to eliminate the need for storing the selection of the papers (I8) and the organization of sessions (I9) since they are only used for the production of O7 and O8. We also reduce input/output transport since we avoid the writing out and the reading in of these inputs in the data base.

4) Processes PI10 and PO9 are grouped into a single process P4. This eliminates the need for storing the invitations lists (I10) since invitations (O9) are produced directly from them. As in the previous groupings we also reduce input/output transport.

5) Finally, PI11 and PO12 are grouped into a single process P5. This does not eliminate the need for storing the registrations (I11), since they are required for the production of O10 and O11, but we reduce input/output transport.

Now the data base design performed in the previous step needs to be refined, since the above groupings affect the data base contents. We repeat the previous step with the new system structure and we arrive at the contents depicted in figure 24. The new conceptual schema is the same as that of figure 23, but removing the SESSIONS and INVITATION-LIST relation schemes, attribute SESSION of PAPERS and attribute LIST of PERSONS.

$B_{PCS}(d) = \{$IFIP GROUPS MEMBERS: If $d \geqslant$ ANNOUNCEMENT-PLANNING then
        MEMBERS,

  PERSONS: If $d \geqslant$ ANNOUNCEMENT-PLANNING then
    PERSONS (PERSON$\epsilon$Y),

  LETTERS: LETTERS-OF-INTENT (DATE-RECEIVED $\leqslant d$) * LOI-COAUTHORS,

  PAPERS: PAPERS (DATE-RECEIVED $\leqslant d$) * PAPERS-COAUTHORS,

  ASSIGNMENTS: If $d \geqslant$ ASSIGNMENT-OF-REFEREES then
    ASSIGNMENTS,

  REPORTS: REF-REPORTS (DATE-RECEIVED $\leqslant d$) * QUALIFICATIONS$\}$

$B_{OCS}(d) = \{$IFIP GROUPS MEMBERS: If $d \geqslant$ BEGN (INVITATIONS-PLANNING) then
        MEMBERS,

  PERSONS: If $d \geqslant$ BEGN (INVITATIONS-PLANNING) then
    PERSONS (PERSON$\epsilon$Y),

  AUTHORS: If $d \geqslant$ BEGN (INVITATIONS-PLANNING) then
    PAPERS [AUTHOR],

  REGISTRATIONS RECEIVED: REGISTRATIONS (DATE-RECEIVED $\leqslant d$) $\}$

  with Y = MEMBERS [PERSON] U LETTERS-OF-INTENT (DATE-RECEIVED $\leqslant d$) [AUTHOR]
    U PAPERS (DATE-RECEIVED $\leqslant d$) [AUTHOR]

   Figure 24. Revised data base contents.

Once the new data base design has been verified, we define for each process the subset $B\bar{j}(d)$ read from the data base and the subset $Bj(d)$ added to the data base, as described in section 4.2. The result for the PCS system is shown in a narrative form in figure 25.

Then we verify the internal consistency of this structure, by analysing that for every process $Pj$ and for all $d\varepsilon PR(Pj)$ the following conditions hold (section 4.2):

1) The informations $Bj(d)$ added to the data base are derivable from inputs at date $d$ and from the informations $B\bar{j}(d)$ read from the data base.

2) The outputs at date $d$ are derivable from inputs at date $d$ and from the informations $B\bar{j}(d)$ read from the data base.

Once we are sure that both conditions are satisfied, we verify the consistency with specifications, by analysing that (section 4.2):

1) Inputs to the processes correspond to inputs defined in the specifications.

2) Outputs derived by the processes correspond to outputs defined in the specifications.

3) Informations added to the data base agree with the data base contents previously designed.

When this consistency has been verified, we have finished the second iteration of the architectural design. Then it is possible to try other groupings. For instance, process PI4 may be grouped with PO2, by delaying input I4=LETTERS OF INTENT until the whole set of letters of intent is available and then entering it as a batch. This would eliminate the need for storing them. Other feasible grouping is that of PI5 and PO3, but in this case we would not eliminate the need for storing the papers, since they are required for the production of other outputs. However, we would reduce input/output transport. In both cases, the gains appear to be greater than the possible disadvantages of the batch inputs.

We terminate here the architectural design of the example. At this point, the application programmer has to perform the detailed design of the system and its implementation. Among the activities that must be done there are the following:

1) Assign a physical format to each input and output.

2) Perform the physical design of the data base.

3) Determine the sorting criteria of inputs and outputs and insert the required sorting operations into the process structure.

4) Analyse and document the internal structure of the processes.

5) Develop the testing strategy and the test cases.

At present, these activities are not directly supported by DADES.

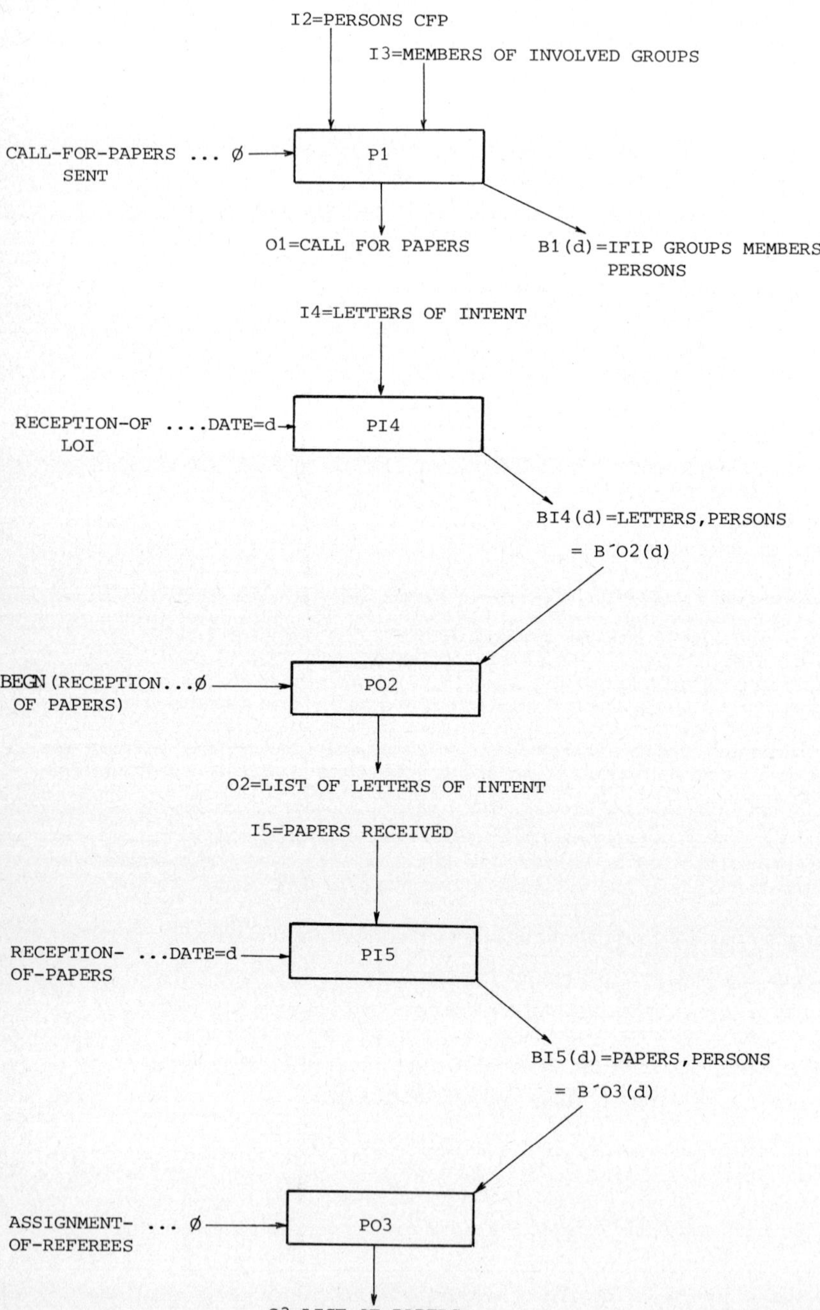


Figure 25. Process structure of the PCS system (Part 1 of 2).

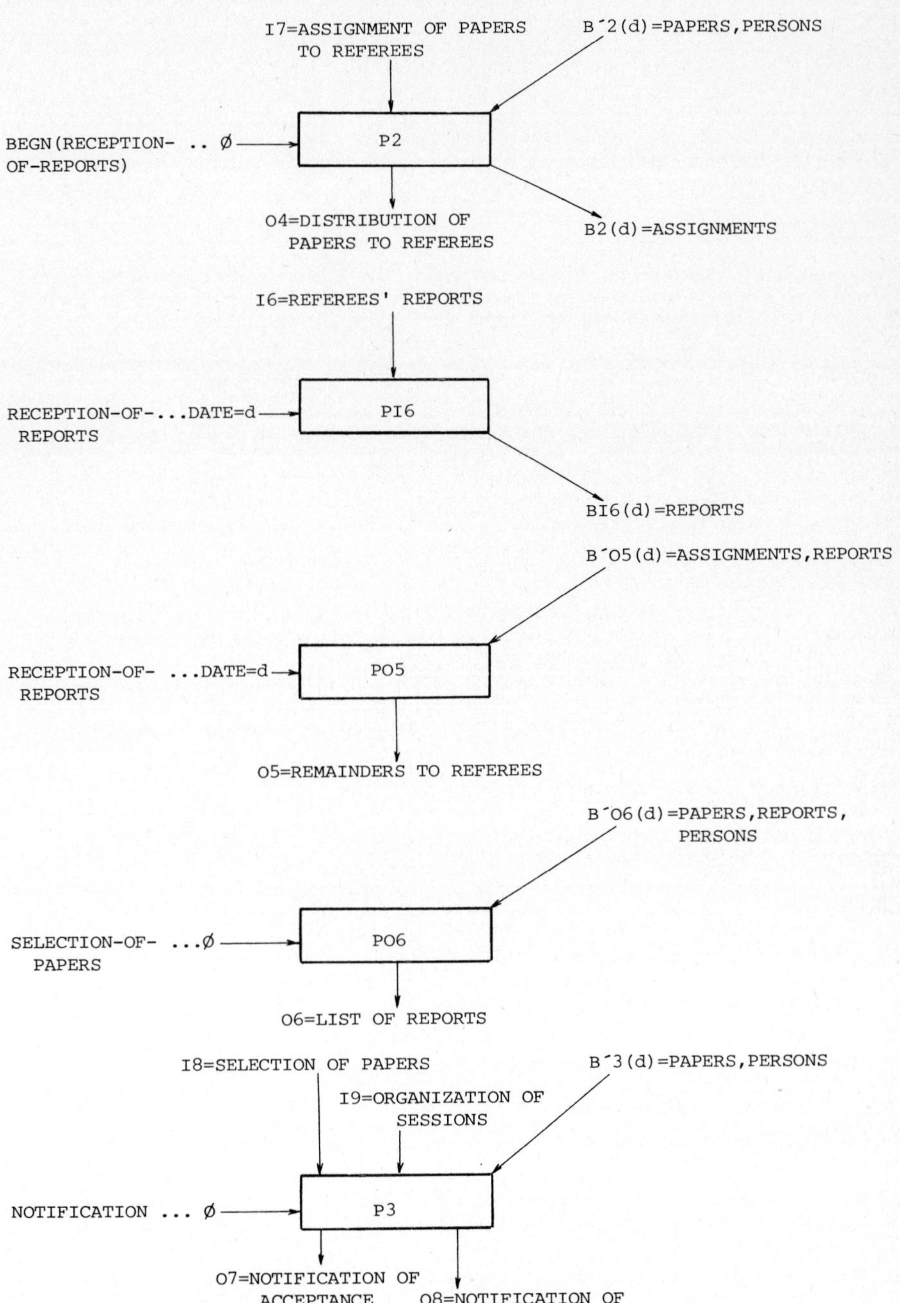


Figure 25. Process structure of the PCS system (Part 2 of 2).

                                          *A. Olivé*

APPENDIX. THE RELATIONAL ALGEBRA.

The relational algebra allows the derivation of new relations from others, by
using a set of operations. These operations are the traditional set operations
(cartesian product (x), union (U), intersection (∩) and difference (-)) and
operations on relations (projection, join, natural join, selection, division).
The notation for the operations on relations that are used in the paper
is defined as follows:

### Projection

Let r be a relation on a set of attributes X. Let Y be a subset of X. We
define  r[Y]  as the relation obtained by removing all the components of the
tuples of r that do not belong to Y and then dropping duplicate tuples.

### Natural join

Let r be a relation on X and s a relation on Y. Let X1 be a subset of X and
Y1 a subset  of Y, such that X1 and Y1 are defined on common domains. The
natural join of r on X1 with s on Y1 is denoted by  r[X1 * Y1]s. It is
the concatenation of tuples of r with tuples of s, removing redundat
attributes, whenever the X1-component of the r-tuple is equal to the
Y1-component of the s-tuple. When X1 = Y1 = A(r) ∩ A(s) we simply write r * s.

### Selection

Let r be a relation on X. Let A be an attribute in X and c a value from the
domain of A. Then the selection r(A=c) is the subset of r having value c
for A. Other comparison operators, such as ≠,≥,≤, may also be used.
If s is an unary relation on attribute B, such that A and B are defined on
common domains, then the selection r(Aεs) is the subset of r such that the
A value is in s. Several selections can be combined in a single operation
r(A1=c,...,Anεs).

ACKNOWLEDGMENTS

The author wishes to thank Rafael Andreu for his work and assistance in the
preparation of this document.

REFERENCES

[1]   BEERI,C.;BERNSTEIN,P. Computational problems related to the design of
          normal form relation schemas. ACM TODS, Vol.4, No. 1, March 1979.

[2]   BRACCHI,G.;FURTADO,A.;PELAGATTI. Constraint specification in evolutionary
          data base design. In [31] , pp. 149-165.

[3]   BUBENKO,J.A.;BERILD,S.;LINDECRONA-OHLIN,E.;NACHMENS,S. From information
          requirements to DBTG-data structures. Proc. of the ACM-SIGMOD/
          SIGPLAN Conference on Data, ACM, N.Y., 1976, pp. 73-85.

[4]   BUBENKO,J.A. The temporal dimension in information modeling. In [20]
          pp. 93-118.

[5]   BUBENKO,J.A. IAM: An inferential abstract modeling approach to design of
          conceptual schema. Proc. SIGMOD Int. Conf. on Management of Data,
          1977, pp. 62-74.

[6]   CODASYL. An information algebra. Comm. ACM, Vol.5, No.4, April 1962,
          pp. 190-204.

[7]   CODD,E.F. A relational model of data for large shared data banks.
        Comm. ACM, Vol.13, N.6, June 1970, pp. 377-387.

[8]   CODD,E.F. Further normalization of the data base relational model.
        In "Data base systems" Rustin,R. (Ed.), Prentice Hall, 1972,
        pp. 33-64.

[9]   FALKENBERG,E. Concepts for modeling information. In [18], pp.95-109.

[10]  FREEMAN,P. The context of design. Tutorial on software design techniques.
        3rd. ed., IEEE, 1980, pp.2-4.

[11]  GANE,C.;SARSON,T. Structured systems analysis: tools and techniques.
        Prentice Hall, Inc.,N.Y., 1979, 241 p.

[12]  GRINDLEY,K. SYSTEMATICS: A new approach to systems analysis. McGraw Hill,
        UK, 1975.

[13]  GRINDLEY,K. The role of the trigger in Systematics. In [31], pp. 233-256.

[14]  INFOTECH. Structured analysis and design. State of the art report.
        Infotech International, 1978.

[15]  LANGEFORS,B. Theoretical analysis of information systems. Studentlittera
        tur. 4 Ed., 1973, Sweden, 489 p.

[16]  LANGEFORS,B. Information systems. Proc. IFIP Congress, 1974, pp.937-945.

[17]  LUNDEBERG,M.;GOLDKHUL,G.;NILSSON,A. Information Systems Development.
        A systematic approach. Technical report. ISAC Group. Dept. of
        administrative information processing. University of Stockholm.

[18]  NIJSSEN,G.M.(Ed.). Modeling in data base management systems.
        North-Holland Pub. Co., Amsterdam, 1976.

[19]  NIJSSEN,G.M. A gross architecture for the next generation database
        management systems. In [18], pp. 1-24.

[20]  NIJSSEN,G.M. (Ed.). Architecture and models in data base management
        systems. North Holland Pub. Co., Amsterdam, 1977.

[21]  NIJSSEN,G.M.;VAN ASSCHE,F.J.;SNIJDERS,J.J. End-user tools for
        information systems requirement definition. In [31], pp. 125-148.

[22]  NUNAMAKER,J.F. A methodology for the design and optimization of
        information processing systems. Proc. AFIPS SJCC, Vol.38,
        AFIPS Press, Montvale, N.J., pp.283-294.

[23]  OLIVE,A. Una àlgebra informacional per al disseny lògic de sistemes
        d'informació. Ph.D. Th. Universitat Politècnica de Barcelona.
        Barcelona, 1978 (in catalan).

[24]  OLIVE,A. Anàlisi de precedències entre conjunts d'informació. Aplicació
        al model informacional. QUESTIIO, Vol.3,N.3, 1979, pp.129-143,
        (in catalan).

[25]  OLIVE,A. Ús de l'àlgebra informacional en el disseny lògic de sistemes
        d'informació. Proc.CIL/79 Congress, Barcelona, 1979, pp.415-427,
        (in catalan).

[26]  OLIVE,A. A logic for logical information systems analysis. Technical
        report. Facultat d'Informàtica, Universitat Politècnica de
        Barcelona, 1980.

[27]    OLIVE,A. Aplicació de l'anàlisi de precedències al disseny del
        contingut de bases de dades. QUESTIIO, Vol.4, N.3, September 1980,
        pp. 147-159, (in catalan).

[28]    OLIVE,A.;SALTOR,F. Formal verification of information derivability
        in databases using precedence analysis. Technical report. Facultat
        d'Informàtica. Universitat Politècnica de Barcelona, 1981.

[29]    OLIVE,A. A method for formal specification of information systems.
        Proc. Int. Comp. Symp. on Systems Architecture, London, 1981.

[30]    ROSS,D.T.;SCHOMAN,K.E. Structured analysis for requirements definition.
        IEEE Trans. on Soft. Eng., January 1977, pp. 6-15.

[31]    SCHNEIDER,H-J. (Ed.). Formal models and practical tools for information
        systems design. North Holland Pub. Co., Amsterdam, 1979, 297 p.

[32]    SERNADAS,A. Temporal aspects of logical procedure definition.
        Information Systems, Vol.5, pp. 167-187.

[33]    STAVELIN,S. Derivability analysis and data modelling. Master Th.,
        Norwegian Institute of Technology in Trondheim, 1980.

[34]    SUNDGREN,B. Theory of data bases. Mason-Charter Pub. Inc.,
        USA, 1975.

[35]    TEICHROEW,D. Problem Statement Analysis: Requirements for the Problem
        Statement Analyzer (PSA). ISDOS Working paper N.43, April 1971.

[36]    TEICHROEW,D. A survey of languages for stating requirements for
        computer-based information systems. Proc. FJCC, 1972, pp.1203-1224.

[37]    TEOREY,T.J.;FRY,J.P. The logical record access approach to database
        design. Computing Surveys, Vol.12,N.2, June 1980, pp.179-211.

[38]    VERRIJN-STUART,A.A. Information algebras and their uses. Management
        Datamatics, Vol. 4, N.5, 1975, pp. 187-197.

[39]    YOUNG,J.W.;KENT,H.K. Abstract formulation of data processing problems.
        The Journal of Industrial Engineering, November-December 1958,
        pp. 471-479.

*INFORMATION SYSTEMS DESIGN METHODOLOGIES: A Comparative Review*
*T.W. Olle, H.G. Sol, A.A. Verrijn-Stuart (editors)*
*North-Holland Publishing Company*
© *IFIP, 1982*

# IML-INSCRIBED HIGH-LEVEL PETRI NETS

Gernot Richter
Reiner Durchholz
Gesellschaft für Mathematik und Datenverarbeitung (GMD)
St. Augustin
F.R. Germany

Premature distribution decisions in the system design process may preclude or at
least impede proper response to requirements gradually evolving during the dialogue with the user. It is therefore important to use a system design
specification tool which allows to postpone any decisions on grouping resources
into local components. Predicate/transition-nets together with an appropriate
information-structure description tool seem to be a proper choice under this
aspect. The paper demonstrates the use of this tool. It shows how it can be used
for relating a detailed, high-concurrency design with overviews as well as with.
designs which approach implementation and thus include localization decisions.

CONTENTS
1. Introduction
2. First overview net
3. High-concurrency net
4. Second overview net
5. Low-concurrency OC net
6. Conclusion
References
Appendix


## 1. INTRODUCTION

This contribution emphasizes the distribution and concurrency aspects in the design of
information systems.

Until recently, information systems were usually thought of as being based on some computing
machinery with a large central memory and a number of more or less distributed terminals
through which the memory was accessed. With the advent of cheap and small, but powerful,
hardware components the attitude has significantly changed. The idea of distributing
processing capacity and data became a realistic requirement since there are some good
reasons for decentralization.

Although hardware development made distribution commercially attractive, there remain still
some engineering problems intrinsically tied to the idea of distributing processing autonomy as
well as to intriguing theoretical ramifications. Integrity and synchronization are well-known
aspects of this kind. The present approach is based on the contention that it will generally not
be possible to develop a well-engineered design for a distributed system by starting from a
centralized solution and gradually extracting distributable parts, but that it is necessary to
identify first the conditions of the application which must be taken care of by a n y
distribution. Such an approach must first exhibit the causal structure of the given problem and
only then proceed to design a system which is compatible with the causal structure.

The trouble with the approach of gradual evolution from a centralized toward a distributed solution is  that the centralized design inevitably obfuscates the causal structure. Because there is no obligation to exhibit the causal structure explicitly, a centralized design incorporates decisions which are adverse to distribution. As such decisions are made very early, the conversion to a distributed design tends to upset the entire architecture. A typical such decision is to bind semantically closely related pieces of information into one data construct, say, a record, although access to it as a whole is never required.

The approach presented in this contribution recommends a tool which allows to elaborate the causal system structure with only minimal data structure. It also allows and supports to proceed from here to a directly implementable software design.

The tool is demonstrated with the example problem as defined for this conference. Of course, a complete and detailed design would be beyond the limits of a conference session. The emphasis is therefore on showing the application of IML-inscribed nets when used in the design process, rather than giving a complete solution to the problem as stated. The major guidelines chosen are:
-   to show interesting features of the tool,
-   to show each feature only once,
-   to avoid any detail or variation which only adds to size, not to sophistication.

The guidelines entail at times omissions and implausible assumptions as far as a realistic information system is concerned. However, it should be clear in each such case how the solution could be made more convincing.

The description tool is based on two independent conceptual systems used in conjunction, predicate/transition-nets (PrT-nets, see [4]) and information management concepts (IMC, see [2] and [3]). PrT-nets are interpreted, inscribed high-level Petri nets, where inscriptions consist of variables for individuals (as opposed to the non-individual token of Petri nets) and truth-valued expressions, preferably in first-order predicate logic. IMC provides a general concep-tual framework to describe information structure in a compositional way (as opposed to operational information structure specification, but reconcilable with it). Both conceptual systems are under development now for some years and represent a substantial body of investigation, practice and insight in handling information flow and structure. For PrT-nets, the results of general net theory (see [1]) provide a solid theoretical background. For IMC a suitable information management language (IML) has been developed ([6], [7]) which allows to describe construction and transformation of information constructs in a general way.

The design of a system requires that the object under consideration is described under various problem aspects and on various levels of detail. Controlling the relationship and the consistency between all those different descriptions is a major issue of design technology. The unique feature of nets which makes them particularly suitable for design purposes is that they lend themselves readily for relating descriptions of the same system from several different points of view. Differences that can be reconciled may be in terms of level of refinement (as occur e.g. in a top-down development), or in terms of abstractions with respect to various aspects (such as abstraction from message variety in causality considerations or abstraction from sequencing conditions for a single actor).

In the literature, a variety of nets have been introduced, the most commonly known of which are probably Petri nets as described in [5]. For practical purposes a descriptional tool on a higher level than Petri nets is required. Of the various net derivates that have been developed so far, we employ two kinds:
-   channel/agency-nets, which are suitable for information flow overviews without sequencing and concurrency specifications
-   predicate/transition-nets, which allow for formal specification of any desired degree of precision and detail.

We will not give a separate and detailed account of these nets, but rather introduce them in parallel to the development of the example problem. Of course, this procedure draws heavily on intuitive insight and it will leave open many questions, but it seems to provide a more direct way to show the applicability of the suggested instrument.


## 2. FIRST OVERVIEW NET

In this section a general overview of the information flow in the conference preparation process is given by means of channel/agency nets. Programme Committee (PC), Organising Committee (OC) and the professional community are considered as agencies on the highest level. The professional community is thought of as an unstructured dialog partner to the committees. PC and OC are built up from several sub-agencies. The sub-agencies are designed from an intuitive understanding of the given problem definition.

An agency is an abstract functional unit charged with the task of using and producing information in a defined way. It is abstract in so far as it is not specified in which way it is conducted by actors (persons, machines, one or several actors for one or several agencies).

A channel is a functional unit that holds information. An arrow from an agency to a channel says that the agency generates information which is deposited in the channel. An arrow from a channel to an agency says that the agency takes information from this channel. Nothing is said about packing information into messages, sequencing, information structure and the details of information transformation. Further, the channel/agency net is unspecific also with respect to disposal of used information, i.e. whether it is retained, eliminated or changed.

Given these remarks, the diagram in Fig. 2.1 should be easy to interpret. Although it does not express sequencing in a strict sense, it is organized from left to right roughly in the direction of information flow. The following considerations outline the conference preparation process along the overview net of Fig. 2.1. They are however not restricted to features expressed in the net, but also take note of aspects to be considered in a later refinement.

First, the PC contacts the professional community by sending out requests for help in the functions of chairpersons and referees (PC-a and PC-b). Calls for paper and letters of intent are omitted in the model since they do not have any effect on the actions of the committees. (The only explicitly stated consequence of a letter of intent we have found is that "Presumably one would not want to invite as referee someone who ... has sent a letter of intent.") It is assumed that information on possible chairpersons and referees is available by some procedure outside the considered system. The PC remembers to which person it has sent requests (**mailed requests to chair** and **mailed requests to referee**). Responses to the requests are checked against the registered requests to detect self-appointments. Confirmations or rejections are then mailed accordingly (PC-c and PC-d). The responses which have passed the test are registered as **chairpersons** or **referees.**

Incoming **contributions** undergo several tests. They are first screened with respect to some formal and practical conditions (PC-e). To make sure that none of the authors of a contribution is also a referee, a comparison with the acknowledged referees has to be performed. Vice versa, any newly received response from a requested referee has to be checked against accepted authors, since we do not want to impose a premature decision on the sequence of referee and author admittance. So we have a mutual test for conflicting applications as referee and as author. A person applying for both will be acceptable in that function only in which he happens to appear first to the PC. These considerations are not reflected in detail in Fig. 2.1, but only the fact is recorded, that some **coordination information** must be traded between PC-d and PC-e.

Another formal check for contributions concerns deadline satisfaction. An incoming contribution is rejected if the postmark does not match the submission deadline. The deadline is incorporated in PC-e as a constant.

There is also a practical reason to reject a contribution for being late. Even if the contribution is mailed in time, one cannot exclude that it will arrive too late for inclusion in the programme. Once the decisions for paper acceptance and rejection are made (in PC-g), any further received contributions must be rejected and should not go into the review process.

The different reasons for rejecting a paper are not made explicit in Fig. 2.1, but they must reappear in a more detailed system as given below in section 3.

PC-e traces the papers that have been sent to referees by recording them as expected referee reports. When a referee report is returned (see PC-f), the recording is changed from "expected" to "received" and the findings of the referee are attached. With the aid of the channel containing the **expected/received referee reports,** the PC is also able to recognize would-be referees, that is, uninvited referee/paper combinations.

Of course, there is a deadline for referee reports. However, it affects the conference preparation process only inasmuch as final decisions on contribution acceptance must wait until after this point in time. (In the unlikely event that a l l referee reports have been returned before the deadline, the decisions could in fact start earlier.) Of course, the PC may send reminders to the referees, but since they do not establish any formal obligation, they have no consequence for the committee work. Hence, reminders to referees are omitted in this model. The referee report deadline is implicitly contained in PC-g as its starting date (plus a reasonable delay time).

The final decision on contribution acceptance (PC-g) needs **paper selection criteria,** which draw on the referee reports and also restrict the total number of acceptable papers. The result for the PC is a register of **accepted contributions.** Both acceptance and rejections are expressed in **notifications to submitters.**

In a final step (PC-h), the PC uses the register of **accepted contributions,** predefined **session grouping criteria,** and the list of ackowledged **chairpersons** to produce a **programme.** This is handed over to the OC.

OC-p distributes **invitations** which contain copies of the **programme.** The necessary information is drawn from a predefined **invitee mailing list** and from the list of all **submitters,** regardless of whether they have been successful or not. The OC keeps a record on the **invitees** to be able to check incoming applications. The requirement of attaining the financial break-even point makes it necessary to invite more people than can be accommodated.

Consequently, the OC must be prepared to reject applications for capacity limitation reasons. There must be a closing date for attendance applications. After this, the OC can decide on admittance (OC-q). The decision results in a **final attendee register** and in notifications to applicants.

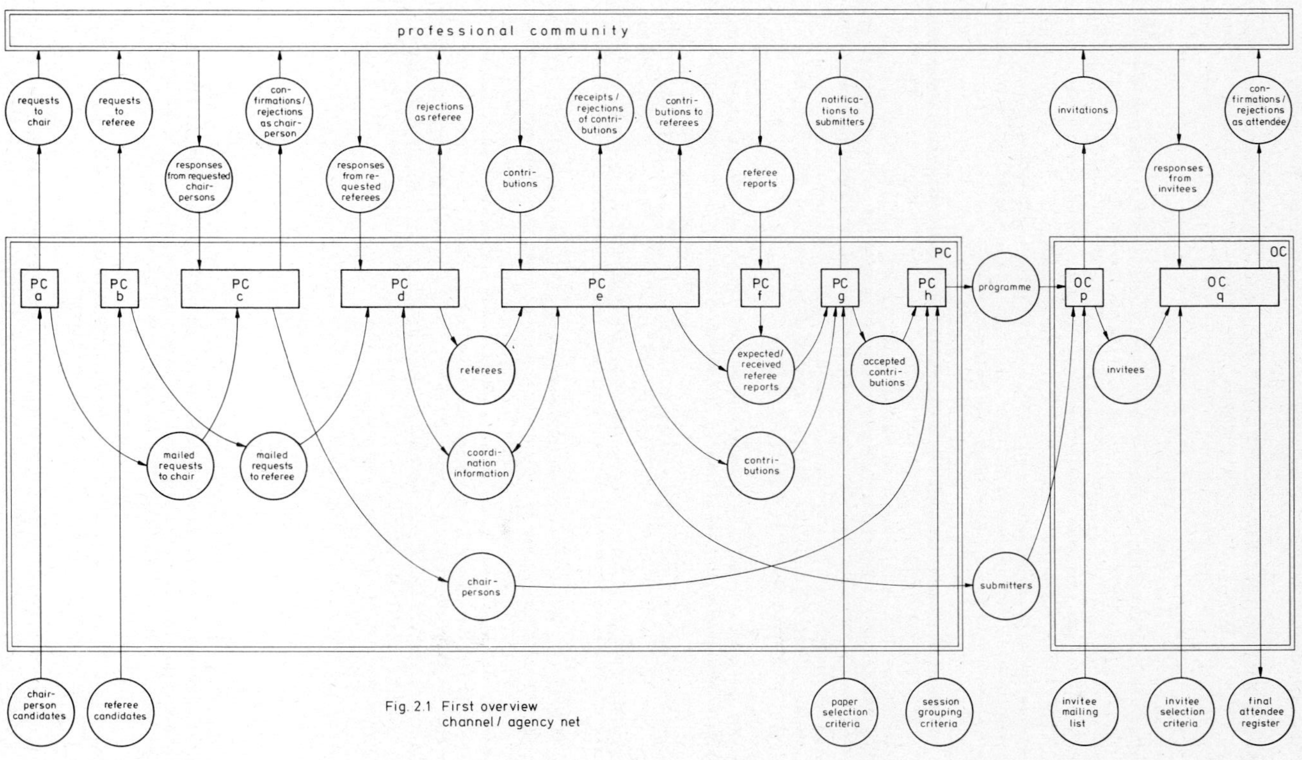


Fig. 2.1  First overview channel / agency net

## 3. HIGH-CONCURRENCY NET

To arrive at a more detailed description of the information flow we introduce a stricter interpretation of nets, thus arriving at predicate/transition-nets (PrT-nets). Although we do not want to give a systematic treatment of PrT-nets (see [1] and [4]), a few introductory explanations are necessary.

In a PrT-net, a channel represents a predicate. The contents of the channel is interpreted as the extension of the predicate (that is, the set of things for which the predicate holds). The predicate can be regarded as saying of any of its individuals "..." in its extension, that "... is in such and such a processing state". Clearly, the processing state changes for an individual as the system carries on. Thus the predicates have "time-varying" extensions. Subsequently we will use the words "predicate" and "channel" interchangeably, depending on whether we want to emphasize the truth-value aspect or the information content aspect. We will also allow for the sloppy wording "predicate" for "extension of predicate".

An agency is considered as representing all possibilities of coincident (i.e. indivisible) change of the adjacent predicate extensions. It is called a "transition" in this context. In a PrT-net description, predicates with a direct causal dependency  m u s t  be linked by a common transition. For example, a predicate **unregistered contribution** may be allowed to lose an individual only if simultaneously a predicate **registered contribution** is augmented by the same individual. There must then be a transition which directly links both predicates. Indirect causal dependency is expressed by linkage of direct causal dependencies. It is claimed that any causal dependency can be expressed this way.

PrT-nets can be treated in a linearly written language, but they are particularly suited for a natural graphical representation. Following established conventions, a transition is depicted by a rectangle which is linked by arrows to the predicates between which it establishes direct causal dependencies. The specification for predicate changes is composed by a so-called "transition formula" written into the rectangle, and by inscriptions of the linking arrows. The predicates are given by circles. A predicate inscription indicates the "-arity" of the predicate along with the construct type (sort of individuals) required at each position.

An arrow leading to a predicate means that the predicate is augmented by an individual (or an n-tupel of individuals) as indicated by the inscription of the arrow. An arrow coming from a predicate means that the predicate is diminished by an individual (or n-tupel of individuals) as indicated by the inscription of the arrow. A transition is "enabled", that is, the changes can take place, only if a l l  of the adjacent predicates can be changed in the manner indicated. A predicate can be diminished by an individual if the individual is in its extension. It can be augmented by an individual only if the individual is n o t  in its extension. (In general, PrT-nets allow for multiple identical individuals. We found it convenient for the present exercise to restrict ourselves to maximum multiplicity 1.)

The inscriptions of arrows indicate variables local to the transition to which they are attached. The variables normally appear in the transition formula. Identical variables mean identical individuals. Thus, in the example below, the two "p" at the upper two arrows stand for the same individual.

The change of a predicate need not be one individual (or n-tuple of individuals) at a time. A transition is enabled as many times as assignments of individuals from the predicates can be made to the variables. The entire net develops in steps. In each step, the predicates of each enabled transition may, but need not, change according to the transition specification, the only restriction being that the same individual from one predicate extension may not participate in two transitions or in two occurrences of the same transition. An arbitrary number of changes by a multiply enabled transition may occur in one step.

To make net-representations more perspicuous, we introduce two abbreviations: A double arrow is a simplified notation for taking information from and putting information into the same predicate. For our purpose we establish the convention shown in Fig. 3.1 (other conventions could be established).

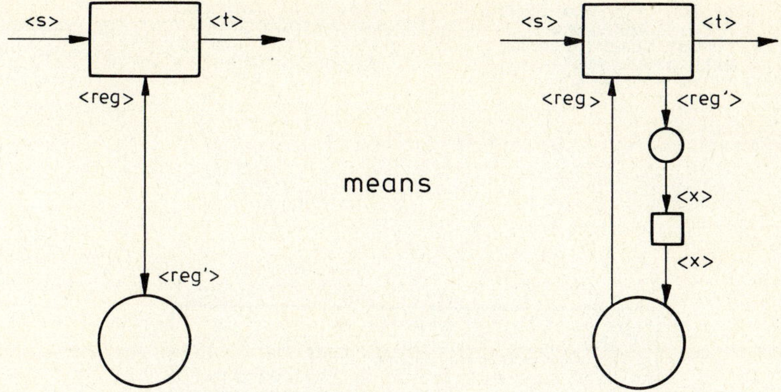



Fig. 3.1        Double arrow convention for PrT-nets

The transition expressed by the small rectangle simply turns over the individual from its input to its output channel. Mind that the returned individual reg' is not available to the original transition before the "little" transition has done its work. This takes an unspecified number of steps of the system.

If arrowheads are omitted this means return of the same information that has been used. Thus

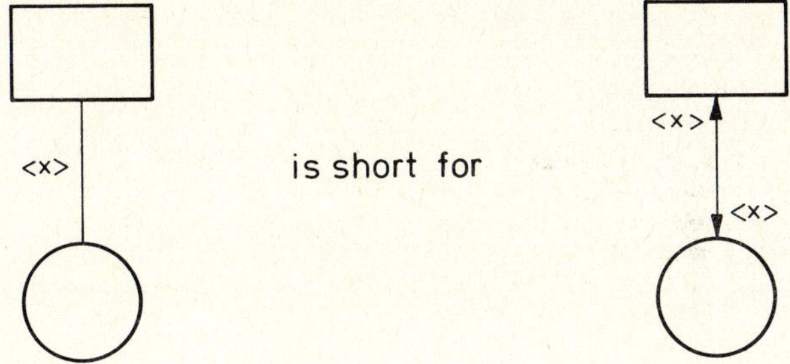



Fig. 3.2        Convention for non-destructive read operation
               ("side condition")

The following examples (Fig. 3.3 and 3.4) illustrate the main concepts of PrT-nets and already make use of the above conventions.

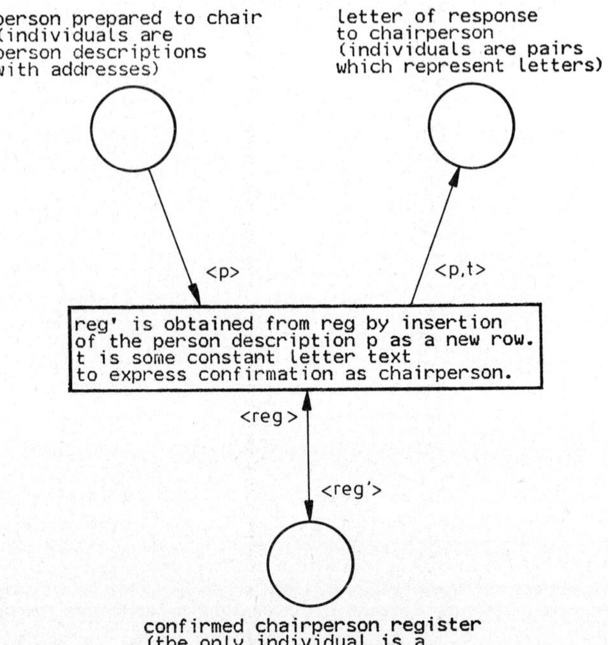


Fig. 3.3     Example for the demonstration of PrT-net conventions with informal inscriptions.

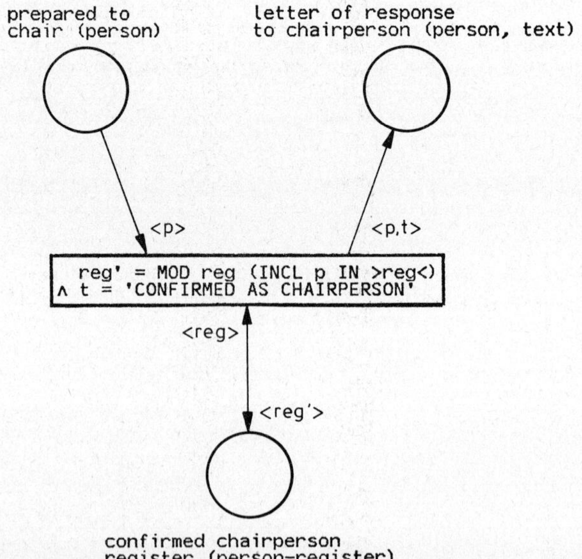


Fig. 3.4     Example for the demonstration of PrT-net conventions
with formal inscriptions.

The example of Fig. 3.3 uses an informal inscription. (A more extensive example for a PrT-net with informal inscriptions can be found in [7].) If the individuals are formally specified, it is possible to make the transition formula more concise and also more precise by using a suitable formal language. We use here IMC for defining individuals and IML imbedded in predicate logic to specify transitions. Fig. 3.4 above provides a formal version of the little example of Fig. 3.3.

Apart from net interpretation rules, we need a few purely graphical conventions: Because of its size, the total high-concurrency net given in Fig. 3.5 is distributed over several "sheets", each containing a partial net. The sheets are referenced by numbers. The connection between sheets is by channels which are identified by numbers. Circles with the same number are meant to represent the same channel. The in- and outgoing arrows again have numbers, which refer to the sheet on which the arrow appears together with its predicate and transition.

With the above comments on PrT-nets, we are now able to explain the PrT-net description in Figures 3.5 to 3.7. The net is intended as a complete specification of the process of conference preparation on a chosen level of detail and under the assumption of a certain given inscription language. As such, it should not need separate explanations. But as we did not detail the exact rules for PrT-nets nor give an account of the inscription language used, and as it is also sometimes difficult to guess how such a net is to be read, some guidance should be appropriate. We shall go through the net, explaining each predicate and each transition, initially rather detailed, later on more in outlines, spending some time on special features as they turn up.

The work of the PC naturally begins with recruiting chairpersons and referees. However, "begins" is to be understood in a causal, not in a temporal sense. In fact, the design of the system is such that it does not prevent receiving contributions before any request is issued formally.

Right from the start we have also an opportunity to show that nets can readily be adapted to changing emphasis on aspects. Whereas in the information flow overview (Fig. 2.1) it was natural to distinguish between requests to chair and to referee, we now want to make apparent the similarity of both processes. For this we "fold" the two partial nets together and make the necessary distinction with appropriate individuals. The channels **requests to chair** and **requests to referee** become a single predicate **letter of request to referee/to chair.** Similarly, the pairs (**mailed requests to chair, mailed requests to referee**), (**responses from requested chairpersons, responses from requested referees**) and (**confirmations/rejections as chairperson, rejections as referee**) are folded together. The agencies PC-a and PC-b become one transition (1.1), PC-c and PC-d are partially folded together (onto transitions 1.2, 1.3, and 1.6; transitions 1.4 and 1.5 represent the not folded parts).

The assumption that the information about possible referees and chairpersons is predefined is expressed by specifying "$M_0$" for predicate **referee/chairperson candidate.** $M_0$ refers to the "initial marking" of the net, that is, the assumed initial extension of the predicates. For predicates for which no $M_0$ is specified, an empty initial extension is assumed. The initial marking of the predicate **referee/chairperson candidate** consists of pairs (charge, person), where "charge" is either of the constants "REFEREE" or "CHAIRPERSON" and "person" is a unique description of a person including a mailing address. The three dots indicate that any number of (different) such pairs may be in the extension of the predicate. In each occurrence of the transition 1.1, the extension of this predicate is diminished by any number of such pairs and the predicates **letter of request to referee/to chair** and **mailed request** are augmented by the same pairs. A pair that is already in the extension of either of the two latter predicates cannot participate in the transition. However, since they have no initial markings, this cannot occur.

Please note that the style of naming channels is slightly different for the channel/agency-net and for the PrT-net. Whereas the plural for the former emphasizes the view of a totality of individuals, the latter rather supports the idea of a predicate that does or does not apply to an individual or tuple of individuals.

**Mailed request** represents the memory of the system which holds information on which person is requested for which charge. Obviously such pairs represent all the information that is necessary for the purpose. The same is true from a system point of view for a **letter of request to referee/to chair**, although such a letter must of course be more elaborate because it is to be understood by the receiver in an entirely different context.

The diamond-shaped partial net on the left side of sheet 1 is a device to decide whether a response conforms to the memory of mailed requests and to dispose of it accordingly. The essence of a response is a triple ⟨person, charge, decision⟩, where "decision" is "NEG" or "POS". A negative response is just ignored (transition 1.3). A positive response is tested against the **mailed request** predicate. Transitions 1.4 and 1.5 take care of acceptable positive responses from referees or chairpersons, respectively. They are enabled only if a corresponding pair is in **mailed request**. If a response is actually processed by a transition, it disappears from **mailed request** and reappears there later (this is the meaning of the line without arrowheads). In the same step the pair is put into **locked response** for reasons that will become clear shortly.

A positive response that is not expected by virtue of **mailed request** is to be rejected. The detection of this situation is based on the fact that **mailed request** can accommodate a pair if and only if it is not already there. Therefore, if transition 1.2 is able to put a pair into the extension of **mailed request**, it coincidently produces a **letter of rejection**. Of course, the pair must eventually be removed so that 1.2., 1.4. and 1.5 do not come to false conclusions. Removal is done by 1.6 via **locked response**.

As its name says, the **locked response**-predicate has the task to exclude accidental errors. If a self-appointed referee writes two response letters, the first one processed causes a corresponding pair to be included in **mailed request**. If there were no lock, the second letter would enable transition 1.4 and the person could pass as a referee. A detailed verbal explanation of how the lock is set and how it is released would be somewhat tedious, but playing a little with the graph should convince the reader that it does work.

A negative response does not preclude acceptance of a positive one. A positive response cannot be revoked. This is not realistic indeed, but since we show revocation in another context (attendance), we decided to leave it out here. An oddity may result if a positive response from an expected sender comes in twice. The second processed response produces a rejection. Therefore the rejection text allows for this possibility. The oddity can easily be removed if it is considered inadequate.

Transitions 1.4 and 1.5 distribute responses according to their different charges into separate channels. The person description for a chairperson goes into the extension of predicate **prepared to chair.** Whether the person will actually be accepted as a chairperson depends on whether there are still more chairpersons desired and whether the programme is not yet constructed. The maximum number of chairpersons is assumed to be known in advance and is given as the initial marking of **number of chairpersons still desired**. Transition 1.7 represents chairperson acceptance. It is enabled only if **number of chairpersons still desired** is positive. Each chairperson acceptance decreases this number by one and a letter of confirmation is sent to the respondent. Further, the fact of confirmation is registered in the **confirmed chairperson register**. This predicate has an extension of only one individual, which is initially the empty table. "reg' = MOD reg (INCL p IN ⟩reg⟨ )" means that reg' is the modification of reg obtained by inclusion of p.

**Confirmed chairperson register** gives rise to a discussion of a repeatedly encountered design decision problem with PrT-nets. If a number of things must be expressed as being simultaneously in a channel, one has the option of either viewing them as individuals of an extension or of introducing a single compound individual which encompasses the things, e.g. a set. In the latter case the predicate's extension has only one compound individual.

Each of the options has its merits. An extension allows for concurrent processing of several of the individuals by one as well as by several adjacent transitions. Thus it does not impose unnecessary sequencing conditions, the typical kind of overspecification with sequential programming languages. Its drawback is that the transition formula cannot refer to global properties of an extension. For instance, if the number of individuals in an extension is required, or, in particular, a transition is to be enabled when an extension is empty, this cannot be expressed by a transition formula. In this case, a solution with one compound individual is preferable, in some sense it is even unavoidable.

The obligation to decide between the two options often reveals causal dependencies which are easily overlooked. For instance, the test for a set to be empty cannot be made while set elements are accessed. On the other hand, it is in many cases rather a matter of convenience and design comprehensibility to give up some unimportant concurrency for the sake of a more compact net.

In the case of the **confirmed chairpersons register** one must be prepared that transition 1.10 needs the totality of confirmed chairpersons to be able to make proper groupings and chairperson assignments. Therefore, the solution with one compound individual is chosen. A small amount of concurrency could be saved for the penalty of considerably increased complexity. Later on we will have a case were it seemed desirable to use even both options in parallel (**invitation record** and **final invitee register** on sheet 5).

Once the **number of chairpersons still desired** is counted down to zero, transition 1.7 is no more enabled. Instead, transition 1.8 now transforms respondent information from **prepared to chair** into very polite negative acknowledgements.

Even if the desired number of chairpersons is never attained, there must be  s o m e  event which closes acceptance for any further chairperson. In the present design the construction of the programme is chosen to be this event. It can take place when transition 1.10 is enabled.

Transition 1.10 is enabled when **accepted contribution register** has received the result from the refereeing process (in channel 11). The function PROG-EDIT incorporates the edition of the programme. (It can be detailed if required.)

Transition 1.10 can occur only once and when it does, it disables transitions 1.7 and 1.8 by taking the only individual from **number of chairpersons still desired**. At the same time, it enables 1.9, via **programme closed**, which remains alive to handle late chairperson responses. The predicate **programme** is given the resulting programme, which is the precondition for the OC to come into full action.

With **programme closed** we have an example of a "nullary" predicate. A nullary predicate holds if a so-called "token" is in the channel. It does not hold in absence of a token. Movement of the token is indicated by an empty pair of brackets ("**< >**") at an arrow.

We now proceed with explaining how the information on the persons **prepared to referee** and further interaction with the professional community eventually lead to the **accepted contribution register** that is needed by transition 1.10. First, a pre-check for incoming contributions is described on sheet 2. Then, a device to ensure that the same person does not become author and referee is treated on sheet 3. The final decision on acceptance of contributions is described on sheet 4.

The two topmost predicates on sheet 2 are links to the professional community. A **submitted contribution** is handled by one of the four transitions 2.1 through 2.4. Transition 2.1 is the only one which retains a paper for further consideration. The other ones return letters of rejection. Transition 2.3 treats contributions which have a postmark that does not match the deadline. Transition 2.2 handles those which are mailed in time but for some reason are received after the final programme construction step is initiated. Transitions 2.1 and 2.2 are mutually exclusively enabled. The initial marking of the **contribution in time**-predicate enables 2.1, the initial (empty) marking of the **contribution not in time**-predicate disables 2.2. Transition 2.1 uses the token of **contribution in time**, but returns it. Transition 2.5 removes the token from **contribution in time** and puts a token into **contribution not in time**. At the same time, it enables the final decision on paper acceptance by putting a token into the **programme to be closed**-predicate. Transition 2.5  must be thought of as occurring when a given deadline is reached. This is not made explicit to reduce complexity, although it can be expressed with PrT-nets.

Transitions 2.2, 2.3 and 2.4 deal with contributions that have to be rejected for reasons as indicated. Transitions 2.1, 2.2 and 2.3 include the authors of contributions in a **submitter register**, so that they can be invited by the OC, no matter whether they are successful or not.

There must be some event after which invitations of submitters are no more possible. This condition is expressed in the nullary predicate **submitter register closed for invitations.** The OC disables transitions 2.1, 2.2 and 2.3 by taking the only individual from **submitter register** coincidently with putting a token into **submitter register closed for invitations.**

For each paper that has passed the checks on sheet 2, a counter for the number of papers that have to be further processed is increased by one (channel 3). This counter is used later to decide whether each contribution has actually been either mailed to a referee or returned to its authors.

The partial net on sheet 3 checks for collisions between authors and referees. This task is somewhat more sophisticated than may be expected at first glance. The following reasons account for the complexity:
- The possibility of concurrent treatment of referee responses and contributions shall not be oppressed by the system design.
- It must be made sure that simultaneous consideration of conflicting responses from the same person does not by chance result in a double role assignment.
- A paper may have several authors, the conflict of any of which with referee assignment must cause rejection of the entire contribution.

Obviously some coordination between referee confirmation and contribution acceptance is necessary. For this, a scheme analogue to the locking device on sheet 1 is applied. It only becomes more complex because more situations have to be distinguished. The coordination device is on the lower half of sheet 3. Its details are not explained here, but left as an exercise to the reader. Only one new feature needs some explanation: Transition 3.3 occurs if a person is completely new, that is, if it is yet neither referee nor author. This situation is indicated by the possibility to augment the extension of the **registered person**-predicate by both a pair <REFEREE,person> and a pair <AUTHOR,person>. The "+"-sign in the inscription of the arrow from transition 3.3 to **registered person** indicates that both pairs together are put coincidently into the extension of the predicate. After transition 3.3 has tentatively put both pairs into **registered person,** integrity is restored coincidently with the lock release by transition 3.6, which removes the "wrong" pair <AUTHOR,person>. The same feature is used with transitions 3.7. and 3.10.

Transitions 3.13, 3.14 and 3.15 are concerned with making the authors of one paper individually available to the collision test and deriving a decision on the paper from the findings for the individual authors. Transition 3.13 extracts a table of authors from a contribution and provides for a "tag" for each author. The tags are initially empty and are then changed step by step through occurrences of the transitions 3.7, 3.8 and 3.9. Only when all tags are treated, **authors to be checked** is cleared by transition 3.14. Coincidentally, 3.13 is enabled to process the next contribution (predicate **ready for analysis of next contribution**). The entire contribution is handed on from **contribution under analysis** to **contribution for response.** Transitions 3.10, 3.11 and 3.12 release locks and untag the **checked authors**-table. The result of the whole analysis process is crystallized in the **finding**-predicate on sheets 3 and 4 (channel 8).

Transition 3.7 through 3.12 have a variable ("y") which is not in any of the arrow inscriptions. This means that the variable may have assigned an arbitrary individual. The effect is the same as if the entire formula were preceded by an existential quantifier for this variable.

The partial net on sheet 4 has only one new feature that requires explanation: Transition 4.4 is specified with a CASE-expression. One may find this unnecessary and expect that the simpler formula without the CASE- and the ELSE-line will suffice. The trouble with this however is, that undefined expressions result if $dec=\emptyset$. An expression which can be undefined for a combination of individuals from adjacent predicates is not admissible for a transition. "CASE $dec\neq\emptyset$ (...) ELSE (...)" means that the first parenthesis is not evaluated if $dec\neq\emptyset$ is false and the second paranthesis is evaluated instead.

It should be mentioned that the selection criteria used by transition 4.5 are thought of as containing information on the maximum number of admissable contributions and the maximum number of acceptable conference authors. The latter condition is necessary to guarantee each author the possibility of attendance.

The working of the OC is described on sheets 5 and 6. PC and OC interact on the three channels shown on sheets 1 and 2 and repeated on sheet 5: **programme** (12) and **submitter register** (5) are generated by the PC for use by the OC, **submitter register closed for invitations** (13) conveys the message from the OC to the PC that submitters can no more be considered for attendance invitation.

The OC can already start working before it has a programme by preparing letters to priority invitees. This is expressed in transition 5.7. Once the programme is available, the **conference author register** can be extracted from the programme by transition 5.2. This also enables transition 5.4. Transition 5.10 remains disabled until for all priority invitees and all conference authors a personal invitation and a record indicating attendance guarantee have been put into the respective predicates **invitee** and **invitation record**. Transitions 5.5 and 5.8 take care of this condition and enable 5.12, which in turn composes the register of all other invitees and then enables 5.10.

The left column of transitions (transitions 5.3, 5.6, and 5.9) is to remove duplicate invitee information. The **invitation check register** is the common memory to coordinate invitations.

After the **non-priority register** is fully exploited, transition 5.11 closes down any activity on sheet 5 except transition 5.1, which continues to compose invitation letters from the **invitee**-predicate and the **programme for enclosure**.

The result of sheet 5 is gathered up in the **invitation record**-predicate. Its main information, the totality of invitees, is also made available in the **final invitee register.** The duplication is made for convenience. On sheet 6, the **final invitee register** is used conservatively, that is, without change, whereas the extension of the **invitation record**-predicate is gradually consumed as incoming letters of application are processed.

Such a letter either triggers a rejection (transitions 6.1 and, after closing registration, 6.2), or is ignored (transition 6.3), or is used to make provisions for subsequent treatment (transition 6.4).

A deadline for invitee acceptance is incorporated in transition 6.5. If this transition occurs, it enables apart from transition 6.2 also transitions 6.6. and 6.7, which proceed to count declined and accepted invitations, respectively, at the same time producing an ordered **list of accepted invitations.** The order is priority invitees and conference authors first, the rest according to the invitee response mailing date. Transition 6.8 compares the number of processed invitation records with the number of entries in the **final invitee register** and causes termination of transitions 6.6 and 6.7. It constructs tables of **rejected invitees** and **confirmed invitees.** Finally, a **letter of notification to invitee** for each invitee having responded is produced by transitions 6.9 and 6.10, the latter one generating thereby the desired **attendee register.**

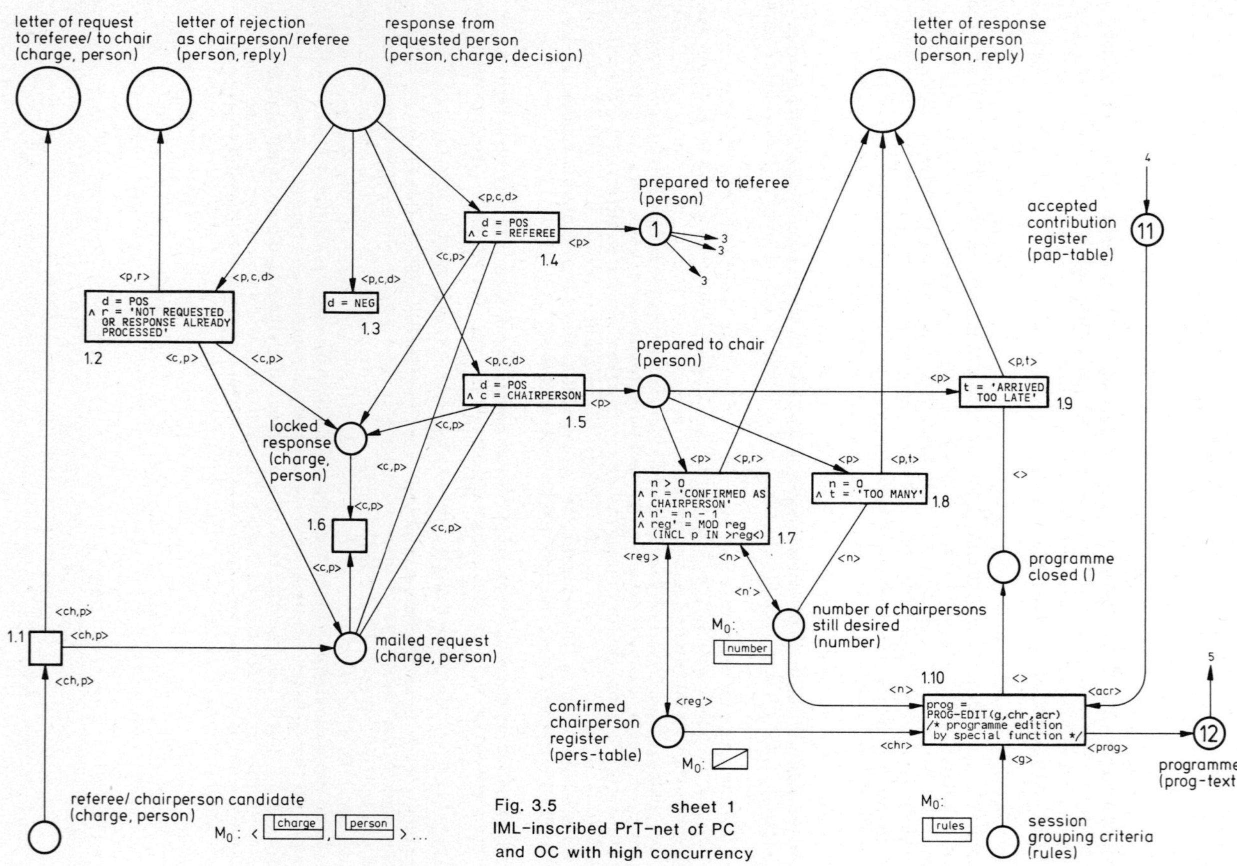


Fig. 3.5          sheet 1
IML-inscribed PrT-net of PC and OC with high concurrency

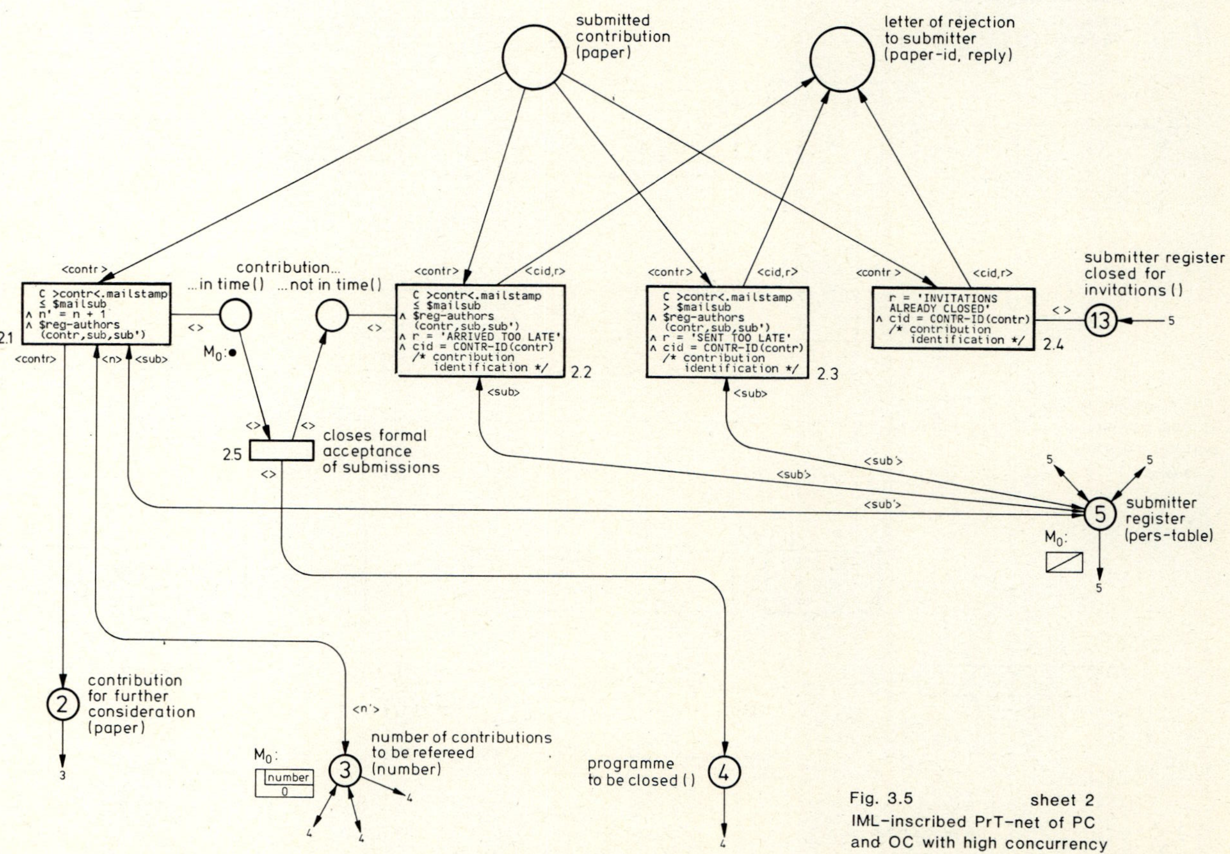


Fig. 3.5     sheet 2
IML-inscribed PrT-net of PC and OC with high concurrency

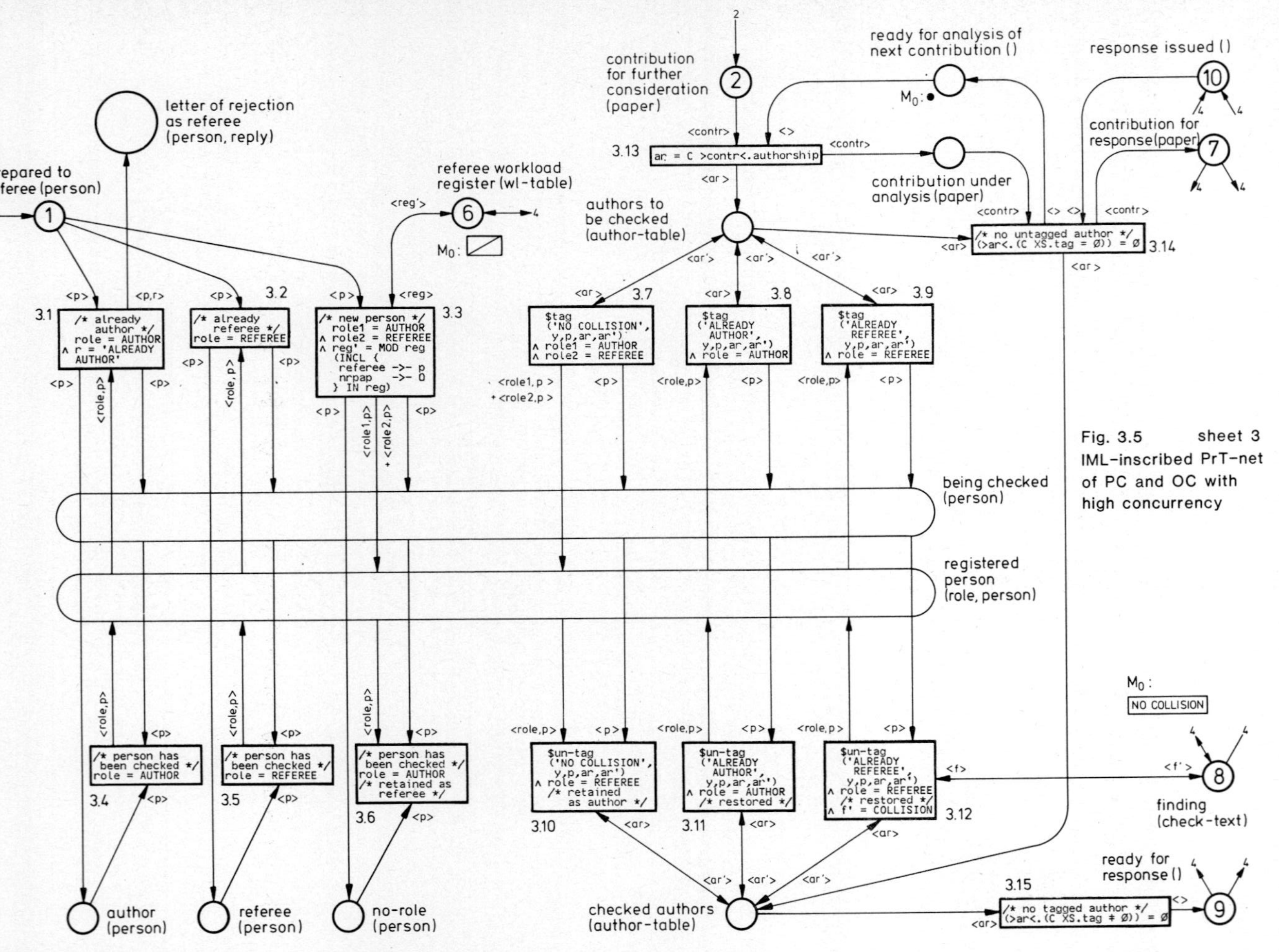


letter of rejection as referee (person, reply)
prepared to referee (person)
contribution for further consideration (paper)
ready for analysis of next contribution ( )
response issued ( )
contribution for response (paper)
referee workload register (wl-table)
authors to be checked (author-table)
contribution under analysis (paper)
3.13  ar = C >contr<.authorship
/* no untagged author */ (>ar<.(C XS.tag = Ø)) = Ø  3.14
3.1  /* already author */ role = AUTHOR ∧ r = 'ALREADY AUTHOR'
3.2  /* already referee */ role = REFEREE
3.3  /* new person */ role1 = AUTHOR ∧ role2 = REFEREE ∧ reg' = MOD reg (INCL { referee ->- p nrpap ->- 0 } IN reg)
3.7  $tag ('NO COLLISION', y,p,ar,ar') ∧ role1 = AUTHOR ∧ role2 = REFEREE
3.8  $tag ('ALREADY AUTHOR', y,p,ar,ar') ∧ role = AUTHOR
3.9  $tag ('ALREADY REFEREE', y,p,ar,ar') ∧ role = REFEREE
being checked (person)
registered person (role, person)
Fig. 3.5  sheet 3  IML-inscribed PrT-net of PC and OC with high concurrency
3.4  /* person has been checked */ role = AUTHOR
3.5  /* person has been checked */ role = REFEREE
3.6  /* person has been checked */ role = AUTHOR /* retained as referee */
3.10  $un-tag ('NO COLLISION', y,p,ar) ∧ role = REFEREE /* retained as author */
3.11  $un-tag ('ALREADY AUTHOR', y,p,ar,ar') ∧ role = AUTHOR /* restored */
3.12  $un-tag ('ALREADY REFEREE', y,p,ar,ar') ∧ role = REFEREE /* restored */ ∧ f' = COLLISION
NO COLLISION
finding (check-text)
author (person)
referee (person)
no-role (person)
checked authors (author-table)
3.15  /* no tagged author */ (>ar<.(C XS.tag ≠ Ø)) = Ø
ready for response ( )

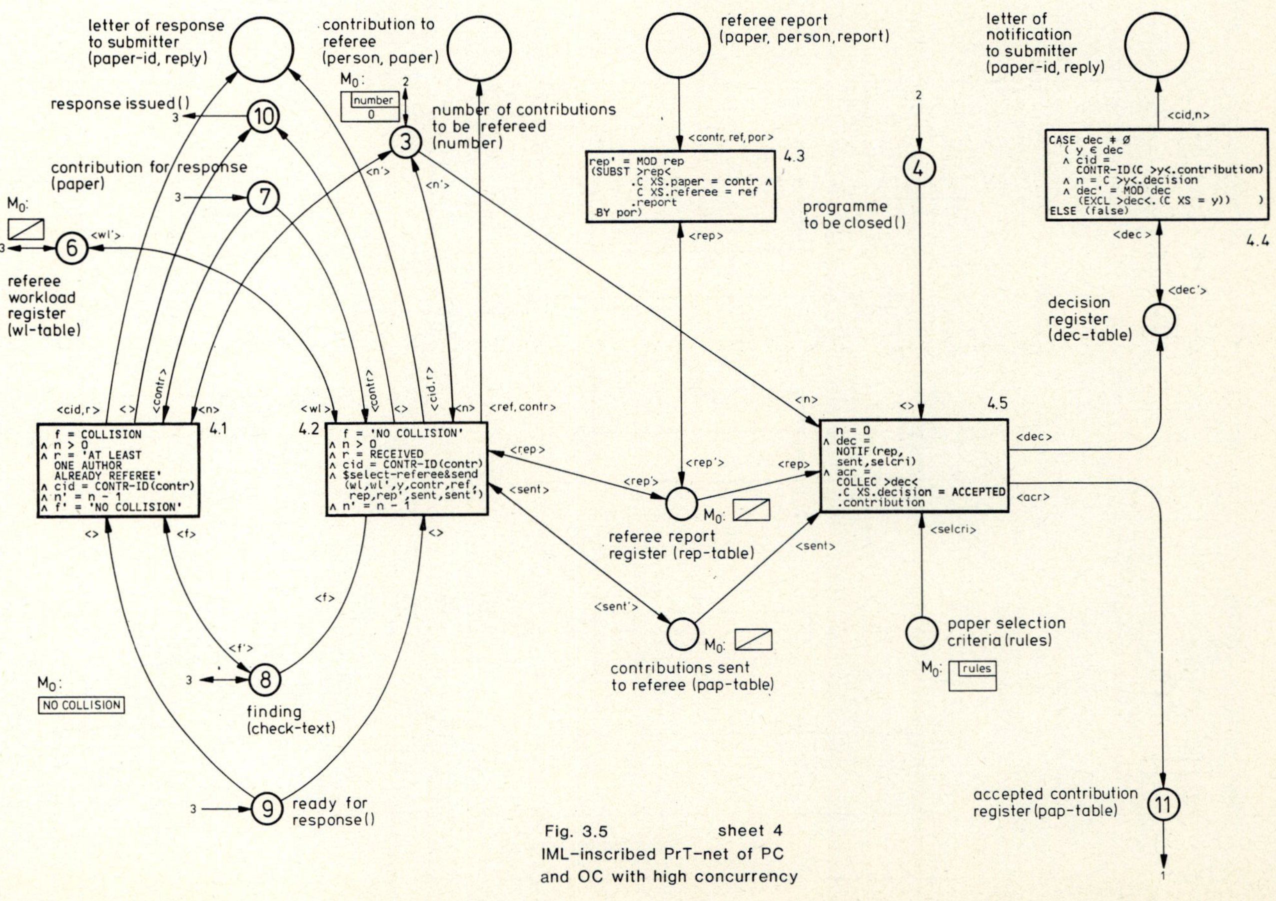


Fig. 3.5     sheet 4
IML-inscribed PrT-net of PC
and OC with high concurrency

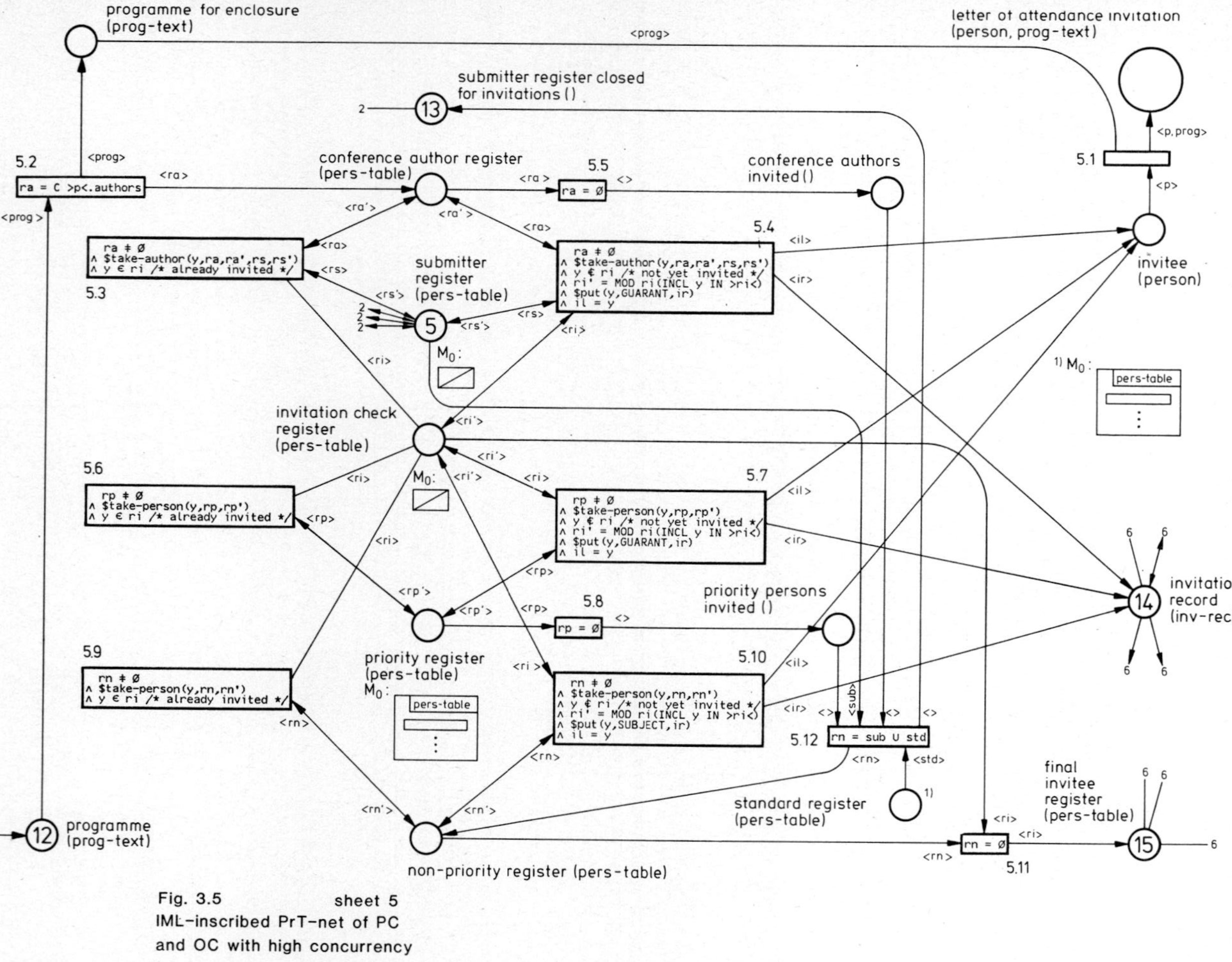


Fig. 3.5     sheet 5
IML-inscribed PrT-net of PC
and OC with high concurrency

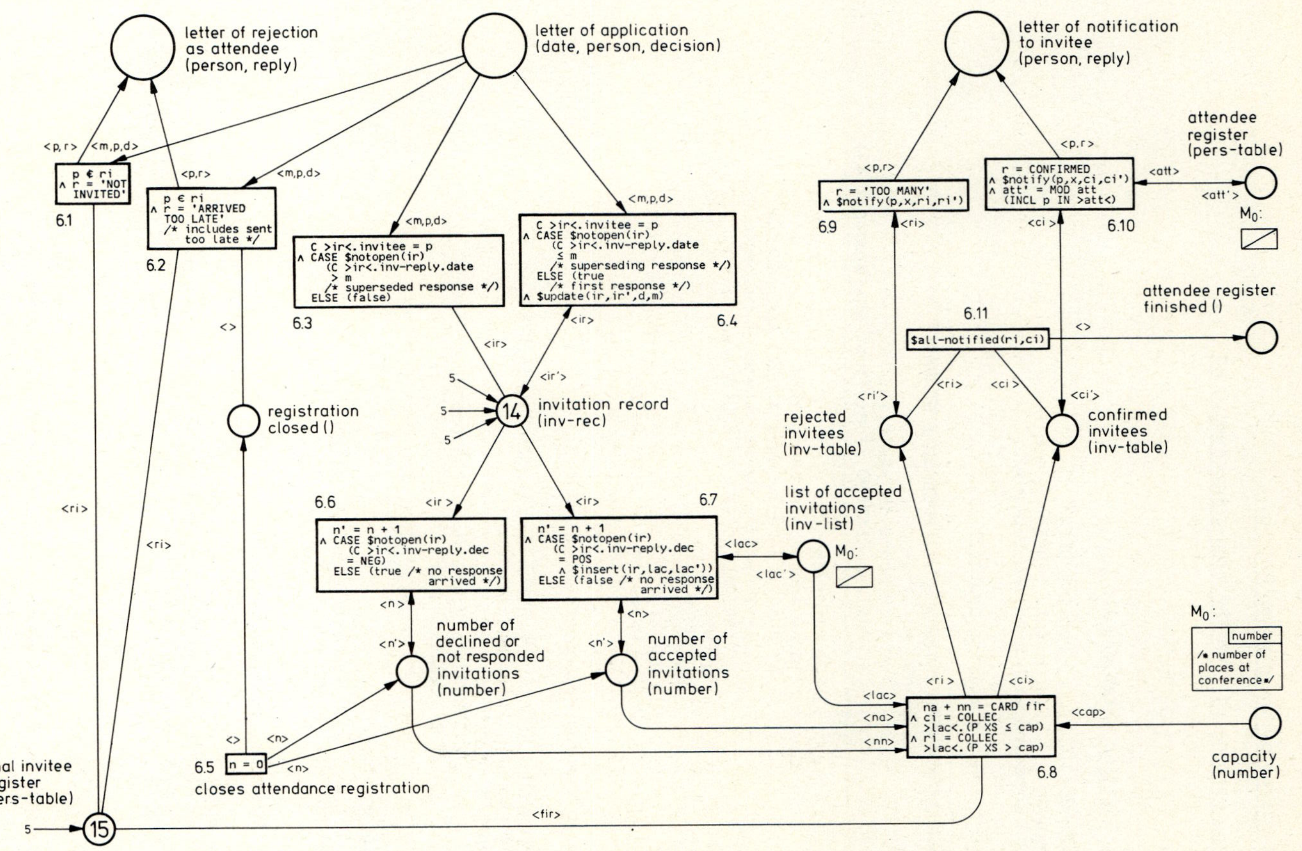


Fig. 3.5        sheet 6
IML-inscribed PrT-net of PC
and OC with high concurrency

<u>Definition of inscription macros</u>

<u>being referenced from the high-concurrency net</u>


<u>all-notified</u> (rtab,ctab) :

```
( >#rtab<.(C XS.org-reply = OPEN)
U >#ctab<.(C XS.org-reply = OPEN) ) = Ø
  /* no record with open org-reply */
```

<u>insert</u> (record,oldlist,newlist) :

```
#newlist = CASE C >#record<.attendance = GUARANT
             (1(MOD #oldlist
                (INCAT #record IN >#oldlist<
                 BY ARRIVAL DESCEND /* at first position */) )1)
           CASE C >#record<.attendance = SUBJECT
             (2(MOD #oldlist
                (INCAT #record IN >#oldlist<
                 BY C XS.inv-reply.date ASCEND ACC calendar
                    /* insertion by mailstamp of response */,
                    ARRIVAL ASCEND /* duplicates last */) )2)
           ELSE (false)
```


<u>mailsub</u> : /* mailing deadline for submission */


<u>notify</u> (person,record,oldtab,newtab) :

```
  #record ∈ COLLEC >#oldtab<.(C XS.org-reply = OPEN)
∧ #person = C >#record<.invitee
∧ #newtab = MOD #oldtab
            (SUBST >#oldtab<.(C XS = #record).org-reply
             BY GIVEN)
```


<u>notopen</u> (record) :

```
C >#record<.inv-reply ≠ OPEN
```


<u>put</u> (invitee,attendance,record) :

```
#record = { invitee    ->- #invitee
            attendance ->- #attendance
            inv-reply  ->- OPEN
            org-reply  ->- OPEN }
```


<u>reg-authors</u> (paper,oldreg,newreg) :

```
#newreg = #oldreg U COLLEC >#paper<.authorship..author
```

**Fig. 3.6**                          **sheet 1**

**Inscription macros to figure 3.5 (in IML)**

```
select-referee&send (oldwlreg,newwlreg,line,contribution,referee,
                     oldrepreg,newrepreg,
                     oldsentreg,newsentreg) :

  #line ∈ COLLEC >#oldwlreg<.(ALL WITH MIN C XS.nrpap)
  /* any referee among those with lowest workload */
∧ #newwlreg = MOD #oldwlreg
              (SUBST >#oldwlreg<.(C XS = #line).nrpap
               BY C TS + 1) /* increment workload */
∧ #newrepreg = MOD #oldrepreg
               (INCL { paper    ->- #contribution
                       referee  ->- C >#line<.referee
                       report   ->- Ø                  }
                IN #oldrepreg) /* inclusion of new entry */
∧ #newsentreg = MOD #oldsentreg
                (INCL #contribution IN #oldsentreg)
∧ #referee = C >#line<.referee


tag (tag,line,person,oldreg,newreg) :

  #line ∈ #oldreg
∧ C >#line<.tag =  Ø
∧ #person = C >#line<.author
∧ #newreg = MOD #oldreg
            (SUBST >#oldreg<.(C XS = #line).tag
             BY #tag)


take-author (line,oldconf,newconf,oldsub,newsub) :

  #line ∈ #oldconf
∧ #newconf = MOD #oldconf
             (EXCL >#oldconf<.(C XS = #line))
∧ #newsub = MOD #oldsub
            (EXCL >#oldsub<.(C XS = #line))


take-person (line,oldreg,newreg) :

  #line ∈ #oldreg
∧ #newreg = MOD #oldreg
            (EXCL >#oldreg<.(C XS = #line))


un-tag (tag,line,person,oldreg,newreg) :

  #line ∈ #oldreg
∧ C >#line<.tag = #tag
∧ #person = C >#line<.author
∧ #newreg = MOD #oldreg
            (SUBST >#oldreg<.(C XS = #line).tag
             BY Ø)


update (oldrec,newrec,decision,mailstamp) :

#newrec = MOD #oldrec
          (SUBST >#oldrec<.inv-reply
           BY { dec  ->- #decision
                date ->- #mailstamp } )
```

**Fig. 3.6       sheet 2
Inscription macros
to figure 3.5 (in IML)**

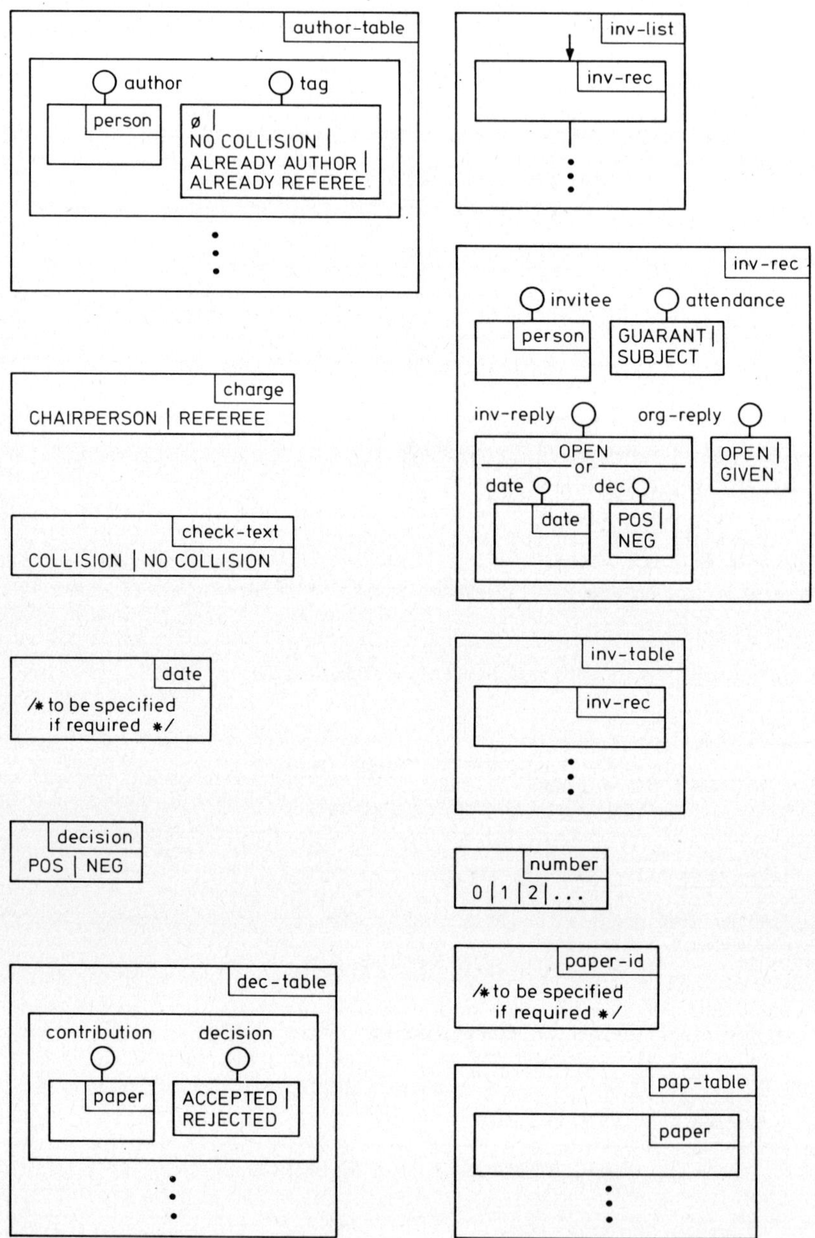

**Fig. 3.7**                                        sheet 1
**Construct types to figure 3.5 (in IMC box representation)**

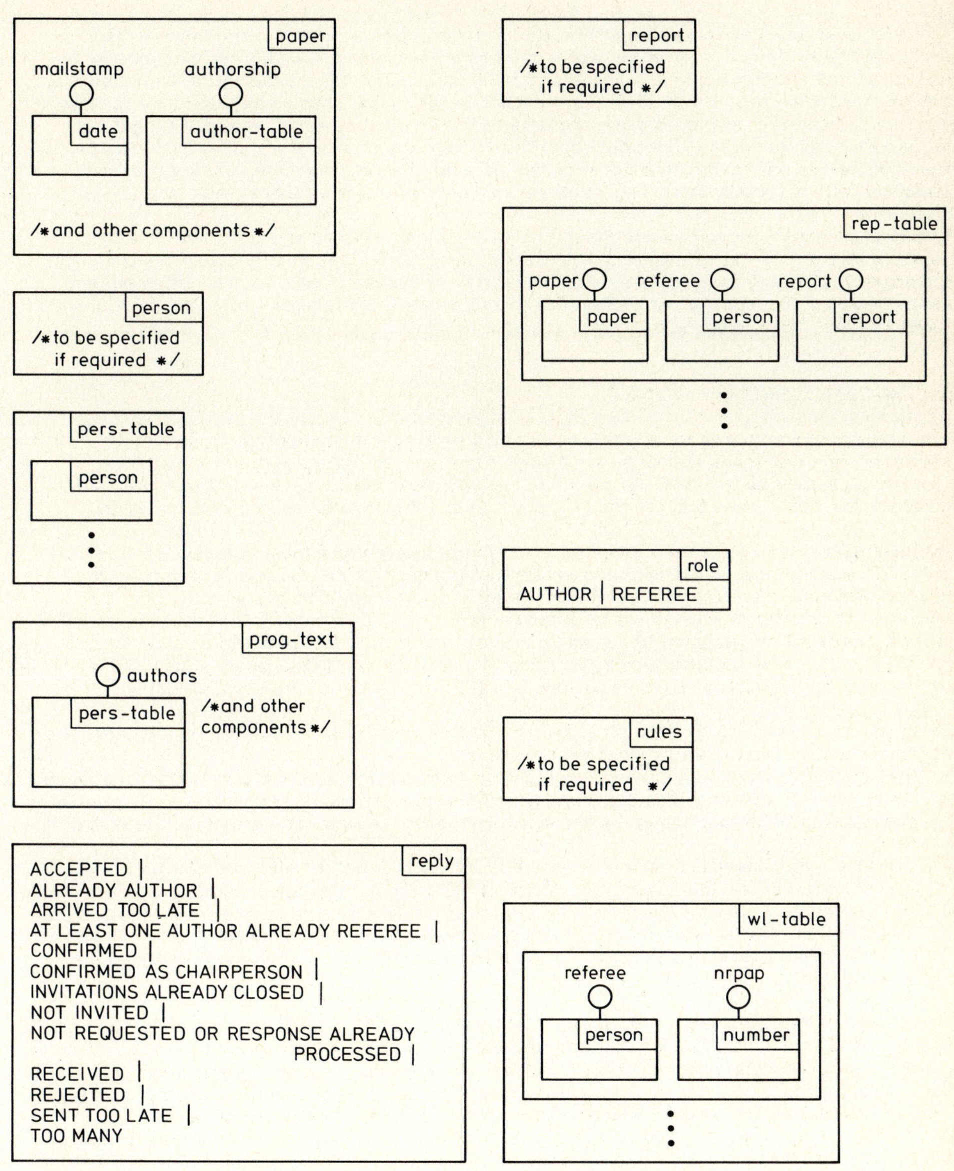


Fig. 3.7     sheet 2

**Construct types to figure 3.5 (in IMC box representation)**

## 4. SECOND OVERVIEW NET

The first overview net served to outline the information flow for an initial approach to designing the system. The detailed high-concurrency net obviously calls for guidance in understanding and surveying its overall organization. Such guidance cannot be expected from the first overview net. The second overview net in Fig. 4.1 is specifically designed for this purpose. It has been developed from the detailed net by coarsening. The resulting net is no more a PrT-net, because it does not specify in which way channels are affected by actions of the agencies. In particular, it is not required that all channels adjacent to an agency are coincidentally affected. So this net is to be considered a channel/agency-net.

The inscriptions of the net should make Fig. 4.1 self-explanatory and also make it easy to relate it to the PrT-net of Figure 3.5. It shows major functional units and also the graphical distribution of the PrT-net on sheets as an overlay of broken lines. The predicate numbers which serve to connect the net of Fig. 3.5 across sheets are repeated in this figure. Channels which connect the system with the professional community are indicated by larger circles.

## 5. LOW-CONCURRENCY OC NET

The high-concurrency net of chapter 3 will not directly be implemented. For an implementation one will make decisions as to what functions and data are grouped into local functional units. One possible and plausible such decision would be to establish one local database for the PC and one for the OC, and connecting them by appropriate channels.

In this chapter, we give a description of an example design for a local database for the OC only. Although almost all information is represented here in one compound data construct which constitutes the processing state of the local system component, we still chose to distinguish transitions. This allows to postpone sequencing decisions. The next step towards software production would be to sequence actions and to fold all transitions into a single large one, which may then be described by a conventional programming language along with suitable consistency and persistency specifications (see [6]) linked to the resulting database.

There are many ways to develop local system components from a high-concurrency net. The design principles for the solutions given here are:
- The channels connecting the local component with its environment correspond to channels in the high-concurrency net. By identification of corresponding channels a partial net of the latter may be substituted by the local component without any effect on the rest of the net.
- The local component is maximally centralized. That is, almost all inner channels are concentrated in one big channel (**database of OC**). Exceptions are **programme for enclosure** and **invitee** (same predicate as in Fig. 3.5, sheet 5). These could have been integrated but the idea was, that an automated system prints out letters to invitees and, after copies of the programme become available, a person puts letters and programme into envelopes (transition 1).

The construct representing the database contents is shown in the big channel on the bottom of Fig. 5.1. The construct types of the database and its components are given in Fig. 5.3. The central part of the db-construct is a file (named **inv**), in which the processing state for each candidate invitee is registered. For each invitee there is an entry (record) which contains the invitee's identification (under **invitee**), his invitation priority (i.e. his **attendance** is GUARANTeed or SUBJECT to capacity restrictions), a remark on his reply status (**inv-reply**), and whether and how the OC has responded to the invitee's reply (**org-reply**). The invitee's reply is either not yet received (OPEN) or its mailing **date** and **decision** on participation is given. Similarly, either the OC's reply has not yet been issued (OPEN), or the invitee has been notified (CONFIRMED, REJECTED).

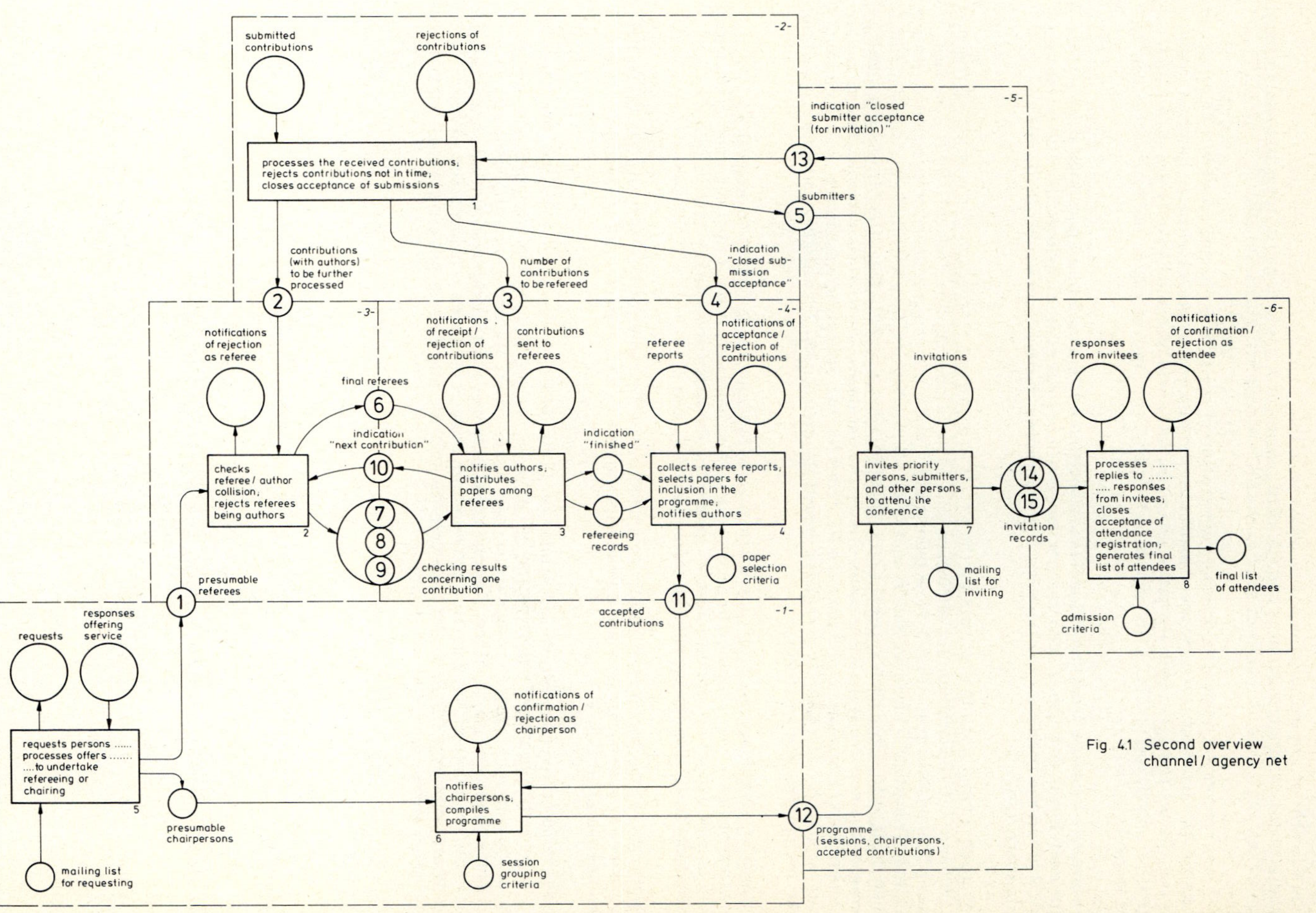


Fig. 4.1  Second overview channel / agency net

The file **prio** of the database contains all persons that must have priority invitations. Conference authors are listed in the file **conf**, submitters (including unsuccessful ones) in **subm** and other invitees (WG members etc.) in the OC's standard mailing file **std**.

The **reg**-component indicates whether registration of application is still possible (OPEN) or not (CLOSED). The **capacity**-component expresses the maximum number of participants. Finally, in the file **att** the attendees are gathered up. Initially **prio, std** and **capacity** are given (and never altered), **reg** is OPEN, **inv** and **att** are empty, and **conf** and **subm** are missing (as opposed to empty).

Before any message from the PC arrives, transition 4 is enabled to prepare invitation letters. For each letter it finishes, a corresponding record is entered into the **inv**-file. The letters are withheld in the predicate **invitee** until the **programme for enclosure** is available for transition 1.

The **programme** is made available by the PC. If it is present, transition 2 is enabled. Transition 2 copies it into **programme for enclosure** and, in addition, supplies the **conf**-file to the data base. This enables transition 3. Now transitions 3 and 4 may both proceed to prepare invitation letters. Transition 5 however has to wait until all priority invitees and conference authors have been dealt with. Only then is transition 6 enabled, which accepts from the PC the **submitter register** and creates from it the **subm**-file of the database, which in turn enables transition 5. Coincidently, transition 6 prevents the PC from further accepting submitters as invitees by putting a token into **submitter register closed for invitations**. Transition 5 can now prepare the remaining letters of invitations.

Transition 7 deals with applications from not invited persons. It cannot do so until all invitations have been recorded in the **inv**-file. This, however, is not true for transition 9, which may accept expected applications and update the database accordingly even during the invitation activities represented by transitions 3, 4, and 5.

Transition 10 incorporates an application deadline in the same manner as transition 2.5 of Fig. 3.5, sheet 2. It sets the database component **reg** to CLOSED, which disables transition 9 and enables transitions 8, 11 and 12.

After registration has been closed, transition 11 produces letters of confirmation, first to invitees with guaranteed participation (priority invitees and conference authors) and then to other invitees as long as the capacity is not exhausted. At the same time the final list of attendees (file **att**) is generated. As soon as all attendees are recorded in file **att**, transition 13 indicates its availability by putting a token into channel **attendee register finished** (same predicate as in Fig. 3.5, sheet 6). Concurrently, transition 12 sends letters of rejection to those who could not be accepted as attendees.

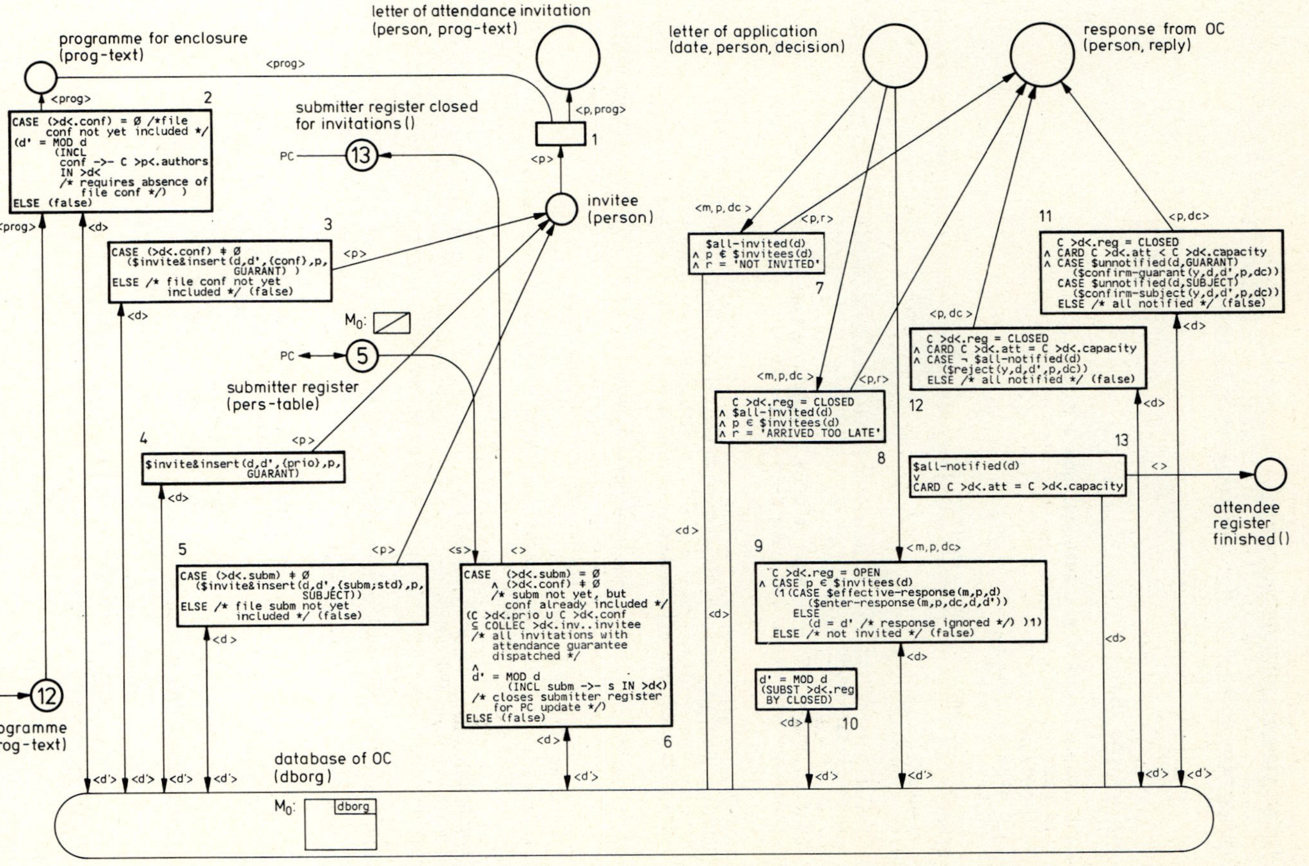


Fig. 5.1    IML-inscribed PrT-net of OC with low concurrency

<u>Definition of inscription macros</u>

<u>being referenced from the low-concurrency OC net</u>


<u>all-invited</u> (base) :

```
CASE >#base<.conf ≠ Ø ∧ >#base<.subm ≠ Ø
  (C >#base<.prio U
   C >#base<.conf U
   C >#base<.subm U
   C >#base<.std
   = COLLEC >#base<.inv..invitee)
ELSE
  (false)
```


<u>all-notified</u> (base) :

```
(>#base<.inv.(C XS.inv-reply ≠ OPEN ∧ C XS.org-reply = OPEN)) = Ø
 /* all arrived responses have been answered */
```


<u>confirm-guarant</u> (record,oldbase,newbase,person,decision) :

```
  #record ∈ COLLEC >#oldbase<
                 .inv
                 .( C XS.inv-reply ≠ OPEN
                  ∧ C XS.org-reply = OPEN
                  ∧ C XS.attendance = GUARANT)
∧ #newbase = MOD #oldbase
            (SUBST >#oldbase<.inv.(C XS = #record).org-reply
             BY CONFIRMED
             INCL C >#record<.invitee IN >#oldbase<.att)
∧ #person = C >#record<.invitee
∧ #decision = CONFIRMED
```


<u>confirm-subject</u> (record,oldbase,newbase,person,decision) :

```
  #record ∈ COLLEC >#oldbase<
                 .inv
                 .(ALL WITH MIN C XS.inv-reply.date
                    /* earliest mailstamp */
                   AMONG  C XS.inv-reply ≠ OPEN
                        ∧ C XS.org-reply = OPEN
                        ∧ C XS.attendance = SUBJECT)
∧ #newbase = MOD #oldbase
            (SUBST >#oldbase<.inv.(C XS = #record).org-reply
             BY CONFIRMED
             INCL C >#record<.invitee IN >#oldbase<.att)
∧ #person = C >#record<.invitee
∧ #decision = CONFIRMED
```


## Fig. 5.2                                        sheet 1
## Inscription macros to figure 5.1 (in IML)

```
effective-response (mailstamp,person,base) :

  C >#base<
    .inv
    .(C XS.invitee = #person)
    .inv-reply                 = OPEN /* first arrived response */
v >#base<
  .inv
  .(C XS.invitee = #person)
  .inv-reply
  .(C XS.date ≤ #mailstamp) ≠ Ø     /* superseding response */


enter-response (mailstamp,person,decision,oldbase,newbase) :

#newbase = MOD #oldbase
           (SUBST >#oldbase<.inv.(C XS.invitee = #person).inv-reply
            BY {dec  ->- #decision
                date ->- #mailstamp})



invitees (base) :

COLLEC >#base<.inv..invitee



invite&insert (oldbase,newbase,filenames,person,attendance) :

  #person ∈ COLLEC >#oldbase<
                   .N XS ∈ #filenames
                  .(C XS ∉ COLLEC >#oldbase<.inv..invitee
                     /* a person not yet invited */
  /* yields false if all persons invited */
∧ #newbase = MOD #oldbase
             (INCL {invitee    ->- #person
                    attendance ->- #attendance
                    inv-reply  ->- OPEN
                    org-reply  ->- OPEN }
                    /* new invitation entry */
             IN >#oldbase<.inv)



reject (record,oldbase,newbase,person,decision) :

  #record ∈ COLLEC >#oldbase<
                  .inv
                  .( C XS.inv-reply  ≠ OPEN
                    ∧ C XS.org-reply  = OPEN
                    ∧ C XS.attendance = SUBJECT)
∧ #newbase = MOD #oldbase
             (SUBST >#oldbase<.inv.(C XS = #record).org-reply
              BY REJECTED)
∧ #person = C >#record<.invitee
∧ #decision = 'TOO MANY'


unnotified (base,attendance) :

(>#base<.inv.( C XS.inv-reply  ≠ OPEN
             ∧ C XS.org-reply  = OPEN
             ∧ C XS.attendance = #attendance)) ≠ Ø
/* true if at least one person not yet notified */
```

**Fig. 5.2        sheet 2**
**Inscription macros**
**to figure 5.1 (in IML)**

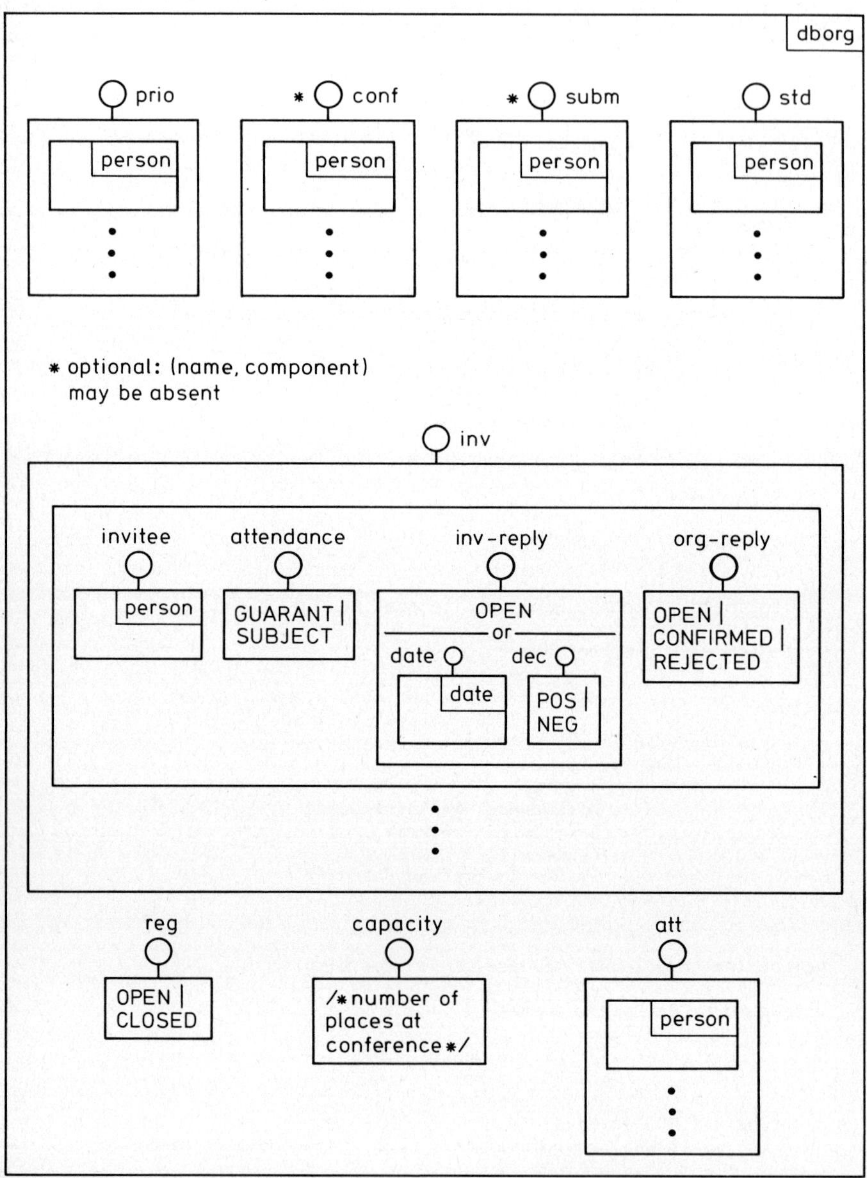



**Fig. 5.3**          **sheet 1**
**Construct types to figure 5.1 (in IMC box representation)**

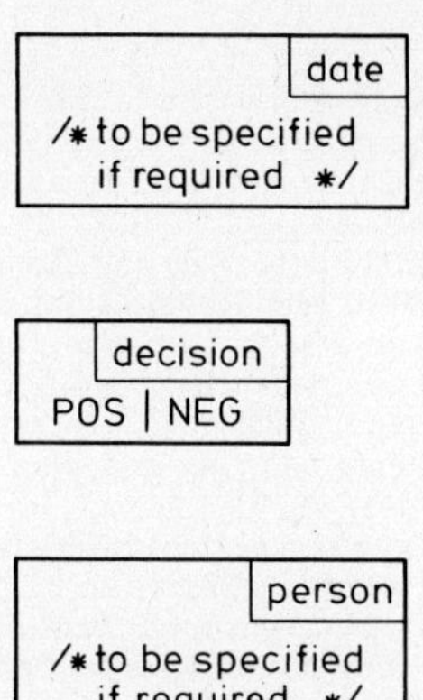


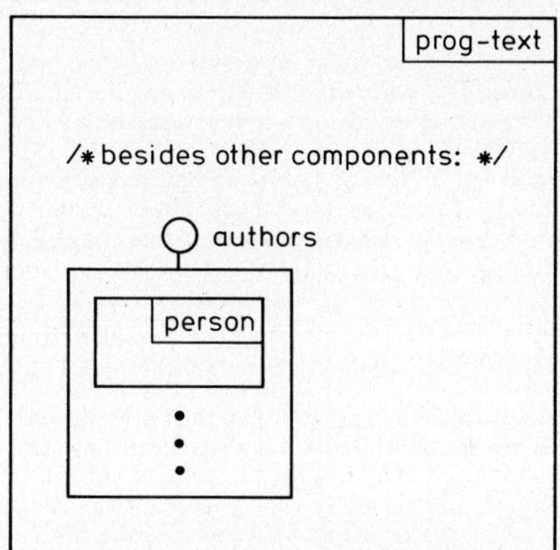

Fig. 5.3                    sheet 2
Construct types to figure 5.1
(in IMC box representation)

## 6. CONCLUSION

The era where software engineers impose their inventions onto users seems to be gradually, but definitively coming to an end. User participation in the system development process entails new requirements for system design methods and tools, the most conspicuous requirement probably being a very high emphasis on modifiability of design due to interface adaptation and evolution. The consequence of this is that at any stage in the system development process, the design and implemented products must be alterable and hence mentally manageable on any level of detail. Well designed change-control mechanisms are of paramount importance, and a suitable design documentation language plays a key role. "Suitable" means, apart from traditional language quality criteria, that it facilitates changes, exhibits consequences of changes and is applicable on many or - ideally - all levels of detail.

The present contribution does not present a complete system design methodology, but is restricted to discussing a specific design tool which is deemed to be particularly responsive to the above requirements. Nets have been used for system specification in practical cases and have shown considerable potential for precise, comprehensible and adaptable system descriptions (see [8], [9]). A cautionary remark is however necessary: Nets are relatively new in practical use. As a tool they are not yet developed to a degree that they can unconditionally be given to system designers in real production environments. It seems that some substantial research and development is still afforded to make nets a tool for routine application.

With this precautionary remark in mind, one can safely say that nets have properties that justify favourable expectations. The following features are particularly relevant:
- avoidance of premature localization of data and processes by providing a natural way to postpone decisions on distribution,
- support for transition between different levels of detail and points of view, e.g. support for stepwise refinement, support for coarsening to obtain overview documentation,
- harmonious composition of partial descriptions on different levels of detail,
- avoidance of overspecification, in particular of sequentialization where concurrency is sufficent or required,
- theoretical results which allow for formal derivation of system properties and for formal checks on certain design errors.

In this paper, we have not discussed the merits of nets with respect to all of these aspects, but the issue of the first point shall be explained: If a distributed system is designed by first developing a centralized system and then trying to identify distributable parts, one will inevitably incorporate decisions, particularly with respect to data structure, that defeat later distribution. It is only slightly better to start with identifying the distributed components and then to design their interaction and the local (locally centralized) structures. The gain will be moderate because it is not easy to find out at the very beginning the best distribution of resources. Later redistribution will encounter problems similar to those of starting from a centralized solution. Significant improvement can be expected if the design first lays open the causal structure that must be taken care of in a maximally distributed system. If a system is designed that way, grouping of functions and of information for local implementation should be relatively easy. Moreover, if later changes of localization requirements afford redistribution, relatively little effort is necessary, because the functional architecture is rather stable as it reflects the intrinsic causal structure only thus avoiding any additional restriction for later implementation.

ACKNOWLEDGEMENTS

The authors thankfully acknowledge the very efficient support in the preparation of the paper. Gertrud Breuer patiently and skilfully helped us through all stages of typing and correcting. Martina Bogen competently advised us with laser-printer character fonts and produced the inscriptions. Elisabeth Münch made the professional drawings, the careful design of which, we trust, will largely contribute to exhibit the merits of graphical representation.

REFERENCES

[1]   Brauer, W. (ed.), Net Theory and Applications, Lecture Notes
      in Computer Science 84 (Springer, Berlin, 1980).

[2]   Durchholz, R., and Richter, G., Concepts for Data Base Management
      Systems, in: J.W. Klimbie and K.L. Koffeman   (eds.), Data
      Base Management (North-Holland, Amsterdam, 1974) 97-120.

[3]   Durchholz, R., and Richter, G., Information Management Concepts
      (IMC) for use with DBMS Interfaces, in: Nijssen, G.M. (ed.),
      Modelling in Data Base Management Systems (North-Holland,
      Amsterdam, 1976) 49-69.

[4]   Genrich, H.J., and Lautenbach, K., System modelling with
      high-level Petri nets, Theoretical Computer Science 13 (1981) 109-136.

[5]   Peterson, J.L., Petri Nets, ACM Computing Surveys, Vol. 9,
      No. 3 (September 1977) 223-252.

[6]   Richter, G., Utilization of data access and manipulation in
      conceptual schema definitions, Information Systems, Vol. 6,
      No. 1 (1981) 53-71.

[7]   Richter, G., IML-inscribed nets for modeling text processing
      and data(base) management systems, in: Proceedings of the
      7th International Conference on VLDB, Cannes, Sept. 81, 363-375.

[8]   Shapiro, R.M., Towards a design methodology for information
      systems, in: Petri, C.A. (ed.), Ansätze zur Organisationstheorie
      Rechnergestützter Informationssysteme, GMD Bericht Nr. 111, 107-118
      (Oldenbourg, München, 1979).

[9]   Shapiro, R.M., The application of general net Theory -
      a personal history, in [1] 401-440.

APPENDIX

HINTS FOR THE READER OF THE PRT-NETS.

An introductory description of IML, which is used for transition inscription in this exercise, is given in [6], section 4, and [7], sections 3 and 5. It is expected that this background would suffice to understand the inscriptions. However, the full inscription of a transition is only obtained after having expanded the IML-macros, that is after substituting a string "$ macro-id (parameter-list)" by the identified macro-text (given in Figs. 3.6 and 5.2), where the supplied parameters have been inserted. Nesting of macros has been avoided in order not to overstress language aspects.

When evaluating a transition formula the reader should be aware that the sequence of evaluation is only given by the familiar precedence rules of boolean operators and not by inscription layout.

The three ad hoc operators PROG-EDIT (in transition 1.10), CONTR-ID (in transitions 2.2, 2.3, 2.4, 4.1, 4.2, 4.4) and NOTIF (in transition 4.5) have not been detailed. PROG-EDIT yields a construct of type "prog-text" (see Figs. 3.7 and 5.3), CONTR-ID yields a construct of type "paper-id" (see Fig. 3.7) which uniquely identifies a contribution according to the needs of the PC, and NOTIF creates a construct of type "dec-table" (see Fig. 3.7) which contains the PC's decisions to all submitted contributions.

The construct types, occurrences of which appear as individuals in the PrT-nets, are given in Figs. 3.7 and 5.3 using IMC box representation. Graphical representation of IMC constructs and construct types has been introduced and applied in [2], [3], [6], sections 1 and 2, and [7], section 3. Additionally, the symbol

is introduced for the empty construct in graphical representation, and $\emptyset$ for the empty construct in string notation. A formal definition of all construct types using IML is possible as has been shown in [6], section 5.

The type designations of the construct types not only appear in the "type plates" of the IMC boxes, but also as variables of the predicates which label the PrT-channels.

*INFORMATION SYSTEMS DESIGN METHODOLOGIES: A Comparative Review*
*T.W. Olle, H.G. Sol, A.A. Verrijn-Stuart (editors)*
*North-Holland Publishing Company*
© *IFIP, 1982*

# THE REMORA METHODOLOGY FOR INFORMATION SYSTEMS DESIGN AND MANAGEMENT

Colette ROLLAND                                          Christian RICHARD
Professor                                                Engineer
Université de PARIS-I                                     THOMSON-CSF

ABSTRACT

The Remora methodology proposes to organize the IS design process in two steps : a conceptual step and an internal step.

The first step is centered on the semantic description of the real world system. Its solution we name information conceptual schema is a formal representation of the natural structure of facts percieved in their static and dynamic dimensions. The IS conceptual schema simultaneously represents the organization components structure (as a data schema) and the organization behaviour structure (as a dynamics schema).

The second step includes the technical aspects of the solution ignored in the first one and takes into account the particularities of utilization the users planned to make of the IS. It complements the initial solution through the introduction of parameters that were not previously necessary.

For each step, the solution is :

   1) obtained through a modeling using theoretical concepts and methodological rules
   2) expressed through a formal language.

The paper presents the models, languages and tools associated to the conceptual level (first section) and to the internal level (second section).

Otherwise, we propose a computer aided system to help the designer during the IS design process. This system grounded upon a particular tool named Pilot controls the design process performing and calls in men or tools according to noteworthy situations. The piloting (that has given its name to the project, as the Remora is a pilot fish) is presented in section 3.

<u>I N T R O D U C T I O N</u>

## 1. THE METHODOLOGICAL TRENDS

It is rather difficult to classify the IS design and implementation methods.
However, we identify two main trends that are nowadays parallely developed and
that we name the "functional trend" and the "structuralist trend".

The functional trend is the oldest. It has predominated during the first IS
elaboration period and remains the most used in the organizations. Its main design
principle is to build up a system through an analysis of its functions leading to
an implementation of technical solutions that work out these functions. The functions are defined as the needs of the future IS users. They are often identified
by a list of messages the IS has to produce. Moreover, the analysis methods, such
as CORIG [14], MINOS [31], PROTEE [34], MARK IV [29], S-2000 [49], ISDOS [51],
MERISE [30], MACSI [33], [see [50] for an overwiew], developed and widely used by
the organizations in the frame of the functional approaches propose computer and
data processing concepts such as procedures, data structures, data sets and data
flow diagrams. Finally, these approaches result in IS partitioned in applications
that can only grow in the course of time (a new functional unit for each new requirement). They accumulate data, processes and messages redundancies in such a way
that the users requirements are defined in "solution oriented" terms [7]. This
issues in an important reduction of the admittable solutions field.

The structuralist trend is more recent. It corresponds to the development of data
bases (DB) and data bases management systems (DBMS). It aims to build up a system
through a definition of its structure. Many propositions nowadays rejoin the
ANSI-SPARC report [1] and suggest the introduction of a conceptual schema in the
IS design process. This schema constitutes both an abstract view of the IS data
system and an integrated view of the organization entities system. This approach
more emphasizes the semantic representation of the facts occuring in an IS. It
provides formal tools to validate the representation qualities (redundancy elimination [3], [13], consistency, integrity [5], [19], [32] and it allows a real
independence between the users requirements expression and the technical solutions.

## 2. OUR POINT OF VIEW ABOUT IS DESIGN

Both our research work and our industrial experience have lead us to retain a
structuralist type approach. But our structuralist approach is more complete than
the data base one. Indeed, we think that, for large and integrated IS, consistency
and completness become today operational objectives for designers. But generally
they disconnect strongly the design of the data systems and the design of the
programs systems. So they primary ignore the time interrelations between programs,
between data and between data and programs. Consequently synchronization problems
in IS are not correctly presented and solved. We claim that consistency and
completness require the integration of dynamic aspects in IS design and our work
is a contribution towards this.

This approach we have supported for several years [40] gains nowadays the adhesion
of a large part of the data base scientific community as some recent publishings
indicate [20], [25].

## 3. THE IS CONCEPTUAL SCHEMA

We define at the conceptual design step an IS conceptual schema. It allows a
complete, consistent, not redundant and economical representation of the universe
of discourse. It has the same role and advantages as the data base conceptual
schema in the design of a data base but it is more complete. We make the hypothesis that the complete aspects of real phenomena must be represented in IS design.
Not only static aspects of the organization (as in a database) must be represented,

but also the evolution of the items in the course of time : the transformations of
the organization components must complete the static struture expressed by the
data schema.

From our point of view, the IS conceptual schema is a unique schema wherein the
static structure, the transformations of the organization components and their time
interrelations must be represented. Our IS conceptual schema is the integration of
these three aspects.
4. THE IS DESIGN STEPS

The IS conceptual schema is the result of the real phenomena analysis and modeling
step. But it also constitutes the starting point for the next design step (figure 1).

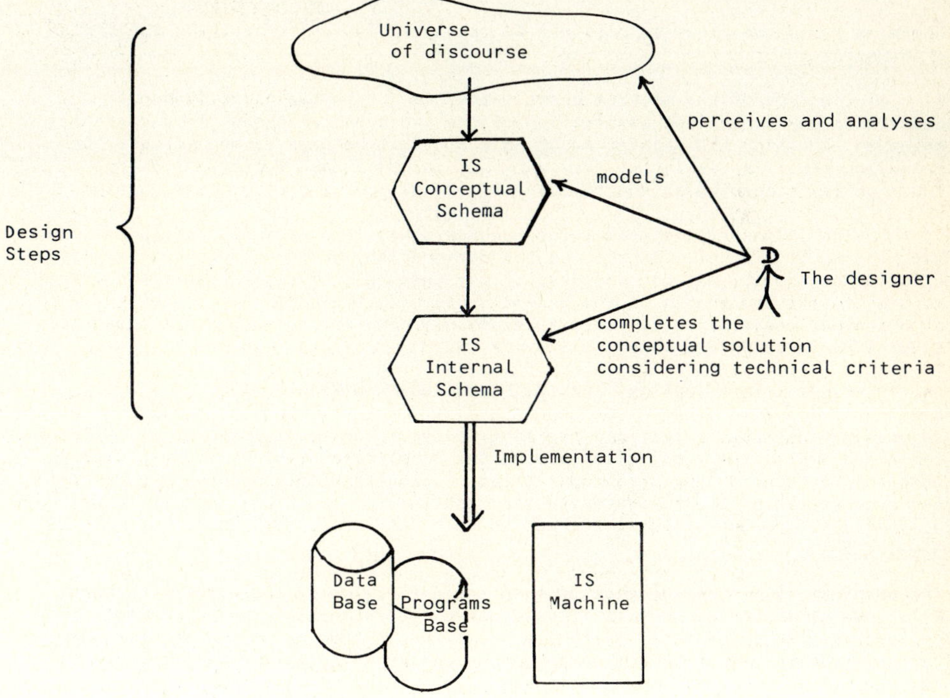


Figure 1 : The IS design steps

We propose to organize the design process in two interdependent steps : the conceptual step and the internal step. For each step, the solution is :

   1) obtained by a modeling through theoretical concepts and methodological
      rules
   2) expressed through a formal language

The first step is centered on the semantic representation of the universe of discourse.
The second step includes the technical aspects of the solution ignored in the
first one. It complements the initial solution in introducing parameters that
were not necessary before. The resulting internal schema is used for the imple-

mentation of the IS. The implemented IS consists then of a collection of data structured in a data base, a collection of programs and transactions stored in a programs base and a collection of commands activated by an IS machine that controls the triggering of programs and transactions upon data. Consequently, from our point of view an IS is a 3-uple (data base, programs base, IS machine).

## 5. THE IS MACHINE

The  IS machine is the set of means to manage the IS, i.e. the set of means that intervene at the end of the design process

> 1) in the implementation step
> 2) in the IS evolution, operating and use stage.

There is a wide spectrum of possible IS machines. Two criteria allow their discrimination :

1) the type of the machine means : they can be software tools, manual procedures or any convenient combination of the two previous types. In a current solution, in which the machine involves a DBMS, it belongs to men to work out some functions. Particularly, they work out the data base evolution control function in triggering at the relevant times the updating programs execution.

2) The IS description level the machine takes into account. The IS machine may be brought into play as soon as the designer has built up a conceptual description of the IS. On the contrary, it may require a physical description. According to the hypothesis of the previous example, the DBMS may work either from a conceptual description if it is a relational DBMS or from a physical description if it is a CODASYL one.

## 6. THE PILOT : AN AUTOMATON  FOR IS DESIGN AND MAINTENANCE AID

We make the hypothesis that all the IS life cycle can be assisted by an IS Computer-Aided System (CAS) organized around the pair (automaton, man). This system combines both human heuristic capabilites of complex problems solving and solutions generated by the automaton to the problems for which the complexity was dominated. It rejoins solutions recommended by other projects such as [17], [33], [54].

The originality of the solution lies in the definition of the automaton named Pilot. We have considered that it was possible both to build up the inventory of the problems to solve in IS design, and from those that we are now able to solve, to decide which will be given to an automaton and which will remain to the designer. Furthermore in order to treat each problem in IS design and maintenance process, there is a permanent and complex interaction between the functions carried out by the designer and those worked out by the automaton. As our research work has lead us to determine in which conditions and according to which sequence each one of these functions must be carried out, we decided to work out and to control the execution and linkage of the functions by a tool we name "Pilot". This tool must carry out the coordination of the functions all over the IS computer aided design and maintenance process. We name this coordination "Piloting". Consequently, the Computer Aided design System (CAS) we propose consists in a set of tools controlled by the Pilot.

## 7. PRESENTATION OF THE REMORA METHODOLOGY

This paper is organized in three sections. The first one presents both the conceptual level and the IS machine we have associated to this level. The second one presents the internal level in a given IS machine environment. The third part introduces the Computer-Aided System.

## FIRST SECTION : THE CONCEPTUAL LEVEL

The definition of the IS conceptual schema requires :

- a conceptual model (a set of concepts and formal rules called constraints)
- a formal language.

The model must provide elements for the definition of the data set, the programs set and the control of the time interrelations between data and programs. There are many data models [see [26] and [48] for a survey and comparative analysis] but very few proposals attempting to integrate data, programs and dynamic commands. To build the IS conceptual schema, we have developed an IS conceptual model. In this section, we present both the model (section 1.1) and its application to the IFIP conferences management case (section 1.2).

The language must allow a formal description of the IS conceptual schema. Consequently it must involve both constructions to describe the data structures and constructions to describe the processes and their synchronization. We have defined a relationally complete language that we name ISDEL .IS DEfinition Language . ISDEL partially derives from SEQUEL [8] and from the recent programming languages such as PASCAL [55], PLAIN [53] or PASCAL-R [47]. We present both the language and its application to the IFIP example in section 1.3.

Section 1.4 is an introduction to the IS relational machine we have defined at this level.


## 1.1 THE PROPOSED MODEL

### 1.1.1 What do we need to represent ?

The model has been defined by an analysis of the real world phenomena, which lead to the two following conclusions :

1) In a dynamic perspective we have to represent three categories of phenomena, described according to their properties as objects, events, and operations ;

2) The dynamic dimension is completely represented by three categories of associations between the three categories of phenomena : modify (operation, object) ascertain (object, event), and trigger (event, operation).

An object is a durable, concrete or abstract component of the organization that can be particularised. Examples might be the customer DURAND or the product number 33.

An operation is an action that can be executed at a given time in the organization and that modifies the state of one or more objects. For example, the operation "order analysis" number 312 creates the object "accepted order" number 202.

A modify association is an association connecting an operation and one or more objects. In it the operation modifies the objects.

An event is anything that can happen at a given time. It is the ascertainment of the state change of one or more objects by means of operations execution. For example, the event "order arrival" is the acknowledgement of the creation of the object order number 44 which triggers the operation "order analysis".

An ascertain association is an association connecting an event and one or more objects. It expresses that the state changes of objects are events.

A trigger association is an association connecting an event and one or more operations. It expresses that an event triggers one or more operations.

We propose a causal definition for the organization dynamics : the events cause the execution of operations issuing state changes of objects that could become events (see Figure 2).

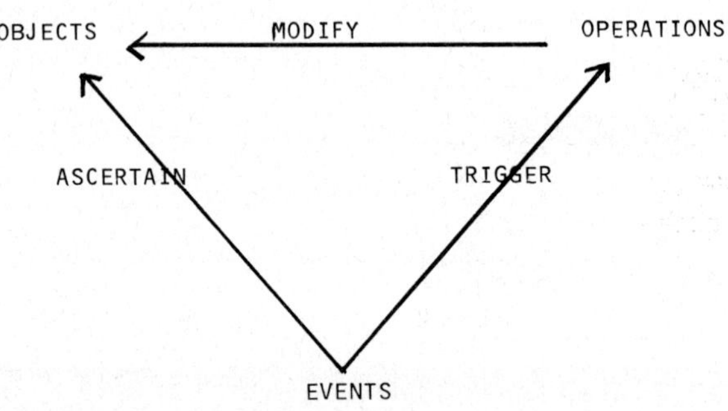


<u>Figure 2</u> : <u>Definition of organizational dynamics</u>

Our representation is based upon a clear difference between state, state change, and event. A state change is different from a state. The state of an object can be durable, but a state change is instanteneous. A state change expresses the passage from one state to another one. An event is different from a state change ; not all state changes of an object are events. For example, any modification affects the stock and generates a multitude of state changes of the stock, but only some of them are events issuing restock orders. A state change describes a change, an event is a state change that triggers determined operations.

It should be noted that the phenomena of one category belong to classes, for example, the customer class or the order arrival class. In a class all the phenomena are described by the same collection of properties.


1.1.2 How to represent it ?

The conceptual model must satisfy two main requirements : to be formal and to represent easily and homogeneously the classes of facts previously defined.

    1) We choose a typed relational model [12]
    2) We introduce types for relations in order to represent different
       categories
    3) We introduce time.

The correspondence between reality and conceptual representation is that :

    1) each class of phenomena and each class of associations is represented by
one or several relations ;
    2) each property of a class of phenomena is represented by an attribute of
relation ; and
    3) the category of a class of phenomena is represented by its relation type
(denoted C-object, C-operation, or C-event).

The three types of relations, c-object, c-operation, and c-event can be expressed
in a normal form we name temporal normal form. We give the definition of concepts
below.


## The c-object concept

A c-object relation type is a permanent relation, i.e. a third normal form (3NF)
relation [15] where each attribute is in a permanent dependency [42] with the
relation's identifier. A permanent dependency between two attributes A and B
(denoted A ⟶ B) is an elementary direct and canonical dependency where ∀ a
(occurence of A) and the dependent b (occurence of B), a and b have the same life
duration. For example the 3NF relation CUSTOMER (NCUS, NAME, FIRSTNAME, ADDRESS,
IDENTNUM, CA) is decomposed into the three c-objects.

. CUSTOMER-PER (NCUS, NAME, FIRSTNAME, IDENTNUM),
. CUSTOMER-AD  (NCUS, DATEM, ADDRESS) and
. CUSTOMER-ACTIVITY (NCUS, DATE, CA)

because the name, the first name and the identification number of the customer are
permanent ; the address can be modified and the turnover (CA) increases for each
order of the customer.

We can interpret a c-object as being the biggest set of properties of an object
having identical dynamic behaviour, that is to say, properties created, modified
or suppressed at the same time. A c-object represents a time-consistent aspect of
the real-world objects class. Several c-objects represent a real world objects
class. We name c-class the gathering of all these c-objects.

A c-object  represents an atomic state of the information system.

## The c-operation concept

A c-operation relation type is a permanent relation. The normalization of a c-
operation must satisfy the following constraints :

. C-OP ⟶ C-OB
. C-OP ⟶ TYPE-CHANGE
. C-OP ⟶ TEXT-OP

We express the constraints using functional dependency notation [15]. We make C-OP,
C-OB the identifiers of c-operations and c-objects ; we make TYPE-CHANGE the designation of the three state change types of objects (creation-destruction-modifica-
tion) and TEXT-OP the name of texts of c-operations.

We define the c-operation by reference to the c-object concept. The c-operation is
the expression of the smallest transformation that can happen to a c-object. More
precisely, the first two constraints express the fact that the occurrences of the
c-operation represent the operations that modify, in the same way, the states of
objects corresponding to the same c-object. In other words, a c-operation modifies
in a unique way the state of one and only one c-object. The third constraint
expresses the fact that a c-operation represents an organization management rule.

As a c-object, a c-operation represents a temporal aspect of a real world operations class and several c-operations represent the complete real operations class.
For example, the real operations class "order analysis" is represented by three
c-operations

    1) EXECUTION-ORDER-ANALYSIS      (NOR-AN, DATE-EXEC, NOR)
    2) PERMANENT-ORDER-ANALYSIS      (NOR-AN, TYPECRE), and
    3) MANAG-RULE-ORDER-ANALYSIS     (NOR-AN, DATETEXT, TEXTOP),

because there are many executions of "order analysis" operations (1), several
management rules used at different periods of the c-operation life (3), and only
one type modification of objects corresponding to the c-object order (NOP) for all
the life of the c-operation (2).

A c-operation represents an elementary transformation of the information system.


## The c-event concept

A c-event relation type is a permanent relation. The normalization of a c-event
must satisfy four constraints :

. C-EV $\longrightarrow$ C-OB
. C-EV $\longrightarrow$ TYPE-CHANGE
. C-EV $\longrightarrow$ PRED
. C-EV $\longrightarrow\!\!\!\!\rightarrow$ C-OP

We express the constraints using functional dependency notation (3) and multiva-
lued functional dependency (3). We denote by C-OB, C-EV, and C-OP identifiers of
c-object, c-event, and c-operation relations ; we make TYPE-CHANGE the designation
of the three change types of objects and PRED the designation of predicate that
expresses the state change of a c-object.

We define the c-event by reference to the c-object concept. The c-event is the
expression of the smallest noteworthy state change of a c-object. More precisely,
the two first constraints express that a c-event represents the class of events
that ascertains only one type of state change  of objects corresponding to the
same c-object. The third constraint expresses that the state change that is the
event is defined by the initial state and the final state expressed with a predicate. For example, the events belonging to the c-event "restock" are connected
with the modification of the c-object "stock" defined by the predicate

. PRED : Previous state of stock $\gg$ limit and actual state of stock $<$ limit.

The fourth constraint expresses that the events of a c-event trigger the operations corresponding to one or several determined c-operations. In other words,
a c-event is the state change type ascertainment of only one c-objet, which triggers one or more c-operations.

A c-event represents a temporal aspect of a real events class, and several c-events
represent the complete real events class. For example, the real events class
"order arrival" is represented by the following three c-events :

        1) ORDER-ARRIVALS            (NOR-ARR, DATE-ARR, NODER)
        2) PERMANENT-ORDER EVENT     (NOR-ARR, PRED, TYPECRE)
        3) TRIGGER-ORDER EVENT       (NOR-ARR, NOR-AN, DATE-TRIG)

Relation (1) describes the arrivals of the event type "order arrival". Relation
(2) describes the state change that defines the event. Relation (3) describes the
triggering of the operations belonging to the type "order analysis" associated
with the events "order arrival".

The triggering of the operations issuing from an event arrival can be conditional
and/or iterative.

If the triggering is conditional, the associated operation is executed if and
only if the condition (that expresses the required state of the system) is fulfilled. An iterative triggering corresponds to a repetition of the associated
operation execution for all the triggering factor occurrence.

1.1.3 What do we obtain in modeling reality through the model ?

The conceptual schema issued from the conceptual modeling is a collection of relations belonging to the three types : c-object, c-operation and c-event. This
collection of relations is completed by a set of convenient integrity constraints.
It can be split up in two sub-schemas :
- the c-objects collection corresponds to the current data schema. It constitutes
a static view of the organization representing the entities, properties and relationships of interest in the enterprise [48].
- The c-operations and c-events collection, named dynamic sub-schema corresponds
to a dynamic view of the organization. It represents the organization behaviour
rules through the interrelations between c-objects, c-operations and c-events.

Not many approaches define the IS in a dynamic way and attempt to integrate the
data, the transformations and the transformations command actions. Our originality lies in the capability to structurally analyze the interrelations between
these three aspects. We give the opportunity to define through a complete description the functional behaviour of the IS to be built. The following example
in chapter I-2 points out the mutual dependencies connecting the c-objects,
c-operations and c-events of the IFIP conferences management case.


1.2   THE CONCEPTUAL SCHEMA OF THE PROPOSED IFIP CASE


We present now both the c-objects relations collection in specifying the hypothesis we have retained and an explained graphic representation of the dynamic
sub-schema that better highlights the dynamic interrelations between the different activities of the two committees than the c-operations and c-events relations collection.

   1.2.1  Static sub-schema

OB 1    TECHNICAL-COMMITTEE (NTC, LIBTC)
OB 2    WORKING-GROUP (NWG, NTC, LIBWG)
OB 3    WG-MEMBER (NMEM, NWG, MBNAME, MBADDR, MBCOUNTRY, MBTYPE)
        * the set of the technical committee members is the union of the sets of
          the technical committee working groups members
OB 4    DECISION-CONFERENCE (NTC, DECDATE, NCONF)
OB 5    CONFERENCE (NCONF, CONFBEGDATE, CONFENDDATE, CONFDESIG, CONFLOCATION,
                    TOPICS)
OB 6    INVOLVED-TC (NCONF, NTC)
        * Several technical committees may jointly organize a conference
OB 7    PROGRAM-COMMITTEE (NPROGCOM, NCONF, PCCREATDATE, PCSUPPDATE)
OB 8    ORGANIZATION-COMMITTEE (NORGCOM, NCONF, OCCREATDATE, OCSUPPDATE)
OB 9    PROG-COM-MEMBER (NMEMB, NPROGCOM, MBRTYPE)
OB 10   ORG-COM-MEMBER (NMEMB, NORGCOM, MBRTYPE)
OB 11   COMMITTEE-MEMBER (NMEMB, MBCNAME, MBCADDR, MBCCOUNTRY)
        * a person can be a member of several committees
OB 12   CALL-FOR-PAPERS (NCALL, NCONF, TOPICS, LETTERDEADLINE, PROPDEADLINE,
                         ACCEPTDATE, PAPERDEADLINE)
OB 13   TIME-SCHEDULE (NCONF, ACTIVDATE, ACTIVITY, ACTIVTYPE)
        * The time schedule defines the meetings directory of the TC involved in
          a given conference
OB 14   RESEARCHER (NRES, NCONF, RESNAME, RESADDR, RESCOUNTRY)
OB 15   INVITED-PERSON (NINVIT, NCONF, INVNAME, INVADDR, INVCOUNTRY, INVSTATE)
OB 16   INSCRIPTION (NINSCR, NCONF, INSCRNAME, INSCRADDR, INSCRCOUNTRY)
OB 17   WAITING-SQUATTER (NSQUAT, NINSCRIPT)
                             NINSCRIPT : = NINSCR, NCONF
OB 18   ATTENDEE (NINVIT, NCONF, ACCEPTDATE)
        * The system simultaneously manages several conferences

             * a squatter is someone who has sent a registration form without beeing
             invited to the conference
OB 19  LETTER-OF-INTENT (NLETINT, NCONF, LETINTDATE, TITLE)
OB 20  LET-INT-AUTHOR (NLETINT, NCONF, AUTHNAME, AUTHADDR, AUTHCOUNTRY)
OB 21  PROPOSITION (NPROP, NCONF, RECEPTPROPDATE, TITLE, ABSTRACT)
OB 22  PROP-AUTHOR (NPROP, NCONF, AUTHNAME, AUTHADDR, AUTHCOUNTRY)
       * letters of intent and propositions can be submitted by several authors
       and all the authors are not necessarily known by the system
OB 23  REFEREE (NREF, NCONF, REFNAME, REFADDR, REFCOUNTRY)
OB 24  REFEREE-OF-A-PROP (NREF, NCONF, NPROP)
OB 25  REFEREE-PROP-RESPONSE (NREF, NCONF, NPROP, RESPDATE, MARK)
OB 26  PROP-RESULT (NPROP, NCONF, RESULTDATE, GENMARK, RESULTSTATE)
OB 27  REFUSAL (NREFUS, NCONF, REFUSDATE, REASON)
                         NREFUS : = NLET V NPROP
OB 28  INVITED-PAPER (NINVPAP, NCONF, NRES)
OB 29  INVITED-PAPER-RECEIPT (NINVPAP, NCONF, RECEIPTINVPAPDATE, TITLE, ABSTRACT)
       * A proposition of communication is read by several referees. Each one
       appraises the paper and transmits his mark to the program committee of
       the relevant conference
OB 30  SESSION (NSESS, NCONF, NMEMB, SESSDATE, SESSBEGTIME, SESSENDTIME)
       * NMEMB refers the chairman of the session
OB 31  COMM-SESSION (NSESS, NCONF, NCOM, COMTIME)
                      COM : = NPRO V NINVPAP
       * The communications are distributed over the different sessions of the
       related conference
OB 32  TIMER (TIMDATE)


### 1.2.2 Dynamic sub-schema

The decision made during a T.C. meeting is an event (EV1) that triggers
the identification of both the conference (OP1) and the involved TC
(OP2), the definition of both program committee (OP3) and organization
committe (OP4), the choice of their chairmen (OP5, OP6, OP7), the selection of an invited persons list (OPW) from the WG and TC members and the
choice of the date of the two chairmen first meeting (OP8).

The first meeting day arrival is an event (EV2) leading to the determination of the two committees members (OP9, OPA, OPB) and the choice of
a meetings directory.

The arrival of the program committee first meeting day is an event (EV3)
that triggers the elaboration of a call for papers (OPD), the choice of
the referees (OPE), the invited papers (OPF) and the determination of
a researchers list to which the call for papers will be sent (OPG).

A letter of intent author entry is an event (EV4) issuing in the adjunction of a researcher to the list (OPH) if both the author is not yet
known by the system (condition C1) and the letter of intent deadline
is not reached (condition C2).

The entry of a communication proposition author is an event (EV5) that
leads both to the adjunction of the author to the invited persons list
(OPI) and to the adjunction of a researcher to the list (OPJ) if both
the author is not yet known (condition C1) and the communication proposition deadline is not reached (condition C3).

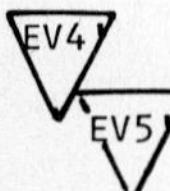

A letter of intent (respectively communication proposition) is an event
EV4' (respectively EV5') that triggers a refusal (OPK, respectively OPL)
if the corresponding deadline has been reached (condition C2, respectively C3).

 The arrival of the program committee foreseen day to analyze the propositions is an event (EV6) issuing in the apportionment of the propositions over the referees (OPM).

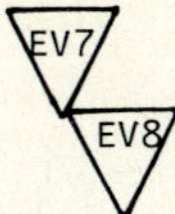 The arrival of the program committee deliberation foreseen day is an event (EV7) issuing in the communications evaluation and selection operation (OPN). When all the propositions have been examined (EV8 and condition C4), the program committee decides the sessions (OPO), the sessions chairmen (OPP) and the communications distribution over the sessions (OPQ) for the retained communications (condition C6).

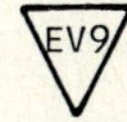 The arrival of the organization committee meeting foreseen day to select the invited persons is an event (EV9) that updates the invited persons list (OPR).

 An inscription arrival is an event (EVA) issuing in either the attendees list updating (OPS) if the registering person is an invited one (condition C5) or his adjunction to a waiting list (OPT) in the contrary (condition C5).

 The arrival of the organization committee meeting foreseen day to build definitively the attendees list is an event (EVB) that updates both the invited persons list (OPU) and the attendees list (OPV) from the waiting squatters list.

Figure 3 presents now a graphic representation of the IFIP conferences management system dynamic sub-schema based on the following conventions :

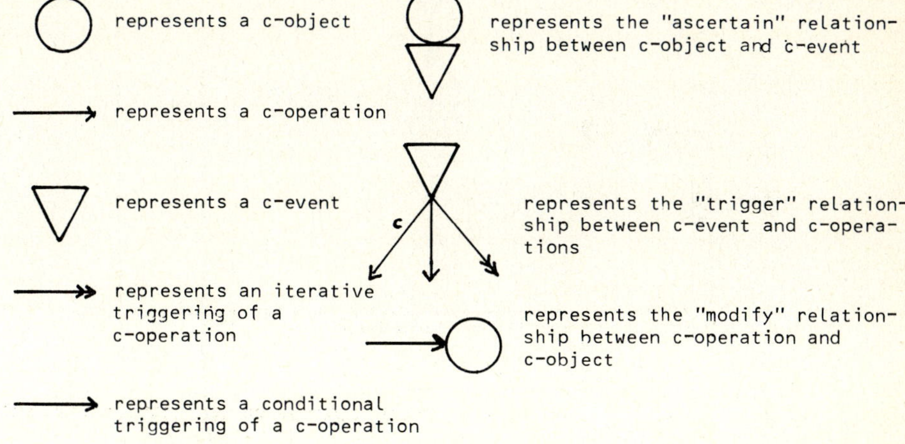

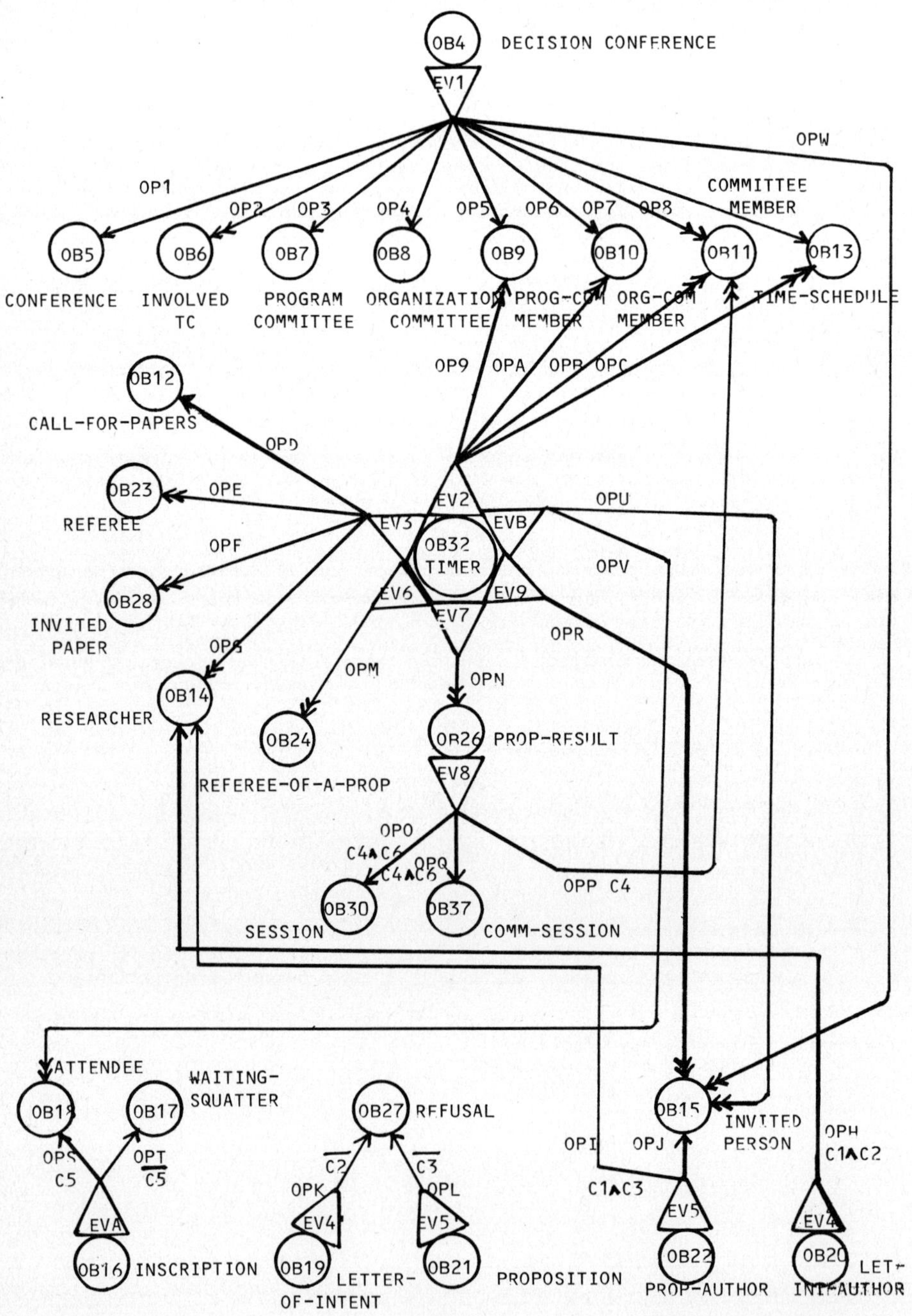


<u>Figure 3</u> : <u>The IFIP conferences management system dynamic sub-schema</u>

## 1.3 THE ISDEL LANGUAGE

ISDEL must satisfay two main objectives :

1) to allow dynamic conceptual schema description, i.e. description of both relations collections and associated integrity constraints
2) to be the central input of a relational IS machine.

To reach the first objective, we have chosen a relational complete language which is both the description and manipulation language of the  DB. To reach the second objective, ISDEL includes constructions derived from programming languages, and namely PASCAL [55] and extensions close to those developed by Schmidt in PASCAL-R  47  and Wasserman in PLAIN [53]. With these constructions, we can define through assertional expressions the c-operations texts, the predicates, triggering conditions and factors associated to c-events. These expressions are interpreted and afterwards generated under the shape of processing modules stored in the programs base and workable by the processors. We will limit our presentation to four basic constructions of ISDEL (assertional expressions, RELATION predefined type, FOREACH control structure and language extensions) and to the DDL description architecture in introducing in the example frame the most characteristic clauses.

### 1.3.1 Four ISDEL basic constructions

#### 1.3.1.1 Assertional expressions

ISDEL assertions are built under the general shape of current relational expressions. The usual logical operators are refered by the key words AND, OR, NOT, EXIST, ALL.

Examples :

a) provide all the conferences of the system

$$(x) : conference \langle x \rangle$$

b) provide all the english referees of the conference named "formal models and practical tools for IS design"

$$(x.nref) : referees \langle x \rangle \text{ AND conference } \langle y \rangle$$
$$\text{AND EXIST } \langle y \rangle \text{ (y. confdesig = 'formal models and practical tools for IS design'}$$
$$\text{AND EXIST } \langle x \rangle \text{ (x.nconf = y.nconf AND x.refcountry = 'England')}$$

#### 1.3.1.2 RELATION predefined type

This type has been introduced to allow local and temporary relations building from IS relations and their manipulation without IS modification. It has the same structure as a PASCAL RECORD. The declaration of a RELATION type variable obeys the following syntax (we systematically use BACCKUS notation) :

```
⟨ relation type ⟩    ::=    RELATION    ⟨ field  list ⟩ END ;
⟨ field list ⟩       ::= ⟨ identifier ⟩ : ⟨ type ⟩ |
                      ⟨ identifier ⟩ : ⟨ type ⟩ ; ⟨ field list⟩
```

Example : declaration of an intermediate relation describing the conferences of a given TC : tc-conference (ntc, nconf, conflocation, confbegdate, confenddate).

```
VAR tc-conference : RELATION ntc : INTEGER ; nconf : INTEGER ; conflocation :
CHAR (80) ; confbegdate : DATE (8) ; confenddate : DATE (8) END.
```

The t-uples set of a RELATION variable is built from the t-uples of existing
relations.

<u>Example</u> : build the "tc-conference" relation from the t-uples of the "conference"
relation corresponding to TC 08.

```
tc-conference : < (y.ntc, x.nconf, x.conflocation, x.confbegdate, x.confendate) :
involved-tc < y > AND conference < x > AND EXIST < y > (y.ntc = 08 AND EXIST < x >
(x.nconf = y.nconf)).
```

### 1.3.1.3 FOREACH control structure

The FOREACH control structure has been introduced to express manipulation of
t-uples of one relation. It is analogous to constructions of (8), (15), (46),
and it obeys the following syntax :

```
FOREACH < variable > IN < relation > [ UNTIL < expression > ] DO < instruction > END;
```

This structure expresses the repetition of < instruction > either as many times as
there are t-uples in < relation > or until the stop condition described by < expression > is fulfilled. For every repetition of < instruction > a new t-uple of
the relation is allocated to < variable > . We consider that < variable > has the
same relation type as the relation refered by < relation > and consequently the
same attributes. This is its only declaration and its range is the < instruction >
group following the DO clause. < Relation > refers either a relation defined in
ISDEL or a variable of RELATION predefined type.

<u>example</u> : compute the number of conferences organized by TCO8.

```
VAR number : INTEGER ;
number : = 0 ;
FOREACH w-conference IN tc-conference DO number : = number + 1 END ;
```

### 1.3.1.4 Language extensions

To make easier relations manipulation, ISDEL involves embodied usual functions
(8), (15), (46) : TOTAL (adding up of    attribute values), COUNT (counting of
the t-uples of a relation) AVERAGE (arithmetic average of a list of values),
MAX (greatest value of an attribute), MIN (smallest value of an attribute),
UP and DOWN (order functions).

### 1.3.2 ISDEL description architecture

An ISDEL description of a dynamic conceptual schema is constituted of the successive and non ordered descriptions of the schema relations. The description of
a relation is worked out through description clauses leading

    1) to assign a type to every relation
    2) to name it and to provide the list of all its attributes
    3) to specify every attribute
    4) to identify and to describe every integrity constraint :

〈relation-description〉:: = IS-TYPE 〈is-type-ident〉〈relation-specification〉 END

                                                    expression of (1)

〈relation-specification〉 :: = 〈rel-spec〉|〈rel-spec〉 ; 〈 relation-specification 〉

〈rel-spec 〉:: = 〈relation-name〉(〈field-name-list〉)〈 domain-spec 〉|〈relation-name〉

                                                                   expression

        ( 〈 field-name-list 〉) 〈domain-spec 〉 〈assertion-spec 〉

                    of (2)                expression of (3) expression of (4)

We now review aspects (1), (3), (4) in introducing the main characteristic
clauses.

      1.3.2.1 Relations types and modes

 〈is type-ident〉 :: = COBJECT MODE COB | COPERATION MODE 〈 cop〉| CEVENT MODE 〈cev〉
 〈cop〉 :: = COPPER | COPTEXT
 〈cev 〉 :: = CEVPER | CEVASCERT | CEVPRED | CEVTRIG

Every relation described through ISDEL is identified by an IS-TYPE, associating
the relation with one of the three phenomena categories represented : C-OBJECT,
C-OPERATION, C-EVENT. This type is completed by a MODE to specify the particular
aspect of the phenomenon described by the relation.

      1.3.2.2 Domains

 〈domain-spec 〉 :: = DOMAIN 〈domain-spec-def 〉;
 〈 domain-spec-def 〉 :: = 〈domain-def〉|〈domain-def 〉 ; 〈 domain-spec-def 〉
 〈domain-def 〉 :: = 〈field-name 〉: 〈domain-exp〉|〈field-name 〉:   SAME OF〈relation
   name〉
 〈 domain-exp〉 :: = CHAR (integer) | INTEGER (integer) | REAL  (integer, integer) |
                     DATE (integer) | BOOLEAN

The DOMAIN clause specifies the domain of values associated to every relation
attribute. In addition to usual predefined domains (INTEGER, REAL, BOOLEAN, CHAR),
ISDEL allows DATE type use. This type is defined with regard to a calendar [27] :
a date is a projection over the calendar. Moreover, an attribute domain can be
defined as that of another attribute (SAME OF).

      1.3.2.3 Assertional expressions of integrity constraints

Integrity constraints are introduced by the ASSERT clause :

<assertion-spec> ::= ASSERT <ident-spec-list>
<ident-spec-list> ::= <spec-list-elem>|<spec-list-elem> ;<ident-spec-list>
<spec-list-elem> ::=<identifier>: <static assert>|<identifier>: <dynamic assert>
                    |<identifier>: LIKE<identifier>


I-3231 Static integrity constraints


<static assert> ::= <field-name-list> COMPOSKEY <field-name> ;|<field-name>
                    KEY; | CONSTRAINT (<field-name-list>) :<text-constraint> ;


KEY defines the relation key field ; COMPOSKEY expresses the composition in fields
of a key identifier ; CONSTRAINT defines an integrity constraint over or between
terms of attributes specified by <text-constraint>, whose result is transmitted by
the assertion identifier.

Example : description of the c-object "conference"

IS-TYPE  C-OBJECT  MODE COB conference (nconf, confbegdate, confenddate,
confdesign, conflocation, topics)
DOMAIN nconf : INTEGER (5) ; confbegdate : DATE (8) ; confenddate : DATE (8) ;
confdesign : CHAR (80) ; conflocation : CHAR (80) ; topics : CHAR (40)
ASSERT  as1 : nconf KEY ;
        as2 : CONSTRAINT (confbegdate, confenddate) :
             BEGIN IF confbegdate > confenddate THEN as2 : = FALSE
                                                ELSE as2 : = TRUE
             END ;
END ;


I-3232 Dynamic integrity constraints


<dynamic assert> :: = <fieldname> <id-text> <dyn-assert-end>
<dyn-assert-end> :: = (<relation-name>) : <constraint-text>
<id-text> :: = CONDITION | FACTOR | OPERATION | PREDICATE


All the constraints are expressed under a same description schema. <Text-
constraint> is an assertion block framed by BEGIN and END symbols. It corresponds
to a procedure block whose imput parameter is a relation (relation of the schema
or RELATION type variable) referred by <relation-name> and whose result (if
existing) is transmited by the assertion identifier <field-name>.

Key word CONDITION refers an  integrity constraint describing a c-event triggering
condition whose result (true or false) is transmitted by the assertion identifier.
Key word OPERATION refers a constraint describing a c-operation text. Key word
FACTOR refers a constraint describing the set of the t-uples for which there will
be an iterative operation triggering. This set is allocated to the corresponding
<field-name> . In this case, the assertion identifier takes the same part as a
RELATION type variable.  Key word PREDICATE represents the description of a constraint defining the state change associated to a c-event.

Example :

1) description of the triggering conditions associated to the c-operation OPI
triggered by the c-event EV5

```
IS-TYPE CEVENT
ev5opi   TRIGGER (nev5, nopi, copi)
         DOMAIN nev5 : SAME OF ev5per ;
                nopi : SAME OF opiper ;
                copi : CHAR (5) ;
         ASSERT asev5opi1 : nev5, nopi COMPOSKEY ev5opi ;
                asev5opi2 : copi CONDITION (prop-author)
                VAR bool : BOOLEAN
                    prop : RELATION dateprop : DATE (8) END ;
                    call.: RELATION deadline : DATE (8) END ;
                BEGIN bool : = FALSE ;
                    prop :< (x.receptpropdate) : proposition < x >
                         AND EXIST < x > (prop-author.nconf = x.nconf AND prop-
                         author.nprop = x.nprop)
                    call :< (x.propdeadline) : call-for-papers < x >
                         AND EXIST < x > (prop-author.nconf = x.nconf)
                    FOREACH elem IN researcher UNTIL bool
                         DO IF elem. resname = prop-author.authname
                            AND elem.resaddr = prop-author.authaddr
                            AND elem.rescountry = prop-author.authcountry
                               THEN bool : = TRUE ;
                END ;
                IF NOT bool AND prop.dateprop < call.deadline
                         THEN copi : = TRUE
                         ELSE copi : = FALSE ;
         END ;
```

2) <u>description of the predicate defining the c-event EV7</u>

```
IS-TYPE CEVENT
ev7 PRED (nev7, predev7)
    DOMAIN nev7 : INTEGER (4) ;
           predev7  : CHAR (5) ;
    ASSERT asev71 : predev 7 PREDICATE (timer) :
           VAR workingrel : RELATION evdate : DATE (8) ; wactivity : CHAR (30) ;
                           wactivtyp': CHAR (30) END ;
           BEGIN
               workingrel : < (timer.timdate, y.activity, y.activtype) : TIME-
                           SCHEDULE < y >
                   AND EXIST < y > (y.activdate = timer.timdate
                   AND y.activity = 'deliberation'
                   AND y.activtype = 'Program Committee meeting')
IF COUNT (x.workingrel) ⌐ = 0   THEN predev 7 : = TRUE
                                ELSE predev 7 : = FALSE ;
END ;
```

3) <u>description of the triggering factor associated to the c-operation OPN triggered by the c-event EV7</u>

```
IS TYPE CEVENT
    ev7opn   TRIGGER (nev7, nopn, factev7opn)
             DOMAIN nev7  : SAME OF ev7
                    nopn  : SAME OF opnper
                    factev7opn : CHAR (10)
             ASSERT asev7opn1 : nev7, nopn COMPOSKEY nev7nopn ;
                    asev7opn2 : factev7opn FACTOR (timer)
                    VAR workingrel : RELATION wnconf : INTEGER (5) ; wnprop :
                                    INTEGER (5) END ;
                    BEGIN
```

```
            workingrel : < (x.nconf, x.nprop) : prop-author <x >
                    AND time-schedule < z >
                    AND EXIST < z > (z.activdate = timer.timdate
                    AND EXIST < x > (x.nconf = z.nconf))
        END ;
```

4) <u>description of the text of the c-operation OPN</u>

```
IS-TYPE COPERATION
   Texopn (nopn, datopn, textopn)
   DOMAIN nopn : SAME OF opnper ;
          datopn : DATE (8) ;
          textopn : CHAR (10) ;
   ASSERT astexopn 1 : nopn, datopn, COMPOSKEY nopndatopn ;
          astexopn 2 : textopn TEXT (VAR factopn : RELATION fnconf :
                    INTEGER (5), fnprop : INTEGER (5) END ;)
          VAR propmark : RELATION pmprop : INTEGER (5) ; pmmark :
                    REAL (4,2) END ;
            statvar : CHAR (16) ;
            datvar : DATE (8) ;
            propaverage : REAL (4,2) ;
          BEGIN
            propmark : < (x.nprop, x.mark) referee-prop-response < x >
                    AND EXIST < x > (x.nconf = factopn.fnconf
                       AND x.nprop = factopn.fnprop) ;
            datvar : = TIME (8) ;
            IF COUNT (x.propmark) = 0 THEN
               INSERT (factopn.fnconf, factopn.fnprop, datvar, '99.99',
                    'not reviewed') IN prop-result
                                 ELSE
               BEGIN propaverage : = AVERAGE ((x.pmmark) propmark < x >) ;
                    IF propaverage > 14 THEN statvar : = 'accepted'
                                    ELSE statvar : = 'to be discussed' ;
                    INSERT (factopn.fnconf, factopn.fnprop, datvar, p-opave-
                          rage, statvar) IN prop-result ;
               END ;
END ;
```

## 1.4 THE IS CONCEPTUAL MACHINE

### 1.4.1 The DBMS approach

In data management field, the DBMS approach has introduced a very important change in the designer's tasks. DBMS are tools that create and manage data bases
starting from an appropriate description of the data structure given by the designer. Globally, the DBMS makes easier two functions at the use time of the
data base : the data manipulation and the automatic execution of control operations over the data in order to maintain both the data base integrity and consistency.
But the DBMS differ [15] by the nature of the data description they need and the
action aid they develop at the design time. For many DBMS [11], [22], [23],
the data base description they need must include the data implementation structure.
In this case, the designer is more deeply embedded in the data structuration. He
must define the access path to the data and many manipulation actions must
include the navigation in the logical access structure. For others DBMS [2], [9],
[16], [20], [28], [45], [32], the data base description is limited to the semantic
dimension. The task of the designer is to give a very complete representation of

the reality without any reference to the data implementation structure. Conversely,
the task of the DBMS is very complex.
At the design time it automatically chooses the data implementation structure and
automatically generates by interpretation of the declarative description all the
control and manipulation programs. In this solution, the error risks are minimized
particularly in the generation of the control programs. At the use time, the end
user communicates by non procedural languages with the data base. Any action on
the data is on the total control of the DBMS reducing the inconsistent actions
that could alterate the data.

### 1.4.2 Extension of the approach to the IS management

We postulate that it is pertinent and profitable to apply the previous approach
to IS management.
The IS we define is a more complete representation of the reality than a data
base because simultaneously it includes a static schema (equivalent to the data
schema) and a dynamic schema representing the interconnection between objects,
operations and events. The more complex the reality the designer wants to represent completely the more difficult the IS design and use without an automatic aid.
So we propose to realize an Information System Management System (ISMS) analogous
to the DBMS. The Information System Management System will assume several functions : at the design time, it chooses the physical implementation, it generates
the physical structure and controls the creation of the information system. This
generation implies the creation of the algorithms corresponding to the operations
classes and to the commands controlling the interactions between the events
classes and the operations classes.

At the use time, it controls the dynamic evolution of the IS by the selection and
the execution of the operations related to any object state change recognized as
a real event.

If the scope of the ISMS is the same than for any DBMS one must admit that its
functions are more complete. Its functions include not only the consistent manipulation of the data but also the control of the operations on the data and the
control of the events that trigger these operations.

The ISMS works with an ISDEL description of the IS. Consequently the designer
using such ISMS will only provide a semantic description without any reference
to a physical implementation.

We examine now the ISMS functions.

### 1.4.3 ISMS functions and architecture

In our point of view, to manage the IS is to choose a technical solution to implement it, to make sure and to control the IS creation according to that solution and to manage the IS evolution over the time. Moreover, it is to give to
users the means to easily query and manipulate the IS.

The tool carries on four functions :

- IS internal structure generation,
- IS creation,
- IS evolution management,
- IS utilization.

Each function corresponds to a particular module M0, M1, M2, M3[*].

* We develop an ISMS prototype. It is designed as an extension of the SYNTEX [16]
DBMS. Modules M0, M1, M3 are operational (M1 only under some simplifying hypothesis). Module M2 is being developed. It will be operational by december 1981.


### 1.4.3.1 IS internal structure generation (Module M0)

The IS schema is described by a relations collection : the objects, the operations
and the events represented in the IS are described in a same way. Thus, we can
implement in the same way the c-objects, the c-operations, the c-events and their
links. The internal structure of the IS is the physical structure chosen for the
relations implementation. The ISMS utilizes one physical structuration model
and mapping rules between the external (relational) model and the internal model.
But the real choice depends on the relation range and the frequency and volume
of the modifications that may occur on these relations. The module M0 chooses an
internal structure for the considered IS and generates the description of this
structure in an appropriate language. This generation is carried out after a
consistency and completness  control of the IS description provided by the designer. The consistency controls bear upon the concepts use correctness. These
controls are implicitly described by the type definition of a relation. The completness  controls verify logical rules of synchronized presence of c-events and
c-operations acting upon a given c-object.


### 1.4.3.2  IS creation (Module M1)

The module M1 works out the IS creation from the collection of the real objects,
operations and events. This creation is controlled by the integrity constraints
verification. It is followed by the generation of the c-operations texts, the
triggers conditions and the c-events predicates in a programming language compatible with the data implementation choice according to the SYNTEX [16] DBMS.


### 1.4.3.3  IS evolution management (Module M2)

Our aim is to build an automaton able to represent the reality evolution. We name
this automaton "dynamics automaton". In this way, the IS is the permanent image
of the organization it represents. As an extension, we say that the IS and the
reality have the same behavior : once the automaton percieves a state change it
takes it into account, verifies if this state change is an event and triggers
the execution of the operations that correspond  to this event. Those operations
are the image of the organization reactions to real events. The automaton manages
the change from one IS state to another one. It manages the IS evolution in the
course of time.


### 1.4.3.4 IS use (Module M3)

We intend to define an user oriented language so that users can query and manipulate the IS without knowledge of its implementation. We have retained a predica-
tive type language, well conformed to the IS relational expression. It will be
possible to make queries on present and past objects states, on executed operations, on events that triggered these operations. Chiefly, it will pe possible
to inform the managers about the causes and consequences of any state change.
The passage from the data base to a more complete representation of real phenomena through an information system extends users information and increases their
capability to resolve problems. The module M3 generates access to IS contend from
user query declarations.
Consequently, the ISMS constitutes the interface between IS and the real world
perceiving of its users :

- a state change in the users universe of discourse will be submitted to module M2
(IS evolution management) that will effect the appropriate change in the IS if
this state change corresponds to the behaviour rules of the system expressed
through the conceptual schema. If not, the IS will remain completely unchanged.

- every query or manipulation of the IS must be submitted to module M3 (IS use)
that constitutes the only way to access IS contend.


### 1.4.4 The event processor

The event processor is composed of a set of mechanisms under the control of a
scheduler that activates them at the right moment. The scheduler operates according to the automaton functioning structure, i.e. the IS conceptual description.
In order to accomplish its task, the scheduler manages itself an informations
set that we name "reference data base".

These references are created either by the IS users and correspond to the description of the external events they perceived or by the automaton itself in the
case of internal events. By this way, the event processor constitutes the interface between IS and the real world evolution perceived by its users.

Two kinds of mechanisms are controlled by the scheduler : control mechanisms and
operating mechanisms [18]. The scope of the control mechanisms is :

- to recognize an object state change as an event belonging to a c-event,
- to identify the operations to trigger,
- to control if those operations can be triggered,
- to identify the operation triggering consequences,
- to update the IS.

The scope of the operating mechanism is to start and to control the execution of
the operations communicated to it by the control mechanisms. All these mechanisms
act upon the information system (figure 4).


### 1.4.4.2 The event processor description

To describe the event processor is to describe how it takes the decisions concerning the actions over the IS it has to perform after every produced state-change.
We describe it through its conceptual schema using the graphic conventions we have
introduced for the IFIP conferences management specification.

The event processor conceptual schema drawn in figure 4 represents its functioning
logic through the logical linkage of c-objects, c-events and c-operations causal
interrelations.

- the C-OPERATIONS of that schema represent the operating or the control operations of the automaton

- the C-OBJECTS of that schema are either the c-objects of the reference data
base (we name c-references) either the IS c-operations, c-events.

All the c-references are of the same nature : they describe some particular
states of IS c-objects, c-operations, c-events that concern the automaton.

- the C-EVENTS of that schema describe the c-reference state changes which are
pertinent for the automaton.

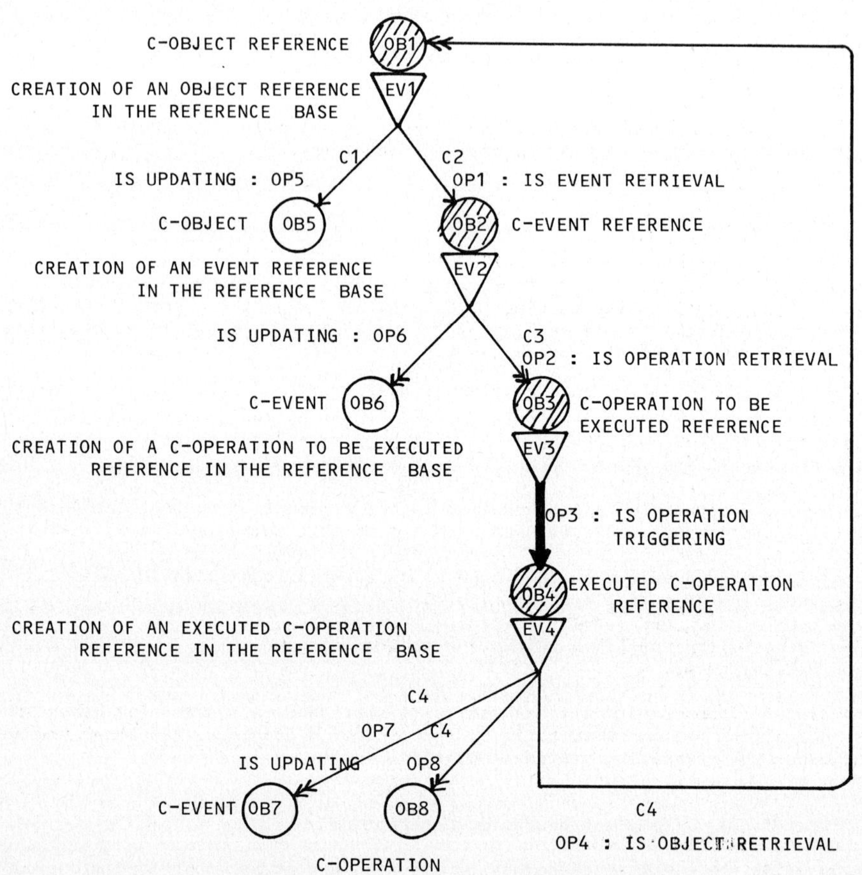


<u>Figure 4</u> : <u>event processor conceptual schema</u>

<u>CONDITIONS</u> :

C1 : the associated integrity constraints are fulfilled
C2 : the state change of the object is an event occurrence
C3 : the triggering conditions are fulfilled
C4 : all the operations associated to the processed event the triggering condi-
     tions of which were fulfilled have been executed.


<u>NOTATIONS</u>

        C-REFERENCE

$\longrightarrow$  Control mechanism

$\blacktriangleright$  Operating mechanism


This conceptual schema defines the functioning logic of the event processor.
It points out :

1) Its working primitives :

    i)      to recognize if a state change is an event (OP1)
    ii)     to determine the operations to trigger (OP2)
    iii)    to trigger the controlled execution of the operations (OP3)


2) Its impact on the system of the representations by the updatings of the information system (OP5, OP6, OP7) which stores the occurrences of C-OBJECTS,
C-OPERATIONS and C-EVENTS.

3) The informations that the event processor has to manage in order to insure a
correct functioning : they are references that describe the created C-OBJECTS,
C-OPERATIONS and C-EVENTS occurrences.

For every C-OBJECT occurrence(expressed by OB1) the event processor determines
which are the consequences in the system in using its conceptual description :

- it determines if the C-OBJECToccurrence can induce a C-EVENT occurrence(OP1)
- if true (OB2 creation) it updates the system (OP5 creates OB6 : creation of a
C-EVENT relation occurrence)and determines which are the C-OPERATIONS to trigger
(OP2)
- it triggers and controls their executions, relfects the consequences of these
operations on the system (OP6, OP7, OP8 : creation of C-EVENT, C-OPERATION, and
C-EVENT relations occurrences and determines if the state changes induced by
these operations are events (conditional triggering of OP1 (C2) by EV1 associated to OB1 created by OP4) and if they are, determines and triggers the resulting
actions.

We limit the ISMS presentation to the previous paragraphs, else the paper should
become too much large. The reader can find in [27] and [41] a more detailed
presentation of the different ISMS elements.

1.5  FIRST PART CONCLUSION

We experiment for several years our research results on the design and implementation of large and integrated information systems for electronics industry
firms, administrations and hospitals.

From our experience of IS design, we can assume the following conclusions :

1) The interest to define a conceptual solution

2) The necessity to dispose of a set of precise concepts allowing a rigourous
analysis and design

3) The advantage for projects management to use a complete method grounded on
a formal model . We have developed such a method based on the IS conceptual
schema which is today used for the design of complex IS implying automatic data
processing, network communication and real time response [36]. As we want to
keep the paper not too large and as the model is the key element of the conceptual level to which all the others elements (language, method, tools) are bound
up, we have not presented the method here.

Our effort is now devoted to the ISMS development to enforce our approach.

SECOND SECTION : INTERNAL LEVEL

The IS physical schema completes the description issuing from the conceptual step
in dealing with :

1. the specificity of the IS utilization its users intend to make
2. the technical parameters.

We assume to work in a current technical environment in which the data are managed
through a navigational type DBMS and the programs are written down through languages compatible with the DBMS. According to this hypothesis, the synchronization is worked out on the one hand by the IS managers that trigger the programs
and transactions executions at the convenient time and on the other hand by the
DBMS that manages the data access concurrency.

The internal schema is constituted by two complementary sub-schemas :

- the data structuration sub-schema
- the processes synchronization sub-schema

Both are presented in this section ( section 2.1   and  2.2 ). The c-objects
collection is the starting point for the data structuration sub-schema definition.
That of the c-operations and the c-events is the starting point for the processes
synchronization sub-schema (see figure 5).

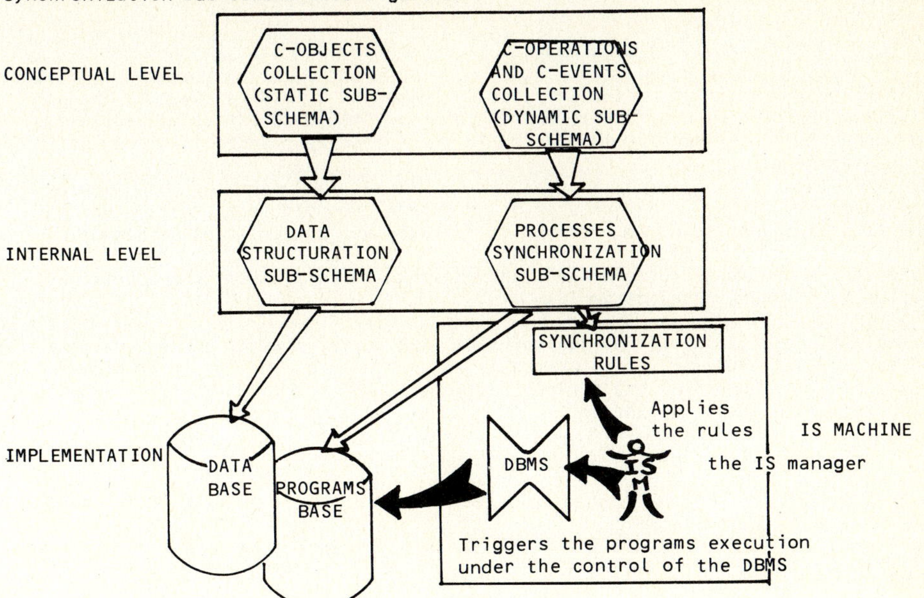


Figure 5 : IS design and implementation process

## 2.1  DATA STRUCTURATION SUB-SCHEMA

The data structuration sub-schema issues from a modeling step that deals with :

- the conceptual static sub-schema (the c-objects collection)
- the permanent or aleatory information needs of the IS users
- the capabilites and constraints of the DBMS that will be used to operate
the data base.

The designer has to define how the data must be stored in the storage space to
correctly and completely answer to the informations requirements of the future
data base users. So he must express the solution through a structure that points
out both the data gatherings and the logical paths among them.

The first difficulty of this step lies in the inventory of the needs to take
into account. This inventory includes those expressed during the analysis by
the future base known users but it must be able to integrate the new requirements.
The second difficulty is related to the amount of feasible solutions. The needs
complexity can lead the designer to multiply the access functions to navigate
more easily in the storage space. This issues in redundancy that he otherwise
has to minimize. So the internal schema constitutes a critical compromise between
the redundancy, the structure complexity and the additional programming charge.
Finally, the third difficulty arises from the DBMS itself, with its particularities, capabilities and constraints.


### 2.1.1   The steps of the method

To increase the solution portability, we recommend to introduce the DBMS characteristics as later as possible to better point out the compromises it implies
independently of the other compromises. So the method we propose involves two
steps (figure 6) :

-the first one allows to define a standard schema grounded on a general logical
model. It is supported by no DBMS but it includes all the existing data models.

- the second one leads to turn the standard schema into a specific one well
adapted to the DBMS characteristics.

We explain these two steps through both the IFIP conferences management example
and the SOCRATE DBMS [10]. This method is fully presented in [4]. It is perma-
nently used in industrial and administrative applications for five years (about
a hundred of implemented systems).

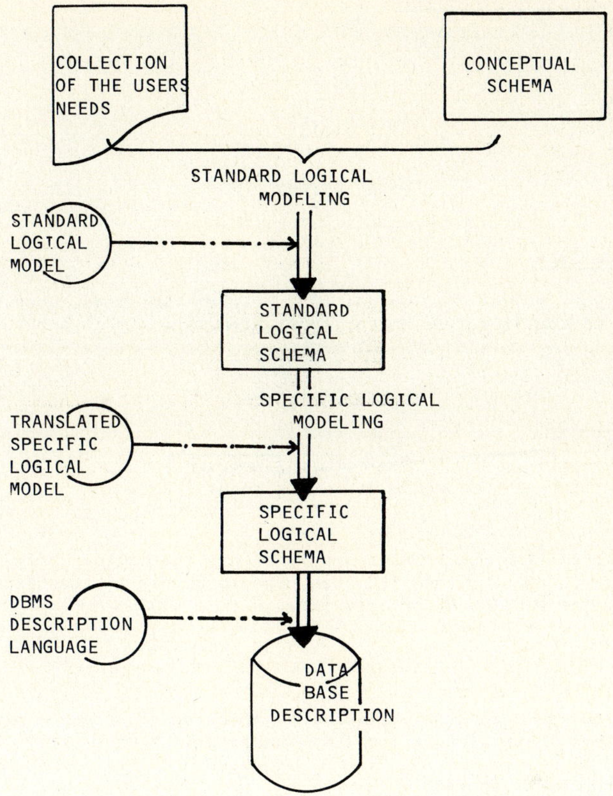



Figure 6 : The logical structuration process

2.1.2  The standard schema definition step

2.1.2.1 The standard model

The standard model is based upon four concepts :

a) the item type
b) the access function type
c) the entry function type
d) the order relation type

a) the item type

It is the elementary gathering of the data stored in the storage space. It is logically accessed as a whole by one time. It corresponds to the DBMS access unit and is therefore equivalent to the file structure notion. It is defined by :

- one entity type that allows the DBMS to refer the item type occurrences and to discriminate them without knowing the contend of their values. So it is equivalent to the surrogate notion [15].
- several data types corresponding to the values stored in the data base.

<u>example</u> : <u>Technical Committee item type</u>

b) <u>The access function type</u>

The access function type defines the logical link between two items types.
It is described by a source item type and a target item type. It is generally
named.

<u>example</u> :

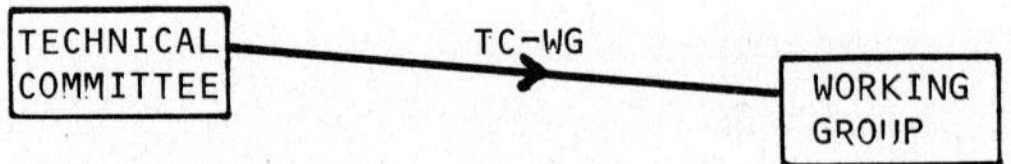


The TC-WG access function type occurrences are functions that allow  from
every occurrenceof the TECHNICAL-COMMITTEE item type to access the corresponding
occurrences (0,1,n) of the WORKING-GROUP item type.

c) <u>The entry function type</u>

The entry function type is an access function type allowing to access a given
item type of the storage space without a previous access to another item type.

   c1) The system entry function type

It is a particular entry function type involving only one element that can be
viewed as the data base name (we name it ENTRY). Then it is possible to define
access functions types of which the sources are ENTRY and the targets are items
types. That amounts to define an item type which is the data base entry point.

<u>Example</u> :

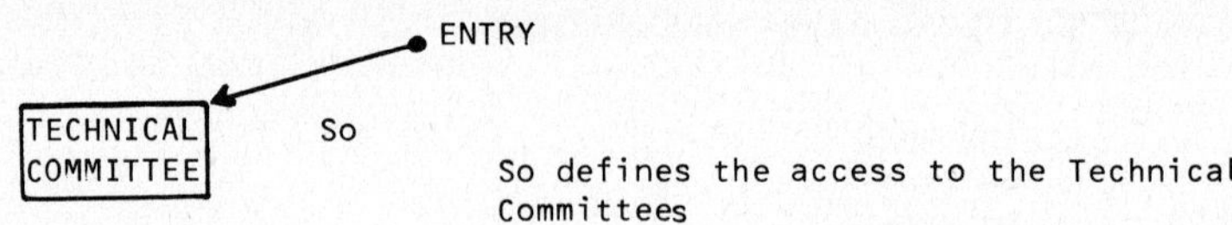


So defines the access to the Technical
Committees

   c2) The entry by data type function type

This entry function type allows to access an item type from data types related
to it either directly or through otheritems types to which it is connected.

Example :

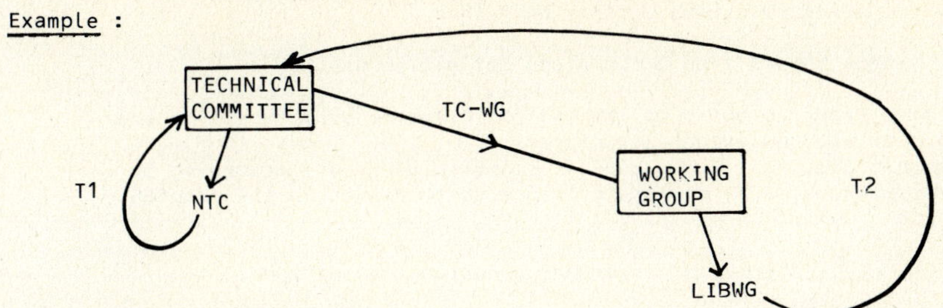


T1 corresponds to the access to the Technical Committee of which the identification number is given.
T2 corresponds to the access to the Technical Committee of which a Working Group
has a given name.


     c3) The entry by data type and item type function type

This entry function type allows to access an item type from on the one hand data
related (directly or not) to this item type and on the other hand items types
connected by access paths to the accessed item type.

Example :

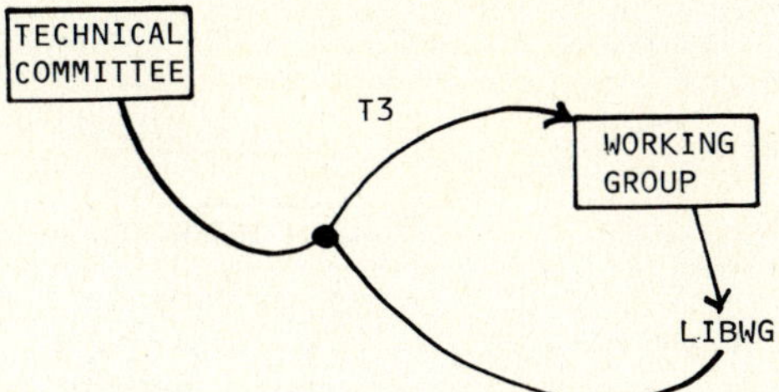


T3 permits to access one occurrence of the WORKING-GROUP item type of which the
system knows its designation and the Technical Committee to which it belongs.


d) The order relation type

The order relation type allows to define an order over the sets of given items
types occurrences. It bears upon an access function type or an entry function
type. It requires to precise both on which criteria or on which data type of
the item type and in which sense the order must be established.

Example : On the TC-WG access function type, we can define the order
          ORD1 : NWG ↗

### 2.1.2.2 The standard schema definition method

The standard schema issues from a two steps definition process :

- the first step leads to build up the maximal standard structure from the interpretation of the conceptual structure
- the second step aims to fit the maximal standard structure according to the users informations needs and their frequence to result in the adapted standard schema.

#### 2.1.2.2.1  The maximal standard structure definition

The maximal standard structure derives from the conceptual structure by the application of three basic rules :

<u>Rule 1</u> : For every c-object, create an item type.

That amounts to define the item type semantics : an item type represents a time-consistent aspect of a real objects class or a real objects associations class.

<u>Rule 2</u> : Examine every item type A and for every data type D which is key of a conceptual schema relation represented by an item type B, both create an access function type from A to B and eliminate the data type D of the item type A.

<u>Example</u> :

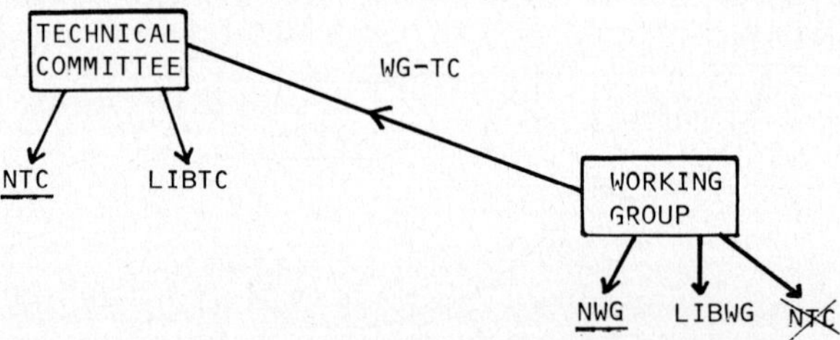


That amounts to define the access function type semantics : it represents at the logical level the links between objects or associations classes expressed in the conceptual schema through the permanent functional dependency between the keys identifiers.

<u>Rule 3</u> : Create an access function type from every item type A to the other items types involving as data type the key identifier of the relation described by the item type A.

<u>Example</u> :

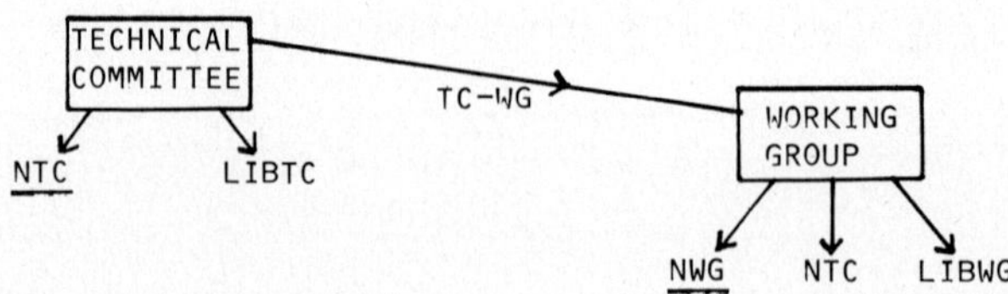


This rule expresses another aspect of the conceptual semantics : the association between an object and n objects of a same class.

### 2.1.2.2.2  Transformation into the adapted standard schema

The modifications of the maximal standard structure belong to the three following
types :

1) Adjunction or suppression of access functions types

2) Introduction of the entry functions types

3) Definition of the order relations types


1) The suppression of an access function type occurs when either no user requirement justifies to keep this function into the adapted standard schema or the
low frequence of a requirement does not justify its integration in the data base
and consequently its permanent cost support.

The adjunction of an access function type is made to increase the data base
access performances. A frequent and urgent informations requirement justifies
to set up a direct access function between two items types whereas the maximal
standard structure leads to fullfil this requirement through a sequence of
access functions issuing in performances decreasing.


2) The entry functions types speed up the access to the occurrences of the item
type on which they are defined. Consequently, we will determine the entry
functions types to introduce in the maximal standard structure according to both
the accesses we have to make to the items types and their frequences.


3) The analysis of both the users needs and the processes we intend to run over
the data base highlights some privileged logical sequences that we will introduce
in the logical structure description.

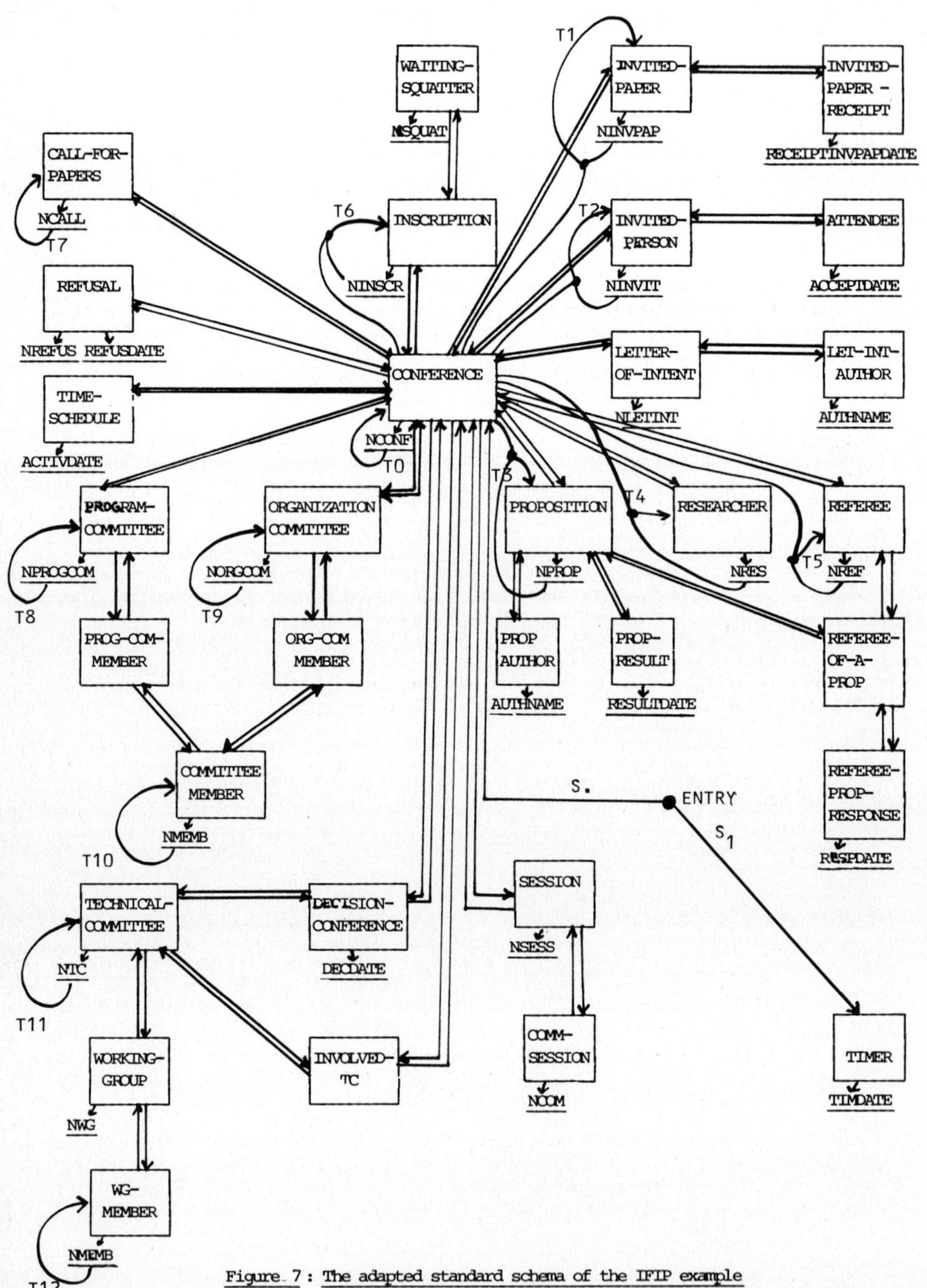


Figure 7 : The adapted standard schema of the IFIP example

### 2.1.3   The specific logical schema definition step

The designer introduces through this step some new compromises due to the DBMS
that involves not necessarily all the capabilities implied by the standard access
model. We propose to deal with this step in two times :

1) to make a comparison between the DBMS data structuration model and the standard model
2) to translate the adapted standard schema into the specific logical schema
according to the previous comparison.

#### 2.1.3.1  Definition of the correspondence board with the DBMS model

The correspondence board between the standard access model concepts and the
studied DBMS concepts points out that the DBMS

1) involves some concepts of the standard access model without any limitation
on these concepts. Sometimes, we dispose of several alternative DBMS concepts
for a same standard access model concept.
2) involves some concepts of the standard access model but with some limitations.
3) does not involve some concepts of the standard access model.

In the first **case,** the adapted standard schema can be translated without any
change into the DBMS description language. In the two other cases, the adapted
standard schema must be modified

- either in introducing some redundancy to palliate the lack of access functions
or entry functions
- either in creating complementary access functions or entry functions
- or in transfering to manipulation programs the entry functions or access functions that cannot be directly supported by the DBMS (access programming in place
of access functions and entry functions).


#### 2.1.3.2 Specific logical schema definition

Let us otherwise notice that the specific logical schema definition must integrate
some parameters that were not considered before, as they were not previously
necessary :

- number of the different items types and description complexity of each one
- frequence and modalities of the access functions and entry functions use. We
intend as modalities the use we make of the accessed item type informations :
creation, modification, deletion or reading.

These parameters can lead to compromises and to a wide solutions range. The
choice and interest of each solution depend upon each case : creation or suppression of entry functions or access functions, suppression of items types
to integrate them in other items types (this is another way to wittingly
introduce some redundancy),etc...

The specific logical schema is the expression of the adapted logical schema
(eventually reduced and transformed) through the DBMS description language.
In the paper continuation, we present the correspondence board with the
SOCRATE DBMS and the data base description through the DBMS language.

2.1.3.3 SOCRATE DBMS case

a) Correspondence board between standard model and SOCRATE model

| STANDARD ACCESS MODEL CONCEPTS | SOCRATE DATA MODEL CONCEPTS |
|---|---|
| ITEM TYPE | ENTITE (entity) |
| DATA TYPE | CARACTERISTIQUE (characteristic)<br>it can belong to the following types :<br>- word<br>- numeric<br>- list of values<br>- text<br>one can otherwise gather the characte-<br>ristics under a same identifier in<br>building imbricated <u>blocks</u> |
| ENTITY TYPE | REPERE (reference) of occurrence (it<br>is implicit) |
| ACCESS FUNCTION TYPE | ANNEAU (ring function)<br>it is an access function connecting<br>one occurrence of a source entity to<br>o or n occurrences of a target entity<br><br>REFERENCE (reference function)<br>it is an access function converse of<br>the ring that connects one occurrence<br>of a source entity to one and only<br>one occurrence of a target entity.<br>The reference function can be declared<br>independently of the ring function.<br>But if the ring function exists, the<br>reference function which is its con-<br>verse function is systematically asso-<br>ciated to it<br><br>IMBRICATION D'ENTITES (entities imbrica-<br>tion) It is an access function implicitly<br>declared in imbricating several entities<br>issuing in an arborescent hierarchical<br>structure |
| ENTRY FUNCTION TYPE<br>SYSTEM ENTRY FUNCTION TYPE | ENTITE DE PREMIER NIVEAU (first level<br>entity)<br>it is an access function implicitly de-<br>clared over every entity which is not<br>imbricated |
| ENTRY BY DATA TYPE FUNCTION TYPE | INVERSE sur UNE valeur d'une caractéris-<br>tique (INVERSE on ONE value of a charac-<br>teristic) |
| . DISCRIMINANT | Characteristic declared CLE UNIQUE (unique<br>key) |
| . NOT DISCRIMINANT | Characteristic declared CLE (key) |
| ORDER RELATION | ORDRE DE CREATION DES REALISATIONS (occur-<br>rences creation order) for the occurrences<br>of a first level entity<br>ORDRE DES VALEURS D'UNE CLE (order of the<br>values of a key) for the occurrences of a<br>ring function. |

b) <u>SOCRATE specific logical schema definition</u>

We present (figure 8) the SOCRATE specific logical schema of the IFIP example
through the following graphic conventions

ENTITE (SOCRATE entity)

IMBRICATION D'ENTITES (entities imbrication) : the arrow
                           points on the imbricated entity

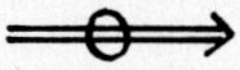

ANNEAU (ring function with its reference function) : the
                           arrow points on the ring function
                           target entity

REFERENCE (reference function) : the arrow points on the
                           reference function target entity

<u>Characteristics</u>          CLE (key)

Value                        INVERSE (inverse)

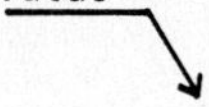

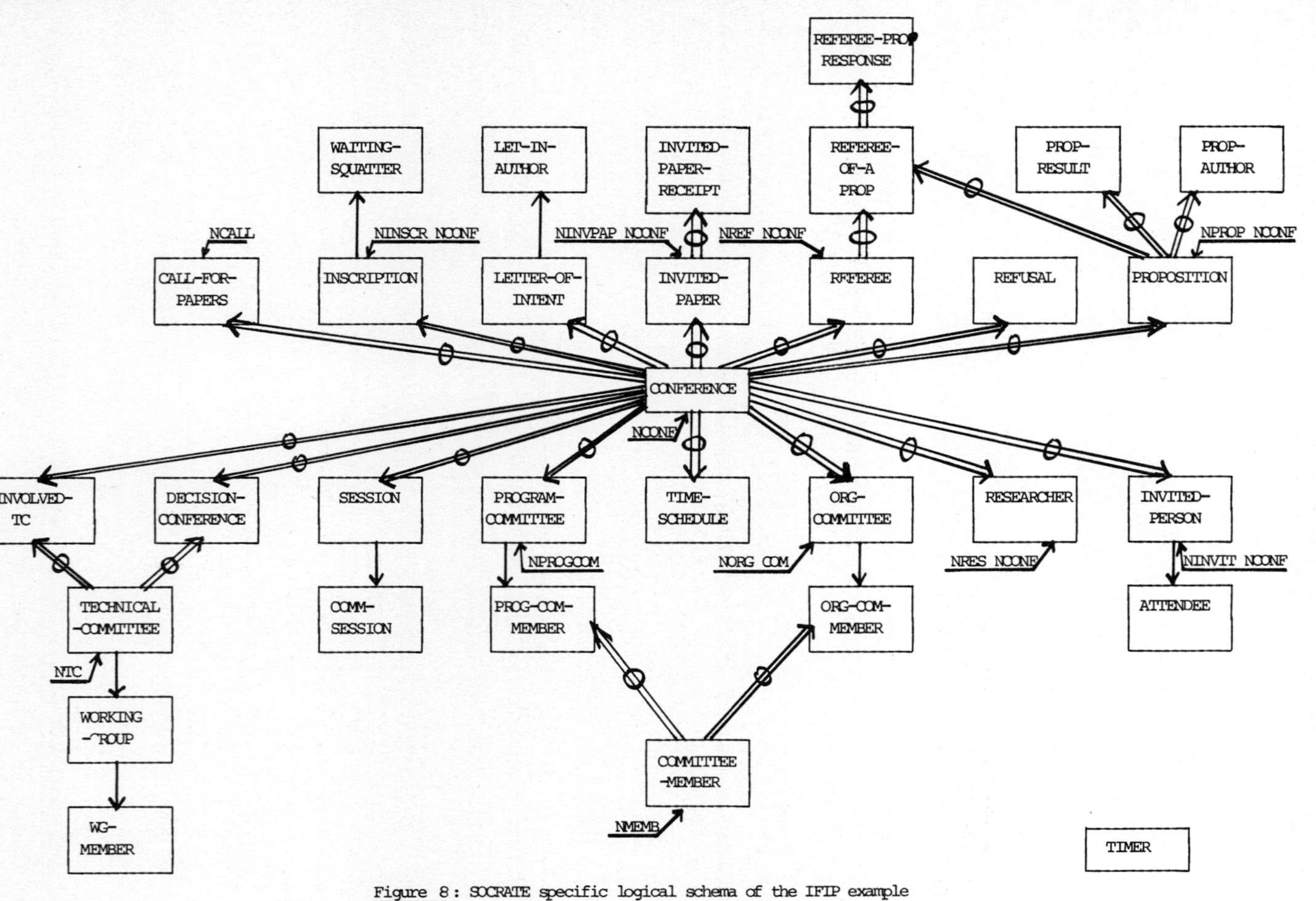



Figure 8 : SOCRATE specific logical schema of the IFIP example

## 2.2 PROCESSES SYNCHRONIZATION SUB-SCHEMA

The processes synchronization sub-schema issues from a modeling step that
deals with :

- the conceptual dynamic sub-schema (the c-events and c-operations sub-schema)
- the IS use conditions defined by the future users
- the technical environment that will support the IS operating.

The designer has to define how the conceptual operations must be gathered into
modules, the triggering conditions of these modules and the sequencing rules of
the modules executions. As we have seen for the static schema, the designer has
to deal with some difficulties issuing in compromises.

The first difficulty is related to the wide range of possible solutions. The
designer has to find a fair compromise between the definition of independent
modules gathering many elementary operations but involving redundancy and the
definition of more elementary modules but strongly interdependent. The second
difficulty lies in the determination of the IS use conditions that must allow
the designer to define the IS operating choices (real time events processing,
delayed events processing, remote batch processing,...).
Finally, the third difficulty arises from the IS technical environment he has
to take into account.

The methodical solution we propose is grounded on a logical processes synchronization model and methodical rules to translate the conceptual dynamic sub-
schema into a logical processes synchronization sub-schema. We present now
both aspects and their use in the IFIP proposed example case.


### 2.2.1 Logical processes synchronization model

This model involves two concepts : the module concept and the trigger concept.

A module is a sequence of statements performed in that order, available by its
name and having one and only one entry point. It is described by a block or a
procedure with ONE input parameter and SEVERAL output parameters. It is represented by a rectangle including its name (the only access way to the module
statements).

Example :

A trigger is a condition (or a predicate) bearing on the IS state and allowing
to trigger the execution of one and only one module. This condition can be named
and becomes by this way available by its name. It is described by a condition
text (expressed through a programming language) or by a boolean function. It can
be fulfilled either after the execution of one or several given modules (internal
trigger) or after the arrival of a stimulus from outside the system (external
trigger). It is represented by a lozenge including its name.

Example :



An edge oriented from a trigger to a module expresses that the trigger causes
the module execution. Conversely, an edge oriented from a module to a trigger
expresses that the module execution contributes to the trigger validation.

A modules synchronization schema (MSS) is a 2-alternate graph over both the modules set and the triggers set, i.e. a graph in which a module type vertex always follows a trigger type vertex and conversely.

The constraints related to the triggers (a trigger bears on <u>one</u> module and can be validated by <u>several</u> modules) and the modules (a module has one and only one access point) imply that every modules synchronization schema is built from three basic structures :


1) the "linear" structure

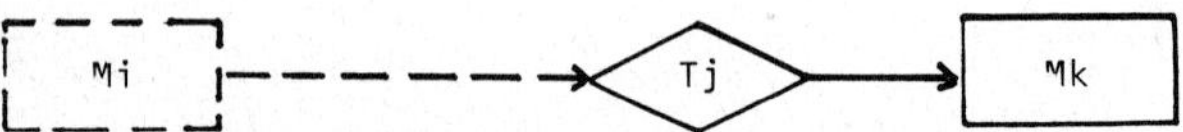

It expresses that a trigger Tj bearing on a module Mk is either an external one or validated by only one module Mi


2) The "fork" structure

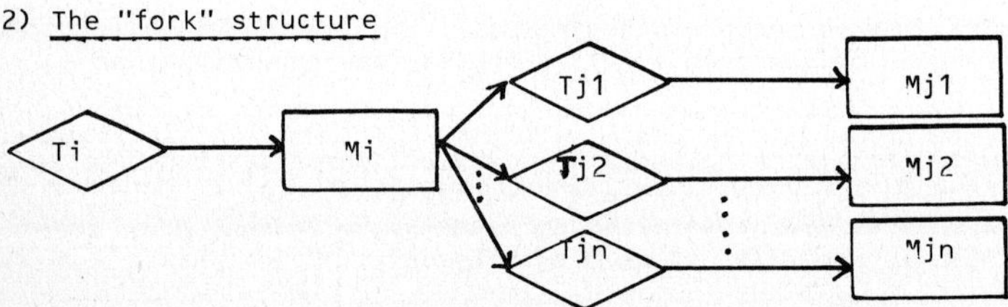

It expresses that the execution of a module Mi induced by the trigger Ti may issue in the triggerings of the executions of modules Mj1 and/or Mj2 and/or ... and/or Mjn by the triggers Tj1, Tj2,..., Tjn.


3) The "join" structure

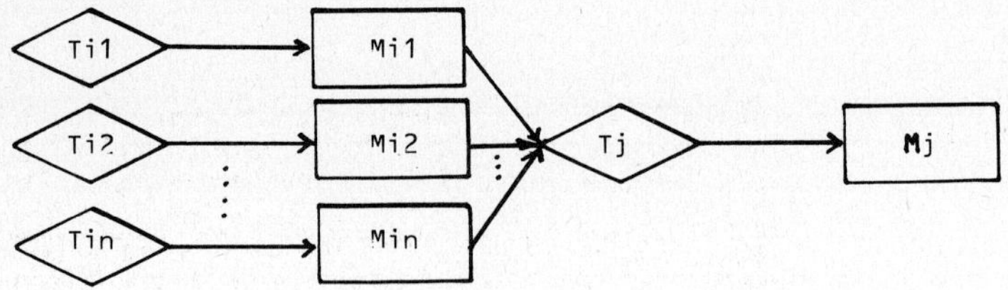

It expresses that the trigger Tj bearing on the module Mj can be validated by the execution of either a module Mi1 due to the trigger Ti1, either a module Mi2 due to the trigger Ti2,..., or a module Min due to the trigger Tin.


2.2.2  The definition rules of a modules synchronization schema

We propose five rules to translate the dynamic conceptual schema into a modules synchronization schema.

### 2.2.2.1 Rule 1 : elementary modules definition

We name "dynamic cycle" the sequence of the dynamic conceptual sub-schema involving

- a c-event EVj
- the c-operations $OP^k j$ it triggers
- the c-objects these c-operations modify

Then an <u>elementary module</u> Mj is constituted by the statements implementing all the c-operations of a dynamic cycle. Its input parameter is the c-object associated to the c-event of this cycle and its output parameters are the c-objects of the cycle the state changes of which could become c-events.

<u>Example</u> :

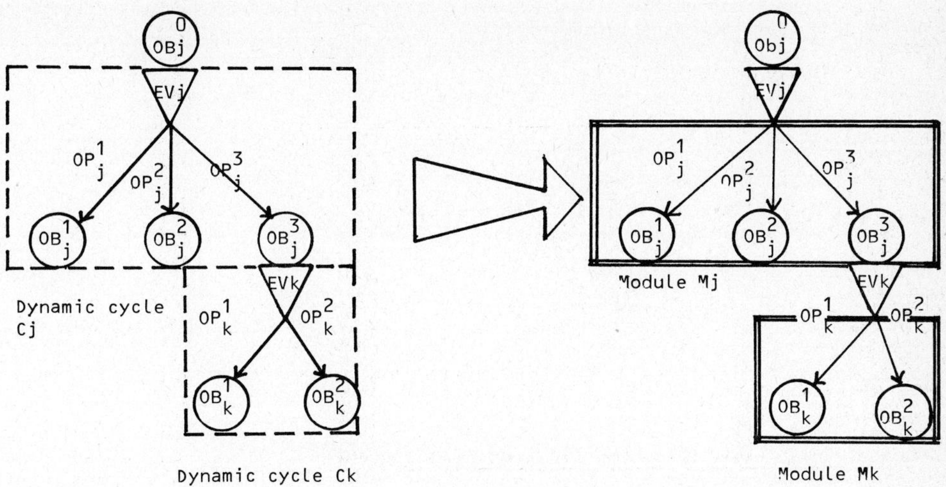


<u>Module Mj specification</u> :
- input parameter : $OBj^0$
- output parameters : $OBj^3$
- procedure body : the statements implementing $OPj^1$, $OPj^2$, $OPj^3$

<u>Module Mk specification</u> :
- input parameter : $OBj^3$
- output parameters : no output parameters
- procedure body : the statements implementing $OPk^1$, $OPk^2$.

### 2.2.2.2 Rule 2 : elementary modules concatenation

When we know a priori that an elementary module $M_j$ is always activated after an elementary module $M_i$ (the trigger of $M_j$ is always validated by the execution of $M_i$) it seems judicious to gather these two modules by concatenation (denoted $M_i.M_j$). So the trigger of $M_j$ has not to be computed after any execution of $M_i$.

We propose a systematic process to determine the modules concatenations we have to set up. It is grounded on the notion of chronological dependency between c-events [35] that we will now present.


A : <u>The graph of chronological dependencies between c-events</u>

1) <u>Direct Systematic Chronological Dependency (DSCD)</u> :

A c-event $EV_j$ is in DSCD with a c-event $EV_i$ if and only if

(i)   $EV_i$ triggers unconditionally a c-operation $OP_i^k$ that induces the state change of a c-object $OB_j$ ascertained by $EV_j$
(ii)  this state change always defines an event belonging to the $EV_j$ type ($EV_j$ always follows $EV_i$)


<u>Example</u> :

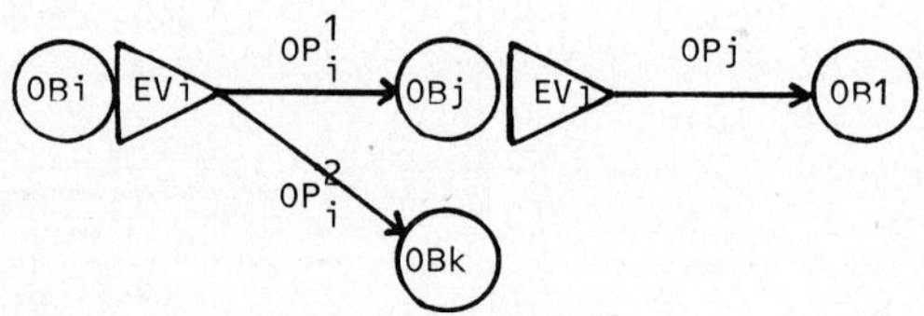


As $EV_j$ is always the state change induced by $OP_i^1$, $EV_j$ is in DSCD with $EV_i$ (denoted $EV_i \xrightarrow{s} EV_j$).


2) <u>Direct Conditional Chronological Dependency (DCCD)</u> :

A c-event $Ev_j$ is in DCCD with a c-event $EV_i$ if and only if

(i)   $EV_i$ triggers a c-operation $OP_i^k$ that induces the state change of a c-object $OB_j$ ascertained by $EV_j$
(ii)  either $EV_i$ triggers conditionally $OP_i^k$, or the state change induced by $OP_j^k$ does not always define an event belonging to the $EV_j$ type ($EV_j$ may follow $Ev_i$).


<u>Example</u> :

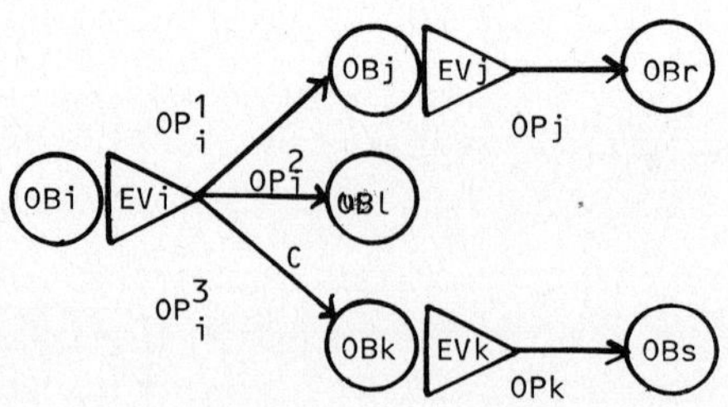

. EVi unconditionally triggers $OP_i^1$ but the state change of OBj induced by $OP_i^1$ is not always an event belonging to the EVj type. Consequently, EVj is in DCCD with EVi (denoted EVi $\xrightarrow{c}$ EVj).

. EVi conditionally triggers $OP_i^3$, consequently EVk is in DCCD with EVi (denoted EVi $\xrightarrow{c}$ EVk).


3) <u>The graph of chronological dependencies</u>

It is the graph that involves all the chronological dependencies (DSCD or DCCD) of a given conceptual dynamic sub-schema.


B : <u>Modules concatenation rule (Rule 2)</u>

<pre>
┌─────────────────────────────────────────────────────────────┐
│  (1)    EVi ───s──→ EVj ⟹  Mi . Mj                          │
│                                                               │
│  (2)    EVi ───c──→ EVj ⟹  Choice : either MI . Tj . Mj     │
│                                    or Mi, Mj separate         │
└─────────────────────────────────────────────────────────────┘
</pre>

(1) If a c-event EVj is in DSCD with a c-event EVi, EVj always follows EVi. Consequently, the module Mj associated to EVj will always follow the module Mi associated to EVi. Therefore it is unnecessary to compute the trigger associated to Mj. That's why we propose in this case the systematic concatenation of Mj to Mi (denoted Mi . Mj).

(2) If a c-event EVj is in DCCD with a c-event EVi, EVj may follow EVi. Consequently, the module Mj associated to EVj may follow the module Mi associated to EVi. In this case, it is necessary to compute the condition defining the trigger of Mj. We are then faced with the following alternative : either we concatene the two modules in inserting the computation of the trigger of Mj between them (Mi.Tj.Mj) or we keep the two modules Mi and Mj separate (a way to solve this alternative is to choose either the less expensive solution or the fastest solution, according to the technical constraints we have to deal with).


C : <u>Consequences of the modules concatenation rule</u>

    C1 <u>Elementary modules duplication</u>

When the graph of chronological dependencies points out that a c-event EVk is dependent of several c-events (for example EVi and EVj), the application of the modules concatenation rule may issue in the duplication of the module Mk associated to EVk.

- <u>First case</u> :There are only direct systematic chronological dependencies. So EVk is in DSCD with both EVi and EVj. That is expressed in the graph by a situation of the following kind

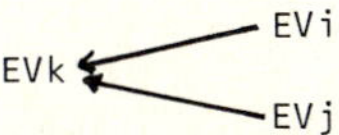

in which ──→ denotes the DSCD relation. The application of the modules concatenation rule implies the concatenation of Mk to Mi (Mi.Mk) and to Mj (Mj.Mk) which is graphically expressed as

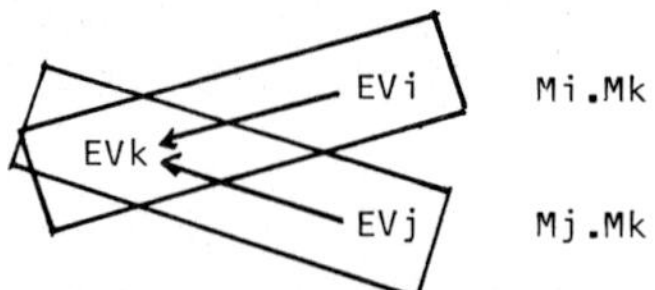


and the module Mk must be duplicated in the modules Mi.Mk and Mj.Mk.


- <u>Second case</u> : There are some direct conditional chronological dependencies. So, assume that EVk is in DSCD with EVi and in DCCD with EVj. That is expressed in the graph by a situation of the following kind.

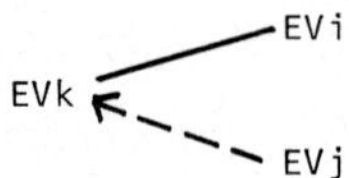


In which————►denotes the DCCD relation. The application of the modules concatenation rule issues in

- either two modules (Mi.Mk) and (Mj.Tk.Mk) implying the duplication of Mk
- or a module (Mi.Mk) and two separate modules Mj and Mk implying the duplication of Mk in (Mi.Mk) :

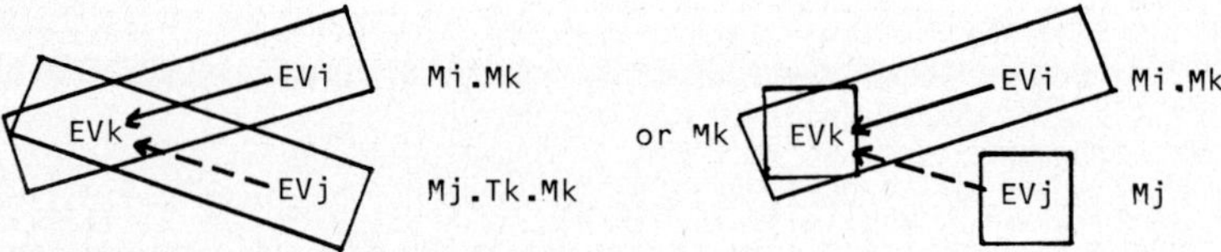


<u>C2) Interdiction of elementary modules duplication</u>

Conversely, as the graph of chronological dependencies points out that a c-event EVi is a source of several dependencies (for example with EVj and EVk) we do not have to duplicate the module Mi associated to EVi. Else, as the condition associated to the trigger of Mi will be fulfilled, Mi will be activated several times (two, in the case of our example : once in (Mi.Mj) and once in (Mi.Mk)). Moreover that will issue in a trigger bearing on several modules, and that is inconsistent with the trigger definition of our model.


<u>D) Successive applications of the concatenation rule</u>

We apply the previously defined concatenation rule  in a recursive way until all the judicious gatherings have been made. That issues in the definitive set of modules that will appear in the modules synchronization schema corresponding to the conceptual description.


### 2.2.2.3 Rule 3 : Triggers definition

The condition associated to the trigger Tj of a module Mj resulting from the application of rules 1 and 2 is the translation of the predicate defining the c-event of the first dynamic cycle of Mj. That justifies that a trigger bears only on one module, as a c-event corresponds to only one dynamic cycle.

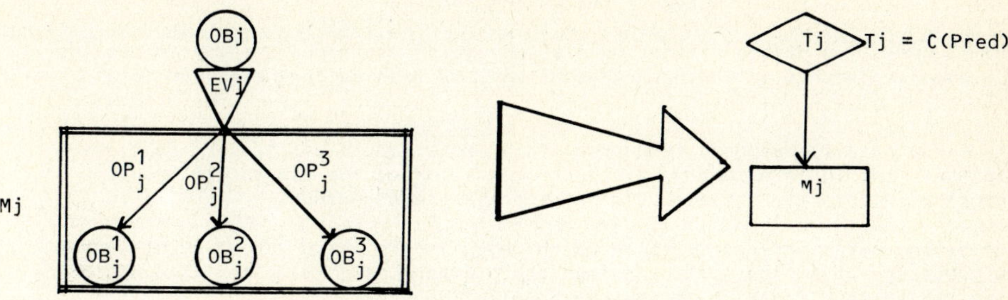


### 2.2.2.4 Rule 4 : Independent modules definition

In a technical environment where the IS machine does not involve synchronization mechanisms, it may be in the designer's interest to build up a set of independent modules. So he can be sure that the triggering of the modules by the users will not induce inconsistencies due to a bad respect of the synchronization rules.

Then,
> to build up a set of independent modules amounts to build a module for every connected component of the graph of chronological dependencies.

A connected component Ci of the chronological dependencies graph is defined as :
A connex component Ci of the chronological dependencies graph is defined as :

$$Ci/EVi = \left\{ EVj \ / \ EVi \xrightarrow{+} EVj \right\}$$

in which $\xrightarrow{+}$ denotes the strict transitive closure of the direct chronological dependency relation defined as the union of the DSCD relation and the DCCD relation.

Example :

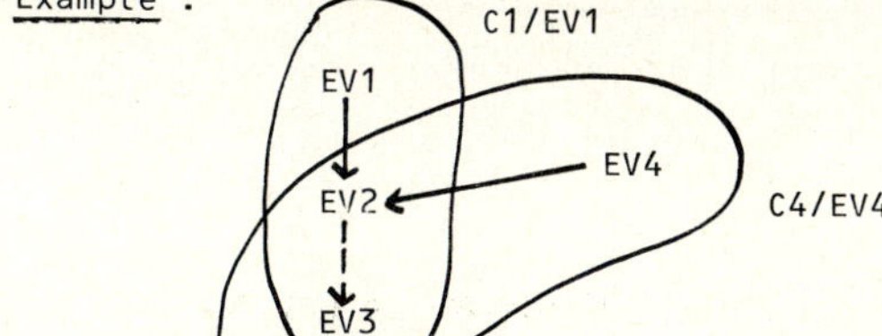


C1/EV1 and C4/EV4 are the two connected components of this graph. The application of the rule 4 implies the definition of two independent modules (M1.M2.T3.M3) and (M4.M2.T3.M3).

This example highlights a general situation : the definition of independent modules often issues in the duplications of a great number of modules.

### 2.2.2.5 Rule 5 : Events processing choices

The IS operating method defined by its end users determines the way to process the events : either in an instantaneous way, as soon as they occur or in a delayed way.

The first case corresponds to a "real time" solution in which every real event expressed through a data base state change validates the convenient trigger inducing by this way the execution of the associated module.

The second case corresponds to a "batch" solution in which a real events batch is processed at a time different from their occurring times. This kind of choice requires the modification of the synchronization schema.

Assume that we have obtained the following synchronization schema.

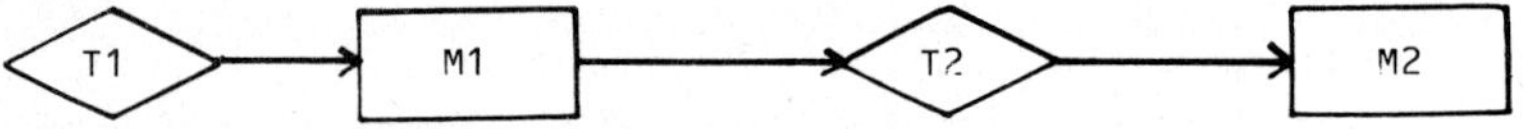


The choice to delay the execution of M1 to a date D leads :

1) To introduce a "calendar" type trigger TC that defines the date to which the events batch will be processed. TC triggers the module M1.

2) To introduce a particular module MS that stores the occurrences of the initial trigger T1 in the waiting file of module M1. MS is triggered by the initial trigger T1.

Then, the final synchronization schema is the following.

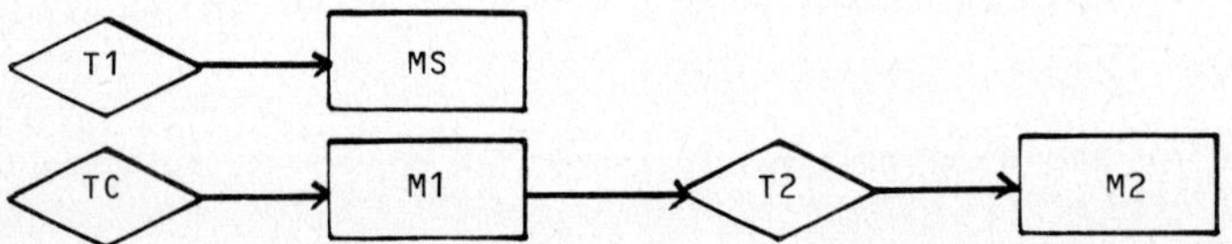


### II-23 Application to the IFIP conferences management case

The analysis of the dynamic conceptual sub-schema issues in the following graph of chronological dependencies between c-events :

| EV1 | EV2 |      | EV6 | EV9 |
|-----|-----|------|-----|-----|
| EV3 | EV4 | EV4' | EV7 | EVA |
|     | EV5 | EV5' | EV8 | EVB |

(EV7 → EV8)

This graph points out that there are really very few interactions between the different tasks worked out by the two committees. Except EV7 and EV8 (EV8 is in DSCD with EV7), all the other c-events are mutually independent. Therefore the logical solution is obvious. It involves twelve independent modules corresponding to the dynamic cycles respectively associated to EV1, EV2, EV3, EV4, EV4', EV5, EV5', EV6, EV9, EVA, EVB, EV7 . EV8. These twelve modules are triggered by twelve triggers associated to the twelve previous c-events (EV8 is gathered with EV7) :

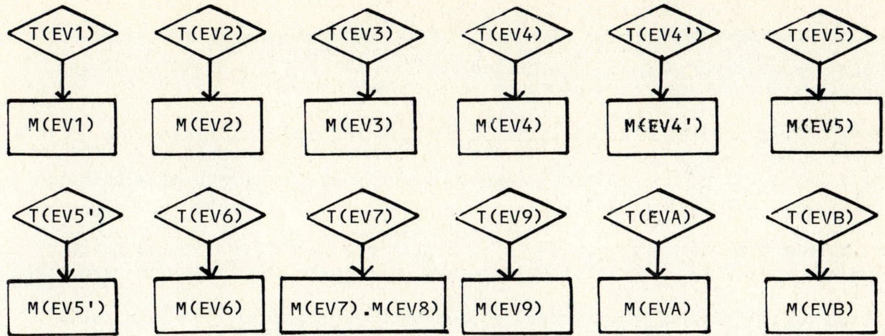

In the frame of the SOCRATE DBMS solution we have introduced in paragraph II-13
every module is a transaction expressed through the SOCRATE query language that
can be pre-compiled and triggered according to the real events arrival by the
application managers. We limit us to the presentation of the transaction  M(EV5)
text.

Assume that PROP-REF is the name of the SOCRATE reference function connecting
the PROP-AUTHOR entity to the PROPOSITION entity (see figure 8). Then the text
of the transaction M(EV5) is the following :

```
D X1 = UN PROP-AUTHOR
* X1 is the name of the "prop-author" entity occurrence the arrival of which
validates the trigger of M(EV5) *


G  UN INVITED-PERSON X2
   M NINVIT DE X2 = NUM DE X2
   M NCONF DE X2 =  NCONF DE X1
   M INVNAME DE X2 = AUTHNAME DE X1
   M INVADDR DE X2 = AUTHADDR DE X1
   M INVCOUNTRY DE X2 = AUTHCOUNTRY DE X1
   M INVSTATE DE X2 = U
FAIRE RECH
   SI RECEPTPROPDATE DE PROP-REF DE X1 < OR = PROPDEADLINE DE
      CALL-FOR-PAPERS AYANT NCONF = NCONF DE X1
      ALORS POUR TOUT RESEARCHER X3
            SI RESNAME ≠ AUTHNAME DE X1
            OU RESADDR ≠ AUTHADDR DE X1
            OU RESCOUNTRY ≠ AUTHCOUNTRY DE X1
               ALORS  M Y1 = 1
               SINON  M Y1 = 0    SORTIE DE RECH
               FIN
      FIN
   FIN
FIN

Si Y1 = 1     G    UN RESEARCHER X3
              M NRES DE X3 = NUM DE X3
              M NCONF DE X3 = NCONF DE X1
              M RESNAME DE X3 = AUTHNAME DE X1
              M RESADDR DE X3 = AUTHADDR DE X1
              M RESCOUNTRY DE X3 = AUTHCOUNTRY DE X1
FIN
```

## 2.3 SECOND SECTION CONCLUSION

Our several years experience in the method application for the building of the
data structuration schema leads us to point out the interest

- of the standard model to the analysis, understanding and evaluation of a
DBMS specific data model
- of the first level of the method (standard level) for the design of a solution
easily portable over several DBMS.

The more recent experience [38], [39] of the method application for the building
of the processes synchronization schema allows us to make the following comments :

- the graph of the chronological dependencies between c-events [35] is a tool
both powerful and simple for the processes structuration
- the methodological rules are sufficient and easy to use to result in all the
cases in a solution adapted to the users needs. Moreover, it guarantees the IS
consistency all over its evolution in the course of time.

### THIRD SECTION :  THE COMPUTER AIDED SYSTEM

The Computer Aided System (CAS) is a system to support the IS design and maintenance. It is controlled by an automaton named pilot that coordonates men and
convenient softwares able both to take the good decisions and to execute the
appropriate actions.

In this section, we will describe on the one hand the functions carried out by
tools and, on the other hand, the pilot and the piloting. In both cases, we
consider that the system intervenes during the conceptual step of IS design that
is to say within the definition of the IS conceptual schema.

## 3.1 FUNCTIONS CARRIED OUT BY COMPUTER-AIDED DESIGN TOOLS

### 3.1.1 What about an aid ?

To define the IS computer-aided design functions we have considered the qualities
that conceptual schema must respect and also the characteristics of any design
process.

We have determined three functions : Control, Integration, Documentation.

i) <u>The conceptual schema qualities</u>

The conceptual schema is an abstract expression of real phenomena to be represented in the IS. Building an IS from its CS is possible only if the latter is
correct. The qualities, which the CS has to respect, must aid the control of this
semantic description. They are :

- fidelity :

a translation of reality without indirect means and distortions,

- consistency :

so that it includes neither contradiction nor ambiguity,

- completness :

all aspects of phenomena are represented (but we take into account only the
part of the organization that is "useful").

ii) <u>The design characteristics</u>

The very nature of the IS design and implementation process leads the designer
to commit errors and to find difficulties all over this process. Indeed, according to the problems to be resolved, it is impossible that the CS should be
built directly, at one time, by one person. We consider that the design process
is modular and sedimentary and that the design is carried out by several designers.

a) <u>Modular</u> :

A module is, from our point of view, a unit of the CS description. A module
definition in the Remora conceptual language is called a "statement" ;

b) <u>Sedimentary</u> :

The different modules are not described only at one time but through successive
strata at different times ;

c) <u>Several designers</u> :

The description of the different modules is often given to different designers.


iii) <u>Functions</u>

Our reasoning, based upon these two components, allows us to determine three functions.

Indeed, to permit a modular description of CS leads us to control each module when it is defined. To control means that we check its consistency and fidelity. The first function to be carried out by CAS, or <u>Control Function</u>, aims to verify that a statement is itself correct.

To permit a sedimentary description of CS prescribes the control, when the modules are all together, of the fact that the set has always the required qualities (fidelity, completness, consistency). The second function, or <u>Integration Function</u>, has an object in view : to verify that the insertion of a statement, controlled by Control Function, into the statements already considered does not overthrow the qualities of the previously defined CS.

Designers describe real phenomena at several moments ; the CS description can be carried out by many designers : tools and men, as we said, interact in turn during IS design. To propose a third function, or <u>Documentation Function</u>, seems necessary ; this function, carried out by any CAS, aims to inform designer <u>and</u> automaton during the design process.


3.1.2 Control function

We have defined two types of control :

- consistency
- fidelity

i) <u>consistency controls</u>

Designers describe modules with the help of the conceptual model that CS must respect. Consistency controls then correspond to a check of the conceptual model integrity  constraints.

For instance, we must :

- control that any component of a C-object is in permanent (see paragraph I-12) functional dependency with the identifier,

- control that a C-operation modifies uniquely the state of one and only one C-object.

Any statement that does not respect these rules is called "unconsistent".


ii) <u>Fidelity controls</u>

To check the consistency of a statement is not enough for its validation. Indeed, a module description result can be consistent and also be a distorted representation of reality.

For instance : Data structure in CS, as we have defined it, is a system of c-objects gathered in c-classes. It can respect model integrity constraints an

yet some functional relation between two real objects can be not represented.
Therefore the description provided is not faithful to the real world.

Fidelity controls are feasible with difficulty and are related to artificial
intelligence. To carry them out, the only solution, in our opinion, consists
of having two descriptions of the same reality and controlling their semantical
equivalence.

For instance : the descriptive model (object, events, operations) permits the
expression of the functional relations between real objects perceived by  the
designer. A data structure based upon the conceptual model corresponds to this
collection of relations. We can control that all the functional relations of the
real world are found there even if they are not explicitly or directly represented.

Such controls are possible in Remora.


3.1.3  Integration Function

Suppose we have a, a collection of real phenomena, represented by A in CS.
A has the required qualities (consistency, fidelity, completeness). Suppose A',
image of the real phenomenon a', to be correct (checked by the control function).
We must now control that the new statement A' combines correctly into the
already described statements A or also that the relations between a and a' are
correctly represented by the relations between A and A', so that A and A' (=A'')
is correct, that is to say consistent, faithful, complete.

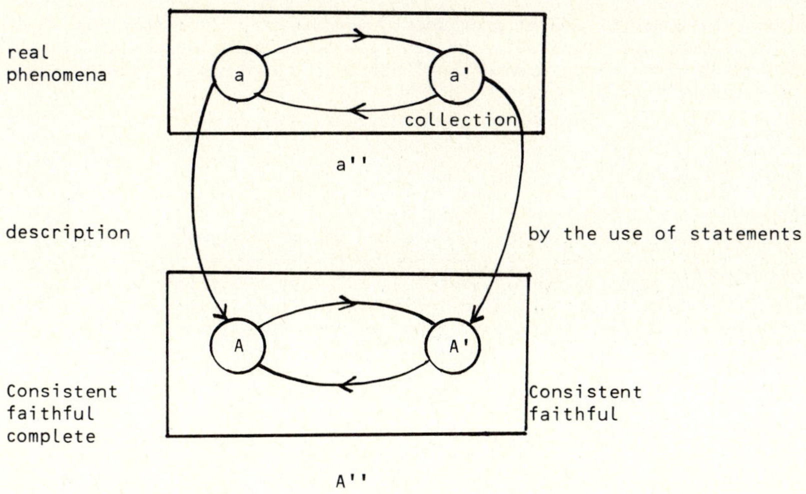


Figure 9 : Integration function


For instance : a C-class can be partially defined at a time to (first set of
C-objects), then completed at a time T1 by the introduction of a new C-object
into the C-class. We must check that the "new" C-class is correct.

Therefore, we find global consistency controls and fidelity controls as in the
Control Function. Here we introduce completness  control for checking that the

"new" built CS is still complete. These controls rely on the definition of completness  rules.

For example, in Remora, we must control that :

- any C-object of a C-class is created by at least one C-operation ;
- any C-operation is triggered by at least one C-event.


### 3.1.4   Documentation Function

Designers always need documentation about archieved and designed programs. This is the role of different documents written up at the different steps of analysis and programming of a problem. But, within big projects, documentation is so important that it is not possible to prescribe its manual update and systematic consultation. That is why much software based upon Data Dictionaries is proposed and we see how much better is the service : the system carries out the update of documentation, the designer can question (often by the use of a conversational language) all or only part of the information. But these dictionaries are in fact archieved during IS accomplishment and give only a technical view of the problem. In order to permit a better design, we think that it is necessary to propose, at the conceptual step, a documentary stock to be questioned at any time.

As the result of the conceptual step is a CS, we have chosen it to be a documentary stock. Also, in Remora, we have built the CS in the shape of a Data-Base managed by the DBMS SYNTEX [16] .

The algebraic query language of SYNTEX provides to the designer interrogation facilities to the documentary stock which he can call up at any time during his design work. Connected with the documentation function, we develop a graphic tool [44] able to draw the conceptual schema by means of a drawing table.


### 3.2 THE PILOT AND PILOTING

Let us recall that the computer aided design system, as we intend it in this paper, is constituted by a set of tools that realize the functions acting during the design and implementation process of an IS. These functions perpetually interact either between themselves or  with the designer according to a dynamic schema managed by a particular tool that we name Pilot.


### 3.2.1   The Pilot

It appears then, according to what we have just recalled, that the Pilot must take a triple part :

- it must recognize some given states which occur during the IS design and implementation process,

- according to those states, it must determine the actions to execute in order to ensure the correct development of this process (i.e. it has to determine which are the tasks that must be executed to carry out the design and implementation process),

- lastly, it must ensure the activation of the execution of these actions (or tasks)previously determined.

Thus, for instance, the Pilot must recognize the state corresponding to the
entry into the system of a statement to be analysed and thereafter according
to this recognized state, it must determine the actions corresponding to the
control function (defined in the previous paragraph), and, when these actions
are well-defined, it must ensure the activation of their execution. At the
same time as the recognition of the presence of a correct statement (i.e. a
statement which has fulfilled the control function), it has to determine the
actions corresponding to the integration function (also defined in the previous
paragraph) and it must ensure the activation of their execution.

In fact, we note, following Glushkov and Letichevskii [18], that the Pilot
defined in this way, is constituted of two parts :

- a Control Part (CP) corresponding to the aforesaid two first attributions,
- an Operational Part (OP) corresponding to the third of these attributions.

More exactly, what is the control part and what is the operational part ?

- The operational part, according to above, has a very simple function : it must
ensure the activation of the execution of the tasks that the Pilot has to activate in order to carry out the design and implementation process of an IS.

These tasks are determined by the control part of the Pilot.

- The control part must recognize some well-defined states, that is to say
that it has to recognize the presence of some events (according to the meaning
of "event" in our model) and, according to the presence (or the absence) of
these events, it must determine which are the actions to be executed in order
to carry out the IS design and implementation process, that is to say that the
control part has to determine both the manual and automatic tasks that must
be executed to carry out this design process.

For example, the CP of the Pilot must recognize the events "end of entry of a
statement to be analysed", "presence of a correct statement" (i.e. a statement
which has fulfilled the control function), and, thereafter, it has to determine
respectively the tasks corresponding to the control function and those corresponding to the integration function.

Since the CP of the Pilot has to recognize events and must consequently determine the tasks to be executed in order to carry out the IS design and implementation process, an axhaustive inventory of events to be recognized by the Pilot
and their consequences must be provided. For example, if we limit ourselves to
the simple case of a statement analysis, this inventory will be :

- the event E1 ascertains the presence of a statement to be analyzed : it triggers the Control function which provides a correct statement (or a statement
that must be corrected) ;

- the event E2 ascertains the presence of a correct statement ; it triggers the
Integration function, providing a statement which is consistent with regard for
integration into this Conceptual Schema ;

- the event E3 ascertains the presence of a statement which is a candidate for
integration into the Conceptual Schema ; it triggers the building function which
inserts this statement into this Conceptual Schema ;

- the event E4 ascertains the insertion of a statement into the Conceptual Schema
and it triggers the Documentation function that provides the designer with the
information about this new insertion into the Conceptual Schema.

The management of this inventory by the Pilot, according to the occurrence of
real events, constitutes the Piloting of the computer aided design process. The
description of this inventory can be reduced to the description of causal relations between events and actions whose results could be events. To describe
this inventory is to describe the dynamics of the Computer Aided System, and
that is to provide a static description of the Piloting.


    3.2.2  The Piloting System

Since it appears that the Piloting system is a particular kind of IS, and
since our problem is to describe this system, then we will provide  on the one
hand a conceptual definition of such a system by the use of the IS conceptual
model (defined in the first part of this paper) giving a conceptual schema of
the Piloting system and on the other hand we will provide a technical (or logical) description of this system. This logical description will be the starting
point of a prototype of the Piloting system.


i) <u>Conceptual definition</u>

As we intend to utilize the IS conceptual model in order to give the conceptual
definition of the Piloting System, it is very important to precisely define
which are the events, the operations and the objects that occur during the
Piloting process.

- All of the objects that constitute the Piloting belong to the same type.
This type is the execution of the tasks ensured by the computer aided design
system tools (which permit the execution of the functions previously defined
and which intervene during the computer aided design process). We point out that
the Piloting is described by the execution of the tasks and not by the means
which ensure these tasks because, in this case, we should describe the Computer
Aided System. The state of an object is equivalent to the result of the execution.

- All of the events necessary to describe the Piloting system belong to the
same type. This type of event is the end of the execution of a task (that is
to say that an event ascertains the end of the execution of a task).

- All of the operations necessary to describe the Piloting system belong to the
same type. This type of operation is the task activation.

By the use of those three concepts, it is possible to define the semantics of the
Piloting system through a conceptual schema which should be described by a collection of relations. We restrain ourselves to give  through a simple example  a
graph representation  in order to make easier the understanding of this schema
(figure 10).

E1    The event E1 is the ascertainment of the end of the entering processing of a
      statement to be analyzed. It triggers the activation of the execution of the
      task T1 corresponding to the Control function.

E2    The end of the execution of T1 is an event E2 that triggers the activation of
      the execution of the task T2 corresponding to the Integration function.

E3    The end of the execution of T2 is an event E3 that triggers the activation of
      the execution of the task T3 corresponding to the Building function of the
      Conceptual Schema (that inserts the statement into this Schema).

E4    The end of the execution of T3 is an event E4 that triggers the activation of
      the execution of the task T4 corresponding to the Documentation function.

(In the case of activation of T4 by the event E4, this task provides the
informations about the statement inserted into the Conceptual Schema to the
designer).

The designer asks for the modification  of a statement and the ascertainment of
the entering of this request is the event E5. It triggers the activation of the
execution of T5 (statement modification) whose end of execution is an event E6
that triggers the activation of the execution of T6 (inventory documentation correction). The end of the execution of T6 is an event E7 that triggers the activation of the execution of T1.

The end of the entering of a documentation request made by the designer is an
event E8 that triggers the activation of the execution of the task T4 corresponding to the Documentation function.

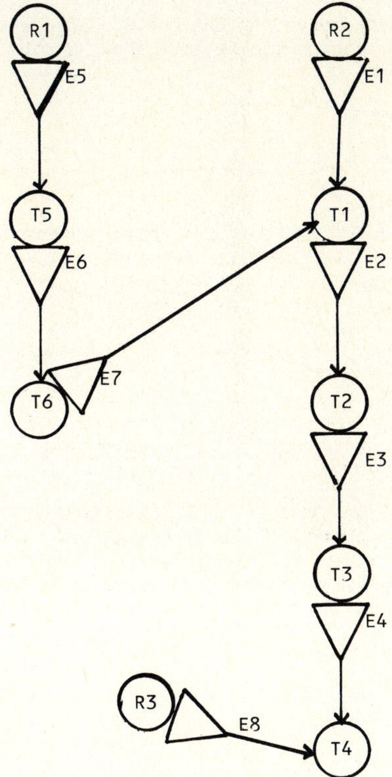


Figure 10 : Conceptual Schema of the Piloting system

ii) <u>Technical definition</u>

Such a description of the semantics of the Piloting by the use of a Conceptual
Schema seems to be indispensable to a good understanding of the Piloting problem
which is necessary to the elaboration of the tool Pilot that will really manage
the Piloting of the Computer Aided Design System. Nevertheless, this step of
description, as well as being necessary, is not sufficient to really implement a
tool Pilot. A more accurate description, by which we shall complete the previous
representation through the introduction of constraints originated by the synchronization and parallelism problems, also seems indispensable. This is what we call
an internal step, in which appear the notions of synchronization and parallelism
[6], [29].

Thus a reasoning based upon the notions of independence and dependence between
events leads us to define what we call the automaton of the piloting. This automaton is a graph defined over the set of the tasks to be activated by the Computer
Aided Design System in order to carry out the IS design process, and it associates
to any given task the set of the tasks that we can activate after this given task
(determined through reasonings based upon the notions of dependence between events
that trigger the tasks). In the case of the example shown at the conceptual level,
the automaton of the piloting should be :

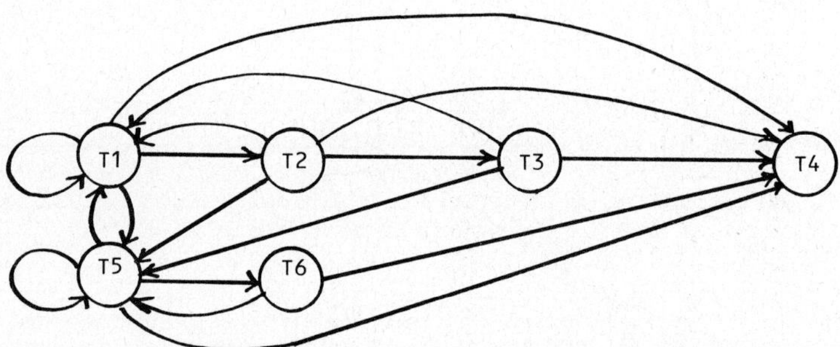


Figure 11 : The automaton of the piloting

Moreover a reasoning based upon the sharing of the objects (our resources) leads
us to define the matrix of parallelism P. This matrix allows us to determine which
are the tasks that could be activated in parallel with any given task. In the case
of the example shown at the conceptual level, this matrix could be :

$$P = \begin{pmatrix} 0 & 1 & 1 & 1 & 0 & 1 \\ 1 & 0 & 1 & 1 & 1 & 1 \\ 1 & 1 & 0 & 0 & 1 & 0 \\ 1 & 1 & 0 & 0 & 1 & 0 \\ 0 & 1 & 1 & 1 & 0 & 1 \\ 1 & 1 & 0 & 0 & 1 & 1 \end{pmatrix}$$

where $P_{ij} = \begin{cases} 1 \text{ iff Ti and Tj could be activated in parallel} \\ 0 \text{ otherwise} \end{cases}$

Then the Piloting System will manage the dynamics of the design and implementation
process of an IS according to the automaton of the Piloting and the matrix of parallelism, which are our solutions respectively to the problem of synchronization
and parallelism.

## 3.3 THIRD SECTION CONCLUSION

Following these proposals, we have developed a prototype that will be fully
operational by december 1981. We have already built tools carrying out partially
the control function, integration function, documentation function and piloting
function.


# CONCLUSION


From both our research work and practical experience of the REMORA method, we have
drawn the two following conclusions :

- The correct tool specification implies a conceptual description of the problem
to manage. We believe that this approach can be used for the design of all computer software tools : we apply it for IS design but also for the design of the
tools associated to our methodology, i.e. for the definition of the event processor and the pilot.

- In many cases the reality can be viewed as a dynamic process. So, the designer
needs a dynamics model similar to the one we have presented to model the reality.
We are now applying successfully our dynamics model to three fields of interest :

    . the distributed data bases for the design of a distributed DBMS [43]
    . the office management for the design of office automation tools [37]
    . the real time technical software design and particularly in french
      telephony industry [36] .

# BIBLIOGRAPHY


[1] ANSI/X3/SPARC, Study group on data base management systems, Interim Report, FDT bulletin of ACM SIGMOD7, Nb 21 (1975)

[2] ASTRAHAN, M.M., et al., System R : a relational approach to data base management, ACM TODBS (1976)

[3] BEERI, C., BERNSTEIN, P.A. and GOODMAN, N., A sophisticate's introduction to data base normalization theory, in : Proceedings of the 4th international conference on VLDB, BERLIN (IEEE eds, 1978)

[4] BENCI, G. and ROLLAND, C., Les bases de données : une conception canonique pour une réalisation extensible (SCM publ., PARIS, 1979)

[5] BRACCHI, G., FURTADO, A. and PELAGATTI, G., Constraint specification in evolutionary data base design, in : SCHNEIDER, H.J. (ed.), Proceedings of IFIP working conference on "Formal models and practical tools in information system design" (NORTH HOLLAND, AMSTERDAM, 1979)

[6] BRINCH HANSEN, P., Operating system principles, Prentice Hall series in automatic computation (PRENTICE HALL, ENGLEWOOD CLIFFS, 1973)

[7] BUBENKO, J.A., Information modeling in the context of system development, invited paper in : LEVINGTON, S.H. (ed.), Proceedings of IFIP conference "Information processing 80" (NORTH HOLLAND, AMSTERDAM, 1980)

[8] CHAMBERLIN, D.D. et al., SEQUEL 2 : a unified approach to data base definition, manipulation and control, IBM journal on research and development, Nb 20-6 (1976)

[9] CII HONEYWELL BULL, Multics relational data store reference manual (CII HONEYWELL BULL, PARIS, 1976)

[10] CII HONEYWELL BULL, SOCRATE II : users manual (CII HONEYWELL BULL, PARIS, 1977)

[11] CODASYL, data base task group report (ACM, NEW YORK, 1971)

[12] CODD, E.F., A relational model of data for large shared data banks , Communications of the ACM, Vol 13, Nb 6 (1970)

[13] COOD, E.F., Further normalization of the data base relational model, in : data base systems (PRENTICE HALL, ENGLEWOOD CLIFFS, 1972)

[14] CORIG, CGI : manuel de présentation CORIG (CGI, PARIS)

[15] DATE, C.H., An introduction to data base systems (ADDISON WESLEY, 2nd edition, 1977)

[16] DEMOLOMBE, R., LEMAITRE, M. and NICOLAS, J.M., the language of SYNTEX-2 : an implemented relational-like DBMS, in : Moneta (ed.), Information Technology, TCIT 3 (NORTH HOLLAND, AMSTERDAM, 1978)

[17] GERO, J.S., Ethics in computer aided design : a polemic, ACM SIGDA newsletters, Vol 5, Nb 4 (1975)

[18] GLUSHKOV, V.M. and LETICHEVSKII, A.A., Theory of algorithms and discrete processors, Advances in information systems science, Vol 1, Ch 1 (1973)

[19] HAMMER, M.M. and MC LEOD, D.J., Semantic integrity in a relational data base system, in : Proceedings of the first international conference on VLDB, FRAMINGHAM (IEEE, 1975)

[20] HELD, G.D. et al., INGRES : a relational data base system, in : Proceedings of the NCC 75 congress (1975)

[21] HOARE, C.A.R., An axiomatic basis for computer programming, Communications of the ACM, Vol 12 (1969)

[22] HONEYWELL BULL, IDS2 users manual (HONEYWELL BULL, PARIS)

[23] IBM, IMS, IBM systems journal, Vol 16, Nb 2 (1977)

[24] IFIP, SCHNEIDER, H.J. (ed), Proceedings of IFIP working conference on "Formal models and practical tools for information system design" (NORTH HOLLAND, AMSTERDAM, 1979)

[25] ISO TC97/SC5/WG3, VAN GRIETHUYSEN, J.J. et al. (ed.), Concepts and terminology for the conceptual schema, Preliminary Report (ISO-ANSI, NEW YORK, 1981)

[26] KERSCHBERG, L., KLERG, A. and TSICHRITZIS, D., A taxonomy of data models, in : LOCKMANN and NEUHOLD (eds.), Systems for large data bases (NORTH HOLLAND, AMSTERDAM, 1976)

[27] LEIFERT, S., Un langage de spécification des systèmes d'information. Un outil pour leur gestion, Thèse de docteur ingénieur, UER de Mathématiques, Université de NANCY-1 (May 1980)

[28] MAC CLEOD, D.J. and HELDMANN, M.J., A generalized minicomputers relational data base management system, in : Proceedings of the NCC 75 congress (1975)

[29] MARK IV Informatics Inc, MARK IV reference manual, Order N° SP-681810 1

[30] MERISE, Introduction a MERISE, journées internationales de l'informatique et de l'automatique (PARIS, 1981)

[31] MINOS, SLIGOS : manuel de présentation MINOS (SLIGOS, PARIS)

[32] NICOLAS, J.M., A property of logical formulas corresponding to integrity constraints on data base relations, in : Proceedings of the international conference on "Formal bases for data bases", TOULOUSE (Université de TOULOUSE, 1979)

[33] PECOUD, F., MACSI : méthode d'aide à la conception des systèmes d'information, Thèse de doctorat d'état, Université de GRENOBLE (1975)

[34] PROTEE, SIS : manuel de présentation PROTEE (SIS, PARIS)

[35] RICHARD, C., Une approche conceptuelle des problèmes de synchronisation, Thèse de 3ème cycle, UER de Mathématiques, Université de NANCY-1 (OCTOBER 1979)

[36] RICHARD, C., Spécification conceptuelle d'un logiciel technique de téléphonie, THOMSON-CSF/S.C.A.G. internal report (THOMSON-CSF/S.C.A.G., PARIS, 1981)

[37] ROLLAND, C., La conception des systèmes de bureau, in : Proceedings of AFCET congress 1979, GRENOBLE (AFCET, PARIS, 1979)

[38]   ROLLAND, C., A methodology for information systems design, in : Proceedings of NCC 81 conference (NCC, CHICAGO, 1981)

[39]   ROLLAND, C. and BENCI, G., Management of information system projects in : Proceedings of the Internet Congress 1979 (Internet, 1979)

[40]   ROLLAND, C. and FOUCAUT, O., Concepts for the design of an information system conceptual schema and its utilization in the Remora project, in : Proceedings of the 4th international conference on VLDB, BERLIN (IEEE, 1978)

[41]   ROLLAND, C., LEIFERT, S. and RICHARD, C., Tools for information system dynamics management, in : Proceedings of the 5th international conference on VLDB, RIO DE JANEIRO (IEEE, 1979)

[42]   ROLLAND, C., LEIFERT, S. and RICHARD, C., A proposal for information system design and management, ACM SIGDA, Vol 20, Nb 2 (1980)

[43]   ROLLAND, C. and RICHARD, C., A distributed information system concurrency control method, in : Proceedings of IFDO-IASSIST 1981 conference (IFDO, GRENOBLE, 1981)

[44]   ROLLAND, C. and THIERY, O., Un outil graphique pour la visualisation de la dynamique d'un système d'information, in : Proceedings of the CIPS' 81 conference, WATERLOO (CIPS, WATERLOO, 1981)

[45]   SCHMID, M.A. et al., The relational data base system OMEGA, Progress Report, University of TORONTO (1976)

[46]   SCHMID, M.A., An analysis of some constructs for conceptual models, in NIJSSEN (ed.), Modeling in data base management systems (NORTH HOLLAND, AMSTERDAM, 1976)

[47]   SCHMIDT, J.W., Some high level language constructs for data of type relation, ACM TODBS, Vol 2, Nb 3 (1977)

[48]   SOLVBERG, A., Software requirement definition and data models, in : Proceedings of the 5th international conference on VLDB, RIO DE JANEIRO (IEEE, 1979)

[49]   SYSTEM 2000, MRI System Corporation, System 2000 general information manual (1972)

[50]   TEICHROEW, D., Improvement in the system life cycle, in : Information processing 74 (NORTH HOLLAND, AMSTERDAM, 1974)

[51]   TEICHROEW, D. and HERSCHEY, E.A., PSL/PSA : a computer-aided technique for structured documentation and analysis of information processing system, IEEE transactions on software engineering, Vol. SE 3 (1977)

[52]   TODD, S.J.P., Peterlee relational test vehicle PRTV : a technical overview, IBM systems journal, Vol 15, Nb 4 (1976)

[53]   WASSERMAN, A.I., USE : a methodology for the design and development of interactive information systems, in : Proceedings of OXFORD IFIP congress (NORTH HOLLAND, AMSTERDAM, 1979)

[54]   WATERS, S.G., Methodologie assistée par ordinateur dans la conception des systèmes informatiques, l'informatique nouvelle (1976)

[55]   WIRTH, N., The programming language PASCAL, Acta informatica, Vol 1, (1971) 35-63.

*INFORMATION SYSTEMS DESIGN METHODOLOGIES: A Comparative Review*
*T.W. Olle, H.G. Sol, A.A. Verrijn-Stuart (editors)*
*North-Holland Publishing Company*
© *IFIP, 1982*

THE EVOLUTIONARY DESIGN METHODOLOGY
APPLIED TO INFORMATION SYSTEMS

G. Rzevski, Kingston Polytechnic, Kingston-upon-Thames, United Kingdom.

D.B. Trafford, Cranfield Institute of Technology, Cranfield, United Kingdom.

M. Wells, Chelmer Institute of Higher Education, Chelmsford, United Kingdom.

The Evolutionary Design Methodology is a general methodology
applicable to a wide variety of systems.  In this paper some
major features of the Methodology are briefly described and
its application to the design of information systems is
illustrated by an example.

INTRODUCTION

The aim of this paper is to demonstrate to the reader how the Evolutionary Design
Methodology [14] can be applied to the design of large information systems.

The Methodology is based on a long-term research carried out at Kingston
Polytechnic whose aim has been to investigate:

1.  Desirable quality parameters of information systems.

2.  Factors which affect these quality parameters and are under direct or partial
    control of those engaged in systems development or maintenance.

3.  Factors which affect the productivity of personnel engaged in systems
    development or maintenance.

4.  Methods for controlling quality and productivity factors with a view to
    achieving required quality of information systems at a minimum cost.

5.  Methods for protecting information systems from faults caused by human
    errors which occur during systems development and maintenance.

The research strategy has been empirical.  Hypotheses were made on the importance
of various factors, one at a time, and then those hypotheses were tested during
information system development projects.  The same approach has been applied to
the development of methods for the control of quality and productivity factors.

Projects were mainly from the areas of engineering applications, e.g. [2], [3],
[4], [5], [8], [12], [17].  There are many more projects which have not yet been
described in publications.  The methodology has also been applied to the design of
engineering products and educational systems.

Some aspects of the Methodology, which emerged from this research, have been
published, e.g. [1], [6], [7], [9], [10], [11], [14], [15], [16].  Other aspects
are still to be published.

Every year since 1974, some 20-30 engineers and computer scientists have taken
part in the research and the development of the Methodology.

PART 1 of the paper briefly describes major characteristics of the Methodology.

PART 2 of the paper gives an example of the application of the Methodology to the design of a small information system.


PART 1    DESCRIPTION OF THE METHODOLOGY

Some Fundamental Concepts

The QUALITY of an information system is measured by means of QUALITY PARAMETERS, such as:-

- reliability
- maintainability
- modifyability
- usability
- relevance
- robustness
- portability
- efficiency

Each quality parameter is defined below:

RELIABILITY is a measure of the system capability to perform as specified for a given period of time.

MAINTAINABILITY is a measure of the system capability to be repaired, after a failure, during a given period of time.

MODIFYABILITY is a measure of the system capability to be modified, when there is a change of requirements, expressed in terms of resources required for modifications relative to resources required for a new system.

USABILITY is a measure of the system capability to enable its users to maximise their performance when using the system.

RELEVANCE is a measure of the system capability to perform as expected by its users (rather than as specified).

ROBUSTNESS is a measure of the system capability to generate permissible outputs in response to inputs outside permissible ranges.

PORTABILITY is a measure of the system capability to be transferred from one computing environment to another.

EFFICIENCY is a measure of system processing speed and storage requirements.

The LIFE CYCLE of an information system consists of the following stages:

- requirement specification
- system environment specification, and
  - design
  - coding
  - testing

. installation

. use

. maintenance and replacement of information systems

The term INFORMATION ENGINEERING is used here to cover all the above activities
with the exception of use and, in addition, it includes management of information
engineering projects.

The PRODUCTIVITY of information engineering personnel is measured in terms of the
time required to complete a given task relative to an agreed norm.


The Aim

The aim of the Methodology is to provide methods and guidelines for the control of

1.   Quality of information systems, as represented by quality parameters.

2.   Productivity of information engineering personnel.


The Scope

The Methodology is concerned with all constituent activities of information
engineering:-

. project management

. requirements specification

. system environment specification

. design

. coding

. testing

. installation

. maintenance and replacement

It must be stressed though that different parts of the Methodology have been
developed up to a different level of completeness at present.  The development of
the Methodology is an ongoing process.


Quality and Productivity Factors

Factors which affect quality parameters of information systems and productivity of
information engineering personnel have been identified and grouped into distinct
classes.  Each class of factors is briefly discussed below.

1.   Human Error Factors

     Productivity and several quality parameters (e.g. reliability, maintainability,
     modifyability, usability) critically depend on human errors which may occur
     at various stages of the system's life-cycle.  A very large number of
     important factors which cause the occurrence of human errors has been
     identified, and also factors which affect the detection and correction of
     faults caused by human errors.

These factors generally tend to be either under control of project managers
(eg. characteristics of the working environment, availability of suitable
tools, etc) or under direct control of system designers/modifyers (eg. module
complexity, interface complexity, etc).  They are therefore considered in
some detail in sections of this paper devoted to project management methods
and design methods, respectively.

2.    Interdependence Factors

The resources required for the modification of an information system when
requirements change (modifyability) depend to a considerable degree upon the
interdependence of various elements of information systems.  A factor which
is found to be of exceptional importance is the interdependence of data
structures and algorithms.  Interdependence factors are under control of
system designers and are discussed further in the appropriate section of
this paper.

3.    Controllability and Observability Factors

The user must be in charge of the computer-based information system.  The
usability, as defined in the first section of this paper, will depend upon
the user's capability to control the system and observe the consequences of
his actions.  Speed of response to the user's commands, angle of the screen,
etc. are examples of these factors.  These factors are under control of
system designers.

4.    Requirements Factors

The relevance of an information system depends on the completeness of the
requirements specification and on changes of user requirements during the
system life-cycle.  Some factors which affect the completeness and changes
are under partial control of information engineering personnel.  Methods for
controlling these factors are described in the section of this paper devoted
to the requirements specification methods.

5.    System Environment Factors, which are:-

5.1.   Computing Environment Factors, ie., factors which cause a system to be
       dependent on its particular computing environment (eg. procedures for
       addressing peripherals) and thus affect system portability, and

5.2.   Data Environment Factors, ie., factors which cause the occurrence of
       incorrect inputs and thus affect system robustness.

In general, system environment factors may differ for each system and thus
the Methodology prescribes that a thorough analysis of the environment should
precede system design.  It also provides methods for isolation of parts of
the system which are dependent on its computing environment and methods for
the protection of the system from incorrect inputs.

6.    Computational Complexity Factors

These are factors which affect computational efficiency of an information
system, ie., its speed of processing and storage requirements.  These factors
are under control of system designers and thus, methods for controlling them
are included in the Design Methodology.

Project Management

A considerable number of factors which cause the occurrence of human errors and thus affect both quality and productivity are under direct control of project managers.  These factors are discussed below.

The research results show, for example, that the occurrence of human errors can be minimised and the detection and correction of faults caused by human error could be maximised if the following conditions are satisfied.

1.    Tasks given to development/maintenance personnel must be:

         .    PERCEIVABLE, ie., structured in such a way that a person who
              performs the task is able to hold, at one and the same time,
              all elements of the task and all their mutual relations.

         .    WELL DEFINED, ie., each task is defined in terms of (a) its
              inputs, (b) its outputs, (c) operations which must be
              performed on given inputs to obtain required outputs.

2.    Physical, psychological and social environments within which information
      engineering tasks are carried out must be conducive to high human
      performance.  Noise level, ventilation, team morale, criteria for
      advancement, attitudes of managers, etc. all these factors are of
      considerable importance.

3.    Tools given to personnel, such as guidelines, standards, and especially
      computer aids, must be of required quality.

4.    Personnel expected to undertake information engineering tasks must be
      trained in accordance with certain criteria.  For example, knowledge, skills
      and attitudes of personnel which play an important part in this subject are:

         .    knowledge of a systematic information engineering methodology

         .    skills of applying such a methodology in practical situations

         .    thoroughness in checking one's work and the work of others

         .    readiness to submit one's work for inspection by colleagues

         .    ingenuity in finding simple solutions to complex problems

      The Methodology provides guidelines for the control of all above factors.
      However, since experience shows that in spite of all precautions human error
      still occurs, the Methodology also includes procedures for:

         .    checking the output of each task

         .    correcting detected faults

         .    reviewing design solutions and modifications

         .    testing and correcting code

Specification of Requirements

Factors which affect the completeness of requirement specifications and changes in user requirements during the information system's life-cycle and are under partial control of information engineering personnel are as follows:

1.    Inability of users to articulate their needs and their expectations.

2.    Lack of appreciation by users of facilities which a computer-based
      information system, under given conditions, can/cannot provide.

3.    Inability of users to anticipate the direction into which their future
      requirements will develop.

4.    Lack of appreciation by system designers of user needs and expectations.

For the purpose of helping to control these factors the Methodology prescribes
that, before any agreement on user requirements is finalised, the designers should
develop, with full participation of users, a model of the TOTAL INFORMATION SYSTEM,
of which the required computer-based information system is a part.

For example, before the design of a computer-aided design system (CADS) begins, it
is necessary to devise with full participation of users, a model of the DESIGN
PROCESS of which CADS will be a part.  The process of modelling of the total
information system gives an opportunity to users and system designers to learn
from each other and thus to come up with a better requirements specification.

The model of the total information system serves as a basis for deciding which
parts of the system will be computerised and the sequence of their design and
implementation.  The Methodology prescribes that all large information systems
must be developed in an evolutionary manner so that both users and designers can
experience practical consequences of specified requirements, and learn from this
experience, as the project progresses.

The user participation in the modelling of the total information system and the
evolutionary strategy for the development of large computer-based information
systems are two main features of the Methodology.  Excellent practical results
have been obtained in some industrial applications [8], [13].


Information System Design

Factors which affect quality and productivity and are under direct control of
information system designers include:-

1.    A subset of human error factors.

2.    Interdependence factors.

3.    Controllability and observability factors.

4.    Computational complexity factors.

The research shows that the occurrence of human errors can be minimised and the
detection and correction of faults caused by human error maximised if information
systems are designed to be:

1.    PERCEIVABLE, ie., structured into hierarchies of models, each performing a
      clearly defined function and each organised such that it is always possible
      to hold in mind at one and the same time all its constituent elements and
      all their interconnections.

2.    WELL DEFINED, ie., each element of an information system (including the
      requirements specification) is completely and unambiguously defined.

Perceivability depends upon psychometric complexity of modules, ie., the complexity as experienced by a person who attempts to understand the function and/or structure of the module with a view to performing a task related to this module (checking for correctness, modifying, etc).

Three aspects of psychometric complexity have been identified as particularly important:

1.   SEMANTIC COMPLEXITY, i.e. the complexity of the operation (function) performed by the module.

2.   SYNTACTIC COMPLEXITY of

   2.1.   the MODULE INTERFACE, ie., the complexity of the data structures addressed by the module.

   2.2.   the MODULE ITSELF, ie., the complexity of the control structure (algorithm) of the module.

3.   PRAGMATIC COMPLEXITY, ie., the complexity of design documentation.

The Methodology provides rules for partitioning of information systems into perceivable modules and specifies standards for design documentation.  These aspects of the Methodology are clearly illustrated by the examples given in Part 2 of the paper.

For applications where a high level of reliability is required there are, in addition, guidelines for the design of fault tolerant modules.


Control of Interdependence

If the only criterion for the design of data structures is to make algorithms more efficient, a situation may arise such that, in response to a change in requirements new algorithms must be introduced which render the old data structure obsolete.  The opposite strategy, ie., to design data structures in anticipation of possible changes, does not make sense because the expected change may never materialise.

To solve this problem, the Methodology prescribes that data structures should be designed using relational data-base concepts irrespective of whether the data will be stored, in a data-base or not.  This approach enables "conceptual" data structures to be designed independently from algorithms (modules).  During the top-down functional partitioning of the system into a hierarchy of modules, designers can design, for each module, required "external schemas" by defining an appropriate relation on data entities contained in the "conceptual schema".  The approach is illustrated in Part 2 of the paper.


Control of Controllability and Observability

In order to avoid the well known tendency of designers to concentrate on the design of software and to hope that the interface with the user will somehow emerge from this process almost as a byproduct, the Methodology specifies that the MAN-MACHINE SYSTEM is to be designed immediately after a model of the total information system is finalised and <u>before</u> any design of software begins. Participation of users in the design of the man-machine system is extremely valuable.

The relationship between the total system, man-machine system and software is illustrated in Figure 1.

A checklist of factors which are found to affect the controllability and observability (and thus to affect usability) of information systems is included in the Methodology.


Control of Efficiency

There is often a conflict between requirements for data independence and for system efficiency.  Very rarely such a conflict exists between requirements for perceivability and efficiency.

Whenever the conflict arises the Methodology prescribes that design for efficiency should be delayed until it is possible to identify critical modules.  Only for critical modules it is permissible to increase efficiency at the expense of perceivability and independence.

A checklist of factors which affect the computational complexity, ie., the complexity as experienced by machine, and thus affect the efficiency is included in the Methodology.


Computer-Aided Design of Information Systems

An important axiom of the Evolutionary Design Methodology is that information system design is a TRIAL AND ERROR process which includes:-

1.   Creation of tentative solutions.

2.   Checking and testing of proposed solutions.

3.   Selecting the best solutions.

4.   Documenting design decisions.

The first and third activities require creativity, inventiveness and capabilities of making value judgements and are thus, best performed by humans.  The second and fourth activities are very often algorithmic and are therefore best performed by computers.

It follows that the design of information systems is best performed interactively by man and machine.  A pilot interactive CAD system has been developed to support Methodology [15].  The system is now being further developed.  The major features are that it enables man to make tentative design proposals and all important design decisions whilst the machine undertakes the following tasks:

1.   Provides the required design information in an appropriate format, whenever requested.

2.   Ensures that design tasks are performed correctly and in a correct order.

3.   Ensures that design solutions are correct and perceivable.

4.   Generates all design documentation.

5.   Generates code (this facility is still under development).

FIGURE 1

TOTAL INFORMATION SYSTEM

MANUAL SYSTEM
MAN/MACHINE SYSTEM

USER
MACHINE-BASED INFORMATION SYSTEM

HARDWARE
SOFTWARE

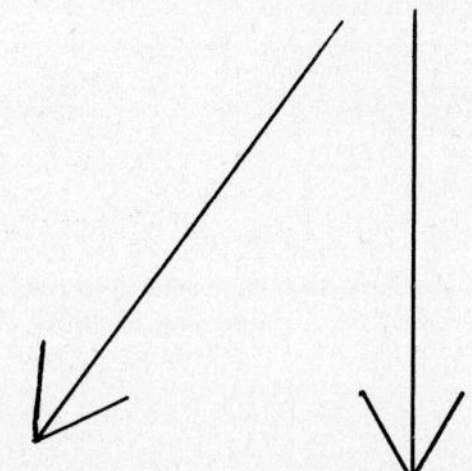

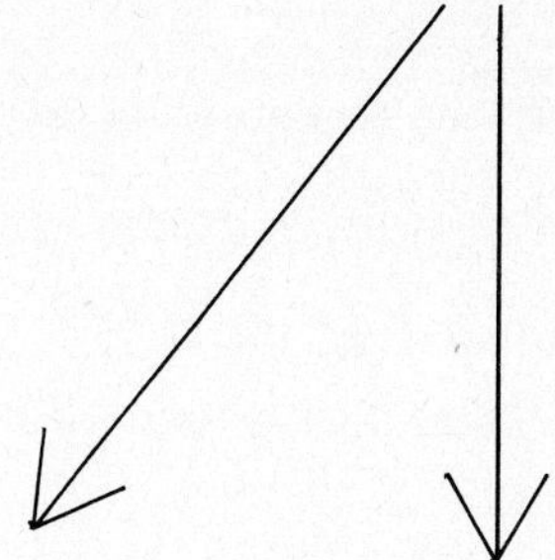

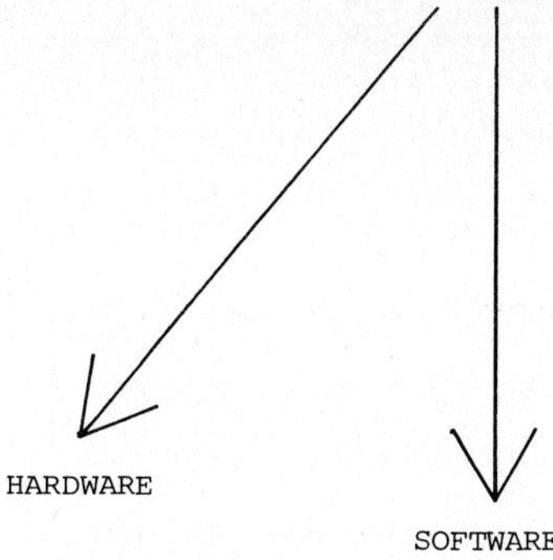

The Defintion of Information Engineering Tasks

There exists a useful analogy between

.    an information system, and

.    an information engineering project.

Both are systems.  Elements of information systems are modules whilst elements of projects are tasks.  To reduce the occurrence of human errors during various stages of an information system life-cycle both modules and tasks must be

.    well defined, and

.    perceivable

Criteria for definition and perceivability of modules and tasks are the same.

There exists, in addition, an asymmetrical relationship between projects and systems:  the way in which a project is organised always affects the structure of the information system (which is being developed by means of the project).

For this reason the Methodology emphasises the importance of organising projects into hierarchies of perceivable tasks.

In this section of the paper two constituent activities of an information engineering project, namely

.    requirements specification, and

.    information system design

are partitioned into unit tasks.  The output of each task is referenced to a set of documents enclosed in Part 2 of the paper.


Requirements Specification

This activity consists of modelling the total information system of which the future computer-based information system is a part (the total information system is a system of activities some of which are to be performed by the future computer-based system whilst others are to be performed without the use of computers).

The modelling of the total information system is partitioned into the following constituent tasks:

1.    Formulate the functional specification of the total system, ie.,

    1.1.    Define inputs into the system from its environment.

    1.2.    Define outputs from the system into its environment.

    1.3.    Define, in broad terms, the function which the total system performs.

    1.4.    Document all decisions on appropriate A4 forms

    1.5.    Check the functional specification for perceivability and correctness
            according to appropriate criteria (not described in this paper).

2.　　Formulate the data-flow structure of the total system, ie.,

    2.1.　　Partition the system function into a number of constituent functions according to guidelines for partitioning (not given in this paper).

    2.2.　　For each newly created function define input and output data.

    2.3.　　Interconnect these functions into a structure which depicts the flow of data.

    2.4.　　Decide, for each newly created function, whether it will be performed by:

        . a man interacting with a machine (interactively), or

        . a man without a machine (manually), or

        . a combination of the two methods.

    2.5.　　Document all decisions on an appropriate A4 form

    2.6.　　Check data-flow structure for perceivability and correctness.

3.　　Apply the above activities to each newly created function, in turn, until all functions are designated to be either manual or interactive (in other words, until there is no function left which needs to be performed by a combination of these two methods).

4.　　Summarise the model of the total system by a diagram depicting its hierarchical structure.

    The model of the total information system provides a statement of requirements for the man-machine (interactive) information system in terms of its inputs, outputs and functions that are to be performed on inputs in order to obtain required outputs.


Information Systems Design

The design of information systems consists of two major activities, the design of the man-machine system and the design of software (assuming that hardware is given).


Man-Machine System Design

Man-machine system design consists of the following tasks:

1.　　Formulate the function specification of the man-machine system based on information contained in the requirements specification, ie.,

    1.1.　　Define inputs into the man-machine system.

    1.2.　　Define outputs from the man-machine system.

    1.3.　　Define the function which the man-machine system is required to perform upon inputs in order to generate required outputs.

    1.4.　　Document all decisions on appropriate A4 forms

    1.5.　　Check results for perceivability, correctness and feasibility.

2.    Design the data-flow structure of the man-machine system, ie.,

    2.1.    Partition the system into a number of man-machine subsystems such that each one can be designed and implemented independently.

    2.2.    For each man-machine subsystem define inputs from the user and outputs to the user.

    2.3.    Document all decisions on an appropriate A4 form

    2.4.    Check data-flow structure for perceivability, correctness and feasibility.

3.    Design the control structure of the man-machine system, ie.,

    3.1.    Decide how the user is going to select the man-machine subsystem which he/she needs (eg., by means of commands).

    3.2.    Design the conceptual control structure for this purpose (eg., a system of commands).

    3.3.    Design the layout of control structures (eg., screen format).

    3.4.    Document all decisions on appropriate A4 forms

    3.5.    Check control structure for perceivability, controllability, correctness and feasibility.

4.    For each man-machine subsystem formulate the functional specification as described in Step 1.

5.    Decide which subsystem is to be designed first.

6.    Design the data-flow structure of the selected man-machine subsystem, eg.,

    6.1.    Partition its function into a number of constituent functions such that each one is performed either by the user or by machine.

    6.2.    For each newly created function define inputs and outputs.

    6.3.    Interconnect these functions into a structure which depicts the flow of data between the user and machine (ie., describes a man-machine dialogue).

    6.4.    Document all decisions on an appropriate A4 form

    6.5.    Check data-flow structure for perceivability, correctness and feasibility.

7.    Design external data structures for the selected man-machine subsystem, ie., for each set of data entities which is transmitted between the user and the machine in one transaction.

    7.1.    Define data entities in terms of constituent data items.

    7.2.    Arrange data entities into data structures (ie., "user views").

    7.3.    Design layouts of data structures (eg., screen formats).

    7.4.    Document all decisions on appropriate A4 forms

7.5.   Check data structures for perceivability, observability,
       correctness and feasibility.

8.   Design control structures for the selected man-machine subsystem,
     ie., for each function which is to be performed by machine:

8.1.   Decide how the user is going to instruct the machine to perform
       the function (eg., by means of commands, by answering questions,etc).

8.2.   Design the conceptual control structure for this purpose
       (eg., a set of commands).

8.3.   Design the layout of control structures, (eg., screen format
       of commands).

8.4.   Document all decisions on appropriate A4 forms

8.5.   Check control structures for perceivability, controllability,
       correctness and feasibility.

9.   Summarise the design of the man-machine system (including subsystems) by
     means of a diagram depicting its hierarchical structure.


Software Design

Software design includes the following tasks:

1.   Formulate the functional specification for the software system which is to
     support the previously designed man-machine system, ie.,

1.1.   Define input and output data sets.

1.2.   Define the function which must be performed on inputs in order to
       obtain required outputs.

1.3.   Document all decisions on appropriate A4 forms

1.4.   Check results for perceivability, correctness and feasibility.

2.   Design the conceptual data structure of the software system such that it may
     be implemented as a system data-base if required, ie.,

2.1.   Identify all data entities.

2.2.   Organise data entities into a conceptual data structure.

2.3.   Document all decisions on appropriate A4 forms

2.4.   Check data structure for perceivability, computational complexity,
       correctness and feasibility.

3.   Design the data-flow structure of the software system, ie.,

3.1.   Partition the system into a number of subsystems, each one supporting
       a previously designed man-machine subsystem.

3.2.   For each newly created subsystem define input and output data sets.

3.3.   Interconnect these subsystems into a structure which depicts the
       flow of data through the system.  ·

3.4.   Document all decisions on an appropriate A4 form

3.5.   Check data-flow structure for perceivability, correctness and
       feasibility.

4.   Design external data structures for each subsystem, ie., for each set of
     input/output data:

4.1.   Define data entities.

4.2.   Arrange data entities into data structure (subsystem views).

4.3.   Design, if required, mappings between the external subsystem data
       structures and the conceptual system data structure.

4.4.   Document all decisions on appropriate A4 forms

4.5.   Check data structures for perceivability, computational complexity,
       correctness and feasibility.

5.   Design the control structure of the software system, ie.,

5.1.   Interconnect constituent subsystems by means of sequences, decisions
       and/or loops in such a way that the systems can perform the specified
       function.

5.2.   Document all decisions on an appropriate A4 form

5.3.   Check the control structure for perceivability, computational
       complexity, correctness and feasibility.

6.   For each subsystem define the functional specification as described in
     Step 1.

7.   Design the software subsystem which supports the first man-machine subsystem
     following exactly the same procedure as for the design of the software system.

8.   Design constituent modules of the subsystem one at a time following Steps 3,
     4, 5 and 6.

9.   Continue this recursive design procedure until all modules are realisable
     in terms of an existing subroutine, function or a block of not more than
     50 statements in the language of implementation.

10.  Carry out implementation design, eg., design of internal data structures in
     a selected data base environment, etc.


## References


(1)   Kaposi, A.A.,  Popovic, L., Rzevski, G.,  An algebra of algorithms and its
      application to program design and maintenance, CAD Jrnl.10 [1978] 74-77.

(2)   Renton, M., Rzevski, G., POLYMARK - A Suite of programs for the computer
      aided solution of stochastic problems, Proc. 3rd Int.Conf.on Computers in
      Engineering and Building Design, CAD 78, [IPC Science and Technology Press,
      1978].

[3]   Amitirigala, E.M.P., Rzevski, G., On the computer-aided assessment of safety
      of Electronic systems, Proc. IEE Conf. on Computer-Aided Design and
      Manufacture of Electronic Components, Circuits and Systems, [IEE
      Publications, 1979].

[4]   Rzevski, G., Walker, C.C., On the computer-aided assessment of reliability
      of large plants and control systems, Proc. of IFAC Symp. on Computer-Aided
      Design of Control Systems, [Pergamon Press, 1979].

[5]   Ferrer, D.R., Rzevski, G., Computer-aided analysis of dynamic behaviour of
      lumped parameter mechanical structures using electrical network techniques,
      in: Adey, R.A. [ed], Engineering Software [Pentech Press, 1979].

[6]   Rzevski, G., On the design of Engineering Software, in: Adey, R.A. [ed],
      Engineering Software [Pentech Press, 1979].

[7]   Rzevski, G., Improving system reliability by the elimination of a class of
      design errors, in: Synthesis and Analysis Methods for Safety and Reliability
      Studies, Plenum Publishing, 1980 .

[8]   Rzevski, G., Woolman, D., Trafford, D.B., A Methodology for the design of
      CAD systems and its implementation in an industrial environment, Proc. of
      4th Int. Conf. on Computers in Design and Engineering, CAD 80, [IPC Science
      and Technology, 1980].

[9]   Rzevski, G., A technique for fault-tolerant reliability assessment, Proc.
      6th Advances in Reliability Technology Symposium [1980].

[10]  Kaposi, A.A., Rzevski, G., On the aims and scope of a system design
      Methodology, Proc. 5th European Meeting on Cybernetics and Systems Research
      [1980].

[11]  Rzevski, G., Systematic design of simulation software, in: Cellier, F.E. [ed],
      Progress in Modelling and Simulation [Academic Press, 1980].

[12]  Rzevski, G., On the use of Markov Processes for the interactive computer-
      aided solution of discrete-state stochastic simulation problems,
      International Journal of Modelling and Simulation, 1980.

[13]  Rzevski, G., Woolman, D., Trafford, D.B., Validation of a Design Methodology
      Design Studies, I [1980].

[14]  Rzevski, G., On the design of a Design Methodology, in: Jacques, R.,
      Powell, J.A. [eds], Design : Science : Method [IPC Business Press, 1981].

[15]  Rzevski, G., Wells, M.J., Computer-aided design of Engineering Software, in:
      Adey, R.A. [ed], Engineering Software II, [CML Publications, 1981].

[16]  Rzevski, G., Recent Advances in Software Reliability Methods, Proc. 3rd.
      National Reliability Conference, [NCSR, 1981].

[17]  Rzevski, G., Patel, R., Research into Computer-Aided Engineering of Micro-
      processor and Application Systems, Proc. of European Conf. on Electronic
      Design Automation, [IEE, 1981].

PART 2    AN EXAMPLE


Overview

The example described in Part 2 is aimed at illustrating the Evolutionary Design
Methodology as applied to the design of Information Systems.  The design of the
System was performed by applying tasks, defined in Part 1 to:-

1.    Requirements Specification          ie.,  Total System Documentation

2.    Information System Design           ie.,  (a)  Man/Machine System Design.

                                                (b)  Software System Design.


Due to the restriction in pages for the submission, certain design documents
prescribed by EDM have been omitted.  In addition, the requirements specification
(total system) is incomplete as certain activities (eg. financial and
accommodation activities performed by the Organising Committee) have been
purposely omitted.

The system was designed using, as a basis, the limited specification provided by
the customer (IFIP), as a result the completed design may not accurately reflect
the expectations of the customer.  This is contrary to EDM which prescribes total
collaboration and consultation with the customer during the drafting of the
requirements specification (total system) and with potential users of the system
during the man/machine system design.


Design Documentation

The design is documented on standard A4 EDM design sheets, each document
describing the output from a design task defined in Part 1.

The standard symbol used to describe the data flow structure and control flow
structure are given in Figure II.

FIG.IIa DATA FLOW STRUCTURE                    FIG. IIb CONTROL FLOW STRUCTURE

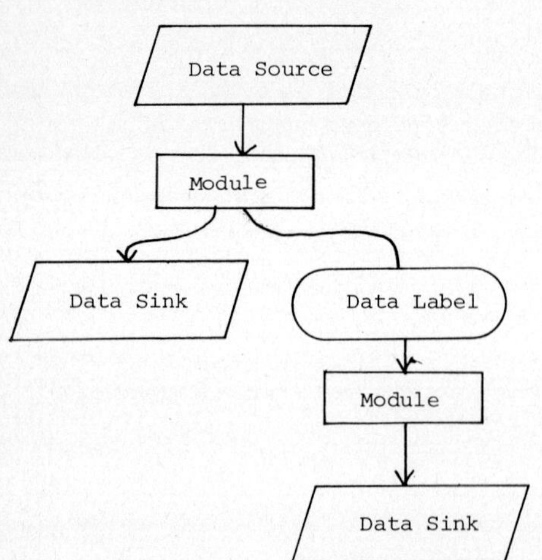

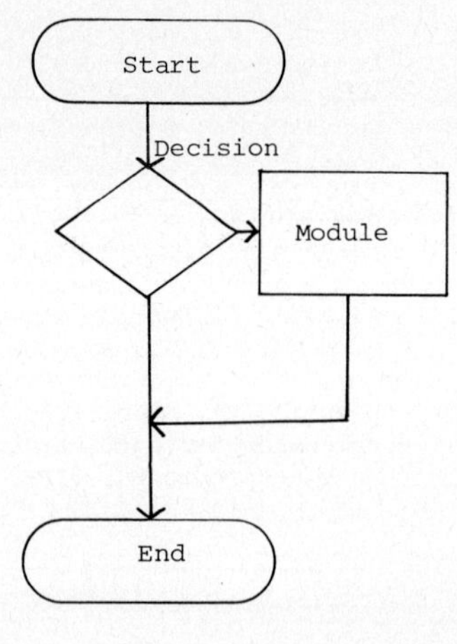

EVOLUTIONARY DESIGN METHODOLOGY

| TOTAL SYSTEM | √ | SYSTEM ID. | IFIP Conference System | SYSTEM REF. | IFIP/T |
|---|---|---|---|---|---|
| MAN/MACHINE SYSTEM | | MODULE ID. | | MODULE REF. | |
| SOFTWARE | | | | | |

| FUNCTIONAL SPECIFICATION | √ | DATA FLOW STRUCTURE | DATA FORMAT/ STRUCTURE | CONTROL STRUCTURE | HIERARCHICAL STRUCTURE |
|---|---|---|---|---|---|

## Functional Description

The function of the IFIP Conference System is to organise an IFIP Working Conference and to invite representatives of IFIP and authors of submitted papers to the Conference.  The system complies with the existing IFIP policy on Working Conferences which suggests that there is a Programme Committee to deal with the technical content of the conference and an Organising Committee to handle financial matters, local arrangements and invitations.

A description of the requirements of the system is given in an IFIP document entitled "Problem Definition - 15th September 1980".  In summary; the Programme Committee issues a call for papers; acknowledges the letters of intent; receives the submitted papers; ensures that they are refereed; selected and grouped into sessions with a Chairman.  The Organising Committee invites the priority representatives of IFIP and the selected and rejected authors; registers their acceptances (and rejections) and produces a final list of attendees.

### Input/Output Data

| Data Ref. | I/P | O/P | Description |
|---|---|---|---|
| 1 | √ | | Possible Contributors List (i.e. possible authors, referees, chairmen) |
| 2 | √ | | Priority Attendees List |
| 3 | √ | | Correspondence In |
| 4 | | √ | Conference Programme |
| 5 | | √ | Conference Attendees List |
| 6 | | √ | Correspondence Out |

EVOLUTIONARY DESIGN METHODOLOGY

| TOTAL SYSTEM √ | SYSTEM<br>ID. | IFIP Conference System | SYSTEM<br>REF. | IFIP/T |
|---|---|---|---|---|
| MAN/MACHINE<br>SYSTEM | MODULE<br>ID. | | MODULE<br>REF. | |
| SOFTWARE | | | | |
| FUNCTIONAL<br>SPECIFICATION | DATA FLOW<br>STRUCTURE √ | DATA FORMAT/<br>STRUCTURE | CONTROL<br>STRUCTURE | HIERARCHICAL<br>STRUCTURE |

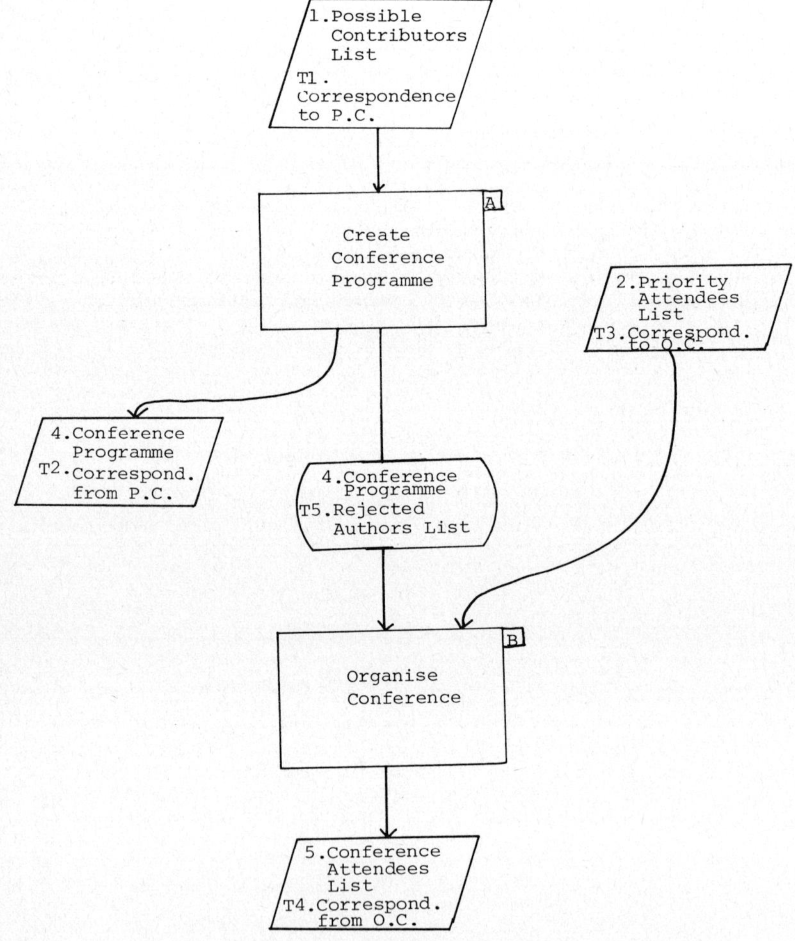


NOTES:      (a)  Correspondence In (ref.3) is partitioned into
                 .    correspondence to P.C. (ref T1), and
                 .    correspondence to O.C. (ref T3).
            (b)  Correspondence Out (ref.5) is partitioned into
                 .    correspondence from P.C. (ref T2), and
                 .    correspondence from O.C. (ref T4).

EVOLUTIONARY DESIGN METHODOLOGY

| TOTAL SYSTEM ✓ | SYSTEM ID. | IFIP Conference System | SYSTEM REF. | IFIP/T |
| MAN/MACHINE SYSTEM | MODULE ID. | Create Conference Programme | MODULE REF. | TA |
| SOFTWARE | | | | |
| FUNCTIONAL SPECIFICATION ✓ | DATA FLOW STRUCTURE | DATA FORMAT/ STRUCTURE | CONTROL STRUCTURE | HIERARCHICAL STRUCTURE |

Functional Description

The Programme Committee deals with the technical content of the Conference and creates the Conference Programme.  The creation of the Conference Programme includes the following activities:-

     (i)    Preparing a list of possible contributors;

    (ii)   Issuing the call for papers;

   (iii)   Registering the letters of intent;

    (iv)   Registering the contributed papers on receipt;

    (v)   Inviting acknowledged people in the field of the Conference to act as Referees and/or Session Chairmen;

    (vi)   Distributing the papers to the Referees;

   (vii)   Selecting the papers for the Conference from the Referee reports;

  (viii)   Grouping the selected papers into Conference Sessions;

    (ix)   Selecting a Chairman for each Conference Session;

    (x)   Producing the Conference Programme.

Input/Output Data

| Data Ref. | I/P | O/P | Description |
| --- | --- | --- | --- |
| 1 | ✓ | | Possible Contributors List |
| T1 | ✓ | | Correspondence to PC |
| 4 | | ✓ | Conference Programme |
| T2 | | ✓ | Correspondence from PC |
| T5 | | ✓ | Rejected Authors List |

EVOLUTIONARY DESIGN METHODOLOGY

| TOTAL SYSTEM ✓ | SYSTEM ID. | IFIP Conference System | SYSTEM REF. | IFIP/T |
| MAN/MACHINE SYSTEM | MODULE ID. | Create Conference Programme | MODULE REF. | TA |

SOFTWARE

| FUNCTIONAL SPECIFICATION | DATA FLOW STRUCTURE ✓ | DATA FORMAT/ STRUCTURE | CONTROL STRUCTURE | HIERARCHICAL STRUCTURE |

EVOLUTIONARY DESIGN METHODOLOGY

| TOTAL SYSTEM | ✓ | SYSTEM ID. | | IFIP Conference System | | SYSTEM REF. | IFIP/T |
|---|---|---|---|---|---|---|---|
| MAN/MACHINE SYSTEM | | MODULE ID. | | Organise the Conference | | MODULE REF. | TB |
| SOFTWARE | | | | | | | |

| FUNCTIONAL SPECIFICATION | ✓ | DATA FLOW STRUCTURE | DATA FORMAT/ STRUCTURE | CONTROL STRUCTURE | HIERARCHICAL STRUCTURE |
|---|---|---|---|---|---|

Functional Description

The Organising Committee deals with the administrative aspects of organising the Conference.  The activities include:-

    (i)    Sending out invitations for the Conference;

   (ii)    Registering the acceptances and rejections, and producing a list of Conference attendees;

  (iii)    Making all necessary accommodation arrangements;

   (iv)    Financial arrangements, ie., ensuring that all Conference attendees are invoiced, etc.

    NOTE:  Activities (iii) and (iv) are not further considered in this paper.

Input/Output Data

| Data Ref. | I/P | O/P | Description |
|---|---|---|---|
| 4 | ✓ | | Conference Programme |
| 2 | ✓ | | Priority Attendees List |
| T3 | ✓ | | Correspondence to OC |
| 5 | | ✓ | Conference Attendees List |
| T4 | | ✓ | Correspondence from OC |
| T5 | ✓ | | Rejected Authors List |

EVOLUTIONARY DESIGN METHODOLOGY

| TOTAL SYSTEM ✓ | SYSTEM ID. | IFIP Conference System | | SYSTEM REF. | IFIP/T |
| MAN/MACHINE SYSTEM | MODULE ID. | Organise the Conference | | MODULE REF. | TB |
| SOFTWARE | | | | | |
| FUNCTIONAL SPECIFICATION | DATA FLOW STRUCTURE ✓ | DATA FORMAT/ STRUCTURE | CONTROL STRUCTURE | HIERARCHICAL STRUCTURE | |

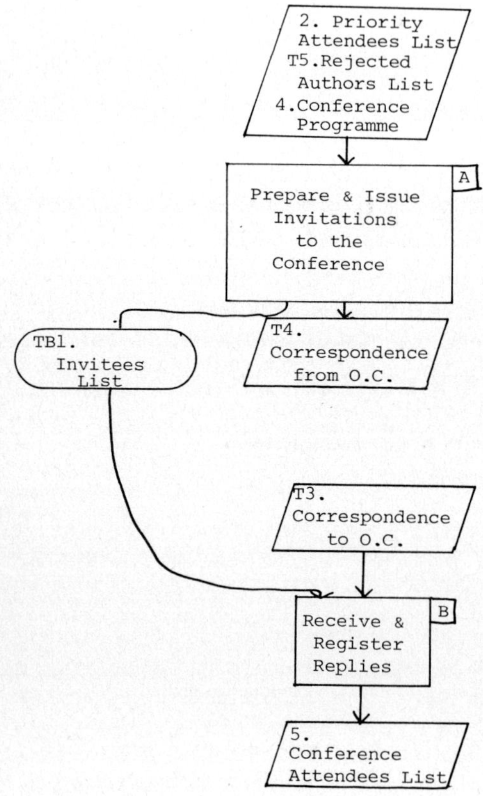

EVOLUTIONARY DESIGN METHODOLOGY

| TOTAL SYSTEM | √ | SYSTEM ID. | IFIP Conference System | | SYSTEM REF. | IFIP/T |
|---|---|---|---|---|---|---|
| MAN/MACHINE SYSTEM | | MODULE ID. | Commission Papers | | MODULE REF. | TAA |
| SOFTWARE | | | | | | |

| FUNCTIONAL SPECIFICATION | √ | DATA FLOW STRUCTURE | DATA FORMAT/ STRUCTURE | CONTROL STRUCTURE | HIERARCHICAL STRUCTURE |
|---|---|---|---|---|---|

Functional Description

The activities within this function include:

    (i)    Preparing a list of possible contributors;

   (ii)    Issuing the call for papers to the list
          of possible contributors;

  (iii)    Receiving and Registering the letters of intent,
          ie., recording:

        (a)    Paper Title;

        (b)    Author(s);

        (c)    Addresses of Author(s);

   (iv)    Receiving and Registering the submitted papers.

Input/output Data

| Data Ref. | I/P | O/P | Description |
|---|---|---|---|
| TA1 | √ | | Prospective Authors List |
| TA2 | √ | | Correspondence from Prospective Authors |
| TA5 | | √ | Correspondence to Prospective Authors |
| TA7 | | √ | Authors List |
| TA8 | | √ | Submitted Papers List |

EVOLUTIONARY DESIGN METHODOLOGY

| TOTAL SYSTEM ✓ | SYSTEM ID. | IFIP Conference System | SYSTEM REF. | IFIP/T |
| MAN/MACHINE SYSTEM | MODULE ID. | Commission Papers | MODULE REF. | TAA |
| SOFTWARE | | | | |

| FUNCTIONAL SPECIFICATION | DATA FLOW STRUCTURE ✓ | DATA FORMAT/ STRUCTURE | CONTROL STRUCTURE | HIERARCHICAL STRUCTURE |

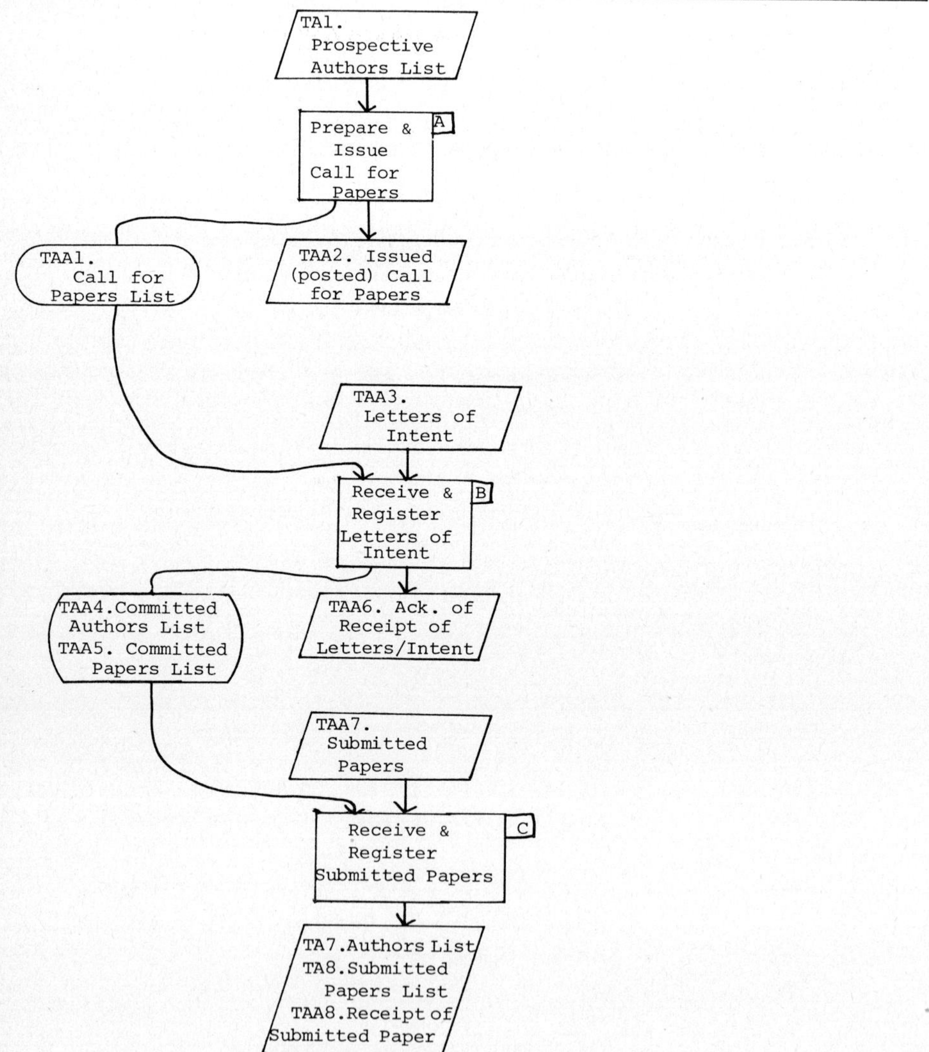

EVOLUTIONARY DESIGN METHODOLOGY

| TOTAL ✓ SYSTEM | SYSTEM ID. | IFIP Conference System | SYSTEM REF. | IFIP/T |
|---|---|---|---|---|
| MAN/MACHINE SYSTEM | MODULE ID. | Prepare and Issue Call for Papers | MODULE REF. | TAAA |

SOFTWARE

| FUNCTIONAL ✓ SPECIFICATION | DATA FLOW STRUCTURE | DATA FORMAT/ STRUCTURE | CONTROL STRUCTURE | HIERARCHICAL STRUCTURE |
|---|---|---|---|---|

## Functional Description

The function is to prepare a list of people to which a call for papers is to be sent.  When the list is prepared the addresses are printed on the envelopes; the "call for papers" inserted in the envelopes and the envelopes posted.

## Input/Output Data

| Data Ref. | I/P | O/P | Description |
|---|---|---|---|
| TA1 | ✓ | | Prospective Authors List |
| TAA1 | | ✓ | Call for papers List |
| TAA2 | | ✓ | Issued (Posted) call for papers |

EVOLUTIONARY DESIGN METHODOLOGY

| TOTAL SYSTEM ✓ | SYSTEM ID. | IFIP Conference System | SYSTEM REF. IFIP/T |
| MAN/MACHINE SYSTEM | MODULE ID. | Prepare and Issue Call for Papers | MODULE REF. TAAA |
| SOFTWARE | | | |

| FUNCTIONAL SPECIFICATION | DATA FLOW ✓ STRUCTURE | DATA FORMAT/ STRUCTURE | CONTROL STRUCTURE | HIERARCHICAL STRUCTURE |

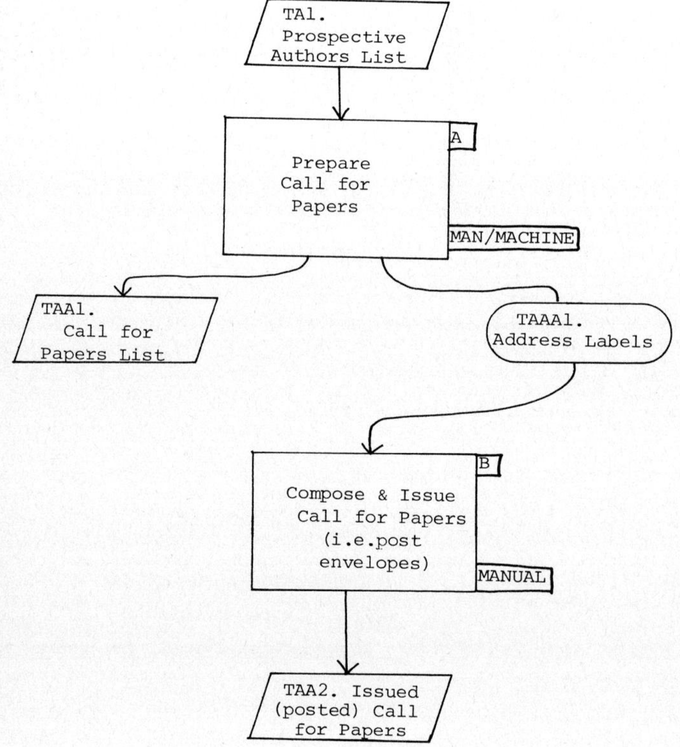

EVOLUTIONARY DESIGN METHODOLOGY

| TOTAL SYSTEM | √ | SYSTEM ID. | | IFIP Conference System | | SYSTEM REF. | IFIP/T |
|---|---|---|---|---|---|---|---|
| MAN/MACHINE SYSTEM | | MODULE ID. | | Receive and Register Letters of Intent. | | MODULE REF. | TAAB |
| SOFTWARE | | | | | | | |

| FUNCTIONAL SPECIFICATION | √ | DATA FLOW STRUCTURE | DATA FORMAT/ STRUCTURE | CONTROL STRUCTURE | HIERARCHICAL STRUCTURE |
|---|---|---|---|---|---|

Functional Description

The function is to receive from the prospective authors their letters of intent; to register their intention to submit a paper and forward a letter of acknowledgement.

In registering the letter of intent the following information is recorded:

    (i)    Paper Title

   (ii)    Authors

  (iii)    Addresses of Authors

The letter of acknowledgement is sent only to the principal author.

Input/Output Data

| Data Ref. | I/P | O/P | Description |
|---|---|---|---|
| TAA1 | √ | | Call for Papers List |
| TAA3 | √ | | Letters of Intent |
| TAA4 | | √ | Committed Authors List |
| TAA5 | | √ | Committed Papers List |
| TAA6 | | √ | Acknowledgement of receipt of letter of intent |

EVOLUTIONARY DESIGN METHODOLOGY

| TOTAL SYSTEM ✓ | SYSTEM ID. | IFIP Conference System | SYSTEM REF. | IFIP/T |
| MAN/MACHINE SYSTEM | MODULE ID. | Receive and Register Letters of Intent. | MODULE REF. | TAAB |
| SOFTWARE | | | | |

| FUNCTIONAL SPECIFICATION | DATA FLOW STRUCTURE ✓ | DATA FORMAT/ STRUCTURE | CONTROL STRUCTURE | HIERARCHICAL STRUCTURE |

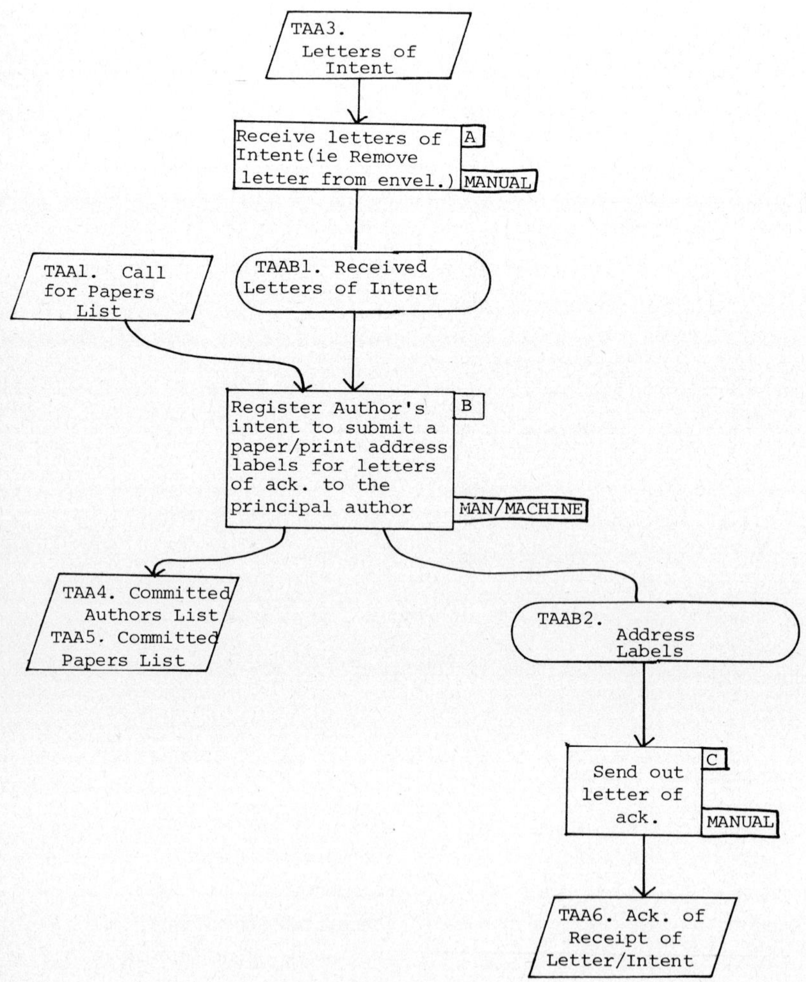

EVOLUTIONARY DESIGN METHODOLOGY

| TOTAL SYSTEM ✓ | SYSTEM ID. | IFIP Conference System | | SYSTEM REF. | IFIP/T |
| MAN/MACHINE SYSTEM | MODULE ID. | Prepare Call for Papers | | MODULE REF. | TAAAA |
| SOFTWARE | | | | | |
| FUNCTIONAL SPECIFICATION ✓ | DATA FLOW STRUCTURE | DATA FORMAT/ STRUCTURE | CONTROL STRUCTURE | HIERARCHICAL STRUCTURE | |

Functional Description

The function is to prepare a list of persons to whom the call for papers is to be
sent and to produce envelope labels with their names and addresses.

Input/Output Data

| Data Ref. | I/P | O/P | Description |
|-----------|-----|-----|-------------|
| TA1 | ✓ | | Prospective Authors List |
| TAA1 | | ✓ | Call for Papers List |
| TAAA1 | | ✓ | Address Labels |

EVOLUTIONARY DESIGN METHODOLOGY

| TOTAL SYSTEM ✓ | SYSTEM ID. | IFIP Conference System | | SYSTEM REF. IFIP/T |
| --- | --- | --- | --- | --- |
| MAN/MACHINE SYSTEM | MODULE ID. | | | MODULE REF. |
| SOFTWARE | | | | |

| FUNCTIONAL SPECIFICATION | DATA FLOW STRUCTURE | DATA FORMAT/ STRUCTURE | CONTROL STRUCTURE | HIERARCHICAL ✓ STRUCTURE |
| --- | --- | --- | --- | --- |

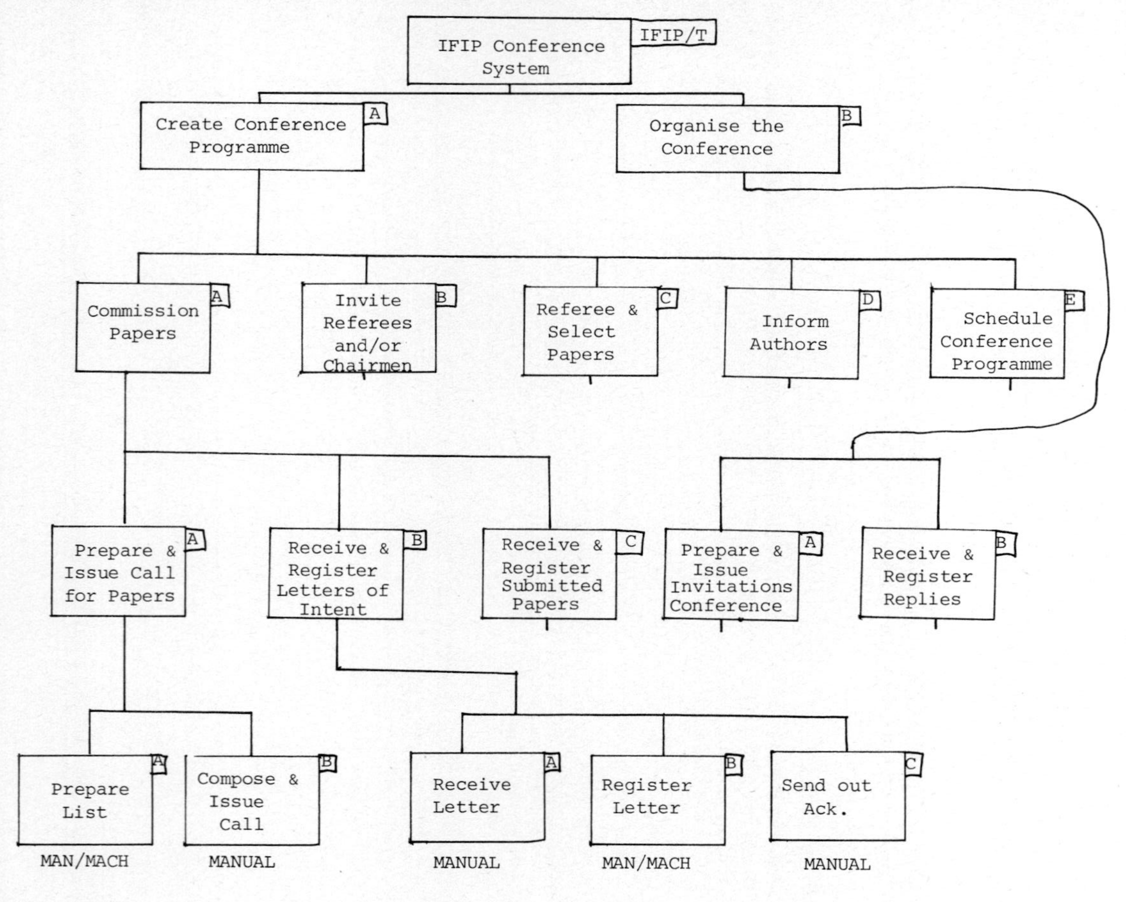

EVOLUTIONARY DESIGN METHODOLOGY

| TOTAL SYSTEM | SYSTEM ID. | IFIP Conference System | | SYSTEM REF. | IFIP/M |
|---|---|---|---|---|---|
| MAN/MACHINE SYSTEM √ | MODULE ID. | Conference System | | MODULE REF. | M |
| SOFTWARE | | | | | |

| FUNCTIONAL SPECIFICATION √ | DATA FLOW STRUCTURE | DATA FORMAT/ STRUCTURE | CONTROL STRUCTURE | HIERARCHICAL STRUCTURE |
|---|---|---|---|---|

Functional Description

The function of the man/machine system is as described in the functional
specifications of those modules of the total system which are labelled MAN/MACHINE.
Due to restrictions on the volume of documentation only one such functional
specification is included in this paper, namely ref. TAAAA.

In addition the man/machine system provides facilities for storing, editing,
printing, retrieving of all relevant Conference information.  It also provides a
comprehensive help to the user for operating the machine.

Input/Output Data

| Data Ref. | I/P | O/P | Description |
|---|---|---|---|
| M1 | √ | | Requests for Conference Data |
| M2 | √ | | Received Correspondence |
| M3 | √ | √ | Conference Data |
| M4 | | √ | Address Labels |

EVOLUTIONARY DESIGN METHODOLOGY

| TOTAL SYSTEM | | SYSTEM ID. | | IFIP Conference System | | SYSTEM REF. | IFIP/M |
|---|---|---|---|---|---|---|---|
| MAN/MACHINE SYSTEM | √ | MODULE ID. | | Conference System | | MODULE REF. | M |
| SOFTWARE | | | | | | | |

| FUNCTIONAL SPECIFICATION | DATA FLOW STRUCTURE | √ | DATA FORMAT/ STRUCTURE | CONTROL STRUCTURE | HIERARCHICAL STRUCTURE |
|---|---|---|---|---|---|

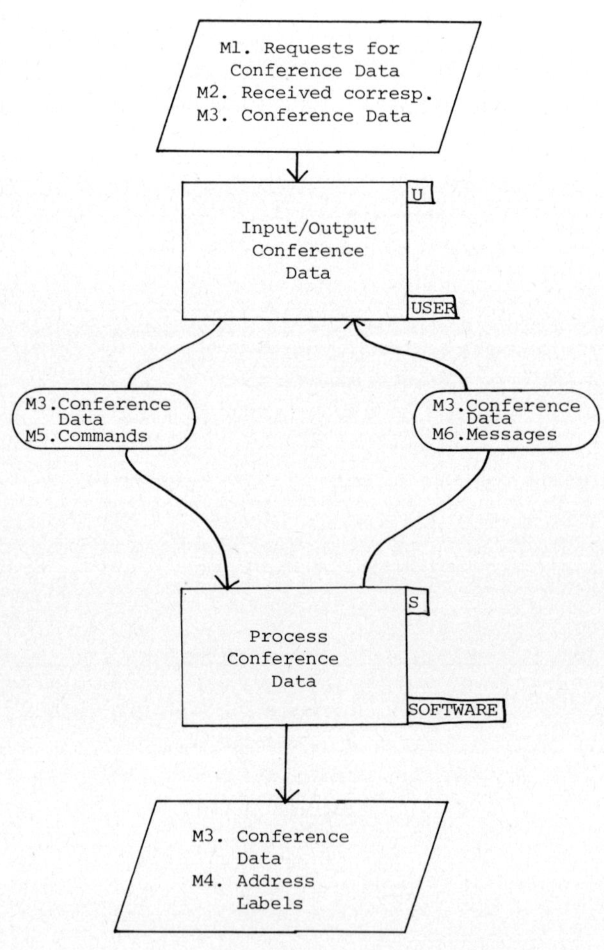

EVOLUTIONARY DESIGN METHODOLOGY

| TOTAL SYSTEM | SYSTEM ID. | IFIP Conference System | | SYSTEM REF. | IFIP/M |
|---|---|---|---|---|---|
| MAN/MACHINE SYSTEM √ | MODULE ID. | Conference System | | MODULE REF. | M |
| SOFTWARE | | | | | |

| FUNCTIONAL SPECIFICATION | DATA FLOW STRUCTURE | DATA FORMAT/ STRUCTURE | CONTROL STRUCTURE √ | HIERARCHICAL STRUCTURE |
|---|---|---|---|---|

The Man/Machine system is controlled by a simple command language by means of which the user selects available facilities.

The structure is hierarchical.  The first level of hierarchy is shown below.  At this level the user either selects facilities related to the work of Programme Committee, or those related to the work of Organising Committee.

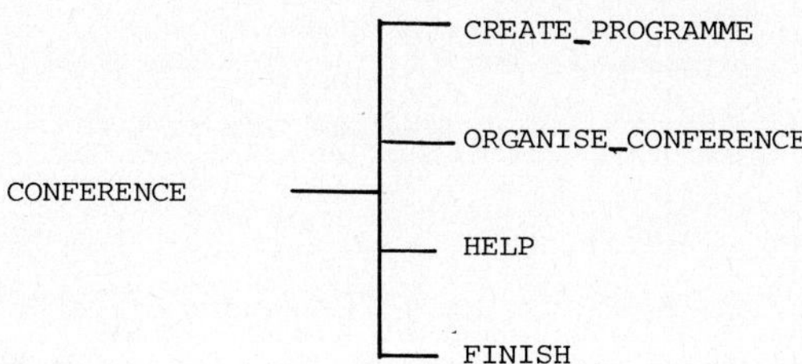


NOTES:

1.  Commands are entered in response to the machine
    prompt:  COMMAND PLEASE?

2.  The user may enter only the first three characters
    of any command.

EVOLUTIONARY DESIGN METHODOLOGY

| TOTAL<br>SYSTEM | SYSTEM<br>ID. | IFIP Conference System | | SYSTEM<br>REF. | IFIP/M |
| --- | --- | --- | --- | --- | --- |
| MAN/MACHINE √<br>SYSTEM | MODULE<br>ID. | Conference System | | MODULE<br>REF. | M |
| SOFTWARE | | | | | |
| FUNCTIONAL<br>SPECIFICATION | DATA FLOW<br>STRUCTURE | DATA FORMAT/<br>STRUCTURE | CONTROL<br>STRUCTURE | √ | HIERARCHICAL<br>STRUCTURE |

The hierarchical structure of commands for creating Conference Programme is shown below:

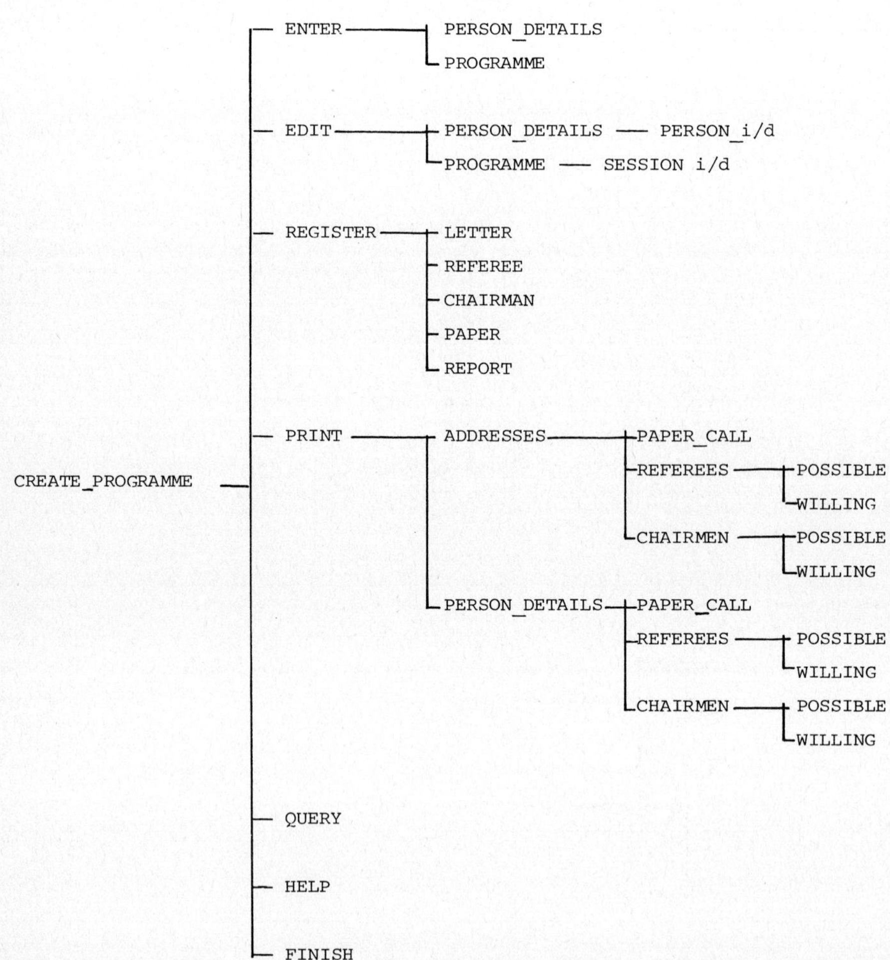

EVOLUTIONARY DESIGN METHODOLOGY

| TOTAL SYSTEM | SYSTEM ID. | IFIP Conference System | SYSTEM REF. | IFIP/M |
| --- | --- | --- | --- | --- |
| MAN/MACHINE SYSTEM √ | MODULE ID. | Conference System | MODULE REF. | M |
| SOFTWARE | | | | |
| FUNCTIONAL SPECIFICATION | DATA FLOW STRUCTURE | DATA FORMAT/√ STRUCTURE | CONTROL STRUCTURE | HIERARCHICAL STRUCTURE |

In response to commands CREATE_PROGRAMME ENTER PERSON_DETAILS the following form is displayed for the user to fill.

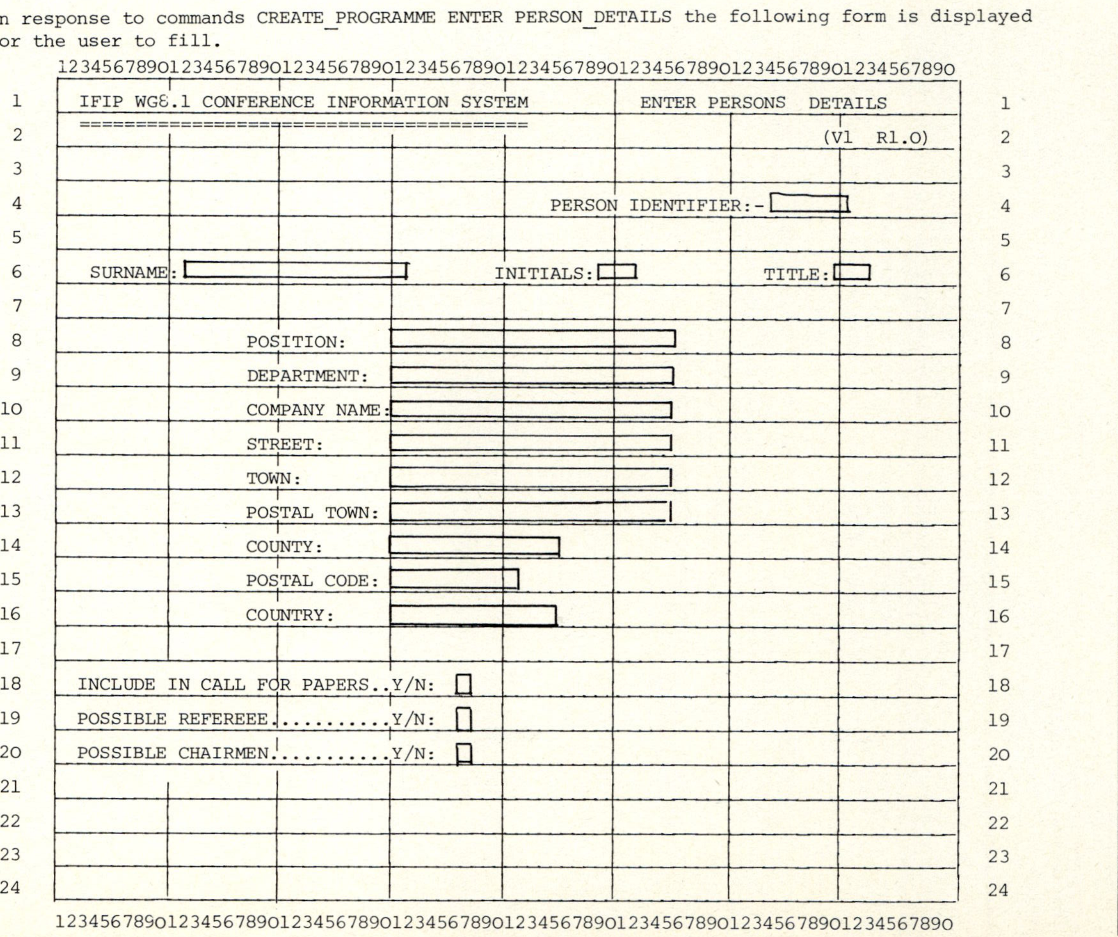

```
          1234567890123456789012345678901234567890123456789012345678901234567890

 1    IFIP WG8.1 CONFERENCE INFORMATION SYSTEM        ENTER PERSONS  DETAILS
 2    ========================================                        (V1  R1.0)
 3
 4                                        PERSON IDENTIFIER:-[      ]
 5
 6    SURNAME:[            ]        INITIALS:[   ]        TITLE:[   ]
 7
 8                 POSITION:      [                    ]
 9                 DEPARTMENT:    [                    ]
10                 COMPANY NAME:  [                    ]
11                 STREET:        [                    ]
12                 TOWN:          [                    ]
13                 POSTAL TOWN:   [                    ]
14                 COUNTY:        [        ]
15                 POSTAL CODE:   [      ]
16                 COUNTRY:       [        ]
17
18    INCLUDE IN CALL FOR PAPERS..Y/N:[ ]
19    POSSIBLE REFEREEE..........Y/N:[ ]
20    POSSIBLE CHAIRMEN..........Y/N:[ ]
```

EVOLUTIONARY DESIGN METHODOLOGY

| TOTAL SYSTEM | SYSTEM ID. | IFIP Conference System | SYSTEM REF. | IFIP/S |
| MAN/MACHINE SYSTEM | MODULE ID. | Process Conference Data | MODULE REF. | S |

SOFTWARE √

| FUNCTIONAL SPECIFICATION √ | DATA FLOW STRUCTURE | DATA FORMAT/ STRUCTURE | CONTROL STRUCTURE | HIERARCHICAL STRUCTURE |

---

Functional Description

This interactive program provides the following facilities:-

 (i) Displays forms for the user to fill in Conference Data and enables the user to edit displayed data;

 (ii) Displays messages for the user such as command prompts, help messages and error messages;

 (iii) Stores Conference Data for further use;

 (iv) Retrieve requested Conference Data and displays/ prints them;

 (v) Prints requested Address Labels.

Input/Output Data

| Data Ref. | I/P | O/P | Description |
|-----------|-----|-----|-------------|
| M3 | √ | √ | Conference Data |
| M4 |   | √ | Address Labels |
| M5 | √ |   | Commands |
| M6 |   | √ | Messages |

EVOLUTIONARY DESIGN METHODOLOGY

| TOTAL SYSTEM | SYSTEM ID. | IFIP Conference System | SYSTEM REF. | IFIP/S |
| MAN/MACHINE SYSTEM | MODULE ID. | Process Conference Data | MODULE REF. | S |
| SOFTWARE √ | | | | |

| FUNCTIONAL SPECIFICATION | DATA FLOW STRUCTURE | DATA FORMAT/ √ STRUCTURE | CONTROL STRUCTURE | HIERARCHICAL STRUCTURE |

Conceptual data structure (relational notation) for CONFERENCE DATA


ENTITY_SETS
___________


    PERSON(PERSON_ID,SURNAME,INITIALS,TITLE,POSITION,DEPT,COMPANY_NAME,

            STREET,TOWN,POSTAL_TOWN,COUNTY,POSTAL_CODE,COUNTRY)


    PAPER(PAPER_ID,PAPER_TITLE)


    PAPER_AUTHOR(PAPER_ID,AUTHOR_ORDER,PERSON_ID)


    SESSION(SESSION_ID,SESSION_TITLE,PERSON_ID[of Chairman],DATE,TIME)


    SESSION_PAPER(SESSION_ID,PAPER_ORDER,PAPER_ID,START_TIME_OF_PAPER)


RELATION_SETS
_____________


    GROUP_PERSON(PERSON_GROUP,PERSON_ID)


    PERSON_GROUP(PERSON_ID,PERSON_GROUP)


    GROUP_PAPER(PAPER_GROUP,PAPER_ID)


    PERSON_PAPER(PERSON_ID,PAPER_ID)

EVOLUTIONARY DESIGN METHODOLOGY

| TOTAL SYSTEM | SYSTEM ID. | IFIP Information System | SYSTEM REF. | IFIP/S |
| MAN/MACHINE SYSTEM | MODULE ID. | Process Conference Data | MODULE REF. | S |
| SOFTWARE √ | | | | |

| FUNCTIONAL SPECIFICATION | DATA FLOW STRUCTURE | DATA FORMAT/ √ STRUCTURE | CONTROL STRUCTURE | HIERARCHICAL STRUCTURE |

Conceptual data structure (table notation) for Conference Data

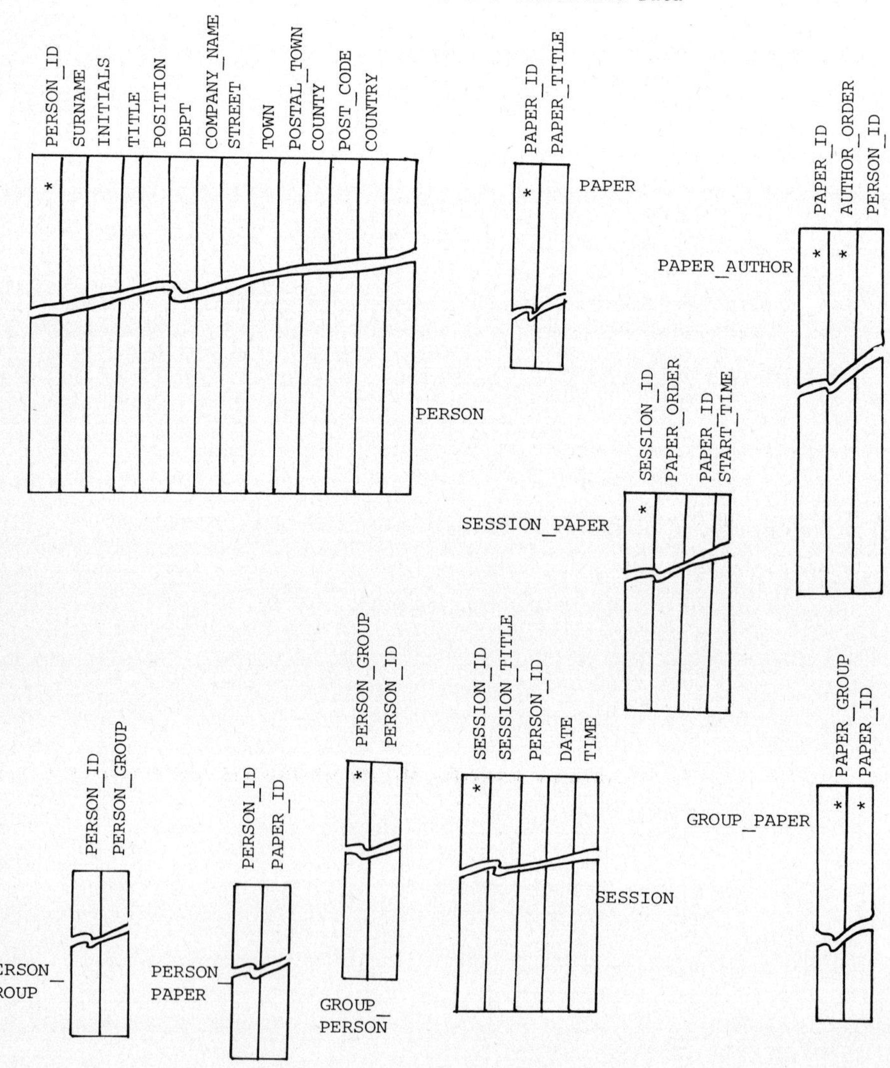


* denotes Primary Key

EVOLUTIONARY DESIGN METHODOLOGY

| TOTAL SYSTEM | SYSTEM ID. | IFIP Conference System | SYSTEM REF. | IFIP/S |
| MAN/MACHINE SYSTEM | MODULE ID. | Process Conference Data | MODULE REF. | S |

SOFTWARE √

| FUNCTIONAL SPECIFICATION | DATA FLOW STRUCTURE | DATA FORMAT/ √ STRUCTURE | CONTROL STRUCTURE | HIERARCHICAL STRUCTURE |

ATTRIBUTE - DOMAIN DEFINITIONS

| I.D | DESCRIPTION | DATA TYPE | RANGE | COMMENT |
|---|---|---|---|---|
| PERSON_ID | Unique identifier of each person in the D/B | CHAR (6) | alpha-numeric | |
| SURNAME | Surname of person | CHAR (20) | " | |
| INITIALS | Initials of person | CHAR (4) | " | |
| TITLE | Title of person eg. Mr, Dr, etc. | CHAR (4) | " | |
| POSITION | Position held in Company | CHAR (30) | " | |
| DEPT | Department in Company | CHAR (30) | " | |
| COMPANY_NAME | Name of Company | CHAR (30) | " | |
| STREET | Part of Address | CHAR (30) | " | |
| TOWN | Part of Address | CHAR (30) | " | |
| POSTAL_TOWN | Part of Address | CHAR (30) | " | |
| COUNTY | Part of Address | CHAR (20) | " | |
| POST_CODE | Part of Address | CHAR (6) | " | |
| COUNTRY | Part of Address | CHAR (20) | " | |
| PAPER_ID | Unique identifier of each paper | CHAR (6) | " | |
| PAPER_TITLE | Title of Paper | CHAR (60) | " | |
| AUTHOR_ORDER | The order of the authors of a Paper | Numeric | Positive Integer | |
| SESSION_TITLE | Title of the session | CHAR (60) | alpha-numeric | |
| DATE | Date of the session | CHAR (6) | alpha-numeric | Day:Day:Month:Month:Year:Year |
| TIME | Start time of session | CHAR (4) | alpha-numeric | Hour:Hour:Min:Min |
| SESSION | Unique identifier of conference session | CHAR (6) | alpha-numeric | |
| PAPER_ORDER | Order of the paper within a session | numeric | positive integer | |

EVOLUTIONARY DESIGN METHODOLOGY

| TOTAL<br>SYSTEM | SYSTEM<br>ID. | IFIP Conference System | SYSTEM<br>REF. | IFIP/S |
| MAN/MACHINE<br>SYSTEM | MODULE<br>ID. | Process Conference Data | MODULE<br>REF. | S |

SOFTWARE   √

| FUNCTIONAL<br>SPECIFICATION | DATA FLOW<br>STRUCTURE | DATA FORMAT/ √<br>STRUCTURE | CONTROL<br>STRUCTURE | HIERARCHICAL<br>STRUCTURE |

ATTRIBUTE- DOMAIN DEFINITIONS (continued)

| I.D. | DESCRIPTION | DATA TYPE | RANGE | COMMENT |
|---|---|---|---|---|
| START-TIME_<br>OF_PAPER | | CHAR (4) | alpha-numeric | Hour:Hour:<br>Min:Min |
| PERSON_GROUP | Name of groups to<br>which individuals<br>belong | CHAR (12) | CALL/INTENT/<br>SUBMIT/ACCEPT<br>POSS_CHAIR/<br>POSS_REF/<br>ATTEND_LIST | |
| PAPER_GROUP | Name of groups to<br>which papers<br>belong | CHAR (10) | INTENT/<br>SUBMIT/<br>ACCEPT | |

EVOLUTIONARY DESIGN METHODOLOGY

| TOTAL SYSTEM | SYSTEM ID. | IFIP Conference System | SYSTEM REF. | IFIP/S |
| MAN/MACHINE SYSTEM | MODULE ID. | Process Conference Data | MODULE REF. | S |

SOFTWARE √

| FUNCTIONAL SPECIFICATION | DATA FLOW STRUCTURE √ | DATA FORMAT/ STRUCTURE | CONTROL STRUCTURE | HIERARCHICAL STRUCTURE |

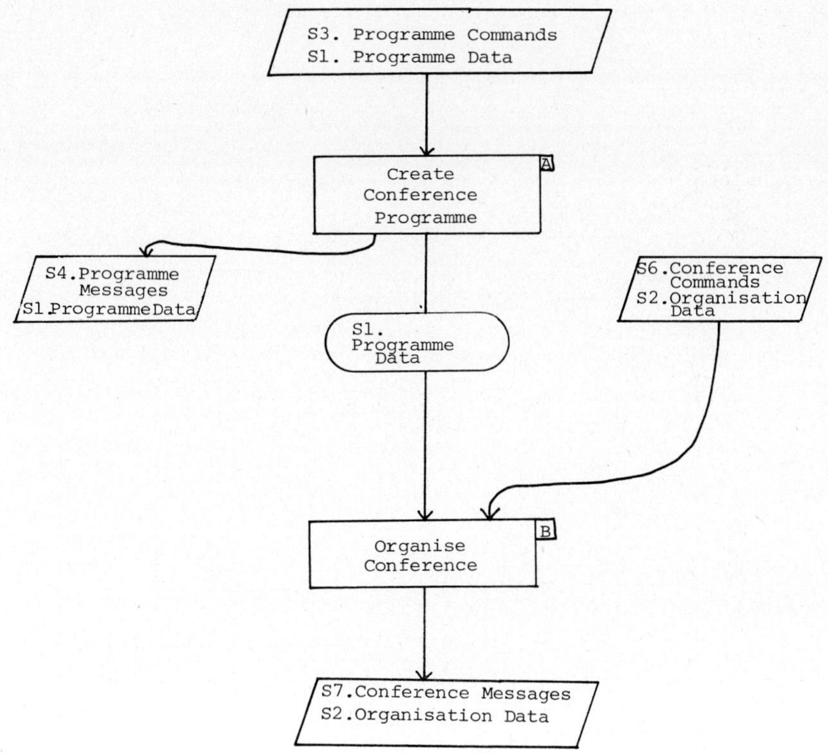

*G. Rzevski et al.*

EVOLUTIONARY DESIGN METHODOLOGY

| TOTAL SYSTEM | SYSTEM ID. | IFIP Information System | SYSTEM REF. | IFIP/S |
|---|---|---|---|---|
| MAN/MACHINE SYSTEM | MODULE ID. | Process Conference Data | MODULE REF. | S |
| SOFTWARE √ | | | | |

| FUNCTIONAL SPECIFICATION | DATA FLOW STRUCTURE | DATA FORMAT/ STRUCTURE | CONTROL STRUCTURE √ | HIERARCHICAL STRUCTURE |
|---|---|---|---|---|

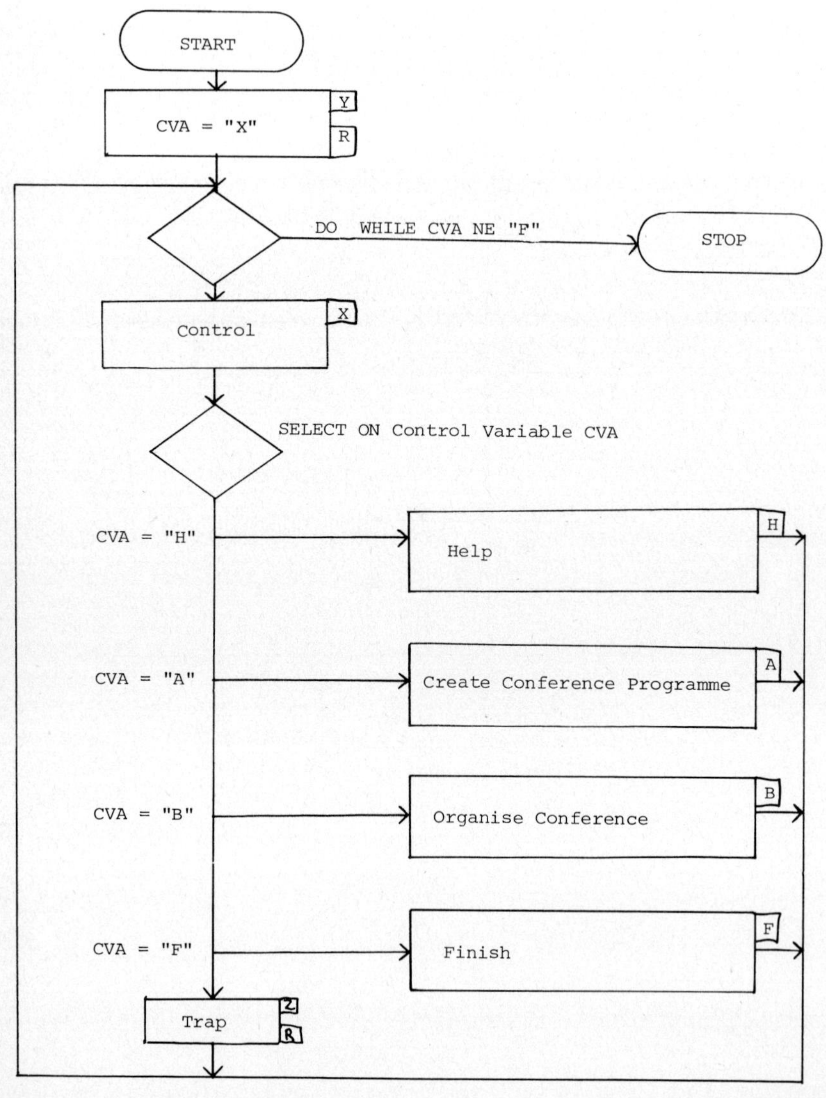

EVOLUTIONARY DESIGN METHODOLOGY

| TOTAL SYSTEM | SYSTEM ID. | IFIP Conference System | SYSTEM REF. | IFIP/S |
| MAN/MACHINE SYSTEM | MODULE ID. | Create Conference Programme | MODULE REF. | SA |
| SOFTWARE √ | | | | |

| FUNCTIONAL SPECIFICATION √ | DATA FLOW STRUCTURE | DATA FORMAT/ STRUCTURE | CONTROL STRUCTURE | HIERARCHICAL STRUCTURE |

Functional Description

This module provides facilities for the user to create the Conference Programme. These facilities include:

    (i)    entering, editing and displaying the programme data by means of screen forms;

    (ii)    displaying of messages to the user, eg. command prompts, help messages and error messages;

    (iii)    storing of programme data;

    (iv)    retrieving programme data for displaying and printing;

    (v)    printing requested address labels.

Input/Output Data

| Data Ref. | I/P | O/P | Description |
|-----------|-----|-----|-------------|
| S3 | √ | | Programme Commands |
| S1 | √ | √ | Programme Data |
| S4 | | √ | Programme Messages |

EVOLUTIONARY DESIGN METHODOLOGY

| TOTAL SYSTEM | SYSTEM ID. | IFIP Information System | SYSTEM REF. | IFIP/S |
| MAN/MACHINE SYSTEM | MODULE ID. | Creat Conference Programme | MODULE REF. | SA |

SOFTWARE √

| FUNCTIONAL SPECIFICATION | DATA FLOW STRUCTURE | DATA FORMAT/ STRUCTURE √ | CONTROL STRUCTURE | HIERARCHICAL STRUCTURE |

PROGRAMME DATA comprises the following sets:


        A.PERSON          =    PERSON, ie. all tuples of the PERSON
                                    entity set


        A.PAPER           =    PAPER, ie. all tuples of the PAPER
                                    entity set


        A.PAPER_AUTHOR    =    PAPER_AUTHOR, ie. all tuples of the
                                        PAPER_AUTHOR entity set


        A.SESSION         =    SESSION, ie. all tuples of the SESSION
                                    entity set


        A.SESSION_PAPER   =    SESSION_PAPER, ie. all tuples of the
                                        SESSION_PAPER entity set


        A.GROUP_PERSON    =    GROUP_PERSON, ie. all tuples of the
                                        GROUP_PERSON relation set


        A.PERSON_GROUP    =    PERSON_GROUP, ie. all tuples of the
                                        PERSON_GROUP relation set


        A.GROUP_PAPER     =    GROUP_PAPER, ie. all tuples of the
                                        GROUP_PAPER relation set


        A.PERSON_PAPER    =    PERSON_PAPER, ie. all tuples of the
                                        PERSON_PAPER relation set

EVOLUTIONARY DESIGN METHODOLOGY

| TOTAL SYSTEM | SYSTEM ID. | IFIP Information System | SYSTEM REF. | IFIP/S |
| MAN/MACHINE SYSTEM | MODULE ID. | Create Conference Programme | MODULE REF. | SA |

SOFTWARE √

| FUNCTIONAL SPECIFICATION | DATA FLOW STRUCTURE | DATA FORMAT/ STRUCTURE | CONTROL STRUCTURE √ | HIERARCHICAL STRUCTURE |

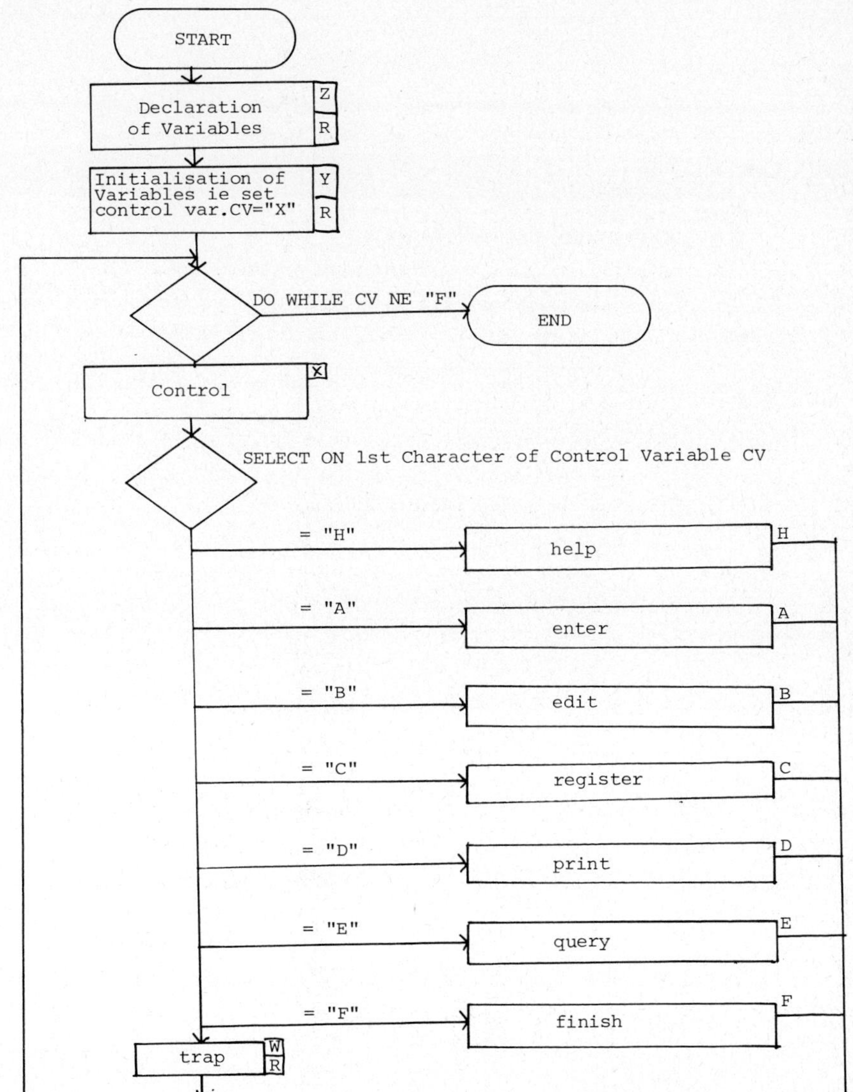

EVOLUTIONARY DESIGN METHODOLOGY

| TOTAL SYSTEM | SYSTEM ID. | IFIP Information System | SYSTEM REF. | IFIP/S |
|---|---|---|---|---|
| MAN/MACHINE SYSTEM | MODULE ID. | Organise Conference | MODULE REF. | SB |
| SOFTWARE ✓ | | | | |

| FUNCTIONAL SPECIFICATION ✓ | DATA FLOW STRUCTURE | DATA FORMAT/ STRUCTURE | CONTROL STRUCTURE | HIERARCHICAL STRUCTURE |
|---|---|---|---|---|

Functional Description

This module provides facilities for the user to organise the Conference.
These facilities include:

- (i)    displaying programme data;
- (ii)   entering, editing and displaying organisational data by means of screen forms;
- (iii)  displaying of messages to the user, eg. command prompts, help messages and error messages;
- (iv)   storing of organisational data;
- (v)    retrieving of organisational data for displaying and printing;
- (vi)   printing requested address labels.

Input/output Data

| Data Ref. | I/P | O/P | Description |
|---|---|---|---|
| S1 | ✓ | | Programme Data |
| S2 | ✓ | ✓ | Organisational Data |
| S6 | ✓ | | Conference commands |
| S7 | | ✓ | Conference messages |

EVOLUTIONARY DESIGN METHODOLOGY

| TOTAL<br>SYSTEM | SYSTEM<br>ID. | | SYSTEM<br>REF. | IFIP/S |
|---|---|---|---|---|
| MAN/MACHINE<br>SYSTEM | MODULE<br>ID. | Organise Conference | MODULE<br>REF. | SB |
| SOFTWARE √ | | | | |

| FUNCTIONAL<br>SPECIFICATION | DATA FLOW<br>STRUCTURE | DATA FORMAT √<br>STRUCTURE | CONTROL<br>STRUCTURE | HIERARCHICAL<br>STRUCTURE |
|---|---|---|---|---|

Programme Data consists of the following sets:

(i)      B.PERSON  =  {PERSON

$\exists$ GROUP_PERSON(GROUP_PERSON.PERSON_ID=PERSON.PERSON_ID
& (GROUP_PERSON.PERSON_GROUP="SUBMIT" OR "CHAIRMAN" OR
"IFIP_REP"))}

ie. Only those tuples in the PERSON entity set which are defined in
the GROUP_PERSON relation set to be <u>submitted authors</u> or <u>Chairmen</u>
or <u>IFIP Representatives</u>

(ii)     AB.PAPER  =  {PAPER

$\exists$ GROUP_PAPER(GROUP_PAPER.PAPER_ID=PAPER.PAPER_ID
& GROUP_PAPER.PAPER_GROUP="ACCEPT")}

ie. Only those tuples in the PAPER entity set which are defined in
the GROUP_PAPER relation set to be <u>accepted paper</u>

(iii)    AB.PAPER_AUTHOR  =  {PAPER_AUTHOR

$\exists$ GROUP_PAPER(GROUP_PAPER.PAPER_ID=PAPER_AUTHOR.
PAPER_ID & GROUP_PAPER.PAPER_GROUP="ACCEPT")}

ie. Only those tuples in the PAPER_AUTHOR entity set which are defined
in the GROUP_PAPER relation set to be <u>accepted papers</u>

(iv)     AB.SESSION  =   SESSION ie. all tuples of the SESSION entity set

(v)      AB.SESSION_PAPER  =   SESSION_PAPER ie. all tuples of the
SESSION_PAPER entity set

EVOLUTIONARY DESIGN METHODOLOGY

| TOTAL SYSTEM | SYSTEM ID. | IFIP Conference System | | SYSTEM REF. | IFIP/S |
|---|---|---|---|---|---|
| MAN/MACHINE SYSTEM | MODULE ID. | | | MODULE REF. | |
| SOFTWARE √ | | | | | |

| FUNCTIONAL SPECIFICATION | DATA FLOW STRUCTURE | DATA FORMAT/ STRUCTURE | CONTROL STRUCTURE | HIERARCHICAL STRUCTURE √ |
|---|---|---|---|---|

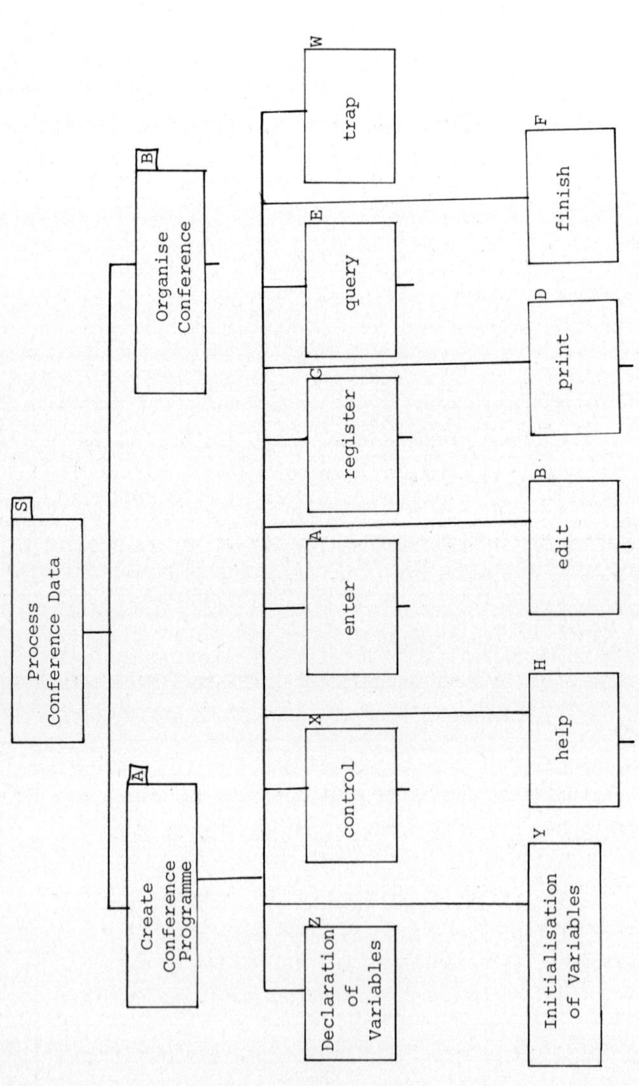

*INFORMATION SYSTEMS DESIGN METHODOLOGIES: A Comparative Review*
*T.W. Olle, H.G. Sol, A.A. Verrijn-Stuart (editors)*
*North-Holland Publishing Company*
© *IFIP, 1982*


# A DRAFT PROPOSAL FOR INTEGRATING
# SYSTEM SPECIFICATION MODELS

Arne Sølvberg

Dept. Computer Science
University of Trondheim
The Norwegian Institute of Technology


SUMMARY

The report is divided in two main parts.  The first part is
concerned with describing system modelling elements, ranging
from requirements specifications to program specification.
It is demonstrated through an example how a requirement
specification is gradually transformed into a computer program
solution which satisfy the requirements.  The second part shows
the results of the proposed method applied on the IFIP-Working
Conference example case.


## 1.  INTRODUCTION

One major difficulty in information systems design and maintenance, is the lack of
coherence between the requirement definition activity and the implementation and
operation activities.  This is partly due to a cultural collision between people
who are concerned with analysis "in the large", and people who are concerned with
programming "in the small".  But the main reason for our present difficulties is
probably the lack of a coherent set of methods and systems models, which offers a
continuous and smooth transition from "in the large" problems to "in the small"
problems.

To be able to produce maintainable systems, this lack of a sufficient methodological basis has had to be counteracted by administrative means e.g. project
management controls, documentation standards.  The majority of administrative tools
which are available, are independent of specific methods, models or implementation
tools.  So we feel that we can divide the systems development problem into

> one administrative problem,
>> concerned with project management tools, and

> one technical problem,
>> concerned with system models, analysis methods,
>>> design methods, implementation methods

This paper is concerned only with the technical aspect of the information systems
design problem.

We try to contribute to bridging the gap
between analysis "in the large" and programming "in the small".

We have examplified our approach by using the IFIP WG8.1 example case for
designing an information system for supporting IFIP Working Conference
arrangements.

The paper is organized in two parts:

    . chapter 2 contains

           . definitions of, and suggestions for, modelling tools for terminology definition, process requirement definition, data definition, and their relationships

           . a detailed examplification of the process of developing a requirement specification into a computer program solution which satisfy the specification

    . chapter 3 contains

           . excerpts from a solution of a conference management system, adapted to the IFIP example case

           . a detailed analysis of the first phases of requirement definition, with special emphasis on terminology definition

## 1.1.  Information systems modelling

Systems are designed to perform tasks which are useful to the system's environment.  Information processing systems perform information processing tasks for some other systems.  The basic requirements for an information processing system to be useful, is that it performs the right tasks, that it is reliable, and that it interacts properly with its environment.  Information processing tasks can only be performed if information processing resources are assigned to the tasks. Reliability can only be achieved if there is some mean of controlling that tasks have been performed on time.

When designing an information processing system, we are thus faced with determining the tasks to be performed, the interaction with the environment, the assignment of processing resources to tasks, the task control system, the process resource control system, the rules for operating the system.

An implemented, operational information processing system is a part of the organization in which it is imbedded.  So by implementing an information system in an organization, we change the organization.  This can severely interupt the operation of the organization, if the information system is not properly designed. To minimize this danger, we resort to building a model of the information processing system, so that the system can be evaluated prior to implementation.

For any model to be useful, its objecttypes and relationtypes must be so chosen, that each of the types is a useful classification of the phenomena which are studied.  The "usefulness" of a classification is dependent both on the characteristica of the system being modelled, and on the properties of the system design process (the development method).

## 1.2.  Basic approach

Systems development methods are usually divided into two subgroups:

    . requirement definition methods, aiming at specifying WHAT the information system should do, and

    . design methods, aiming at specifying HOW the requirement specifications shall be satisfied.

We are not in complete agreement with this point of view, although we acknowledge that this is a natural division as seen from a project management point of view.

Our basic approach is that

> . requirements are always formulated in the form of solutions to problems,
>   and
>
> . the solution of one problem on one level, leads to a requirement for
>   solutions of some new problems on a next level (the HOW of one level is
>   the WHAT of the next level).

System development must therefore be viewed as a continuous design process, where
the solution alternatives on one level must satisfy requirements imposed by design
decisions on previous levels. We further believe that knowledge about some
specific information system, is distributed among several groups of people. The
systems specifications must therefore be understandable for all persons who are
involved in the development work.

The major activities in systems design, excluding the project administrative
activities, are

> . developing a common terminology which cover the most important concepts in
>   the system and its environment.
>
> . developing a specification of the information processing tasks ("primary"
>   tasks) which are the raison d'etrê of the information system, including
>   a specification of the flow of messages among the tasks, and between the
>   tasks and the system environment.
>
> . definition of the contents of, and operations on, the information resources
>   which must be available during the operation of the system.
>
> . analysing error conditions, and specifying appropriate actions.
>
> . analysing the responsibility aspect for the task performance e.g. what
>   should happen if some task has not been performed correctly.
>
> . allocating processing resources to tasks, communication channels to message
>   flows, and data storage locations (e.g. archives) to information resources.
>
> . designing the man - machine interfaces.
>
> . designing the resource management system.
>
> . operational design (e.g. procedures for initialization and restart).
>
> . data base design.
>
> . program structure design (subroutines, program modules).

In chapter 2, we illustrate how one proceeds from one design activity to the next,
in a smooth continuous fashion. We suggest features of a basic formalism to be
used for specification purposes. We have tried to use as much of commonly used
methods and techniques as possible.
This is because we believe that a lot of common sense and usefulness is reflected
by commonly used methods for e.g. programming, flowcharting etc.

One conclusion to be be drawn from the presentation of chapter 2, is that it is
impossible to keep track of all the specification details by manual methods alone.
Some type of computer support is necessary. We have therefore chosen to present
the system solution in chapter 3 by rather conventional means (task structure
diagrams and program module diagrams) which are suited for manual documentation.

In the paper we have used a number of techniques which have appeared in the
literature.  Some features of the graphical presentation of diagrams have been
borrowed from Gane and Sarson's book "Structured Systems Analysis:  tools &
techniques", Prentice Hall [1].  The ideas on specification of communication
channels are taken from Lesser, Serrain, Bonar's paper "PCL:  a processoriented
job control language".  (Proc. 1st Int. Conf. Distr. Computing Systems, 1979) [2].

The solution which is presented in chapter 3 is based on a complete specification
and implementation of a conference management system, developed by students of the
Computer Science Department of The Norwegian Institute of Technology, as a term
project.  Only when having seen a complete, well documented, implemented solution
of such a system does one recognize that the number of details is so large, that
it is impossible to fit it into the format prescribed by the IFIP example system.


2.  BASIC OBJECT-TYPES AND RELATIONTYPES

The major purpose of an information system is to collect and transmit knowledge
about phenomena, which (quite often) exist independently of the information system
e.g. a person exists independently of an IFIP Working Conference.
An information system usually interacts with some of the phenomena which it
carries information about e.g. a program committee interacts with authors of
papers.  We need concepts which enable us to model phenomena, both external and
internal to the information system.

2.1.  General model-concepts

A complete account of model concepts can be found in [3].

2.1.1.  Entities and connections

The concept of entity is undefined.  An entity can be anything.  Nevertheless, we
need an object type in our model which we can use to represent whatever we wish
to represent, without being forced to do a premature classification in types which
are relevant only to the information processing system.

So we introduce the object-types

     entity  and  entitytype

where an entitytype-object represent a collection of entities which are perceived
to have some similar features.

Example:

     entitytype PC_MEMBER;

     entity PC_CHAIRPERSON;

These object-types are no more and no less general than are the concepts of
discrete mathematics.

The objecttypes

 connection and connectiontype

represent entities which have the properties of mathematical relations, i.e. they
are subsets of cartesian products of sets of entities (entitytype-objects and/or
connectiontype-objects).

Example:

 entitytype PAPER, POTENTIAL_PARTICIPANT;

 connectiontype AUTHOR (from PAPER to POTENTIAL PARTICIPANT)

The concept of AUTHOR is regarded as a mathematical relation between the
mathematical sets PAPER and POTENTIAL_PARTICIPANT.

### 2.1.2.  Organization-objects and the system-object

Some of the entities in an information system (IS) have characteristica which are
common to most IS's.  For example, IS's are usually divided in organizational
units.  The concept of organization-entity is a useful concept.

Example:

 organization WCM, PC, OC;

WCM  -  working conference management
PC   -  program committee
OC   -  organization committee

There is only one system object, e.g. system WORKING_CONFERENCE;

### 2.1.3.  The component-relationtype

To support hierarchical representations of systems structures, we introduce the
component-relationtype.

Example:

 component (WCM):  PC, OC;

Both the program committee and organization committee are parts of (components
of) the working conference management system.

All of the organization objects are components of the system object.

## 2.1.4.  General Relationtypes

Working on this rather general conceptual level, it is convenient to introduce
relationtypes of similar generality.

| Relationtype name | Definition | Example |
|---|---|---|
| subset<br>alias subtype<br>alias role | role (Y) : X<br>$\Rightarrow X \subset Y$ | subtype (REFEREE):PC_MEMBER; |
| member | member (Y) : Z<br>$\Rightarrow Z \in Y$ | member (PC_MEMBER):PC_CHAIRPERSON; |
| element | element (Y) : y<br>$\Rightarrow$ Let $y \in Y$ | element (REFEREE): Referee; |
| isa | isa $\equiv$ member$^{-1}$ | entity PC_CHAIRPERSON (isa PC_MEMBER); |
| from<br><br>to | connectiontype<br>Y (from X to Z)<br>$\Rightarrow Y \subset X \times Z$ | connectiontype<br>PANELIST (from SESSION<br>        to PARTICIPANT); |
| coordinate | connectiontype<br>A (coordinate<br>    B, C, D, E)<br>$\Rightarrow A \subset B \times C \times D \times E$ | coordinate (DATE): DAY, MONTH, YEAR; |
| domain | domain (A) : B<br>$\Rightarrow$ every $b \in B$<br>appears as first<br>coordinate in the<br>pairs (x,y) of<br>A = {(x,y)} | domain (AUTHOR): PAPER; |
| range | range (A) : C<br>$\Rightarrow$ every $c \in C$<br>appears as second<br>coordinate in the<br>pairs (x,y) of<br>A = {(x,y)} | range (PANELIST): DISCUSSANT; |
| classification | classification (X):Y<br>$\Rightarrow$ Y is a mathematical<br>partion of X | classification (PERSON):<br>        SEXGROUP (member MALE, FEMALE) |
| category | category (X): A,B,C<br>$\Rightarrow A \cup B \cup C = X$<br>$A \cap B \cap C = 0$ | category (PERSON): MALE, FEMALE; |

Fig. 1  Concepts for terminology modelling

### 2.1.5. Graphical representation

The graphical symbols for object-types are

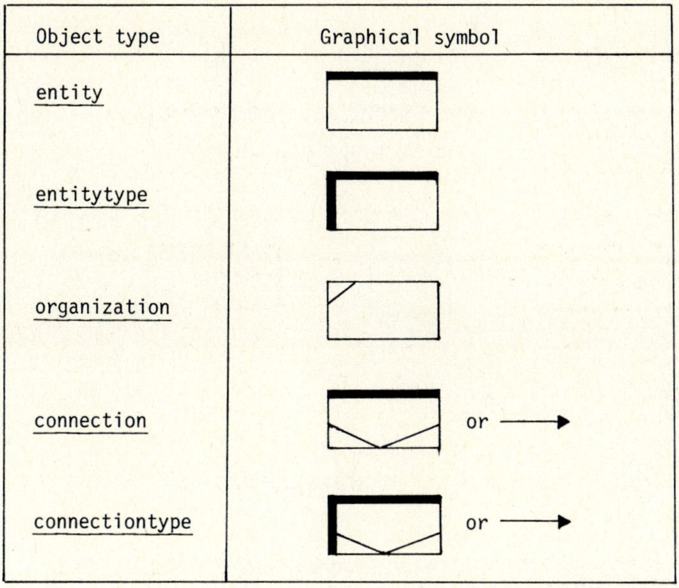

| Object type | Graphical symbol |
|---|---|
| entity | |
| entitytype | |
| organization | |
| connection | or $\longrightarrow$ |
| connectiontype | or $\longrightarrow$ |

Fig. 2.  Graphical symbols for representing terminology models

### 2.1.6. Example of crude terminology definition for an IFIP working conference

The first part of a modelling effort is usually concerned with the classification (and naming) of entities which are of importance for the later stages of systems development.

The general modelling concepts which we have introduced so far, are mainly aimed at being used for terminology definition.

Example (fig. 3):

| | |
|---|---|
| system | WORKING_CONFERENCE, |
| organization | WCM, OC, PC; |
| entitytype | PAPER, POTENTIAL_PARTICIPANT, SESSION, PC_MEMBER, OC_MEMBER; |
| component | (WCM): OC, PC; |
| entity | PC_CHAIRPERSON (isa PC_MEMBER), OC_CHAIRPERSON (isa OC_MEMBER); |
| connection | AUTHOR (domain PAPER to POTENTIAL_PARTICIPANT); |

The last statement implies that any paper has one or more authors.

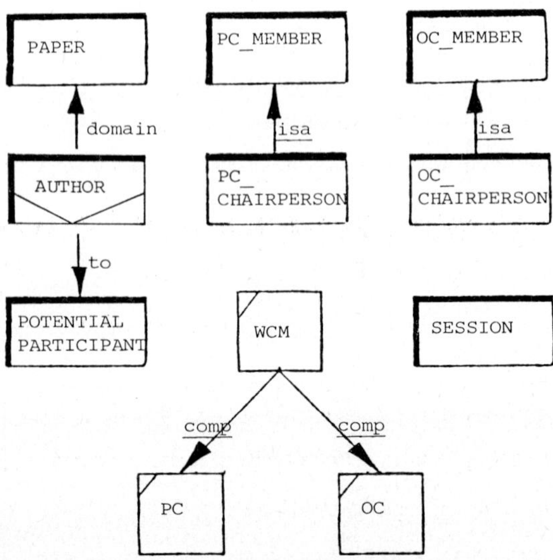


Fig. 3.   Graphical representation of objects and relationships in the
          WORKING_CONFERENCE system.

2.1.7.   The problem of assigning names to entities.  The alias-relationtype.

If we insist on a unique naming scheme, we will end up with so many different
names that we will have small chances of creating an effective language for
communicating about the system's features.

Example:   Papers have authors, which are persons.  These persons are authors
           because they are connected to papers.  In the example of 2.1.6, we
           defined a connection named AUTHOR from PAPER to POTENTIAL PARTICIPANT.
           But it is also natural to talk about persons as authors, if they have
           written papers.  So we also want to use the term AUTHOR to denote a
           subtype of POTENTIAL_PARTICIPANT.

Example:   Papers are submitted to the program committee, they are sent to
           referees, returned from the referees, sent to the publisher, etc.
           Because we have to specify the features of papers in different stages
           of processing, we have a need for distinguishing between different states
           of the papers.  If insisting on a globally unique naming scheme, we would
           have to invent a rather large number of unique names e.g. PAPER1,
           PAPER2, SUBMITTED_PAPER, PAPER_IN_REVIEW, etc. etc. in addition to the
           "root"-name PAPER.

The examples show that unique naming schemes are quite impractical.

So we introduce the alias-relationtype.

Example:   <u>range</u> (AUTHOR) : (<u>alias</u> AUTHOR);
           which means that the subset of POTENTIAL PARTICIPANT which is AUTHOR-
           related to PAPER, will also be called AUTHOR.  Whenever it is necessary
           to distinguish between the AUTHOR-connection-object and the AUTHOR-
           entity-object we shall have to do this explicitly.

Any object can be <u>alias</u>-related to the name of any other object, or to any string
of characters which can serve as a name.

Example:  <u>entitytype</u> PC (<u>alias</u> 'Program Committee');

## 2.2.  <u>Special model-concepts for functional specification</u>

The main object-types which are intended to be used for functional specifications
of information systems are

   <u>datatype</u>, <u>message</u>, <u>datastore</u>, <u>task</u> and <u>signal</u>

Datatypes, messages and datastores are used to specify the content and structure
of the data which are transmitted and stored in the information system.

Signals are used to store information about events in the information system e.g.
a certain message has been produced.
Tasks communicate via messages and signals.  Tasks can be interpreted as mappings
among messages.

### 2.2.1.  <u>Datatypes and messages</u>

A datum is an alfanumerical symbol.

A <u>datatype</u>-object is a (time-independent) set of data with similar characteristica e.g. AGE = {1, 2, 3..., 120}.

A message is a collection of data which exists over a limited interval of time,
and which is transmitted collectively from one entity to another.

A <u>message</u>-object represents a link for transmitting messages between entities.
A <u>message</u>-object can only contain one message at a time.  A <u>message</u>-object thus
<u>represents</u> the set of all messages that are transmitted through the <u>message</u>-object
link, over an unspecified span of time.  (e.g. a mathematical variable is a
<u>message</u>-object.)

So the basic difference between <u>datatype</u>-objects and <u>message</u>(type)-objects is
their relationship to time.  A <u>datatype</u>-object has a time-independent definition,
while a <u>message</u>-object is defined to consist of data which have time-limited
existence ("occurrences", "instantiations").

The graphical symbols for

     datatypes are circles           ◯

     messages are romboids           ▱

            or arrows       ───────▶

## 2.2.2.  Attributes, identifiers and qualities

A datatype-object can be attribute-related to an object (e.g. entitytype-object)
which represent a set of entities, if the data of the datatype-object can be used
to represent properties of individual members of the e.g. entitytype.

Example:

    attribute (PERSON):  NAME, ADDRESS;

The relationtype identifier is used to represent that a datatype-object is a
unique identifier with respect to the members of a set-type object e.g.
identifier (PERSON):  SOCIAL-SECURITY-NUMBER;

Objects can be quality-related to datatypes.  A quality-relation represents a
variable property of the object, which is specific for the (e.g.) entitytype,
rather than for the individual members of the set.

Example:

    quality (PERSON):    AVERAGE-AGE;
    attribute (PERSON):  AGE;

    While the AGE-property is individually descriptive of each X ∈ PERSON, the
    AVERAGE-AGE property is descriptive of the PERSON-object itself, and is
    consequently shared by every X ∈ PERSON.

A datatype-object which is attribute, identifier or quality related to another
object, represent all those values which can possibly be used to characterize the
intended property of this object.

Example:

    The AGE-attribute of PERSON must represent all possible values of the age of a
    person, given som scale of measurement.

## 2.2.3.  Messages, tasks and signals

A message is characterized by its content, its sender and its addressee.  A message
consists of data.  A datum may be a member of some datatype.
So a message is a (structured) collection of occurrences (instantiations) of datatypes.

Messages are realized (implemented) on storage media (e.g. paper, electromagnetic
media display) in prespecified forms (e.g. purchase order form), and transmitted
through communication channels (e.g. radio, mail, telephone).  The storage medium,
the form and the mode of transmission characterize the implementation of a message.

A task is a function which maps input messages into output messages.  A task is
realized by processors e.g. human information processors, programmed computers.
A task is active while its associated processor(s) perform the mapping of input
messages into output messages.

The graphical representation of a task is 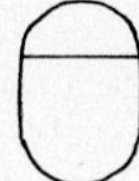

## 2.2.4.  Implementation aspects.  Responsibility, processing and transmission

The responsibility for having a task performed, resides with an entity, a collection of entities or an organizational unit.  The tasks are carried out by processors e.g. human processors, computers, whose operations might be the responsibility of some other organizational unit(s).  We thus distinguish between task management and resource management.

Relations between organizations, messages, tasks, processing resources and transmission resources are shown in figure 4.  Task $T_1$ maps message $M_1$ onto message $M_2$, which is mapped by task $T_2$ onto $M_3$.  The organization-entity $Org_1$ is responsible for having task $T_1$ performed, $Org_2$ is responsible for task $T_2$.  Task $T_1$ is performed by a group of clerks i.e.
entitytype CLERK, while task $T_2$ is performed by the organization-object COMPUTER-SYSTEM.  Processor objects entitytype CLERK and organization COMPUTER-SYSTEM, communicate via a channel-object TERMINAL, which transmits the message-object $M_2$.

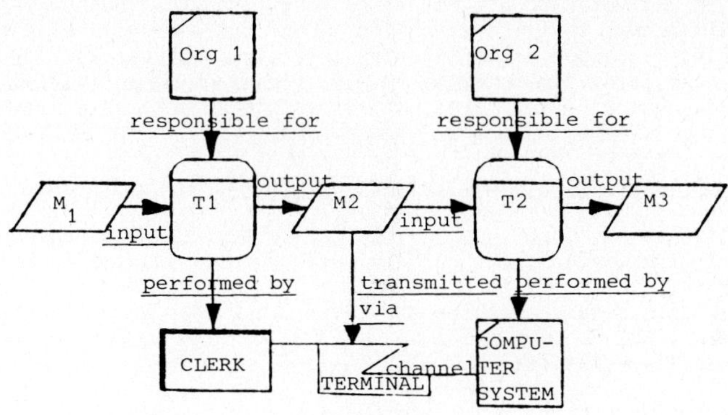


Fig. 4   Relations between messages, tasks, processors, responsible organisations

## 2.2.5.  Message-objects are datalinks between task-objects

A message-object represents a link for transmitting symbols e.g. values, between task objects.

The states of a message-object are:

    the message-object contains a message (is "full")

    the message-object does not contain a message (is "empty")

The states of a <u>task</u>-object are:

>   the <u>task</u>-object performs a mapping (is "active")
>
>   the <u>task</u>-object does not perform a mapping (is "passive")

A task-object can start to perform a mapping, when all of its input-related
message-objects contain messages (are "full").  When a task-object is through
with its mapping, the output-related message-objects will contain the messages
which are results of the mapping process.

An event is defined to be a change of state (of an object).  The events of a
<u>message</u>-object are

>   . the <u>message</u>-object changes state from "empty" to "full"
>
>   . the <u>message</u>-object changes state from "full" to "empty"

The events of a <u>task</u>-object are

>   . the <u>task</u>-object changes state from "passive" to "active"
>
>   . the <u>task</u>-object changes state from "active" to "passive"

### 2.2.6.  <u>Activation of task-objects</u>

<u>Task</u>-objects can be activated on pre-specified conditions.  If nothing else has
been said, we shall assume that a task-object is activated when its input is
ready for processing i.e. when all of its input-related messages are "full".
But sometimes we need to give more detailed specifications of activation conditions:  e.g. a task cannot be activated until some other tasks have been
passivated.

### 2.2.7.  <u>Transfer of information about triggering events</u>

Some events are of special importance in information systems, from the point of
view of activating tasks.  The event of terminating one task, usually results in
starting up other tasks.  The event of sending a message from one task to another
task, usually implies a requirement for the latter task to become active.

### 2.2.7.1.  Next-activity relations

So we need a descriptive mechanism for stating transfer of control.  The next-
activity relation <u>next</u> is defined to be a relation from tasks and/or messages
to tasks.  The graphical symbol is a broken arrow − − − − ≫

Example:

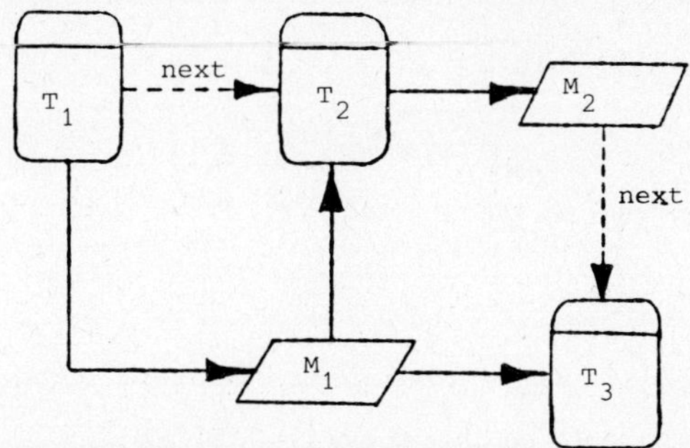



T₁ activates T₂ on termination of T₁
T₂ produces M₂ based on M₁, which was produced by T₁
M₂ activates T₃, when M₂ has been produced

Fig. 5.  Specification of control transition structure

## 2.2.7.2.  Signal-objects

Sometimes it is inconvenient to specify transfer of control directly, as shown above.

For example, if task $T_1$ and $T_2$ both have $T_3$ as a next-activity, it is not clear from the specification if $T_3$ has one or two "entry-points" i.e. if $T_3$'s actions should be different if triggered by termination of $T_1$ or $T_2$.

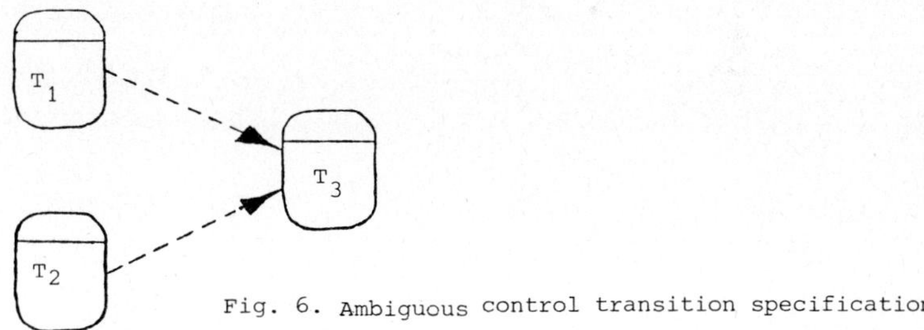



Fig. 6.  Ambiguous control transition specification

The signal-object provides a descriptive mechanism for stating such situations clearly.  (Fig. 7).

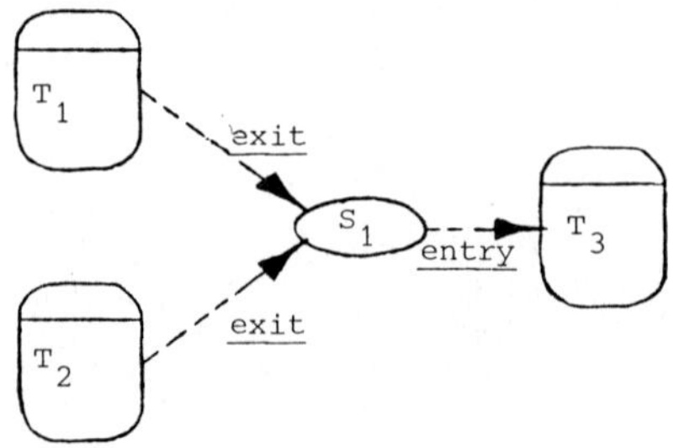


Fig. 7.   Unambiguous control transition specification

In the example, the diagram should be interpreted as follows:
$T_1$ and $T_2$ both produce a termination signal to the signal-object $S_1$, which serves
as an exit-point for the two tasks.  $S_1$ triggers task $T_3$ whenever there is a signal
in $S_1$, and thus serves as an entry-point for task $T_3$.

The graphical symbol of a signal-object is an ellipsoid $\bigcirc$

The states of a signal-object are

    . the signal-object contains a signal (is "on")

    . the signal-object does not contain a signal (is "off")

A signal-object has the property that it requires action by ("triggers") all of its
succeeding tasks, if it is "on".  The semantics of the model is thus different from
the semantics of state-transition-nets e.g. Petri-nets [4].

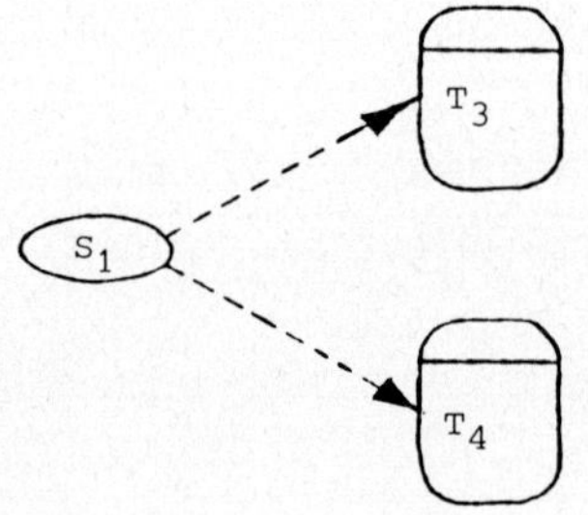


Fig. 8.   Triggering of parallell

task-performance

When all of its succeeding tasks have been activated, the signal-object is put in
an off-state.
A signal-object thus represents a link between tasks, for transmitting messages
about events.

### 2.2.8.   Specification of decisions

A decision-object is a special type of task-objects.

A decision-object has the property that it has at least two different termination
signals, and that the termination signals are mutually exclusive.

The graphical symbol is a diamond $\diamondsuit$

Example:

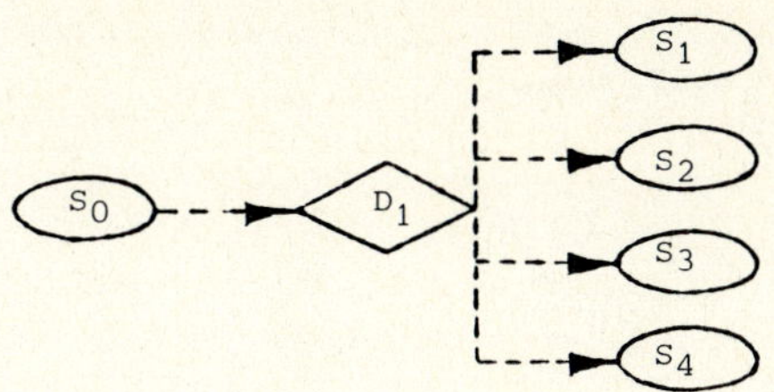

Fig. 9.   Specification of branching


If no termination signals are explicitly specified, all outcomes of a <u>decision-</u>object are considered to be mutually exclusive.

Example:

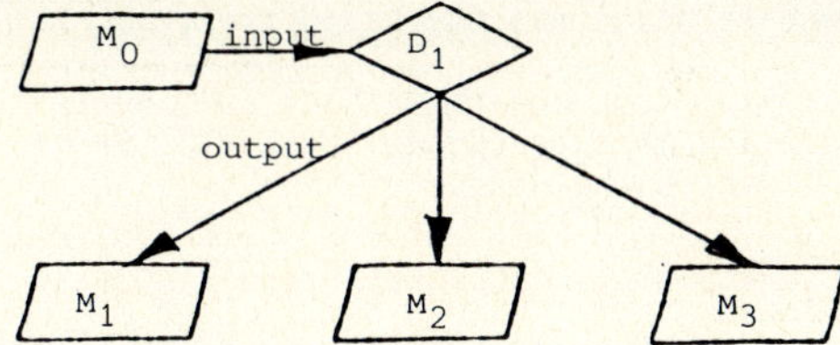


Fig. 10.   Decision tasks produce mutually exclusive
control transfers

Interpretation of fig. 10:

The occurrence of a $M_0$-message is considered to trigger $D_1$, which produces mutually exclusive outcomes $M_1$, $M_2$ and $M_3$.

### 2.2.9.   <u>Transmission of state-information</u>

So far we have only supported the specification of transmission of message  and control signals among tasks (<u>input</u>, <u>output</u>, <u>next</u>, <u>exit</u>, <u>entry</u> relations).

It is quite common that we have to check the state of system-objects, to determine if certain actions shall be performed; e.g. if we have not received any answer on our request within such and such a date, then we are going to perform some follow-up task.

So we need to support the specification with some means for testing the states of objects.

The relations offered are called

    <u>existence</u>-relation, graphical symbol

    <u>non-existence</u>-relation, graphical symbol

The state-information is transmitted in the direction of the arrow.  The values transmitted are true or false.  The (final) receiver of the state-info should be a decision-object.

490                      *A. Sølvberg*

Example:

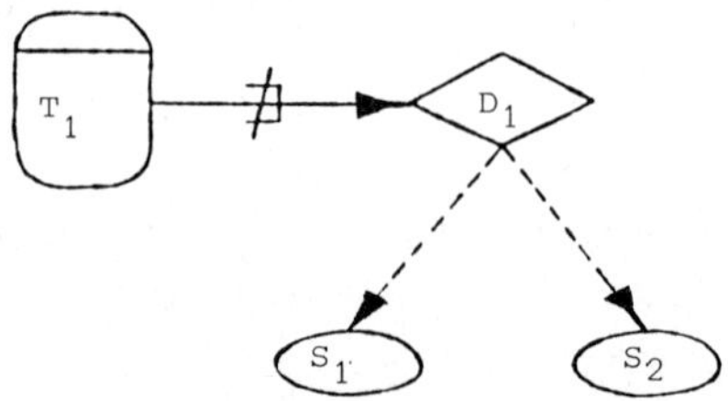



Fig. 11.   Decisions might be based on state information

Interpretation of fig. 11:

Depending on the state of $T_1$ ("active" or "passive") decision $D_1$ terminates in $S_1$ or $S_2$.

The existence-relation has the value true, if

     the relevant <u>task</u>-object is "active", or if
     the relevant <u>message</u>-object is "full", or if
     the relevant <u>signal</u>-object is "on".

## 2.2.10.   The structure of message-objects

Two basic aspects of a message are its content and its distribution.

### 2.2.10.1.   The message content aspect

Two or more messages can have the same content.

Example:

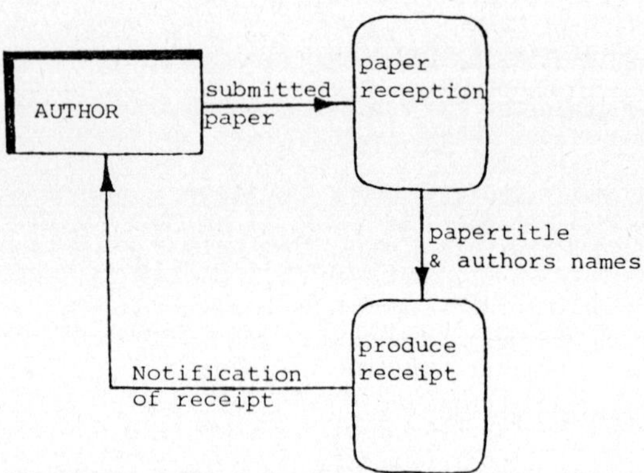



Fig. 12.   Example of tasks interacting with
external entities

In the example of fig. 12, we see that the message object "submitted paper" delivers a message (e.g. the submitted paper) to the task-object "paper reception", which produces a message of type "papertitle & authors names", which is used by the task "produce receipt", to produce a message "Notification of receipt", to be sent to the submitter of the paper.  The contents of the messages are strongly

overlapping.  The "Notification of receipt" message must contain the contents of
the "papertitle & authors names" message, which in its turn must be a copy of some
part of the "submitted paper" message.
Let us assume that the content of a "submitted paper" message is a "manuscript-
text", a "title", and "authors name".

The relations between the three messages are shown in fig. 13.

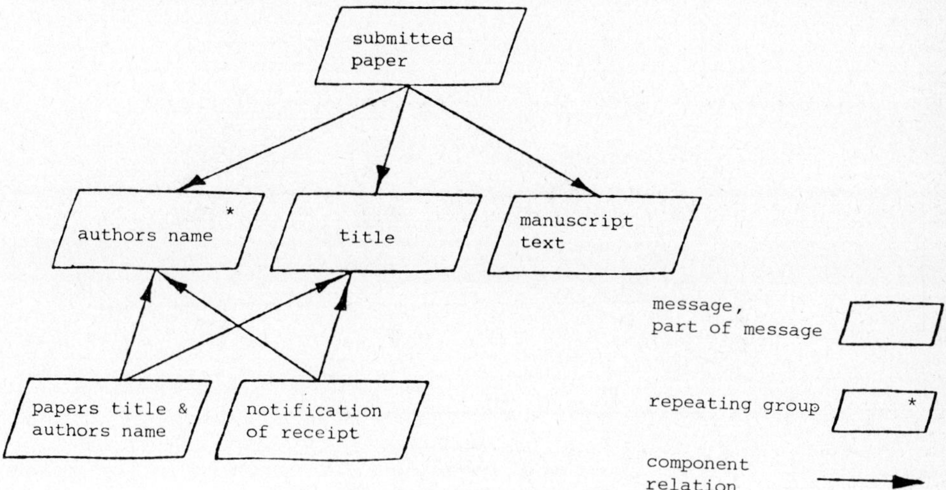


Fig. 13.  Overlap of contents of messages

It is important to note, that if the three messages are to be transmitted on
different transmission channels, and/or stored on different forms, this calls
for <u>copying</u> of e.g. "title" from "submitted paper" to the other two messages.

2.2.10.2.  Simple distribution and broadcast distribution

The <u>message</u>-objects represent transmission between entities, which are either

 <u>simple distribution</u>:  every message is intended for one receiver only

or

 <u>broadcast distribution</u>:  every message is intended for every member of
           the receiving set

An addressee-component of the message, is necessary for simple distribution,
only if the receiving entity is a set, or if several simple links to different
receivers share the same transmission channel.  An addressee-component is
necessary or not necessary for broadcast distribution depending on the choice
of implementation e.g. radio, telephone, mail:

 <u>message</u>-objects represent simple distribution

 <u>broadcast message</u>-objects represent broadcast distribution

## 2.2.10.3.  Default specifications

It happens quite often that the distribution of messages are dependent on the existence of the data which are to be transmitted, e.g. in the example we stated that the addressee of the "Notification of receipt" should be the sender of the "submitted paper".  But who should be the receiver of the receipt, if the sender has not identified himself?  We then have to decide upon a receiver of the receipt, and we have to specify that the receiver is determined by default.

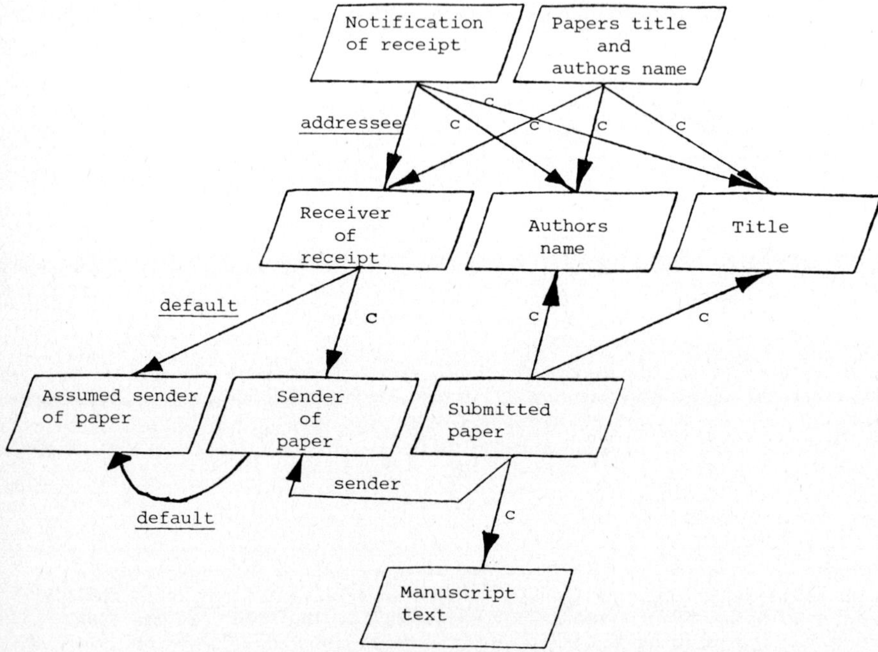


Fig. 14.   Message structure with default specification

The systems specification of fig. 14 is not complete until a task-object which map into (i.e. produce a value for) the message-component "Assumed sender of paper", has been specified.

## 2.2.10.4.  Compound message-objects: the alternative-relation

We have stated that message-objects represent transmission links between entities. Systems are modelled on varying levels of detail.  It would therefore be useful to have a concept for expressing that a message-object represents several "elementary" links (fig. 15).

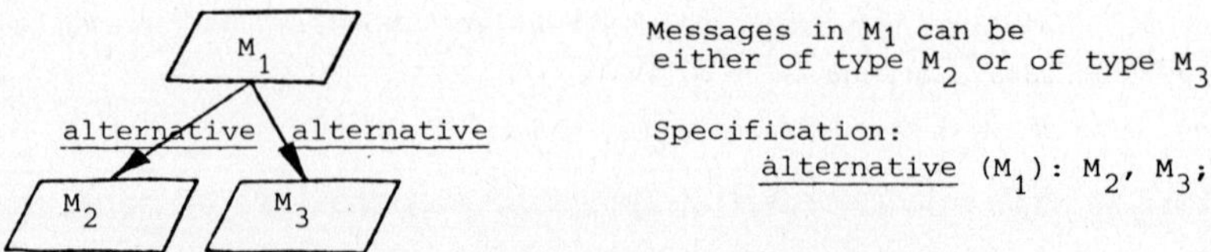


Fig. 15.   Specification of compound messages

In this case it is necessary that each alternative message, carry some "identification" so that the receiver of the compound message can determine which alternative he is receiving.  This "identification" can be implemented in different
ways e.g. by using different forms for each alternative or by attaching a tag to
each message, the tag being unique for each message type.

### 2.2.11.  Implementation of messages.  Forms

When messages are implemented they must be stored on some medium e.g. paper, and
they must be assigned some form.   Storage on paper is indicated by adding a
graphical symbol of "letter" (in the mail) to the main graphical symbol.

Examples

Blank document (pre-printed)

Duplicates of blank documents

Package of different blank documents

Message on paper                                          or

Duplicated messages on paper

Document-entitytype

A form object has a name.  Its graphical representation is its layout.

### 2.2.12.  Storage and retrieval of information

Data about system entities are stored in data store-objects.

The graphical symbol for a
data store-object is

A document archive is graphically
represented by the symbol

### 2.2.12.1.  The specification of contents of data stores

The contents of data store-objects are specified by relating the data store-objects
to the entities which they carry information about, and to their attributes [2,5].

The relations are

reference     from data store-objects to system objects (entities)
restriction   from data store-objects to attributes
projection    from data store-objects to attributes

494  A. Sølvberg

Example:

        entitytype POTENTIAL_PARTICIPANT (attribute NAME);
        entitytype PAPER (attribute TITLE);
        connection AUTHOR (domain PAPER to POTENTIAL_PARTICIPANT
                        range (alias AUTHOR));

        data store SUBMISSIONS
                (reference PAPER
                projection TITLE, AUTHOR_NAME);

Graphical representation

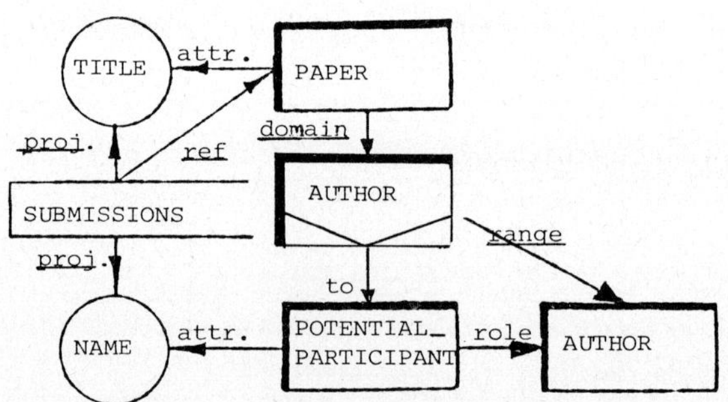


Fig. 16.   Contents of data stores are specified by
           relating data store objects to datatypes
           and entitytypes (and/or entities).


Let us assume that the selection of papers has been done.  The papers have been
classified in accepted and rejected papers.  We want to store data (title and
authors names) of the accepted papers.

Specification statements:

        category (PAPER):  ACCEPTED_PAPER, REJECTED_PAPER,
        data store ACCEPTANCES (reference ACCEPTED_PAPER
                        projection TITLE, AUTHOR.NAME)

Because ACCEPTED_PAPER is a subset of PAPER, the data store-object ACCEPTANCES is
included in SUBMISSIONS, and all the necessary data can be retrieved from
SUBMISSIONS provided that a proper retrieval criterion (restriction) can be given.

Restrictions are written like e.g.

        restriction AUTHOR.NAME = 'EINSTEIN';
        that is, only titles of papers by the author EINSTEIN are stored in
        ACCEPTANCES.

### 2.2.12.2.  Operations on data stores

The basic operations are the well known get, insert, modify and delete.  Common
for all of the operators are that they operate on one data store (a "target") and
that they operate on some subset of the information contained in the "target".
The subsets can be specified in the same way as the data stores are specified,
i.e. by

>     referencing the appropriate system object
>     restricting on the attributes of the system object
>     projecting on the attributes of the system object

Example:

>     get (from ACCEPTANCES
>
>         reference PAPER
>
>         restriction AUTHOR.NAME = 'EINSTEIN'
>
>         projection TITLE);

Less explicit specifications can be stated by e.g. omitting the reference-
statement, and only referring to the data types of the data store, e.g.

>     get (from ACCEPTANCES
>
>         restriction NAME = 'EINSTEIN'
>
>         projection TITLE);

In the former case we can test (at compile-time) if the get-statement specifies
a possible subset of the ACCEPTANCES data store-object.  In the latter case we
get whatever data that the data store contains,which are consistent with the
restriction statement, e.g. if the target contains data about persons and their
titles, we will retrieve that data instead of the intended information about the
author 'EINSTEIN' and the title(s) of his accepted paper(s).

The get, modify, delete and insert operators are specified within this general
frame work, that is, by using reference, restrict, project relations.

The data base operators contain too much detail to be easily represented in
diagrams.
So we choose to compromize on generality and detail.
The graphical symbol is an arrow.  Details are displayed in the following way:
The restriction datatypes are written within paranthesis, and the projection
data types are written behind the paranthesis.  In the case that we have not
decided on projection and/or restriction details, we write ++ behind the
paranthesis, and/or leave the restriction paranthesis empty.

The type of data base operator is indicated by the symbols get, delete, insert,
modify.
If a $\nabla$-symbol succeeds the data base operator, this means that the operator shall
be applied on the next record in the data store which satisfy the restriction
criterion.

Example:

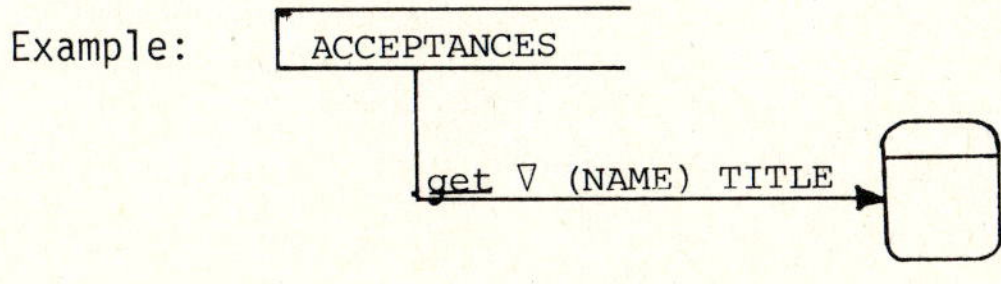


Fig. 17.  Retrieve TITLE
information of the next paper
of an author with a given
name.

The arrow is pointing <u>from</u> the data store for <u>get</u> and <u>delete</u> operators, <u>to</u> the data store for <u>insert</u> and <u>modify</u> operators.

All of the operations have to perform a common first task, before thay can proceed.  This is to find if the data specified by the <u>restriction</u> relation are stored in the data store.

If the specified data are not present in the data store, then the data can not be retrieved (<u>get</u>, <u>modify</u>, <u>delete</u>).  It it is present, then it can not be inserted (<u>insert</u>).

So all four operators must have a standard "error" exit, for the case that the intended operation can not be completed.

### 2.2.13.   Example:  PAPER-SOLICITING

Paper soliciting is usually done by mailing call-for-papers to persons who are assumed to be possible contributors to a conference, by advertizing the conference in professional journals, and by soliciting from individuals (based on personal interaction through mail, telephone etc.)  Advertizements and distribution of call-for-papers are initiated some time ahead of the planned conference date. A diagrammatic representation of the PAPER-SOLICITING task is depicted in figure 18.  Diagrammatic representations of the PAPER-SUBMISSION task are shown in figs. 19 and 20.  This task will be elaborated later in the paper.

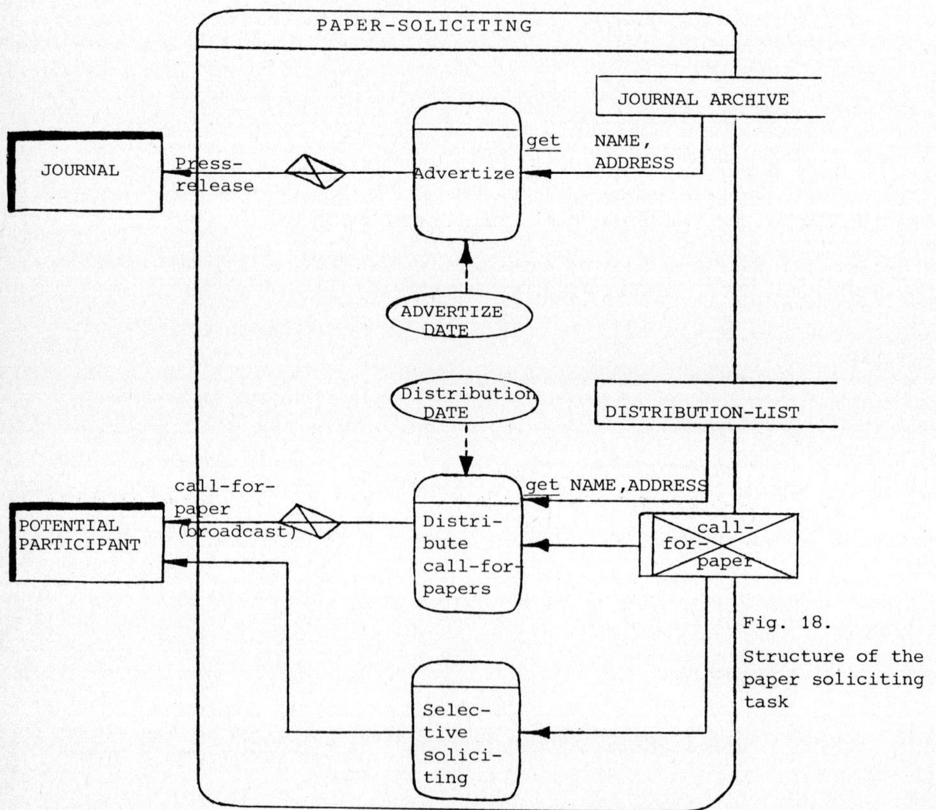


Fig. 18.

Structure of the paper soliciting task

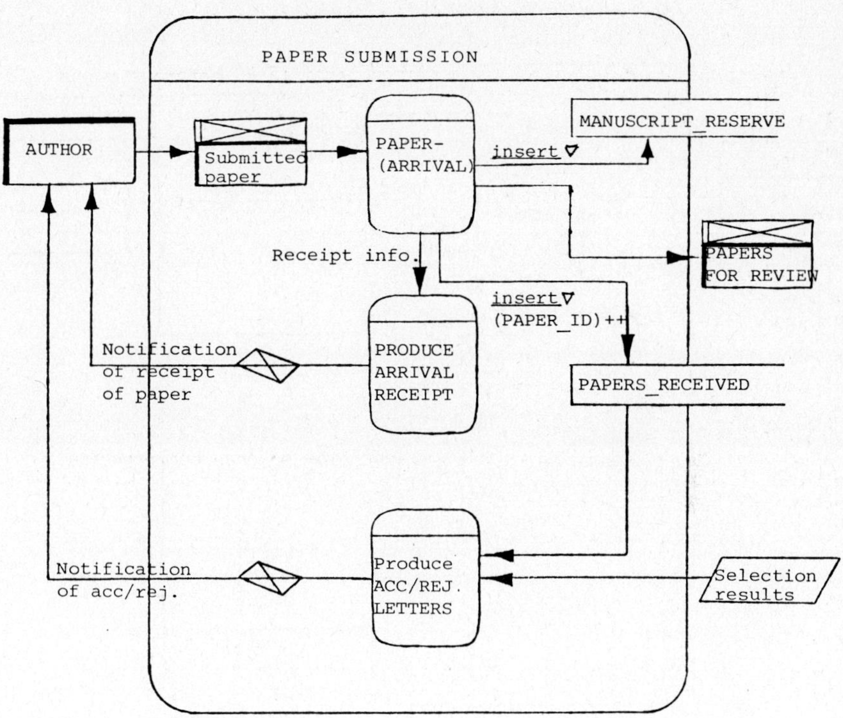


Fig. 19. Structure of the paper submission task

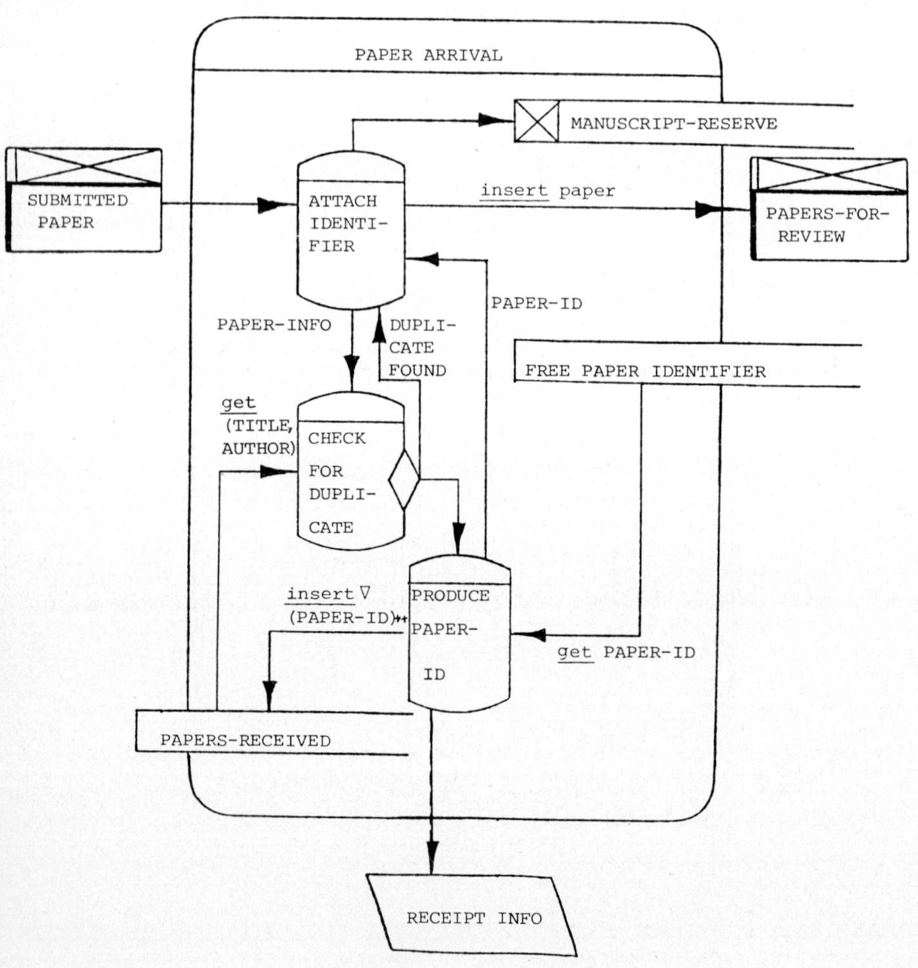


Fig. 20.   Structure of the PAPER_ARRIVAL component of the
           PAPER_SUBMISSION task

## 2.3.  <u>Allocation of processing resources</u>

We assume that the functional base line has been specified within the frame work
of sect. 2.2.  The next step of the systems design is to allocate processing
resources for performing the tasks, and to determine responsibility for controlling
if the tasks have been performed properly.

The processing resources allocation consists of

>     assigning processors to tasks
>     assigning communication channels to messages

Note that the detailed determination of message-formats depends on channel selection for message-transmission.  Note also that the selection of storage media for
data stores should not be done until the logical data base structure has been
determined.  This can not be done until we have decided upon intermediate storage
of data in the data base.  This decision depends on the choice of processing mode
e.g. batch processing or interactive processing.  The task management system must
also be designed.

Example:

>     In the PAPER-SUBMISSION task (fig. 19) we have specified that we are going
>     to insert information into the data store PAPERS-RECEIVED, with the restric-
>     tion that PAPER-ID has a certain value.  What are we going to do if PAPERS-
>     RECEIVED already contains a non-empty set of information restricted by
>     PAPER-ID having this value?  We need to have a fallback position.  In general,
>     we must be able to specify what should be done in such situations.

Example:

>     What are we going to do if we have selected a paper with a given PAPER-ID
>     value, and there is no data about this paper in the PAPERS-RECEIVED data
>     store?  We will not be able to get the name and the address of the person
>     to which the notification of acceptance should be sent.  Have we lost some
>     data in PAPERS-RECEIVED?  Is the "selection result" message wrong?  Which
>     action should we take to correct the situation?

The point we want to make here, is that every design decision that we make, has
the potential of leading to the definition of new tasks to be performed.  Resources have to be allocated to these new tasks.  Consequently we might interfere
with design decisions already made.  And there we are, in the middle of an iterative design procedure, where each design decision potentially results in new
requirements for information processing.

Task management and allocation of processing resources, can be looked upon from a
subcontracting-analogy point of view.  The task to be performed, is given to a
subcontractor, together with all of the data which are necessary for the task to
be done.  The subcontractor (e.g. the computer) returns the required results to
the contractor when the task has been performed.  The responsibility for checking
the results, and for checking that the results come back in due time, resides
with the contractor.

Let us do a small design exercise, to make the main points more clear.

Assume that we shall work out an implementation design for PAPER-SUBMISSION
(figs. 19 and 20).

The design decisions are highlighted in the table of fig. 21, e.g. the task
PRODUCE_PAPER_ID is the responsibility of the PC_CHAIRPERSON, but is to be
performed by the COMPUTER.  Graphical presentations of the design decisions
applied on the task structure, are given in figures 22 and 23.

| Message/task/data store | Task-responsibility | Task, data store, message allocation to performance resources |
|---|---|---|
| **Tasks** | | |
| PAPER-SUBMISSION | PC-CHAIRPERSON | |
| ATTACH-IDENTIFIER | " | PC-CHAIRPERSON |
| CHECK-FOR-DUPLICATES | " | COMPUTER |
| PRODUCE-PAPER-ID | " | " |
| PRODUCE-ARRIVAL-RECEIPT | " | " |
| PRODUCE-ACC/R-LETTERS | " | " |
| | | |
| **Message interfaces:** | | |
| PAPER-INFO | Not applicable | DISPLAY-TERMINAL |
| SELECTION-RESULTS | " | " |
| duplicate-found | " | " |
| PAPER-ID (to ATTACH IDENTITIER) | " | " |
| Notification-of-receipt-of-paper | " | PRINTER |
| Notification of acc/rej | " | " |
| | | |
| **Data stores** | | |
| PAPERS-RECEIVED | " | COMPUTER |
| FREE-PAPER-IDENTIFIERS | " | " |

Fig. 21.    Design decisions concerning task responsibility, task performance,
            message communication and data storage.

Detailed Graphical representation of design proposal, concerning the allocation of tasks to resources:

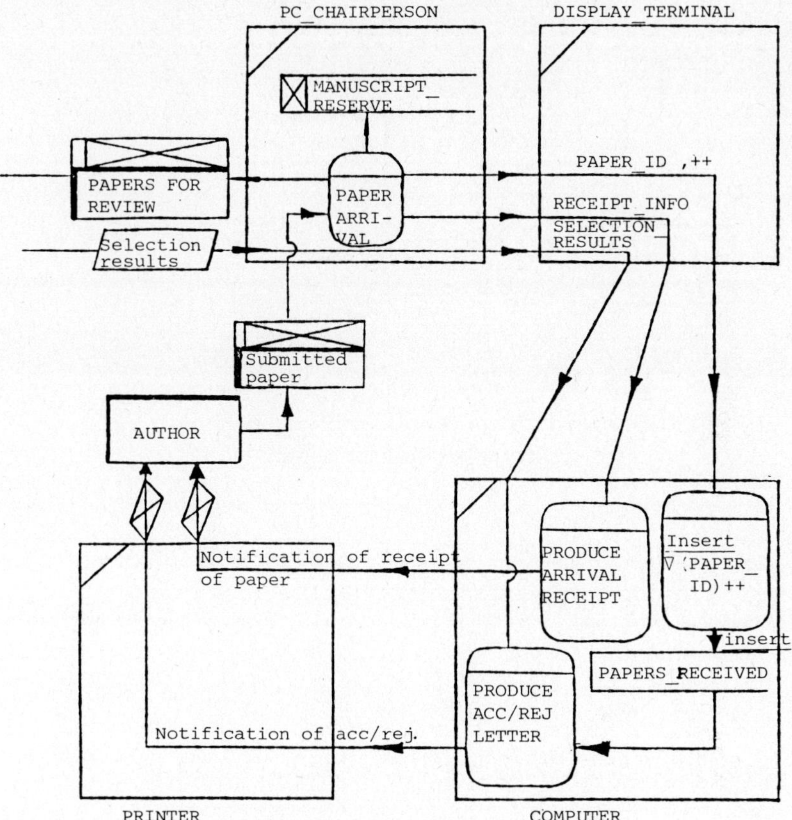


Fig. 22. Graphical presentation of the PAPER_SUBMISSION task modified by design decision of fig. 21

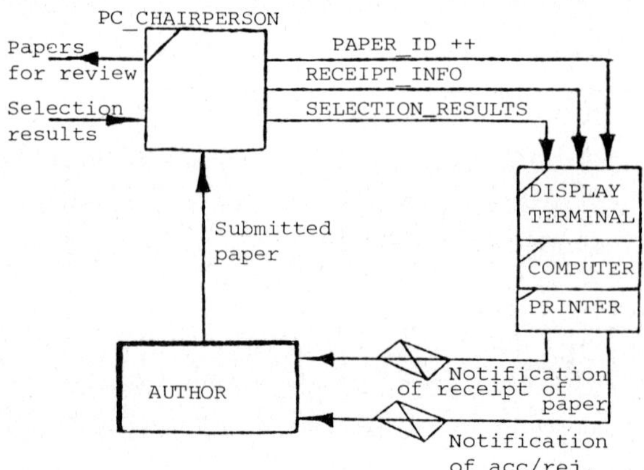


Fig. 23.  Simplified presentation of man-machine interfaces
of the PAPER_SUBMISSION task

## 2.4.  The responsibility aspect.  Task management

The PC_CHAIRPERSON is responsible for all of the tasks being performed correctly
and on time.

What can go wrong?  Which security features should we have?  Which additional
information is needed by the PC_CHAIRPERSON for him to feel that he is in control?

a)  It would probably be very useful for the PC_CHAIRPERSON to be able to browse
    in the PAPERS_RECEIVED datastore.

b)  Back-up storage of the PAPERS_RECEIVED datastore might be considered, in case
    of a computer fall-out, loss of the database etc.  Reloading procedures should
    be considered.

c)  What should happen if the SELECTION_RESULT messages refer to papers which are
    not represented in PAPERS_RECEIVED?

d)  What should happen if some of the papers represented in PAPERS_RECEIVED are
    not mentioned in the SELECTION_RESULT message?

All of these cases (and probably more) have to be analysed, decisions on procedure
must be made, new information processing tasks must be formulated and specified,
the allocation of tasks to resources must be decided upon.

An analysis of the responsibility aspect will add more tasks to the example.
However, this addition of detail does not contribute in either negative or posi-
tive sense to the discussion of program design.
So we shall not elaborate the aspect of responsibility further.

2.4.1.  <u>Performing the tasks</u>

We shall concentrate on the computer aspect of task performance.

Our design decisions so far are:

     Tasks   CHECK_FOR_DUPLICATES, PRODUCE_PAPER_ID,

           PRODUCE_ARRIVAL_RECEIPT, PRODUCE_ACC/REJ_LETTERS

           shall be performed by a computer.

    Interaction with the computer-environment shall be via

       . DISPLAY_TERMINAL

              for messages PAPER_INFO, Duplicate_found,

              PAPER_ID, Selection_results

       . PRINTER

              for messages Notification_of_receipt

              and Notification_of_acc/rej.

These design decisions require additional information processing tasks to be performed, for example:

a)  The communication channel between COMPUTER and DISPLAY_TERMINAL transmits
    several messages.  The messages must be represented on the display terminal.
    This requires that display-forms be designed, and that procedures for display-
    form generation be specified i.e. some new information processing tasks which
    are the result of choosing a display terminal for transmission of messages
    have to be specified.

b)  The computer has to decide upon which task to perform, by analysing the
    message which it receives from the display terminal.  This is an additional
    information processing task, resulting from the decision to do several diffe-
    rent primary tasks within the same computer.

2.4.1.1.  Transaction management

The point of view which is applied during the design of the task performance
system, is quite different from the point of view which is applied during task
analysis and task design.  During the task design phase, messages are viewed as
carriers of information about some external entities.  During design of the task
performance system, the messages are themselves entities of primary importance:
message entities are transported between task performers, message-entities are
sent through different communication channels.  The messages which are transmitted
through a channel must contain additional information about their own properties,
such as type (and format), so that the receiver can transmit the message to the
appropriate task performer e.g. program.

The general structure of message processing is shown in figure 24.

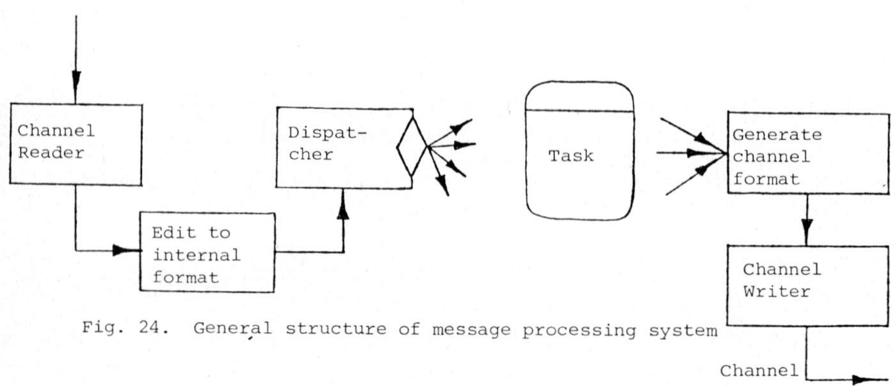

Fig. 24.   General structure of message processing system

Communication channels are connected to <u>ports</u> of the task performers [2].

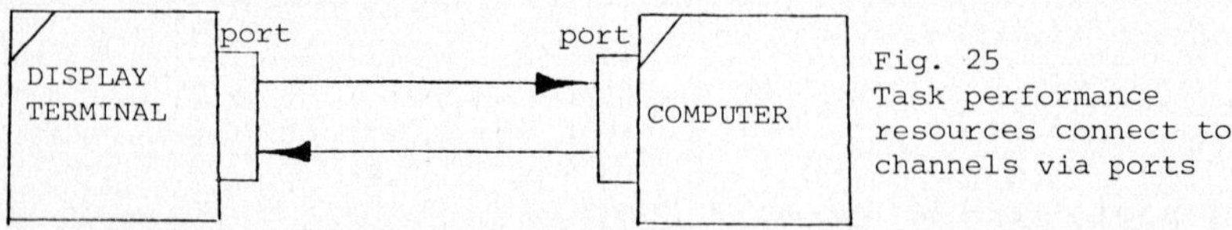



Fig. 25
Task performance
resources connect to
channels via ports

Each port contains a channel reader and a channel writer, as well as appropriate
formatters (fig. 25).

The dispatchers are considered to be task-components of the task performers (fig. 26).
To indicate that the dispatcher is a "secondary level" task belonging to the
computer entity alone, the task-symbol is drawn with <u>two</u> horisontal lines in
fig. 26.  Each dispatcher has to be designed according to its intended use, so
its properties depend on the task-structure of the task-performer, and on the
type variety of messages to be transmitted through the relevant channel.

The previous example system as expanded with the dispatcher is shown in fig. 26.

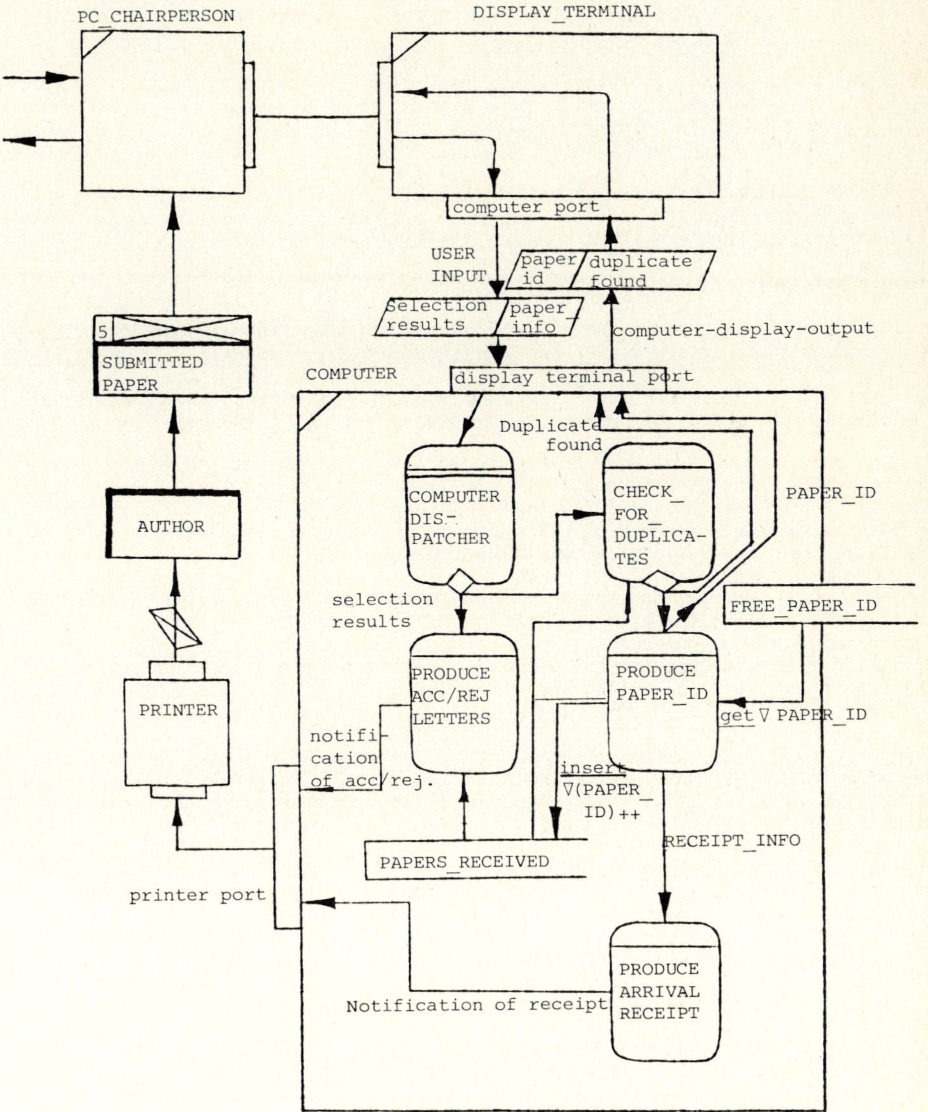


Fig. 26. The PAPER_SUBMISSION task modified by message management tasks

### 2.4.1.2.  The man - machine interaction

The interaction mode, and message formats, have to be determined.  In our case,
the PC_CHAIRPERSON interacts with the DISPLAY_TERMINAL, and AUTHOR get letters
produced by the PRINTER.  The latter is no problem, because the obvious solution
is to design standard letters like

>     "We regret that.....................Many good papers had to be rejected
>      for this conference".
>     "We are pleased to inform you..........."
>     "We have received your submission......."

For the PC_CHAIRPERSONs interaction with the DISPLAY_TERMINAL we have several
design options.  Before selecting one design alternative, we have to choose which
level of systems knowledge that the user shall be expected to possess.

The extremes are:

(1)  the user is expected to have perfect knowledge about formats and about the
     processing of messages i.e. the user knows his user manual.

(2)  the user is expected to have no knowledge whatsoever about the operation of
     the system, about the transaction repertoire etc.

The assumption of perfect user knowledge leads to a minimal design of the interaction system.  The user is expected to enter correct transactions in a correct
format.  To capture the few cases where the user makes an error, a transaction
analyser with appropriate error exits must be inserted in the terminal, prior to
the dispatcher, or as a part of the dispatcher.
The extreme consequences of the no-knowledge assumption, is the design of a
computer aided instruction type of support system, and a menu-driven interaction
system, which forces the user to enter his data step by step while being detailed
supervised by the computer.
Obviously some balanced compromise must be developed.  Additional information
processing tasks will be introduced in any case.
In fig. 27 we have chosen an alternative in which the computer system presents an
empty screen format on the display, after the user has sent a transaction telling
which message-type he wishes to enter next.  The GENERATE_DISPLAY_FORM task has
been defined to be a component of COMPUTER (i.e. a task performance design
decision).  An alternative design decision might have been to let an "intelligent"
DISPLAY_TERMINAL perform this task.

The next design task is to decide upon the details of the screen layout, and to
determine the details of the user command structure.  These design decisions will
determine the internal details of the COMPUTER DISPATCHER and GENERATE_DISPLAY_
FORM tasks, and the contents of the SCREEN_LAYOUT datastore.  We shall, however,
not develop those details further here.

### 2.4.1.3.  Operational design.  Initiation and restart.

By looking at fig. 27 we find that data stores SCREEN_LAYOUT and FREE_PAPER_ID
have no insertion commands specified.  The data store PAPERS_RECEIVED is associated with an <u>insert</u> command, but initial contents is not specified.

Design decisions; initialization:

>     . PAPERS_RECEIVED shall be empty.
>
>     . SCREEN_LAYOUT shall be fitted with appropriate layout definitions.
>
>     . FREE_PAPER_ID initialisation requires a definition for the paper

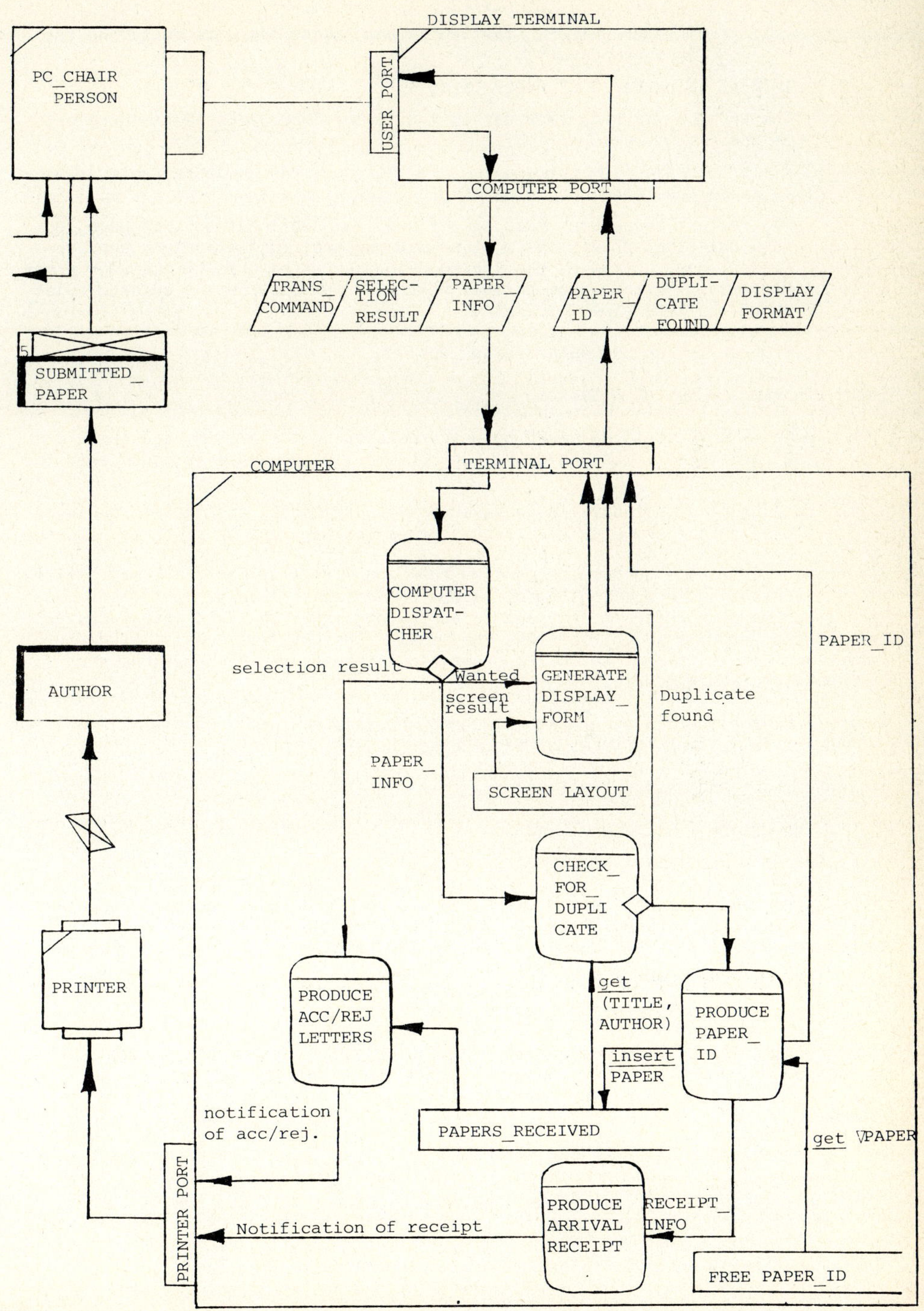



Fig. 27.   PAPER SUBMISSION by message management and form generation

identifier.  One solution is to let PAPER_ID be a positive
integer number, starting at one, being incremented by one for
each new paper:

. Initial value for FREE_PAPER_ID is 1.

. The PRODUCE_PAPER_ID task has to modify the FREE_PAPER_ID in increments
  of one.

. A start transaction command must be designed, and an appropriate initialization function must be defined.

. The restart procedures must be defined.  We shall not do that here, but
  only note that provisions must be made so that initialization and subsequent destruction of the stored data can not be done by operator error.
  Provisions must be made so that selection results are not entered twice
  about the same paper etc. etc.

2.4.1.4  Program design and data storage design

There are two classes of data:

. data which have to be saved between restarts of the system, and therefore
  must be stored in the database (any interaction sequence is considered to
  be a restart).

. data which do not have to be saved between restarts, and therefore can be
  stored in the computer's working storage (primary and/or secondary storage).

Design decisions have to be made on structure and format of both of these classes
of data, resulting in workingstorage layout and database layout.
The structure of working storage and database determines the data interfaces
between the programs which implement the tasks.  The programs consist of code
(which implements tasks), which are organized in procedures (subroutines etc.),
and encapsulated in modules.

We shall sketch the design procedure, using the task structure of fig. 27 modified
by the initialization features of fig. 28 as a starting point.

The outcome of the design shall be

. the database structure, and

. program modules with interface definitions

Because programs communicate via (working) storage locations, we shall also have
to design the data working storage.  There are some details missing in the task
structure specifications.  We shall fill in the details as we go along with the
design.

2.4.1.4.1.  Relations between contents of messages

Our first step is to find out how the message contents of the task structure relate
to each other, and to specify these relationships.

Example:

    RECEIPT_INFO (output of PRODUCE_PAPER_ID) contains the PAPER_INFO message
    which is used by PRODUCE_PAPER_ID.  This PAPER_INFO message has the same
    contents as the PAPER_INFO message which is input to CHECK_FOR_DUPLICATE,
    which in its turn has the contents of USER_TRANSACTION's PAPER_INFO message.

The content-relationships are graphically represented in fig. 29.

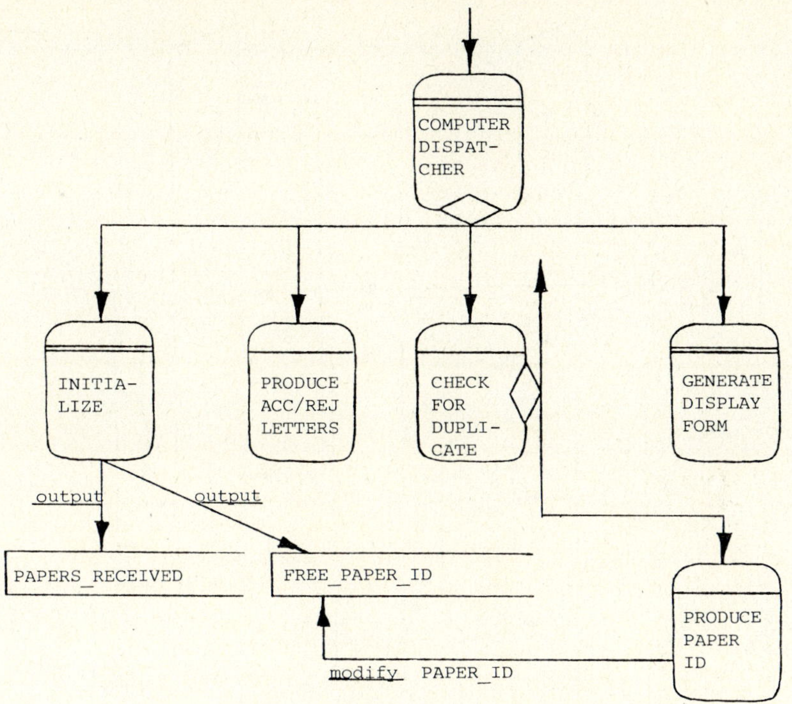

Fig. 28.   The initialization component of the performance
           of the PAPER_SUBMISSION task


2.4.1.4.2.   Choice of data interfaces between processes.

We shall limit the discussion to the production of the 'notification of receipt'
message.
By analyzing the content diagram (fig. 29) and the task diagram (fig. 28), it is
easy to see that the 'notification of receipt' message includes the contents of
all of the messages which flow between the tasks which are involved i.e. PRODUCE_
ARRIVAL_RECEIPT, PRODUCE_PAPER_ID, CHECK_FOR_DUPLICATE.
One variable length data field with the structure

        (paper-id, manuscript title, sender, *author)

will therefore be sufficient to support the production of 'notification of receipt'.
(An asterics preceeding a name, indicates that the name represents a repeating
group).
To keep in line with common programming practice, we shall choose the acronym
PAPSUB for this field (PAPSUB is abbreviation for PAPer SUBmitted).

It is easy to see, from the message content diagram, that 'Notification of acc/rej'
contains data of the same type as PAPSUB.  One might therefore be tempted to store
also these messages in a slightly sxpanded PAPSUB, especially because the processing of selection results and the processing of paper reception are mutually exclusive.  However, this would introduce an implementation coupling between the two
(independent) processes.   This might later on make it difficult to change one
process without changing the implementation of the other process, and should
therefore be discouraged.

A. Sølvberg

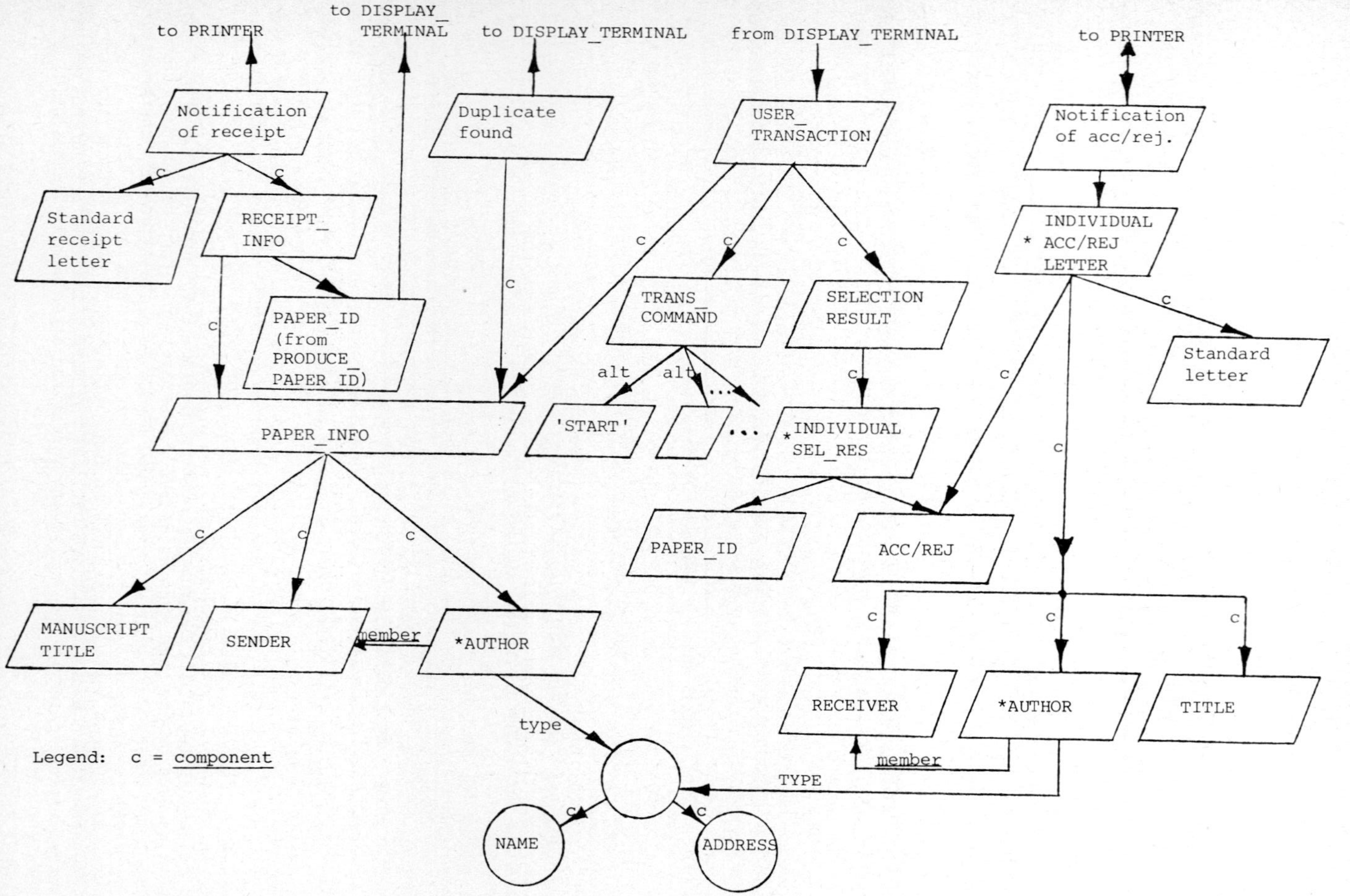


Fig. 29. Relations between the contents of the messages in the task structure of fig. 27

Our basic point is that designers judgement is necessary to make good choices, so
that also intangibles (like maintainability) are properly taken care of.

2.4.1.4.3.  Database design

The basis for database design is a statement of the contents and the use of the
data which has to be stored between restarts of the system [6].

In our example, neither contents nor use have been detailed specified so far.
Our example problem is too small to show the scope of the database design problem,
and the scope of the problem is too large to permit a design procedure to be easily
explained in a few sentences.

We shall therefore limit ourselves to a short discussion of the PAPERS_RECEIVED
data store.

The PAPERS_RECEIVED datastore supports the production of acceptance/rejection
letters, and the check to prevent that the same paper is submitted several times.
Data is inserted in the store by the PRODUCE_PAPER_ID task, one record for each
submitted paper.

A short analysis of the use of PAPERS_RECEIVED, shows that it must contain data of
the type (PAPER_ID, sender-of-paper, *author, manuscript title), one record for
each submitted paper.

Definition:

    <u>datastore</u> PAPERS_RECEIVED

        <u>reference</u> PAPER

        <u>projection</u> PAPER_ID, SENDING AUTHOR, *AUTHOR, TITLE;

The detailed specification of use will be of the form (e.g. for the CHECK_FOR_
DUPLICATE task):

    <u>get</u> (<u>from</u> PAPERS_RECEIVED

        <u>reference</u> PAPER

        <u>restriction</u> TITLE = PAPER_INFO·TITLE

            <u>and</u> (*AUTHOR ∩ PAPER_INFO. *AUTHOR)$\neq$0

        <u>projection</u> *AUTHOR, TITLE ;

and so on for the other tasks.
It is implicitly understood that PAPER_INFO represents the current PAPER_INFO
content of the task which request the data.  The number of records in PAPERS_
RECEIVED is rather low, in the order of a couple of hundreds.  Sequential search
therefore seems to be quite sufficient.  Our design decision is that PAPERS_
RECEIVED be implemented by an unordered sequential file, named PPSQRC (=papers
sequentially recorded).
The data store FREE_PAPER_ID shall only contain the value of the identifier of the
next paper to be submitted, according to previous decisions.  (Sect. 2.3.4.4.1.)
This datafield will be called NPAPID (=Next PAPer IDentifier).

2.4.1.4.4.  Program code for the tasks

Each task is to be implemented by a sequence of program statements.

The code "chunks" are specified by e.g. pseudocode.

Example:

```
code (PRODUCE_PAPER_ID):
        name PRPAPID;
        arguments NPAPID, PPSQRC, PAPSUB
        pseudocode
                PAPSUB (PAPER_ID) = NPAPID;
                display NPAPID;
                write PAPSUB into PPSQRC;
                increment NPAPID with 1;
        end code;
```

Example:

```
code (CHECK_FOR_DUPLICATE):
        name CHDUPL;
        argument PAPSUB, PPSQRC;
        pseudocode
            search PPSQRC for match
                between PAPSUB (TITLE) and PPSQRC (TITLE)
            and (between some PAPSUB (*AUTHOR) and some PPSQRC (*AUTHOR));
            if match then display PAPSUB (except PAPER_ID)
                    else go to PAPER_INFO exit;
        end code;
```

All of the tasks on the most detailed decomposition level will be associated with
a chunk of code.

It becomes quite complicated to present these relations in a pictorial form.  We
have, nevertheless, tried to show some of these implementation relations in fig. 30.
It is quite obvious that these relations can only be kept updated by using some kind
of computer assisted tool.

2.4.1.5.  Program design

The next design step is to create the procedural structure and the program module
structure.  Let us assume that CHDUPL and PRPAPID are going to be implemented by
subroutines (procedures), and that all of the other tasks are going to be implemented by subroutines as well.  The control flow of a possible implementation is
shown in fig. 31.  Each box represents one call of a subroutine.
This picture of the control flow is rather complicated, and will become more so,
as the complexity of the implementation increases.

The usual way of implementing the control flow, is to create a "monitor", whose
only task is to take care of the correct sequencing of the "sub-programs".
One commonly used graphical presentation of the relationship between the "monitor"
(MAIN_PROGRAM) and the other programs, is shown in fig. 32 [1].

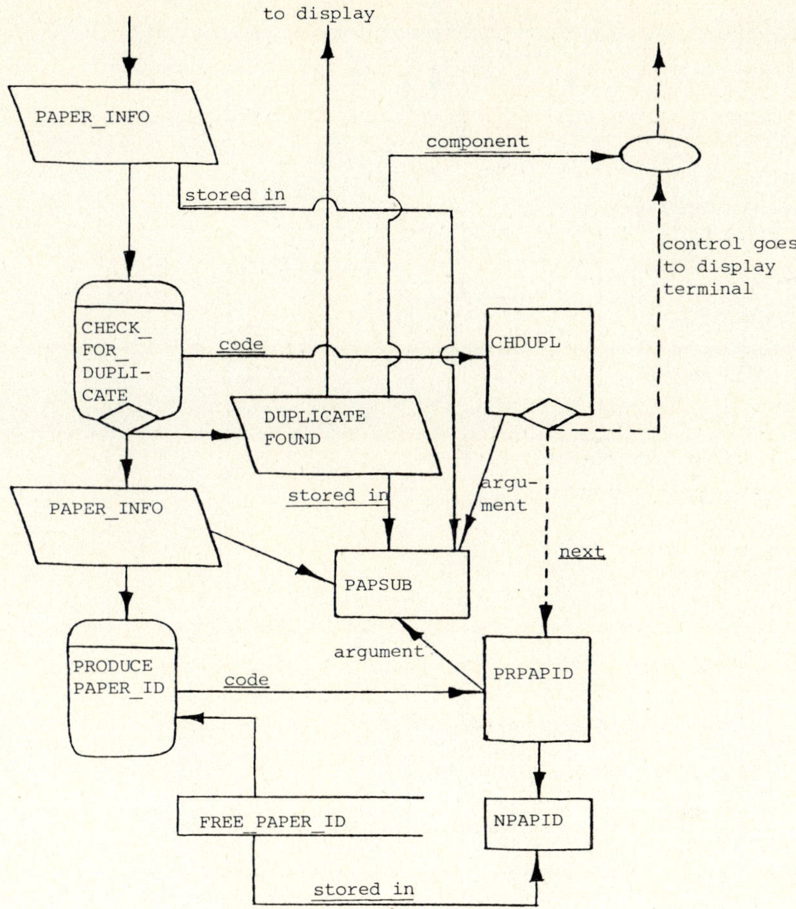


Fig. 30.   Relations between tasks, messages and working
storage, data bases, program code

In diagrams like the one depicted in fig. 32 the control logic is usually implemented (and hidden) in a MAIN PROGRAM.  One would also usually hide the dispatcher
by making it a part of the main program.

These kinds of diagrams, supported by detailed specification of control flow and
data flow as shown earlier, might well serve as a programming and implementation
basis.

We see, however, that most of the details of sequencing and interfacing are hidden.
So this kind of diagrams serves as a rather highlevel "highlighting" of the implementation design.

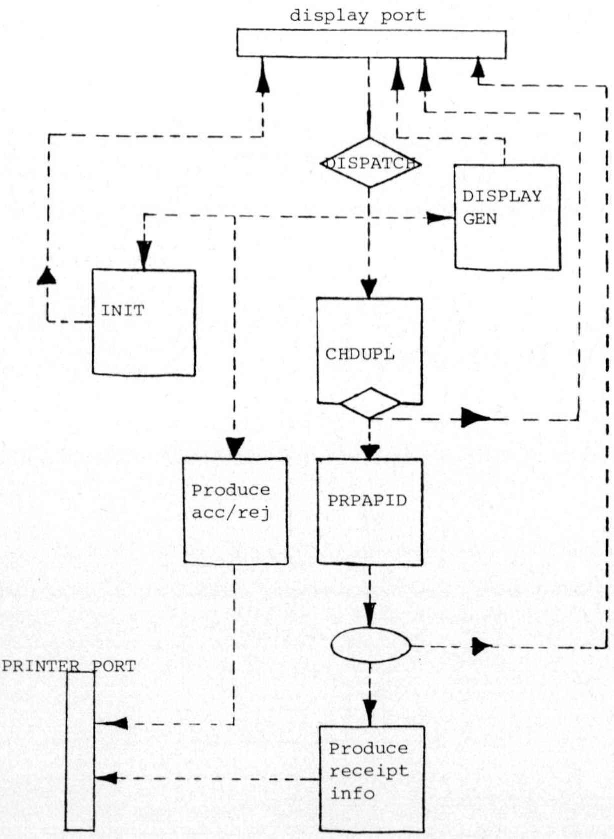


Fig. 31.    Control flow of implementation of the COMPUTER subsystem

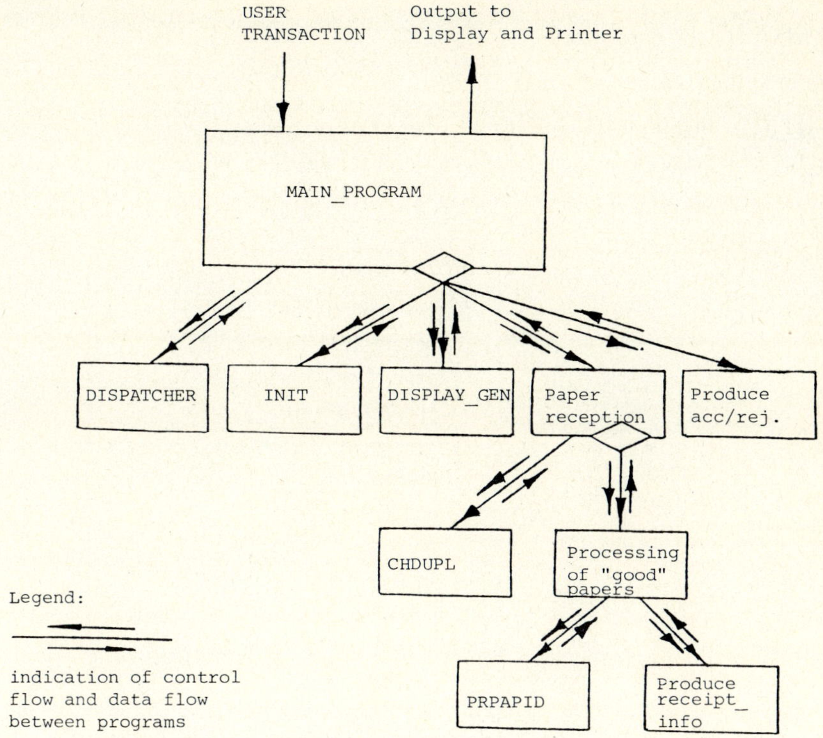


Fig. 32.   A program module structure of the implementation design of
the PAPER_SUBMISSION task.

## 2.4.1.4.6.   Encapsulation of programs in program modules.   Abstract datatypes

So far we have discussed the development of program specification from the point
of view of task performance.  The main emphasis has been put on administration of
dataflow and control flow, to support the performance of some predefined task
structure.

A consequence of this is that the implementation design will be specialized to
support the wanted systems behaviour.  But wishes about systems behaviour change
over time, so implementation changes will be initiated.  To prepare for this
(inevitable) change process, the different parts of the implementation should be
insulated from each other.

One useful technique is to encapsulate programs in modules, so that implementation
details which are common for the programs in one module, are hidden in that module,
and not seen by the user of the programs of that module.

The programs (procedures, subroutines) of a module are interpreted as computational
resources (e.g. operators) which can be freely used by other programs outside of
that module.  A module is therefore merely a syntactical structure, and will never
be instantiated.  Only the programs of a module can be instantiated.

An example of a modularization in our example could be to create a program module
which initializes, and increments the paperidentifier, i.e. we define an abstract
datatype with suitable operators.

The operators might be called

    create_id - initialization of first identifier value
    new_id    - get current identifier and create the next identifier

The NPAPID-implementation of FREE_IDENTIFIER will be hidden within the module:

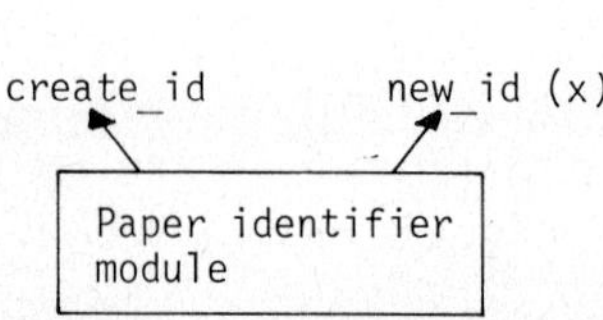


```
Module definition:
    module PAPER LABEL;
    export create-id, new-id(x);
    integer NPAPID;
    procedure create-id;
    NPAPID = 1;
    end create-id;
    procedure new-id(x);
    integer x;
    x = NPAPID;
    NPAPID = NPAPID + 1;
    end new-id;
    end PAPER_LABEL;
```

Suitable connections between the modules and the programs and the tasks must be
defined.  We shall not go into any kind of further detail on this.  Our only
purpose is to point out that the modularization concepts of modern programming
languages can be rather easily fitted into our framework.


## 3.   SYSTEM:   IFIP WORKING CONFERENCE

Lack of space prohibits a description of a detailed solution of the IFIP Working
Conference case.  We have therefore decided to emphasise the terminology development aspect.  We show how policy decisions and design decisions in the early
phases of requirement definition influence the choice of terminology, and thereby
the choice of a "conceptual database".  We further describe the functional
specification and the definition of datastores, using the systems terminology.
The development of program system design and database design, based on the
functional specifications, is only very briefly sketched.

Some purposes of Working Conferences (WC):

   . enhancing personal contact between knowledgable persons who are in the forefront of furthering the-state-of-the-art

   . providing a forum for debate on professional issues

   . disseminate technical/scientific knowledge

   . providing a forum for researchers to test their ideas.

Common features of Working Conferences:

   . limited attendance (to provide for effective professional contact and debate)

   . presentation of prepared scientific papers, in limited time (typically 20 min,1/2 hour, 1 hour), followed by a discussion of each paper

   . discussion sessions on predetermined themes, including prepared presentation of short statements of professional opinion on the theme of the discussion session (position papers, panel sessions)

   . preprints of presented papers are available at start of WC

   . social "sessions" to encourage informal professional discussions and "getting-to-know-you" atmosphere

   . conference participants are encouraged to stay on the conference site, preferrably at the same hotel(s), to obtain an air of "closeness" with the WC.  So hotel-accommodation is usually arranged by the WC-management

   . conference proceedings are published after the conference (might sometimes be available at conference start, replacing the preprints)

   . conferences should be financially self-supporting, either through sponsorship or through conference fees or a combination of these

   . conference fees should be as low as possible

   . the individuals which are involved in the conference arrangements are doing voluntary, non-paid work

   . organizational responsibilities are normally split between a program committee (PC) and an organization committee (OC).  The main responsibility of the PC is to organize a high quality professional program for the conference.  The main responsibility of the OC is to ensure that everything runs smoothly during the conference.


ORGANIZATION:  WORKING CONFERENCE MANAGEMENT SYSTEM (WCM)

The major responsibilities are

   . to get high quality papers for the WC

      . solicit papers from selected experts

      . advertise the WC to the general public e.g. distribute "Call for Papers"

      . select high quality papers for presentation at the WC

   . to develop the conference program

      . appoint persons to be responsible for the professional part of the program (session chairpersons, panel chairpersons etc.)

      . ensure that the participants in the professional program (speakers, session chairman, panel participants) get sufficient information about their duties

. to ensure proper attendance to the WC

    . issue invitations for attending the WC

    . select attendees (if over-booking)

    . inform selected attendees about registration matters (hotel etc.)

. to take care of WC-participants

    . register participants

    . distribute pre-prints (proceedings)

    . distribute material on social events, etc.

    . provide necessary physical resources (rooms, projectors, etc.)

. to take care of the money flow

    . collect conference fees from participants

    . book-keeping

    . get sponsors

. to reschedule conference program

    . take proper action on "no-shows" of speakers and/or session chairmen.

## 3.1.  Classification of important entities.  Terminology

### 3.1.1.  Basic terminology

The two major organizational units of the system are the

    PC - program committee

    OC - Organization committee

Important entity sets are

| | |
|---|---|
| AUTHOR | - persons who are authors of one or more manuscripts received by the PC |
| PAPER | - manuscripts received by PC |
| ATTENDEE | - persons who attend the conference, but have no other pre-planned role |
| REFEREE | - persons who review papers for the paper selection process |
| PC_MEMBER | - persons who are members of PC |
| OC_MEMBER | - persons who are members of OC |
| SESSION | - preplanned meetings at the conference, with the purpose of discussion and/or presentation of papers. Each session starts at a given time, and lasts for a given interval of time |
| SESSION_CHAIRPERSON | - persons who are responsible for chairing one or more sessions |
| CONTRIBUTOR | - persons who have a preplanned active role in the conference, except of attending, e.g. PC-members, OC-members, referees, authors of papers which are presented at the conference, session chairpersons etc. etc. |
| PARTICIPANT | - persons who attend the conference, i.e. the attendees, and those of the contributors who show up at the conference |

SPEAKER — persons who are authors of one more accepted papers

DISCUSSANT — persons who are to have preplanned (by the PC) contributions to a session (usually a panel-session)

JOURNAL — publications used for conference advertisements

SPONSOR — organizations which officially give money and/or services to the WC

HOTEL — organizations used for accomodating participants

REJECTED_AUTHOR — authors which have got no paper accepted by the PC, i.e. SPEAKER and REJECTED_AUTHOR are disjunct subsets of AUTHOR

INVITEE — persons who are being invited to participate in the working conference

POTENTIAL-PARTICIPANT — persons who should be contacted for contributions to the working conference.

## 3.1.2. Relationships between the systems entities

The system entities are related in several ways. The entity sets partly overlap with each other, and partly include each other. There are other types of relationships between entities, e.g. the connection between authors and papers. The somewhat lengthy discussion on terminology development that follows, is intended to demonstrate the close connection between terminology and policy/design decisions.

### 3.1.2.1. Terminology development

A number of the terms introduced so far, denote persons in different roles, as represented by membership in entity sets, e.g. CONTRIBUTOR, SPEAKER, etc.

a) Definition of terminology

   i) CONTRIBUTOR = PC_MEMBER $\cup$ OC_MEMBER $\cup$ REFEREE $\cup$ SPEAKER $\cup$ SESSION-CHAIRPERSON $\cup$ DISCUSSANT

This is the definition of the entityset CONTRIBUTOR. So CONTRIBUTOR is the union of the entitysets mentioned above, nothing more, nothing less. The subsets might be partly overlapping, e.g. a PC_MEMBER might also be a SESSION_CHAIRPERSON. The subsets are consequently subset-related to CONTRIBUTOR.

   ii) AUTHOR = SPEAKER $\cup$ REJECTED_AUTHOR
SPEAKER $\cap$ REJECTED_AUTHOR = 0

The entity-set AUTHOR consists of the two disjunct entity-sets SPEAKER and REJECTED_AUTHOR. The two objects are consequently specified to be categories of AUTHOR.
Remark: SPEAKER denotes persons which are authors of one or more accepted papers. Even if only one of the authors, in case of co-author ship, is chosen to present the paper at the conference, all of the authors will normally be treated as equals by the conference managers.

   iii) PARTICIPANT = ATTENDEE $\cup$ subset (CONTRIBUTOR)

Not all of the contributors will participate in the conference, e.g. referees might choose not to participate, only one of the co-authors of a paper might participate.

b) <u>Policy decisions</u>

    i)      <u>Policy rule 1</u>

         All contributors shall be invited to participate in the conference:
            CONTRIBUTOR $\subset$ INVITEE

    ii)     <u>Policy rule 2</u>

         Participation is by invitation only:
            PARTICIPANT $\subset$ INVITEE

         Consequence:
            ATTENDEE $\subset$ PARTICIPANT $\subset$ INVITEE

         i.e. all attendees must be invitees.

    iii)    <u>Policy rule 3</u>

         All rejected authors shall be invited to participate:
            REJECTED_AUTHOR $\subset$ INVITEE

         Consequence:

            AUTHOR = SPEAKER $\cup$ REJECTED_AUTHOR
            SPEAKER $\subset$ CONTRIBUTOR $\subset$ INVITEE
            REJECTED_AUTHOR $\subset$ INVITEE
            AUTHOR $\subset$ INVITEE
         This means that everybody who submits a paper, no matter how bad the
         quality of the paper, will be invited to participate in the conference.

c) <u>Definition of terminology</u>

    i)      INVITEE is not well defined. According to the specification statements
         so far, we have only mentioned some of the subsets of INVITEE, but not
         defined the whole set. Definition of INVITEE will be done later in the
         analysis.

    ii)     INVITEE $\subseteq$ POSSIBLE_PARTICIPANT

         This statement implies that the persons to be invited are selected from
         a (possibly) larger group of candidates for participation.

    iii)    The conference management system WCMS is an organizational unit, i.e.
         it is a member of the pre-defined model object class <u>organization</u>

            WCM   $\in$    <u>organization</u>
            OC, PC $\in$  <u>organization</u>

d) <u>Specification of system structure (Design decisions)</u>

    i)      <u>System definition</u>

         The working conference system consists of several entity sets e.g.
         POTENTIAL_PARTICIPANT, and of organizational units, e.g. PC, OC.
         Specification statement:

            <u>component</u> (WORKING_CONFERENCE):
                 JOURNAL, SPONSOR, PAPER, POTENTIAL_PARTICIPANT,
                 SESSION, HOTEL, WCMS;

    ii)     <u>Design decision 1</u>

         <u>component</u> (WCM):  PC, OC;

All of the other entitysets which have been mentioned earlier are subsets of the POTENTIAL_PARTICIPANT set.

iii)   Design_decision_2

Referees and PC-members are the major processing resources of the
program committee, and OC-members are the major processing resources
of the organizing committee.
Specification statements:

> resource (PC) : REFEREE, PC-MEMBER
>
> resource (OC) : OC-MEMBER

e)   Policy-Design

i)   Policy_rule_4

One of the policy decisions which has to be made, is to decide if
program committee members shall be permitted to submit papers.
Opinions differ on this policy problem.
(Specification of denial:

> PC_MEMBER ∩ AUTHOR = 0
> i.e. disjunct sets.)

Because of the differing opinions, we prefer to let PC-members have
the possibility of being authors.  This is formally stated by the
specification,

> PC_MEMBER ⊂ CONTRIBUTOR
>
> SPEAKER   ⊂ CONTRIBUTOR

which does not rule out any overlap between the sets.

## 3.1.2.2.  Entity-connections

a)   Authors and papers

Every author must submit one or more papers.  Every paper has one or more
authors.
Specification statement:

> mandatory connection  (alias AUTHOR  from PAPER onto AUTHOR
>                        correspondance (many:many))

Remark:  The connection and its range-set are denoted by the same name (AUTHOR).

b)   Sessions and contributors

A session is normally chaired by one person only.  Even if there are
examples of shared chairpersonship, we shall require that one and only one
person is responsible for each session.

i)   Policy_rule_5

Every session must have one and only one responsible session chairperson.  Every chairperson is responsible for one or more sessions.
Specification statement:

> mandatory connection SESSION_RESPONSIBLE
>                       (from SESSION onto SESSION_CHAIRPERSON
>                       correspondance (many:one))

Graphical representation:

ii)  <u>Definition of PANEL</u>

A session can consist of prepared discussions.  Such discussions are usually called panel discussions.  A session can have one or more panelists.  A discussant must participate in one or more panels. Specification statement

<u>connection</u> PANEL MEMBER
              (<u>from</u> SESSION <u>onto</u> DISCUSSANT
              <u>correspondance</u> (<u>many</u>:<u>many</u>))

### 3.1.2.3.  Terminology, summing up

We have established a basic vocabulary to be used in the next phases of the systems analysis and design.  The terms introduced denote important system entities.  Relationships between the entities have been established (section 3.1.2.3. and 3.1.2.2.)  Some of the relationships are depending on policy decisions, which determine properties of the system e.g. participation by invitation only.  The relationships among the terms introduced so far, are depicted in fig. 33. Reference to policy rules e.g. (PR 1), and design decisions e.g. (DD 1), are given where appropriate.

Note that the specific relationships are static relationships, e.g. an author is either a rejected author or a speaker.  This specification implies that an author can be sub-classified to be only a rejected author or a speaker.  The specification does not imply that every author shall have such classification at all times.  A complete systems description must contain a specification of the events which initiate the classification of an entity e.g. what is the condition for an author to become a speaker?  Because we do not have a well-tested formalism for specifying temporal conditions, we refrain from suggesting modelling concepts for this part of the specification.

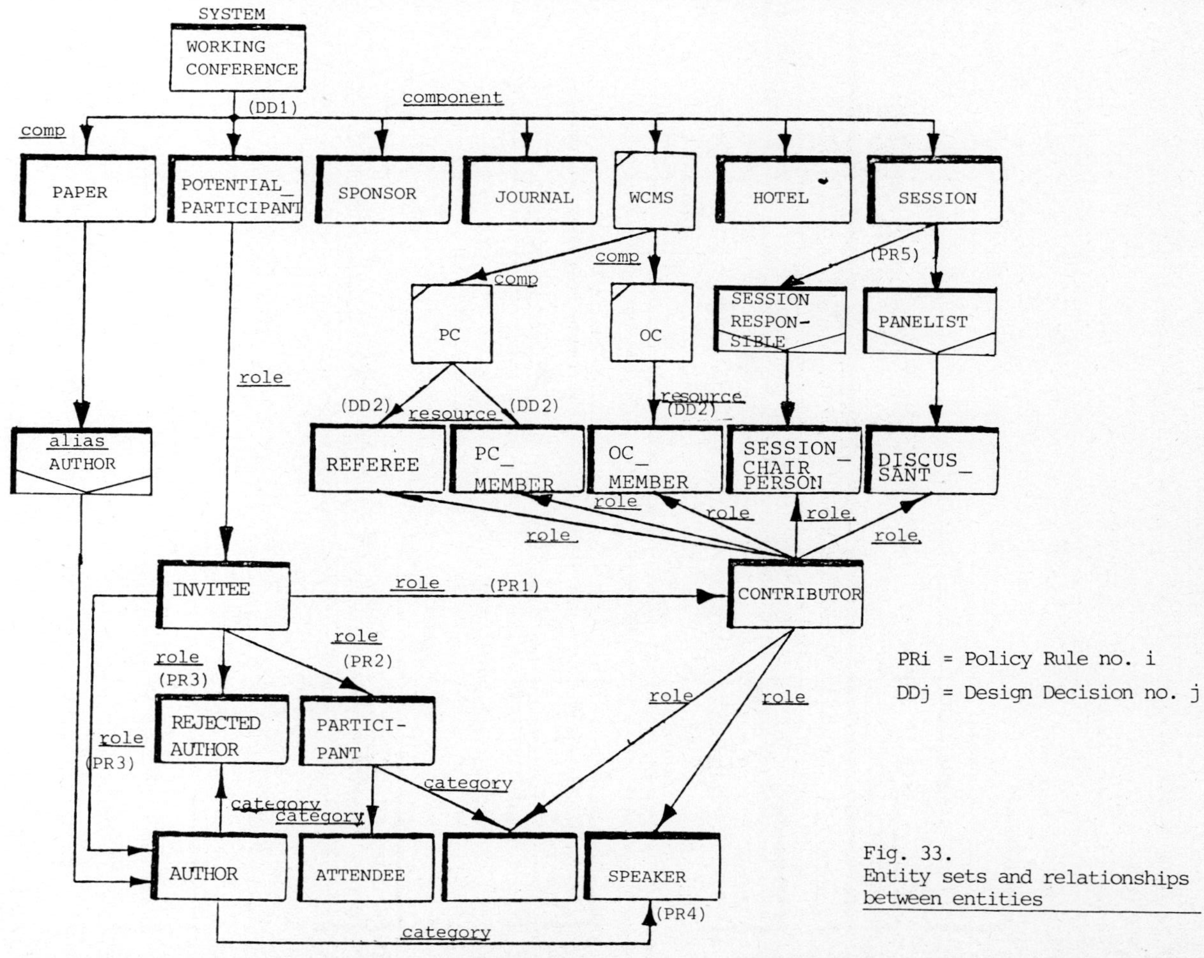


Fig. 33.
Entity sets and relationships between entities

524                               *A. Sølvberg*

## 3.2.  Analysis of tasks and interactions

The WCM-system is interacting with several external entities e.g. authors, hotels, journals.

An overview diagram of the dataflow in the system is given in fig. 34.

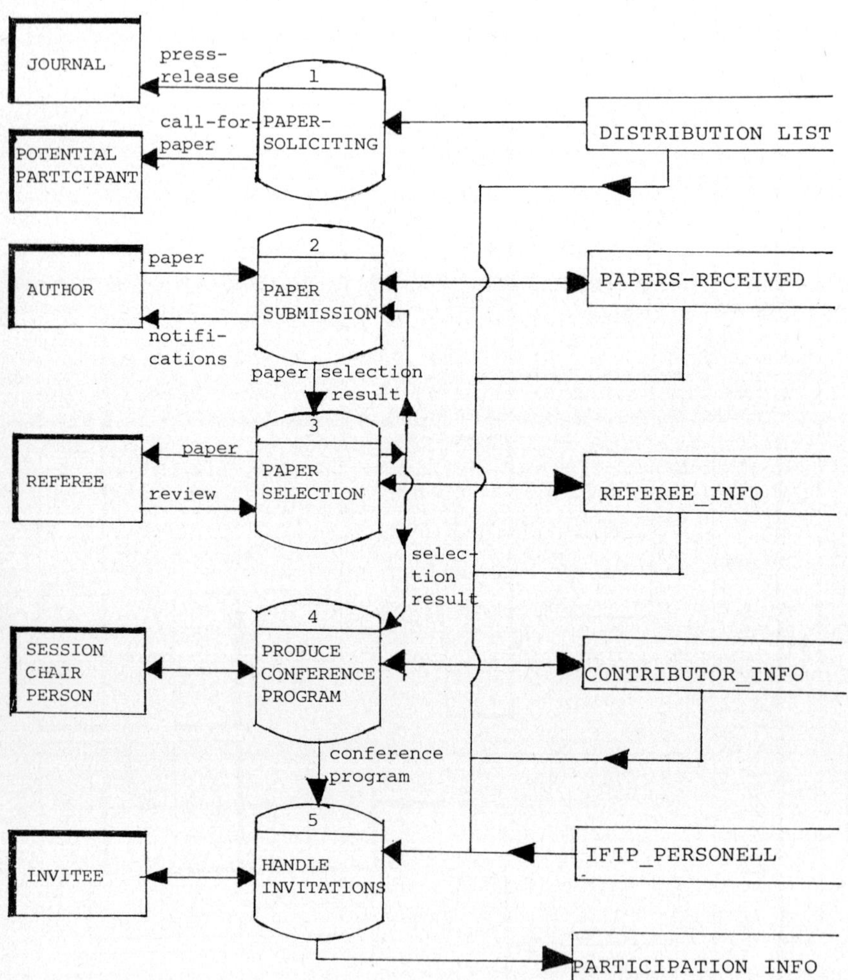


Fig. 34.  Overview diagram.  Data flow in WCMS.

To keep within reasonable limits of length of this paper, we can not explain the design of the system in any detail.  We do therefore concentrate on giving functional specifications, and on defining the contents of appropriate datastores, with respect to the terminology which has been developed so far.  A few excerpts of a total design are given in section 3.4.

The major tasks to be performed by the WCM-system are:

### 3.2.1.  Paper-soliciting

A "call-for-paper" is distributed to potential authors, the conference is advertised in selected professional journals, "press-releases" are sent to selected journals, personal solicitation is done by phone, by letter etc.
Output:  "call-for-paper", "press-release", advertisement
Production-basis:  "call-for-paper", adresses of potential authors and of journals.

Datastore definition:

        datastore  DISTRIBUTION_LIST

            reference  POTENTIAL_PARTICIPANT

            projection NAME, ADDRESS

Time:  Should be done 4-12 months before the deadline for paper submission.

Diagram:  Fig. 18

### 3.2.2.  Paper-submission

Papers are received from authors, notification of receipt of paper should be sent immediately to the author(s).  The papers are sent for review.  When the paper selection process is over, notification of acceptance/rejection of the papers must be sent immediately to the respective author(s).
For those of the accepted papers which are not ready for publication, instructions for preparing camera-ready papers should accompany the notification-of-acceptance message.

 Input:    Submitted papers (from authors).

 Output:   Submitted papers (for review, and for paper selection)
           Notification of paper receipt (to authors)
           Notification of acceptance/rejection (to authors)

 Produc-   Addresses of authors, selection result for each paper (acceptance/
 tion      rejection), instructions for preparing camera-ready papers, standard
 basis:    acceptance/rejection letters

Datastore definition:

        datastore  PAPERS_RECEIVED

            reference (connection between PAPER and AUTHOR)

            projection PAPER_ID, PAPER.NAME,
                       AUTHOR.NAME, AUTHOR.ADDRESS,
                       SENDER.(NAME, ADDRESS);

Diagram:  Figure 19

### 3.2.3.  Paper-selection

The submitted papers are accepted/rejected by decision of the Program Committee members in a plenum meeting.

a)  The referees

The formal basis for the selection is one or more reviews of each submitted
paper (normally 3-4 separate reviews).  The responsibility for reviewing the
papers are distributed among the PC-members, so that each PC-member will be
responsible for reviewing a set of papers, and each paper is read by several
PC-members.  Additional referees are quite often appointed, if there are many
submitted papers.  Referee-appointments are normally made on suggestion of the
PC-members.  PC-members quite often use "personal" referees, e.g. to check
their own judgement if they do not feel fully competent on the subject area
of a paper.
The use of "personal" referees is usually considered to be the PC-members'
own business, so a "personal" referee is not considered to be a REFEREE-member,
and is therefore not being entitled to an invitation to the working conference.
Based on this discussion we formulate

### Policy rule 6

    a)  Referees must be officially appointed by the PC
    b)  PC-members are referees i.e. PC_MEMBER $\subset$ REFEREE
    c)  Each paper must be sent to at least two PC-members
    d)  Each paper must be reviewed by at least three referees, which can
        be PC-members.

b)  Distribution of papers to referees

Because PC-members and reviewers usually live in different countries around
the world, the papers have to be transmitted by mail, stored on paper.
(As opposed to e.g. electronic mail, storage on some electronic medium.)
To avoid copying costs for the PC, one requires that authors submit their
papers in several copies (usually 4-6 copies).  Of security reasons, one of
the copies must always reside with the program committee, in case of papers
being sent to the referees are lost.  Because of geographical spread, one must
also assure that referee-reports will be stored on paper and returned by mail
to the PC.
Based on this discussion, we formulate

### Design decision 3

    a)  Papers shall be submitted by the author in 5 copies, stored on
        paper-medium.
    b)  One copy of each paper shall be stored by the program committee
    c)  The additional copies are to be sent to referees
    d)  Referee reports are stored on paper-medium

c)  Anonymous reviewing

The problem of anonymous reviewing is handled differently by program
committees.  Anonymous reviewing means that the names of the authors of a
paper are not known by the reviewers of the paper.  In the case of anonymous
reviewing, it is useful if each paper is identified by a unique identifier,
to avoid possible confusion during final selection because of similar paper-
titles.  Based on this discussion, we formulate

### Design decision 4

Each paper shall be given a unique identifier, (by the PC) at arrival of
the paper from the authors to the PC.

d) <u>Missing referee-reports</u>

The next problem to be discussed is the problem of referee-reports not being returned in due time (delayed in the mail, not done, PC-member got delayed in travelling (foggy airports), and so on).  In such cases it is extremely useful to know who was supposed to review each paper, so that e.g. telephone contact can be established,if necessary to clear up disagreement in the PC-meeting. This leads us to formulate

> <u>Design decision 5</u>

> A record shall be kept by the PC on who reviews each paper

e) <u>Matching papers and referees</u>

The last problem to be discussed is the problem of determining which referee shall review which paper.  We assume this to be done at the PC-chairman's discretion, constrained by a rule of not overloading any reviewer.

The PAPER SELECTION task is diagrammed in fig. 35.

Datastore definition:

> <u>datastore</u>  REFEREE_INFO
>
> > <u>reference</u>  REFEREE
> >
> > <u>projection</u> REFEREE.(NAME, ADDRESS), PAPER_ID;

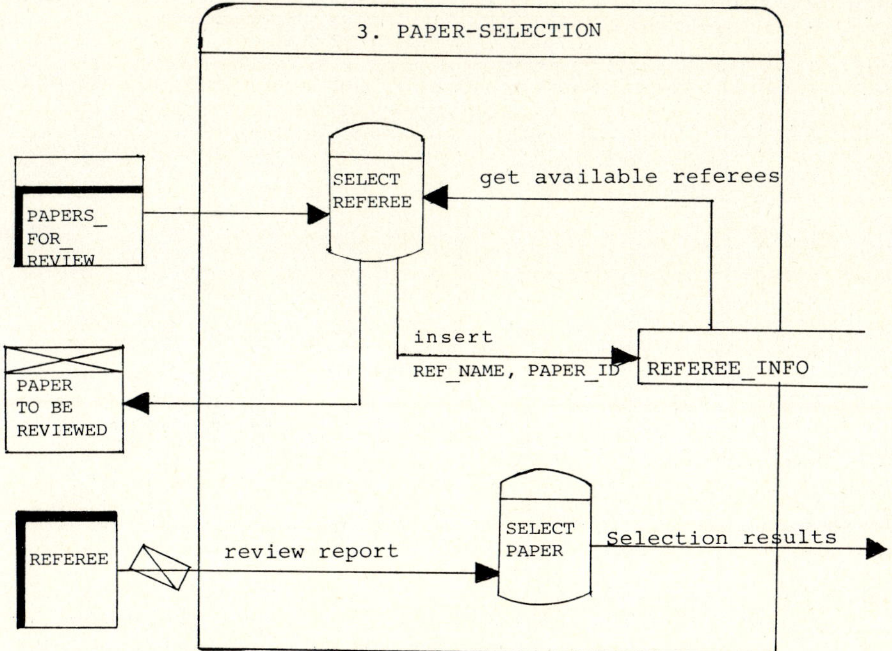


Fig. 35.  Data flow of PAPER_SELECTION

### 3.2.4. Produce conference program

The accepted papers are grouped in sessions, and given a time on the conference
program. Each session is given a name. Panel sessions are decided. Session-
chairpersons are selected. Session chairpersons are usually charged with the
responsibility of suggesting discussants for the session of which they are
responsible, within some time-limit. In the case of parallell sessions, it is
seen to that no persons are supposed to be at more than one session at the same
time.
The final program can not be decided until all of the suggested chairpersons have
accepted to contribute. To speed up the finalization of the conference program,
it is quite common to ask authors, PC-members and others who are supposed to
attend the conference, to serve as chairperson.

Input:          Selection results

Output:         Conference program, including list of chairpersons and discussants

Production      List of known contributors (authors, etc), list of probable partici-
basis:          pants, PC-members' general knowledge, list of persons who have been
                asked to contribute.

Datastore definition:

        datastore  CONTRIBUTOR_INFO
           reference  CONTRIBUTOR
           projection CONTRIBUTOR.(NAME, ADDRESS), CONTRIBUTOR_ROLE;

Diagram: Figure 36

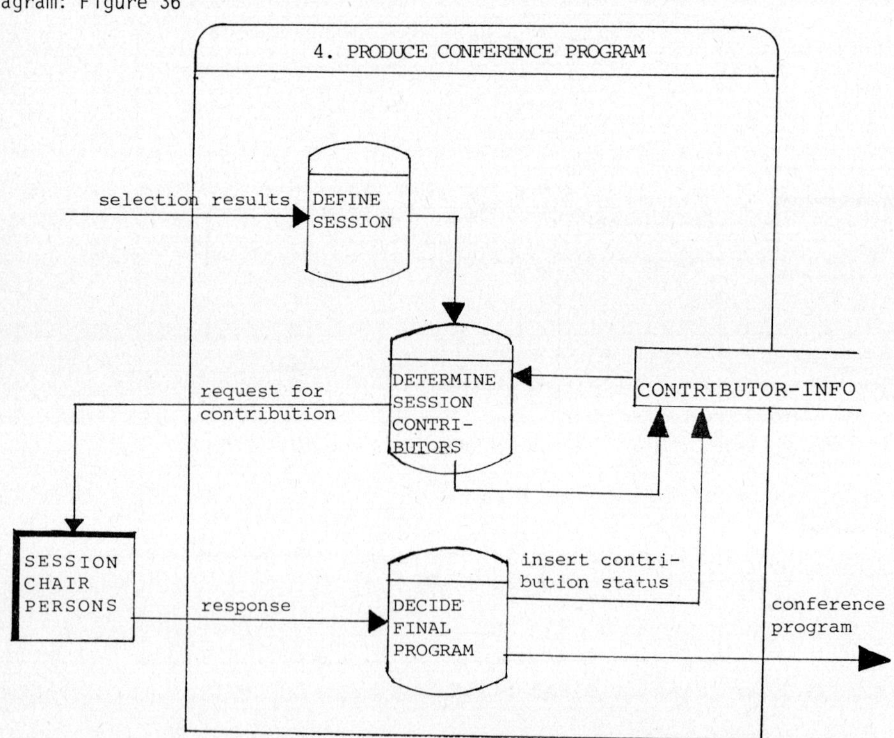


Fig. 36.  Data flow diagram of PRODUCE_CONFERENCE_PROGRAM.

## 3.2.5.  Handle invitations

Working conferences have limited attendance.  First priority is given to those
who contribute to the WC in some capacity (PC-members, OC-members, speakers,
discussants etc).  Second priority is given to authors who did not get any paper
accepted.  Third priority is given to persons associated with the IFIP technical
committee(s) and working group(s) which sponsor the working conference.  All the
members of these groups will receive "priority invitations".
NB!  IFIP-associated persons are not defined in the vocabulary of the WCMS
     (fig. 33).
Some time after the answers of the priority invitations are due, additional
prospective participants will be selected, and will be given an invitation to
attend the WC.

Input:   CONTRIBUTOR_INFO, IFIP_PERSONELL, PAPERS_RECEIVED, DISTRIBUTION_LIST
Output:  PARTICIPANT_INFO

Datastore definitions:

        datastore  IFIP_PERSONELL
            reference?
            restriction ?
            projection NAME, ADDRESS;
        datastore  PARTICIPANT_INFO
            reference  PARTICIPANT
            projection NAME, ADDRESS, PARTICIPATION_ROLE;


Diagram:  Fig. 37


## 3.3. Analysis of the contents of the datastores

By comparing the terminology definition of fig. 33 with the datastore definitions
of section 3.2, we can see that

    REFEREE_INFO [NAME, ADDRESS]⊆ CONTRIBUTOR_INFO[NAME, ADDRESS]

It is also easy to see that

    CONTRIBUTOR_INFO/CONTRIBUTOR_ROLE = 'SPEAKER' [NAME, ADDRESS]
        ⊂ PAPERS_RECEIVED [AUTHOR.(NAME, ADDRESS)]

where [ ] denotes projection
and / denotes restriction

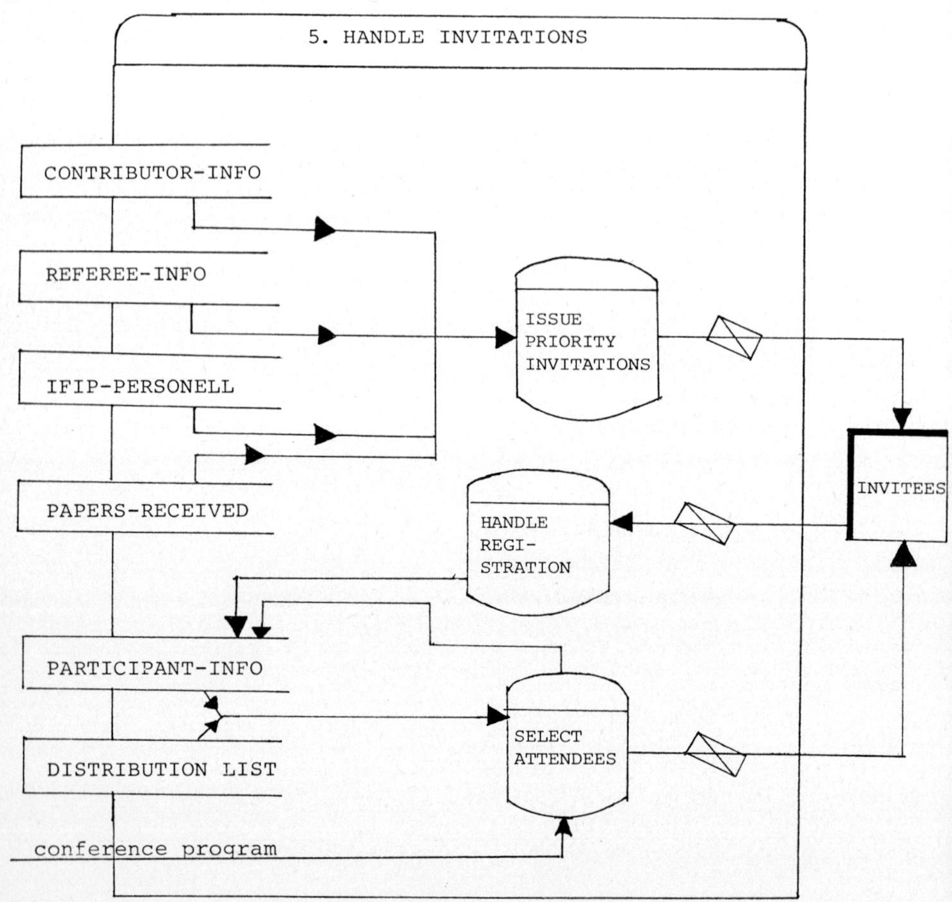



Fig. 37.   Data flow diagram.   HANDLE_INVITATIONS.

### 3.4.  System design

By pursuing this analysis, we end up by proposing a solution where we have

> one record class containing information about persons, their names, addresses, and roles

> one record class containing information about papers

> one record class containing information about sessions

A proposal for a logical database design is depicted in fig. 38.

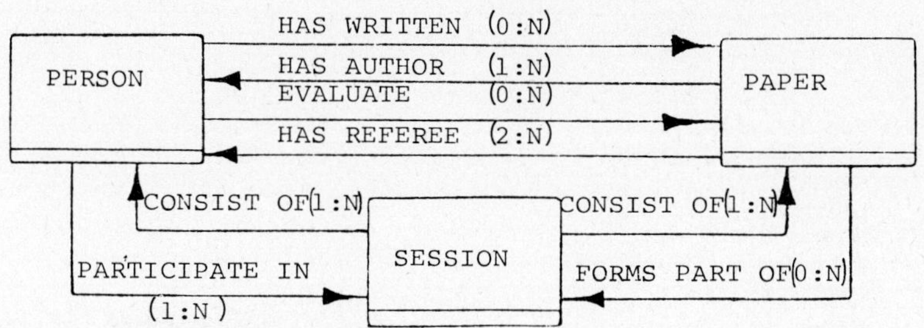

Fig. 38.  Data base logical structure

The user interface has to be designed.  The basis for this design is the data-store interactions as specified in the dataflow diagrams.
A "menu" of appropriate users' commands is depicted in fig. 39.

```
*MENU


        MENU : COMMANDS CONCERNING OPERATIONS ON :
        PERSONS :
            - REGISTRATION OF A NEW .....................  *PREG
            - LISTING/UPDATING .........................  *POLD
            - CENSORED PAPERS ..........................  *PCEN
            - WRITTEN PAPERS ...........................  *PWRI
            - DELETING .................................  *PDEL
        PAPERS :
            - REGISTRATION OF A NEW ....................  *MREG
            - LISTING/UPDATING .........................  *MOLD
            - DELETING .................................  *MDEL
        SESSIONS :
            - REGISTRATION OF A NEW ....................  *SREG
            - LISTING/UPDATING .........................  *SOLD
            - LIST PARTICIPANTS ........................  *SPAR
            - DELETING .................................  *SDEL
        COMMANDS FOR :
            - REGISTRATION OF HOTELS ...................  *HREG
            - PRICES ON SOCIAL ACTIVITIES ..............  *COST
            - TERMINATION ..............................  *EXIT
```

Fig. 39.  The users main menu

The screen-formats have to be designed.  Examples of proposals for screen forms are depicted in figs. 40-42.

```
*PREG GRØSTAD


          PERSONNUMBER: 000010                    CATEGORY: .
          LASTNAME : GRØSTAD                       FIRSTNAME: ....................
          STREET   : ................................
          DISTRICT : .........................
          COUNTRY  : ...................
          TELEPHONE: ................
          WORK     : .........................
          HOTEL    : 00                               HOTEL CATEGORY: 00
          REGISTERDATE: ....   CONFIRMDATE: ....      ARRIVAL: .
          REGISTER TO ACTIVITIES:
          ACT. NR.: 01 02 03 04 05 06 07 08 09 10 11 12 13 14 15 16 17 18
          NUMBER   :
          TOTAL PRICE:      0        HAS PAID:      0
MANUSCRIPT WRITTEN:         ......   ......   ......   ......   ......   ......
MANUSCRIPT SENSOR :         ......   ......   ......   ......   ......   ......
                            ......   ......   ......   ......   ......   ......
                            ......   ......   ......   ......   ......   ......
PARTICIPATE SESSIONS:       ......   ......   ......   ......   ......   ......
```

Fig. 40.   Person screen formular, example

```
     MANUSCRIPT NUMBER: ......

     TITLE  : ..............................
     TOPIC  : ....................                ACCEPT/REJECT: .

     SESSION : ....................               AUDIO VISUAL AIDS: .. .. ..

     AUTHOR NAME            NUMBER                CONFIRMATION SENT
                                                  RECEIVE   REFEREE
     ...................    ......                ....      ....
     ...................    ......                ....      ....
     ...................    ......                ....      ....
        ---
        ---

     REFEREE NAME           NUMBER                RESULT

     ...................    ......                ....
     ...................    ......                ....
        ---
        ---
     UPDATE THE REQUIRED FIELDS. GIVE NEW MANUSNUMBER OR COMMAND.
```

Fig. 41.   Paper screen formular

```
  SESSION NUMBER : ......
  SESSION NAME   : .................                DATE: ....

  PLACE          : .............                    TIME: .........

  SESSION LEADER : .................                NR  : ......
  PANEL LEADER   : .................                NR  : ......

  LECTURE:
  MANUSTITLE                         MANUSNR    SPEAKER                 PERSON NUMBER

  ..........................         ......     .................       ......
  ..........................         ......     .................       ......
  ..........................         ......     .................       ......
  ..........................         ......     .................       ......
  ..........................         ......     .................       ......


  UPDATE THE REQUIRED FIELDS.   GIVE NEW SESSION NUMBER OR COMMAND.
```

Fig. 42.  Session screen formular

Modularizations of the programs have to be decided upon.  Examples of program
structures are shown in figs. 43, 44.

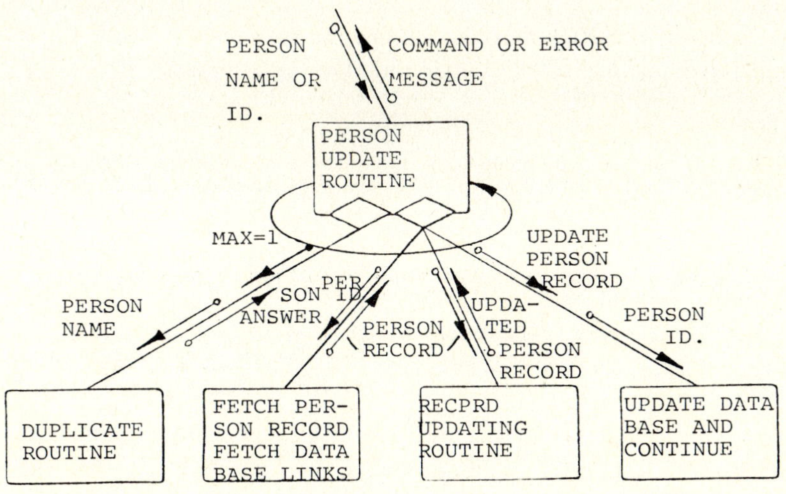


Fig. 43 .  Person updating routine structure chart

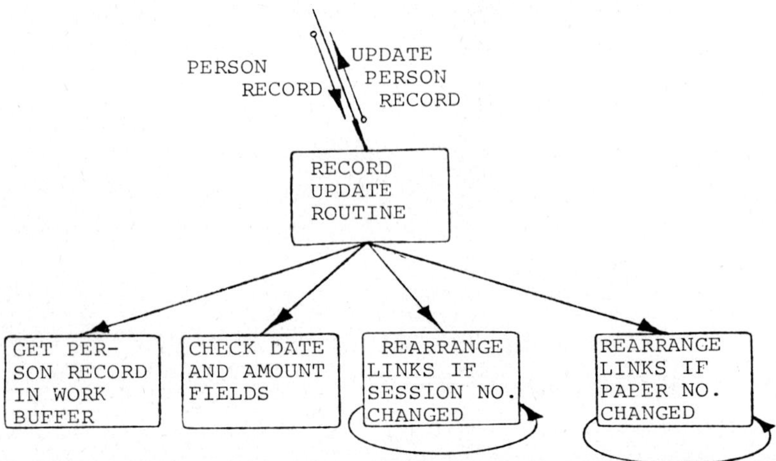



Fig. 44 .   Record updating routine structure chart

The way of reasoning to proceed from the functional "requirement" specification to a program system design proposal, has been explained in detail in chapter 2 of this paper. We do feel that a detailed discussion of design issues within the space given to us, will not add additional information to the reader.

ACKNOWLEDGEMENTS

The model and method which are proposed in this paper, can not be easily applied without software support for developing the documentation, especially the diagrams.

The report could not have been finished without the hard work of Svein Stavelin and

Geir Skylstad, who extracted part of the solution of chapter 3 from the documentation of a complete solution[7],

Gong Chen Ho,  who made most of the artwork, and

Norun Brembo, Rannveig Kristensen, Anne Sørvik who patiently did the typing and retyping of ever changing drafts of the report.

Ref.


[1]  Gane & Sarson:  "Structured Systems Analysis:  tools & techniques", Prentice Hall 1978

[2]  Lesser, Serrain, Bonar:  "PCL: a processoriented job control language". Proc. 1st. Int. Conf. Distr. Computing Systems, 1979

[3]  Sølvberg, A:  "A contribution to the definition of concepts for expressing users' information systems requirements" in P.P.Chen(ed):  "Entity-Relationship Approach to Systems Analysis and Design", North-Holland Publ. Co., 1980

[4]  Peterson, J.L.:  "Petri-nets" Computing Surveys, Vol. 9, pp 223-252, 1977

[5]  Stavelin, S:  "Derivability analysis and data modelling",
                 Masters thesis, Dept. Computer Science, The Norwegian
                 Institute of Technology, Trondheim, Norway, 1980

[6]  Oftedal, Sølvberg:  "Database design constrained by traffic load estimates",
                 Information Systems, no. 4, 1981

[7]  Otnes W.,     "Structured systems analysis applied in analysis of a
     Stavelin S.:  conference information system",
                 Technical Report No. 13/80, Dept. of Computer Science,
                 The Norwegian Institute of Technology, Trondheim, Norway.

*INFORMATION SYSTEMS DESIGN METHODOLOGIES: A Comparative Review*
T.W. Olle, H.G. Sol, A.A. Verrijn-Stuart (editors)
*North-Holland Publishing Company*
© IFIP, 1982


NIAM: AN INFORMATION ANALYSIS METHOD


Verheijen, G.M.A. and Van Bekkum, J.
Information Systems Department
CONTROL DATA B.V.
Rijswijk, The Netherlands


NIAM[1] is a method to perform information analysis, based on a
general framework for information systems in which terms like
information, information flows and information systems are
explained. In this framework the conceptual grammar is an essential part which describes the static and dynamic aspects of
the object system accurately and completely. Although formal,
the conceptual grammar is perfectly understandable for users,
enabling them to participate fully in the development of an
information system. The basic concepts and the associated graphical
formalism will be described and attention will be paid to supporting software.
The second part of the paper demonstrates the application of the
NIAM-approach by specifying an information system, which supports
the organization of an IFIP working conference.


PART I: NIAM THEORY


1. OVERVIEW

In this paper we present NIAM[1], an information analysis method. Information
analysis is an inevitable step to be taken when developing an information system.
We will outline the framework in which terms like information, information system
and information analysis are explained. Next we will study information systems in
more detail to find the basic aspects which are essential for any information
system. Concepts like function, information flow and information base will then be
introduced to describe the function model of NIAM. Subsequently we will deal with
the NIAM sentence model. From this we notice the emergence of NIAM-concepts like
object type, idea type, constraint, etc. and we will introduce RIDL, a Referential
IDea Language.

To apply information analysis successfully, undisturbed communication between
analysts and users is a prerequisite. NIAM solves this problem by using a graphical
notation, both for dynamic and static properties of information systems.

Information analysis should be supported by automated tools to avoid being drowned
in an endless stream of documentation. For NIAM such a tool was developed. It is
commercially available and called ISDIS[2]. Besides its function as an information
dictionary, it verifies the information system specifications and is equiped with
software generators, simplifying the implementation of the information system.

Finally, we discuss NIAM in the light of project management. NIAM may be incorporated in any project management approach, provided the approach recognizes the
need and importance of information analysis.

The second part of this paper is dedicated to the elaboration of the -by now well
known- IFIP-case. In a number of steps (which are enumerated in chapter 6 of part
I) we apply NIAM to end up with a conceptual grammar for the IFIP information
system. It will be obvious that the lack of communication with the users of the
information system to be, is an insuperable handicap. Instead of a user's opinion,
we have to satisfy with presumptions, one of the most dangerous pitfalls of information system development. Nevertheless, we believe that the elaboration suffices
as a demonstration of NIAM's capability as an information analysis method.

## 2. OBJECT SYSTEM, INFORMATION SYSTEM AND ENVIRONMENT

### 2.1. INTRODUCTION

A method for specifying an information system should -above all- be based on properties of information systems and communication, instead of properties of computer
systems. Therefore, a clear definition of information, information systems and
communication, together with their connections, is indispensable. The framework
given by Dr. G.M. Nijssen [ref. 5-7], which also turns out to be very close to
concepts of the preliminary report of ISO, TC97/SC5/WG3 [ref. 2], will be our
guide in this.

### 2.2. THE FRAMEWORK

In this framework, three major components are distinguished, being:

- the object system

- the information system

- the environment

An object system is that part of the observable reality, for which we want to collect
information and retrieve -possibly derived- information. The object system aims at
goals, to be reached by performing activities. An activity may deal both with goods
and with information. For instance, in the IFIP-case there exists an activity
called "distribute papers among referees", which involves shipment of goods (= papers) and information (= request to referee). Information is needed by an activity
either to perform the activity or to control it. In this view, an information
system is merely a tool, which delivers the information needed to run the object
system, which in its turn is needed to attain the predefined goals.

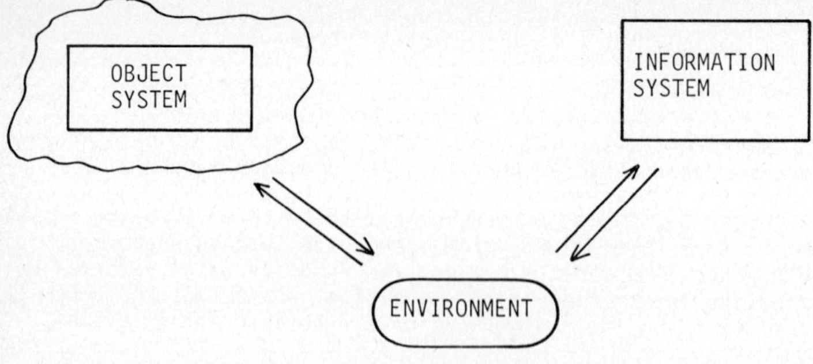


Figure 2.1
Object- and Information System
and the Environment

The information system describes -in a predefined formalism- the state of the object system. It is informed about phenomena happening in the object system by what
we call the environment. This could be the information system users, but also some
kind of machinery. It is assumed that the environment is able to observe the object system and to translate the phenomena happening there into messages. As a
reward for this activity, the environment will in its turn receive messages from
the information system, enabling it to perform and control the activities of the
object system.

Note, that in this view an object system is always part of the observable world
and is considered separate from the information system and the environment.


## 2.3. THE ABSTRACTION SYSTEM

Observation of the behaviour of an object system may convince its environment that
all possible states and transitions, occurring in the object system, can be characterized by an abstraction system. The abstraction system is a mental model of the
object system, consisting of object- and activity classes and rules. To guarantee
an efficient and effective communication between members of a particular environment, it is crucial that all agree about one abstraction system and conform to one
interpretation of it. Here we encounter the hazards for the successful development
of an information system: the environment (read: users and analysts) cannot agree
about one abstraction system or they cannot express it unambiguously and completely.


## 2.4. THE CONCEPTUAL GRAMMAR

The name commonly used for the formal description of the abstraction system is
conceptual grammar [ref. 5]. This conceptual grammar is part of the information
system. The part of the information system reflecting the state of the object system is called the information base. Now we have treated all elements acting in
figure 2.2.

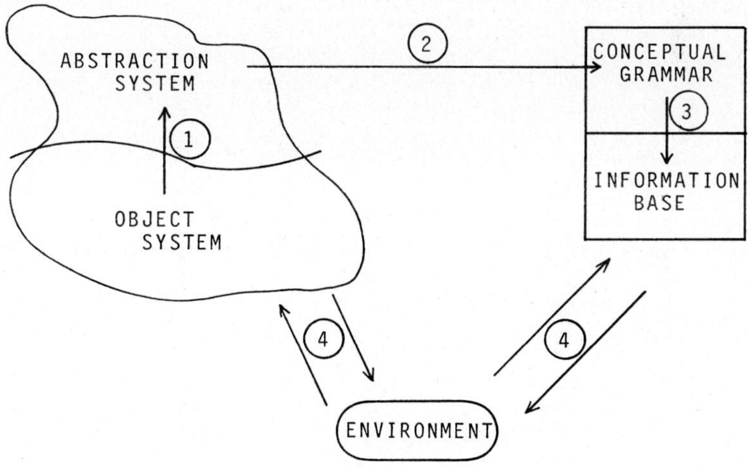


Figure 2.2

## 2.5. INFORMATION ANALYSIS

In figure 2.2 each arrow represents a process, namely:

- Process 1: Classification, generalization, establishing rules, etc. In short, the
            modelling of the object system.

- Process 2: Translates the abstraction system into formal propositions. The result
            is a representation of the abstraction system in some kind of language.

- Process 3: Enforces the rules of the conceptual grammar upon the contents of the
            information base and enables the deduction of new information from
            the existing information base contents.

- Process 4: The recording of facts and the delivery of messages by the information
            system from and to its environment plus intervention in the object
            system by the environment.

It will be clear, that the results from process 1 and 2 are decisive for the performance and success of the information system. Information analysis is the exercise which must lead to an unambiguous, complete and correct conceptual grammar.
It should be obvious now, that an information analysis method, which does not stimulate the modelling process, or which is too poor to express an abstraction system
properly, is an insuperable obstacle when applied to the development of information
systems.


## 3. INFORMATION SYSTEM ASPECTS


### 3.1. INTRODUCTION

The previous chapter depicted the area in which we will encounter information systems. An information system was described as a communication partner for its environment, where the communication was restricted to affairs concerning a particular object system. This chapter discusses the basic aspects of information systems,
in order to determine the goals for information analysis.

### 3.2. PURPOSE OF INFORMATION SYSTEMS

The main purpose of each information system is that of acting as a communication
partner for its environment. Often, this environment will consist of persons,
communicating with each other via the information system (figure 3.1).

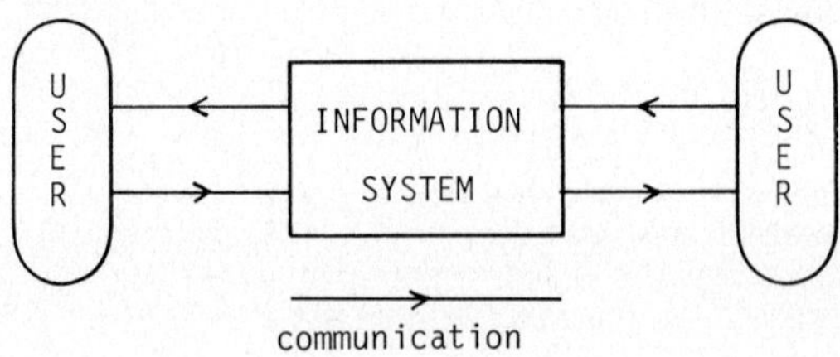


Figure 3.1
Communication via Information System

An information system is not merely a tool to exchange messages, but fulfils other essential duties. We expect information systems to retain messages, enabling us to consult them the moment it is considered opportune. In the IFIP information system we register a person only once. From that moment on, we may consult all messages known about that person when needed, like his name and address. Another service that we demand from an information system is the deduction of new messages from existing ones and deduction rules. An example of this can be found in the IFIP information system, which deduces from the referee reports for a paper, whether the paper is accepted or not.


## 3.3. INFORMATION SYSTEM ASPECTS

We will now introduce a terminology for those aspects that we consider to be essential for any information system:

- Information flows

- Functions

- Information base


### 3.3.1. Information Flow

An information flow denotes a stream of messages, representing a communication between two partners. Each information flow has therefore an origin as well as a destination. An information flow is not a flow of messages conveying information on arbitrary subjects; on the contrary, the messages occurring in a particular information flow are dedicated to certain subjects. Such a subject could be a paper or an invitation to attend an IFIP-conference. A message in such a stream would inform about a particular paper or represent an invitation for a certain person and conference.


### 3.3.2. Function

Function is the name we give to the capability to transform information flows. Transformation of information flows implies that the outgoing flows deal with subjects which differ from the ingoing flows. Often such a transformation may be characterized by a verb. The IFIP information system includes a function called "select callees", resulting in a flow of messages about persons to be called. The ingoing information flows however, contained messages about persons and selection criteria. The performance of a function may be known, in which case we call it a formalizable function. Unformalizable functions are functions for which we do know the in- and outgoing information flows, although we are ignorant about the mechanism achieving the transformation. It is obvious that only formalizable functions can be part of an automated information system.


### 3.3.3. Information Base

Information flows may originate from or terminate in an information base. As a consequence, the information base acts as a store for messages. We learned from chapter 1 that the contents of the information base should reflect the state of the object system. Conceptually speaking, there exists only one information base.


## 3.4. INFORMATION ANALYSIS GOALS

Information analysis should -in our opinion- result in a complete and accurate description of information flows, information base and functions. NIAM fulfils these requirements by building its concepts upon the following principles [ref. 5]:

- Communication involving an information system can be considered
  to consist of special natural language sentence instances (elementary sentences).

- Each communication can be described completely by a conceptual
  grammar.

- All functions performed by a formal information system can be
  described completely by a conceptual grammar.

The NIAM concepts, which enable us to describe the information system aspects in a
conceptual grammar, are a direct consequence of the above mentioned principles.


## 4. NIAM CONCEPTS


### 4.1. NIAM FUNCTION MODEL

To perform the activities of an object system, we need information. This information
results from an information system, which in its turn receives information about
the facts and events that happen in the object system. The information received by
the information system will be transformed into information that is of direct use
to us. An information system may therefore be conceived as a function, transforming
information flows.


### 4.2. FUNCTIONAL DECOMPOSITION

The transformation of information flows accomplished by an information system is
often very complex. To reduce its complexity, decomposition is applied. Decomposition means dividing the transformation capability of one function over more than
one function; the so-called subfunctions. Each subfunction in its turn may be decomposed, until we encounter functions for which we can:

- Describe its transformation in full detail.

- Define its information flows, for instance by giving a sample
  of such a flow.


### 4.3. INFORMATION FLOW DIAGRAMS (IFD)

Having established the functions by applying functional decomposition we must show,
for each level of decomposition, the information flows involved. To do so, we use
the concepts and graphical notation as shown in figure 4.1.
As an example of an IFD, we refer to figure 4.2, which shows part of the IFIP information system. The functions acting in this IFD, result from the decomposition
as shown in figure 4.3.

An IFD may contain formalizable functions and non-formalizable ones. Only the first
category will be a candidate for automation. An information flow always has a function as its origin or destination. Communication between, for instance, the program-
and organizing committee not running via the information system is not considered
in IFDs. An IFD does not show the path of a particular message. These aspects,
known as control of flows, are reveiled when describing the performance of each
function in a formal language. Although this control is also part of the conceptual
grammar, we will postpone this exercise. After analyzing all information flows, it
will turn out to be very trivial, whereas at this stage, it only obscures important

aspects. Note that the environment cannot send its messages straight to the information base. A function should mediate to prevent illegal messages reaching the information base.

Now that we defined the information flows on a level where the users of the information system can provide samples, we may start the next phase: that of analyzing information flows.

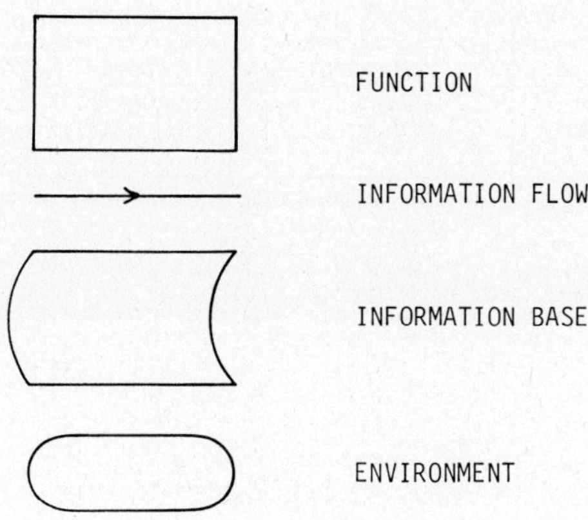


Figure 4.1
NIAM  Concepts

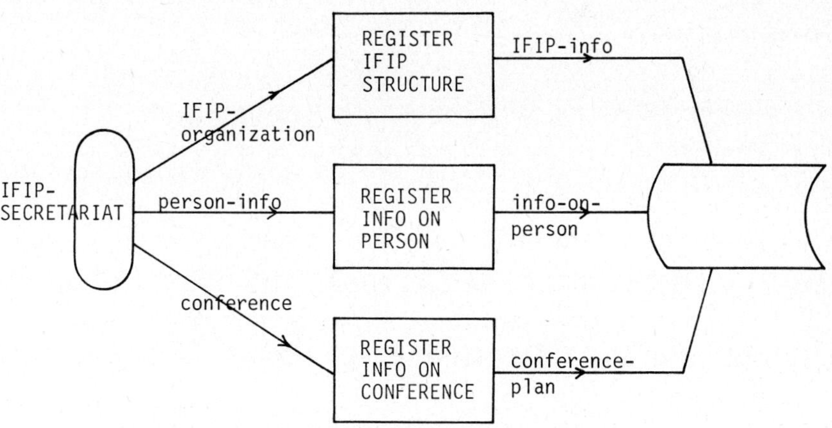


Figure 4.2

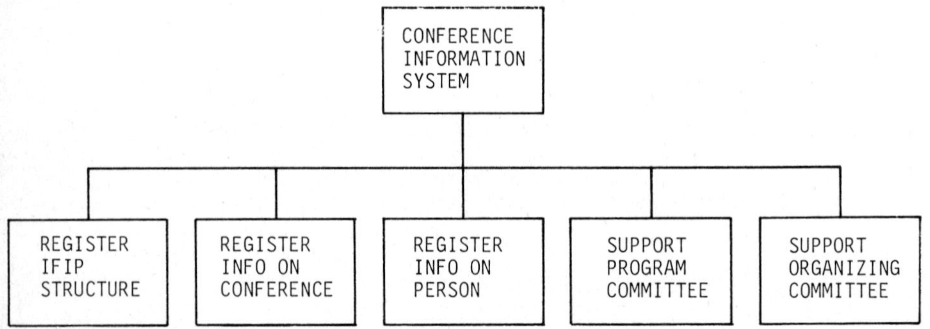


Figure 4.3
Functional Decomposition


## 4.4. NIAM SENTENCE MODEL

In the previous paragraphs we encountered three NIAM-concepts: function, information flow and information base. Further, it was stated that information flows and
-as a consequence of that- the information base consist of elementary sentences,
which are a special case of natural language sentences.

A natural language sentence like

    "Pieters lives in Amersfoort"

lacks a lot of information. Nevertheless, it will be perfectly understandable by a
receiver, who knows the context in which the sentence was used. To be independent
from context-bound communication, we must make the lacking information explicit.


### 4.4.1. Lexical- and Non-Lexical Objects

A sentence conveys information about objects (real or abstract things) in the object system. However, the sentence does not show the objects involved, but refers
to them by names ("Pieters", "Amersfoort"). We conclude that we have to deal with:

   - Lexical objects: Strings that can be uttered and which refer to an  object.

   - Non-lexical objects: Real or abstract things in the object system which are
     non-utterable.

It is quite possible to have different kind of names for one object, e.g. we may
refer to a paper for a conference by its paper number or by the name of its submitter plus its title.


### 4.4.2. Object Classifications

We already used the expression: kind of name. It will be obvious that we mean a
class of names, which includes all lexical objects that refer to non-lexical objects of a particular class. In NIAM-terms, we distinguish:

- Lexical object types (LOT): Classes of lexical objects like surname,
  title, town-name, etc.

- Non-lexical object types (NOLOT): Classes of non-lexical objects
  like person, town, paper, etc.

Classifying lexical- and non-lexical objects is one of the first steps in the
modelling process (paragraph 2.5).

From the example given, we may now conclude:

"Pieters" is an occurrence of the LOT surname.

"Amersfoort" is an occurrence of the LOT town-name.

Note that we cannot show occurrences of NOLOTs, as they are -by definition- not
utterable. An occurrence of the NOLOT person could be the reader of this paper or
one of its authors.
The sentence

"Pieters lives in Amersfoort"

may now be transformed in one that bears a deeper structure:

"The person with surname Pieters

lives in

the town with town-name Amersfoort".

Or:

"The town with town-name Amersfoort

is residence of

the person with surname Pieters".

Both sentences express the same association between two objects. For each object,
the sentence states the class that it belongs to, the naming that is used to reference it and the actual lexical objects ("Pieters", "Amersfoort"). The sentence
is completed by the predicates (lives-in, is-residence-of) which are called roles
in NIAM.


## 4.4.3. Sentence Type

Not only can lexical- and non-lexical objects be classified, classification applies
to sentences as well:

"The person with surname Pieters lives in the town
with town-name Amersfoort"

and:

"The person with surname Van Gool lives in the town
with town-name Schiedam"

are both sentences belonging to a sentence type, described by:

A person, referred to by a surname

   lives in

a town, referred to by a town-name.

Or:

A town, referred to by a town-name

   is residence of

a person, referred to by a surname.

This NIAM sentence type model can be described by:

$$ST = \langle NOLOT1,LOT1,R1 \rangle \quad \langle NOLOT2,LOT2,R2 \rangle \quad \ldots \ldots \quad \langle NOLOTn,LOTn,Rn \rangle$$

where

| | | |
|---|---|---|
| ST | = | sentence type |
| NOLOTi | = | non-lexical object type i |
| LOTi | = | lexical object type i |
| Ri | = | role i |

## 4.5. DECOMPOSITION OF A SENTENCE TYPE

The previous paragraphs demonstrated that each sentence has a deeper structure and this deeper structure specifies:

- Association between non-lexical objects. We will call such an association an idea, or an instance of an idea type.

- Association between a non-lexical object and a lexical object. We will call such an association a bridge, or an instance of a bridge type.

This observation justifies the decomposition of a sentence type into idea types and bridge types.

   Person is referred to by surname

   Town is referred to by town-name

are examples of bridge types, whereas

   Person lives in town

is an idea type.

NIAM decomposes sentence types into binary associations, i.e. binary idea types and bridge types. This will sometimes lead to the specification of new non-lexical object types, not suspected at first (e.g. a request which is defined as an invitation to one referee to judge one particular paper). This approach is usually called pseudo-binary [ref. 3].

## 4.6. CONSTRAINTS

To describe an abstraction system we need more concepts than those introduced sofar. The abstraction system will include rules, which prescribe the behaviour of the object system. In NIAM these rules are called constraints. The constraints are part of the conceptual grammar. Their purpose is to prevent discrepancies between the contents of the information base and the phenomena in the object system. As an example of a constraint we mention:

> A request (= invitation for referee to judge a paper) results in at most one report.

We will discuss constraints in more detail in paragraph 4.8.2.


## 4.7. SUBTYPES

A NOLOT is a class of non-lexical objects, about which the information system may exchange sentences belonging to one or more sentence types. For instance, for every paper the information system will record its title and submitter. However, only for submitted papers requests for referees are made.

We just introduced the NIAM concept called subtyping. From the example we conclude that subtyping depends on shared and non-shared properties (idea type and bridge types) of the object type. Subtyping is a very natural and hence strong concept in describing an abstraction system.

To explore subtyping a little more, let us consider a NOLOT person with subtypes wg-member and national representative. The subtyping indicates that wg-members and representatives are persons, and therefore bear a surname. Only for persons qualified as representatives, the information system records the country and IFIP-TCs they represent. Only for persons qualified as wg-members, the information system records the IFIP-WG of which they are a member. NIAM applies strong typing, which implies that each occurrence of a (sub) object type could occur in the idea- and bridge types related to the (sub) object type.


## 4.8. GRAPHICAL NOTATION


### 4.8.1. Symbols

The NIAM concepts introduced in paragraphs 4.4. until 4.8. may be visualized by using the following convention:

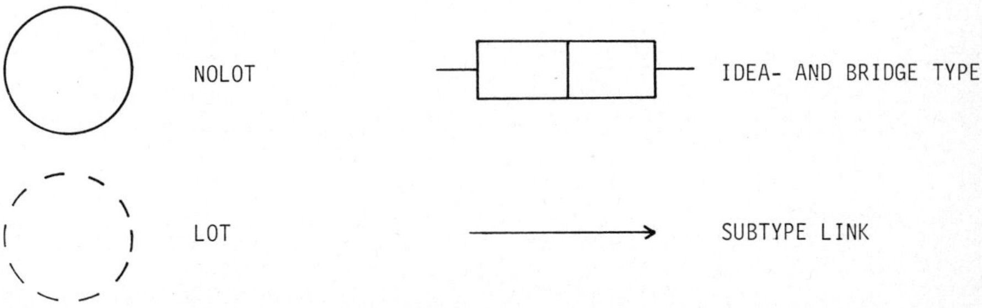


Figure 4.4
Graphical Representation for NIAM Concepts

The diagrams constructed by these symbols are called Information Structure Diagrams (ISD). The basic constructs for ISDs are shown below.

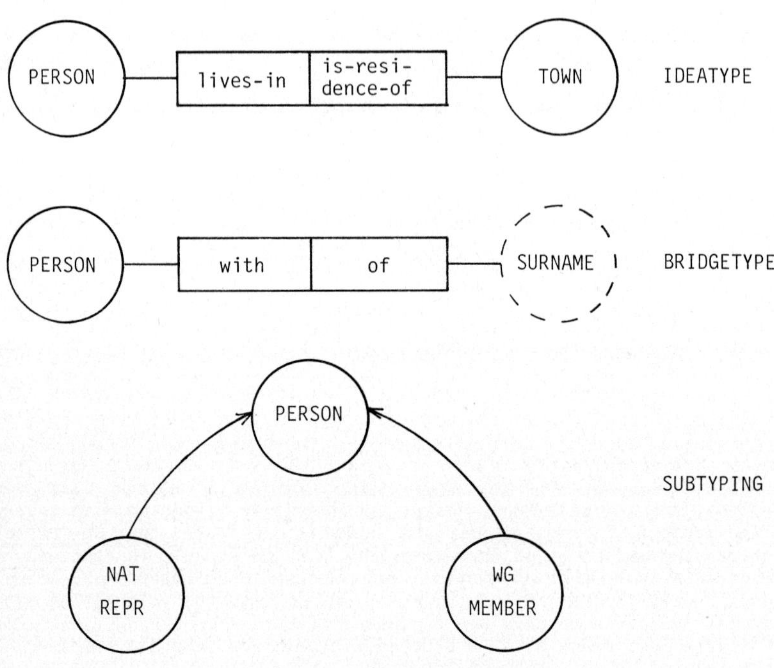


Figure 4.5
Examples of Elements from NIAM-diagrams

## 4.8.2. Constraints having a Graphical Notation

Most of the NIAM constraints have a graphical notation. These are:

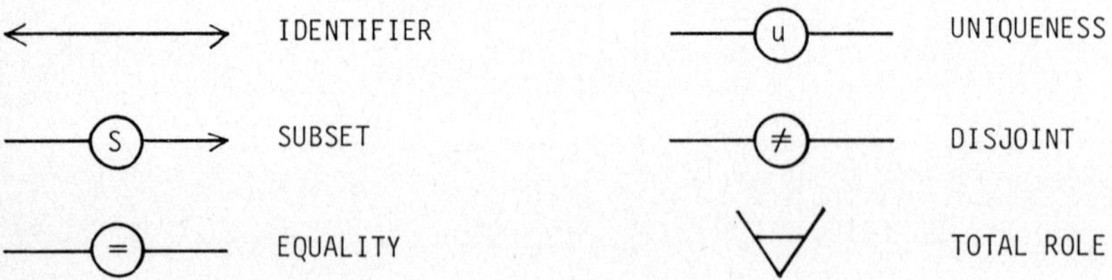


We will treat these constraints in the subsequent paragraphs.

## 4.8.2.1. Identifier Constraint

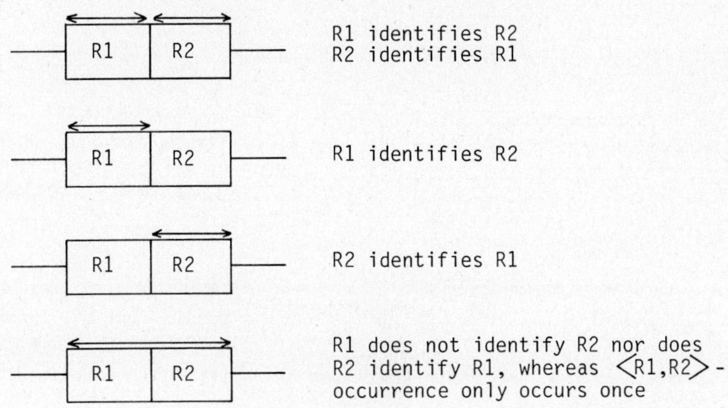



Figure 4.6
Identifier   Constaints in binary
Idea- or Bridge Types

Above we listed the four possible cases for identifier constraints. An identifier constraint is dedicated to one idea- or bridge type only. An identifier constraint limits the population of idea- or bridge type roles, e.g.

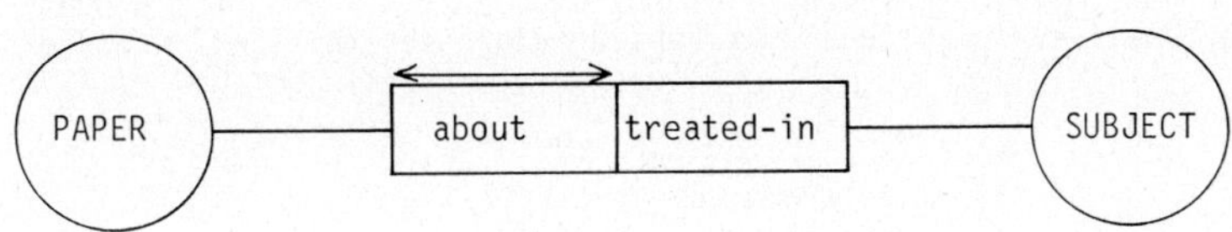



Figure 4.7
Identifier Constraint

declares that a paper may treat only one subject, but a subject may apply to more than one paper. Dealing with bridge types, the identifier constraint causes the following namings:

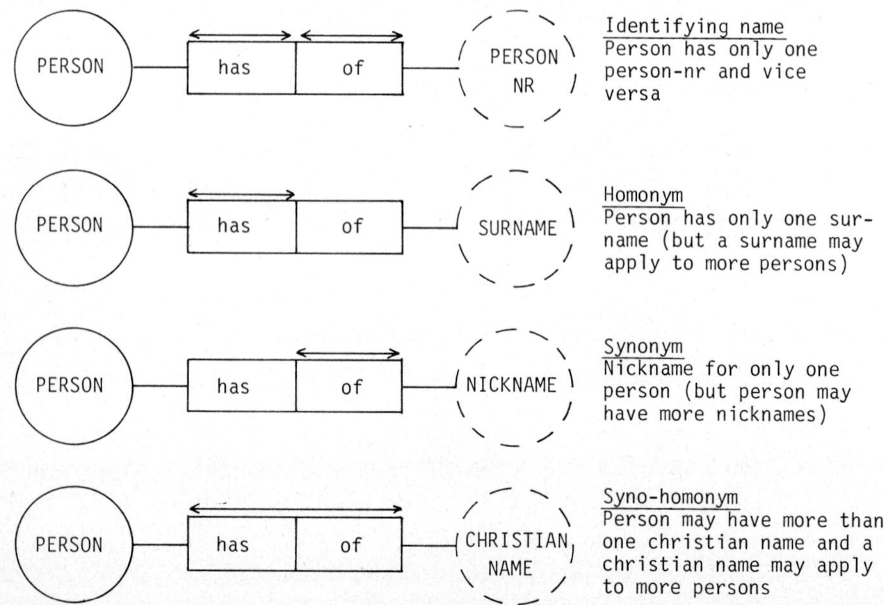



Identifying name
Person has only one person-nr and vice versa

Homonym
Person has only one surname (but a surname may apply to more persons)

Synonym
Nickname for only one person (but person may have more nicknames)

Syno-homonym
Person may have more than one christian name and a christian name may apply to more persons

Figure 4.8
Identifier Constraints in Bridge Types

## 4.8.2.2. Subset Constraint

The subset constraint takes care that the population of one or two roles (from one idea- or bridge type) are a subset of the population of one or two other roles (also from one idea- or bridge type) which originate from similar object types.

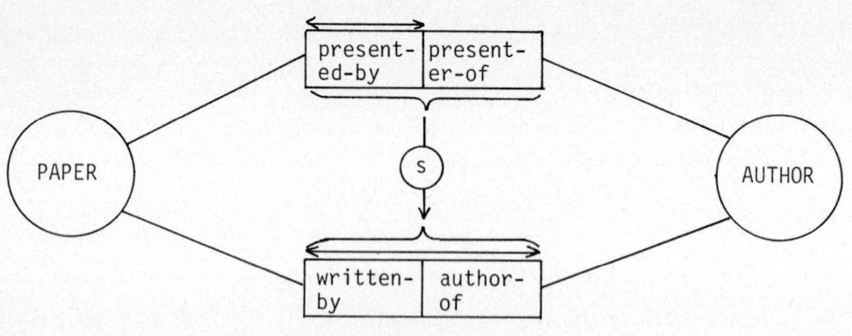



Figure 4.9
Subset Constraint

In the example above, the subset constraint asserts that the presenter of a paper must be one of its authors.

## 4.8.2.3. Equality Constraint

With the equality constraint we express that the population of one particular role
is equal to that of another role for the same object type.

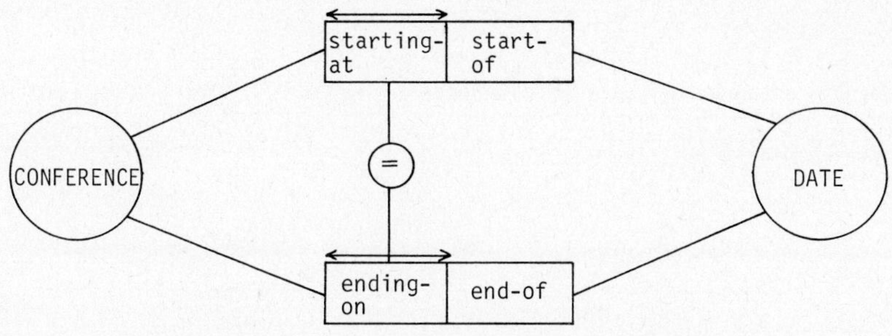


Figure 4.10
Equality Constraint

For a conference both the start- and end date must be registered, or neither of
them.


## 4.8.2.4. Uniqueness Constraint

The uniqueness constraint asserts, that a combination of role occurrences (always
from different idea- and/or bridge types) uniquely identify a certain non-lexical
object.

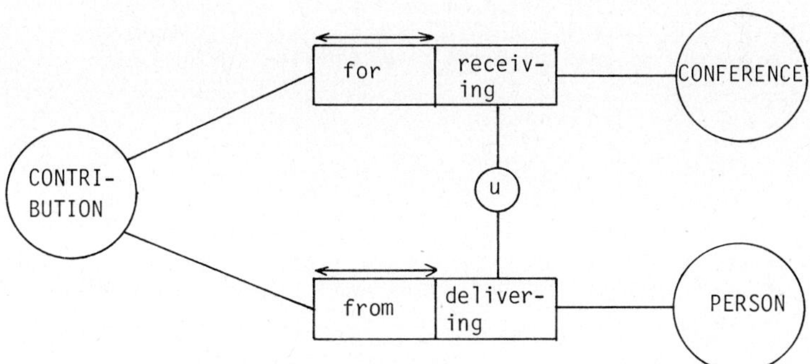


Figure 4.11
Uniqueness Constraint

A contribution occurrence is identified by the person delivering a contribution and
the conference for which the contribution is made. The uniqueness constraint implies an equality constraint between the corresponding roles of the NOLOT which
is identified by the uniqueness constraint. In figure 4.11 the uniqueness constraint
implies an equality between the populations of the roles "for" and "from".

## 4.8.2.5. Disjoint Constraint

The disjoint constraint asserts that the population of two subtypes exclude each
other, like accepted and rejected papers do. The subtypes should belong to the same
nolot-family.

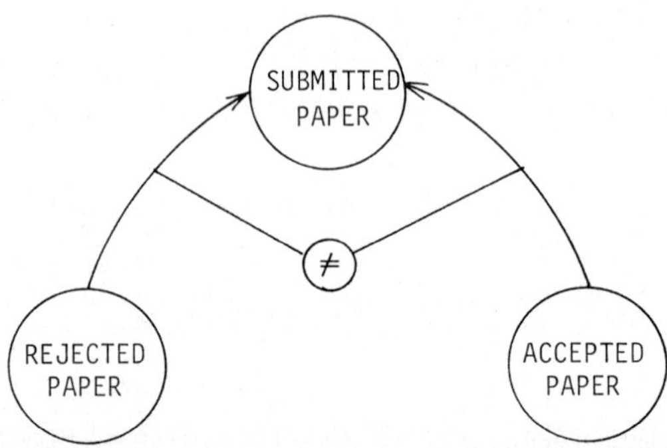


Figure 4.12
Disjoint Constraint

## 4.8.2.6. Total Role Constraint

Until now, we said that an object could act in a certain role, related to the object type for that object. A total role constraint compels that every object of the
object type does act in a certain role.

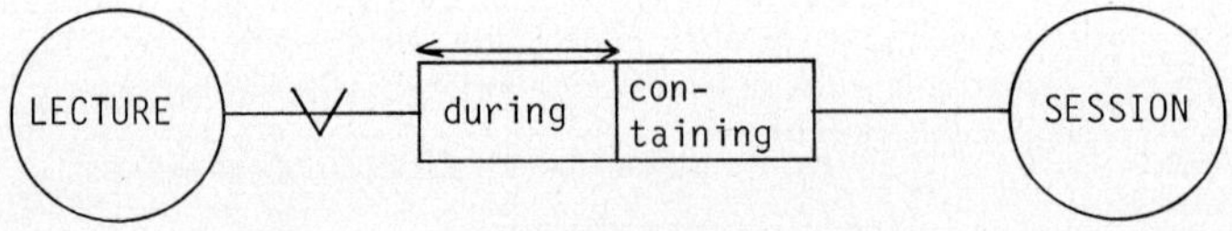


Figure 4.13
Total Role Constraint

In the example above, the constraint (⊥) denotes that a lecture is always during
a session. The information base does not record information on lectures for which
the session is not specified first.


## 4.9. INFORMATION BEARING NAMES

NIAM makes a distinction between things and their names, or -more formally- between
non-lexical and lexical objects. A natural language sentence is decomposed into
binary ideas and bridges. The information conveyed by the sentence is found in its
ideas, whereas the bridges enable the information exchange; they do not convey information themselves!

However, there exist names which do bear information. For example, the name for a
certain lecture could be

```
     "0120301"
```

which means that this lecture takes place during the session with session-nr "03"
of conference with conference-nr "012". Further, the last two digits indicate that
it is the first lecture during the session.

In NIAM we speak of information bearing names in such a case, and the diagram for
it reads:

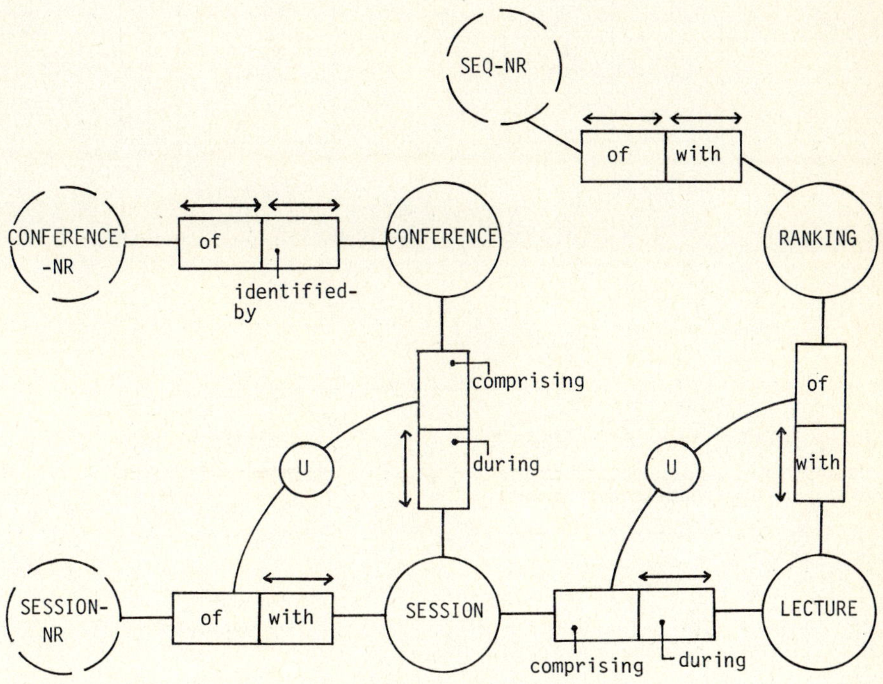


Figure 4.14
Information Bearing Names

## 4.10. POPULATION DIAGRAM AND SET-ORIENTED DIAGRAMS

In a NIAM-diagram one may combine constructs on the type level (idea type, nolot,
etc.) and constructs on the occurrence level (object, idea, etc.). This is an extremely powerful tool to validate the correctness of the conceptual grammar. We
call this kind of diagram: population diagram (figure 4.15).

The occurrence level is represented by lexical objects ("UK", "36", "6"), whereas
the type level consists of nolots and idea types.

Another option to combine both occurrences and types is offered by set-oriented
diagrams. The equivalent for the population diagram is shown in figure 4.16.

*G.M.A. Verheijen and J. van Bekkum*

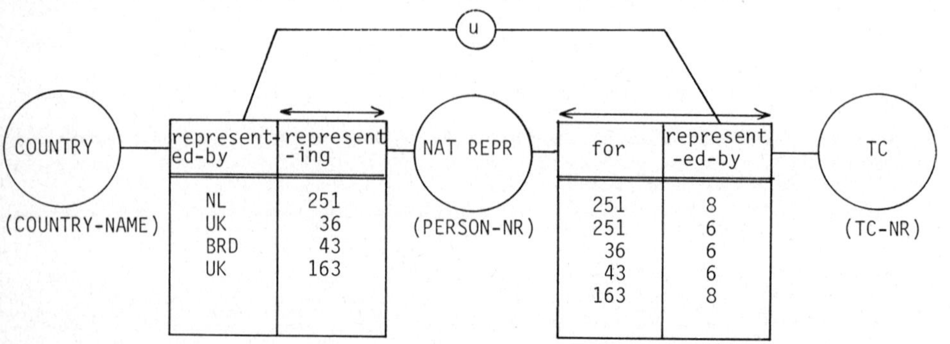


Figure 4.15
Population Diagram

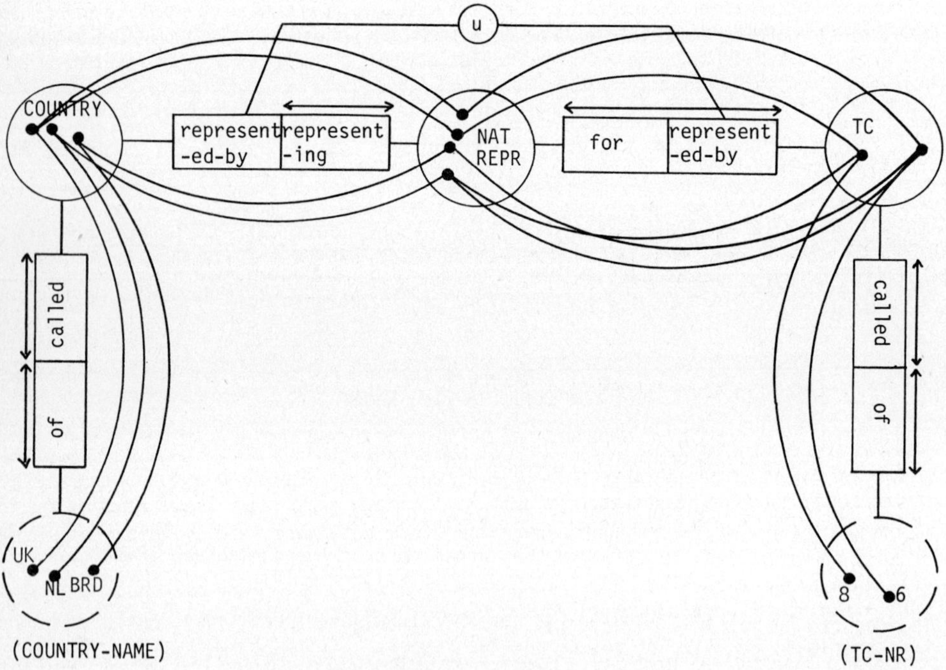

Figure 4.16
Set-oriented Diagram

## 4.11. CONCEPTUAL GRAMMAR LANGUAGE

Until now, we introduced NIAM-concepts, their meaning and the graphical notations. The information flow diagrams (IFDs) and information structure diagrams (ISDs) describe the abstraction system in a formal, yet very attractive manner. The diagrams are a good medium when the implications and consequences of the abstraction system are discussed. In fact, they stimulate the modelling, which is often an iterative process: a model is proposed, expressed in a NIAM-diagram, examined and discussed, resulting in an adjusted abstraction system and so on.

In short, diagrams are extremely beneficial for communication about the abstraction system between humans. Validation of the abstraction system could also be enhanced by computers. The abstraction system must then be expressed in a formal language which supports all the NIAM-concepts. Such a language would not be hampered by limitations characteristic of graphical notations. The language developed for this purpose, is called RIDL[3], which allows:

- Specification of IFDs and ISDs.

- Specification of constraints which cannot be specified by a graphical notation. These kinds of constraints are called procedural constraints.

- Specification of procedures. A procedure specifies the performance of a function.

A conceptual grammar expressed in RIDL may be compiled and generation of information system software is possible. We will return on this subject in chapter 5.


## 5. A META INFORMATION SYSTEM


## 5.1. INTRODUCTION

In chapter 2 we outlined the function of an information system and in chapter 3 we postulated the basic aspects of information systems. Then, we introduced the NIAM-concepts. Now, we must fuse all these aspects of information systems in order to describe meta-information systems, or -less cryptic- information systems which support the development (= modelling, specification and implementation) of information systems.


## 5.2. PURPOSE OF THE META-INFORMATION SYSTEM

The meta-information system should be able, like all information systems, to communicate with its environment. However, the subject of this communication is restricted to information systems. To be more specific, the communication is dedicated to the exchange of sentences about information systems. The sentences could, for instance, convey information about the conceptual grammar deduced from an object system.


## 5.3. INFORMATION SYSTEM ARCHITECTURE

Besides a conceptual grammar and an information base, an information system needs a function which will enforce all rules of the grammar upon the contents of the information base. We will call this function: the enforcer. Further, we distinguish another function, the application, which acts as:

- Interpreter between environment and enforcer.

- Collector of requests from the environment to enable the enforcer
  to process them as a conceptual update.

- Presenter of information according to the requirements of the
  environment.

As figure 5.1 represents the architecture of any information system, it applies to meta-information systems as well. The information base of a meta-information system contains the conceptual grammar of the information system specified by means of the meta-system. The conceptual grammar of a meta-information system is the expression in a formal language of the abstraction model for an object system "performing information analysis".
Integration of a meta-information system with the information system under investigation in one picture, results in figure 5.2.

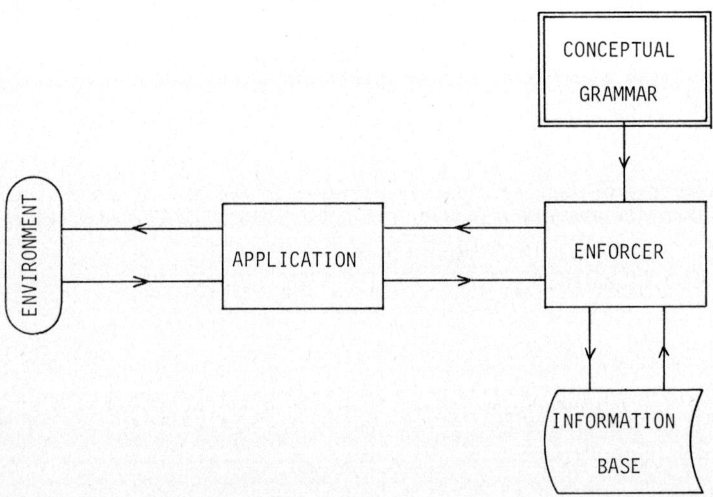


Figure 5.1
Information System Architecture

The information base of the meta-information system (the meta-information base), is equivalent with the conceptual grammar of the information system under development. Therefore, the conceptual grammar of the meta-system must be an information base also, containing the meta conceptual grammar.

The special symbol that was used for the conceptual grammar in figure 5.1 may be dropped now, as every conceptual grammar turns out to be an information base in its own right (see figure 5.2) [ref. 5].

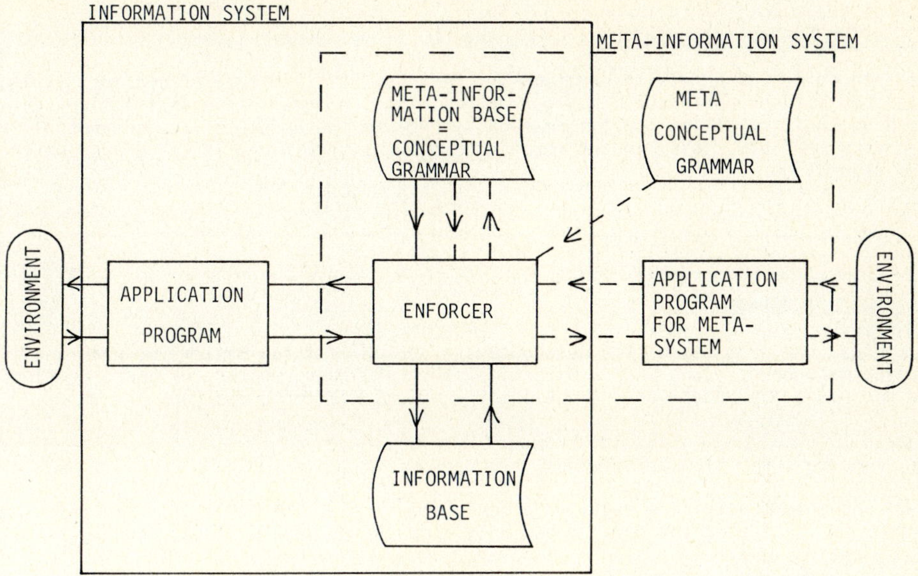


Figure 5.2
Meta-Information System with respect to
Information System, specified by the Meta-System

## 5.4. ISDIS

ISDIS is the meta-information system (also called information dictionary) that supports NIAM analysis. During the development of an information system like that of IFIP, both users and analyst produce:

- Functional decompositions

- Information flow diagrams

- Information structure diagrams (including constraints)

- Description of function performances

All these results are part of the conceptual grammar for the information system to be. They may be expressed in a formal language called RIDL, which is the communication vehicle between ISDIS and its users.

ISDIS will perform the following functions:

- Store and update a conceptual grammar using NIAM-concepts (functional decompositions, IFDs, ISDs, function performances, constraints).

- Show the implications and consequences of the specified conceptual grammar.

- Compile the conceptual grammar to make it suitable for the enforcer of the implementation system. For IMF[4] applications, ISDIS will

generate most of this conceptual grammar, whereas for applications
using Codasyl or relational DBMS, the DDL is produced.

The integration of a meta-information system like ISDIS and the information systems
developed with support from ISDIS guarantees, that changes in the abstraction system have their effect on the information system via the update of the conceptual
grammar with ISDIS. This kind of meta-information system rings in the era of software generation.


## 6. NIAM AND PROJECT MANAGEMENT


### 6.1. PROJECT MANAGEMENT

To control the progress of the development of an information system, we need a
project management plan. Such a plan will prescribe when reports, reviews, meetings
and decisions are opportune and outline the milestones to be reached.


### 6.2. INFORMATION SYSTEM DEVELOPMENT

We do not intend to give a detailed description of the life cycle of an information
system. In the subsequent paragraphs, only a coarse outline will be shown.


### 6.2.1. Business Analysis

Whenever an organization feels inclined to improve its performance, it should start
analyzing the object system. It needs no argument that knowledge of the ins and
outs of the business performed is required. NIAM will help now to model the abstraction system. Essential for business analysis is, that it results in an advice how
and where to improve the object system activities. One such advice could be to develop or enhance an information system.


### 6.2.2. Information Analysis

If the business analysis concludes that an information system will be beneficial
for the performance of the organization, information analysis should be the next
step. Now all aspects of NIAM become useful. First, an inventory is made of all
functions that the information system is expected to support. These functions will
be decomposed to functions to a level of detail where information flows and the
transformation achieved by the functions become clear. Every level of decomposition
is accompanied by an IFD, resulting in a hierarchy of IFDs. As previously mentioned,
the ultimate level of decomposition shows information flows which are subjected to
a thorough analysis. Every information flow gives rise to an ISD. The ISDs produced
this way may (and will) overlap. As soon as the information structures are reveiled,
all constraints and functions may be described formally. Note, that we first determine what a function achieves, in a later phase how it accomplishes the transformation.

All results must be expressed in one formal language to avoid a confusion of tongues.
Additionally, one needs an information dictionary, preventing an avalanche of un-
controllable documents. All the efforts done during the information analysis contribute to the conceptual grammar.

The second part of this paper will show all steps to be executed according to this
paragraph. To recapitulate:

   - Determine the desired information system functions.

- Decomposition of functions accompanied by:

- Construction of IFDs

- Analyzing information flows resulting in ISDs

- Expressing all ISDs in one conceptual grammar

- Formalizing constraints and function performances.

## 6.2.3. Implementation, installation and exploitation

The conceptual grammar produced by completing the information analysis should now be examined to decide:

- The part to implement.

- The part to be automated.

It is quite possible to refrain from implementing all functions of the information system. Moreover, implementation could be done with computers, but other implementation techniques may be considered more advantageously, or a mixture of techniques is applied. The latter option will often be the chosen one, and it is important that we implement with care all parts of the information system. This could mean that we must produce work instructions as well as computer programs, design forms and suitable data structures for the computer, etc.

The previous chapter showed that information dictionaries equiped with software generators will simplify the implementation task.

## 6.3. PROJECT MANAGEMENT FOR NIAM

NIAM does not dictate a particular project management plan. In fact, it may be incorporated into any project management approach, provided this approach recognizes the importance of information analysis.

## PART II: NIAM PRACTICE

## 7. OVERVIEW

In the previous part, we introduced the NIAM-concepts. Now we will elaborate the IFIP-case to demonstrate the capabilities of NIAM. For that very reason, we will not confront the reader with mere results, but rather show him step by step how a NIAM analysis is performed. To keep the size of the elaboration within limits, we will narrow the scope of the analysis more and more while proceeding.

Under normal circumstances, a NIAM analysis requires a substantial user involvement. They should answer questions emerging during the analysis. This exercise however, allowed only one round of written questions, a contact far too meagre to guarantee an effective information system. Consequently, we had to make presumptions, which is the pitfall of successful information system development. Nevertheless we believe, that we achieved our objective: showing how NIAM is applied.

The elaboration comprises a number of steps, executed subsequently. Each step con-

tributes to the ultimate goal: producing a conceptual grammar for an information
system that supports the organization of an IFIP working conference.
In the last chapter, we will repeat the user requirements and show how they are fulfilled by the conceptual grammar.


## 8. FACTS AND PRESUMPTIONS

Organizing an IFIP working conference is done by executing a number of predefined
activities. The facts that are in force of these activities, were established by
submitting an enquete, to be filled in by the user. Facts not checked this way are
reported here as presumptions.

FACTS

- The information system supports the activities of an IFIP program and organizing
  committee, comprising the establishment of a conference program and ensuring conference attendance.

- An IFIP conference is organized by one or more IFIP TCs.

- A working group is part of only one TC.

- A TC always comprises one or more WGs.

- Letters of intent from persons not called are acceptable, likewise a paper without foregoing letter of intent is acceptable.

- Referees and chairmen are already qualified as such. The program committee may
  select from these groups at will.

- Papers may be qualified as intended, submitted, accepted or rejected. Each paper,
  no matter its qualification, may be cancelled by its submitter.

- Persons acting as program committee member or referee for a particular conference
  may not be the author of a paper for that conference.

- The subjects covered by a conference are predefined. A paper must deal with exactly one subject from this list.

- Every conference is bound to a timeframe. Several deadlines exist. A deadline is
  a date on which a certain event for a particular conference should have happened,
  e.g. calls sent, intentions received, etc.

- A referee-report bears a judgement about one paper by one referee, expressed in
  terms like accepted, undecided or rejected.

- A conference comprises at least one session, each of which is lead by exactly one
  chairman.

- A chairman may not present a paper during the session he leads, nor may he be
  author of one of the papers presented during his session.

- A session is an uninterrupted sequence of lectures.

- A person may contribute more than one paper per conference.

- Reminders for referees to deliver their reports are sent when appropriate.

- The information system must be a single conference system.

PRESUMPTIONS

- The presenter of a paper must be one of the authors of that paper.

- The submitter of a paper may be one of the authors, but this is not required. However, the submitter will always act as the contact person for that paper.

- For a particular conference, a person may not contribute papers, bearing the same title. However, papers from different persons may bear the same title.

- A person can be national representative for only one country. However, for that country he may represent more than one IFIP TC. A TC has at most one representative per country.

- There is only one secretariat per conference, receiving mail for both the program- and organizing committee.

- A conference may comprise parallel sessions.

- A lecture is always about one and only one paper, which is qualified as accepted and not cancelled.

- A session is dedicated to one conference subject only. Only papers covering this subject are presented during the session.

- A chairman may lead more than one session per conference.

- The acceptance of a paper is decided by majority vote.

- A person is identified by a person number. This is the only way to refer uniquely to a person. The IFIP information system users are responsible for a correct person registration.

- Referees, submitters, chairmen, WG-members and national representatives must have a correspondence address. For authors, not qualified in one of the mentioned categories, there is no need to register their address.

- Registration of a new conference requires registration of the title, subjects, location, period and TCs  organizing the conference. Optionally, deadlines and start- and end dates may be registered.

- Registration of a person requires specification of the person number, surname and titles.

- Registration of a paper, whether it is intended or submitted, requires specification of the person who made the contribution, the conference, the title and the subject covered by it.

- Registration of a lecture requires specification of the paper's ranking and estimated duration (the ranking specifies the sequence of presentation during a session).

- Per session one should register the date and time announcing the commencement of the session, plus the duration of the opening address by the chairman. Every session is referred to by a session number which is unique within a conference.

## 9. ELABORATION OF IFIP-CASE

### 9.1. ACTIVITY STUDY:  STEP 1

We enlist all activities performed in the object system. Activities are shown in
an activity decomposition. The activities, represented in figure 9.1 originate from
the IFIP problem definition.

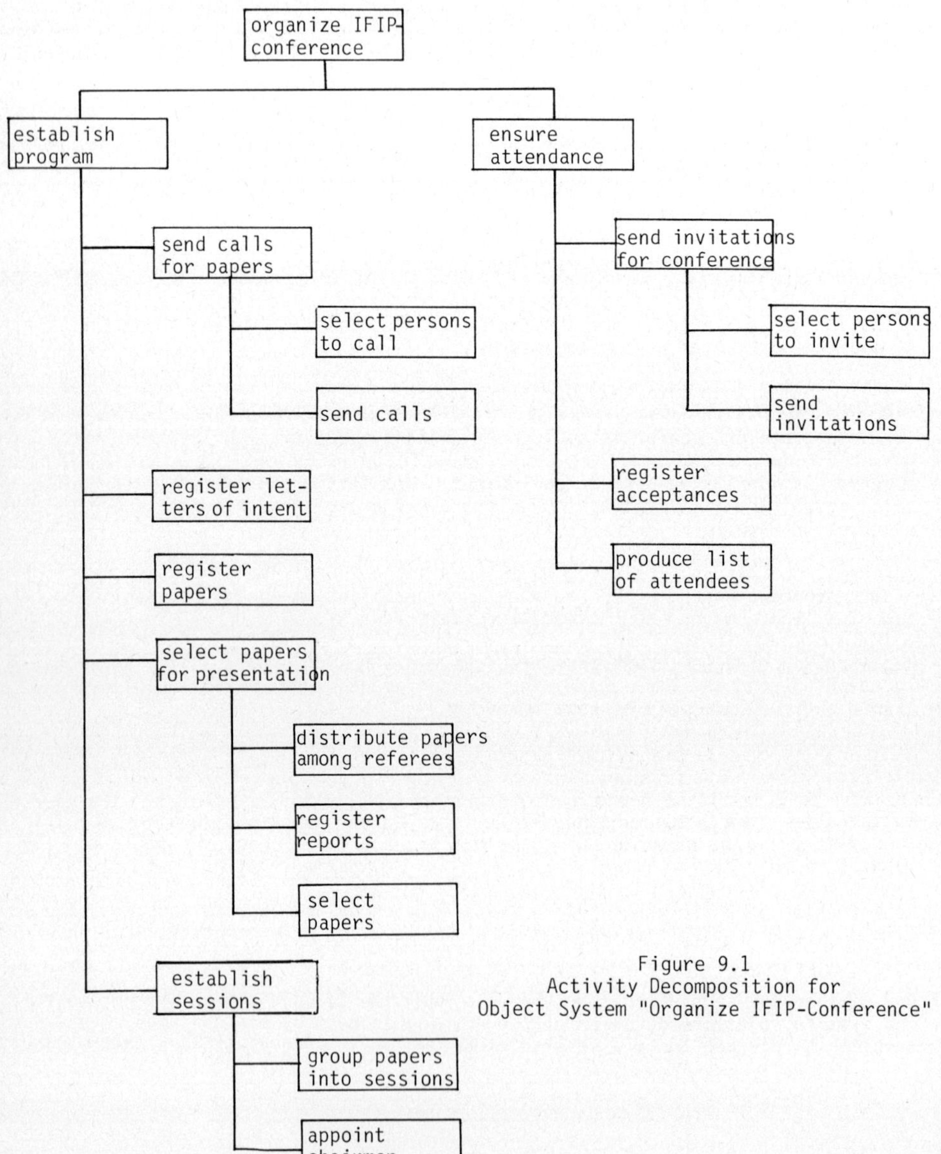


Figure 9.1
Activity Decomposition for
Object System "Organize IFIP-Conference"

The activities mentioned in the IFIP-case like "ensure invitations are sent to ..." are not included in the activity decomposition. They are considered as requirements to be taken into consideration by the activity called "select persons to invite". The same argument holds for the activity called "avoid duplicate invitations".

## 9.2. INFORMATION REQUIREMENTS:  STEP 2

Information is needed to perform and control the activities happening in the object system. We made an inventory of information sets needed per activity. For demonstration purposes we mention in figure 9.2 the information sets for three activities.

| <u>Activity</u> | <u>Information needed</u> |
|---|---|
| Send calls | - Information on callees |
| | - Information on conference |
| | - Information on call-layout |
| Distribute papers among referees | - Information on papers |
| | - Information on referees |
| | - Information on conference |
| Select papers | - Information on reports |
| | - Information on papers |
| | - Information on conference |
| | - Acceptance criteria |

Figure 9.2
Information Sets per Activity

## 9.3. FUNCTION PROPOSAL:  STEP 3

To supply the information needed by the activities, an information system is required. This information system will exhibit information flow transformation capabilities; so-called functions. In fact, the information system itself may be considered as one overall function, which can be decomposed into less complex subfunctions. The functional decomposition is done in such a way that each level performs the same transformation, the only difference being the extent of detail, used to describe the transformation. The functional decomposition should reflect the activity decomposition as close as possible, thus ensuring that the users recognize the functions as necessary to perform their jobs.

Figure 9.3 shows the IFIP information system as a single function, enabling the:

- IFIP secretariat

- Program committees

- Organizing committees

- IFIP relations (wg-members, referees, etc.)

to communicate with each other.

                  *G.M.A. Verheijen and J. van Bekkum*

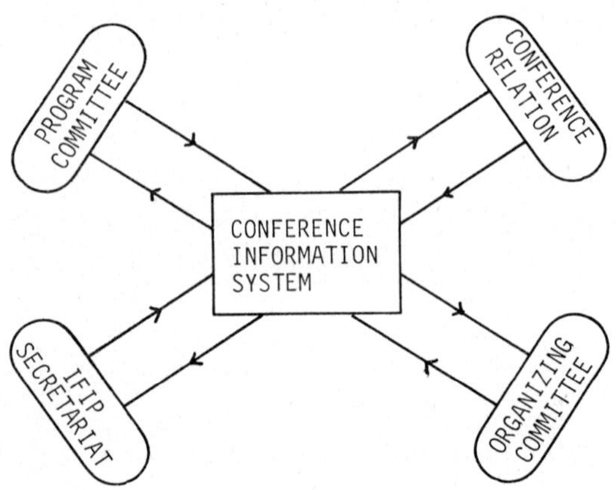



Figure 9.3
IFD for Conference Information System

The authority called "IFIP secretariat" will be responsible for registering wg-members, national representatives, the IFIP-organizing structure, potential referees and chairmen. Further, it will register conference plans, consisting of conference title, subjects, location, period and timeframe.

The program committee is responsible for the registration of the conference program, comprising sessions and lectures, The program committee will correspond with sub-mitters of papers, referees and chairmen.

Finally, the organizing committee takes care of recording all attendees, after having sent invitations.

The first decomposition of the "Conference Information System" is shown in figure 9.4. The corresponding IFD is represented in figure 9.5.

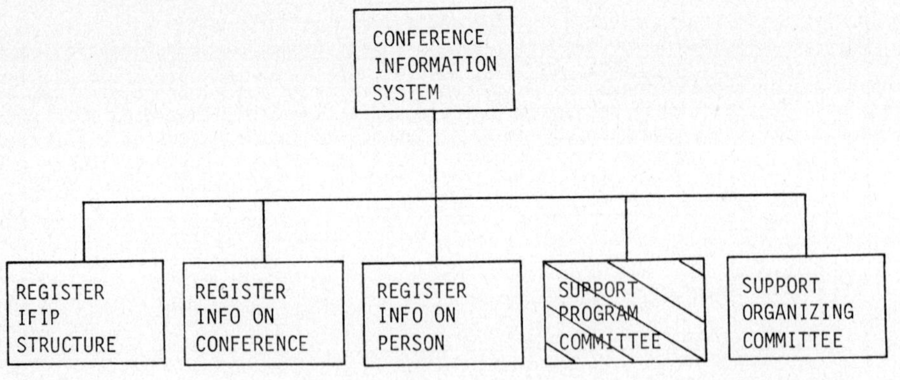



Figure 9.4
Decomposition of Conference
Information System

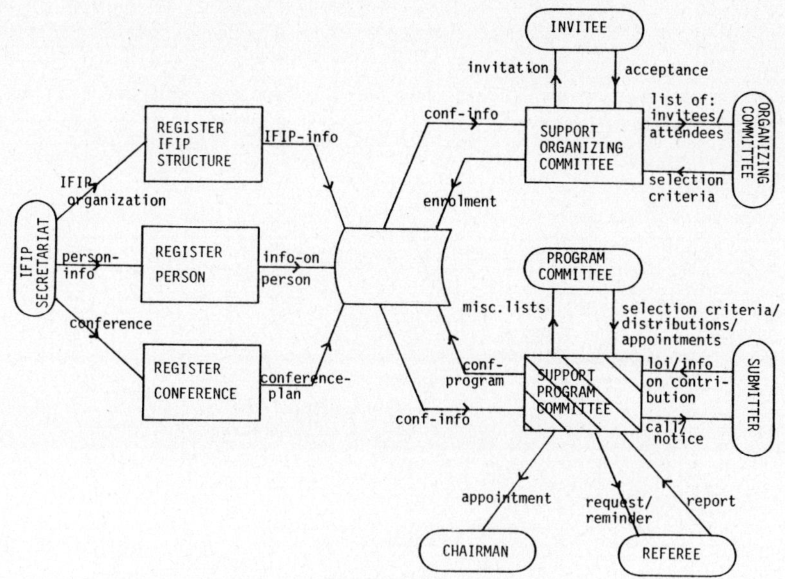


Figure 9.5
IFD for Subfunctions of
Conference Information System

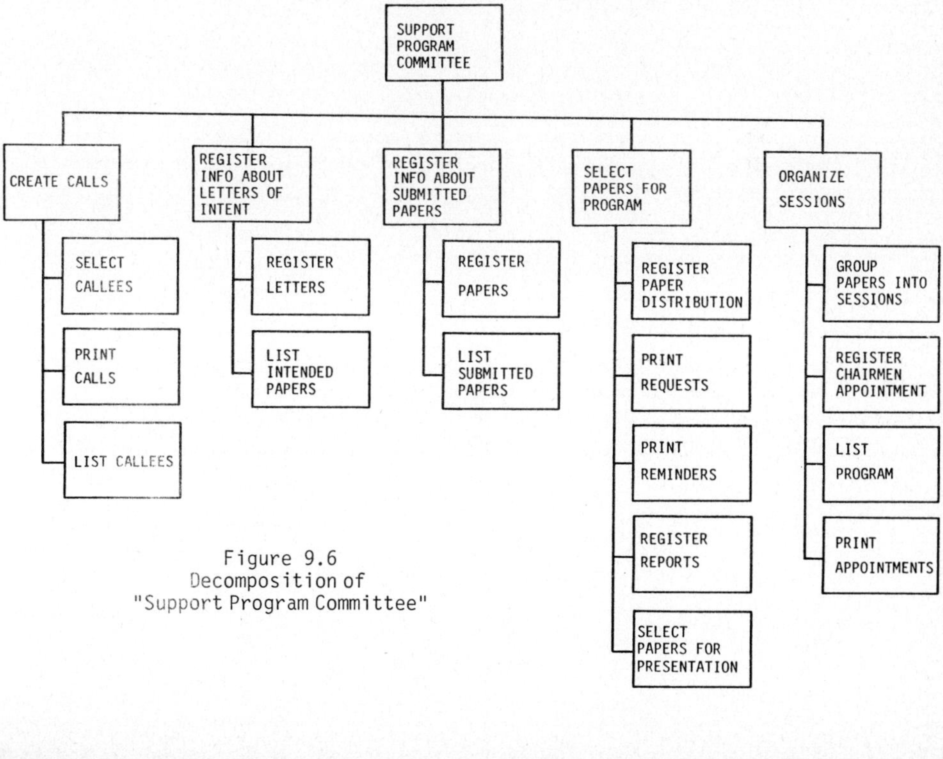

SUPPORT
PROGRAM
COMMITTEE

CREATE CALLS

SELECT
CALLEES

PRINT
CALLS

LIST CALLEES

REGISTER
INFO ABOUT
LETTERS OF
INTENT

REGISTER
LETTERS

LIST
INTENDED
PAPERS

REGISTER
INFO ABOUT
SUBMITTED
PAPERS

REGISTER
PAPERS

LIST
SUBMITTED
PAPERS

SELECT
PAPERS FOR
PROGRAM

REGISTER
PAPER
DISTRIBUTION

PRINT
REQUESTS

PRINT
REMINDERS

REGISTER
REPORTS

SELECT
PAPERS FOR
PRESENTATION

ORGANIZE
SESSIONS

GROUP
PAPERS INTO
SESSIONS

REGISTER
CHAIRMEN
APPOINTMENT

LIST
PROGRAM

PRINT
APPOINTMENTS

Figure 9.6
Decomposition of
"Support Program Committee"

The decomposition of functions has to be performed until we reach a level on which
the corresponding information flows can be described by an Information Structure
Diagram.

We will show the decomposition process only for the function "Support Program Committee" (shaded in figures 9.4 and 9.5). The result is shown in figure 9.6, whereas figure 9.7 shows the IFD for a subset of the constituating functions.

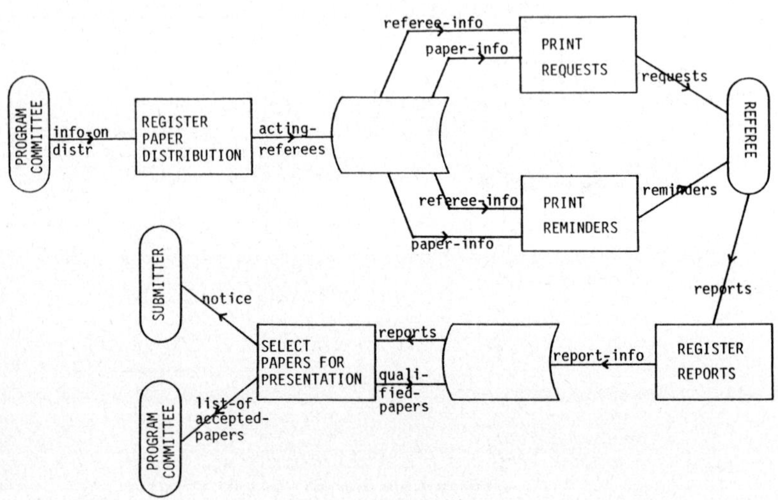


Figure 9.7
IFD for subfunctions of
"Select Papers for Program"

It should be checked, by making a cross reference, that each function supports one
or more activities enlisted in Step 1.
Applying the decomposition process, we now have reached a level of functions, on
which a user can supply samples for each information flow. These samples will be
the basis for constructing Information Structure Diagrams.


9.4. ANALYSIS OF INFORMATION FLOWS:  STEP 4

Samples from the information flows, as depicted in the IFDs of Step 3 will now be
analyzed. The following samples will be examined:

- Call for paper

- Letter of intent

- Request to referee plus his report

- Invitation to attend a conference plus confirmation

- Conference program

Note, that our choice of samples is somewhat arbitrary. Normally, one should study

all information flows. As we are only interested in the instructive element of such
an analysis, we confine ourselves to the  enumerated samples.


9.4.1. Call for Paper

A sample of a call for paper is shown in figure 9.8.


*SAMPLE:   CALL*


*May 25, 1981*


*Mr. L. Modderman*
*Goeverneurkade 35*
*2274 KK VOORBURG*
*The Netherlands*


*Dear Colleague,*

*We hereby notify you of TC8's intention to organize an IFIP*
*conference entitled:*

*"Future Trends in Information Analysis",*

*to be held in Venice, Italy, during June 1982.*

*./. Please fill in enclosed form if you intend to submit one or more*
*papers. Your intentions should reach us before August 1, 1981.*


*With kind regards,*


*The Program Committee*


*Enclosure: 1.*


Figure 9.8
Sample  Call


The call for paper shows a lot of cosmetics. If we ignore these, we discover sentences with a deeper structure like:

"The person with surname Modderman
        is invited for
the conference with title Future Trends in Information Analysis"


"The conference with title Future Trends in Information Analysis
        is held in
the location with name Venice, Italy",

etc.

These sentences give rise to the conceptual grammar, shown in figures 9.9 and 9.10.
Figure 9.9 concentrates on conference information, whereas figure 9.10 describes
the contribution of a person to a conference. Note, that we use a "macro" in the
ISDs for an identifying name. The LOT-symbol is drawn around the NOLOT, indicating
an identifying name for this NOLOT. The LOT-name is enclosed within parentheses.

It will be clear that the LOT surname cannot be used as an identifying name. This
would prohibit the registration of more than one person bearing a certain surname.
The same argument holds for the initials. Even a combination of surname and initials
does not offer an identifying name. As each non-lexical object must bear an identifying name, and this naming must be expressed in the conceptual grammar, we introduce a LOT person-nr. A similar situation is encountered for the NOLOT conference. The title of a conference is not considered to be identifying, so a LOT conference-nr emerges.

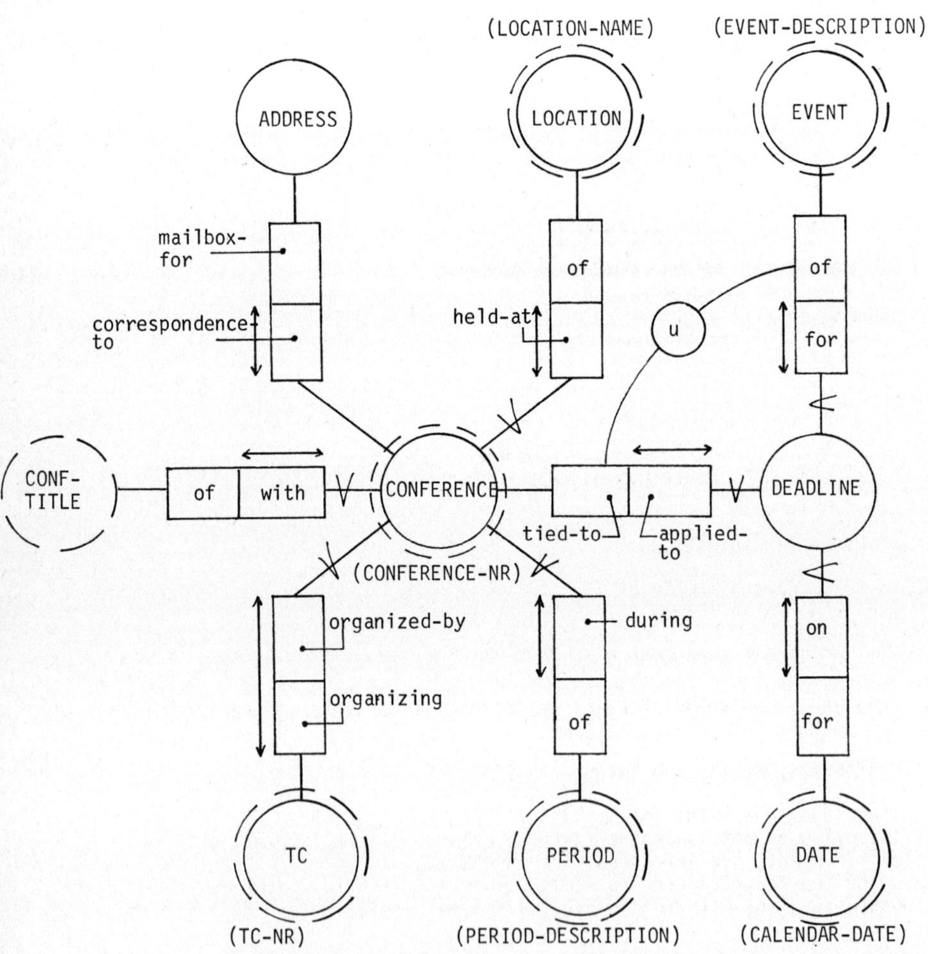


Figure 9.9
Conference Information in Call for Paper

From the ISD of figure 9.10, we observe that a contribution is identified by the
person and the conference involved. A contribution may be an invited one, resulting
from a call. We may define:

    Callee: Person invited to deliver a contribution.

The identification of address will be shown in the total-ISD (paragraph 9.4.6.).

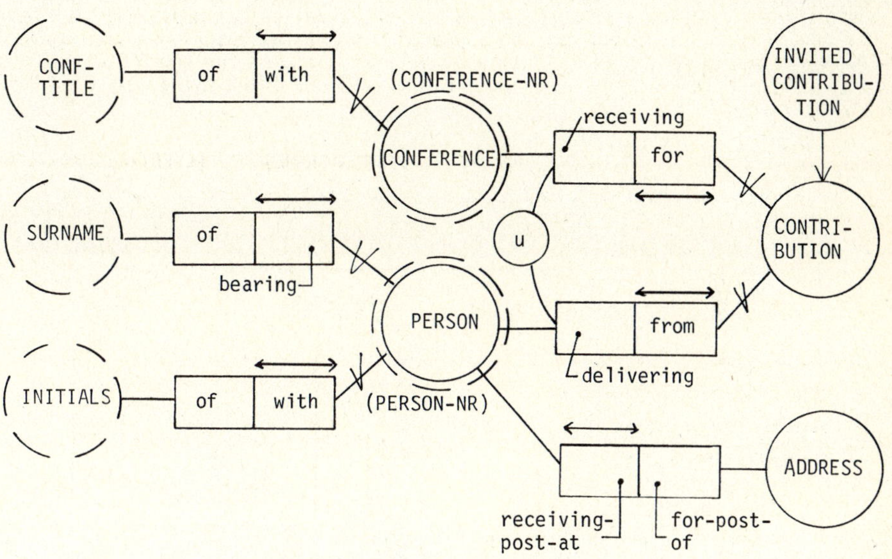


Figure 9.10
Contribution Information in Call for Paper

## 9.4.2. Letter of intent

Figure 9.11 shows a sample of a letter of intent. The corresponding conceptual
grammar is shown in figure 9.12.

A letter of intent announces a paper to be submitted for a conference in due time.
The subject and title for the coming paper are specified, so are the authors and
the presenter. Note, that a contribution may result into zero or more papers. We
may now define:

    Intendant: Person who intends to contribute one or more papers.

A callee sending a letter of intent is thereby an intendant. Whether he effects
his intention or not is another matter. Persons not called, but still sending a
letter of intent, are intendants too. However, their contribution is not qualified
as an invited one. Callees not sending a letter of intent, nor submitting papers
without foregoing letter of intent, cause contributions (even invited ones) without papers.

Interesting is the identification of a paper. We presume that a person, who contributes more than one paper for a certain conference, will use different titles.
So, a paper may be identified by:

```
- Conference-nr  ⎫ identification for      ⎫
- Person-nr      ⎬ contribution            ⎬   identification for
- (Paper) title  ⎭                         ⎭   paper
```

This way of identifying a paper is very clumsy, so we decided to introduce a LOT
paper-nr. Now, a paper may be identified by both its paper-nr (which is a very efficient identification) and the concatenation of conference-nr, person-nr plus
title (clumsy, but very informing).


*SAMPLE: LETTER OF INTENT*

*Submitter*

    *Name   : _______________________________________*

    *Address: _______________________________________*

             *_______________________________________*

             *_______________________________________*

*I intend to submit a paper on (mark exactly one):*

    *Specification languages          O*

    *Meta information systems         O*

    *Information systems architecture   O*

    *Project management             O*

*Preliminary title: ______________________________*

*______________________________________________*


*Author(s): 1) ___________________________________*

        *2) ___________________________________*

        *3) ___________________________________*


*Presented by (one of authors): ___________________*


*Please return form to: Conference "Future Trends in Information*
*                          Analysis"*
*           24, Rue Grande*
*           2780 Brussels, Belgium*

*Note: In case you wish to contribute more than one paper, please*
*      send us a filled-in copy of this form for each one.*


Figure 9.11
Sample of Letter of Intent

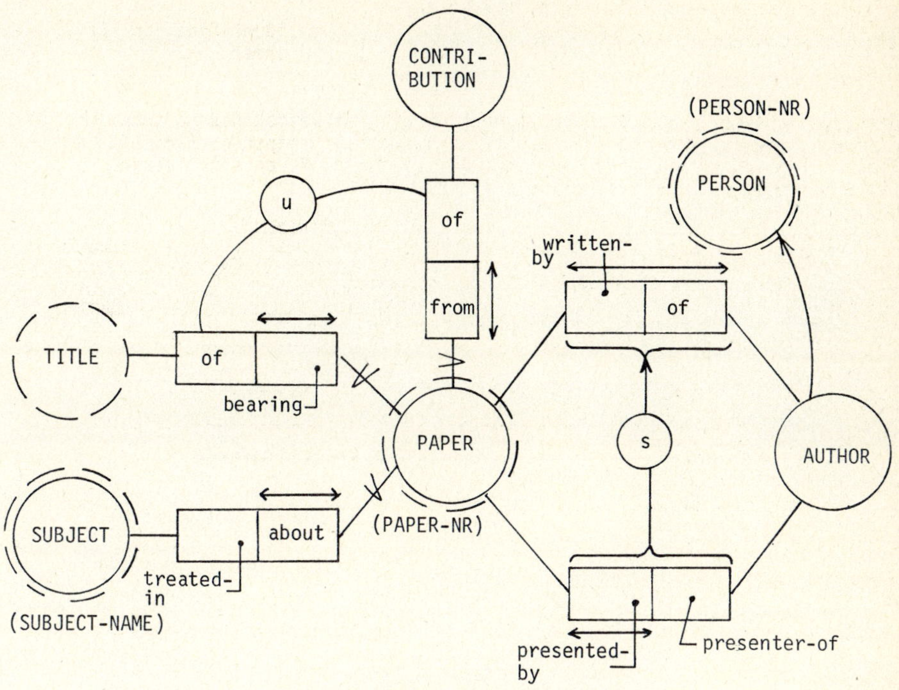


Figure 9.12
ISD from Letter of Intent

### 9.4.3. Request to Referee and his Report

A referee receives a request to judge a paper. The paper must be a "real" paper, not a "paper" paper. This justifies the subtyping for NOLOT paper. We define:

Submitters:　　　　Persons delivering contribution of submitted.
　　　　　　　　　paper.

Intended papers: Papers minus submitted or cancelled papers.

A referee is a person, qualified as referee by the IFIP secretariat. This explains the subtyping for NOLOT person. Note, that a request is identified by the referee and the submitted paper involved.

The report received by the program committee from a referee contains the judgment for a particular paper by that referee.
Figure 9.15 shows the conceptual grammar resulting from the request and report sample.

SAMPLE:   REQUEST

                                              September 7, 1981

Mr. N.E. Pieters
Lorentzstraat 17
3817 XJ AMERSFOORT
The Netherlands


Dear Colleague,

In view of the IFIP conference entitled:

    "Future Trends in Information Analysis",

we would like you to evaluate the following paper:

    Paper-nr: 27

    Subject : Meta-information systems

    Title   : "Formal Specifications for Information Systems"

Please send us your opinion before October 31, 1981 on the
./. enclosed evaluation report.

                                      With kind regards,

                                      The Program Committee

Enclosure: 1.


Figure 9.13
Sample Request to Referee

SAMPLE:   REPORT

Referee:  37
Name    :  Mr. N.E. Pieters

Paper   :  27
Title   :  "Formal Specifications for Information Systems"

| Judgement:<br>(cross one) | accepted | rejected | undecided |
|---|---|---|---|
|  |  |  |  |


Comment:  __________________________________________

          __________________________________________

          __________________________________________


Please send to: Conference "Future Trends in Information Analysis"
                24, Rue Grande
                2780 Brussels, Belgium


Figure 9.14
Sample Report of Referee

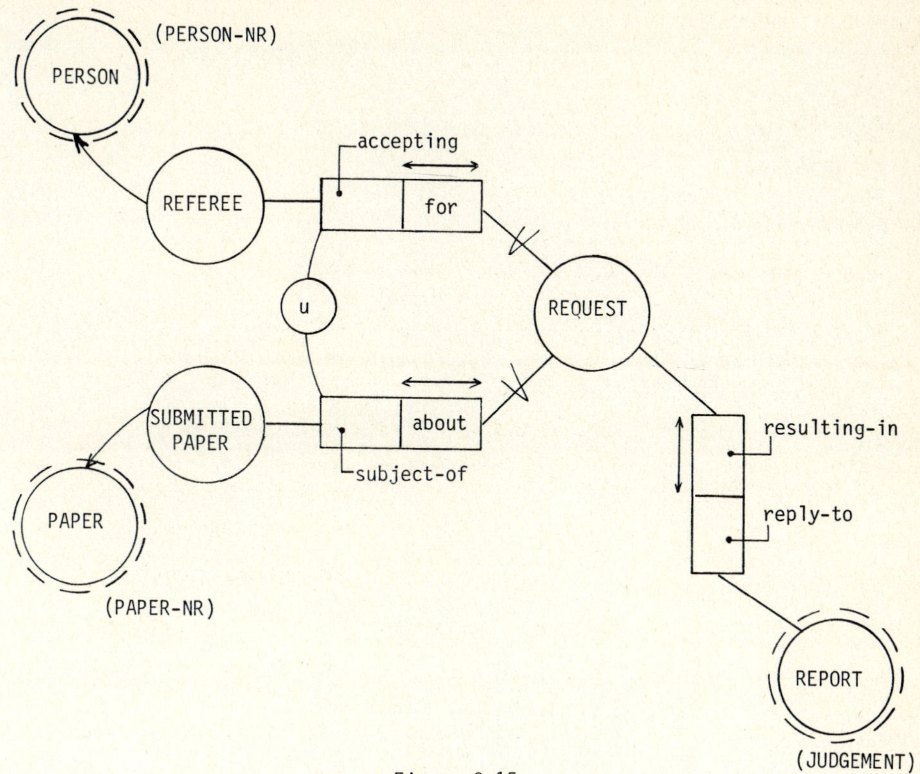



Figure 9.15
ISD from Request and Report

## 9.4.4. Invitation and Confirmation

An invitation applies to one conference only and is intended for one particular person. Note, that this is also the identification used for invitations. We define:

Invitees: Persons receiving an invitation.

Invitees who intend to visit the conference, send confirmations to the organizing committee.

Invitations that were accepted are qualified as confirmations, expressed by subtyping of NOLOT invitation. We define:

Attendees: Persons receiving invitations qualified as confirmations.

*SAMPLE:   INVITATION*

*April 19, 1982*

*Mr. R.A.M. van Gool*
*Schubertplein 148*
*3122 NJ SCHIEDAM*
*The Netherlands*


*Dear Colleague,*

*We invite you to attend the IFIP conference entitled:*

*"Future Trends in Information Analysis",*

*to be held in Venice, Italy, from June 9 to June 11, 1982.*
*./. Further details on the conference can be found in the enclosed*
*./. leaflet. The confirmation of your attendance should reach us*
*before May 22, 1982.*

*With kind regards,*

*The Organizing Committee*

*Enclosures: 2.*


Figure 9.16
Sample Invitation


*SAMPLE:   CONFIRMATION OF ATTENDANCE*


*Invitation nr: 012-81*

*Name            : Mr. R.A.M. van Gool*


*I intend to visit the conference entitled:*

*"Future Trends in Information Analysis".*


*( Enquete about fees and hotel reservations could appear here,*
*but are out of scope in this exercise )*


*Please send to: Conference "Future Trends in Information Analysis"*

*24, Rue Grande*
*2780 Brussels, Belgium*


Figure 9.17
Sample Confirmation

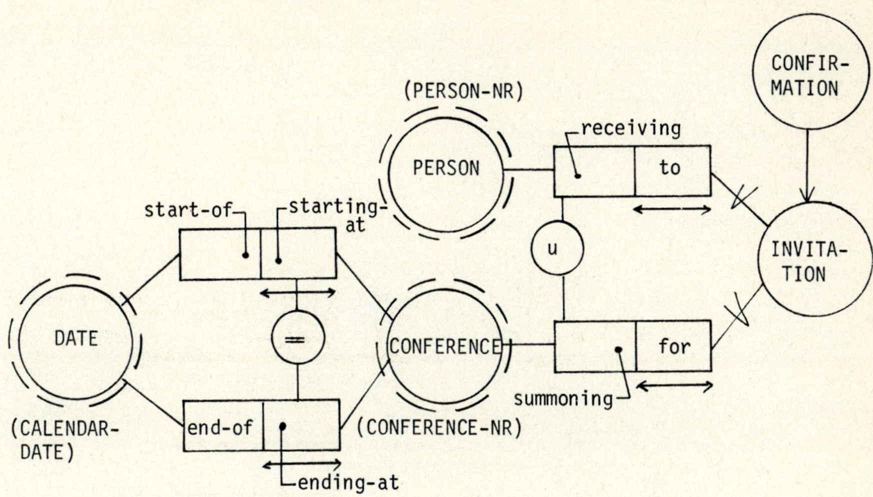


Figure 9.18
ISD from Invitation and Confirmation

## 9.4.5. Conference Program

*SAMPLE:   CONFERENCE PROGRAM*

*Program for conference "Future Trends in Information Analysis"*

*Location: Venice, Italy*

*Dates    : June 9 to June 11, 1982*


*Session nr 3: June 10, 1982 at 09.00 hours*

*Subject     : Meta-Information Systems*

*Chairman    : G.M. Nijssen*


| *Lecture* | *Presenter* | *Title* |
|---|---|---|
| *0  09.00 – 09.30 hrs* | *Chairman* | *Openings-address* |
| *1  09.30 – 11.15 hrs* | *R. Meersman* | *RIDL* |
| *2  10.15 – 11.00 hrs* | *F. van Assche* | *ISDIS* |
| . | . | . |
| . | . | . |
| . | . | . |

Figure 9.19
Sample Conference Program

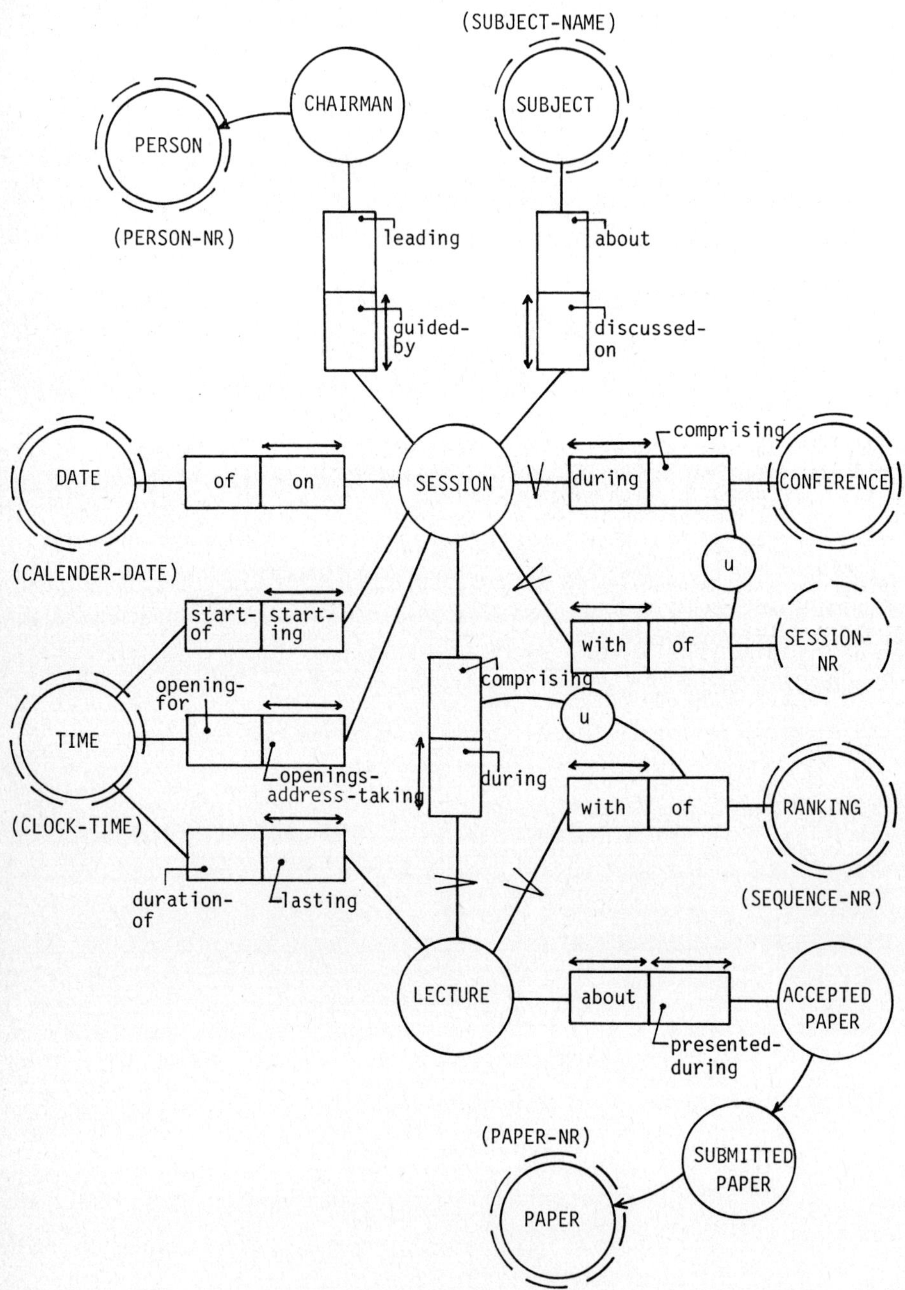


Figure 9.20
ISD for Conference Program

The conference program is published after the program committee finished its task. It will reach attendees before the conference starts; it is possibly enclosed in the invitation sent by the organizing committee.

A session deals with only one subject and comprises lectures. A lecture has a ranking within a session, indicating the sequence of presentation. During a lecture, one and only one paper is presented. Each lecture has a duration. In the program, we observe a deduced sentence: time on which a certain lecture starts. We may deduce this information from the sentences:

- Start of session

- Ranking of lecture

- Duration of lecture

## 9.4.6. Integration of ISDs

The previous paragraphs showed the construction of ISDs for a selection of information flows, occurring in the IFD of the Conference Information System. This process has to be performed for each information flow. The resulting ISDs have to be integrated into one ISD for the information system.
In this paragraph we show the result of the integration in two steps.

Figure 9.21 gives an overview of the ISD. Only the most important NOLOTs and IDEA TYPEs are shown, resulting in a skeleton of the information structure for the information system. In the following figures the details are added, each time for a part of the total ISD. The resulting ISDs concentrate on person-, conference- and paper info. The details for request, invitation and session were already specified in figures 9.15, 9.18 and 9.20.

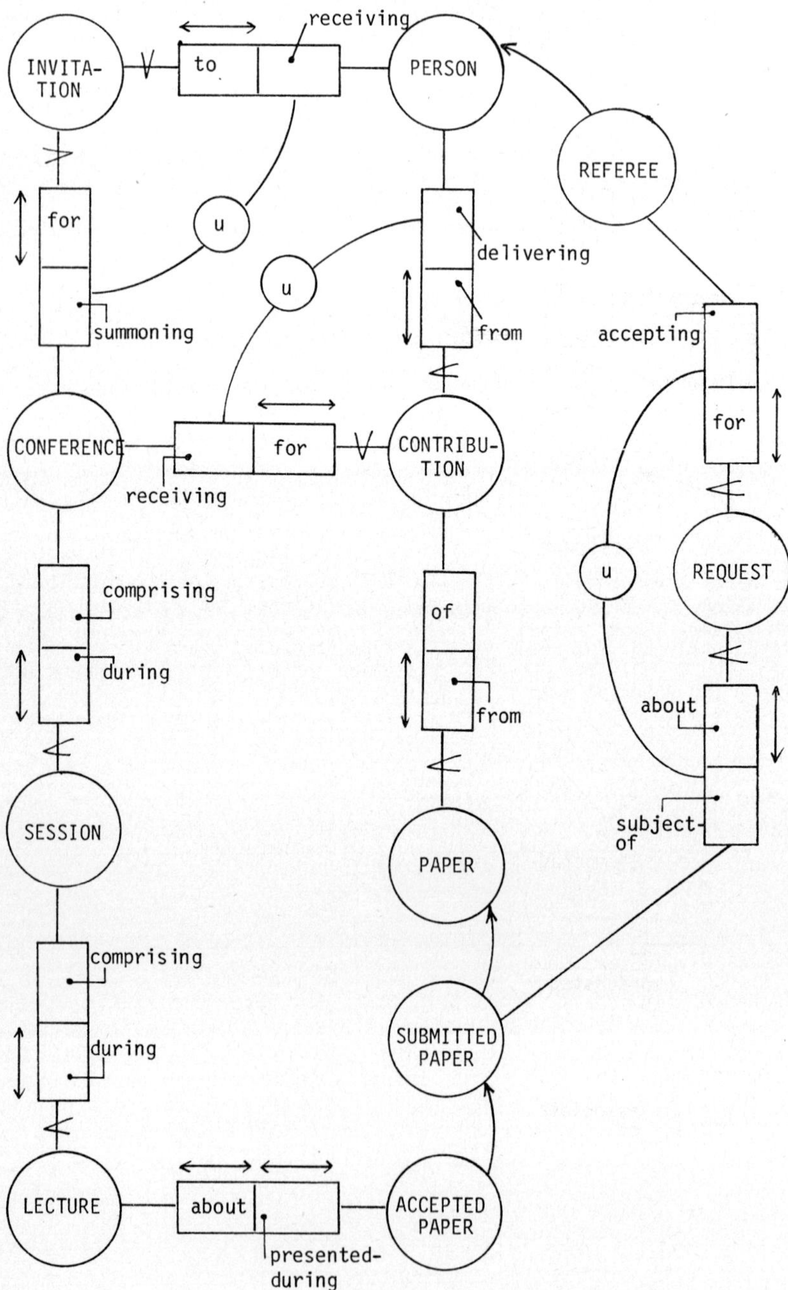


Figure 9.21
ISD Overview. The Skeleton of
the Conference Information Structure

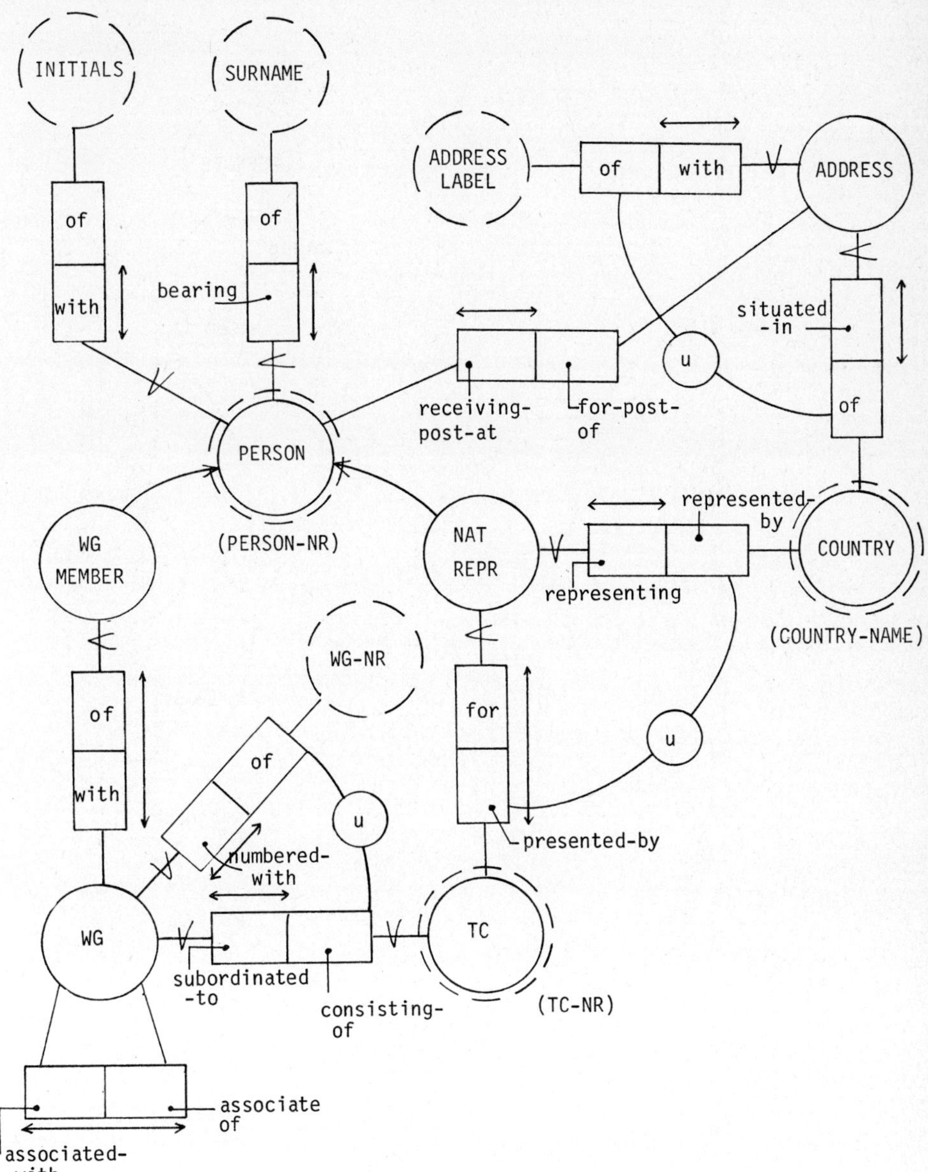


Figure 9.22
ISD "Person-Info"

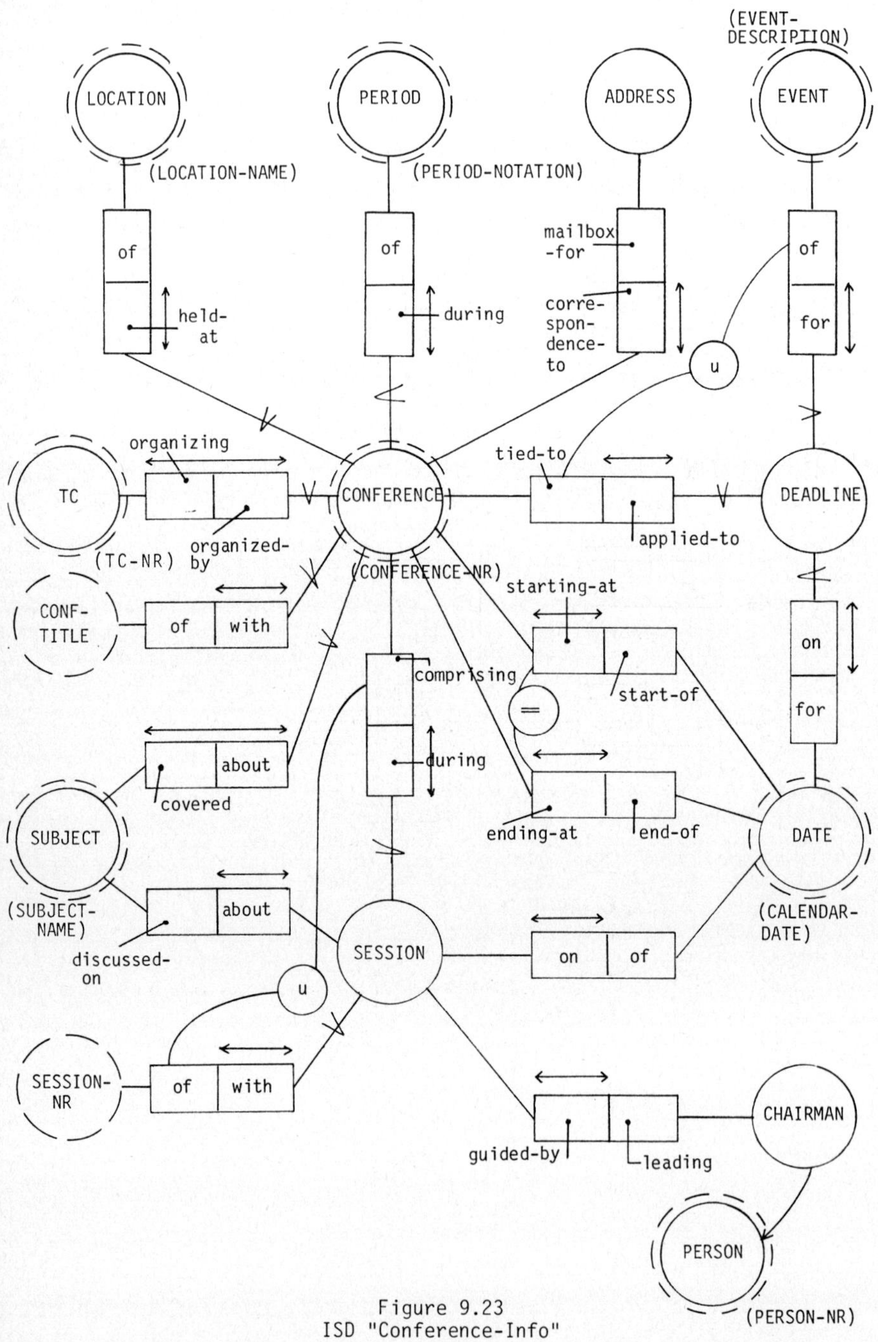


Figure 9.23
ISD "Conference-Info"

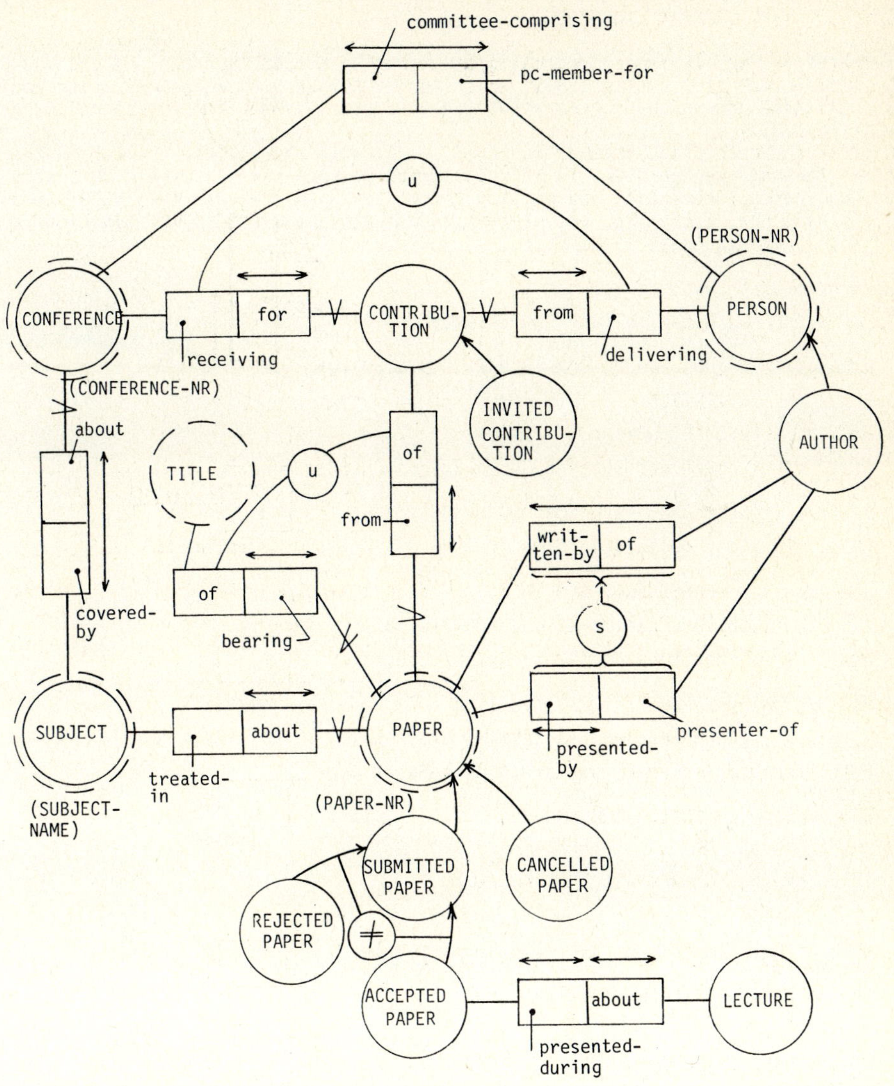


Figure 9.24
ISD "Paper-info"

## 10. CONCEPTUAL GRAMMAR LANGUAGE

As stated in Part I, the conceptual grammar can be stored, updated and checked by
the meta-information system ISDIS, which serves not only as a documentation tool,
but will also add value by generating the conceptual schema for relational or coda-
syl-type DBMS.
To store the conceptual grammar in ISDIS, we have to express the grammar in the
formal language called RIDL. In this paragraph we show parts of the RIDL source for
the Conference Information System. Note, that all NIAM concepts like NOLOT (plus
subtyping), LOT, IDEA TYPE, BRIDGE TYPE, CONSTRAINT, and PROCEDURE (function description) are expressed in RIDL.

```
begin grammar
   add conceptual grammar IFIP-CONFERENCE;
   :
   add nolot PERSON, PAPER, CONFERENCE, CONTRIBUTION,
            INVITATION                                              ...   ;
   add nolot REFEREE subtype of PERSON;
   Note: other nolot and subtype declarations omitted here.
   :
   add lot    PERSON-NR, PAPER-NR, SURNAME, TITLE,                  ...   ;
   Note: other lot declarations omitted here.
   :
   add idea type CONFERENCE-SOMEWHERE
      roles (CONFERENCE held-at and LOCATION of);
   Note: other idea type declarations omitted here.
   :
   add bridge type PERSON-IDENTIFICATION
      roles (PERSON bearing and SURNAME of);
   Note: other bridge type declarations omitted here.
   :
   add constraint PERSON-SURNAME
      condition
          PERSON bearing only one SURNAME
      holds;
   Note: other identifier-constraints omitted here.
   :
   add constraint CONFERENCE-IN-PERIOD
      condition
          CONFERENCE always during PERIOD
      holds;
   Note: other total-role constraints omitted here.
   :
   add constraint SESSION-IDENTIFICATION
      condition
          SESSION is identified by
              SESSION-NR of SESSION
          and
              CONFERENCE comprising SESSION
```

*holds;*
Note: other uniqueness constraints omitted here.
.
.
*add constraint* BOTH-START-AND-END-DATE
   *condition*
      CONFERENCE starting-at DATE
        *is equal to*
      CONFERENCE ending-at DATE
   *holds;*
Note: other equality constraints omitted here
.
.
*add constraint* REFEREE-EXCLUDES-AUTHORSHIP
   *for each* CONF in CONFERENCE
      *do*
         *condition*
            AUTHOR of PAPER from CONTRIBUTION for CONF
              *is disjoint of*
            REFEREE accepting REQUEST about SUBMITTED-PAPER
            from CONTRIBUTION for CONF
         *holds*
      *end for*;
*add constraint* PC-MEMBER-EXCLUDES-AUTHORSHIP
   *for each* CONF in CONFERENCE
      *do*
         *condition*
            AUTHOR of PAPER from CONTRIBUTION for CONF
              *is disjoint of*
            PERSON pc-member-for CONF
         *holds*
      *end for*;
Note: the previous two constraints are not present in the ISDs, because there
     is no graphical representation for them. We refrain from listing all pro-
     cedural constraints.

*add constraint* ACCEPTED-OR-REJECTED
   *condition*
      ACCEPTED-PAPER *is disjoint of* REJECTED-PAPER
   *holds;*
Note: other disjoint constraints omitted here.
.
.
*add constraint* PRESENTER-AMONG-AUTHORS
   *for each* DOCUMENT in PAPER
      *do*
         *condition*

```
            AUTHOR presenter-of DOCUMENT
                is included in
            AUTHOR of DOCUMENT
          holds
        end for;
  Note: other subset constraints omitted here.
    :
  add constraint SINGLE-CONFERENCE-SYSTEM
      condition
        number of CONFERENCE is <= 1
      holds;
  Note: other cardinality constraints omitted here
    :
  add procedure MAJORITY-VOTE
      in CONF: CONFERENCE-NR;
        begin
          for each DOCUMENT in SUBMITTED-PAPER from CONTRIBUTION for CONFERENCE
                            identified-by CONF minus CANCELLED-PAPER
          do
            POSITIVE:= REQUEST (about DOCUMENT and resulting-in
                          REPORT voting 'ACCEPTED');
            NEGATIVE:= REQUEST (about DOCUMENT and resulting-in
                          REPORT voting 'REJECTED');
            if cardinality (POSITIVE) <= cardinality (NEGATIVE)
              then
                  add DOCUMENT is a REJECTED-PAPER
              else
                  add DOCUMENT is an ACCEPTED-PAPER
            end if
          end for;
        end;
        :
  Note: the above described procedure performs part of the function "select papers
        for presentation" (figure 9.6).
end grammar
```

## 11. JUSTIFICATION OF GRAMMAR

The conceptual grammar will now be confronted with the original requirements to check the effectiveness of the grammar. The activities enlisted in the IFIP problem definition will act as touchstones.

## 11.1. PREPARING A LIST TO WHOM THE CALL FOR PAPERS IS TO BE SENT

The persons who are called to submit papers for a particular conference can be listed according to procedure:

*procedure* LIST-CALLEES

   *in* CONF: CONFERENCE-NR;

     *begin*

        CALLEES:= PERSON delivering INVITED-CONTRIBUTION for

            CONFERENCE identified-by CONF;

      *sort* CALLEES *on* SURNAME of PERSON;

      *for* CALLEES

        *list* (PERSON-NR of, INITIALS of, SURNAME of)

     *end;*


## 11.2. REGISTER THE LETTERS OF INTENT RECEIVED IN RESPONSE TO THE CALL

For each letter of intent, the IFIP information system will record:

- The conference

- The person

- The paper: subject
             title
             authors
             presenter


## 11.3. REGISTERING THE CONTRIBUTED PAPERS ON RECEIPT

On receipt of a paper, it will be registered. It is possible that the submitted paper was announced in a letter of intent. If so, it needs only to be qualified as submitted. If the information about the submitted paper differs from the information on the letter of intent (e.g. authors or presenter), an update of paper information should happen. If no letter of intent was sent before, the paper information is recorded from scratch.


## 11.4. DISTRIBUTING THE PAPERS AMONG THOSE UNDERTAKING THE REFEREEING

The distribution of papers among referees is registered as requests. This enables us to create reminders in case a referee delays his report:

*procedure* REMINDER-FOR-REFEREE

*in* CONF: CONFERENCE-NR;

   *begin*

     *for each* REQ *in* REQUEST (about SUBMITTED-PAPER from

              CONTRIBUTION for CONFERENCE identified-by CONF

                  *and*

               *not* resulting-in REPORT)

  *do*

    PRINT-REMINDER (*in* REQ)

    *end for*

*end;*

## 11.5. COLLECTING THE REFEREES' REPORTS AND SELECTING THE PAPERS FOR INCLUSION IN THE PROGRAM

The result of the referee-report is registered. Per request the report-result reads 'accepted', 'rejected' or 'undecided'. To establish the acceptance for a paper, a sound democratic procedure is executed. This procedure may be found in the conceptual grammar of chapter 10, called "majority-vote".

## 11.6. GROUPING PAPERS INTO SESSIONS AND SELECTING CHAIRMEN

Accepted papers will be presented during a lecture, which takes place during a particular session of the conference involved. Per session the program committee may registrate a timeframe.

Registering the results of this grouping plus recording the chairmen for each session means the fulfilment of the program committee's task.

## 11.7. PREPARING A LIST OF PEOPLE TO INVITE TO CONFERENCE

The persons who are invited for a particular conference may be listed according to the following procedure:

*procedure* LIST-INVITEES

 *in* CONF: CONFERENCE-NR;

  *begin*

   INVITEES:= PERSON receiving INVITATION for CONFERENCE identified-by CONF;

   *sort* INVITEES *on* SURNAME of PERSON;

   *for* INVITEES *do*

    *list* (PERSON-NR of, INITIALS of, SURNAME of)

   *end for*

  *end;*

## 11.8. ISSUING PRIORITY INVITATIONS TO NATIONAL REPRESENTATIVES, WG-MEMBERS AND MEMBERS OF ASSOCIATED WORKING GROUPS

The priority-invitations for persons with a special qualification may be issued with the support of the following procedure:

*procedure* PRIORITY-INVITATIONS

 *in* CONF: CONFERENCE-NR;

  *begin*

   PRIO:= (WG-MEMBER of WG subordinated-to

    TC organizing CONFERENCE identified-by CONF) *union*

    NAT-REPRESENTATIVE *union*

    (WG-MEMBER of WG associate-of WG subordinated-to TC

    organizing CONFERENCE identified-by CONF);

   *for each* VIP *in* PRIO

    *do*

     REGISTER-INVITATION (*in* PERSON-NR of VIP,CONF)

```
            end for
   end;
```

## 11.9. ENSURING ALL AUTHORS OF ACCEPTED AND REJECTED PAPERS RECEIVE AN INVITATION

Here too we may define a procedure to guarantee authors to be invited:

```
procedure AUTHOR-INVITATIONS
   in CONF: CONFERENCE-NR;
      begin
         AUTHORS:= AUTHOR of SUBMITTED-PAPER from CONTRIBUTION
                   for CONFERENCE identified-by CONF;
         for each WRITER in AUTHORS
            do
               REGISTER-INVITATION (in PERSON-NR of WRITER, CONF)
            end for
      end;
```

## 11.10. AVOIDING SENDING DUPLICATE INVITATIONS TO INDIVIDUALS

The uniqueness constraint for an invitation in the conceptual grammar prevents duplicate registration of planned invitations. By applying a procedure, which prints the invitation registered in the information system, sending of duplicate invitations is avoided.

```
procedure PRINT-INVITATIONS
   in CONF: CONFERENCE-NR;
      begin
         for PERSON receiving INVITATION for CONFERENCE
                           identified-by CONF
         (*INVITATION IS PREPRINTED EXCEPT FOR NAME AND ADDRESS OF INVITEE*)
            list (INITIALS of, SURNAME of, ADDRESS-LABEL of,ADDRESS for-post-of,
               COUNTRY-NAME of,COUNTRY of,ADDRESS for-post-of)
      end;
```

In case the address is missing and the involved person is an author, then the address of the submitter of the corresponding paper should be printed. This strategy is not embodied in the procedure.

## 11.11. REGISTERING ACCEPTANCE OF INVITATIONS

Upon receipt of an acceptance, the registered invitation will be qualified as confirmation.

## 11.12. GENERATING FINAL LIST OF ATTENDEES

For this activity, we exploit the following procedure:

```
procedure LIST-ATTENDEES
   in CONF: CONFERENCE-NR;
      begin
         for PERSON receiving CONFIRMATION for CONFERENCE identified-by CONF;
         list (PERSON-NR of, INITIALS of, SURNAME of)
      end;
```

ACKNOWLEDGEMENT

We are in debt to our colleagues within CDC for their valuable advice and to HIO
"De Maere" for their study on the IFIP-case.

FOOTNOTES

[1]   NIAM: Nijssens Information Analysis Method: Dr. G.M. Nijssen is leader of
      CDCs research team on information systems development.

[2]   ISDIS: Information Systems Design and Implementation System: CDC-product.

[3]   RIDL: Referential IDea Language: CDC-product. [Ref. 4].

[4]   IMF: Information Management Facility: CDCs DBMS.

LITERATURE

[1]   Falkenberg, E., "Foundations of the Conceptual Schema Approach to Information
      Systems". In: Lecture Notes, Nato Advanced Study Institute, Data Base Manage-
      ment and Applications, (June 1981, Portugal).

[2]   ISO TC97/SC5/WG3, "Concepts and Terminology for the Conceptual Schema", pre-
      liminary report, (February 1981).

[3]   Kent, W., "Data and Reality", (North Holland, Amsterdam 1978).

[4]   Meersman, R., and Vermeir, D., "RIDL Reference Manual". In: Data Management
      Research Report, (January 1980, Control Data Belgium S/A).

[5] Nijssen, G.M., "A Framework for Advanced Mass Storage Applications". In: Medinfo 1980, Proceedings of the Third World Conference on Medical Informatics, Tokyo 1980, (North Holland, Amsterdam, 1980).

[6] Nijssen, G.M., "The Next Five Years in Data Base Technology". In: Data Base Technology, Volume 2, (Infotech State of the Art Report, London, 1978).

[7] Nijssen, G.M., "On the Gross Architecture for the Next Generation Data Base Management Systems". In: Information Processing 1977, Proceedings of the 1977 IFIP Congress, Toronto, Canada, (North Holland, Amsterdam, 1977).

*INFORMATION SYSTEMS DESIGN METHODOLOGIES: A Comparative Review*
*T.W. Olle, H.G. Sol, A.A. Verrijn-Stuart (editors)*
*North-Holland Publishing Company*
© *IFIP, 1982*

# THE USER SOFTWARE ENGINEERING METHODOLOGY:
## AN OVERVIEW

Anthony I. Wasserman

Medical Information Science
University of California, San Francisco
San Francisco, CA 94143 USA

The User Software Engineering methodology is an approach to the specification and development of interactive information systems. The methodology focuses equally on aspects of systematic software development and user participation in system specification. The USE methodology is supported by a set of tools (Unified Support Environment) in the Unix$^{TM}$ environment specifically directed to the needs of interactive information systems. This paper provides an overview of the methodology and tools, with emphasis on the innovative aspects of the USE methodology. Attention is also given to some of the decisions made in the evolution of the methodology. The USE methodology is demonstrated through the example of creating an interactive information system to support the management of IFIP Working Conferences.

## INTRODUCTION

Many computer-based systems may be described as interactive information systems (IIS), providing their users with conversational access to data. Such users are frequently unfamiliar with the technical details of computer hardware and software and view the computer system only as a tool that may be of help to them (or may possibly be required) in doing their jobs. Trends toward distributed systems, lower hardware costs, and the criticality of user/program interfaces all indicate the importance of developing tools and techniques specifically for this class of systems.

Accordingly, the User Software Engineering project was undertaken in 1975 with the objective of creating a methodology to support the specification, design, and implementation of interactive information systems, including the construction of tools that would support the developer of such systems. Attention was specifically focused on the application program developer, who had been traditionally squeezed between the realistic needs of users and the lack of suitable tools for meeting those needs. At that time, virtually all interactive systems were being developed in a haphazard, *ad hoc* manner, and the emerging techniques for software engineering did not adequately address this very important class of programs. The goals of the project combined notions of software engineering and systematic program development with those of user involvement in the early stages of the software development process.

After considerable study of the state-of-the-art in interactive information systems and tools for their construction, it became possible to identify some requirements for the methodology and tools. These requirements included the following key points:

(1)  SPECIFICATION OF USER/PROGRAM INTERACTION
The user/program interaction is a key aspect of an interactive information system. It should be easy to produce a representation of the dialogue that was both comprehensible to the user and sufficiently precise for the developer.

(2)  DESIGN GUIDELINES FOR USER/PROGRAM DIALOGUE
Such guidelines could assist the application developer in creating a dialogue between the user and the program; ideally, it should be possible to identify several types of dialogues, where the appropriate dialogue type for a given application can be determined from a study of user, organization, and hardware characteristics.

(3)  EXPERIMENTATION WITH USER/PROGRAM DIALOGUE
Users needed the chance to work with a "breadboard" of the system to help create a hospitable user interface before full-scale development of the production version of the system was begun; availability of such a tool would assist the user in thinking more carefully about how the system would work and how it would be used; this tool could thus also serve as an effective analysis tool, leading to a better specification and eventually to a better system.

(4)  LANGUAGE FOR IMPLEMENTATION OF INTERACTIVE INFORMATION SYSTEMS
Available programming languages either lacked support for the needs of interactive programs or for the objectives of structured programming (or both!) [1].

(5)  ASSISTANCE IN MAINTENANCE OF PROGRAM PRODUCTION LIBRARY
An automated tool could help keep track of the documentation associated with the specification, design, implementation, and testing of interactive information systems; such a tool could also help keep track of versions of the system and its individual modules.

(6)  ORIENTATION TO SMALL AND MEDIUM-SIZED MACHINES
The methodology and tools should take advantage of hardware trends toward distributed systems and mini- and microcomputers; it was assumed that application programs would probably run on such computers and that the development would take place on such computers, regardless of the target machine.

(7)  INTEGRATION OF THE TOOLS INTO A SUITABLE EXISTING DEVELOPMENT ENVIRONMENT
Support tools for the methodology should be built on top of other tools for common tasks such as program editing, text formatting, language development, and other common software development activities, since it was not sensible to build these tools from scratch.

These seven requirements were above and beyond more general requirements for a software development methodology, which includes the following points:

(1)  SUPPORT FOR PROBLEM SOLVING
The methodology should support problem-solving techniques. It should encompass intellectual processes such as abstraction, partitioning (modularization), classification, and hierarchical decomposition.

(2)  LIFE CYCLE COVERAGE
The methodology should cover the entire software development cycle. It does relatively little good to have a methodology for software design if there is no systematic procedure to produce the specification used for the design and/or the executable program that must be created from the design. Thus, a methodology must assist the developer at each of the stages of the development cycle.

(3)  SUPPORT FOR TRANSITIONS
The methodology should facilitate transitions between phases of the development cycle. When a developer is working on a particular phase of a project (other than requirements analysis), it is important to be able to refer to the previous phase and to trace one's work. At the design stage, for example, one must make certain that the architecture of the software system provides for all of the specified functions; one should be able to identify the software module(s) that fulfill each system requirement. During implementation, it should be easy to establish a correspondence between modules in the system design and program units, and between the logical data objects from the design stage and the physical data objects in the program. It is important to note that one must be able to proceed not only forward to the next phase of the life cycle, but also backward to a previous phase so that work can be checked and any necessary corrections can be made. This phased approach to software development makes it clear that information lost at a particular phase is generally lost forever, with an impact on the resulting system. For example, if an analyst fails to document a requirement, it will not appear in the specification. Eventually, during acceptance testing (or perhaps during system operation), that failure will be recognized and it will be necessary to make modifications to the system.

(4)  SUPPORT FOR VALIDATION
The methodology must support determination of system correctness throughout the development cycle. System correctness encompasses many issues, including not only the correspondence between the system and its specifications, but also the extent to which the system meets user needs. Accordingly, the methodology must not only be concerned with techniques for validation of the complete system, but also must give attention to obtaining the most complete and consistent description of user needs during the early stages of the project. For example, the methods used for analysis and specification of the system should aid problem understanding by the developers, the users, and other concerned parties, and make it possible to trace later system development back to the requirements and specification.

(5)　SUPPORT FOR THE SOFTWARE DEVELOPMENT ORGANIZATION

The methodology must support the software development organization. It must be possible to manage the developers and the developers must be able to work together. This requirement implies the need for effective communication among analysts, developers, and managers, with well-defined steps for making progress visible throughout the development activity. The intermediate products generated by the methods and tools, such as a detailed design or an acceptance test plan, can be reviewed by the organization so that progress can be effectively measured and so that quality can be assured.

(6)　GENERAL APPLICABILITY

The methodology must be repeatable for a large class of software projects. While it is clear that different methodologies will be needed for different classes of systems and for different organizational structures, an organization should be able to adopt a methodology that will be useful for a sizeable number of programs that they will build. Certainly, it makes little sense to develop a methodology for each new system to be built.

(7)　TEACHABILITY

The methodology must be teachable. Even within a single organization, there will be a sizeable number of people who must use the methodology. These people include not only those who are there when the methodology is first adopted, but also those who join the organization at a later time. Each of these people must understand specific techniques that comprise the technical aspects of the methodology, the organizational and managerial procedures that make it effective, automated tools that support the methodology, and the underlying motivations for the methodology.

(8)　AUTOMATED SUPPORT

The methodology must be supported by automated tools that improve the productivity of both the individual developer and the development team. This collection of tools, and the way in which they are used, constitute a "programming support environment."

(9)　SUPPORT FOR SYSTEM EVOLUTION

The methodology should support the eventual evolution of the system. Systems typically go through many versions during their lifetimes, which may last eight to ten years or more. New requirements arise from changes in technology, usage patterns, or user needs, and these changed or additional requirements must be reflected in a modified system. In many ways, the evolution activity is a microcosm of the development process itself. The development methodology can assist this evolutionary activity by providing accurate external and internal system documentation, and a well structured software system that is easily comprehended and modified by those making the system changes.

These objectives led to development of the User Software Engineering methodology for the creation of interactive information systems and to the creation of tools that support the methodology.

## OVERVIEW OF THE USE METHODOLOGY

An important initial consideration in developing the User Software Engineering methodology was to support a systematic approach to software development. The potential benefits of such an approach include:

1.　improved reliability;

2.　verifiability, at least in an informal sense;

3.　improved evolvability, including portability and adaptability;

4.　system comprehensibility, as a result of improved structure;

5.　more effective management control of the development process;

6.　higher user satisfaction.

In general, a systematic approach to software development increases effort in requirements analysis, specification, and design. This increase is balanced by expected lower costs for testing and system evolution, since the implemented system will represent a better fit to the user's needs and will operate more reliably than would otherwise be the case.

We found much to commend such a systematic approach to software design and development, but also found one extremely serious flaw: when developing information systems, there may be a long period of time between the early stages of analysis and specification and the actual availability of the system while the systematic procedure is followed. During this time, the user's needs may change significantly, and the user has no system to use in the interim. When the system finally becomes operational, it may do what was originally specified, but user experience with the system may show that what is needed is quite different. As a result, a large part of the systematic development effort may have been wasted as it becomes necessary to redesign and reimplement a system that meets the newly identified needs of the user.

In short, we found some merit to the traditional idea of "let's build one of these and see how it works". If such a system is conceived as a "throwaway" system, intended only to identify user needs or to serve those needs during an interim period while development of a production system is in progress, *and* it can be built quickly and inexpensively, then there is ample justification for proceeding with this approach.

USE attempts to combine the systematic approach to software inherent in the life cycle approach with the rapid construction approach successfully used in the INTERLISP [2] and Smalltalk [3] environments. USE tries to strike a balance by building a partial system as an aid to *analysis and specification*, and making that system useful to users throughout subsequent stages of a life cycle approach until a production version of a system is completed.

The steps of the USE methodology may be summarized as follows:

(1)  Requirements analysis -- activity and data modelling, identification of user characteristics

(2)  User/program dialogue design

(3)  Creation of a "façade", a mockup of the user/program dialogue with revisions as needed

(4)  Informal specification of the system operations using narrative text

(5)  Preliminary relational database design

(6)  Creation of a "precursor", or partial, system, providing at least some, and possibly all, of the system's functions

(7)  Formal specification of the system operations using behavioral abstraction

(8)  System design at the architectural and module levels

(9)  Implementation in PLAIN

(10) Testing and verification

Some of these stages are handled by existing techniques, while others have been developed for the methodology. The USE methodology is supported by a set of tools called the Unified Support Environment. Five principal tools have been developed to date:

(1)  TDI (Transition Diagram Interpreter) -- a tool for encoding transition diagrams that permits the rapid construction and modification of prototype user/program interfaces, as well as the creation of system prototypes

(2)  Troll -- a tool that provides a relational algebra-like interface to a small relational database system, used both as the runtime support of PLAIN and as the "backend" of TDI in the construction of partial systems

(3)  RAPID (RApid Prototypes of Interactive Dialogues) -- a tool combining TDI and Troll that permits the rapid construction of (partial) systems; one can link data manipulation and/or routines written in high-level languages to the user/program dialogue, thereby providing useful system functions

(4)  PLAIN (Programming LAnguage for INteraction) -- a procedural programming language derived from Pascal that contains features for building interactive information systems, including strings, patterns and pattern-matching operations, exception-handling, and relations, with a set of operations to support definition and manipulation of relational data bases

(5)  USE Control System -- a tool that supports a modular organization of the software system, provides a unified framework for developer activities, provides version control, and automatically logs developer activities

The interactive information system is modelled and specified using a combination of formal and informal methods. The dialogue is built using TDI, and functionality may be provided with a partial system through the use of RAPID. The system may then be implemented in PLAIN, with the entire development and evolution process controlled by the USE Control System.

The remainder of this paper describes the User Software Engineering development methodology and tools in greater detail, giving an historical perspective on the project. We also show the application of the methodology and tools to the design and development of an interactive information system for the management of a technical conference.

## REQUIREMENTS ANALYSIS IN THE USE METHODOLOGY

Requirements analysis and specification are the first steps in the software life cycle. As such, they are a principal determinant of system quality, including reliability, usability, and fit to user needs. Errors introduced at the early stages are often not caught until acceptance testing, if then. Similarly, functions not requested during this process are likely to be omitted from the operational system.

As a result, many methods for requirements analysis and specification have been developed during the past few years. Among these techniques are Structured Systems Analysis (SSA) [4,5], SADT$^{TM}$ [6], Information Systems and Analysis of Change (ISAC) [7], and many, many others. A lengthy desription of such techniques is beyond the scope of this paper; some of them are briefly described in [8].

In short, requirements analysis deals with problems of understanding the problem and of communicating that understanding among the concerned individuals and organizations. This step is often achieved through the construction of a model of a system. The requirements then form the basis for a system specification, which also includes information on the planned use of the system, development constraints, cost constraints, and user considerations.

The analysis and specification process typically also results in the creation of user documentation, based upon design of the user/program dialogue. This dialogue may be interactive, or may simply be batch-oriented, with a deck of user input producing a file of program output. The input and output may be alphanumeric characters, or may involve a variety of non-alphanumeric characters and devices, such as light pens, graphics, plotters, and audio.

The biggest difficulty with analysis and specification of interactive information systems is that the user (or user representative) and developer must reach agreement on system capabilities and operation at a very early stage. If the user has little or no previous experience with computer-based systems, the user is not likely to have a good understanding of what a computer system can do, let alone be able to decide upon a suitable form of user/program interaction or even to specify a complete set of desired system capabilities.

The likely outcome of this situation is that the user and the developer are unable to communicate effectively with one another and that the user is unable to convey to the developer the information that would result in a totally satisfactory system. The resulting system will then be at best partly satisfactory, necessitating an ongoing process of evolution, as the user comes to understand the functions of the system as compared to the evolving information processing needs of his organization.

Accordingly, any assistance that can be provided in the requirements analysis and specification activity is likely to have a large payoff in terms of reducing the need for maintenance activities and in reducing the cost of the information system over its lifetime. In particular, a means for involving the user in the analysis phase and in the design of the user/system interaction can provide a significant amount of this necessary assistance [9,10,11,12,13]. User involvement in the USE methodology is enhanced through the use of prototypes of the user/program dialogue, and, where feasible, the system itself.

The analysis process is iterative, with the first iteration attempting to reach a reasonable (definitely *not* perfect) understanding of the problem from the user's perspective. The goal here is to gather enough information about the problem and expected usage patterns to be able to construct a prototype of the user interface to the system. Thus, the analyst must understand the kinds of functions (or transactions) to be performed by the user (or by each class of users) and must use this information to create a user/program dialogue that allows the user to request these functions, with any needed options, as easily as possible.

One or more of the above mentioned analysis techniques can be used for this analysis process. In this regard, we have been extremely pragmatic, and have not chosen to develop our own analysis methods, relying instead on effective use of techniques created by others. Furthermore, we have found that it is possible to be flexible concerning the use of a process-oriented versus a data-oriented approach to analysis.

Indeed, we view these approaches as being complementary. If one identifies operations (process-oriented approach), one cannot then help but identify the objects upon which the operations are performed. Conversely, using principles of data abstraction, identification of operations must follow directly from identification of data objects.

In short, we are not prescriptive about the method(s) used for analysis. The goal of the analysis activity is to be able to write the specification, for which we *have* prescribed a format.

In our previous analysis work, we have been most successful using Structured Systems Analysis and the principles of conceptual database design and data abstraction as put forth by Smith and Smith [14,15]. Structured Systems Analysis not only provides a way of modelling systems through data flow, but also leads to a relational data base design and the creation of a data dictionary. The data abstraction ideas help to refine the data base design, as well as providing a framework for formalizing the specification at a later stage and establishing different views of the system.

Our approach to data base design, carried out informally at the early stages, is to follow a multi-level approach, along the lines of the ANSI/SPARC framework. The conceptual model is intended to capture the semantics of the data. The external model defines the view of the data for different classes of users, so that a given system may contain several external models reflecting a single conceptual model; these are all mapped into a single internal model. We create a conceptual model of the application database objects and their relationships, then define a set of "views" of the database, corresponding to the external models for each user class, and then later define a set of normalized relations as the internal model.

The overall structure of our analysis procedure can then be described as a sequence of five steps, where steps 2 and 3 may be interchanged or performed in parallel.

1.  Identify system objectives and constraints, including conflicts of interest among user groups, based upon the problem statement

2/3.  Model the existing system using a requirements analysis method (Structured Systems Analysis)

2/3.  Construct a conceptual model of the data base, using the Semantic Hierarchy Model of Smith and Smith

4.  Produce a system dictionary containing the names of all operations, all data items, and all data flows

5.  Review the analysis results within the development group and, insofar as possible, with the user(s) and/or customer(s)

At this point, we can either carry out additional analysis based upon the review, proceed to build a prototype of the user/program dialogue, or proceed with the complete system specification. It should be noted that the latter alternative is taken only if the prototype stage is omitted. Our presentation of the methodology will, of course, include the role of prototypes.

Before proceeding further, though, we can examine the application of these analysis ideas to a particular problem.


## THE IFIP WORKING CONFERENCE PROBLEM

The problem that we will use to exemplify the USE methodology has been proposed by IFIP Working Group 8.1 (Design and Evaluation of Information Systems) as a standard problem to compare various methodologies for information system design. Briefly summarized, it calls for the development of an information system to support the organization of a small technical conference, providing primarily for the activities of the technical program committee, but also for the general organizing activities. The information system requirements are shown in Figure 1. We decided, though, to ignore the second requirement for the Program Committee, since our previous conference planning experience had shown relatively little correlation between the letters of intent and the actual papers received.

> The information system that is to be designed shall support the activities of both the Programme Committee and the Organizing Committee for an IFIP Working Conference, excluding activities of conference budgeting, hotel arrangements, and production of the conference proceedings.
>
> The following Programme Committee activities shall be supported:
>
> 1.  Preparing a list of persons to whom the Call for Papers is to be sent.
> 2.  Registering the letters of intent received in response to the Call.
> 3.  Registering the contributed papers on receipt.
> 4.  Distributing the papers among referees.
> 5.  Collecting the referee reports and selecting the papers for inclusion in the conference program.
> 6.  Grouping selected papers into sessions for presentation and selecting a chairman for each session
>
> The following Organizing Committee activities shall be supported:
>
> 1.  Preparing a list of people to invite to the conference.
> 2.  Issuing priority invitations to national representatives, Working Group members, and members of associated working groups.
> 3.  Ensuring all authors of each selected paper receive an invitation.
> 4.  Ensuring authors of rejected papers receive an invitation.
> 5.  Avoiding sending duplicate invitations to any individual.
> 6.  Registering acceptance of invitations.
> 7.  Generating final list of attendees.

Figure 1 -- Summary of IFIP Working Conference Problem

## ANALYSIS OF THE IFIP CONFERENCE PROBLEM

Beginning with the brief problem statement, the analysis effort focused on achieving a deeper understanding of the connections between the various activities, the reporting and communication requirements of the various organizers, and, to a lesser extent, the relationship between the aspects of conferences addressed in the problem and the broader aspects of conference organization.

The approach to problem understanding was multifaceted, involving reading of books on technical conferences to obtain general background [16,17], reading of professional society (ACM and IEEE Computer Society) guidelines for conference organization, interviews with the potential users of the system, and personal experience with such conferences.

Throughout this analysis process, though, the goal was to produce a model of the conference organization activity, using Structured Systems Analysis, and a conceptual data base design. As with most analysis activities, there was some difficulty in bounding the scope of the problem and in understanding the details that distinguished the IFIP conference problem from other conference organization problems. This effect may have been exaggerated in our experience, since early efforts at building an SSA model were far too broad.

Eventually, though, a model of the conference organizational structure was produced. A small excerpt of this model is depicted in Figure 2.

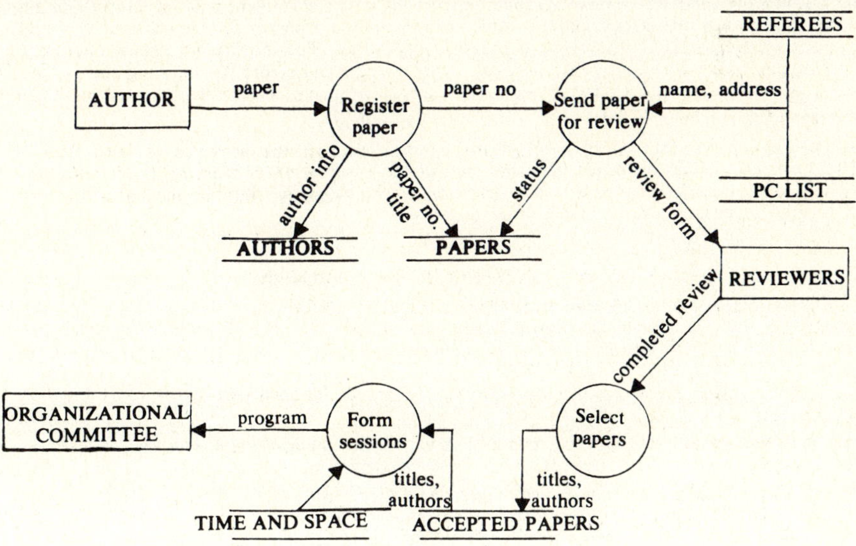


Figure 2 -- SSA overview diagram of Program Committee activities

A system dictionary (not shown) was also made as part of these analysis activities. It should be noted that the model is regarded as preliminary and highly subject to change at this point in the development cycle. From this point, though, the next step involves the construction of a prototype of the user/program dialogue. Prototype construction requires design of the dialogue itself, which necessitates making numerous assumptions about program functions and the way in which they will be used, then experimenting with those assumptions and making changes as necessary.

## THE ROLE OF PROTOTYPES

In our earlier development of the USE methodology, as described in [18] for example, we went directly from our analysis to a system specification, as described below. While that approach worked successfully on a couple of applications, the potential users didn't really seem to get a true sense of how the system would actually work in practice.

Accordingly, we sought a way to provide the user with that necessary understanding, and identified a prototype of the user/system dialogue as an effective way to achieve that goal. Our idea was to produce a façade of the system, a program whose external behavior mimicked that of planned system, but which didn't actually perform any other system functions.

There were four reasons for building such a façade:

1.   it would enable to user to evaluate the interface in practice and to suggest changes to the interface;

2.   it would enable the developer to evaluate user performance with the interface and to modify it so as to minimize user errors and improve user satisfaction;

3.   it would facilitate experimentation with a number of alternative interfaces and modification of interfaces; furthermore, it would be possible to generate the dialogue quickly and to make minor revisions in a matter of minutes;

4.   it would give the user a more immediate sense of the proposed system and thereby encourage users to think more carefully about the needed and desirable characteristics of the system.

This last goal was seen as being particularly significant, since it creates a "bonding" between the user and the emerging system, helping to overcome the abstract nature of a system described on paper.

With an automated tool, though, the user would be able to simulate the interaction at a very early stage in the development cycle. Even though the functionality of the system is minimal, the user is still forced to think more closely about the task being automated and about the way in which operations will be requested. The result of that thinking should be a more accurate understanding of the problem and improved communication between the user and the analyst/developer.

An even more significant result of this process would be that the original IIS would be a better fit to user needs than was previously possible. The user interface would have been thoroughly tested, and a larger set of desired operations would have been implemented. Thus, the amount of needed system evolution would be reduced, with a corresponding reduction in the cost of the IIS over its lifetime.

Before proceeding further with construction of the interface, it is necessary to discuss guidelines for the construction of user/program dialogues, then the method for specification of these dialogues, and then their automation. That discussion then leads to a lengthier discussion of the specification method and construction of partial systems rather than just prototypes of the dialogue.


## DESIGN AND MODIFICATION OF USER/PROGRAM DIALOGUE

In many respects, creation of user/program dialogue is the most critical aspect of designing an IIS, since the user's satisfaction with the system is strongly determined by the ease with which it is possible to request operations. If it is difficult to interact with the IIS, then the user will be less likely to use it and may reject it entirely.

Of course, the user interface is determined not only by the dialogue itself, but also be diverse environmental factors such as terminal type, output speed, readability of user input, hard vs. soft copy, noise level, terminal placement, and input mode (keyboard vs. non-keyboard). These human factors have been the subject of a significant amount of recent research [19,20,21,22,23,24] involving psychologists, industrial engineers, computer scientists, and others, and the discussion of this research is beyond the scope of this paper.

Our approach has been to glean from this research and from our own empirical observations a set of guidelines that we can follow in making a preliminary user/program dialogue. We are aided in this process by the requirements analysis process, which has provided us with information on user characteristics, environmental considerations, legal constraints (e.g., the need for a hard copy), and application needs.

The actual dialogue design process, though, remains largely *ad hoc*, with only our general guidelines to aid the design process. These guidelines, discussed at greater length in [25], may be summarized as follows:

(1)   Interactive systems should be interactive, and should not require the user to input lengthy strings conforming to a precise syntax.

(2)   Underlying aspects of the computer system should be hidden as fully as possible.

(3)   Users should not be able to cause abnormal program termination.

(4)   Users should be notified if any request can have major consequences.

(5)   Systems should provide online assistance.

(6)   Input requirements should be tailored to user characteristics.

(7)   Output messages should be tailored to characteristics of terminals.

(8)Different user skill levels should be distinguished.

(9)User errors should not require a large amount of additional user effort.

(10)Response time should be consistent for the same request, and meaningful feedback should be provided to the user.

In many interactive information systems, the permissible operations (transactions) are defined in the specification, so that it is frequently possible to build such systems around a series of user commands. Even so, the process of determining the desired set of operations and then the appropriate commands is not well defined.

The process of dialogue design is basically an iterative one and involves a certain necessary amount of experimentation before developing a set of commands (or other dialogue format) that both provides the desired set of operations and satisfies the user's requirements for ease of use. In many system developments, though, it is difficult to iterate and to experiment with various possible dialogues, for two major reasons. First, the modification of the dialogue may involve major structural changes to the software system, particularly where the addition of new transactions is involved. Second, the interaction may not be testable until the entire IIS has been built, making the cost of experimentation and subsequent modification inordinately high.

Because of the criticality of the user/program dialogue in the overall design of an IIS, though, such iteration and experimentation is essential. Thus, we have given attention to the development of tools and techniques to facilitate the design of the user interface, and to the creation of program development methods that simplify the evolution of that interface.

We have developed a user-centered technique for the specification of an IIS that treats the user/program dialogue as a key component of the system specification and as a starting point for system decomposition [26]. As noted, an interactive program may be viewed as a set of transactions between a user and the program. Each transaction consists of a set of messages transmitted between a user and the program. Furthermore, each transaction results in some "operation", typically involving retrieval from or modification to data in a data base. Thus the specification method consists of specifying the data base, the operations, and the dialogue that comprises each transaction.

From this standpoint, it can be seen that these operations can be organized (perhaps aggregated) to form transactions. Then, appropriate dialogue can be defined for each of these transactions. Such an approach permits separation of the program structure from the particulars of the user/program dialogue, but also makes the dialogue a cornerstone of the specification process, rather than relegating it to a secondary role.

The IIS user interface provides the user with a language for communicating with the system. The interface can take many forms, including multiple choice (menu selection), a command language, a database query language, or natural language-like input. In all cases, however, the normal action of the program is determined by user input, and the program may respond in a variety of ways, including results, requests for additional input, error messages, or assistance in the use of the IIS.

The critical observation, though, is that the semantics of the IIS, i.e., its actions, are driven by raw or transformed user input. As with programming languages, the user language in its runtime context determines the semantic actions to be performed; the resemblance between such a user language and an interpreted programming language is quite strong.

Accordingly, an effective specification technique for programming languages can be used effectively for specifying user interfaces. One can write down the grammar of the user input, and associate program actions with the successful recognition of "words" or "phrases" in the grammar.

A variety of language definition techniques are applicable in this setting. One of the key goals for defining the dialogue was the ability to associate the actions with specific inputs. Thus, some of the highly formal language definition schemes or the report format used for Algol 60 and Pascal were not ideal. Two techniques seemed equally useful: language specification as given to a translator writing system such as YACC [27] and transition diagrams [28]. We chose the latter primarily because of its pictorial representation.

Transition diagrams have been used for a variety of language translators, and are used as the formal specification of the MUMPS programming language [29]. Our own experience has indicated that they are well suited to the construction of interpreters and that they make the sequence of language processing quite visible. In short, they are useful both to the implementers who can build an interpreter directly from the diagram and to the computer-naive users who can easily see what actions will result from the recognition of specific inputs.

A transition diagram is a network of nodes and directed paths. Each path may contain a token, corresponding to a character string in the primitive alphabet (such as ASCII), or the name of another diagram. If the path is blank, it will be traversed as the default case, i.e., if all other paths leaving a given node fail. Scanning of the diagram begins at a designated entry point and proceeds until reaching an exit node or a dead end (no successful match on the paths from a given node). A semantic action may be associated with any path; traversal of the path causes the associated action to occur.

As a brief example, consider Figure 3, showing part of a transition diagram. The diagram is initially in state START, as shown by the double circle. The message associated with START is displayed. If the input string is 'quit', the path from START to BYE will be traversed and the associated action 1 will be taken. Also, the message associated with the node BYE will be displayed. Similarly, if the input string is 'help', the path from START to INFO will be traversed, and the message associated with the node INFO will be displayed. Control then returns directly to START. If the input string is 'enter', the subconversation NEWENTRY, represented by another transition diagram (not shown here), will be invoked. NEWENTRY may return with either the value 0 or 1, which then determines the path followed and the action to be taken next.

Intuitively, one can see that paths may contain arbitrary strings, and that the state transitions can invoke arbitrary actions. The distinguished inputs then lead to different states from which other input symbols may cause yet additional actions.

In this manner, one may specify the user/program dialogue. Indeed, one may specify an entire IIS, showing the dialogue and associated actions as a set of transition diagrams, accompanied by specifications of the actions and a conceptual data base design. The user may review these diagrams and see the valid inputs and the actions that occur as a result of those inputs.

Experience with this technique showed that users were indeed able to review the transition diagrams and to observe the nature of the user interface. Furthermore, the diagrams served as a good basis for system design and subsequent implementation. However, it seemed that the users did not really get a true sense of how the system would actually work from the diagrams alone.

We originally tried to incorporate all of the error handling and all of the online assistance information in the transition diagrams. Although that approach worked, it could lead to extremely complicated diagrams, particularly if one wanted to provide extensive diagnostic messages and to support a user-oriented dialogue. For example, if one wanted to give a user three tries at providing some input, and wanted to then take some default action or wanted to provide different messages for each occurrence of the error, it would be necessary to add extra nodes to the diagrams above those needed for "normal" processing. It can be seen that such diagrams could easily become unwieldy.

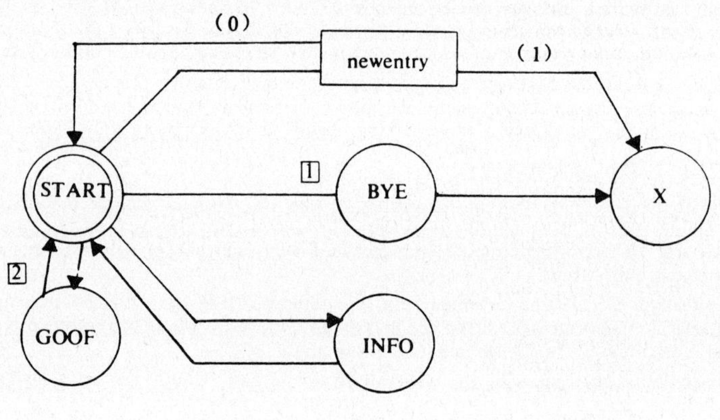


<table>
<tr><td>MESSAGES</td><td>ACTIONS</td></tr>
<tr><td>START = 'Please type a command'<br>BYE = 'Byebye'<br>INFO = 'Valid commands are ...'<br>GOOF = 'Illegal command'</td><td>1 Close database.<br><br>2 Update user error log.</td></tr>
</table>

Figure 3 -- Sample transition diagram

As a result, the diagrams that are shown to the user for review only contain the "normal" case, that of providing "correct" input. This approach represents a compromise between showing the entire dialogue with its possible complexities and showing a subset of the dialogue, with increased comprehensibility. (It is, of course, necessary to specify the entire dialogue for the developer.)

Accordingly, we sought to automate the transition diagrams. The primary intent of such automation was to be able to encode the diagrams quickly and to generate the user interface so that the prospective user could interact with it. Another advantage would be the ability to encode the error-handling and online assistance parts of the more-detailed diagrams so that the users could gain experience with those aspects of the dialogue.

## THE TRANSITION DIAGRAM INTERPRETER

These goals motivated the design and implementation of the Transition Diagram Interpreter (TDI). The TDI accepts the encoding of one or more transition diagrams as input and produces an executable program simulating the specified interface. An action can be associated with each arc on the transition diagram, so that it would be theoretically possible to implement the entire IIS in this manner. In practice, such an implementation strategy is not likely to be used; however, it is very useful to provide a sample of the user interface or a rapidly built prototype of the system.

Input to the TDI is specified in four sections:

1.	Conversation name definition section -- identifies the diagram and its starting point

2.	Variable definition section -- permits the specification of names corresponding to lexical elements that may be described as strings of alphanumeric or numeric characters

3.	Node message section -- associates a message with a node in the diagram

4.	Body section -- describes the structure of the diagram and its transition conditions (see below)

The body section contains information on the arcs of the transition diagram. For each arc, one may specify

1.	source name -- the name of the source of the arc

2.	input selectors -- for each arc leaving the node, one of the following: a "Unix regular expression", a returned value from a subconversation (another transition diagram), a variable name defined in a variable definition declaration, or an empty field, representing the default situation;

3.	destination name -- the name of the destination of the arc (possibly the same as the source node)

4.	action -- if supplied, this item causes the execution of an action prior to entry to the destination. This action may be any executable program or routine, thus permitting a wide variety of semantic actions.

In this way, the set of diagrams can be encoded, and a running (partial) system produced. The encoding of the transition diagram of Figure 3 is shown in Figure 4.

In addition to providing a "mockup" of the user/program dialogue that serves to familiarize the user with the functions of the system, TDI can provide some other useful capabilities. First, it can check the encoded diagrams for consistency, making sure, for example, that there is a path from each node. (The problem of checking to see that there is a path from entry to exit becomes combinatorially large as the number of nodes and paths increase.)

Second, it can be used to *measure* user performance with the interface. It is a very straightforward task to capture information on keystrokes, errors, and other aspects of use to determine the ease of use, the error rates for various user classes, and other key measures of user performance with the system.

One can easily extend this notation to support a variety of input devices in conjunction with the TDI. The input selector, for example, could be defined for graphics primitives, such as the selection of alternatives with a light pen. Such a selection could cause a state transition in much the same way as is done here with characters and character strings.

Furthermore, a more sophisticated positioning of output messages can be supported. In simplest form, the output is simply produced beginning at the point where the output device cursor is positioned. TDI, however, allows general cursor positioning and related features to support user/program dialogue on a screen oriented device. Thus, the message "R2,C15,'Hi there'" could put the message 'Hi there' on row 2 of the screen beginning in column 15.

DIAGRAM Figure_3 ENTRY START EXIT X

NODE START
  CS, 'Please type a command'

NODE BYE
  'Byebye'

NODE INFO
  R$-2, 'Valid commands are ... '

NODE GOOF
  R$,RV, 'Illegal command',SV

ARC START
  ON 'enter' TO <newentry>
  ON 'quit' DO 1 TO BYE
  ON 'help' TO INFO
  ELSE DO 2 TO GOOF

ARC BYE SKIP TO X

ARC INFO SKIP TO START

ARC GOOF SKIP TO START

ARC <newentry>
  WHEN 0 TO START
  WHEN 1 TO X

Figure 4 -- TDI encoding of transition diagram of Figure 3

## DIALOGUE DESIGN FOR THE IFIP CONFERENCE EXAMPLE

The conference management system, named CONMAN, would support two classes of end user: a Programme Committee chairman and an Organizing Committee Chairman. (Of course, those individuals could authorize others to use the system in the same capacities.)

Our approach, in this case, was to define two similar command language based dialogues. In both cases, the user would request a given kind of operation with a command, and the program would then elicit any additional information. We have found this approach to be successful in the past, and it can do an excellent job of meeting our general guidelines for dialogue design.

We begin, then, by creating a transition diagram for the "top" level of the dialogue, the command level, as shown for the Programme Committee in Figure 5. From this diagram, it can be seen that the Programme Committee chairman has the following transaction types available:

(1)   Invite someone to submit a paper.

(2)   Receive a paper

(3)   Add a name to referee list

(4)   Assign a paper to a referee for review

(5)   Form a conference session

(6)   Provide help in the use of the system

(7)   Quit

Each of these transaction types is shown in a rectangular box, designating a subconversation, shown by another transition diagram. In most cases, the path leading to the subconversation is not a string literal, but is rather a name, again designating the name of another transition diagram. If there were simply a single string to cause the transition to the subconversation, this could be shown without using another diagram. However, our desire to support both novice and expert users has led to providing several ways to make the transition, and it is more convenient to show this situation with the additional diagram. Furthermore, this approach makes the top level

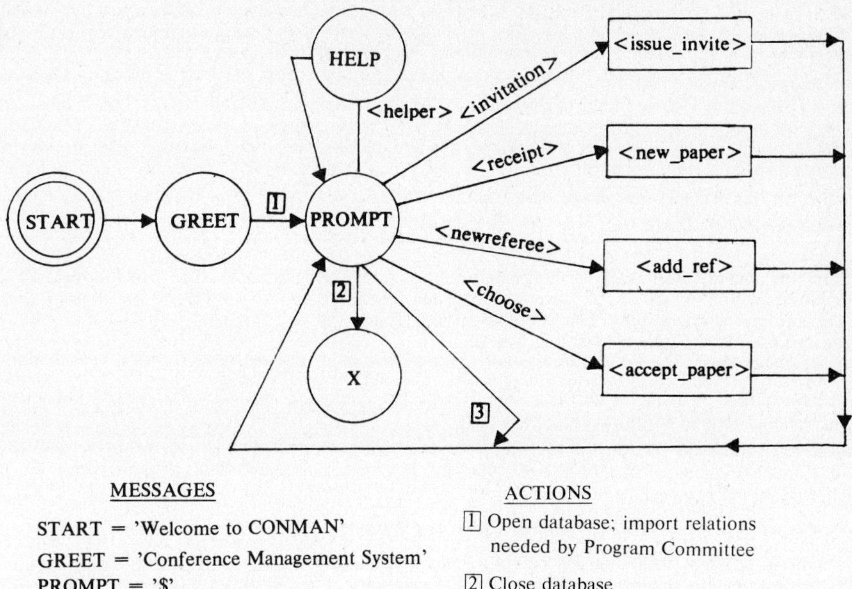



**MESSAGES**

START = 'Welcome to CONMAN'

GREET = 'Conference Management System'

PROMPT = '$'

HELP = 'Valid commands are ...'

X = 'Byebye'

**ACTIONS**

1 Open database; import relations needed by Program Committee

2 Close database

3 Write 'illegal command'; update user error log

Figure 5a -- Transition diagram for "transaction level"
of CONMAN for Program Committee

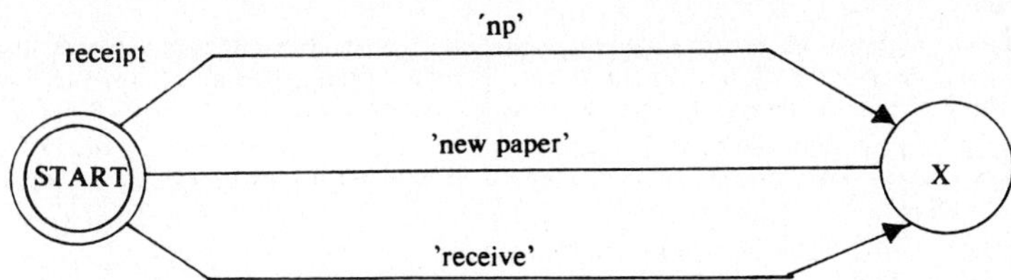



Figure 5b -- Transition diagram showing valid inputs
to cause transition receipt in Figure 5a

diagram almost entirely independent of the actual input text, thereby isolating the design decisions concerning the dialogue to the greatest extent possible. The disadvantage to this approach is that it creates additional diagrams that must be reviewed and incorporated into the prototype.

Now, the diagrams shown in Figure 5 may be encoded for the TDI. This encoding is shown in Figure 6.

It can be seen from the transition diagram named receipt that three different inputs, 'np', 'new paper', and 'receive', are treated similarly, causing the initiation of the subconversation <new_paper>. Experienced users can use the terse notation, while other users can use one of the other two equivalently. Numerous alternatives can be provided to accommodate different user preferences as long as there is no conflict in the grammar.

The flavor of this dialogue can also be seen from the diagrams in Figure 5. The system begins by typing

    Welcome to CONMAN
    $

The user then types a response. If the response is 'quit', the program will reply with the message 'Byebye', carry out semantic action 3 of closing the database, and quit. If the response causes one of the subconversations to begin, the CONMAN system will prompt the user for input. Thus, in the <new_paper> subconversation, the system will respond first with

    Enter paper title:

It will subsequently prompt for author names and mailing addresses, then assign a paper number and display this information to the user for confirmation.

It can be seen from the structure of the transition diagrams and the TDI input that it is very easy to alter the diagrams and the input as the users work with the prototype and show their preferences for specific input formats and output messages.

## SPECIFICATION OF INTERACTIVE INFORMATION SYSTEMS

The results of analysis, including use of the prototype dialogue, is used to develop the specification for the interactive information system. As the first detailed statement of system functions, specifications play a critical role in the development activity, providing a foundation for future work and a link between the user's concept of the system and its actual implementation.

Specifications are of critical importance in the USE methodology, since:

(1) The specification is a means for precisely stating the system requirements. The specification can be compared against the requirements definition to ascertain the correspondence between the specification and the user's needs.

(2) The specification provides insight into the system structure and is used during the design phase as a checkpoint against which to validate the design. Typically, there will be an iteration between specification and design, as insight into some of the system construction problems helps to clarify the specification.

(3) The specification is the basis against which testing and verification are performed. Clearly, one cannot prove that a program is correct in the absence of a clear understanding of the program's behavioral characteristics. Similarly, although certain kinds of testing can locate clerical errors and other low-level problems, system testing and acceptance testing require comparison of the system against an objective specification.

(4) Modifications and enhancements to a system throughout its operational lifetime require an understanding of the system functions, as documented in the specification. During this phase, the specification can help to locate those system functions that must be changed, and can then be revised accordingly.

The implication of this multifaceted role for specifications is that a specification must be able to serve (to a greater or lesser degree) each of these four different functions. We identified some desirable goals for specifications, including:

(1) completeness -- capturing all of the features of the system

(2) comprehensibility -- ensuring that the specification can be understood by those who must approve it and work with it

(3) testability -- attempting to quantify system requirements and to be sufficiently precise so that the correctness of the implemented system can be tested and/or verified

(4) traceability -- ensuring that the system specification meets the requirements, and writing the specification in such a way that it can be used to check the subsequent design

(5) consistency -- determining that different parts of the system description do not impose inherently conflicting requirements, and that consistent nomenclature is used in the description

(6) unambiguity -- assuring that the specification has a unique interpretation in order to eliminate any confusion

```
DIAGRAM CONMAN
  ENTRY START
  EXIT X

NODE START
  CS, 'Welcome to CONMAN'

NODE GREET
  R2, 'Conference Management System ... '

NODE PROMPT
  R5, '$'

NODE HELP
  R$-2, 'Valid commands are ...'

NODE X
  R$, 'Byebye'

ARC START SKIP TO GREET

ARC GREET SKIP DO 1 TO PROMPT

ARC PROMPT
  ON <helper> TO HELP
  ON <invitation> TO <issue_invite>
  ON <receipt> TO <new_paper>
  ON <newreferee> TO <addref>
  ON <choose> TO <accept_paper>
  ON 'quit' DO 2 TO X
  ELSE DO 3 TO PROMPT

ARC <issue_invite>TO PROMPT

ARC <new_paper> TO PROMPT

ARC <addref> TO PROMPT

ARC <accept_paper> TO PROMPT


DIAGRAM receipt
  ENTRY START
  EXIT X

NODE START

NODE X

ARC START
  ON 'np','new paper','receive' TO X
```

Figure 6 -- Encoding of diagrams in Figure 5 for TDI

(7)  writeability -- providing a scheme that simplifies the process of expressing the specification, and encouraging its production

(8)  modifiability -- structuring the specification so that the system functions can be changed to fit changing user requirements

(9)  implementability -- determining that the system can be feasibly, i.e., within technological and economic boundaries, built

## TWO VIEWS OF A SPECIFICATION

The USE approach to specification attempts to address these goals and to provide for the diverse uses of the specification. We produce a *user view* and a *developer view* of the specification. Our model is depicted in Figure 7 and shows that the user view is intended for the computer-naive user while the developer view is intended for the computer-knowledgeable user.

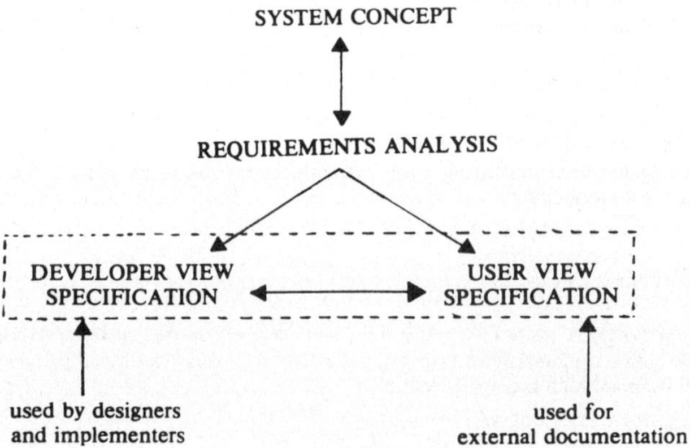


Figure 7. The USE model of specifications.

The *user view* specification is a detailed, but informal, description of the system function formulated by the developer working closely with the user. This informal description can serve as a contract between the developer and the users, and can also serve as the starting point for more formal specifications. It is often the case that more than one class of user will have access to a given information system, frequently with different privileges and operations. In such a case, it is necessary to specify a separate view for each user class.

The user view specification is aimed at meeting the specification goals of comprehensibility for the reader and completeness of the system description. It is written using the terminology of the application environment, reflecting the user's view of the problem.

The need for comprehensibility implies the need to impose some structure upon the user view specification. As we have seen, a system can typically be decomposed into a number of functions, which can in turn be decomposed into subfunctions, and so on. Such a hierarchical decomposition, combined with gradual refinement of the system requirements, is a particularly effective way to present the narrative portion of such a specification.

The *developer view* specification provides a view of the system functions for a computer-knowledgeable reader. It is intended to aid the system designers, and those who are responsible for testing and/or verifying the implemented system. This view defines a high level program structure, identifies program modules to the greatest extent possible, and shows the logical data flow between the modules. Note that there will frequently be a correspondence between the hierarchical decomposition achieved in the user view specification and the design view specification.

The developer view specification is used to aid the software designer in implementing the system, easing the transition between the specification and design phases of the software life cycle. This specification describes the behavior of the system and its modules without overly constraining the activities of the system designers and implementers, who fill in the detail and produce the algorithms and storage structures. The developer view is primarily addressed to the specification goals of implementability and consistency.

The developer view also concentrates on the correctness issues of the specification, making it possible to establish testing and verification procedures for the implemented system. The developer view uses a formal notation that is amenable to rigorous checking so that one may, in fact, prove formally or informally the correspondence between the specification and its realization.

The formal notations used for this view makes it possible to utilize automated aids for consistency checking. Names, value ranges, and module interfaces can all be checked from such a specification approach.

Thus, there is a balance between these views of a specification, intended to meet the diverse needs to which specifications are put. We are able to link the two views of the system to one another so that it is possible to achieve "traceability," linking the appropriate part of each specification view to the requirements.

## COMPONENTS OF THE IIS SPECIFICATION

Our discussion of interactive information systems to this point makes it clear that an IIS consists of three components: the user interface to the system, the operations upon the data objects, and the database used by the system. The USE specification method leads to a specification of each of these components. We have already seen the use of transition diagrams for specifying the user interface. We specify the database as a set of normalized relations.

There are several reasons for this decision:

(1)   Relations have a underlying mathematical theory and therefore support formal definition of systems for purposes of testing and verification;

(2)   Both procedural (algebra-like) and non-procedural (predicate calculus-like) operations are defined upon relations, so that one can precisely specify the data base operations in terms of the defined relations

(3)   The existence of several relational database management systems (including Troll) simplifies the implementation of prototype systems;

(4)   Relations are conceptually straightforward and users can easily understand their structure and use with minimal training.

(5)   Structured Systems Analysis leads to a set of relations, and we use the Semantic Hierarchy approach to data modelling to define a hierarchy of relations. Use of relations in the specification therefore simplifies the transition between analysis and specification.

For all of these reasons, then, relations seem to be the best method of specifying the content and structure of the database.

The relations for the IFIP Working Conference problem are shown in Figure 8. Note that each attribute has a defined domain showing the set of values that it may assume and that some of these domains are defined along with the relations themselves.

The final step of the specifications is to create a tie between the semantic actions of the transition diagrams and the operations on the data base. Each semantic action must be specified and the method of specification may be chosen from a variety of alternatives. Our preference is to use a narrative form for the user view specification, and then to use a more formal approach for the developer view specification. The specification language can include the semantic actions, including the data base operations.

The specification of the semantic actions in this way is a powerful tool for several reasons:

(1)   Each of the semantic actions is quite small, since it is associated with the traversal of a single arc of a transition diagram. Thus, an effective decomposition of the system is produced in this way.

(2)   One may continually rework the individual semantic actions, beginning with a prose description and proceeding through a specification language, a program design language, and finally code. Comparison and tracing from one stage of the software life cycle to another is simplified in this way.

(3)   The relational data base definition and the syntax of the paths on the transition diagram are extremely well suited to implementation in PLAIN, so that the transformation from the specification of an interactive information system to its realization in a PLAIN program is as straightforward as possible.

The user view and the developer view of the specifications for each semantic action are easily tied together, as it is possible to describe the user view with text, and then to provide the more precise formal specification as well.

The formal specification method that we have chosen to use is based on the axiomatic approach developed for Alphard [30] and extended to information systems by Leveson [31]. Leveson's methodology supports the specification and verification of information systems, and permits the enforcement of semantic integrity constraints on a data base. The formal specification, termed an operational specification, gives a description of the *behavior* of the system, including a complete description of the semantics. The semantics include the names of the objects, the operations defined on each object, and the effect of each operation.

```
domain paperrange: integer (1..100);

domain sessionrange: integer (1..30);

domain weekday: scalar (Mon, Tue, Wed, Thu, Fri);

domain clock: integer (800..2000);

domain date: integer (0..3112);

domain money: float (0.00..200.00);

domain paperstatus: scalar (received, inreview, accepted, insession, rejected);

domain person: string;


relation accepted_papers [key paperno] of
    paperno: paperrange;
    title: string;
    sessionnum: sessionrange;
end;

relation attendance [key name] of
    name: person;
    amtpaid: money;
end;

relation author_list [key name, paperno] of
    name: person;
    paperno: paperrange;
end;

relation mailing_list [key name] of
    name: person;
    affiliation: string;
    detail_address: string;
    postcode: string;
    city: string;
    country: string;
end;

relation papers [key paperno] of
    paperno: paperrange;
    title: string;
    resp_pc_member: person;
    status: paperstatus;
end;

relation pc_list [key name] of
    name: person;
    papercount: integer (0..10);  {no PC member handles more than 10 papers}
end;

relation priority_list [key name] of
    name: person;
    role: string;
end;
```

**Figure 8 -- Relational database design for IFIP Working Conference problem**

```
    relation referee_list [key name] of
        name: person;
        number_assigned: integer (0..6);  {limit on papers to be refereed}
    end;

    relation reviewing [key refname, paperno] of
        refname: person;
        paperno: paperrange;
        datesent: date;
        dateofreply: date;
    end;

    relation sessions [key sessionnumber] of
        sessionnumber: sessionrange;
        title: string;
        timeslot: sessionrange;
    end;

    relation session_chair [key sessionnumber] of
        sessionnumber: sessionrange;
        chairman: person;
    end;

    relation times [key timeslot, room] of
        timeslot: sessionrange;
        room: string;
        day: weekday;
        starttime: clock;
    end;
```

Figure 8 (cont.) -- Relational database design for IFIP Working Conference problem

The notions of data abstraction are used to define the objects, so that the permissible operations are defined upon each object.  As with a narrative text description of the semantics, there is no statement of *how* the operations will actually be carried out, but only a description of *what* will be done.

The formal development methodology, called **BASIS** (Behavioral Approach to the Specification of Information Systems), includes a semantic integrity specification consisting of three parts: the abstract image, the invariant, and input and output constraints for each operation defined on the abstract object.  In the context of the IFIP Working Conference problem, objects include paper, referee, session, and author.

In Figure 9, we show part of the BASIS specification for the abstract object paper.

The operations defined on the object paper shows that the specification must include not only creation and updating operations, but also retrieval operations, including those that permit access to individual pieces of an abstract object.

If we consider the operation "assign_paper_to_session", we can identify some pre-conditions on the operation, including:

-- the paper has been accepted
-- the paper has not already been assigned to another session
-- the session does not have more than some maximum number of papers

Postconditions might specify:

-- the session is noted as containing that paper
-- the paper is noted as having been assigned to a session

The specification of the object session is not shown here, but one can see that its abstract image contains such things as a session chairman, a set of papers, a time slot, and a location.  Furthermore, it has an abstract invariant requiring that the cardinality of the set of papers for a given session is less than some defined constant **MAXPAPERS**.

```
object paper
    abstract image
        title: text
            authors: set of author
            status: paperstatus
            paperno: 1..300
    abstract invariant

    operations
        receive_paper (papertitle: text, submitters: set of authors) returns p:paper
            post
                        title  = papertitle
                        authors  = submitters
                        status  = received
                        paperno  = cardinality (paper)
        review_paper (p:paper)
            pre p.status  = received
            post p.status  = inreview
        accept_paper (p: paper)
            pre p.status  = inreview
            post p.status  = accepted
        assign_paper_to_session (p:paper, s: session)
            pre p.status  = accepted  & s.papercount < MAXPAPERS
            post p.status  = insession
        reject_paper (p: paper)
            pre p.status  = inreview
            post p.status  = rejected
        accepted? (p: paper) returns b: boolean
            post b  = (p.status  = accepted | p.status  = insession)
        change_paper_title (newtitle: text, p: paper)
            post p.title  = newtitle
        change_authorship (newauthors: set of authors, p:paper)
            post p.authors  = newauthors
```

Figure 9 -- Specification of the object "paper"

The preconditions, postconditions, and invariants make it possible to enforce integrity constraints, a set of rules that determine which configurations of the data base are reasonable. There are two major types of semantic invariants: value constraints and inter-object constraints. The value constraints are the set of legal values of instances of the object. We have already seen how the domain definitions of our relations above serve to enforce value constraints.

The inter-object constraints define constraints on the relationships allowed between objects. An example of an inter-object constraint in the IFIP Conference problem is that no paper may be assigned to more than one session. As another example, a particular conference organizing committee could impose the constraint that no person who is a member of the Programme Committee shall be the author of a paper.

In order to prevent integrity violations, it is necessary that all operations defined on the abstract objects preserve the invariants. Integrity problems can arise from faulty operations or from illegal sequences of legal operations. The preconditions are aimed at eliminating illegal sequences of operations, and verification techniques can be used to show the truth of the postconditions. Furthermore, these preconditions, postconditions, and invariants may be implemented with type definitions and assertions in the programming language PLAIN.

The formal specifications for "assign_paper_to_session" would be used in conjunction with a narrative description of the operation, which would be as follows:

> "An accepted paper should be assigned to one and only one session. An effort should be made to place the paper in a session dealing with the major theme of the paper. The paper should not be assigned to a session that already has a full set of papers."

The definition of the abstract objects and operations normally occurs as part of the analysis process, with the specification of the invariants, preconditions, and postconditions being developed as part of the specification process. Each abstract operation can usually be associated with part or all of an action in a transition diagram, thereby providing the formal component of the specification of system operations.

This association can be accomplished most effectively by relating the "data stores" identified through Structured Systems Analysis or the "database abstractions" of the Semantic Hierarchy Model to the abstract objects of the BASIS approach.

## STRUCTURE OF THE COMPLETE SPECIFICATION

The dialogue design, the database design, and the formal and informal approaches to description of the operations are united in the complete specification. The specification consists of:

(1)   a set of transition diagrams, representing the entire dialogue, with brief descriptions of the actions

(2)   the database specified as a set of normalized relations

(3)   the operations, with each operation linked to the diagram and action number, and described both formally and informally.

The specification of the operations may be seen in the IFIP Conference example. Figure 5 includes a subconversation new_paper. Within the diagram for new_paper (not shown), there is a subconversation select_refs. The diagram select_refs is shown as Figure 10, and the operations are shown as Figure 11.

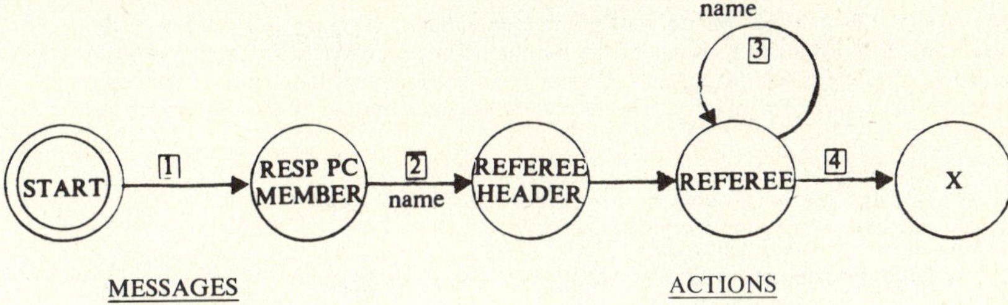


MESSAGES

START = 'CONMAN - New paper processing'

RESP_PC_MEMBER = 'Name of responsible
    'Program Committee member'

REFEREE_HEADER = 'Referee selection for'
    'paper number', paper_no,
    'Title: ', title,
    'Please select at least three referees'
    'Type one referee name on each line,
    'ending with an empty line'

REFEREE = 'Referee name: '

X = countrefs, ' referees assigned'
    'Paper ', paper_no, ' in review'

ACTIONS

[1] Display paper title and authors; countrefs := 0

[2] Verify Program Committee member name; store Program Committee name with paper

[3] Verify referee name; increment number_assigned for that referee; associate referee with paper; enter date sent; increment countrefs

[4] Verify sufficient number of referees; paperstatus := inreview

Figure 10 -- Transition diagram for select_refs subconversation

Note that the operation is given a name, in this case "Assign_referees", and that the name is linked to an action in the transition diagram, in this case action 3 of select_refs. In a complete specification document, the action items in the transition diagram can include a reference to the page where the operation is described.

The name of the operation is subsequently used in module design and implementation, and is entered into the development dictionary that supports the project. This consistency of name usage is valuable in validating the eventual source code module against the specification.

We have found the discipline of the formal specification to be extremely helpful as another way of looking at the problem, and have seen that it helps in defining database attributes and the necessary checks that must be made to assure integrity of the operations.

In summary, then, our specification includes the user/program dialogue, shown with transition diagrams including the semantic actions, the data base design, expressed as a set of normalized relations with domain definitions, and the operations, shown in both narrative text and, where appropriate, with a formal specification based on axioms and verification conditions.

Note that the dialogue serves to determine the operations that can be performed by a given user. With reasonable kinds of login and database authorization mechanisms, this predetermination of operations is extremely valuable for protection and security of the IIS. Furthermore, this process of enumerating operations, combined with the specification of the relations in the database, makes it possible for the system designer to define relations and secondary indexes upon those relations that make the most critical operations execute efficiently.

This complete specification then serves as the basis for system design and implementation, as well as for user/customer approval. In the past, we have found this specification technique (even in the absence of the formal specification part) to be satisfactory for this purpose and have used it to specify several medical information systems [32].

*operation* select_refs [3]

*name* Assign_referee (p: paper)

*informal*

> Assign_referee prompts the user to assign a referee name r, checking the validity of the referee name and maintaining counts of the number of papers handled by the referee and the number of referees for the paper p. Assign_referee also enters the date that the paper was sent to the referee for review. The referee should not be one of the authors of the paper.

*formal*

> **pre** p.countrefs $>$ = 0 & p.countrefs $<$ MAXREFS
>     & r.number_assigned $<$ MAXPAPERS
>
> **post** is_referee (r,p) & p.countrefs' = p.countrefs + 1
>     & date_sent (r,p) = [today's date] & ˜(r.name **in** p.authors)

Figure 11 -- Operation "Assign_referees" from select_refs subconversation

## RAPID CONSTRUCTION OF PARTIAL SYSTEMS

Even with this specification technique, though, we had the impression that the written specification alone was not sufficient for complete understanding by computer-naive users. We sensed that this was particularly true with respect to completeness of IIS functions, and that there was a strong chance that useful functions would be omitted.

Also, we wanted to be able to produce more realistic messages as sample output when users worked with the TDI. Although, it is possible to program all of the system through the action part of the TDI input, the intended use of the TDI was to simulate the user/program dialogue and not to perform the functions. We normally created some fixed messages that would be typical of the expected system output, which could be output as actions associated with the traversal of a path on the transition diagram. Although this approach is an adequate first approximation to reality, it doesn't provide any useful function for the user.

However, since many of the IIS operations involve access to and modification of data in a database, it is possible to provide this desired functionality by using the TDI in conjunction with a database management system. As noted above, one can add functionality to the TDI by providing those functions as actions in the TDI; these actions can be *any* program that the user of the TDI is allowed to execute. By writing actions that call a database management system, it becomes possible to store either actual or typical data in the database so that the user input can cause actual operations to be performed. In that way, a realistic partial system can be created.

The high-level data definition and manipulation facilities provided by the Troll relational database management system in the USE environment makes it possible to achieve this objective quite easily. The relations defined in the database design stage of the specification can be defined for the database, and data may be added as part of initial experimentation with the system.

The basic mechanism for constructing these systems consists of two tools, TDI and Troll, connected via the Unix pipe mechanism, which permits the output of one process to be given directly as input to another process. The prototype construction tool uses two such pipes, one as input from TDI to Troll and another as output from Troll to TDI. This organization is shown in Figure 12.

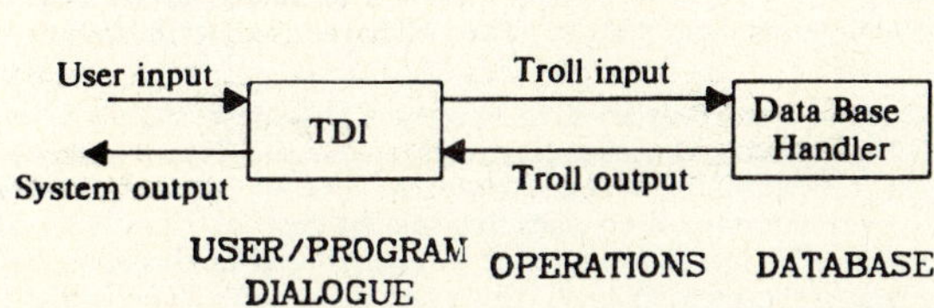


Figure 12. Organization of functional prototype system

The database manipulation facilities in Troll are similar to those of the relational algebra, and include:

(1)  Formation of data base expressions using the following relational algebra-like operations:

-selection of a set of tuples satisfying a certain constraint

-projection on some attributes

-joining two relations on attributes of the same type

-set operations: union, intersection, and difference

(2)  Assignment of a data base expression to a variable

(3)  Individual tuple operations: - associative access using key-attribute values - insertion/deletion of tuples - modification of non-key attribute values

(4)  Iteration through the set of tuples with a foreach clause

(5)  Aggregation operations count, sum, min, max, and avg

Troll also provides some transaction support, including the ability to back out of an unsuccessful transaction. These operations, along with some examples, are described further in Reference 33.

Although many system functions can be performed with nothing more than the parsing of TDI and the database management of Troll, it is necessary to provide additional programming facilities to take advantage of the full power of TDI. Accordingly, we created the tool RAPID (RApid Prototypes of Interactive Dialogues) that integrates TDI, Troll, and routines written in one of several different programming languages (C, Fortran 77, Pascal, and PLAIN). In this way, the actions of the TDI can be programmed in the Troll data manipulation language *and* in some other procedural programming language. Thus, with RAPID, one can truly construct a fully functional IIS, providing all of the functions specified for the system.

The ability to perform IIS functions has several significant advantages over the non-functional approach:

1.  it permits a rapid implementation of a significant portion of the IIS specification with tools that provide a close match to the specification method itself

2.  it allows the database design to be evaluated experimentally in much the same way as the dialogue is evaluated, using a prototype database design as the first step in the design of the production version of the database schema

3.  it can give the user a far more accurate picture of the actual behavior of the production system

4.  it can serve as a workable system version while the production version is being designed, implemented, and tested.  (Indeed, if one creates a complete working prototype system with these tools, it may obviate the need to construct a production version of the system in some cases.)

An important difference between this prototype method and the rapid construction of systems using a programming system such as MUMPS is that these tools are *non-procedural* and that one must only do "programming" for the database manipulation operations. Furthermore, the partial system is primarily constructed from thoroughly tested components, the TDI and Troll, thereby reducing the number of errors that one would normally expect to find in a preliminary version of a system.

One potential disadvantage with the functional prototype scheme is that the user may not understand the reasons for proceeding with a carefully designed and systematically implemented production version which can perform the complete set of integrity checks, provide more extensive diagnostics and online assistance, and optimize the format of system output.

An associated potential disadvantage is that too much effort might be put into the prototype construction effort, to the point of diminishing returns. There appears to be a limit at which the effort to provide functions with RAPID exceeds the additional benefits to be gained. The developer must recall that the goal is only to build a preliminary version and not a production version, with the intent of aiding the user in evaluating the suitability of the specification.

Our feeling is that use of linkage with other programming languages should be sharply limited and that the partial versions built using RAPID should rely almost exclusively on TDI and Troll. However, we do not yet have sufficient experience with the combined use of these tools, so that we cannot determine the extent to which they are an improvement over interface prototypes for the purpose of identifying necessary system functions. Because we have used the USE methodology prior to the addition of this step, we are certain that functional prototypes are not *essential* to the methodology. However, we strongly believe that they will provide a significant advantage for the user and the developer, particularly for larger systems and for those applications being automated for the first time.

The use of the TDI with Troll may be seen for the IFIP Working Conference example. We may assume that the relations defined above are stored in a database named conference. Following standard Troll practice, comments are enclosed in braces.

We shall show the Troll script that carries out the operation named "Assign_referee". Troll scripts can be seen as transactions that may be parameterized and invoked with a **call** statement. Thus, one could invoke the script with the statement

    **call** Assign_referee (name, paper_no, today)

The parameter notation is positional. Within the Troll script, $0 serves as the formal parameter for name, $1 for paper_no, and $2 for today.

```
{assign_referee}
open conference;
import referee_list;
import reviewing;
{preliminary version -- omit checks on number of papers assigned
and on self-refereeing}
if ~exists (referee_list [$0]) then
        begin print 'Unknown referee name'; end
        else  {valid referee name}
        begin
                referee_list [$0].number_assigned := referee_list [$0].number_assigned +1;
                insert reviewing [$0,$1,$2];
        end;
export referee_list, reviewing;
quit;
```

This Troll script will operate upon the relational database subschema defined above, and may be modified and enhanced to perform some of the additional checking specified for the Assign_referee operation.

It can be seen that the various specified operations for the Program Committee can be provided in a similar fashion and that the TDI input, containing the appropriate set of calls, along with the Troll scripts, can be used to build a preliminary version of the Conference Management System.

## ARCHITECTURAL AND DETAILED DESIGN

The specification is followed by two stages of design, termed architectural design and detailed design. The process of design involves developing a program structure and logic that describes *how* to build the system described in the specification subject to any stated constraints. The stage of architectural design involves the creation of an overall program structure and the logical data design. This stage leads to the decomposition of the system into a set of modules with well-defined input and output interfaces and accurately specified functions.

The stage of detailed design involves working out the details of the logic for each module, as well as performing any further needed refinements on the data design. After these design steps have been completed and reviewed, the implementation can be undertaken.

Design may be treated as an implicit part of the specification process or as an explicit phase of the overall system development process. Although we follow the latter approach, it is clear that much of the work in system decomposition and data base design has been carried forth as part of the system specification activity.

The process of architectural design is extremely straightforward in the USE methodology, since much of the necessary work has been accomplished at earlier stages. We follow the general ideas of Structured Design [34], constructing a structure chart to show the overall design. It is normally quite easy to construct the top levels of the structure charts, since the top level of the transition diagram maps almost directly into the transaction model of Structured Design. Alternatively, one could create a structure chart from the SSA Data Flow Diagrams, but that approach seems to be less effective for us, since it tends to obscure the interactive nature of the system.

The major contribution of the structure chart is that it makes the program structure and the module interconnections explicit. We feel, though, that Structured Design is not ideal for our purposes, since it is relatively weak for showing operations on databases. However, the strengths of the method seem to outweigh the weaknesses, particularly since our design is quite apparent from the specification. We would like to improve or extend the structure chart approach, though, to cover the database aspects of architectural design more completely.

In the IFIP Conference problem, we decided to create two separate programs, one for the Program Committee Chairman and one for the Organizing Committee Chairman, using a shared database. We could alternatively have made a single program, using login information to determine the user class, and hence the appropriate dialogue. We decided that the two program approach was more realistic, given the fact that the Program Committee Chairman and the Organizing Committee Chairman are generally at different sites.

We also noted that the relations could be split quite well between the two different programs, and that the amount of sharing was very limited, with only the relation mailing_list being subject to update by both chairmen. The relations pc_list, author_list, papers, referee_list, reviewing, accepted_papers, sessions, session_chair, and times are all created and updated by the Program Committee Chairman, while relations organizers and attendance are exclusively modified by the Organizing Committee Chairman. In addition, the relations are extremely stable, with very few modifications, so that it would be feasible to transfer information between two separate programs running on two different machines at low frequency and at low speed, perhaps even by magnetic tape through the mail. (Indeed, the amount of activity for this problem is sufficiently low that it is probably not economically feasible to design and implement an IIS for conferences the size of the IFIP Working Conferences.)

The top levels of the structure chart for the Program Committee Chairman are shown in Figure 13.

The USE approach to detailed design is to use a program design language, similar to that described by Caine and Gordon [35]. A program design language may be viewed as a "very-high-level" programming language, intended to express the logic of a program module in narrative form, following a format that makes them easily comprehensible to other designers. Program design languages have been widely used with great success as a means of describing the detailed logic of a module, and we have likewise had excellent experience with this approach, finding it preferable to structured flowcharts, and far superior to traditional flowcharts. We especially value the fact that program design languages involve linear text, making them machine processable and easily readable.

These characteristics of program design languages are particularly useful for a methodology, since they improve teamwork by making it possible for developers to gain access to everyone's detailed design information as needed and by greatly simplifying the problem of reviewing designs in a structured walkthrough [36].

Because PLAIN is the implementation language of the USE methodology, we have adapted the program design language notation slightly to take advantage of certain features of PLAIN. The major differences between the Caine/Gordon program design language and the USE Design Language are the following:

(1)   Data modules are permitted in addition to procedure modules.  In that way, it is possible to incorporate data abstraction more effectively at the detailed design stage, since it is present at both the specification and implementation stages.

(2)   Each UDL module contains a list of the modules that it calls, as well as a list of the modules that call it.

(3)   All data objects must have their data types defined.

(4)   Each UDL module provides for an *exception* part, showing the exceptional conditions that can arise in the execution of the module

(5)   The control structures of the *algorithm* section reflect those of PLAIN, rather than PL/1, as was the case in the Caine/Gordon version.

Program design language is written for each module defined in the structure chart, carrying along the module name and the function description.  We are also able to include the calling tree information from the structure chart, along with the input and output information for each module.  We have found the use of this information to be of great assistance in tracing backward from the detailed design to the architectural design in checking our design documents.  Further checking may be performed by comparing the module with the specification of that module.

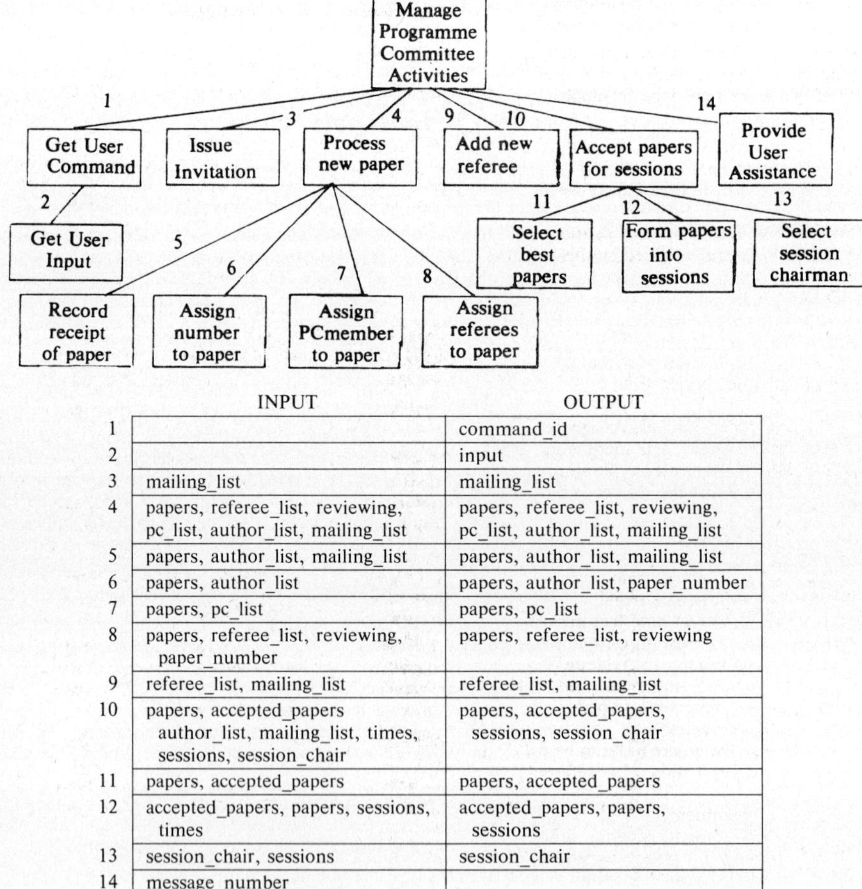


|    | INPUT | OUTPUT |
|----|-------|--------|
| 1  |  | command_id |
| 2  |  | input |
| 3  | mailing_list | mailing_list |
| 4  | papers, referee_list, reviewing, pc_list, author_list, mailing_list | papers, referee_list, reviewing, pc_list, author_list, mailing_list |
| 5  | papers, author_list, mailing_list | papers, author_list, mailing_list |
| 6  | papers, author_list | papers, author_list, paper_number |
| 7  | papers, pc_list | papers, pc_list |
| 8  | papers, referee_list, reviewing, paper_number | papers, referee_list, reviewing |
| 9  | referee_list, mailing_list | referee_list, mailing_list |
| 10 | papers, accepted_papers author_list, mailing_list, times, sessions, session_chair | papers, accepted_papers, sessions, session_chair |
| 11 | papers, accepted_papers | papers, accepted_papers |
| 12 | accepted_papers, papers, sessions, times | accepted_papers, papers, sessions |
| 13 | session_chair, sessions | session_chair |
| 14 | message_number |  |

Figure 13 -- Partial Structure Chart for Program Committee system

The detailed design process also provides an additional measure of module size. At the architectural design stage, we expect that the function of a module can be described in one or two declarative sentences, and use that informal rule of thumb as one basis for splitting modules or modifying the design in some other way. At the detailed design stage, though, we begin to be concerned about the eventual size of each module in lines of code. Because we hope to limit the executable code for each module to 60 lines (one page listing), we try to limit the number of lines in the program design language listing of the algorithm to 20. If the detailed design logic for the module exceeds 20 lines, it is likely that the implemented module will be too large, so we attempt to split the module into two or more modules, revising the architectural design as necessary.

The architectural and detailed designs are each reviewed in walkthroughs to try to find and then correct design errors, since the cost of finding errors at the design stage is far lower than finding and correcting them at a later stage. Our experience is that we review the highest three levels of the structure chart most closely at the architectural design stage, and that we are more selective about reviewing modules at the detailed design level. One approach that we have used successfully for selecting modules for review of the detailed design is to ask designers to each select about 20% of their modules for review, giving preference to those that were difficult to design, or critical in terms of execution speed, space utilization, or user interface. If an inordinate number of problems are found in a designer's work, then we will review additional modules designed by that individual. The detailed design for the Assign_referees module is shown in Figure 14. The end result of the design activity is the production of a *representation* of the system in a form that simplifies implementation.

We are planning to build a checker to analyze the USE Design Language for all of the modules in an IIS. This tool would be of help in checking the interface descriptions, building data dictionaries, and in building calling trees, all of which are now done manually.

```
MODULE Assign_referee
INPUT
    paper_no: paperrange;
    papers, author_list, referee_list, reviewing: relation;
OUTPUT
    papers, referee_list, reviewing: relation;
        {all three relations modified by this module}
CALLS
CALLED BY
    new_paper
LOCAL DATA
    input: string;  {user input of name(s)}
    temp: marking on author_list;
FUNCTION
    For the given paper number, Assign_referee prompts the user to assign
    a referee for the paper.  The module increments the count of
    papers assigned to the referee, limiting the number of papers to six,
    and checks to see that the referee is not an author of the paper.
ALGORITHM
    write 'Referee name: '
    read input;
        Check to see if referee name is in referee_list;
        if not, ask for alternate name.
        {***Design problem: note that minor misspellings of
         referee names or use of last name only may fail to
         find name in referee_list relation***}
    if referee_list[input].number_assigned < 6 then
    referee_list[input].number_assigned := referee_list[input].number_assigned + 1;
    {check for self-refereeing}
    temp := author_list where paperno = paper_no & name = input;
    if count (temp) ~= 0 then reject referee name;

    {OK to make assignment}
    insert reviewing [<input, paperno, today>];
    {the variable today is a system variable with a representation of the current date}
    papers [paper_no].status := inreview;
    else reject referee name;
EXCEPTIONS
END MODULE
```

Figure 14 -- Program design language for "Assign Referee" module

## AN INTRODUCTION TO PLAIN

The implementation language of the USE methodology is PLAIN, which was designed specifically to meet the requirements for constructing interactive information systems. PLAIN was the first of the USE tools to be designed, and the design was carried out in parallel with the design of many other programming languages, including CLU [37], Alphard [30], Gypsy [38], Euclid [39], and Ada [40]. Of these languages, though, only PLAIN addresses the application area of interactive programs and their need for database management facilities.

From the outset, the contribution was seen to be not so much the introduction of new language features, but rather a synthesis of features whose *interrelationships* would lead to a useful tool for such application programs. The approach was to make innovations to support interactive programs and to adhere closely to well-understood approaches for other features.

The design goals of PLAIN fall into two categories: those that support systematic programming practices, and those that support the creation of interactive programs. In practice, these goals mesh in the process of language design, but can be separated when examining the design philosophy.

The design goals for systematic programming were:

(1)   Support for procedural and data abstraction

(2)   Support for modularity

(3)   Control structures to encourage linear flow of control within modules

(4)   Visibility of data flow and data use

(5)   Prevention of self-modifying programs

(6)   Program readability

(7)   Limited language size

Many of the features of PLAIN with respect to systematic programming are derived from Pascal. These goals, and the way that they are addressed in PLAIN, are explained at greater length in Reference 41.

The design goals for supporting the construction of interactive programs were:

(1)   Features for data base management -- the language must deal with data bases and with operations performed on data bases, as well as with more primitive file concepts

(2)   Support for strings and string-handling -- interactive programs involve large amounts of text processing, particularly user-program dialogue

(3)   Facilities for exception-handling -- user errors must be expected, but the user should not be adversely affected

(4)   Availability of a rudimentary pattern specification and matching facility -- many interactive programs depend on a specific text pattern, e.g., a command, to determine program action

(5)   Appropriate input/output features

(6)   Rudimentary timing facilities

With these features, PLAIN programs could be made resilient to user errors, could simplify user interaction with large data bases, and could be made flexible in handling diverse forms of user input. Unlike the case with the systematic programming goals, there were few, if any, languages that had developed a satisfactory solution for achieving the goals for reliable interactive programs. Accordingly, much of the design effort went into the design of features for string handling, exception handling, pattern-matching, and relational data base management.

We now briefly sketch the features of PLAIN that explicitly support interactive programs. The complete language definition is presented in the Revised Report [42].

### Data Base Management in PLAIN

A complete set of relational data base management facilities are part of PLAIN. A relation is a built-in data type, and may be seen as a set of records whose storage persistence is separate from the execution time of the programs accessing them. Relations from one or more data bases may be imported into the execution environment of a PLAIN program to perform the desired data base management operations.

One can routinely create and manipulate relations in PLAIN programs. The data base operations in PLAIN are aimed at providing the programmer with some control over the sequence of data base operations, and therefore at incorporating a set of features that permit the programmer to improve the efficiency of the program's database management [43].

The data base management facilities of PLAIN are those that are incorporated into Troll as described above, including the definition of domains and relations, a relational algebra-like set of operations for relational level operations, tuple processing with the *for each* loop, and item level insertions and modifications.

The Troll interface and the associated PLAIN Data Base Handler were in fact designed and built as part of the PLAIN runtime support system. Thus, the syntax of Troll was strongly influenced by the syntax of the PLAIN data definition and management facilities. We made the decision to separate the Data Base Handler from the remainder of the PLAIN runtime support system, and that decision has made it possible to use the Data Base Handler in conjunction with TDI (as shown above), in conjunction with other programming languages, and as a standalone database management system.

**String Handling in PLAIN**

The key decision in the inclusion of string handling facilities was to permit the generalized use of variable length strings as well as the more traditional use of fixed length strings. It is permissible in PLAIN to declare a variable of type string, with no stated maximum length: as in Pascal, it is also permissible to declare arrays of characters for those instances where the variable-length facility is not needed.

Additional operators and functions were provided to support the use of this data type. The binary operations of concatenation, string, contains, and string follows (lexical ordering) were introduced, along with functions for string insertion, removal, replacement, and extraction. It is also possible to convert between fixed and variable length strings.

The decision to permit variable length strings, with the necessary implementation overhead associated with heap management, was based on the assumption that string processing would not represent a significant bottleneck in PLAIN programs. Instead, it was felt that most of the execution time would be spent either carrying out database and input/output operations involving secondary storage devices, or in waiting for use input. This decision also made it possible to generalize the Pascal array declaration facility to allow dynamic array (using the same heap management) declarations, thereby overcoming a common criticism of Pascal.

**Exception Handling in PLAIN**

Events that occur during the execution of a program may cause an exception to be raised as the result of an exceptional condition, such as an arithmetic overflow. Without explicitly handling these exceptions, a program may fail. The interactive user finds such failures to be extremely undesirable, since they may cause the user to lose some work. Instead, it is necessary to handle such situations gracefully. PLAIN incorporates built-in exceptions and permits the programmer to define additional exceptions. All exceptions may be raised by using a signal statement, and the built-in exceptions may be raised automatically by the run-time system.

When an exception is raised, an exception handler is invoked. This handler is a PLAIN procedure, to which parameters may be passed. The handler may clear the active exception and provide for continued program execution, may clear the exception and provide for repetition of the statement that caused the exception to be raised, may notify the invoker of the module that received the exception signal, or may cause the program for fail.

The exception-handling mechanism makes it possible to trap exceptional conditions and to take actions that can prevent situations that may be harmful to the user. In short, it is possible to write extremely robust programs, capable of dealing with virtually every type of user or software error situation. This exception-handling scheme is described at greater length in Reference 44.

**Pattern Specification and Matching**

The pattern matching facility of PLAIN permits patterns and pattern sets to be declared and used. Pattern matching operators are provided, along with pattern-directed input/output. The pattern declaration facility consists of patterns that are composed of string literals, pattern codes, repetition code, other pattern names, and pattern sets, each consisting of one or more patterns. The pattern codes designate commonly used groupings of characters, such as alphabetic characters or digits. Each pattern code (or group of pattern codes) is preceded by a repetition code, which may be definite or indefinite (O or more, 1 or more). Pattern specifications are static, similar to those of MUMPS, and unlike the dynamic pattern specifications of SNOBOL4.

The binary pattern matching operators "?=" and "?" test a string to determine if it conforms to a pattern. The keywords match and contains are available for pattern sets to determine if a string matches any pattern in a pattern set. In each case, the former operation tests for an exact match between the target string and the pattern, while the latter looks for any occurrence of the pattern in the string.

The programmer may specify any context-free grammar using the facility. Thus, in the construction of an interactive information system, all of the valid user inputs, such as command strings, may be specified in patterns, and the user input string may be compared with various patterns, with appropriate action taken depending on the success of the string pattern match. The pattern-matching and string handling features of PLAIN are described more completely in Reference 45.

## INTERACTIVE SYSTEMS IN PLAIN

It is really the synthesis of these features, rather than any one of them alone, that makes PLAIN a powerful tool for the construction of interactive information systems. For example, relations can be used as the representation mechanism in the declaration of a module (which provides data abstraction facilities) to permit the encapsulation of a set of data base operations that might correspond to a "transaction."

As a more compelling example, consider the scenario of a user of an interactive information system.

(1)   The user repeatedly types some input, e.g., a command.

(2)   This input is decoded and parsed; if it is incorrect, a diagnostic message is presented to the user, who then provides alternate input;

(3)   The input is subjected to various semantic checks, which may also produce diagnostic messages;

(4)   If the input is validated, then some program action is taken, typically an access to or modification of some item(s) in a database, during which time output messages may be provided to the user.

In general, the main program is a loop that reads user input, branches according to the input, calling the appropriate procedures, and terminating if and when the user issues the command to quit. The legal syntax for the various commands are each specified as patterns, and the patterns are collected into a pattern set. The user input is matched against the pattern set to branch to the appropriate case, including the "illegal command" case. The procedures that are thereby invoked contain data base operations using the data management facilities PLAIN. Any execution time errors result in the signalling of an exception, so that a handler procedure can handle the exceptional condition without causing the program to crash, instead generating an appropriate message and carrying out any necessary recovery activities.

The main program for the Program Committee Chairman is typical of the main program for interactive systems of this nature, and is shown in Figure 15.

```
program conmanpc;
external
     {declare relations with attributes that are used by conmanpc}
     {these are relations accepted_papers, author_list, mailing_list,
      papers, pc_list, referee_list, reviewing, sessions,
      session_chair, and times}
     {declarations follow those of Figure 8}
var input: string;
     {other global declarations, including exceptions}
pattern cmdset = [invitation, receipt, newreferee, choose, helper, finish];
      invitation = ['i','invite'];
      receipt = ['np','new paper','receive'];
      newreferee = ['nr','referee','add ref'];
      choose = ['a','accept','select'];
      helper = ['h','help','?','H','HELP'];
      finish = ['q','quit','Q', 'QUIT'];
begin
   write 'Welcome to CONMAN', \n;
   loop
     write '$'; {prompt symbol}
     read input ![ioerr: abort]; {terminate on hardware I/O error}
     case cmdset match input of
        when invitation: issue_invite;
        when receipt: new_paper;
        when newreferee: add_ref;
        when choose: accept_paper;
        when helper: first_aid (1);
        when quit: exit;
        when others: write 'illegal command' {pattern match failed}
     end case;
   repeat;
   write 'Byebye'
end conmanpc.
```

Figure 15.  PLAIN main program for conmanpc

It is important to note the correspondence between the PLAIN code and the specification for the system. If one compares the code in Figure 15 with the transition diagram of Figure 5, one can observe the mapping:

(1)    a diagram name given on an arc (permitting several different inputs to cause a transition) is represented as a pattern set, where the different possible inputs are the elements of the set

(2)    these diagram names are also the case branches in the main program loop

(3)    the procedures invoked as a result of the case branches have the same names as the subconversations that result from traversing the appropriate arc in the transition diagram

(4)    the output messages correspond to the messages in the transition diagram

Thus, it is often possible to go directly from the USE specification to a PLAIN program, since the design is apparent.  Consistent use of the transaction approach in the transition diagrams and PLAIN make the architectural design step trivial.  Similarly, if one has used RAPID to build a partial system, many of the problems of detailed design have been handled as well.  As a result, we are presently examining the feasibility of a limited form of "automatic programming," based upon design of a USE specification language, leading to generation of code in PLAIN.

The program design language segment shown in Figure 14 also converts almost directly into PLAIN.  The major difference is in the procedure heading, which is shown in PLAIN in Figure 16.

```
procedure Assign_referee (paper_no: paperrange);
imports referee_list, reviewing: modified;
     author_list, MAXREFS, MAXPAPERS: readonly;
var
  input: string;
  countrefs: integer;
  temp1: marking on reviewing;
  temp2: marking on author_list;
handler badname;
begin
  write 'Unknown referee name. Please try again.';
  retry
end badname;

begin {Assign_referee}
  {check number of referees for paper}
  temp1 := reviewing where paperno = paper_no;
  countrefs := count (temp1);
  assert countrefs < MAXREFS; {precondition}
  write 'Referee name: ';
  read input;
  referee_list% := referee_list [input] ![undefined: badname];
  {undefined exception will be raised if input name is not good;
  if referee_list%.number_assigned > = MAXPAPERS
    then write 'Referee has too many papers.  Try again.'
    else
      {check for self refereeing}
      temp2 := author_list where paperno = paper_no & input = name;
      if count (temp) ~= 0
        then write 'Author cannot serve as referee.'
        else
          referee_list%.number_assigned := referee_list%.number_assigned +1;
          reviewing :+ [<input, paper_no, today>];
          {insertion not made if input and paper_no are duplicates
           so that a referee cannot be assigned twice to the same paper}
          temp1 := reviewing where paperno = paper_no;
          assert count (temp1) = countrefs + 1 &
             exists (reviewing [input, paper_no]); {postcondition}
      end if
  end if
end Assign_referee;
```

Figure 16. Assign_referee procedure in PLAIN

The PLAIN facilities for string handling, pattern matching, exception handling, and data base management make it quite straightforward to write programs that conform to this extremely common scenario. This reason is why PLAIN was designed: to provide the application programmer with an appropriate tool for this important class of software systems. This is not to say that PLAIN is not well suited for other kinds of applications, but simply to observe that PLAIN is addressed to a type of application that is not well treated by other programming languages.

## THE USE DEVELOPMENT ENVIRONMENT

As we have noted, the USE methodology is a collection of methods and automated tools for the design and development of interactive information systems. To this point, we have focused on the sequence of steps involved in going from the problem definition to system implementation in a procedural programming language, and have described some of the significant characteristics of some of our tools. We now turn to the *software development environment* in which systems are designed and implemented in the USE methodology. As before, we shall omit any further discussion of human factors, and concentrate on the collection of tools available to the IIS development organization.

We began by selecting Unix as the best possible existing software support system for the USE methodology. Unix was selected for several reasons, including the following:

1. It was developed to run on small systems, and variants of Unix, Mini-Unix and LSX [46], had been developed to run on even smaller systems.

2. Unix already possessed a good collection of tools that would assist not only the eventual application developer, but would also assist in the construction of the USE tools. Among the most useful of the Unix tools for our purposes are:
   a) the text editor (ex), with the vi option to provide full-screen editing;
   b) the nroff and troff formatting programs, for typewritten and phototypeset output respectively
   c) the tbl program for producing tables, and usable with both nroff and troff
   d) macro packages (me and ms) to simplify the formatting of text, and to permit the standardized formatting of various documents
   e) a fully hierarchical file system, permitting distribution of the various specification, design, and code files into separate directories
   f) a systems programming language (C), along with a type checking program (lint) and a source code debugger (sdb)
   g) a lexical analyzer generator (Lex)
   h) a parser generator (YACC)
   i) a standard I/O library that could be used to implement the I/O operations of PLAIN
   j) the "shell" which permits one or more Unix commands to be packaged (in a macro-like way) and executed as if it were a single command
   k) a program (make) for combining files and preparing them for execution
   l) various programs for checking writing style and spelling (style, diction, spell) in documentation and reports (including this paper)
   m) an excellent collection of games, including chess, bridge, and adventure, to occupy the developer during less productive interludes

3. The Unix command language (shell commands) are very easy to learn, and the user of the application programs, as well as the application programmer, would not have to learn a complicated operating system command language; indeed, most of the features of Unix could be made completely invisible to the end user.

4. Unix was in widespread use so that the USE tools could be exported to other organizations.

The basic idea was to build our tools, e.g., TDI, Troll, and the PLAIN system, in the Unix environment, and then to use that environment for the subsequent development of interactive information systems. The only problem with this approach is that we wanted to achieve better integration of the tools and their usage from the standpoint of the developer. We wanted to go beyond the facilities provided by the Programmer's Workbench (PWB) version of Unix [47].

We observed that an additional tool could serve to integrate all of the other tools, as well as to assist in project organization. The specification, design, and development of interactive information systems requires the effort of a group of developers over a period ranging from several months to several years. The resulting IIS may contain hundreds of modules. There will almost certainly be multiple versions of these modules and the IIS itself during the lifetime of the IIS, covering development and evolution of the system, as it is modified and enhanced to accommodate new user and hardware requirements.

These development and evolution activities will generate many documents of different types, including:
- Initial problem statement
- Requirements definition (possibly with analysis reports)
- Software specification
- Project schedule information
- Architectural design, showing overall software structure
- Data dictionary
- Detailed design (in a program design language)
- Source code for each module (perhaps in several versions)
- Object code (or intermediate code) for each module,
    perhaps in several versions
- One or more versions of the executable program
- Scripts for various common activities, e.g., printing,
    compiling, and executing the program
- Test data cases and test results
- User documentation
- Trouble reports and change requests

It is apparent from this list that there is a need for some kind of organized information management, not only to keep track of the emerging software product, but also to manage all of the associated documentation. It is this need that motivated the creation of the USE Control System.

We identified requirements for the USE Control System, including the following:

1.  Support for versions of modules -- make it possible to maintain two or more versions of the specification, source code, and object code for a given system module

2.  Support for versions of systems -- make it possible to maintain two or more versions of a fully linked object version of a software system

3.  Simplify the process of compiling, linking, and loading a number of source modules into a single object program

4.  Make it possible to maintain information on module interfaces

5.  Support the production of a data dictionary

6.  Support other important tasks of system development, such as detailed module design and module testing

7.  Provide management information, including the status of modules and systems and data on the development process itself

8.  Support evolution of existing systems under the USE Control System

9.  Permit different users of the USE Control System to encourage or enforce various sets of rules or guidelines concerning the development process

10. Execute on a small computer to support the concept of personal development systems [48,49,50]

11. Utilize, to the greatest extent possible, other tools in the environment of the USE Control System, in order to maximize integration of the USE Control System with those tools and to minimize the size of the running system.

While our other methods and tools are intended to support the technical activities associated with the development of interactive information systems, the USE Control System is aimed more directly at the managerial and organizational issues in software creation. Information on the status of every module can be maintained online so that it is possible to monitor project progress and to identify problems. Furthermore, various members of a project team have access to the information, so that some of the traditional communication and interface problems between members of a group can be overcome.

The USE Control System is a command driven tool that permits the user to create modules and systems, to modify aspects of a module, to compile one or more modules, to examine the status and history of the development, and to run the current version of the system.

Users of the USE Control System may incorporate policies that may be associated with specific commands to permit the execution of an arbitrary program before or after execution of the command. In this way, the USE Control System can be tailored to the needs of specific development environments and can be used to enforce development methodologies, to limit access to parts of a system, and to capture development effort on specific projects.

As the name implies, the basic system building block is the module.[*] Associated with each module are several "documents":

1.    external documentation of the module, possibly a specification;

2.    information on the interfaces of the module to other modules in the system;

3.    detailed design of the module, possibly written in a program design language [35];

4.    source code for the module;

5.    object code for the module;

6.    test data for the module;

7.    a log to record activities involving the module.

Note that, with the exception of the last item, it is necessary to provide for multiple copies of these documents, representing successive versions of the documents.

At the system level, it is necessary to maintain information to govern the system development and to bind the modules together. One may therefore also visualize some system level documents, including:

1.    policies governing the development of the system;

2.    a log of important system events, such as the creation of a new object version;

3.    a directory of modules that comprise the system;

4.    directories of versions of modules that comprise each version of the system.

The IIS developer uses the USE Control System throughout the project and can issue various commands that control different functions, including:

1.    definition of a system, to have the system establish a directory to hold information about the various modules that comprise the system, along with other administrative information.

2.    definition of a module, to have the system create files to store a specification, program design language, source code, object code, and test data for that module. For example, the program design language shown in Figure 11 and the PLAIN code fragment shown in Figure 13 are stored in the USE Control System file hierarchy associated with both the module name "Assign_Referees" and the version number.

3.    editing of a file to create or modify some aspect of the information stored about a module; the old version will be saved and the new version will be saved as a set of changes to the old version (except for an object module, where the newest is saved and older versions must be specifically recreated)

4.    definition of a version, consisting of a named set of object modules and associated date

5)    linking together of a set of object modules to produce an executable load module for Unix

6)    display of statistics about the system and the development effort associated with various phases of the system or with specific modules.

The USE Control System may be seen as imposing discipline on the use of the various tools. When one wants to create a new system, one issues either the

    build system

or

    new system

command, depending on whether or not parts of the system already exist. (We used "new system" for conman.pc and conman.oc.)

The USE Control System then prompts for the names of modules, data files, and "include files," creating a hierarchical file system that is used as the project "data base", containing what has been termed the Production Program Library [51].

The USE Control System can be used to assist in tasks of specification, architectural and detailed design, coding, and testing. During specification, the

    modify doc

command is used to edit documentation for modules. There is no required format for such documentation, which can range from narrative text to a formal specification language such as SPECIAL [52]. The documentation may then be displayed using the

    print

command.

The USE Control System provides more assistance at the design stage.  Apart from forcing a decomposition into modules, the USE Control System will collect information on module interfaces that can be displayed with the

    make dictionary

command, and provides a template for a Program Design Language that is automatically inserted into the files in the pdl subdirectories for each module.  Instead of simply invoking the requested editor, the USE Control System explicitly elicits the interface information so that it can be stored in an easily retrievable format.

Source code is entered through the

    modify src

command, which simply invokes the editor, possibly executing some programs first as a result of existing policies.  When one or more modules have been coded, the developer types

    compile

and the USE Control System will ask whether the developer wants to compile the entire system or just a single named module, but the developer will not need to know the details of the system call to the compiler.

When all of the modules have been completed, the developer simply types

    run system

and the USE Control System automatically compiles any files for which there is no current version of the object code, and links all of the object modules with any needed libraries into an executable version of the system. The information needed to carry out these steps is stored in a "make" file, which is generated by the USE Control System and used as input to the Unix Make program.  Note that the developer is relieved of the tedious details of remembering which files need to be recompiled, and the need to create a script to carry out the needed compilation and linking.

The USE Control System uses many of the Unix tools directly, as well as giving the user direct access to them through a shell "escape" feature.  The details of the USE Control System are described at greater length in Reference [53].

The Unix tools, combined with PLAIN, Troll, the USE Control System, TDI, and RAPID, form the development environment for the IIS developer.  In this way, it can be seen that the Unix tools have been valuable throughout the USE project, and are of further use in system development and future tool building.

## CONCLUSIONS AND FUTURE DIRECTIONS

The USE methodology is quite new and has been evolving rapidly as the methods have been used and as the tools have been built.  Accordingly, there is relatively little experience with the methods and tools together.  To some extent, that situation is a reflection of the rapid changes in the nature of software development and the character of software engineering environments.  It is also a characteristic of methodologies in general -- they must evolve and improve as one gains experience in their use.

The development of the USE methodology has been gradual and we have spent considerable time experimenting with our methods and tools, evaluating them informally as we have applied them to specific projects.  Indeed, the IFIP Working Conference exercise provided an excellent opportunity to evaluate our approach, and we have made some minor refinements to our approach as a result of work on this problem.

Our efforts in the near future will focus principally on refining the existing tools and on developing new tools to produce a better integrated development environment.  We are using the existing tools to specify, design, and build an automated development dictionary system, and plan to build a checker for our USE Design Language as a subsequent tool.

We have also been exploring the area of personal development systems to provide proper support for these tools.  If an IIS developer can be provided with a personal machine that includes these tools, along with suitable facilities for communication with other users and systems, then it becomes much more practical to support high-bandwidth interfaces such as color graphics and audio input/output.  The small size of the USE tools and the availability of Unix on several small machines makes it practical to create a "USE development machine".

Although we have identified specific needed improvements for the various tools we have developed, we are especially interested in graphics.  Within the USE methodology, several of the methods (SSA, Structure Charts, and transition diagrams) rely upon pictorial representations, and we have observed that system developers in general frequently represent their ideas with pictures, e.g., flow charts, data structures, data base designs.  Yet there is almost no automated support for these methods.

In summary, the USE methodology is an attempt to provide the developer of interactive information systems with a method and tools that improve the quality of the systems that are built and the process by which they are built. We regard the present state of the USE methodology as a significant step toward our goals, but feel that there is a great deal of room for further work. Accordingly, we would like to develop graphical tools as part of the USE toolkit, using some of the powerful graphics packages that already exist in the Unix environment.


## ACKNOWLEDGMENTS

Many people and organizations have assisted in the development of the USE methodology. The basic ideas underlying the methodology have been strengthed by discussions with Peter Freeman and Nancy Leveson, who, along with Susan Stinson, also provided valuable comments on an earlier draft of this paper. Reind van de Riet, Martin Kersten, Mark Dippé, and David Sherertz played a significant role in the design of PLAIN. Amnon Meyers led the PLAIN implementation effort. Martin Kersten was instrumental in the design of Troll and the implementation of the Data Base Handler. Susan Stinson helped in working out the details of the specification method. David Shewmake implemented TDI and RAPID. Dan Keller and Shu-huar Yeh were of great help in the design and implementation of the USE Control System. The work of Thomas W. Booster, Esther F. Handa, Karl Lew, Tom Murphy, Gabriela Novy, Carl Resnikoff, Harry Rubin, and Harpreet Sandhu has also contributed to the design and development of the USE tools. Susan Richter did the artwork and the layout of the final version of this paper. Finally, Tina Walters and Marina Gordillo have been invaluable in keeping the logistical aspects of the project in good order.

This work has been supported by the National Library of Medicine (LM 00153), the National Science Foundation (MCS78-26287), and the Netherlands Organization for the Advancement of Pure Research (ZWO) (grant 62-139). Initial development of the USE Control System was partly supported by the National Bureau of Standards under contract NB79KACA1059. Computing facilities have been provided by the Computer Science Division, Electrical Engineering and Computer Sciences Department, University of California, Berkeley, in particular, the VAX-11/780 system supported by the National Science Foundation under grant MCS78-07291, and by a Corporate Research Sponsorship from Digital Equipment Corporation that supported the acquisition of the VAX-11/750 by the Section on Medical Information Science, University of California, San Francisco. Additional computing support was provided by National Institutes of Health grant RR-1081 to the UCSF Computer Graphics Laboratory and by the Vakgroep Informatics, Vrije Universiteit, Amsterdam, the Netherlands.


## FOOTNOTES


[1] The USE Control System is completely neutral with respect to the definition of a module, although policies could be used to impose various kinds of size restrictions. The concept of a module within the USE Control System is some fragment of a system that has well defined interfaces (assuming that these are specified by the developer) and that is separately compilable (one or more subprograms).

[TM] Unix is a trademark of Bell Laboratories. SADT is a trademark of SofTech, Inc. Ada is a trademark of the U.S. Department of Defense.

# REFERENCES


[1] A.I. Wasserman, "Online Programming Systems and Languages: a History and Appraisal," Technical Report #6, Laboratory of Medical Information Science, University of California, San Francisco, 1974.

[2] W. Teitelman and L. Masinter, "The INTERLISP Programming Environment," *Computer*, vol. 14, no. 4 (April, 1981), pp. 25-33.

[3] A. Kay and A. Goldberg, "Personal Dynamic Media," *Computer*, vol. 10, no. 3 (March, 1977), pp. 31-41.

[4] C. Gane and T. Sarson. *Structured Systems Analysis.* Englewood Cliffs, NJ: Prentice-Hall, 1979.

[5] T. DeMarco. *Structured Analysis and System Specification.* Englewood Cliffs, NJ: Prentice-Hall, 1979.

[6] D.T. Ross and K.E. Schoman, Jr., "Structured Analysis for Requirements Definition," *IEEE Transactions on Software Engineering*, vol. SE-3, no. 1 (January, 1977), pp. 6-15.

[7] M. Lundeberg, G. Goldkuhl, and A. Nilsson, *Information Systems Development -- a Systematic Approach.* Englewood Cliffs, NJ: Prentice-Hall, 1981.

[8] A.I. Wasserman, "Information System Development Methodology," *Journal of the American Society for Information Science*, vol. 31, no. 1 (1980), pp. 5-24.

[9] A.I. Wasserman, "Some Principles of User Software Engineering for Information Systems," *Digest of Papers, COMPCON 75 Spring*, IEEE Computer Society, pp. 49-52.

[10] E. Mumford, "Participative Systems Design: Structure and Method," *Systems, Objectives, Solutions*, vol. 1, no. 1 (January, 1981), pp. 5-19.

[11] L. Rudawitz and P. Freeman, "Client-Centered Design: Concepts and Experience," *Systems, Objectives, Solutions*, vol. 1, no. 1 (January, 1981), pp. 21-32.

[12] G.M. Nijssen, E.J. van Assche, and J.J. Snijders, "End User Tools for Information System Requirement Definitions," in *Formal Models and Practical Tools for Information System Design*, ed. H.-J. Schneider. Amsterdam: North-Holland, 1979, pp. 125-148.

[13] M. Lundeberg, "An Approach for Involving the Users in the Specification of Information Systems," in *Formal Models and Practical Tools for Information Systems Design*, ed. H.-J. Schneider. Amsterdam: North-Holland, 1979, pp. 195-217.

[14] J.M. Smith and D.C.P. Smith, "Database Abstraction: Aggregation and Generalization," *ACM Transactions on Database Systems*, vol. 2, no. 2 (June, 1977), pp. 105-133.

[15] J.M. Smith and D.C.P. Smith, "Conceptual Database Design," in *Tutorial: Software Design Techniques*, 3rd edition, ed. P. Freeman and A.I. Wasserman. Los Alamitos, CA: IEEE Computer Society, 1980, pp. 333-356.

[16] R.H. Drain and N. Oakley. *Successful Conference and Convention Planning.* Toronto: McGraw Hill Ryerson Ltd., 1978.

[17] H.S. Kindler. *Organizing the Technical Conference.* New York: Reinhold Publishing Corp., 1960.

[18] A.I. Wasserman, "USE: a Methodology for the Design and Development of Interactive Information Systems," in *Formal Models and Practical Tools for Information System Design*, H.-J. Schneider (Ed.), North Holland, Amsterdam, pp. 31-50.

[19] S.K. Card, T.P. Moran, and A. Newell, "The Keystroke-Level Model for User Performance Time with Interactive Systems," *Communications of the ACM*, vol. 23, no. 7 (July, 1980), pp. 396-410.

[20] *IBM Systems Journal*, vol. 20, no. 2 (1981).

[21] H.T. Smith and T.R. Green (eds.) *Human Interaction with Computers.* London: Academic Press, 1980.

[22] B. Shneiderman. *Software Psychology.* Cambridge, MA: Winthrop Publishers, 1980.

[23] T. Gilb. *Humanized Input.* Cambridge, MA: Winthrop Publishers, 1977.

[24] S.K. Card, T.P. Moran, and A. Newell. *The Psychology of Human-Computer Interaction.* Hillsdale, NJ: Erlbaum, 1982, in press.

[25] A.I. Wasserman, "User Software Engineering and the Design of Interactive Systems," *Proc. 5th International Conference on Software Engineering*, pp. 387-393.

[26] A.I. Wasserman and S.K. Stinson, "A Specification Method for Interactive Information Systems," *Proc. IEEE Computer Society Conference on Specifications of Reliable Software*, Cambridge, MA, 1979, pp. 68-79.

[27] S.C. Johnson, "Language Development Tools," *Bell System Technical Journal*, vol 57, no. 6 (July-August, 1978), pp. 2155-2175.

[28] M.E. Conway, "Design of a Separable Transition-Diagram Compiler," *Comm. ACM*, vol. 6, no. 7 (July, 1963), pp. 396-408.

[29] J.T. O'Neill (Ed.), *MUMPS Language Standard*, ANSI Standard X11.1, American National Standards Institute, 1977.

[30] W.A. Wulf, R.L. London, and M. Shaw, "An Introduction to the Construction and Verification of Alphard Programs," *IEEE Transactions on Software Engineering*, vol. SE-2, no. 4 (December, 1976), pp. 253-265.

[31] N.G. Leveson, "Applying Behavior Abstraction to Information System Design and Integrity," Ph.D. dissertation, University of California, Los Angeles, 1980. (Available as Technical Report #47, Laboratory of Medical Information Science, University of California, San Francisco)

[32] A.I. Wasserman and S.K. Stinson, "A Specification Method for Interactive Medical Information Systems," *Proc. 3rd Symposium on Computer Applications in Medical Care*, Washington, DC, 1980.

[33] A.I. Wasserman, "The Data Management Facilities of PLAIN," *Proc. ACM 1979 SIGMOD Conference*, Boston, May, 1979, pp. 60-70.

[34] E. Yourdon and L.L. Constantine, *Structured Design*. Englewood Cliffs, NJ: Prentice-Hall, 1979.

[35] S.H. Caine and E.K. Gordon, "PDL -- a Tool for Software Design", *Proc. AFIPS 1975 NCC*, vol. 44, pp. 271-276.

[36] E. Yourdon. *Structured Walkthroughs*. 2nd ed. Englewood Cliffs, NJ: Prentice-Hall, 1979.

[37] B. Liskov *et al.. CLU Reference Manual*. Berlin: Springer Verlag, 1981.

[38] D.I. Good *et al.*, "Report on the Language Gypsy -- Version 2.0," Report ICSCA - CMP -10, Certifiable Minicomputer Project, University of Texas at Austin, 1978.

[39] B.W. Lampson *et al.*, "Report on the Programming Language Euclid," *ACM SIGPLAN Notices*, vol. 12, no. 2 (February, 1977), pp. 1-79.

[40] J.D. Ichbiah *et al.. Reference Manual for the Ada Programming Language*. Berlin: Springer Verlag, 1981. Arlington, VA, 1980.

[41] A.I. Wasserman, "The Design of PLAIN -- Support for Systematic Programming," *Proc. AFIPS 1980 National Computer Conference*, vol. 49, pp. 731-740.

[42] A.I. Wasserman, D.D. Sherertz, M.L. Kersten, R.P. van de Riet, and M.D. Dippé, "Revised Report on the Programming Language PLAIN," *ACM SIGPLAN Notices*, vol. 16, no. 5 (May, 1981), pp. 59-80.

[43] R.P. van de Riet, A.I. Wasserman, M.L. Kersten, and W. de Jonge, "High-Level Programming Features for Improving the Efficiency of a Relational Database System," *Transactions on Database Systems*, vol. 6, no. 3 (September, 1981), pp. 464-485.

[44] M.D. Dippé, "Exception-Handling in PLAIN," Technical Report #52, Laboratory of Medical Information Science, University of California, San Francisco, 1981.

[45] A.I. Wasserman and T.W. Booster, "String Handling and Pattern Matching in PLAIN," Technical Report #50, Laboratory of Medical Information Science, University of California, San Francisco, 1981.

[46] H. Lycklama, "UNIX on a Microprocessor," *Bell System Technical Journal*, vol. 57, no. 6, part 1 (July, 1978), pp. 2087-2101.

[47] E.L. Ivie, "The Programmer"s Workbench -- A Machine for Software Development," *Communications of the ACM*, vol. 20, no. 10 (October, 1977), pp. 746-753.

[48] S. Gutz, A.I. Wasserman, and M.J. Spier, "Personal Development Systems for the Professional Programmer," *Computer*, vol. 14, no. 4 (April, 1981), pp. 45-53.

[49] N. Wirth, "Lilith: a Personal Computer for the Software Engineer," *Proc. 5th Int'l Conference on Software Engineering*, San Diego, March, 1981, pp. 2-15.

[50] S. Zeigler , *et al.*, "The Intel 432 Ada Programming Environment," *Digest of Papers, COMPCON Spring 81*, IEEE Computer Society, San Francisco, 1981, pp. 405-410.

[51] F.T. Baker, "Structured Programming in a Production Programming Environment," *IEEE Transactions on Software Engineering*, vol. SE-1, no. 2 (June, 1975), pp. 241-252.

[52] O. Roubine and L. Robinson, "SPECIAL Reference Manual", Technical Report CSG-45, SRI International, Menlo Park, CA, 1978.

[53] A.I. Wasserman, H. Rubin, S. Yeh, and D.S. Keller, "The USE Control System," in preparation, 1982.

As indicated at the end of the introductory paper to this proceedings, the Review Committee selected seven of the thirteen methodologies included for presentation at a half day plenary session.

In order to stimulate the discussion at the meeting, selective members of the Review Committee were invited to present a short discussion paper on each of these seven methodologies.

These short papers indeed had the desired effect and the discussion at the Conference was stimulating and provocative.  The papers are included at the end of this proceedings in the hope that they will have the same effect on the readers of the proceedings as they had on the attendees at the Conference.

The sequence of the papers corresponds to the sequence in the first part of the proceedings.  There is a reference to the page of the reviewed methodology in the heading of each paper.

*INFORMATION SYSTEMS DESIGN METHODOLOGIES: A Comparative Review*
*T.W. Olle, H.G. Sol, A.A. Verrijn-Stuart (editors)*
*North-Holland Publishing Company*
© *IFIP, 1982*


ACTIVE AND PASSIVE COMPONENT MODELLING: ACM/PCM


by Michael L. Brodie and Erico Silva
(see Page 41)

Reviewed by

Roland Traunmüller
Johannes-Kepler-Universität
Linz, Austria


## 1.  CHARACTERISTICS OF THE METHODOLOGY

ACM/PCM is characterized by its authors as a Modelling Methodology for moderate
to large size database-intensive applications.  In terms of the whole information
systems life cycle, the methodology focusses on specification.  ACM/PCM starts
with a pronounced database view, but proceeds with detailed analysis of the behavioural aspects.  The procedure is heavily influenced by the concept of abstract
data types.


## 2.  RELATIONSHIPS TO OTHER METHODOLOGIES

As a database design method, ACM/PCM has many aspects in common with present day
database systems.  The principal feature of modelling events using triggers has
been proposed and implemented earlier.  The following other methodologies have
many similar features, but the emphasis is on different aspects of the overall
design process.

-    CIM (Conceptual Information Modelling) places heavy emphasis on the early
     stage of provisional modelling;

-    USE puts the accent on dialog modelling;

-    TAXIS may be viewed as a database for expert systems;

-    REMORA includes an infological view of events;

-    Smith and Smith mainly refer to semantic modelling via aggregation and
     generalization.

ACM/PCM might be judged to be unique on grounds of its very precise and elaborate
modelling of behaviour.

There is a broad spectrum of ideas about abstract data types.  Many authors
suggest a merger of databases and abstract data types.  Some authors have the
application to practical information systems in mind.  ACM/PCM may be rated highly
as a successful step in both directions.


## 3.  STRONG POINTS

ACM/PCM is a formal, in principle provable methodology, leading to a detailed
specification.  The resulting document leaves no problem oriented design decisions to the application programmer.  The quality of the document is high,
providing checks for completeness and for consistency.

The test case is well handled and helpful in understanding the procedure of abstracting objects, thereby giving a clear indication of different specification steps.

## 4.  WEAK POINTS

The methodology covers only one phase of the design life cycle, namely specification.  The preceding phase of requirements definition is not treated explicitly.  In the test case, requirements are taken into account implicitly.  The even earlier stages, such as stating the objectives, analyzing for organizational change, conceptual modelling, seem to be totally outside the scope of the methodology.

The methodology needs very detailed elaboration and produces very voluminous design (111 actions and 42 transactions) for the test case.  A level-by-level breakdown is missed.  In practice, it might be a problem if such detailed level of description has to be used so early.

## 5.  UNANSWERED QUESTIONS

The methodology ignores the environment in which an information system should be used.  As a result, some questions are difficult to answer.

In the case of a complex enterprise, how will the processes of the enterprise in question be broken down to processes on the database level?  There is a big gap between processes on the enterprise level and processes on the level of database maintenance operations.

How useful will the methodology be to the systems analyst in charge of the design? How useful in practice will ACM/PCM be in terms of understanding and learning by the average analyst/designer?  How well will it serve to achieve consistent communication between designer and user?

*INFORMATION SYSTEMS DESIGN METHODOLOGIES: A Comparative Review*
*T.W. Olle, H.G. Sol, A.A. Verrijn-Stuart (editors)*
*North-Holland Publishing Company*
© *IFIP, 1982*


THE ISAC APPROACH TO SPECIFICATION OF INFORMATION SYSTEMS AND ITS
APPLICATION TO THE ORGANIZATION OF AN IFIP WORKING CONFERENCE


by Mats Lundeberg
(see Page 173)

Reviewed by

Alfred G. Dale
University of Texas at Austin
Austin, Texas


## 1. INTRODUCTION

The ISAC methodology represents a particularly well-developed instance of the
"classic" approach to information system analysis and design.  It incorporates
a graphic description technique, and is particularly strong in carrying the
design process through diffcrent levels of abstraction, leading from activity
analysis (A-graphs) to information subsystem analysis (I-graphs) to component
(data) analysis (C-graphs).

Of major interest is the methodology developed for initial requirements analysis
(termed change analysis in the ISAC approach).  This phase is frequently ignored
or treated very informally in other methodologies.  In ISAC there is a well-
structured methodology incorporating problem analysis, identification of affected
groups, and the generation of high-level activity graphs, which together form
the basis for the identification of alternative activities to be considered as
candidates for more detailed study in the subsequent phases of the design process.


## 2. MAJOR CRITERIA

In assessing the overall effectiveness of a requirements and design methodology,
there are a number of criteria generally recognized as important:

1.  The process should ensure that system limitations are identifiable early in
    the development cycle with respect to performance parameters such as pro-
    cessing capacity and response characteristics.

2.  The methodology should lend itself to the verification of requirements and
    the design, in the sense that conflicts, omissions, and ambiguities can be
    detected in the requirement specification, and that the ensuing system design
    can be tested for completeness and consistency.

3.  The process should support modular development and hierarchical problem
    definition.

4.  Unambiguous communication of requirement statements to users and design
    specifications to implementers should be possible.

5.  The methodology should be responsive to the need to modify components of a
    system design as requirements change.

6.  The design process should utilize aids which support, in particular, the
    analysis of potential performance characteristics and the verification of
    the design.

## 3.  REVIEW OF ISAC APPROACH

Viewing the ISAC approach in the context of these criteria gives rise to the
following observations and questions:

### 3.1  Identification of system limitations

The activity analysis phase of the ISAC methodology includes, as part of the study
of each information subsystem, consideration of "levels of ambition", i.e. the
specification of performance criteria.  Mention is made in the paper of testing
such criteria, but no details are given.  More information on this point would be
useful.

### 3.2  Verification of requirements

The methodology does not explicitly address this concern.  The decomposition
strategy generates potentially large volumes of information-graphs, supplementary
text pages, property tables.  Thus there appears to be sufficient data to support
a verification procedure.  On the other hand, decomposition inherently multiplies
the possibilities for inconsistency.  The applicability of an explicit verification mechanism (for example, verification graph analysis) to the ISAC domain
is an interesting question, and hopefully can be explored further.

### 3.3  Modular development

The methodology rates highly on this dimension.  However, one review of the paper
noted that the decomposition process carries the design to the level of very
small subsystems, and it is not entirely clear how these can then be aggregated
to larger units that may be required in an implementation.

### 3.4  Communication of requirement and design specifications

Unlike some other methodologies to be presented at this conference, the ISAC
approach terminates at a somewhat high conceptual level (I-graphs and C-graphs),
whereas other methodologies carry the specification a further step and generate
pseudo-code to be used by application programmers as a specification for subsystem implementation.  Discussion of the suitability of the ISAC end-product as
an input to computer-based implementations would be valuable.

### 3.5  Responsiveness to change

The methodology explicitly addresses this problem, and this is one of its strongest
features.

### 3.6  Incorporation of design aids

The issue here relates to the use of, or the potential applicability to, computer-
based design aids.  It can be argued that the ISAC methodology, with its extensive
cross-referencing mechanisms, provides a mutual design-aid environment.  However,
if the methodology is to be applied to large and complex systems, it appears that
the information generated would saturate a purely manual process.  Discussion of
the desirability, or the practicality, of interfacing the methodology to a
computer-based support environment would be enlightening.  In particular, discussion of issues such as the use of modelling techniques to explore dictionary/
directory system to assist in design verification, would be enlightening.

*INFORMATION SYSTEMS DESIGN METHODOLOGIES: A Comparative Review*
*T.W. Olle, H.G. Sol, A.A. Verrijn-Stuart (editors)*
*North-Holland Publishing Company*
© *IFIP, 1982*

SYSTEM DEVELOPMENT IN A SHARED DATA ENVIRONMENT
THE D2S2 METHODOLOGY


by I. G. MacDonald and I. R. Palmer
(see Page 235)


Reviewed by

Thomas Skousen
Information Systems Research Group
Handelshøjskolen
Copenhagen, Denmark


## 1.  INTRODUCTION

The methodology claims to be  pragmatic in the sense that it uses a variety of
concepts in combination.  The choice of concepts is not guided by an underlying
theory but rather by practical experience.

The reviewers felt that this paper represented a good traditional methodology and
that the paper was written with a great sense of practicality.  They suspected
that the evolution of the methodology was highly influenced by the needs observed
in practical user projects.

This fact must be borne in mind in the discussion.  Another point is that to a
certain extent the paper covers only the specification part of the systems work.
The criteria presented by Dale (1) plus some others provide the basis for the
review of this methodology.


## 2.  DISCUSSION OF DALE'S CRITERIA

1.  The systems limitations should be clear early in the development process.

    The D2S2 methodology has a starting point called "strategy stage".  This
    stage leeds to the definition of a number of application areas defined by
    functions, entities and relationships which give a good delineation of
    each area in question.

2.  The methodology should offer a possibility of verification - e.g. consistency
    and completeness of specifications.

    The methodology is based on a parallel description of functions and data
    structures/information structures.  It is shown how the interaction between
    the two models can be analysed in three ways.

    1.  State-change matrix (which clarifies missing functions).

    2.  Function-logic diagram (which makes it possible to check whether the
        data structure supports all functions).

    3.  Function-dependency diagram (a low level check for system transactions).

    This seems to be a practical way of verifying the results.


3.  Is modular design supported?

    The main tool is a hierarchical breakdown procedure.  Applications are con-
    sidered as modules, coordinated by the shared data.

4.   Communicatable results from one step to another and to users.

     As a result of the strategy and analyses stages, one gets logical models of
     data structures and function hierarchies.  It is apparently a good communi-
     cation tool.  It is not quite clear whether the methodology gives an adequate
     basis for the design stage.

5.   Responsive to need to change components of the design.

     The documentation size (apparently about 500 pages for the specification of
     the test case) indicates a problem area.  The methodology gives no indication
     of how to survey and maintain documentation.  How is it possible to track
     the consequences of any changes to the system?

6.   To what extent does the methodology utilise design aids (computers, modelling
     techniques, data dictionary, etc.)?

     Interactive use of a data dictionary for the development work is claimed as
     a focal point.  The relationship between the modelling techniques and a data
     dictionary system is not shown in the paper.


3.   FURTHER CRITERIA

Does the methodology provide guidelines on how to perform the specification and
design activities?

The methodology provides a sequence of main activities, a checklist of points to
have in mind and some documentation tools.  How to do the job is left to intuition
or experience of the designer.

How easy is it to learn to use the methodology and to introduce it in organisations?

The methodology seems easy to grasp and use.  There is an emphasis on simple
diagrams with standard specification.


4.   QUESTIONS RAISED

Based on this discussion, the methodology gives an opportunity of raising the
following more general questions:

A.   Starting point of methodology.

     Strategy should be interpreted more broadly than "giving analysts and de-
     signers a much fuller understanding of a complex environment", with the aim
     of designating applications areas.  It is not clear whether there should have
     been earlier activities which state the objectives and limitations of each
     application area.

B.   Emphasis on simple diagrams with standard specifications.

     It is stated that dialogue with users plays an important role in the approach.
     What is the experience with user dialogue?  Where is the balance between
     simple diagrams with inconsistent or incomplete specifications, understand-
     able by all users, and powerful complex diagrams needed as formal specifi-
     cations, but unreadable?

C.   What guidelines are available for functional decomposition?

It is stated that this should be done independently of the organisation
structure.  Is that possible?  Does the decomposition not in fact reflect
the way in which the organisation works?

D.  Decision analysis.

What is a decision?  Are managers and other users able to express decisions
and information needs clearly?

E.  Design stage.

Analysis and design stage should be completely separated.  The number of
steps from analysis to technical design and the separation between them is
more or less an organisational problem.  If one has separated analysis and
design groups, one has the separation of tasks - and the communication
problems - following.  If one does the whole work in the same group or
organisational unit, it is almost impossible to keep the activities separate.

F.  Documentation problems - computational aids.

How is the documentation maintained?  What documentation is used to describe
the actual designed systems?  How are computers a help in the documentation
and design process?

G.  Methodology implementation.

How is the methodology implemented in organisations, and what experience is
available?


Reference

1.  A. G. Dale.  Review of "The ISAC Approach to Specification of Information
    Systems and its Application to the Organisation of an IFIP Working
    Conference".

*INFORMATION SYSTEMS DESIGN METHODOLOGIES: A Comparative Review*
*T.W. Olle, H.G. Sol, A.A. Verrijn-Stuart (editors)*
*North-Holland Publishing Company*
© *IFIP, 1982*


THE REMORA METHODOLOGY FOR INFORMATION SYSTEMS DESIGN
AND MANAGEMENT


by C. Rolland and C. Richard
(see Page 369)

Reviewed by

Colin Tully
University of York
York, England


# 1. INTRODUCTION

Remora proposes a set of models describing information systems from the first
stage of formal conception through to implementation, and describing the
activities of information system management.  Upon these models, which set out to
be complete and frugal, are based notations for the designer's use, and software
tools for his assistance.

The paper has the following structure, the main sections of which correspond to
the broad structure of the methodology.

Introduction

Section 1: conceptual level

Section 2: internal level

Section 3: computer-aided system

Conclusion

The methodology appears to be the fruit of effective collaboration between
academic and industrial partners.  Certainly it gives evidence, on the one hand,
of trying to analyse from first principles the nature of information systems,
and some of the very difficult problems that arise in their design; and, on the
other hand, of a determination to produce methods and tools that will be of
practical benefit to systems designers.

It was these considerations, among others, that led the Review Committee to
discount two obvious shortcomings in the methodology.  First, it is written in
a heavy "Frenglish" dialect (to coin a word analogous to "franglais").  Second,
only the most perfunctory attention is given to the test case.  This  is a more
serious objection.

Perhaps inevitably, given the scale of the enterprise, the limited space available, and the two shortcomings just mentioned, there are a number of criticisms
and questions which arise.  These are discussed here based on the belief that the
high quality of the project demands that it be given careful and critical
attention.


# 2. BASIC MODEL

The basic model of real-world phenomena is difficult to grasp.  The distinction
between <u>events</u> and <u>operations</u> is insufficiently clear.  It seems to depend upon

the relational statement "events <u>ascertain</u> objects".  Even a repeated study of
the context does not remove the difficulty of assigning meaning to this assertion.
What seems to be meant is that the state-change of an object is an event.  One
could further re-express the model by saying that operations cause stage-changes
of objects, and that operations are a class of events.  Justification for each of
these statements can be found in the text; but together they represent a fairly
radical  reformulation of the model as summarised in Figure 2 of the paper.

There could be benefit in discussing the distinction between objects, events and
operations in the real world, and objects, events and operations within an
information system.  That is not done.


3.   USE OF NOTATION

There is a variety of notations for different purposes.  As shown in the paper,
there are formal (programming- and schema-like) languages for the static and
dynamic sub-schemas at the conceptual level, and alternative graphical notation
for the dynamic sub-schema, and graphical notations for the standard and specific
schemas at the internal level.  Is this the complete set of languages and
notations?  It has to be said that the impression is not given that there is a
well engineered interface for the designer, although cosmic surgery could no
doubt go a long way towards removing this objection.

The notational examples are made unnecessarily hard to read and understand by an
insistence on using programming style abbreviations in name formation.  This
should surely be avoided.


4.   INTER-RELATIONSHIPS BETWEEN SYSTEMS

The relationship between ISMS (information system management system - Section 1),
CAS (computer-aided system - Section 3) and the Pilot (also Section 3) is obscure.


5.   USE OF DATA BASE MANAGEMENT SYSTEMS

Two data base management .systems are mentioned, SOCRATE and SYNTEX.  Little is
said about either.  Even though references are given, the reader would benefit
from rather more information about each, and particularly about their respective
roles in the overall methodology.

*INFORMATION SYSTEMS DESIGN METHODOLOGIES: A Comparative Review*
*T.W. Olle, H.G. Sol, A.A. Verrijn-Stuart (editors)*
*North-Holland Publishing Company*
© *IFIP, 1982*

A DRAFT PROPOSAL FOR INTEGRATING
SYSTEM SPECIFICATION MODELS


by Arne Sólvberg
(see Page 475)

Reviewed by

B. K. Brussaard
Ministry of the Interior
The Hague, Netherlands


## 1.  INTRODUCTION

This review is limited to the methodology as presented and <u>does not</u> digress into
the handling of the test case.  This was highly rated, a fact which had an
influence on the selection of the methodology.  The overall judgment of the
Review Committeed was that

- the methodology covers a great deal of the total design process, from the
  modelling of very high level activities down to detailed structuring of
  program modules and offers a smooth development path;

- the approach is very realistic.  It does not pretend to be entirely new,
  but is built on proven ideas;

- it presents a realistic and sound philosophy on the nature of requirements,
  summarized in the statement: "The solution of one problem on one level leads
  to a requirement for solutions of new problems on another level".


## 2.  ADMINISTRATIVE AND TECHNICAL PROBLEMS

The author distinguishes between the "administrative problem" (project management,
etc.) and the "technical problem" within the system development problem.  The
methodology deals only with the technical problem.  Operationally both problems
have to be solved simultaneously.  A methodology, which solves one of the problems,
but obstructs the solution of the other, would not be useful.  The view of this
methodology, i.e. "system development as a continuous design process", may be in
conflict with the requirements of project management (phases, mile-stones, etc.).
If the interests (especially the freedom) of the designer and the need for
control of the project manager are in conflict, the methodology favours the
former.  The designer has many modelling concepts at his disposal (maybe too
many) and he seems rather free to use and combine them.  The resulting models
may show the information system (here the system of all activities needed to
organize a working conference) from several points of view at each level of
detail.  One interesting example is the explicit modelling of the interaction
between the user and the technical system.  In that sense, the models can reflect and support the process of thinking.  However, the paper barely specifies
which models are needed and which modelling concepts are allowed within each
model.  It is therefore not so surprising that some schemes are rather complex
and overloaded with modelling elements.  Making and maintaining them must be an
expensive affair.

3.  COMPUTER SUPPORT

Computer support cannot offer a solution because it automatically presupposes a
formalized process, and thus strict rules and guidelines.  There would be no
real possibility to check the consistency and quality of the models automatically.

On the other hand, the same modelling concepts are used on each level of detail,
which seems to be some guarantee for quality, since no information can be lost
during a translation from one model to another.  It is difficult to weight this
kind of choice in a methodology.  Especially in an environment with relatively
little variation in type of information systems (applications), one could be
inclined to have different preference.


4.  DATA ANALYSIS

Little emphasis is given to data analysis and data base design, but that may be
caused by the limited scope of the test case (as the author claims).


5.  CONTROLLING THE REAL WORLD SYSTEM

Another more fundamental aspect is the following.  It has been more or less
accepted nowadays, that if one wants to design an information system (IS), the
real system (RS) to be controlled has also to be taken into account.  Even if
one has decided in a preceding analysis that a new or improved IS is required,
the objective of the IS remains linked inseparably with the RS.  A special case
of this is when the RS itself is an IS for another level RS.  The test case
offers an example.  The real process to be controlled, that of organizing a
conference, consists mainly of information processing.  If a methodology does
not distinguish clearly between the RS and the IS, there will be the possibility
that

-   either certain processes of the IS will be neglected in designing, because
    they are seen as given real processes, or

-   certain real processes will be designed anew, because they are wrongly seen
    as processes of the IS.

This is an old problem.  How should one limit the field of investigation, and
how should one limit the IS to be designed?  Neither from the methodology's
description nor from the details of the test case can it be determined whether
this method uses this distinction and, if so, whether it is done correctly.
If this is not the case, the conclusion would have to be that the methodology
distinguishes not just a "technical problem" and an "administrative problem",
but also - by implication - an "organizational problem", i.e. the problem of
defining the scope of the IS to be designed (built) and the RS for which the
IS is intended as the controlling system.

One can wonder to what extent the proposed basic concepts, which now seem
somewhat abundant, are useful in solving this problem of defining the IS's
scope or whether they actually hamper communication with the user management
through their formalism and abstraction.


6.  CONCLUSION

In spite of the critical comments and question marks, this methodology seems
very promising.  The problems mentioned can be solved, at least to some extent.
It would then be a good and workable method for the average designer.

*INFORMATION SYSTEMS DESIGN METHODOLOGIES: A Comparative Review*
T.W. Olle, H.G. Sol, A.A. Verrijn-Stuart (editors)
*North-Holland Publishing Company*
© IFIP, 1982


NIAM: AN INFORMATION ANALYSIS METHOD


by G. M. A. Verheijen and J. van Bekkum
(see Page 537)

Reviewed by

J. Roger S. Kistruck
SRI-Europe, Ltd.
Croydon, Surrey
England


## 1.  GENERAL

The information analysis method "NIAM" as described in the paper, is an interesting and advanced example of applying formal methods to the difficult subject
of systems analysis and design.  From one point of view, it falls into the main
stream of systems design methodologies, as it depends upon a top-down decomposition of systems functions, followed by an analytical study of information
flows and data relationships.  Further, the functional decomposition and the
information analysis are aided by diagrammatic representations in a specially
developed notation.  It even shares with several other methodologies the use of
a meta-data base and some actual or potential code generator to assist with the
construction of the final information system.  Within this general agreement on
the structure of the approach, however, NIAM has several features of its own.

Perhaps the most important is the attempt to build the semantics of the object
system into the syntax of the data structure.  Thus, the Information Structure
Diagrams at the heart of NIAM express the meaning in the real world of the concepts named.  A paper has to have a title, a subject and an author because that
is what we have chosen to mean by the lexical object "paper".  The aim of NIAM
is then to enforce these meanings by building them into the structure of the data
base and into the syntax of any statements defining the information system.

Another very important feature of the method is the definition language RIDL which
appears to be a way of translating the specialised notation of the ISD's into
machine processable form and extending it with what are effectively procedure
definitions.  The transformations accomplished in this way may provide very considerable assistance in the time, labour and accuracy of developing the information system itself.

A number of points in the method seem to be important to discuss in the areas
of:

> the conceptual structure;

> the graphical notation of the diagrams;

> some characteristics of the RIDL language.


## 2.  CONCEPTS

Within the concepts of NIAM, a very strong distinction is made between lexical
and non-lexical objects.  This is an important distinction and one that is easy
to grasp in the case of objects.  The definition of verbs ("predicates" in NIAM
terminology) is not so straightforward, and the limitation to binary relationships

through a predicate seems an unfortunate restriction.  In natural language
sentences, it is common to find predicates linking at least three objects,
for example:

    "X  gave $ Y to Z", or

    "X informed Y of Z"

In some circumstances, it is likely to give a lot of trouble (and very voluminous
diagrams) to decompose such sentences into their binary components when all the
real-world options are to be covered.

A second point of concern in the formal expression of constraints is that NIAM
makes no apparent distinction between absolute constraints, "law of nature" if
you will, and constraints that are chosen by the users or the systems designer
("rules of this game").  The users' or designers' choice may be intended in the
object system to enforce a particular policy through the implementation of the
information system.  It can be important to recognise the difference, since laws
of nature (and double-entry bookkeeping) are virtually unchanging, whereas
policies may change frequently in response to changing circumstances.

The reader will wonder, too, whether the restriction to a single conceptual
data base is fundamental.  In these days of physically distributed data bases,
it would be interesting to hear more of the problems at the boundary where a
NIAM-designed system interacts with others which have their own conceptual and
physical data structures already established.


3.  DIAGRAMS

One of the most prominent features of NIAM is the set of graphical conventions
used in the Information Structure Diagrams.  As suggested above, this notation
is a way of capturing information about the objects and relationships in the
"real world" or object system.  For NIAM to be successful in practice it is
important that these diagrams should be relatively easy to draw and should encourage a complete definition of all the relevant relationships.  How can one,
using a NIAM diagram, be sure that it is not just consistent, but also correct?
"Correct" in this context would also imply that it is complete, so that all the
relevant relationships had been correctly included.  A second point arising from
this is whether the notation can itself be demonstrated to be sufficiently
powerful to express all the relationships between objects that are important for
the information systems design.  What about quantitative relationships and volumes
for example, not to mention stochastic relationships?  Third, the permanent
problem with diagrams is that they need to be modified as the analyst's information grows and changes.  It can be a very cumbersome process to bring up to
date several hundred detailed diagrams, particularly when a change in one implies
corresponding changes in many others.  Perhaps the authors could comment on how
modifications to the diagrams are handled in practice?


4.  THE RIDL LANGUAGE

The RIDL language appears to be a very valuable extension to the Information
Structure Diagrams, but it introduces a lot of questions too.  First, the
interpretation of a diagram into RIDL statements appears to be a purely manual
process, absorbing skilled effort.  Second, it is not clear how one could be
sure that all of the features of the diagram have been correctly expressed in
RIDL statements.  If this cannot be done, there is always a risk that although
the diagram and RIDL code are each internally consistent, they may not be consistent with each other.  Historically, this seems to have been a fruitful

cause of design errors as conventional programming block diagrams are translated
into procedural language statements in, for example, COBOL.  Third, the RIDL
language does not appear to be completely consistent with the concepts expressed
in the ISD's.  It is stated in the paper that all the NIAM concepts can be expressed in RIDL, but the converse does not appear to be the case.  Extensive
procedure definitions are included in the RIDL examples at the end of the paper,
but none appear in the ISD's.  The implication must be that RIDL provides an
opportunity for generating the procedural code as well as the data definitions
in the data base.  This immediately raises questions about the procedure definitions themselves; where do the prescriptions come from for timing and control
so that the information system effectively supports its users?

Finally, it is worth noting the parallel between the structure of RIDL definitions and some of the work being done elsewhere in the field of machine
intelligence.  Some success has been achieved with interactive systems for
gathering meta-data about the object system and the information structures that
should represent it.  Are there any plans to make RIDL an interactive system
which could reflect back to the analyst the current state of its "understanding"?
If that line were taken, it might reduce the need for translating Information
Structure Diagrams into a different medium, as they could be generated on a
plotter on demand from a RIDL system.

Taking all these discussion points into account, I believe the paper is a useful
contribution to our understanding of information systems design methods.  It
shows some important pointers for future developments, and is worth a very
careful study.

*INFORMATION SYSTEMS DESIGN METHODOLOGIES: A Comparative Review*
*T.W. Olle, H.G. Sol, A.A. Verrijn-Stuart (editors)*
*North-Holland Publishing Company*
© *IFIP, 1982*

THE USER SOFTWARE ENGINEERING METHODOLOGY:
AN OVERVIEW


by Anthony I. Wasserman
(see Page 591)

Reviewed by

Peter J. H. King
Birkbeck College
University of London
London, England


## 1.   INTRODUCTION

A major comment must be that the methodology does not present an information
analysis and design method in the commonly accepted sense.  Instead, it argues
for an "experimental approach" to the development of interactive information
systems by the extensive use of prototypes.  The position taken is that, provided
sufficiently good software tools are available to create prototype systems, then
this experimental approach becomes feasible.

The author does accept that some form of requirements analysis and specification
is required as a first step, but takes the view that adequate methods already
exist and cites Structured Systems Analysis (SSA), SADT, and Information Systems
and Analysis of Change (ISAC) as approaches which might be used for this first
step.  There is no detailed or comparative discussion of these methods given
in the paper, nor any suggestion that any one of these methods is to be preferred
for the experimental approach, although in fact SSA is used in the subsequent
illustrations in the paper.  The absence of such a discussion is surprising
for it might be supposed that the prototyping approach may make particular demands on the requirements analysis and specification method used.


## 2.   EMPHASIS ON USER DIALOGUES

The paper argues that with interactive systems, specification of user dialogues
is of central importance and that therefore a software tool for the ready
creation and modification of such dialogues is of particular importance.
Accordingly, the USE method provides for the specification of these dialogues
using transition diagrams and includes a Transition Diagram Interpreter (TDI)
for their implementation as one of the major software tools.  The paper illustrates how these transition diagrams can be used with examples from the IFIP
working conference problem.


## 3.   GOALS FOR SYSTEM SPECIFICATION

Following this interesting and important discussion of the TDI and its use,
the paper contains a lengthy and somewhat discursive section referring to such
desirable goals for system specifications as: completeness, comprehensibility,
testability, traceability, consistency, unambiguity, writeability, modifiability
and implementability.  Indeed, this section seems to lack purpose since no one
is likely to dispute this exhaustive list of truisms.  Indeed, in parts of this
discussion, the reader almost ˍexpects to encounter some sentences on the

importance of motherhood!

This discussion concludes by suggesting that it has been demonstrated that an
interactive information system consists of three components: the user interface
to the system, the operations which take place upon the data object of the
system, and on the data base used by the system.


4.  USE OF RELATIONAL MODEL

It is then stated that the data base should be specified as a set of normalised
relations since relational data base software is now available.  The other
arguments given for using the relational model are merely a repetition of some
of the original discussion of Codd in support of his conjective that the simple
tabular view is an adequate data model for data base design.  Whilst the relational approach seems sound enough for the test case and the relational data
base design for this case given in the paper satisfactory, it does not follow
from the arguments and discussion in the paper that it will always be so.
Indeed, the adequacy of the relational view in general practice is simply an
assumption made in the paper.


5.  LEVEL OF DETAIL

A criticism of this paper made by several of the reviewers is that it is
essentially a somewhat lengthy presentation of the USE development environment
and that in parts it is excessively detailed.  The discussion of the string
handling facilities of PLAIN, essentially the incorporation of Snobal 4 string
handling facilities into a version of Pascal, cannot really be regarded as
relevant to the topic under consideration.  The possible argument that higher
level languages facilitate quick implementation and hence the prototyping
approach, through time, would be somewhat spacious as a justification for the
inclusion of this material in the paper.


6.  HANDLING OF TEST CASE

It was regarded by all reviewers that it was an unfortunate failing of the paper
not to treat the IFIP conference test case fully in a separate section as was
requested.  In fact, only parts of the test case were used as illustrative
material in the exposition of the USE software tools.

It could well be argued that this paper is premature in that the USE environment
is not yet sufficiently developed for a full prototype of the test case to have
been produced.  The validity of the prototyping approach has thus not been
demonstrated.  It has been simply argued that such an approach seems promising
and therefore justifies the development of an environment in which it can be
tried in practice, at the same time reporting the current state of development
of this environment.

However, because of the importance of the prototyping viewpoint and of the
radically different nature of this experimental approach from many other systems
analysis and design methods, the Review Committee felt it was justified in including it in the programme, notwithstanding the incompleteness of the work and
the somewhat sketchy treatment of the test case.